3rd Edition

Contemporary Tax Practice

Research, Planning and Strategies

John O. Everett
Cherie Hennig
Nancy Nichols

Wolters Kluwer
CCH

EDITORIAL STAFF
Production: Linda Barnich, Jennifer Schencker
Design: Kaitlyn Bitner

ISBN 978-0-8080-3483-4

4025 W. Peterson Ave.
Chicago, IL 60646-6085
800 248 3248
CCHGroup.com

Printed in the United States of America

Certified Chain of Custody
Promoting Sustainable Forestry
www.sfiprogram.org
SFI-01268

SFI label applies to the text stock

Preface

This is not your parents' tax textbook.

This was the first sentence in the Preface to the first edition of this textbook, and continues to be a guiding principle in this third edition.

Our purpose in writing this text was to provide a comprehensive resource for a second course in taxation that touches all bases of contemporary tax practice: research, planning, and compliance. As a result, this text looks quite a bit different from other second-course tax textbooks in the market.

The combination of the 150-hour accounting program and increasing student interest in a tax specialty has created somewhat of a quandary in planning for a second or advanced course in the tax sequence. Historically, a second undergraduate course in taxation has been devoted to comprehensive coverage of corporations, along with an overview of other tax entities and a brief introduction to federal transfer taxes. If these two courses were required, then a follow-up, general-purpose graduate tax course was usually devoted to tax research, or perhaps to a more theoretical transactional approach to tax planning.

With the advent of the 150-hour program, many accounting programs limit tax coverage to just two courses for the non-tax specialist. Then the question becomes exactly what should be in this second course? This inevitably leads to a push and pull between a comprehensive corporate course using a legal treatise, or some variation of the typical tax research course plus limited coverage of special topics. As a result, some basic coverage of other entities in current second undergraduate courses falls through the cracks.

Contemporary Tax Practice: Research and Planning Strategies is designed to close the gap between these two approaches for a second course, and at the same time provide a solid tax foundation for beginning an accounting career. Our text provides comprehensive coverage of tax research and tax planning strategies, as well as special topics such as the financial accounting tax accrual and tax reform proposals. And for those basic tax topics that might fall by the wayside due to the constraints of a two-semester sequence, we offer a number of comprehensive tax tutorials on our webpage.

When developing this text, our vision was a simple one: *This will be a research text, and much, much more.* First of all, we have included all the features that you would expect in a tax research text:

- A comprehensive introduction to tax authorities, with separate chapters examining legislative, administrative and judicial authorities in detail (Chapters 1, 2, and 3).
- A thorough discussion of locating tax authority with various online tax services, and assessing the relative value of such authority (Chapter 4).
- Numerous research questions that test the research skills of the user; every chapter includes sets of research questions.
- An informative introduction to tax procedures, administration, and sanctions, including current reporting and disclosure controversies (Chapter 9).
- An overview of a typical tax engagement, with a special emphasis on written tax communications (Chapter 10).

But *Contemporary Tax Practice: Research and Planning Strategies* includes much, much more. By moving some of the basic coverage of various tax entities to the web tutorials, we are able to shift gears and provide a much deeper understanding of the legal underpinnings of our tax law and related planning strategies. This coverage includes a number of topics you would *not* expect in the typical tax research text:

- A thorough review and analysis of the leading judicial decisions involving gross income, deductions, property transactions, and accounting periods and methods, including a review of tax principles applicable to each topic and commentary on the importance of each decision and events subsequent to each decision (Chapters 5, 6, 7, and 8).
- An extensive discussion of tax planning opportunities related to individuals, retirement planning, closely-held businesses, and gift and estate taxes (Chapters 11, 12, 13, 14, and 16).
- A unique chapter devoted solely to the choice of business entity decision, from both a tax and a non-tax perspective, with a comprehensive Case Study and Excel model that brings to life the tax factors involved in such a decision (Chapter 15).
- A concise and insightful introduction to the tax accrual for financial accounting purposes, including coverage of ASC Topic 740, formerly FASB 109 and FIN 48, and book-tax reconciliations on Schedule M-3 (Chapter 17).
- An introduction to current proposals for reforming the tax laws, including the Fair Tax, the flat tax, the USA tax, and the value-added tax (Chapter 18).

To quote a Chinese proverb, *"I hear and I forget. I see and I remember. I do and I understand."* In order for students to gain a full understanding of the tax research, planning, and compliance processes in today's practice, they must work with examples, case studies, and planning techniques that incorporate the tax law in a meaningful way. And in this regard, *Contem-*

porary Tax Practice: Research and Planning Strategies offers five significant supplemental benefits, all free of charge. Specifically, adopters will be provided free access to:

- *RESEARCH:* **CCH's IntelliConnect®**—the professional research package with fully integrated full-text primary source documents, analysis, and current tax news, including federal, state, and international tax. Users learn how to do tax research on the CCH industry-leading platform and are also able to answer the research questions found in each chapter.

- *COMPLIANCE:* **ProSystem *fx* Tax,** the award-winning tax compliance and preparation software package from CCH—one of the leading tax return preparation packages in the industry.

- *PLANNING:* The text **Website** (*CCHGroup.com/ContemporaryTax*) contains numerous tax planning case studies, with comprehensive Excel spreadsheet models that analyze such topics as the individual alternative minimum tax, choice of business entity, retirement plan projections, fringe benefits, grantor retained annuity trusts, and other planning scenarios discussed in Chapters 11 through 16. And this third edition includes new spreadsheet cases examining C to LLC conversions and estate executor elections. Most chapters also include supplemental tax planning questions for assignment. In addition, **CCH's IntelliConnect®** offers a number of valuable planning aids, including the *Tax Tools* and *Financial and Estate Planning* sections of the website.

- *INTERACTIVE TAX TOPIC TUTORIALS:* The text **Website** (*CCH-Group.com/ContemporaryTax*) includes interactive tutorials for the basic tax laws applicable to individuals, corporations, and other entities, as well as the gift and estate tax, designed to bring students of various tax backgrounds up to speed with current tax law. These interactive tutorials flesh out the fundamentals of various topics covered in the planning chapters of the text, such as corporate formations, corporate distributions, partnership formations, S corporation requirements, and fiduciary income tax issues. These tutorials help ensure that students who take the CPA Examination are exposed to all topics listed in the specified examination content outlines.

- *STUDENT LEARNING AIDS:* The text includes access to a dedicated product **Website** that features online interactive quizzes, tax news updates, and more. The organization of this text is flexible enough so that individual segments can stand alone.

Please visit *http://www.cchgroup.com/Resources* for any periodic updates or clarifications that may become available for Contemporary Tax Practice 3rd Edition as well as CCH's Daily Tax Day News. Tax Briefings and other valuable resources.

This marks the third edition of this text, and the authors are delighted with the response to the first two editions. We wish to thank many of our colleagues and students for their suggestions in designing and improving the presentation of the material. As always, we welcome any comments on the text and ancillaries.

June 2013

John O. Everett
Cherie J. Hennig
Nancy N. Nichols

About the Authors

John O. Everett, Ph.D., CPA, is a Professor of Accounting at Virginia Commonwealth University in Richmond, VA. John began his career as an IRS agent, and he has served as a speaker and instructor for numerous professional education programs, including the national training courses of Ernst & Young and McGladrey & Pullen. A graduate of Oklahoma State University, he has authored or coauthored a number of articles in academic and professional journals, including The *Journal of the American Taxation Association, Journal of Legal Tax Research, Accounting Horizons, Issues in Accounting Education, Journal of Accounting Education, Advances in Accounting, The Journal of Accountancy, The CPA Journal, The Journal of Taxation, Taxes, Tax Notes*, and *The Tax Adviser*. He is the coauthor of several books, including *Tax Point* with Cherie Hennig, the first interactive tax textbook on the Web, and CCH's *Practical Guide to Schedule M-3 Compliance* with Cherie Hennig and William Raabe, a comprehensive reference source. John is an active member of the American Taxation Association and the American Accounting Association. John was recently selected as the Ray M. Sommerfeld Tax Educator of the Year, and is a previous recipient of the American Taxation Association Outstanding Service Award.

Cherie J. Hennig, Ph.D., M.B.A., began her career as an IRS Revenue Agent in Denver, CO. She has taught undergraduate and graduate tax courses at University of North Carolina, Wilmington, Florida International University, Colorado State University, the University of South Florida, and Virginia Tech. She has published articles in leading tax journals, co-authored two tax texts and written and taught numerous continuing professional education courses. Her articles have appeared in such journals as *The National Tax Journal, The Journal of the American Taxation Association, Advances in Taxation, Issues in Accounting Education, Journal of Legal Tax Research, Journal of Accountancy, Advances in Accounting Behavioral Research, Tax Notes, Accounting Horizons, Journal of Taxation, Taxes, Journal of International Taxation*, and *The Tax Adviser*. She is a member of the American Taxation Association and the American Institute of CPAs. She co-authored with John Everett and Nancy Nichols the text, *Contemporary Tax Practice: Research, Planning and Strategies*, published by CCH, a Wolters Kluwer business. She also co-authored with John Everett and William Raabe the text, *Practical Guide to Schedule M-3 Compliance*, published by CCH, a Wolters Kluwer business. Cherie also coauthored with John Everett, *Tax Point*, the first interactive tax textbook on the Web. She has taught numerous CPE courses for professional organizations. Cherie received the American Taxation Association, 2007 Outstanding Service Award. She served on the

Tax Executive Committee of the AICPA and on the Editorial Board of the ATA Journal of Legal Tax Research.

Nancy Nichols, Ph.D., CPA, is the Journal of Accounting Education Research Professor at James Madison University. She also serves as the Director of the Masters in Accounting program. Prior to obtaining her Ph.D. at the University of North Texas, Nancy was a tax partner at Deloitte and Touche. She teaches graduate and undergraduate courses in taxation. With primary research interests in the areas of taxation and segment reporting, she has published numerous articles in such journals as the *Journal of the American Taxation Association, Journal of Legal Tax Research, Accounting Horizons, Journal of Accountancy, Journal of International Accounting, Auditing and Taxation, Issues in Accounting Education, Journal of Accountancy, The CPA Journal, Tax Notes,* and *Journal of Taxation.* Nancy is an active member of American Taxation Association and serves on the Editorial Board of the ATA Journal of Legal Tax Research.

Acknowledgements

Special thanks to Jennifer Codner, Content Acquisition Editor at CCH, for her unyielding faith in and encouragement for this out-of-the-box project. Thanks also to Kurt Diefenbach, Managing Editor at CCH, for his support and invaluable advice in overseeing this project to completion. We would also like to thank Jennifer Schencker, Linda Barnich, and Lynn Kopon for their outstanding work in managing, editing and coordinating this third edition.

Contents

A detailed Table of Contents for each chapter begins on page xiii.

Table of Contents

CHAPTER 1

Legislative Sources of Authority

Learning Objectives

1. Distinguish between primary and secondary tax authority.
2. Understand the historical development of the tax law.
3. Describe the legislative process for a tax bill.
4. Detail the organization of the Internal Revenue Code.
5. Differentiate substantial authority and reasonable basis in tax practice.

¶1001 Introduction

Traditionally, tax practice is divided into three distinct components: research, planning, and compliance. But these are not mutually exclusive categories, and one of the purposes of this text is to demonstrate the relationships of all three activities.

The first half of this course is devoted to tax research, the process of examining various primary and secondary sources to determine the answer to a tax question. The last half of the course is devoted to tax planning, the orderly process of arranging one's affairs to minimize tax liabilities. But successful tax planning strategies often depend on solid research so that the strategy chosen will withstand judicial scrutiny.

Tax research and planning are also a significant part of the compliance work in contemporary tax practice. For example, changing accounting methods may require extensive research to develop a justification to the IRS for the change, and may require a substantial tax planning effort to determine which change is most tax-benefit efficient. Only after these questions are answered can the complex compliance task of completing Form 3115 (Application for Change in Accounting Method) and accompanying schedules describing the change be completed.

This text is devoted primarily to tax research and tax planning. The first three chapters introduce the major sources of legislative, administrative, and judicial authorities, collectively known as **primary authority**. The first type of tax authority, legislative authority, is discussed in the remainder of this chapter. Chapter 4 introduces the various print and electronic tax services that aid practicing tax professionals in locating the answer to a tax research, planning or compliance question. Chapters 5 through 8 expand the discussion of tax authority, and review quite a bit of tax law as well, by examining the landmark judicial decisions involving income; deductions; property transactions; and accounting records, methods, and income allocations.

The last half of the text is devoted to procedural issues and tax planning strategies. Chapter 9 reviews the maze of administrative and procedural constraints dominating contemporary tax practice, including taxpayer and preparer penalties. Chapter 10 provides an anatomy of a tax engagement, from beginning to end, with a special emphasis on tax communications. Chapters 11 through 16 introduce common and not-so-common tax planning strategies related to individuals, retirement, basic and advanced transfer tax issues, choice of business entity, and small closely-held businesses.

Finally, the last two chapters of the text introduce two broader aspects of contemporary tax practice. First, Chapter 17 introduces the role of taxes in financial accounting issues by reviewing the tax accrual and the impact of ASC 740. And lastly, Chapter 18 examines the debate over tax reform by examining the pros and cons of various tax reform ideas proposed in recent years.

¶1003   An Introduction to Tax Authority

.01   PRIMARY VS. SECONDARY TAX AUTHORITY

In researching a tax question, it is extremely important to understand the difference between primary tax authority and secondary tax authority. Although both sources may be consulted in attempting to find the answer to a tax question, the actual answer must always relate to a primary authority.

Primary tax authority, the "official" body of tax law, consists of the Internal Revenue Code as drafted by Congress, Regulations and other pronouncements of the Department of the Treasury, and judicial decisions devoted to tax issues. The answer to a tax question must necessarily be traced back to a primary tax authority.

Secondary tax authority refers to various "unofficial" sources of tax information, such as textbooks, journal articles, commentaries, tax service editorial comments, and even this text. Secondary services are primarily devoted to finding, interpreting and explaining primary authority. These sources, while possibly being very informative and technically accurate, do not represent the tax law and should not be used to justify a position taken on a tax return.

.03   LEGISLATIVE, ADMINISTRATIVE AND JUDICIAL AUTHORITIES

Primary tax authority may be broken into three categories: legislative, administrative, and judicial. **Legislative authority** refers to tax authority enacted by the legislative body, the United States Congress. Tax bills passed by Congress are added to *Title 26* of the U.S. Code and have the force and effect of law, unless they are found to be unconstitutional. As explained later in this chapter, legislative authority also includes the various committee reports issued by the tax-writing committees in Congress, as well as tax treaties involving the United States.

Administrative authority includes all pronouncements of the executive branch of the federal government. Most tax administrative authority is drafted by the Department of Treasury and one of its major divisions, the Internal Revenue Service (IRS). The primary administrative authority is the tax Regulations, the official interpretations of the tax law by the Treasury and the IRS. Other sources of administrative authority, discussed in Chapter 2, are revenue rulings, revenue procedures, letter rulings, and various other notices and announcements.

Judicial authority refers to decisions of the federal courts on tax matters. As discussed in Chapter 3, a number of courts are asked to decide tax controversies, and these interpretations of the tax law are important components of tax authority. One court, the U.S. Tax Court, is devoted solely to tax cases, while other courts, such as the U.S. District Court and the Court of Claims, hear all kinds of civil and criminal cases, including some tax cases. U.S. Circuit Courts of Appeal, and to a lesser extent the U.S. Supreme Court, may hear tax cases as well.

¶1005 Legislative Authority: A Historical Perspective

The power to tax is specifically defined in the Constitution. Article 1, Section 8, Clause 1 states that "*The Congress shall have the power to lay and collect taxes, duties, imports and excises, to pay the debts and provide for the common defense and general welfare of the United States.*" But this power has not always been exercised by Congress. The following discussion provides a chronological record of taxation in the United States and highlights several concepts that remain important in contemporary tax practice.

- *1643.* The first attempt to tax incomes in the United States was in 1643, when several colonies instituted what was called a *faculties and abilities tax*. This was a modest tax, with tax collectors literally going door to door and asking if the individual had income during the year. If so, the tax was computed on the spot. Needless to say, there were substantial compliance problems with this system.
- *1700s–1800s.* In the early 1700s and well into the 1800s, a number of the southern colonies and states adopted an income tax modeled on the tax instituted in England. This was basically a tax on income, and not on property. The British theory was that you tax the income from property, and not the property itself (i.e., "tax the fruit, but not the tree.") Thus, gains or losses on sales of property were not subject to taxation.
- *1861–1873.* In 1861, the Union enacted the first federal income tax, designed to help finance the civil war. Tax rates were three percent on income exceeding $600 and less than $10,000, and five percent on income exceeding $10,000. The tax, though modest, did provide substantial funds for the war effort. After the war when the need for federal revenues decreased, Congress let the tax law expire in 1873.
- *1880.* During the 1870s, a number of individuals had challenged the validity of the federal income tax. In 1880, one of these cases had worked its way to the U.S. Supreme Court. In *Springer vs. U.S.,*[1] the taxpayer contended that the income tax on his professional earnings and personal property income violated the "direct tax" requirement of the Constitution. At this time, it was hard for the Supreme Court to be interested in a case involving a tax that expired seven years earlier, and perhaps to avoid the chaos that a decision for the taxpayer would generate, the Court unanimously sided with the government. In effect, the Supreme Court concluded that the income tax was an excise tax, and not a capitation tax (based on population) or a property tax.
- *1894.* By 1894, Congress's appetite for more revenues had increased, so a new tax law was passed that year. This was a controversial provision, and the law passed with the signature of President Grover Cleveland. The tax, though modest, received much more attention during times of peace.
- *1895.* Once again, a taxpayer challenged the legality of the income tax. In *Pollock v. Farmers' Loan and Trust Co.,*[2] a taxpayer sued the corporation in which he owned stock, contending that they should never have paid the income tax because it was unconstitutional. In this case, the tax was paid on income from land, and Pollock argued that since a tax on real estate is a direct tax, a tax on the income from such property must

---

[1]   *Springer vs. U.S.*, 102 US 586.
[2]   *Pollock v. Farmers' Loan and Trust Co.*, 158 US 601.

be a direct tax as well. And since the Constitution prohibits a direct tax unless certain conditions are met, the income tax should be declared unconstitutional. The direct tax argument was also used by *Springer* in 1880, but now the Court focused more closely on the possible conflict with the Constitution. The provision in question was Article 1, Section 9, Clause 4 of the Constitution. This clause stated the following:

1. "But all duties, imposts, and excises shall be uniform throughout the United States."
2. "No capitation, or other direct tax shall be laid, unless in proportion to a census or enumeration herein before to be taken."

In effect, this clause required any direct tax to be based on a census. For example, if the government desired to raise $10 million, and New York had 20 percent of the total U.S. population at that time, then New York would be required to raise $2 million. And if New York had 1 million residents, each resident would owe $2 in taxes. Obviously, a tax based on income could not achieve such proportionality, since incomes differed across individuals. This time, in a 5-4 decision, the Supreme Court ruled that the income tax was unconstitutional. A few days after the initial vote, the Court revoted and reached the same result. Thus, the tax law was ruled unconstitutional, and was effectively repealed.

- *1909.* Congress took two actions in 1909 to deal with their increasing revenue needs. First, they passed a corporate income tax, but labeled it an excise tax on the privilege of doing business. The tax was set at one percent on all incomes exceeding $5,000. Secondly, Congress passed the 16th Amendment, which would eliminate the apportionment requirement. This amendment reads as follows:

  > "The Congress shall have the power to lay and collect taxes on incomes from whatever source derived, without apportionment among the several states, and without regard to any census or enumeration."

- *1911.* The U.S. Supreme Court upheld the corporate "excise tax" as constitutional in *Flint v. Stone Tracey.*[3] The court ruled that the tax was a "special excise tax on the privilege of doing business."
- *1913.* The required three-fourths of the states ratified the 16th Amendment, thus adding the amendment to the constitution. Congress then immediately enacted the first "constitutional" tax law, the *Revenue Act of 1913*. The tax ranged from one percent on income exceeding $3,000 to seven percent on incomes exceeding $500,000. For the first time, this statute introduced the notion of a **progressive tax rate** structure (i.e., the tax rate increases as the base, income in this case, increases).
- *1916.* The U.S. Supreme Court upheld the progressive income tax as constitutional in *Brushaber v. Union Pacific Railroad Co.*[4]
- *1916–1939.* During this period, Congress passed a total of 17 different revenue acts devoted to taxation. These were all independent pieces of legislation, as Congress did not bother to eliminate inconsistencies, deadwood provisions, or modifications contained in prior acts. Thus, a person trying to find the answer to a tax question would need to search all 17 Acts. Congress solved this problem in 1939 by merging all of the acts into one cohesive body of tax law titled the *Internal Revenue Code of 1939*. The term "Code" was used to signify that all prior acts had been "codified" into a single location, with inconsistencies and deadwood provisions eliminated.
- *1954.* Following numerous amendments to the Code after 1939, Congress decided to once again reorganize the Code. Amendments were merged into the Code, the organization was changed to flow more logically, and the title was changed to the *Internal Revenue Code of 1954*.
- *1986.* Following major changes in the Code as part of the Tax Reform Act of 1986, Congress decided to change the name of the Code to the *Internal Revenue Code of*

---

[3] *Flint v. Stone Tracey,* 220 US 107.
[4] *Brushaber v. Union Pacific Railroad Co.*, SCt, 1 USTC ¶4, 240 US 1, 36 SCt 236.

1986. However, the organizational pattern of the 1954 re-codification was retained, so in essence the 1986 change was in name only.

- *1993, 1996, 2001, 2004.* Major tax legislation was enacted in each of these years, amending the Internal Revenue Code

This brief historical review provides insight into a number of current Code provisions encountered in tax practice. For example, when determining "earnings and profits" of a corporation for purposes of classifying dividends, no amounts prior to March 1, 1913, are included (this is the date of enactment for the *Revenue Act of 1913*). Similarly, if a taxpayer is forced by the IRS to make an accounting methods change, the cumulative adjustment to income required for such a change will not include any amounts generated prior to 1954 (the date of the second codification of the Code).

OBSERVATION	The 1954 re-codification involved an extensive reordering and renumbering of the Code. For example, Sec. 17(j) of the 1939 Code is now Code Sec. 1231 under the 1954 reorganization. Practitioners researching questions involving statutes enacted prior to 1954 need to cross-check Code reference numbers between the two codes. Most major tax services furnish tables providing these cross references.

¶1007   The Legislative Process

.01   INTRODUCTION

Benjamin Disraeli, a famous British politician of the 19th century, once commented that *"There are two things one should never watch: sausage-making and tax legislation."* The process is indeed complicated, and the path to final passage is often torturous and filled with back-room deals and hidden agendas. Nonetheless, taxes are an important part of everyday life today, and, as Justice Oliver Wendell Holmes once said, *"Taxes are the price we pay for a civilized society."*

It is important to understand how the legislative process operates, not only from a historical perspective but also from the need to understand how several by-products of the process are important sources of legislative authority. But before examining the process in detail, perhaps one question should be asked: Exactly what *is* a tax? How is a tax defined?

.03   DEFINITION OF A "TAX"

There have been many definitions of a tax over the years, but perhaps the most succinct and accurate definition was coined by Ray Sommerfeld years ago: *A tax is a nonpenal yet compulsory transfer remitted for the public good.*[5]

Each phrase in this definition is important. First of all, a tax is not a penalty; in theory, taxpayers receive something of value in return, such as those elements of a civilized society referred to by Justice Holmes. Secondly, even though we describe our tax system as a "voluntary self-assessment system," in reality the system becomes rather involuntary (fines, jail sentences, etc.) if one does not pay his or her share of taxes. So taxes are indeed compulsory transfers. Finally, the exact use of taxes collected by the government is not specified in advance; rather, such collections are used for the public good. The determination of the public good is made by Congress as part of the separate budget process.

.05   THE LEGISLATIVE PROCESS—ORIGINS OF A TAX BILL

Although individual members of Congress sometimes author important pieces of a comprehensive tax bill, as a practical matter the process is usually driven by the Administration currently in power. Generally, the staffs of the Department of Treasury are heavily

---

[5]   Sommerfeld, Ray, M, Hershel M. Anderson, and Horace Brock, *An Introduction to Taxation* (Harcourt Brace Jovanovich, Inc., 1967), 2.

involved in crafting the wishes of the Administration into tax policy, and the initial draft of the bill is presented by the Secretary of the Treasury to Congress. This large bureaucracy includes a number of highly-skilled economists, attorneys, accountants, statisticians, and other professionals.

There are other important players at the beginning of the legislative process. Perhaps more than any other group, the staffs of the two tax writing committees described below (House Ways and Means and Senate Finance Committees) have a major influence on tax legislation. These are bright, highly-skilled individuals with extensive tax knowledge, though generally not much practical experience. Each of these staffs number in excess of 100. In addition, various think tanks, nonprofit organizations and lobby groups manage to leave their imprints on tax legislation as well.

Another key player in the legislative process is the Joint Committee on Taxation (JCT). This committee has 10 members composed of the 5 ranking members of the House Ways and Means and Senate Finance Committees. But it is really the large and experienced staff of this committee that does the heavy lifting in the tax process. JCT staffers work with the two committees in drafting bills and committee reports. They also draft a final report on the new laws after enactment, generally referred to as the "Blue Book," which is discussed below.

OBSERVATION	All of these players in the tax process are sometimes referred to as the "kitchen bureau," in that all are trying to serve as cooks in the same kitchen.

.07 THE LEGISLATIVE PROCESS—THE HOUSE OF REPRESENTATIVES

Article 1, Section 7 of the Constitution requires that all tax bills originate in the House of Representatives. The first stop is the House Ways and Means Committee, the primary group devoted to revenue measures. This committee has had a varying number of members over the years, and (1) the membership is apportioned based on the relative numbers of the two parties in the house, and (2) the chair is from the majority party. **Figure 1** lists the members of the committee for the 113th Session of Congress, which began its two-year session in January, 2013.

OBSERVATION	Although the Constitution states that all revenue bills must originate in the House, this did not occur in 1982. In that year House Democrats insisted that if the Reagan Administration wanted to raise taxes that year, then they should start the bill in the Senate, which was controlled by the Republicans. Democrats were still smarting from the publicity given the Republicans for cutting taxes in 1981, and when a desperate need for raising revenues occurred in 1982 due to ballooning deficits, they wanted to make sure that the Republicans received "credit" for raising taxes.

The first order of business for the House Ways and Means Committee upon receiving a tax proposal is to call public hearings. Anyone can submit written testimony, but the Committee decides who will provide oral testimony. By tradition, the Secretary of the Treasury is the first person to testify on the proposed legislation.

Following the public hearings, the Ways and Means Committee "marks up" the bill and begins debate on the merits of the bill. These hearings are open to the public (including the cameras of *C-SPAN* and other organizations), although closed sessions are sometimes called for the real horse-trading phase of the process. Eventually, the Committee will vote on the bill, which at this stage may look very different than the "marker" that was laid down at the start of the process. If a simple majority passes the bill, it is sent on to the floor of the full House of Representatives. If the bill is defeated, it is essentially dead for this session of Congress.

Figure 1

Dave Camp, Michigan (Chair)	Sander Levin, Michigan (Ranking Member)
Sam Johnson, Texas	Charles B. Rangel, New York
Kevin Brady, Texas	Jim McDermott, Washington
Paul Ryan, Wisconsin	John Lewis, Georgia
Devin Nunes, California	Richard E. Neal, Massachusetts
Pat Tiberi, Ohio	Xavier Becerra, California
Dave G. Reichert, Washington	Lloyd Doggett, Texas
Charles W. Boustany, Jr., Louisiana	Mike Thompson, California
Peter J. Roskam, Illinois	John B. Larson, Connecticut
Jim Gerlach, Pennsylvania	Earl Blumenauer, Oregon
Tom Price, Georgia	Ron Kind, Wisconsin
Vern Buchanan, Florida	Bill Pascrell, Jr., New Jersey
Adrian Smith, Nebraska	Joseph Crowley, New York
Aaron Schock, Illinois	Allyson Schwartz, Pennsylvania
Lynn Jenkins, Kansas	Danny Davis, Illinois
Erik Paulsen, Minnesota	Linda Sanchez, California
Kenny Marchant, Texas	Diane Black, Tennessee
Tom Reed, New York	Todd Young, Indiana
Mike Kelly, Pennsylvania	Tim Griffin, Arkansas

One important byproduct of the process in the Ways and Means Committee is the *Ways and Means Committee Report*. This detailed report, required of both tax-writing committees in Congress, contains four sections: (1) a draft of the legislation, (2) reasons for the changes, (3) an explanation of the changes, and (4) an estimate of the revenue effects of the change. This report is an important document for purposes of attempting to determine Congressional intent, as it may be years before the IRS gets around to drafting regulations that interpret a particular Code provision.

The full House of Representatives generally debates a bill under a **closed rule**, whereby the only person who may amend the bill is a member of the Ways and Means Committee. If the bill is eventually passed, it is sent on to the Senate; if the bill fails, it is effectively killed for that legislative session.

It is important to recall that the House Ways and Means Committee Report summarizes the activities of the committee up to the point that the bill is sent to the House floor. If a tax researcher wants additional details concerning the debate in the House, reference must be made to the **Congressional Record**. This document has a record of all exchanges on the floor of the House.

.09   THE LEGISLATIVE PROCESS—THE SENATE

The first stop for legislation in the Senate is the Senate Finance Committee, the major revenue committee in the Senate. Once again, representation of the committee is proportionate to the full Senate membership, and the chair is always from the majority party. The current membership of this committee is disclosed in **Figure 2**.

The Senate Finance Committee more or less follows the same procedures used by the House Ways and Means Committee. However, there is no requirement that the Finance Committee start with the same bill that the House passed; in fact, it is a rare occurrence when they do. Public hearings are followed by a debate about the merits of the bill, and eventually a vote is taken. If the bill is passed by the Committee, it is sent to the floor of the full Senate.

Figure 2

113th Congress - Senate Finance Committee	
Democrats	**Republicans**
Max Baucus, Montana (Chair)	Charles E. Grassley, Iowa
John D. Rockefeller IV, West Virginia	Orrin G. Hatch, Utah
Benjamin L. Cardin, Maryland	John Thune, South Dakota
Sherrod Brown, Ohio	Richard Burr, North Carolina
Robert P. Casey, Pennsylvania	
Michael F. Bennet, Colorado	Mike Crapo, Indiana
Ron Wyden, Oregon	Pat Roberts, Kansas
Charles E. Schumer, New York	Johnny Isakson, Georgia
Debbie Stabenow, Michigan	Mike Enzi, Wyoming
Maria Cantwell, Washington	John Cornyn, Texas
Bill Nelson, Florida	Rob Portman, Ohio
Robert Menendez, New Jersey	Patrick J. Toomey, Pennsylvania
Thomas Carper, Delaware	

The Senate Finance Committee also issues a comprehensive report of its activities, the *Senate Finance Committee Report*. This report includes the same four sections as the *House Ways and Means Committee Report*: (1) a draft of the legislation, (2) reasons for the changes, (3) an explanation of the changes, and (4) an estimate of the revenue effects of the change. Just like the *Ways and Means Committee Report*, the *Senate Finance Committee Report* is an important document for attempting to determine Congressional intent, as it may be several years before regulations are issued.

The Senate debates the bill under an **open rule**, whereby any Senator may propose amendments to the bill. Eventually, the Senate will vote on a bill, and this piece of legislation may have little in common with the bill passed by the House. If the bill is defeated, as a practical matter it is a dead issue for the session. If the bill passes, the next series of events depends on how different the two tax bills are. If there are only minor differences in the two bills, the Senate version of the bill may be sent back to the House for a concurring vote, and if approved, this bill is sent to the President for a signature.

As was true with the House, any details regarding amendments made on the floor of the Senate will not be described in the Senate Finance Committee Report. Once again, the *Congressional Record* must be consulted for details.

OBSERVATION
It has sometimes been said the "Representatives represent the people, and Senators represent property." This view is given additional credence when one closely follows the legislative process. Because the Senate operates under an open rule, this may be the first chance for outsiders to influence the bill. Lobbyists are always waiting outside the Senate chamber for a chance to pitch their view of the bill. In fact, this area is sometimes called *Gucci Gulch*, a reference to the favored footwear of the lobbyists.

.11   THE LEGISLATIVE PROCESS—THE CONFERENCE COMMITTEE

In the vast majority of cases, the House and Senate bills are quite a bit different, necessitating a Conference Committee. The chairs of the House Ways and Means and the Senate Finance Committees each appoint representatives to this committee, which has the simple purpose of trying to draft compromise legislation. The Conference Committee has a varying number of members each year.

Until the 1986 Act, the chairs of the two tax-writing committees would generally make appointments to the Conference Committee based on seniority on the respective committees. However, when the 1986 Conference Committee was established, both chairs decided to appoint members that they believed would best represent their committee's interests in Conference. For that reason, two prominent names associated with tax policy, Bill Bradley, a senator from New Jersey, and Jack Kemp, a representative from New York, were appointed to the committee even though both were relatively fresh faces in Congress.

If the Conference Committee eventually crafts and passes a compromise tax bill, it is sent back to the House and Senate for a vote; after all, neither chamber of Congress had actually approved the compromise bill. If both houses pass the compromise, it is then sent to the President for a signature.

The Conference Committee also produces a final report of its work, simply called the *Conference Committee Report*. However, this report is not as comprehensive as the reports issued by the House Ways and Means and Senate Finance Committees. In many cases, the Committee adopts either the House or Senate version of a particular provision, and in such a case the *Conference Committee Report* merely refers the reader to the original committee report for details. If a compromise provision is drafted by the committee, the *Conference Committee Report* will include more detailed explanations.

.13   THE LEGISLATIVE PROCESS—THE PRESIDENTIAL SIGNATURE

Generally, there is a 10-day interval between the time that a bill is delivered to the President's desk and when he or she actually signs the bill. During this interim period, staffers on the Joint Committee of Taxation comb the bill carefully for any errors or inconsistencies, and Congress then votes on a Concurrent Resolution to ratify any needed corrections in the bill. The objective of this process is to make sure the President signs a tax bill that is as clean and error-free as possible.

The *Tax Reform Act of 1986* made major changes in the tax laws, in some cases upsetting members of Congress who saw provisions that they championed for their constituencies go away. When the Concurrent Resolution came up for a vote, a number of these unhappy members of Congress started proposing amendments to put their pet provisions back in the bill. As a result, the Concurrent Resolution started hemorrhaging revenue, which violated the "revenue neutrality" pledge that was part of the process in 1986. Revenue neutrality essentially required that final tax bill raise the same amount of total revenue as the tax law before the changes. So in the end, the Concurrent Resolution was not passed, President Reagan signed a bill with over 100 errors, and it was not until two years later that most of these errors were corrected.

Once the tax bill reaches the President's desk, he or she can take one of three actions: (1) sign the bill, at which point it becomes part of *Title 26* of the U.S. Code, (2) veto the bill, or (3) choose not to sign the bill, in which case the bill becomes law after ten days. If Congress adjourns within the ten-day period and the President does not sign the bill, the effect is the same as a veto; this occurrence is known as a **pocket veto**. In most cases, the effective date of the new legislation is the date that the President signs the bill, although in some cases retroactive dates are established for certain provisions; this is discussed later in this chapter.

.15 THE LEGISLATIVE PROCESS—THE JOINT COMMITTEE REPORT AND TECHNICAL CORRECTIONS

As mentioned earlier, The Joint Committee on Taxation issues a final report on the tax legislative process commonly called the "Blue Book" due to the color of the cover on the paperback edition. The Joint Committee on Taxation Report includes the same four elements that the Ways and Means Committee and Senate Finance Committee reports: (1) a draft of the legislation, (2) reasons for the changes, (3) an explanation of the changes, and (4) an estimate of the revenue effects of the change. All of these elements have changed as the bill moved through the process, so in many respects the Blue Book is the most accurate and comprehensive explanation of the new law. Nonetheless, many courts do not give it much weight as a source for determining Congressional intent, as explained later.

In some cases, major tax legislation is followed in the next year or two with a "Technical Corrections Act." No matter how many times staffers read and review a tax bill, errors will frequently slip through the net. And sometimes legislation has unintended consequences that no one could have foreseen. A technical corrections act is drafted to remedy these deficiencies. For example, the *Technical Corrections Act of 1988* was devoted to cleaning up more than 100 errors in the *Tax Reform Act of 1986* caused primarily by the failure of Congress to pass a Concurring Resolution that year.

¶1009 The Internal Revenue Code: A Closer Look

.01 TRACKING THE STAGES OF A TAX BILL

A tax bill is referred to in various manners as it winds its way through the legislative process. When a bill is first introduced in the House or the Senate, it is assigned a bill number. For example, a 2012 tax proposal when first introduced was referenced as follows in the House:

H.R. 3630, 112th Congress, 2nd Session (2012)

Once the bill passes either house, it can be called an Act and is given an official name. In recent years, the art of naming an Act has become somewhat political, with certain emotionally charged words as Jobs and Tax Relief featured in the title. This was the case in this 2012 legislation:

Middle Class Tax Relief and Job Creation Act of 2012

> **OBSERVATION**   Two recent examples of emotionally-charged names of tax acts:
> *Tax Relief, Unemployment Insurance Reauthorization, and Job Creation Act of 2010*
> *P. L. 110-141, Legislation to Exclude from Gross Income Payments from the Hokie Spirit Memorial Fund to the Victims of the Tragic Event at Virginia Polytechnic Institute & State University, 2007*

When an act becomes law, it is first published as a "slip law," given a Public Law number, and is then bound into the appropriate volume of the *United States Statutes at Large*. This 2012 legislation is titled as follows:

P. L. 112-96

> **OBSERVATION**   The first two digits in a Public Law number represent the session of Congress. These Congressional session numbers may be converted to the second calendar year of the session (each session lasts two years) by multiplying the session

> number by 2 and subtracting 212. For example, the 112th Session of Congress ended in 2012 [(112 × 2) – 212 = 12]. For sessions of Congress before 2000, the subtraction is only 112, and not 212. Thus, the 99th session ended in 1986 [(99 × 2) – 112 = 86].

Once the tax act is finally codified into the U.S. Code, the "official" full citation of the act can be quite cumbersome. For example, a complete citation of the 2012 Act is:

Middle Class Tax Relief and Job Creation Act of 2012, P.L. No. 112-96, 126 Stat. 156

.03 ORGANIZATION OF THE CODE

Just as the official title of a tax act can be somewhat cumbersome to remember, so can the Code location of a particular provision. As mentioned earlier, completed tax bills are added to Title 26 of the U.S. Code. But the Code has many titles, subtitles, chapters, subchapters, parts, subparts, etc. to remember. For example, the complete citation for the tax law devoted to computing tax liability for a married couple is disclosed in Figure 3.

Fortunately for tax researchers, there is one unique Code section for each provision of the federal income tax law. So as a practical matter, tax publications generally just refer to a Code section for reference purposes. For example, the provision illustrated in **Figure 3** would simply be Code Section 1.

Figure 3 also provides two examples of short-hand references for a particular Code section. One is simply an abbreviation (*Sec.*), and the other a symbol (§). And as discussed in Chapter 2, tax Regulations, the official interpretations of Code sections, use the Code section number as part of the referencing procedure for this tax authority.

OBSERVATION Although the unique section numbers in the Code provide for ease of reference, it is important to understand the various divisions within the Code. For example, a particular Code section may use the expression "for purposes of this subtitle" or "for purposes of this subpart". In such a case, it is important to know exactly where you are in the Code to know for sure if the provision is applicable to your tax question. It is a good idea to always refer to the Code index to see exactly what Code sections are included in the "subtitle" or "subpart" you are examining.

.05 GUIDES FOR READING AND INTERPRETING THE CODE

Two cardinal rules should always be followed in attempting to determine the answer to a federal tax question: (1) get the facts (GTF) and (2) read the code (RTC). A tax professional must have a firm grip on the facts of a particular case before beginning the research effort; otherwise, subtle differences or nuances may escape detection and lead to the wrong conclusion.

Figure 3

Organization of the Internal Revenue Code *Referencing the Internal Revenue Code and Regulations*

Internal Revenue Code:
The Internal Revenue Code is Title 26 of the United States Code. This portion of the Code contains the internal revenue laws as enacted by Congress. An example of a complete reference is the following, related to the tax computation of a married couple:

26. Title (Internal Revenue Title)
    A. Subtitle (Income Taxes)
    1. Chapter (Normal Taxes and Surtaxes)
        A. Subchapter A (Determination of Tax Liability)
           I. Subpart (Tax on Individuals)
               1. Section (Tax Imposed)
                   (a) *Subsection (Married individuals . . .)*
                       (1) *Paragraph*
                           (A) *Subparagraph*
                               (1) *Clause*

Example of a common reference for citation purposes:

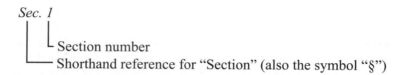

Sec. 1
Section number
Shorthand reference for "Section" (also the symbol "§")

Treasury Regulations:

Treasury regulations are the Department of the Treasury's official interpretation of the Internal Revenue Code. Regulations are numbered to correspond to the section of the Code being interpreted. These regulations are found in Title 26 of the Code of Federal Regulations.

Example of a common reference for citation purposes:

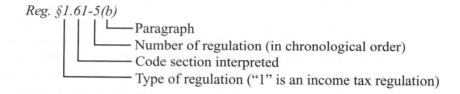

Reg. §1.61-5(b)
Paragraph
Number of regulation (in chronological order)
Code section interpreted
Type of regulation ("1" is an income tax regulation)

The importance of reading the Code cannot be emphasized enough; every answer to a tax question must somehow relate directly to the ultimate primary authority, the Internal Revenue Code. In tax practice there is a temptation to examine the "easy to read" secondary authorities first when trying to find the answer to a question. But these are only interpretations, and if the answer is in the Code itself, the interpretations are irrelevant. Courts have consistently emphasized that their purpose is to interpret the law, and not legislate. This view is illustrated in the following case quotes:

- ***Huntsberry v. Commissioner.***[6] "Unequivocal evidence of legislative purpose is required before the court will override the plain meaning of the statutory language."
- ***Strogoff v. United States.***[7] "The context from which the meaning of a word is taken must be the words of the statute itself."
- ***Woods v. Commissioner.***[8] "To glean the meaning of the words used by Congress, we must first look to the ordinary or settled meaning of the words used to convey its intent."
- ***American Automobile Association.***[9] "The validity of the long established policy of the Court in deferring, where possible, to Congressional procedures in the tax field is clearly indicated in this case."

---

[6] *Huntsberry*, 83 TC 742 (1984).
[7] *Strogoff*, 86-2 USTC ¶9616, 10 ClsCt 584.
[8] *Woods*, 91 TC 11.
[9] *American Automobile Association*, SCt 61-2 USTC ¶9517, 367 US 687.

¶1009.05

- *Eisner v. MaComber.*[10] "And, as this court has so often said, the high prerogative of declaring an Act of Congress invalid, should never be exercised except in a clear case."

When reading and interpreting the Code, it is important to read the language closely, constantly being on the lookout for definitions, cross references, and connectors. For example, *Code Sec. 280A(c)* addresses the office in the home deduction, and one of the key words in that provision is in subsection (c)(1)(B), the word "or". Thus, a home office will qualify if any one of the three conditions is met. This connector was also used as a justification for modifying Code Sec. 280A in 1997; this will be discussed in Chapter 6.

OBSERVATION	Definitions can be extremely important in interpreting the Code. In some cases, the definitions of key terms are contained in the statute; in other cases the researcher may need to check a key word index for the Code to find the definition (e.g., Code Sec. 152 defines a "dependent" for tax purposes). Additionally, *Code Sec. 7701* is titled "Definitions" and contains over 50 definitions of common terms used in the Code, such as "person" and "corporation."

In summary, the words used in the Code must be interpreted in their everyday meaning. Furthermore, if the Code is clear on an issue, there is no need to go any further.

.07 TAX ACT PROVISIONS THAT ARE NOT CODIFIED

A common misperception about the Internal Revenue Code is the notion that every part of a tax act is added to the Internal Revenue Code. In reality, a number of provisions do not make it into the Code; these include transition rules, effective dates, and sunset provisions.

Most of the transition rules affect only a few taxpayers and are of short duration. For example, in order to obtain support from certain members of Congress, special rules may be enacted to "soften" the landing of certain constituents who are losing existing tax benefits because of either new provisions or a repeal of old provisions. This has led to such legislation as the "Gallo Amendment," designed to help the famous vineyard family adjust to a change in the estate tax law.

Also, the transition rules are also the favorite vehicle for Congress to dole out special political favors to constituents. This is an action that members of Congress would prefer to be shielded from public scrutiny.

In some cases, new provisions are effective for only a limited period of time, or an old provision is being phased out over a limited period of time. In these cases, Congress may keep these effective dates out of the Code in order to avoid confusion and to keep the Code relatively clean. In such a case, the researcher must refer to the Act, and not the Code, for the details on these effective dates. These transition rules are often difficult to locate.

Effective Dates

Generally, most provisions contained in a new tax act become effective on the date that the President signs the Act into law. For example, President Obama signed the American Taxpayer Relief Act of 2012 on January 2, 2013, and this is the effective date unless stated differently in the Act.

In some cases, the effective date may be prospective; for example, a new provision may not take effect until the following tax year. In other cases, a provision may be retroactive to a date specified by Congress. In many cases, a retroactive date is the first day the provision was discussed in Congress; that way, taxpayers are prevented from "planning around" the new law before it takes effect.

---

[10] *Eisner v. Macomber*, 252 US 159.

¶1011   Evaluating and Locating Legislative Authority

.01   CONSTITUTION

The Constitution is the ultimate tax authority; if a statute is found to violate the Constitution, it will be declared invalid. Recall the *Pollock* case mentioned earlier in the tax history; this was the only successful challenge to the constitutionality of our tax laws, and this occurred in 1895.

OBSERVATION   There are a number of authors and speakers who make a living by selling products and information that "proves" that the tax law is unconstitutional, and if you will just follow their advice, you will not have to pay taxes. Obviously, none of these schemes have ever worked. Interestingly, the IRS recently did a study on these authors and commentators and found that over 95 percent of them actually do file and pay their own taxes; they know better than to follow their own advice.

The 1895 challenge in the *Pollock* case was the *last* successful challenge on the constitutionality of the federal income tax. And yet, there are always gullible individuals who believe various authors and speakers when they assert that the income tax is unconstitutional and does not have to be paid. A recent case in point was the actor Wesley Snipes, who bought into the notorious "861 argument" of a leading tax protestor. *Code Sec. 861* states that foreign-source wages of U.S. citizens are taxable, and the protest movement argues that since this section does not mention U.S. wages, they must not be taxable! At trial, Mr. Snipes changed his defense to argue that he was "duped" by the tax protestors. Although Mr. Snipes was not found guilty of tax fraud, he was convicted on three counts of failure to file a tax return on income exceeding $10 million (payment for two sequel films in the *Blade* series). The interest and penalties alone on this $10 million deficiency may very well exceed $10 million.

A copy of the Constitution is included in Volume 1 of the U.S. Code. Most tax services, both print and online, also offer copies of the Constitution.

ON THE WEB   The Constitution is available free of charge online at the following locations:
http://www.usconstitution.net
http://www.archives.gov/exhibits/charters/constitution.html

.03   THE INTERNAL REVENUE CODE

As a practical matter, the Internal Revenue Code is the final tax authority for most matters, as long as the Constitution is not violated. As a result, the answer to any tax question must first be tied to a provision of the Code, as statutory authority is always controlling. Interpretations such as Regulations and court cases may help understand how a Code provision is applied, but the ultimate authority is still the Code.

The Internal Revenue Code is available as Title 26 of the United States Code, and is also reprinted in most tax services, both print and online editions. The major publishers also sell hard copy editions as separate volumes, either as one volume by the Research Institute of America (RIA) and two volumes by CCH (a Wolters Kluwer business).

ON THE WEB	The Code is available free of charge online at the following locations:
	http://uscode.house.gov
	http://www.law.cornell.edu/uscode/26

.05   TAX ACTS

As mentioned earlier, not all provisions of a Tax Act are eventually codified. For that reason, it is frequently necessary to examine the full Act, especially for effective dates, transition rules, and sunset provisions. The full text of a tax act is published by the Government Printing Office, and is usually offered as a paperback supplement for most paper tax services.

ON THE WEB	Most tax acts are offered free of charge at the following sites on the worldwide web:
	http://www.loc.gov
	http://thomas.loc.gov

.07   TAX TREATIES

Tax treaties are another source of legislative authority that has not been discussed thus far in this chapter. In general, the President of the United States may enter into a treaty with any other country, and such treaty is considered having the force and effect of law once it is approved with the advice and consent of the Senate (a two-thirds vote is required). Most treaties are designed to eliminate the double taxation of income, either for a U.S. citizen working abroad or for a citizen of another country working in the United States.

The courts generally tend to give equal weight to both the Code and treaties. When the two are in conflict, courts usually assume that the one adopted later controls. In addition, other agreements between the United States and other countries, such as the North American Free Trade Act (NAFTA), though technically not treaties, may have the effect of a treaty for tax purposes.

The full texts of treaties are sometimes difficult to find. Commerce Clearing House and Warren Gorham Lamont offer Tax Treaty Services, and treaties may be found in the United States Code Annotated published by West Publishing Company. The IRS currently provides links to tax treaties at *http://www.irs.gov/Businesses/International-Businesses/United-States-Income-Tax-Treaties---A-to-Z.*

.09   COMMITTEE REPORTS

As discussed earlier, the committee reports of the various tax committees (House Ways and Means, Senate Finance, and Conference) are useful indicators of Congressional intent. These reports may be the only interpretation until regulations are enacted.

However, at all times, it must be remembered that legislative history may be used to solve Congressional ambiguity, and not create it. Committee reports may not be used to overturn the plain meaning of the words in the statute itself. Of the three documents, the Conference Committee Report is usually accorded greater weight since it summarizes the final product of Congress. But in many cases this document merely refers the reader to one of the other two committee reports if the final provision is close (or the same) in wording to the original proposal in one of the houses.

Earlier it was mentioned that the **Joint Committee on Taxation Report (the Blue Book)** is often regarded as the most comprehensive and lucid explanation of a new tax law. Nonetheless, over the years courts have traditionally accorded this document less weight than other sources, since it is not written "contemporaneously" with the legislative process. Recall that the Joint Committee does not have a legislative function; it serves as an interpretive body only. More importantly, there is no opportunity for Congress or anyone else involved in the legislative process to rebut the Blue Book's conclusions.

However, two recent events have tended to provide more authority to the Blue Book. First, the Blue Book is now listed as "substantial authority" for purposes of avoiding the Code Sec. 6662 penalty discussed later in the chapter. Second, the U.S. Supreme Court stated the following in *FPC v. Memphis Light*,[11] concerning the Blue Book: "It provides a compelling contemporary indication of the legislation's effect."

Full-text copies of the various committee reports are printed in the weekly Internal Revenue Bulletin after the tax legislation is passed, and are printed again in the Cumulative Bulletin that is compiled at the end of the year. (There is one exception—the IRS chose not to reprint the 888 pages of the committee reports accompanying the 1954 recodification.) Committee reports for years prior to 1939 are reprinted in the 1939 cumulative bulletin. In addition, most tax services provide all committee reports in paperback form with print services and on their websites.

ON THE WEB   Committee reports may be found on the following websites on the Worldwide Web:
http://www.jct.gov
http://waysandmeans.house.gov
http://finance.senate.gov
http://thomas.loc.gov

There are two other valuable print services that offer access to selected portions of committee reports for legislation enacted prior to 1954. One is J.S. Seidman, *Legislative History of Federal Income Tax Laws, 1861-1938, 1939-1953* (6 volumes).[12] This service organizes pre-1954 legislation by Code section and/or topic, and provides cross-reference tables for converting 1954 code section numbers to 1939 code section numbers and vice versa. A second source is Walter E. Barton and Carroll W. Browning, *Federal Tax Laws Correlated.*[13]

.11   THE CONGRESSIONAL RECORD

The *Congressional Record* is the only source for determining legislative intent on amendments made on the floor of the House or Senate. The relevant discussion must be located by the day of the debate, no easy task. However, there is no other alternative to locating this information.

An important part of this document in regard to a discussion of tax law changes is the presence of *colloquies* and *floor statements*. These represent discussions between members of Congress and the managers (from the Joint Committee) of a tax bill that are intended to clarify specific provisions. These discussions are inserted into the *Congressional Record*. As a general rule, colloquies and floor statements may be relied on only in the event the statute or Committee reports fail to yield any insight into Congressional intent or actions.

There is some question as to how much weight should be accorded to colloquies and floor statements. As a general rule, the following guidelines apply:

- Similar colloquies in both houses is strong affirmation of Congressional intent.
- A colloquy given affirmation by the tax-writing committee chair (or the author of the bill) is given the greatest weight.
- Colloquies and floor statements made *before* a vote are given much greater weight than those given *after* a vote.

Most libraries provide access to the *Congressional Record*, either through print services, microfiche, or online services such as the LEXIS and WESTLAW electronic libraries.

---

[11] *Federal Power Commission v. Memphis Light*, SCt 73-1 USTC ¶9412, 411 US 458, 93 SCt 1723.

[12] J.S. Seidman, *Legislative History of Federal Income Tax Laws, 1861-1938, 1939-1953.* Prentice-Hall, Inc. (Englewood Cliffs, N.J.: 1954).

[13] Walter E. Barton and Carroll W. Browning, *Federal Tax Laws Correlated.* Warren Gorham & Lamont (Boston: 1969).

ON THE WEB	The Historical Congressional Record Index may be accessed through the Government Printing Office (GPO) site at the following location: *http://www.gpo.gov*

.13 CONGRESSIONAL HEARINGS

Public hearings of the House Ways and Means Committee and the Senate Finance Committee yield very little in terms of tax authority. Hearings records typically provide insight into the problems, but not necessarily the legislative solutions. For that reason, hearings records tend to be given little if any weight by the Courts.

Most libraries provide access to Congressional hearings, either with print volumes from the Government Printing Office or online with a LEXIS or WESTLAW subscription.

ON THE WEB	The Historical Congressional Record Index may be accessed through the Government Printing Office (GPO) site: *http://www.gpo.gov*

.15 PENDING LEGISLATION AND UNENACTED LEGISLATION

Questions inevitably arise concerning the weight given to pending legislation, particularly technical corrections that appear certain to be enacted by Congress. The IRS official position is that no reliance can be made on pending legislation until the provisions have actually been signed into law. However, the IRS has sometimes considered pending legislation when issuing private letter rulings.[14]

OBSERVATION	Sometimes the old axiom "No good deed goes unpunished" also applies to tax professionals who try to do the right thing. For example, in 1986 Congress revised the alternative minimum tax (AMT) rules for individuals, and in doing so forgot to continue the required adjustment for personal exemption deductions, since such amounts are not allowed for the AMT. Everyone knew that Congress would eventually correct this oversight and apply the change retroactively, so some firms went ahead and made the adjustment anyway on 1987 returns. Much to their dismay, the returns were bounced by the IRS, who said that the law does not read that way. So the returns were filed a second time, this time without the adjustment, and, oh yes, then refiled a third time in 1988 after Congress made the technical correction!

Unenacted Legislation

At first blush, it is difficult to understand how legislation that was *not* enacted could have any relevance whatsoever to a tax researcher. The answer is that, if nothing else, unenacted legislation tells one what Congress did not intend to enact. There is some value in knowing that Congress considered such an interpretation and consciously decided not to enact that interpretation.

The concept of unenacted legislation is also relevant in explaining an argument sometimes used by taxpayers and occasionally by the IRS. This defense is termed "legislative reenactment," and describes a situation where the IRS or the courts have issued an interpretation of a particular law and Congress has a chance to change the interpretation (in subsequent legislation) but chooses not to. Thus, the IRS or court interpretation is "legislatively reenacted." Generally, taxpayers have had little success in sustaining such arguments, since silence is not necessarily agreement.

---

[14] For example, *see* Ltr. Rul. 88020045.

¶1013   "Substantial Authority" in Tax Controversies

The Internal Revenue Code contains a number of penalties that may be applied to tax professionals for certain actions. However, in some cases these penalties will not apply if the tax professional has "substantial authority" for the position taken on the tax return. This is discussed in detail in Chapter 9.

.01   SUBSTANTIAL AUTHORITY

One of the more common penalties potentially applicable to taxpayers is the "substantial understatement" penalty of *Code Sec. 6662*. This penalty is equal to 20 percent of the understatement; however, it may be reduced if there is "substantial authority" for the treatment of the item.

For purposes of reducing the amount of understatement of income tax subject to the "substantial understatement penalty," *Reg. §1.6662-4(d)* and *Notice 90-20* (1990-1 CB 328) define **substantial authority** to include the following:

1. The Internal Revenue Code and other statutes
2. Regulations (final, temporary, and proposed)
3. Court cases
4. Tax treaties
5. Statements of Congressional intent, including:
   a. House Ways and Means Committee Reports
   b. Senate Finance Committee Reports
   c. Joint Conference Committee Reports
   d. Congressional Record
   e. Joint Committee on Taxation Report (the "Blue Book")
6. Administrative pronouncements, including:
   a. Revenue Rulings
   b. Revenue Procedures
   c. Private Letter Rulings (PLRs)
   d. Technical Advice Memoranda (TAMs)
   e. Actions on Decisions (AODs)
   f. General Counsel Memoranda (GCMs)
   g. Notices, Press Releases, and similar documents

The Internal Revenue Service does have the power to except certain authorities from this list. At least once a year, the IRS must publish in the Federal Register a list of positions it believes lack substantial authority and that affect a significant number of taxpayers. However, this does not mean that substantial authority exists for positions not included on the list.

¶1015   Summary

- A tax bill must work its way through the House Ways and Means Committee, the Senate Finance Committee, the Joint Conference Committee, and passage by both the House and Senate before being sent to the President for his signature.
- The Constitution, Internal Revenue Code, and tax treaties are the three main sources of legislative authority.
- The Internal Revenue Code contains the tax laws passed by Congress and is the highest level of authority in most tax research issues.

Review Questions for Chapter 1

True or False

Indicate which of the following statements are true or false by circling the correct answer.

1. An article in the *Journal of Taxation* is an example of secondary authority.   T   F

2. All answers to a tax question must necessarily be traced back to secondary tax authority.   T   F

3. A decision of the U.S. Supreme Court is an example of administrative tax authority.   T   F

4. The Senate Finance Committee Report is an example of legislative authority.   T   F

5. Under the early British income tax laws that were duplicated in the United States in the 1800s, gains and losses on property were includible in the tax base.   T   F

6. In *Springer vs. U.S.*, the federal income tax was found to be unconstitutional by the Supreme Court.   T   F

7. The corporate income tax enacted in 1909, labeled as an "excise tax on the privilege of doing business," was later ruled unconstitutional.   T   F

8. The U.S. House of Representatives generally debates a tax bill under a "closed rule," allowing amendments only by Ways and Means Committee members.   T   F

9. A Conference Committee bill must generally be voted on once again by both houses of Congress.   T   F

10. *Reg. §1.263-4* refers to the fourth section of the first regulation issued on *Code Sec. 263* of the Internal Revenue Code.   T   F

Fill in the Blanks

Fill in each blank with the appropriate word or phrase that completes each sentence.

11. A decision of the 5th Circuit Court of Appeals is an example of _____ (primary, secondary) tax authority.

12. _____ authority refers to authority as enacted by the U.S. Congress.

13. The first truly national income tax in the U.S. was used to fund the _____.

14. The U.S. income tax was ruled unconstitutional in 1895 because the Supreme Court ruled that it was a _____ tax, requiring apportionment by a census.

15. The _____ Amendment to the Constitution eliminated the apportionment requirement for the federal income tax.

16. The second codification of the U.S. tax laws occurred in _____.

17. The Constitution requires that all revenue bills originate in the _____.

18. For an explanation of changes to a tax bill that occurred on the floor of the Senate, reference must be made to the _____.

19. A(n) _____ occurs if Congress adjourns within the 10-day period that the President is considering a tax bill, and the President does not sign the bill.

20. In the broadest sense, the ultimate tax authority is the _____.

Multiple Choice

Circle the best answer for each of the following questions.

21. Which of the following is not a category of primary tax authority?
    a.   judicial authority
    b.   administrative authority
    c.   procedural authority
    d.   legislative authority

22. Which of the following is not a traditional component of tax practice?
    a.   tax planning
    b.   tax research
    c.   tax compliance
    d.   tax accounting

23. A Revenue Procedure issued by the IRS is an example of:
    a. legislative authority
    b. administrative authority
    c. judicial authority
    d. none of the above

24. The first "codification" of the U.S. income tax laws occurred in:
    a.   1913
    b.   1921
    c.   1939
    d.   1954

25. Which of the following is not a part of the final reports of the Ways and Means Committee or the Senate Finance Committee?
    a.   explanation of the changes
    b.   transcripts of oral testimony to the committee on proposed law changes
    c.   estimate of the revenue effects of the changes
    d.   reasons for the changes

26. A Presidential veto may be overridden only by an affirmative vote of:
    a.   a simple majority of both houses of Congress
    b.   a two-thirds majority of both houses of Congress
    c.   a three-fourths majority of both houses of Congress
    d.   none of the above

27. The final comprehensive report issued that explains recently-enacted tax legislation is the:
    a.   Conference Committee Report
    b.   Congressional Record
    c.   Senate Finance Committee Report
    d.   Joint Committee on Taxation Report

28. P. L. 110-43 would have been enacted in the session of Congress that ended in the year:
    a.   1996
    b.   2000
    c.   2008
    d.   2010

29. The short-hand method of referencing a particular part of the Internal Revenue Code is to cite the:
   a. subtitle number
   b. chapter number
   c. subchapter number
   d. section number

30. Tax Act provisions that may not be added to the Internal Revenue Code itself can include:
   a. effective dates
   b. sunset provisions
   c. transition rules
   d. any of the above

Review Problems

31. Give two examples of each of the following: (a) primary tax authority and (b) secondary authority.
32. List the three basic types of tax authority, and provide an example of each one.
33. What is the importance of each of the following dates in U.S. tax history: 1861, 1895, 1913, 1939, and 1954?
34. What was the U.S. Supreme Court's rationale for declaring the federal income tax unconstitutional in the *Pollock v. Farmers' Loan and Trust Co.* case of 1895?
35. Explain how Congress "fixed" the apportionment problem with regards to the federal income tax in 1909.
36. Define the term "codification," and list the major codifications of the Internal Revenue Code. Why are these dates sometimes important in researching a federal tax question?
37. Explain the basic steps that a tax bill follows in both the House Ways and Means Committee and the Senate Finance Committee. Do both houses of Congress also follow the same procedures when debating a bill on the floor of the entire legislative body? Explain.
38. Why is the Conference Committee Report typically much smaller in size than either the House Ways and Means Committee Report or the Senate Finance Committee Report. Explain.
39. What are the President's options when a tax bill reaches his or her desk?
40. Why are the courts sometimes hesitant to cite the "Blue Book" (Joint Committee on Taxation Report) as authority? Explain.
41. Explain how to convert the following public law numbers to the last year of the legislative session generating the law: P. L. 98-200 and P. L. 107-420.
42. Since each "section" of the Code has a unique Section number, is it necessary to be concerned about broader subdivisions, such as Subchapter, Chapter, and Part?
43. Do all provisions of a tax act eventually end up in the Internal Revenue Code? Explain.
44. "The role of the courts is to interpret the law, and not make the law." Do you agree? Explain.
45. How much weight should be given to colloquies and floor statements? Explain.

Research Questions

46. Which subchapter of the Code contains *Code Sec. 303*?
47. How is a "dependent" defined for purposes of *Code Sec. 119(a)*?
48. *Code Sec. 408* was amended several years ago to allow tax-free distributions from IRAs to charity. Which Act of Congress made this change, and when was the change effective?
49. Refer to Code Sec. 408(d)(8). Is the exclusion from income available for all IRA owners, regardless of their age? What was the initial expiration date for this provision? What is the current expiration date for this exclusion and what most recent Act of Congress made the change to extend the expiration date?
50. *Code Sec. 317* defines the term "property." Is this definition of property to be used for other sections of the Code, such as Code Sec. 1001? Explain.

51. What is the title of Section 5 of *P. L. 110-42*?
52. What was the purpose of *P. L. 110-176*?
53. When was Code Sec. 36B added to the code and what was the Act that added this provision?
54. How did the Technical Corrections Act of 2007 modify Code Sec. 53(e)(2) of the Internal Revenue Code?

CHAPTER 2

Administrative Sources of Authority

Learning Objectives

1. Identify the sources of administrative authority.
2. Differentiate between the different types of Regulations.
3. Describe the various types of IRS pronouncements.

¶2001 Introduction

Administrative sources of authority are a second type of primary authority. This authority is derived from the executive branch, the "Administration." In the tax area, the primary administrative authority is the product of the efforts of the Department of Treasury, primarily through one of its divisions, the Internal Revenue Service. The IRS is specifically charged by the Secretary of the Treasury to enforce the regulations.

The Treasury Department is responsible for the enforcement of tax statutes and the collection of tax revenue. Many of the Treasury's administrative functions are delegated to the Internal Revenue Service. To facilitate the administration of tax law, the IRS issues a variety of official pronouncements, the most important of which are discussed in this chapter.

¶2003 An Introduction to Administrative Authority

.01 DELEGATION OF AUTHORITY

Code Sec. 7805(a) charges the Treasury Department with the overall administration of the Internal Revenue Code:

> Except where such authority is expressly given by this title to any person other than an officer or employee of the Treasury Department, the Secretary shall prescribe all needful rules and regulations for the enforcement of this title, including all rules and regulations as may be necessary by reason of any alteration of law in relation to internal revenue.

The "Secretary" referred to above is the Secretary of the Treasury, a member of the President's cabinet (and not the Treasurer, another official not connected with tax matters). Although the Secretary is granted this broad authority, as a practical matter, most administrative pronouncements are written by staff of the Internal Revenue Service (a division of the Department of Treasury) or the office of the Chief Counsel of the IRS (the Assistant General Counsel of the Treasury Department). The IRS is headed by a Commissioner, who is appointed by the President.

.03 SOURCES OF ADMINISTRATIVE AUTHORITY

The primary sources of administrative authority are the Regulations (published by the government). Other important sources of authority published by the government include Revenue Rulings and Revenue Procedures. Several other administrative pronouncements are produced by the IRS but not published by the government. Chief among these documents are the private letter rulings and technical advice memorandums.

¶2005 Regulations

.01 IMPORTANCE OF REGULATIONS

Final Regulations represent the Treasury and the IRS's ultimate interpretation of the Code. As a rule, Regulations are generally more "readable" than the Code. These are issued under the signature of the Secretary of the Treasury. Because these Regulations are issued with the imprimatur of the Secretary of the Treasury, the IRS Commissioner and staff are bound by the Regulations even if they do not agree with them.

As discussed later, Regulations generally have the force and effect of law, as long as they are reasonable and consistent interpretations of the Code. But since most regulations are interpretive in nature, courts occasionally overturn regulations that they believe do not properly interpret Congressional intent.

.03 CLASSIFICATIONS OF REGULATIONS

Regulations may be grouped by type into one of the three categories:

1. *Interpretive Regulations.* These regulations attempt to clarify the provisions of a particular Code section. The bulk of regulations issued are interpretive in nature.
2. *Legislative Regulations.* In some cases, Congress directs the IRS to in effect perform a law-making function and to specify the substantive requirements of a particular provision. This is generally done when Congress chooses not to delve into highly technical issues. An example would be the detailed requirements found in the Regulations for filing a consolidated tax return. These regulations tend to be accorded a higher level of authority than interpretive regulations.
3. *Procedural Regulations.* These regulations specify detailed procedural rules for various aspects of tax practice, including filing requirements and prerequisites for

making certain elections under the Code. Procedural Regulations are generally denoted with a prefix of "15" or "301" in the citation system for Regulations.

.05 ## REGULATIONS—PROPOSED AND FINAL REGULATIONS

At the beginning of the year, the Treasury schedules Regulation projects for the year. A task force is formed for each Regulation project, consisting principally of attorneys, economists, and CPAs in the Chief Counsel's office. Regulation projects take several years to bear results in most cases, and there is a large backlog of regulation projects (some going back to the Tax Reform Act of 1986 and even earlier).

Once the task force completes a draft of a regulation, it is published in *The Federal Register* as a Proposed Treasury Decision (TD). Interested parties are given 30 days to comment (in writing or orally) on the **Proposed Regulations**. As long as a Regulation is a Proposed Regulation, it does not have the force and effect of law of a Final Regulation. Nonetheless, the Proposed Regulation provides clues as to the IRS position on an issue, and should be considered when contemplating future transactions.

After the comment period, the IRS may (1) issue a final regulation as a TD and publish such in *The Federal Register*, (2) withdraw the proposed Regulation for further work and then reissue as a Final Regulation, or (3) withdraw the Regulation and suspend work on the project. In many cases, lengthy delays develop in the process in the latter two scenarios.

OBSERVATION   Most Regulations include lengthy preambles which "preview" the Regulations and discuss reasons for any changes from the Proposed Regulations. These preambles may provide useful insights, and in some cases have been cited in court cases.

Final Regulations are published in the Federal Register as a Treasury Decision (TD), and then published in the weekly *Internal Revenue Bulletin* (and subsequently in the semi-annual *Cumulative Bulletin*). The date of publication in the *Federal Register* is the release date. An example of a final regulation is illustrated in **Figure 1**.

OBSERVATION   The *Internal Revenue Bulletin* is the primary communications vehicle used by the IRS. For example, new Regulations are published in the weekly bulletin as Treasury Decisions (TDs). At the end of the year, the weekly bulletins are consolidated into a *Cumulative Bulletin*, so that all publications of the same type (e.g., Revenue Rulings, Revenue Procedures, etc.) can be grouped together logically. In terms of print volumes, it usually takes two or three volumes to consolidate the weekly bulletins, and for that reason cites to the Cumulative Bulleting for various authorities such are rulings and procedures may read 2011-1 CB, 2011-2 CB, etc.

.07 ## TEMPORARY REGULATIONS

Temporary Regulations are Regulations issued by the IRS without the normal comment period and are generally effective on the date of issuance. These Regulations are "fast lane" guidance, in that most are drafted in response to a law change or a judicial decision that requires immediate guidance. Generally, such Regulations are issued when the requirements for public notice are impracticable, unnecessary, or contrary to the public interest.

Code Sec. 7805(e), added in 1998, now requires that Temporary Regulations also be issued as Proposed Regulations at the same time, and the Temporary Regulations automatically expire three years after issuance. Temporary Regulations are considered to be authoritative until they are superceded by Final Regulations. As a rule, Temporary Regulations should be treated with the same authority as final regulations.

OBSERVATION   Although there is currently a three-year sunset rule on temporary regulations that are issued as proposed regulations, no such limit applies to old proposed regulations. In some cases, proposed regulations that are more than 20 years old are still around.

Figure 1—Example Regulation

Regulation § 1.61-14. Miscellaneous items of gross income.

(a) In general. In addition to the items enumerated in section 61(a), there are many other kinds of gross income. For example, punitive damages such as treble damages under the antitrust laws and exemplary damages for fraud are gross income. Another person's payment of the taxpayer's income taxes constitutes gross income to the taxpayer unless excluded by law. Illegal gains constitute gross income. Treasure trove, to the extent of its value in United States currency, constitutes gross income for the taxable year in which it is reduced to undisputed possession.

(b) Cross references.
- *(1)* Prizes and awards, see section 74 and regulations thereunder;
- *(2)* Damages for personal injury or sickness, see section 104 and the regulations thereunder;
- *(3)* Income taxes paid by lessee corporation, see section 110 and regulations thereunder;
- *(4)* Scholarships and fellowship grants, see section 117 and regulations thereunder;
- *(5)* Miscellaneous exemptions under other acts of Congress, see section 122;
- *(6)* Tax-free covenant bonds, see section 1451 and regulations thereunder.
- *(7)* Notional principal contracts, see §1.446-3.

(T.D. 6272, 11/25/57 , amend T.D. 6856, 10/19/65, T.D. 8491, 10/8/93)

.09   PRECEDENT VALUE OF REGULATIONS

Generally, Legislative Regulations should be treated as having the force and effect of law, since the law-making function is in effect delegated to the IRS by Congress. Interpretive Regulations should also generally be treated as having the force and effect of law, unless they conflict with the statute. In the latter case, courts have not been hesitant to overturn Regulations if the court believes that the IRS is not correctly interpreting Congressional intent. For example, see *Professional Equities, Inc.,*[1] where the Tax Court overturned Regulations concerning the treatment of wraparound mortgages in determining first-year gain on an installment sale.

In some cases, the IRS may continue to follow a Regulation that has been ruled invalid by a court; since the only decision that the IRS *must* absolutely follow is a U.S. Supreme Court decision. The IRS may continue its interpretation in hopes of winning the issue in another circuit so that perhaps the Supreme Court will consider the issue.

OBSERVATION   In April and October of each year, the IRS publishes a *Semi-Annual Agenda of Regulations*. This document indicates all Code sections for which new regulations are under development or existing regulations that are to be reviewed. In addition, this summary provides information on the current status of all Regulations projects in progress. This document is published in the Federal Register each year.

---

[1] *Professional Equities*, 89 TC 165.

¶2005.09

.11   EFFECTIVE DATE OF REGULATIONS

Generally, Code Sec. 7805(b) states that a Regulation should be effective on the date in which such Regulation is filed with the Federal Register. However, the same statute states that Regulations can be applied *retroactively* in the following situations:

- The Regulation is issued within 18 months of the underlying statute being interpreted.
- The Regulation is designed to prevent taxpayer abuse.
- The Regulation corrects a procedural defect in the issuance of a prior Regulation.
- The Regulation relates to internal Treasury Department policies, practices, or procedures.
- The Regulation may apply retroactively by Congressional directive.
- The Commissioner has the power to allow taxpayers to elect to apply new Regulations retroactively.

.13   CITING A REGULATION

In citing a regulation, the first number (to the left of the decimal) represents the type of Regulation. The most common types are:

1. Income Tax
20. Estate Tax
25. Gift Tax
31. Employment Tax
301. Procedural Matters

Generally, a Regulation is cited in the following manner:

Treas. Reg. Sec. 1.162-1(b)(3)

where "1" represents the type of regulation (Income Tax, in this case), the "162" represents the Code section being interpreted, the second "1" represents the chronological number of the regulation for this Code section (in this case, the first one), and the (b)(3) represents subdivisions (paragraph and subparagraph) within the Regulation (these do not correspond to subdivisions of the Code section being interpreted).

Proposed Regulation cites usually incorporate the abbreviation "Prop," such as:

Prop. Treas. Reg. Sec. 1.263A-3

Temporary Regulations incorporate the abbreviation "Temp." or "T", such as:

Prop. Treas. Reg. Sec. 1T.263A-3

.15   LOCATING REGULATIONS

Most tax services furnish complete sets of Regulations, either separately or incorporated within the codification. Electronic subscription services also provide a Regulations database. Regulations are also available on the Internet at:

http://www.gpo.gov
http://www.irs.gov/Tax-Professionals/Tax-Code,-Regulations-and-Official-Guidance

OBSERVATION   A word of warning: Regulations can easily become outdated, and the IRS is slow to amend such Regulations. It is extremely important to check to see if the regulations have been superceded or modified by subsequent regulations, legislation, or court decisions. Most tax services will prominently display cautionary notes at the top of a regulation if it has been affected by later developments.

¶2007   Revenue Rulings

The rulings process began in 1955 with the objective of consolidating information concerning the internal practices of the IRS. Prior to this time, such interpretations included such documents as Appeals and Review Memoranda (ARMs), Office Decisions (ODs), General Counsel's Memorandum (GCMs), Income Tax Rulings (Its), Internal Revenue Publication Memographs (IR-Mims), and Treasury Department Circulars (DCs). Some of these older documents may still be applicable to current tax situations.

Revenue Rulings are official IRS interpretations of the tax consequences of the Code's application in a specific unnamed hypothetical taxpayer's situation (i.e., a specific set of facts). Unlike Regulations, they are not general statements of authority. An example of a Revenue Ruling is provided in **Figure 2**.

Figure 2—Revenue Ruling Example

Rev. Rul. 2008-5, I.R.B. 2008-3, December 20, 2007. [Code Secs. 165 and 1091]

Deductions: Losses: Wash sales. —
The IRS has addressed the deductibility of losses from wash sales of stocks and securities. Where an individual, who is not a dealer in stocks or securities, sells their stocks or securities from an IRA or Roth IRA, and causes the IRA to purchase the same or substantially similar stocks or securities within 30 days of the sale, the loss will be disallowed pursuant to Code Sec. 1091. Furthermore, the individual's basis in the IRA or Roth IRA will not be increased by virtue of Code Sec. 1091(d).

ISSUE
If an individual sells stock or securities for a loss and causes his or her individual retirement account or Roth IRA to purchase substantially identical stock or securities within 30 days before or after the sale, is the loss on the sale of the stock or securities disallowed?

FACTS
A, an individual, owns 100 shares of *X* Company stock with a basis of $1,000. On December 20, 2007, *A* sells the 100 shares of *X* Company stock for $600 (the "Sale"). On December 21, 2007, *A* causes an individual retirement account (within the meaning of §408) or a Roth IRA (within the meaning of §408A), established for the exclusive benefit of *A* or *A*'s beneficiaries, to purchase 100 shares of *X* Company stock for its then fair market value (the "Purchase").

A executes the Sale and the Purchase with different, unrelated market participants.

A is not a dealer in stock or securities.

LAW AND ANALYSIS
Under §408(a), the term "individual retirement account" means a trust created or organized in the United States for the exclusive benefit of an individual or his beneficiaries, but only if the written governing instrument creating the trust meets certain other requirements.

Under §408(e)(1), generally, an individual retirement account is exempt from taxation.

Under §§408 and 72, any amount distributed from an individual retirement account is includible in the distributee's gross income for the year of the distribution unless it is properly allocable to the account owner's basis in the account. Under §408A, a similar income inclusion rule applies to nonqualified distributions from a Roth IRA. An individual has basis in an individual retirement account only to the extent that the account includes nondeductible contributions.

Section 1091(a) provides that in the case of any loss claimed to have been sustained from any sale or other disposition of shares of stock or securities where it appears that, within a period beginning 30 days before the date of such sale or disposition and ending 30 days after such date, the taxpayer has acquired (by purchase or by an exchange on which the entire amount of gain or loss was recognized by law), or has entered into a contract or option so to acquire, substantially identical stock or securities, then no deduction shall be allowed under §165 unless the taxpayer is a dealer in stock or securities and the loss is sustained in a transaction made in the ordinary course of such business.

Section 1091(d) provides rules for determining the basis of stock or securities the acquisition of which resulted in the nondeductibility under §1091 (or corresponding provisions of prior law) of the loss from the sale or other disposition of substantially identical stock or securities.

In *Security First National Bank of Los Angeles* [CCH Dec. 8098], 28 BTA 289 (1933), the taxpayer sold bonds (at a market price) to a corporation of which the taxpayer was the sole shareholder. On the same day, in exchange for land, the corporation transferred the same bonds at the same price to a trust over which the taxpayer had absolute dominion and control. In finding that §214(a)(5), the predecessor to §1091(a), applied to disallow the loss, the court reasoned as follows:

The [taxpayer] did not personally reacquire substantially identical property and, strictly construed, the language of section 214(a)(5), above referred to, might not apply. However, the rule of strict construction should not be unduly pressed to permit easy evasion of a taxing statute. *Carbon Steel Co. v. Lewellyn*, 251 U.S. 501. Unless the respondent is right, a trust like this one could be used deliberately to accomplish the very thing which Congress intended to frustrate…. Although title to the bonds was acquired by the trust, actual command over the property was still in the [taxpayer]….The difference between acquisition by him personally and acquisition by the trust amounts only to a refinement of title and may be disregarded so far as section 214(a)(5) is concerned.

Security First National Bank [CCH Dec. 8098], 28 BTA at 314 - 315.

Applying this reasoning to the facts of this ruling, even though an individual retirement account is a tax-exempt trust, *A* has nevertheless acquired, for purposes of §1091(a), 100 shares of Company stock on December 21, 2007, by virtue of the Purchase. See also *Shoenberg v. Commissioner* [35-1 USTC ¶9333], 77 F.2d 446 (8th Cir. 1935).

HOLDING
The loss on the Sale of stock is disallowed under §1091. *A*'s basis in the individual retirement account or Roth IRA is not increased by virtue of §1091(d). This ruling does not address any issues other than those specifically addressed herein. In particular, this ruling does not address (and no inference should be drawn with respect to) any issue arising under §4975.

DRAFTING INFORMATION
The principal author of this revenue ruling is Roger E. Wade of the Office of Associate Chief Counsel (Financial Institutions & Products). For further information regarding this revenue ruling, contact Mr. Wade at (202) 622-3950 (not a toll-free call).

.01　SOURCES OF RULINGS

Revenue Rulings are issued in response to taxpayer inquiries (usually through Letter Ruling requests discussed below), court decisions (including the announcement of acquiescence or non-acquiescence to specific court decisions), or a perceived need for additional guidance on a specific transaction. Additionally, the IRS will occasionally respond to the requests for technical advice with a ruling.

The IRS intends for its employees and taxpayers alike to follow Revenue Rulings if the facts in the particular case are substantially the same as those in the ruling, and the preface to the Internal Revenue Bulletin states that rulings may be used as precedent. However, in many cases the facts are not the same, and in other cases a ruling may have been revised, revoked or made obsolete by a later ruling, court decision, or legislation.

Since rulings are official interpretations of the Service, they are issued by the National Office and undergo extensive review at the Branch, Division, and Assistant Commissioner levels. Such rulings generally require extensive editing for all possible situations, distinctions, and limitations.

Generally, a Revenue Ruling is limited to one to three pages and is organized in the following manner: (1) issue, (2) facts, (3) law, (4) analysis, and (5) holding. Currently, the IRS issues approximately 60 Revenue Rulings per year.

.03　PRECEDENT VALUE OF RULINGS

Although Revenue Rulings are sometimes referred to as "Junior Regulations," they do not have the force and effect of Regulations. Rulings are responsive to and limited by the stated pivotal facts, and they are not intended to be statements of general applicability (as Regulations are). IRS personnel generally will follow published Revenue Rulings, and sometimes the rulings provide clues as to the IRS's litigation strategy on a particular issue.

The precedent value attached to Revenue Rulings in the courts depends on the Court. For example, the U.S. District Court and the U.S. Claims Court tend to give such rulings more weight than the U.S. Tax Court, generally because the former courts do not have tax specialists. Witness the following two quotes:

- *Dunn v. U.S.*—"Rulings have the force and of legal precedence unless unreasonable or inconsistent with the provisions of the Internal Revenue Code."[2]
- *Stubbs, Overbeck & Associates v. U.S.*—"Revenue Rulings are merely the opinion of a lawyer in an agency."[3]

.05　PUBLICATION AND CITATION OF REVENUE RULINGS

As official interpretations of the IRS, Revenue Rulings are published in the weekly *Internal Revenue Bulletin* and then consolidated into the semi-annual *Cumulative Bulletin* for that particular year. For this reason, there are two different citations for each ruling: one the location in the weekly *Internal Revenue Bulletin*, and the other the location in the annual *Cumulative Bulletin*.

These two formats may be illustrated as follows:

- *Rev. Rul. 99-40, 1999-48 I.R.B. 5* (temporary citation, the 40th ruling in 1999, found in the 48th weekly issue of the 1999 Internal Revenue Bulletin on page 5)
- *Rev. Rul. 99-40, 1999-2 C.B. 60* (permanent citation, found on page 60 of the 2nd Cumulative Bulletin of 1999)

.07　LOCATING REVENUE RULINGS

As mentioned above, Revenue Rulings are found in the IRB and the CB. Most electronic tax services offer full texts of all Revenue Rulings, and these may eventually be added to free World-Wide Web sites as well.

---

[2]　*Dunn*, DC N.Y., 79-1 USTC ¶9295, 468 FSupp 991.
[3]　*Stubbs, Overbeck and Associates*, CA-5, 71-2 USTC ¶9520, 445 F2d 1142.

Unfortunately, the IRS does not withdraw revoked or obsolete rulings from publication. Therefore, a tax researcher should be cautious and always ensure that a ruling is current. This is best done by checking a finding list in a tax service *Citator* volume, which will note any modifications or changes by subsequent events.

A useful tax research resource related to Revenue Rulings is the *The IRS Bulletin Index-Digest System*. This publication by the Government Printing Office provides the ability to identify most Revenue Rulings (and Revenue Procedures, discussed below) by Code Section or topic; in fact, all are grouped by Code Section in the publication. Finding lists are provided, and each ruling or procedure is summarized in short paragraph form. Four separate services are provided: (1) Income Tax (Publication 641), (2) Estate and Gift Taxes (Publication 642), Employment Taxes (Publication 643), and Excise Taxes (Publication 644). Cumulative supplements are also provided.

¶2009 Revenue Procedures

Revenue Procedures are defined in Reg. §601.601 as "statements of procedure affecting the rights or duties of taxpayers or other members of the public under the Code and related tax laws, or of information that should be a matter of public knowledge." These pronouncements essentially describe the internal practices and procedures of the IRS in administering the federal tax laws. These include guidance on filing requirements and special requirements for elections under the Code. For example, the first Revenue Procedure published each year provides detailed requirements for requesting letter rulings (described below), changes of accounting method, or changes of accounting period.

.01 USES OF REVENUE PROCEDURES

The National Office of the IRS publishes these official guidelines regarding tax procedural matters. Two popular uses of Revenue Procedures are to describe the requirements for obtaining a Letter Ruling from the IRS and to specify those areas of tax law in which the IRS will decline to issue Letter Rulings. The IRS issues about 60 Revenue Procedures per year. In some cases, important guidance of a general and permanent nature may be upgraded to a Procedural Regulation. A recent Revenue Procedure is displayed in **Figure 3**.

In recent years, most of the important IRS procedural guidance has been in the form of Revenue Procedures. This is especially true for procedures that tend to change fairly often, such as the steps that must be taken to request a letter ruling or change an accounting method. The Service simply does not want to be constantly changing Regulations for this purpose.

Figure 3—Revenue Procedure Example

Rev. Proc. 2007-57, I.R.B. 2007-36, 547, September 4, 2007. [Code Sec. 3402]

Withholding of tax at source: Gambling winnings: Poker tournaments. --

The IRS has informed poker tournament sponsors, including casinos, of their withholding and information reporting obligations, under Code Sec. 3402(q), regarding amounts paid to tournament winners. Withholding is required when one or more tournament winners are paid in excess of $5,000 apiece over the entry and "buy-in" fees that participants are charged and that comprise a "wagering pool" from which the winnings are paid. The withholding rate is equal to the third lowest rate applicable to single filers, under Code Sec. 1(c), which currently is 25 percent. A sponsor required to withhold on poker tournament winnings must file a Form W-2G, Certain Gambling Winnings, with the IRS on or before February 28 (March 31 if filed electronically) of the calendar year following the calendar year in which the winnings are paid.

SECTION 1. PURPOSE

This revenue procedure informs taxpayers of their obligations under section 3402(q) pertaining to withholding and information reporting applicable to certain amounts paid to winners of poker tournaments. It further sets forth procedures to be used to comply with the relevant requirements of the Internal Revenue Code and Treasury Regulations thereunder.

SECTION 2. FACTUAL BACKGROUND

A business taxpayer ("poker tournament sponsor") may sponsor a poker tournament, charging an entry fee and a "buy-in" fee for each participant. In exchange for the fees, each participant receives a set of poker chips with a nominal face value for use in the specific poker tournament. The poker tournament sponsor pays amounts, which exceed a participant's fees by $5,000, to a certain number of tournament winner(s), out of a pool comprised of all the participants' fees.

SECTION 3. LEGAL BACKGROUND

.01. *Withholding under section 3402.* Section 3402(q)(1) provides that every person who makes any payment of winnings which are subject to withholding shall deduct and withhold from the payment an amount equal to the product of the third lowest rate of tax applicable under section 1(c) and such payment. Section 3402(q)(3) provides that the term "winnings which are subject to withholding" means, in part, proceeds from a wagering transaction, if the proceeds are more than $5,000 from a wager placed in any sweep-stakes, wagering pool, or lottery. The term "wagering pool" includes "all pari-mutuel betting pools, including on- and off-track racing pools, and similar types of betting pools." H.R. Conf. Rep. No. 94-1515, at 488 (1976) (relating to the enactment of §3402(q)). "In common usage the term 'pool' connotes a particular gambling practice, an arrangement whereby all bets constitute a common fund to be taken by the winner or winners." *United States v. Berent*, 523 F.2d 1360, 1361 (9th Cir. 1975). Section 3402(q)(4)(A) provides that proceeds from a wager shall be determined by reducing the amount received by the amount of the wager.

.02. *Information reporting under section 31.3402(q)-1(e).* Section 31.3402(q)-1(e) of the Employment Tax Regulations provides that each person who is to receive a payment of winnings subject to withholding shall furnish to the payer a statement on Form W-2G or Form 5754 (whichever is applicable) made under the penalties of perjury containing certain required information, including the name, address, and Taxpayer Identification Number of the winning payee. Section 31.3402(q)-1(f)(1) provides that every person making a payment of winnings for which withholding is required shall file a Form W-2G with the IRS on or before February 28 (March 31 if filed electronically) of the calendar year following the calendar year in which the payment of winnings is made and shall furnish a copy of the Form to the payee.

SECTION 4. APPLICATION

A poker tournament sponsor is required to withhold and report on payments of more than $5,000 made to a winning payee in a taxable year by filing an information return with the IRS as prescribed by section 3402(q). The poker tournament sponsor must furnish a copy of the information return to the IRS on or before February 28 (March 31 if filed electronically) of the calendar year following the calendar year in which the payment is made, as prescribed by section 31.3402(q) of the regulations.

SECTION 5. SCOPE

This revenue procedure applies to poker tournament sposors, including casinos, which pay amounts to winners in a manner substantially similar to that described in section 2 of this revenue procedure.

SECTION 6. WAIVER OF LIABILITY UNDER SECTION 3402 AND WAIVER OF OTHER PENALTIES OR ADDITIONS TO TAX

The IRS will not assert any liability for additional tax or additions to tax for violations of any withholding obligation with respect to amounts paid to winners of poker tournaments under section 3402, provided that the poker tournament sponsor meets all of the requirements for information reporting under section 3402(q) and the regulations thereunder.

SECTION 7. EFFECTIVE DATE

This revenue procedure is effective for payments made on or after March 4, 2008.

SECTION 8. DRAFTING INFORMATION

The principal author of this revenue procedure is Blaise G. Dusenberry of the Office of Associate Chief Counsel (Procedure and Administration). For further information regarding this revenue procedure, contact Cynthia McGreevy at (202) 622-4910 (not a toll-free call).

.03   AUTHORITY OF REVENUE PROCEDURES

Revenue Procedures generally have the same level of authority as Revenue Rulings. Like Rulings, they may be used as precedent. If nothing else, the tax professional knows that IRS personnel will definitely following the Procedures. In some cases, Revenue Procedures are mandated in certain areas by Congress, and these tend to be given more deference by the courts.

.05   LOCATING REVENUE PROCEDURES

The citation formats for Revenue Procedures are generally the same as Revenue Rulings. The Procedure is first published in the weekly *Internal Revenue Bulletin*, and then again in the annual *Cumulative Bulletin*. The two citation formats are:
- *Rev. Proc. 99-40, 1999-48 I.R.B. 5* (temporary citation, the 40th ruling in 1999, found in the 48th weekly issue of the 1999 Internal Revenue Bulletin on page 5)
- *Rev. Proc. 99-40, 1999-2 C.B. 60* (permanent citation, found on page 60 of the 2nd Cumulative Bulletin of 1999)

Revenue Procedures may be located with generally the same procedures used for Revenue Rulings described above. Revenue Procedures are also categorized and summarized in the *IRS Bulletin Index-Digest System* mentioned earlier.

¶2011   Private Letter Rulings (PLRs)

Private Letter Rulings are issued by the IRS National Office in response to taxpayers' requests for the IRS's position on a particular tax issue. One example would be a request to evaluate the tax consequences of a proposed merger.

OBSERVATION	There are many topics that the IRS will refuse to rule on. This is especially true for areas of the tax law that seem fairly settled. Generally, the first Revenue Procedure issued each year (e.g., Rev. Proc. 2009-1) provides a current list of the areas that may not be the subject of ruling requests. This Revenue Procedure also lists the requirements for submitting a ruling request, the appropriate fees, and other details.

.01   DRAFTING PROCEDURES FOR PLRs

The procedures used for drafting PLRs are much the same as Revenue Rulings, except that (1) such requests receive a more limited review by the National Office of the IRS at the Group or Section levels only, and (2) such rulings are not published (in print) by the IRS. In addition, the IRS lists a number of issues each year that it will not rule on. This list, along with the detailed instructions for requesting a ruling (as well as for requesting a change in accounting period or method) are usually printed in the first Revenue Procedure issued for the calendar year.

.03   PRECEDENT VALUE OF PLRs

The PLR is issued only to the requesting taxpayer, and its reliability is high for that particular taxpayer. The taxpayer must attach the ruling to the relevant tax return when filed, although there is no legal requirement that the taxpayer must actually follow the ruling. If the IRS receives a number of ruling requests on the same issue, or the issue is one of emerging importance, they may decide to publish the PLR as a Revenue Ruling.

Although the IRS insists that PLRs may not be relied on as precedents, other factors tend to mitigate this statement. For example, Code Sec. 6110(f) makes such letter rulings available for inspection by the public under the Freedom of Information Act, and PLRs are included on the list of authorities that may be cited as "substantial authority" for avoiding certain statutory penalties. Because of these factors, several tax publishers now offer digests or complete texts of such rulings. A PLR is illustrated in **Figure 4**.

Figure 4—Private Letter Ruling 200727008

Trade or business expenses—deduction limitations—partnership employee remuneration. Headnote:
Code Sec. 162(m); deduction limitation doesn't apply to partnership with respect to remuneration paid to covered employee as compensation for services performed by covered employee as partnership employee, nor does it apply to corp. with respect to its distributive share of income or loss from partnership that includes compensation expense of covered employees to extent such compensation expense is attributable to services performed by covered employees as partnership employees.

Full Text:
Release Date: 7/6/2007
Dear [Redacted Text]:
This letter is in response to the letter dated October 26, 2006, submitted by your authorized representative, requesting a ruling under section 162(m) of the Internal Revenue Code (Code). Specifically, you requested a ruling that the deduction limitation of section 162(m) does not apply. The facts, as represented, are as follows.

The Corporation owns approximately X percent of the common limited partnership units in the Partnership. The Corporation also owns preferred units of the Partnership. The Corporation's overall ownership interest in the Partnership (both common and preferred units) is Y percent. The Corporation elected to be taxed as a real estate investment trust (REIT) as defined under section 856 of the Code. Virtually all of the Corporation's interests in properties and other assets are held through the Partnership. Both the Corporation and the Partnership have common equity securities that are required to be registered under section 12 of the Securities Exchange Act of 1934 (Exchange Act). The Corporation has employees who are covered employees (Covered Employees) within the meaning of section 162(m) of the Code. Certain Covered Employees of the Corporation are also employees and senior executives of the Partnership. The Covered Employees are compensated for the services they perform for both entities under a variety of arrangements. The Covered Employees provide only a small portion of their services as employees of the Corporation and the vast majority of their time and effort is devoted to managing the Partnership. The Subsidiary is a subsidiary the Partnership, and it manages all payroll activities for the Partnership and the Corporation.

The total compensation of one or more of the Covered Employees will exceed $1 million and will not be qualified performance-based compensation within the meaning of section 162(m) of the Code.

Section 162(a)(1) of the Code allows a deduction for all of the ordinary and necessary expenses paid or incurred during the taxable year in carrying on any trade or business, including a reasonable allowance for salaries or other compensation for personal services actually rendered.

Section 162(m)(1) of the Code, provides that for any publicly held corporation, no deduction shall be allowed for applicable employee remuneration with respect to any covered employee to the extent that the amount of such remuneration for the taxable year exceeds $1 million.

Section 162(m)(2) of the Code defines publicly held corporation to mean any corporation issuing any class of common equity securities required to be registered under section 12 of the Exchange Act. Section 1.162-27(c)(1)(i) of the Income Tax Regulations (Regulations) provides that whether a corporation is publicly held is determined based solely on whether, as of the last day of its taxable year, the corporation is subject to the reporting obligations of section 12 of the Exchange Act.

Under section 1.162-27(c)(1)(ii) of the Regulations, a publicly held corporation includes an affiliated group of corporations, as defined in section 1504 of the Code (determined without regard to section 1504(b), which lists exceptions to the definition). For purposes of section 162(m), an affiliated group of corporations does not include any subsidiary that is itself a publicly held corporation.

Section 162(m)(3) of the Code defines covered employee as any employee of the taxpayer if (A) as of the close of the taxable year, such employee is the chief executive officer of the taxpayer or is an individual acting in such capacity, or (B) the total compensation of such employee for the taxable year is required to be reported to shareholders under the Exchange Act by reason of such employee being among the four highest compensated officers for the tax able year (other than the chief executive officer).

Section 1.162-27(c)(2)(ii) of the Regulations generally provides that whether an individual is a covered employee for purposes of section 162(m) is determined pursuant to the executive compensation disclosure rules under the Exchange Act.

Section 1504(a) of the Code defines affiliated group to mean one or more chains of includible corporations connected through stock ownership with a common parent corporation if the common parent directly owns 80 percent of the total voting power of the stock and has a value equal to at least 80 percent of the total value of the stock of the corporation.

Based solely on the facts presented, we rule as follows:
1. The deduction limitation of section 162(m) of the Code does not apply to the Partnership with respect to remuneration paid to a Covered Employee as compensation for services performed by the Covered Employee as an employee of the Partnership.
2. The deduction limitation of section 162(m) of the Code does not apply to the Corporation with respect to its distributive share of income or loss from the Partnership that includes the compensation expense of the Covered Employees to the extent such compensation expense is attributable to services performed by the Covered Employees as employees of the Partnership.

Except as expressly provided herein, no opinion is expressed or implied concerning the tax consequences of any aspect of any transaction or item discussed or referenced in this letter. In this regard, note that we specifically express no opinion concerning the limited partnership agreement of the Partnership, including any amendments thereto, or the allocation of the compensation between the Partnership and the Corporation.

This ruling is directed only to the taxpayer requesting it. Section 6110(k)(3) of the Code provides that it may not be used or cited as precedent.

A copy of this letter must be attached to any income tax return to which it is relevant. The rulings contained in this letter are based upon information and representations submitted by the taxpayer and accompanied by a penalty of perjury statement executed by an appropriate party. While this office has not verified any of the material submitted in support of the request for rulings, it is subject to verification on examination. In accordance with the Power of Attorney on file with this office, a copy of this letter is being sent to your authorized representative.

Sincerely,
Kenneth M. Griffin
Senior Technician Reviewer

A number of courts have also cited Private Letter Rulings in some fashion. For example, in *Rowan Companies, Inc. v. U.S.*,[4] the U.S. Supreme Court cited such rulings as evidence of inconsistent IRS positions on the issue of FICA and FUTA tax classifications. There is also evidence that the IRS refers to such prior rulings in order to foster consistent tax administration when dealing with similar issues.

.05   LOCATING PLRs

Private Letter Rulings are generally cited in either of the following manners:
- *PLR 8651012*
- *PLR 200727008*

In the first cite, 86 is the year, 51 is the 51st week of the year, and 012 represents the 12th ruling issued that week. The second cite is for the years 2000 and later; 9 digits are

---

[4]   *Rowan Companies*, SCt, 81-1 USTC ¶9479, 452 US 247, 101 SCt 2288.

used for these cites (with the first four used for the year). Most electronic tax services contain complete texts of all Private Letter Rulings.

¶2013　Other Forms of Letter Rulings: Technical Advice Memoranda (TAMs), Field Service Advices (FSAs), and Determination Letters

.01　TECHNICAL ADVICE MEMORANDA (TAMs)

A **Technical Advice Memorandum (TAM)** is another type of letter ruling issued by the IRS. A TAM represents the IRS's response to a request by an IRS District Director or Appeals Officer regarding a technical question that develops during an audit. The response requires a high level of expertise and a consistent approach by the IRS. In contrast to a PLR, a TAM generally involves a completed transaction.

TAMs should be regarded the same as PLRs in terms of scope and authority. Once again, they are based on a specific taxpayer situation, and may be relied upon by that taxpayer as authority. TAMs are cited in the same fashion as PLRs:

- *TAM 9812130*
- *TAM 200411031*

.03　LETTER RULINGS—FIELD SERVICE ADVICES (FSAs)

Field Service Advices (FSAs) are memoranda issued by the National Office of the IRS to IRS Agents, Attorneys, and Appeals Officers who seek advice and guidance for either (1) developing an issue or (2) assessing litigation hazards. The IRS initially sought to keep the FSAs confidential, as they maintained that public disclosure would hamper the IRS in meeting its mission and discourage communication between IRS personnel and the National Office. However, in *Tax Analysts v. IRS,* the Court ruled that such information should be available to the public under the Freedom of Information Act.[5]

The IRS has recently begun releasing prior FSAs, with a citation system similar to PLRs. Most tax services will be including the FSAs in their databases. It appears that FSAs will be treated essentially the same as PLRs and TAMs in terms of authoritative value.

.05　DETERMINATION LETTERS

A **Determination Letter** is issued by the office of a local IRS District Director in response to a request for a formal tax determination concerning a particular situation or transaction. Two of the most common uses for Determination Letters are questions regarding the tax-exempt status of an organization or questions regarding the qualification of a pension plan as a qualified plan under the Code.

These Determination Letters are not published by the IRS, but are available under the Freedom of Information Act. In general, these letters would provide little guidance for other taxpayers.

¶2015　Miscellaneous Technical Guidance

.01　ANNOUNCEMENTS AND NOTICES

The IRS National Office publishes *Announcements* and *Notices* when they believe that it is necessary to provide quick interpretive guidance to the public. These are authorities similar in scope to Revenue Rulings and Revenue Procedures, and in fact, a number of

---

[5]　*Tax Analysts*, District Court D.C., 98-1 USTC ¶50,407.

Announcements and Notices may eventually be issued as Revenue Rulings or Revenue Procedures. In many cases, a Notice serves as the first draft of Regulations, and as such, provides a preview of forthcoming Regulations.

Notices and Announcements are published in the weekly Internal Revenue Bulletin. However, only Notices are republished in the Cumulative Bulletin.

.03   GENERAL COUNCIL MEMORANDUM (GCM)

A **General Council Memorandum (GCM)** is generated by the office of the IRS Chief Counsel in response to an internal IRS request for a legal analysis to be used in preparing such external pronouncements as Revenue Rulings, Private Letter Rulings, and Technical Advice Memorandums. GCMs generally provide an indication regarding the IRS position in an upcoming ruling, but since they are internal documents, they are not binding authority. However, some courts have noted that GCMs must be made available to the public, and as such, may be viewed as statements of current policy by the IRS.[6]

The IRS does not publish GCMs in print form. However, they are publicly available under the Freedom of Information Act and are included in some tax services.

.05   TECHNICAL MEMORANDUM (TM)

A Technical Memorandum (TM) is more or less a letter of transmittal from the IRS Commissioner to the Assistant Secretary of Treasury for Tax Policy that accompanies Treasury Decisions (i.e., Final Regulations). As mentioned earlier, much of the information originally contained in TMs has been transferred to the Preamble of the Regulations. As a result, most TM releases now have little value as tax authority with precedent value.

.07   ACTION ON DECISION (AOD)

This document is also prepared by the Office of the Chief Counsel of the IRS, generally in response to a loss by the IRS in Court. These are prepared by the litigation division of the Chief Counsel's office, and are generally confined to significant issues.

Generally, the text of the **Action on Decision (AOD)** recommends what action the IRS should take in response to the adverse decision, such as acquiescence, non-acquiescence, or simply do nothing at the present time. An acquiescence indicates that the IRS will follow the court decision in similar cases while a non-acquiescence indicates that the IRS disagrees with the adverse decision and will only follow the decision for the specific taxpayer. An example of a famous AOD is provided in **Figure 5** (who says that the Treasury doesn't have a sense of humor?)

Figure 5—Action on Decision (AOD) 1984-022

UIL No. 0162.01-17; 0162.29-00
Headnote:
Reference(s): Code Sec. 162;
Full Text:
CC:TL, CC-1984-022, Br4:DCFegan

HAROLD L. AND TEMPLE M. JENKINS V. COMMISSIONER
Docket No.: 3354-79
Decision: November 3, 1983
Venue: C.A. 6th.
See Tax Notes, November 14, 1983, p. 606-607 for a summary of this case.

---

[6]   *See Falcone*, DC E.D., Mich., 79-2 ustc ¶9683, 479 F. Supp. 985.

T.C. Memo. 1983-667
Distributed: March 23, 1984

ISSUE
Whether Conway Twitty is allowed a business expense deduction for payments to reimburse the losses of investors in a defunct restaurant known as Twitty Burger, Inc. 0162.01-17; 0162.29-00.

DISCUSSION
The Tax Court summarized its opinion in this case with the following "Ode to Conway Twitty":

"Twitty Burger went belly up
But Conway remained true
He repaid his investors, one and all
It was the moral thing to do.

"His fans would not have liked it
It could have hurt his fame
Had any investors sued him
Like Merle Haggard or Sonny James.

"When it was time to file taxes
Conway thought what he would do
Was deduct those payments as a business expense
Under section one-sixty-two.

"In order to allow these deductions
Goes the argument of the Commissioner
The payments must be ordinary and necessary
To a business of the petitioner.

"Had Conway not repaid the investors
His career would have been under cloud,
Under the unique facts of this case
Held: The deductions are allowed.

"Our reaction to the Court's opinion is reflected in the following "Ode to Conway Twitty: A Reprise":

Harold Jenkins and Conway Twitty
They are both the same
But one was born
The other achieved fame.

The man is talented
And has many a friend
They opened a restaurant
His name he did lend.

They are two different things
Making burgers and song
The business went sour
It didn't take long.

He repaid his friends
Why did he act
Was it business or friendship
Which is fact?

Business the court held
It's deductible they feel
We disagree with the answer
But let's not appeal.

RECOMMENDATION
Nonacquiescence.
DAVID C. FEGAN
Attorney
JOEL GERBER
Acting Chief Counsel
By: CLIFFORD M.HARBOURT
Senior Technician Reviewer
Branch No. 2
Tax Litigation Division

.09   INTERNAL REVENUE MANUAL (IRM)

The *Internal Revenue Manual (IRM)* is a compilation of the procedures, policies, instructions and guidelines governing the IRS's organization and operations. The Manual is now available under the Freedom of Information Act.

The IRM may provide insights into how the IRS construes a particular Code provision, or how the IRS requires its personnel to deal with taxpayers in specific situations. Of particular interest are the audit guidelines for various industries. However, the IM itself has little authoritative value.

¶2017   Informational Releases of the IRS

.01   INFORMATION LETTERS

Information letters are issued by the National Office or a District Office to call attention to a well-established interpretation or principle of tax law that the IRS believes will be helpful to the taxpayer or organization making a request for information from the IRS. These letters are advisory only and are not binding because they do not constitute a ruling.

.03   TECHNICAL INFORMATION RELEASES (TIRs)

Technical Information Releases (TIRs) are issued by the IRS to inform the public quickly regarding important technical developments. An example would be quick advice on a tax election that has a limited time frame. TIRs may be relied on when such reliance is stated in the TIR or the TIR announces a mechanical rule. Otherwise, they tend to have little precedent value.

.05 NEWS RELEASES

News Releases issued by the IRS contain only information of a general nature, as opposed to technical guidance. An example would be an announcement of a new filing requirement to be issued as a Regulation or Revenue Procedure. News Releases generally do not contain any substantive information for taxpayers to rely on, and are not properly cited as authority.

¶2019 Audit-Related Releases

.01 CLOSING AGREEMENTS

Code Sec. 7121 provides for a closing agreement process between taxpayers and the Commissioner of the IRS as to specific issues or tax liability. An example would be a determination of estate tax liability in a timely manner so that assets can be distributed to beneficiaries.

Closing agreements are binding on both parties unless fraud or a misrepresentation of material facts is demonstrated. These are not legally binding and are not cited as authority.

.03 AUDIT NO CHANGE LETTERS

No change letters may be issued by the IRS at the conclusion of an audit, indicating that no adjustment will be made in the original tax liability. Although these may provide comfort to the taxpayers for the year in question, they are *not* binding for other years and thus do not constitute authority. No change letters may protect the taxpayers from retroactive adjustments by the IRS, however.

¶2021 Compliance-Related Releases

.01 IRS PUBLICATIONS

The IRS publishes a number of pamphlets and booklets for the public's self-help. Examples include Publication 17, *Your Federal Income Tax* and Publication 334, *Tax Guide for Small Business*. The IRS views such publications as similar to information letters, and should not be relied on by the public as authority. **Figure 6** shows an excerpt from IRS Publication 970, *Tax Benefits for Education*.

In *Adler*,[7] a taxpayer attempted to deduct the cost of dance lessons as medical expenses because he relied on a statement in Publication 17. The court noted that "No interpretation by taxpayers of the language used in government pamphlets can act as estoppel against the government, nor change the meaning of taxing statutes." However, in a dissent to this decision, one judge made the following statement: "*While men must learn to turn square corners when they deal with the government, there is no reason why the square corners should constitute a one-way street.*"

Figure 6—Excerpt from IRS Publication 970—Tax Benefits for Education

Student Loan Interest Deduction

Introduction

Generally, personal interest you pay, other than certain mortgage interest, is not deductible on your tax return. However, if your modified adjusted gross income (MAGI) is less than $75,000 ($150,000 if filing a joint return) there is a special deduction allowed for paying interest on a student loan (also known as an education loan) used for higher education. For most taxpayers, MAGI is the adjusted gross income as figured on their federal income tax return before

---

[7] *Adler*, CA-9, 64-1 USTC ¶9388, 330 F2d 91.

subtracting any deduction for student loan interest. This deduction can reduce the amount of your income subject to tax by up to $2,500 in 2011.

The student loan interest deduction is taken as an adjustment to income. This means you can claim this deduction even if you do not itemize deductions on Schedule A (Form 1040).

This chapter explains:
What type of loan interest you can deduct,
Whether you can claim the deduction,
What expenses you must have paid with the student loan,
Who is an eligible student,
How to figure the deduction, and
How to claim the deduction.

.03   INSTRUCTIONS TO TAX FORMS

The Instructions to Tax Returns and Tax Forms issued by the IRS as guidance to taxpayers do not constitute "authority," as they are viewed similarly to IRS Publications discussed above. In some cases, these instructions may offer advice different from other authorities. Although taxpayers and tax professionals should rely on this "other authority," reliance on the instructions may nonetheless help establish "reasonable cause" to avoid Code penalties.

¶2023   Summary

- Sources of administrative authority include the Regulations issued by the Treasury and IRS pronouncements including Revenue Rulings and Revenue Procedures.
- Regulations are issued as either Proposed Regulations or Temporary (and Proposed) Regulations. Only after a comment period may a Proposed Regulation be issued as a Final Regulation.
- Revenue Rulings are the IRS's official interpretation of the Code, but they do not carry the same authority as Regulations.
- In addition to Revenue Rulings and Revenue Procedures, the IRS issues a number of pronouncements that may be useful to tax researchers.

Review Questions for Chapter 2

True or False
Indicate which of the following statements are true or false by circling the correct answer.

1. Final Regulations generally have the force and effect of law.   T   F
2. A Temporary Regulation issued in 2006 will remain in effect until a Final Regulation is   T   F
    issued.
3. A Proposed Regulation has the force and effect of law until a Final Regulation is issued.   T   F
4. Revenue Rulings may be used as precedent.   T   F
5. Revenue Procedures are official IRS interpretations of the tax consequences of the Code's   T   F
    application in a specific unnamed hypothetical taxpayer's situation.
6. A taxpayer reading a private letter ruling with almost identical facts can rely on the PLR   T   F
    as precedent.
7. The IRS issues either an acquiescence or nonacquiescence regarding every court decision.   T   F
8. A Technical Advice Memorandum (TAM) represents the IRS's response to a request by   T   F
    an Appeals Officer regarding a technical question that develops during an audit.
9. Since a General Counsel Memorandum generally provides an indication regarding the IRS   T   F
    position in an upcoming ruling, it has the same authority as the eventual Revenue Ruling.
10. Taxpayers may rely on the Instructions to an IRS form as authority in determining a tax   T   F
    position on their return.

Fill in the Blanks
Fill in each blank with the appropriate word or phrase that completes each sentence.

11. Taxpayers have _____ days to comment (in writing or orally) on Proposed Regulations.
12. When Congress directs the IRS to in effect perform a law-making function and to specify the substantive
    requirements of a particular provision, the resulting regulations are referred to as _____
    Regulations.
13. A Regulation can be applied retroactively if it is issued within _____ months of the underlying statute
    being interpreted.
14. The _____ is a compilation of the procedures, policies, instructions and guide-
    lines governing the IRS's organization and operations.
15. The detailed instructions for requesting a private letter ruling are usually printed in a(n) _____
    _____.
16. If the first number (to the left of the decimal) in a Regulation cite was a 31, the Regulation would deal
    with _____ tax.
17. If the IRS plans to follow an adverse court decision for similar cases, it will likely issue a(n)
    _____ in response to the decision.
18. When the IRS receives a number of requests for Letter Rulings on the same transaction, it may issue an
    official interpretation in the form of a(n) _____.
19. _____ Regulations are issued by the IRS without the normal comment period and are gen-
    erally effective on the _____.
20. The IRS may issue a(n) _____ to an IRS Appeals Officer who is seeking advice and
    guidance for assessing litigation hazards.

Multiple Choice

Circle the best answer for each of the following questions.

21. The IRS must follow the decision of which of the following court(s)?
    a.   Tax Court
    b.   District Courts
    c.   Circuit Court of Appeals
    d.   Supreme Court
    e.   All of the above

22. Which of the following is not published in the Cumulative Bulletin?
    a.   Private Letter Rulings
    b.   Revenue Rulings
    c.   Revenue Procedures
    d.   IRS Notices

23. After the comment period for a Proposed Regulation, the IRS may
    a. issue final regulations
    b. withdraw the proposed Regulation for further work and then reissue as a Final Regulation
    c. withdraw the Regulation and suspend work on the project
    d. all of the above

24. Which of the following is not printed by the IRS but is available under the Freedom of Information Act?
    a.   Private Letter Rulings
    b.   General Counsel Memorandum
    c.   Internal Revenue Manual
    d.   Determination letters
    e.   None of the above are printed by the IRS but all of the above are available under the Freedom of Information Act.

25. A Final Regulation is effective:
    a.   when it is issued as a proposed regulation.
    b.   30 days after it is filed with the Federal Register
    c.   on the day it is filed with the Federal Register
    d.   on the day the statute became law

26. In the PLR cite PLR 200605067 the 05 represents
    a.   the day of the month the PLR was issued
    b.   the month the PLR was issued
    c.   the week the PLR was issued
    d.   the 5th ruling issued during the year.

27. A Revenue Ruling contains all of the following sections except for:
    a.   Facts
    b.   Analysis
    c.   Taxpayer details
    d.   Issue identification
    e.   Holding

28. These Regulations generally have the force and effect of law, unless they conflict with the statute:
    a. Legislative
    b. Interpretive
    c. Temporary
    d. Proposed

29. A Private Letter Ruling:
    a. Can be cited as precedent by a taxpayer as long as the taxpayer's facts are similar to the ruling.
    b. Only applies to the taxpayer that requested the ruling
    c. Is available free of charge from the IRS
    d. Will be published by the IRS
    e. More than one of the above are correct.

30. In which of the following cases would not allow Regulations to be applied retroactively?
    a. The Regulation is designed to prevent taxpayer abuse.
    b. The Regulation relates to internal Treasury Department policies, practices, or procedures.
    c. The Regulation corrects a procedural defect in the issuance of a prior Regulation.
    d. The Regulation is issued within 24 months of the underlying statute being interpreted.
    e. In all of the above cases the Regulations may be applied retroactively.

Review Problems

31. Why should a researcher note the date on which a Treasury Regulation was adopted?

32. Provide the correct citation for the indicated passage in the following Regulation.

> Reg §1.25A-3. Hope Scholarship Credit.
> **(a) Amount of the credit.**
> > *(1) In general.* Subject to the phaseout of the education tax credit described in §1.25A-1(c), the Hope Scholarship Credit amount is the total of—
> > > (i) 100 percent of the first $1,000 of qualified tuition and related expenses paid during the taxable year for education furnished to an eligible student (as defined in paragraph (d) of this section) who is the taxpayer, the taxpayer's spouse, or any claimed dependent during any academic period beginning in the taxable year (or treated as beginning in the taxable year, see §1.25A-5(e)(2)); plus
> > > *(ii) 50 percent of the next $1,000 of such expenses paid with respect to that student.*

33. Provide the correct citation for the 52nd Revenue Ruling of 2006 that is found on page 423 of the second volume of the Cumulative Bulletin.

34. Provide the correct citation for the 16th Revenue Procedure in 2005, found in the 10th weekly issue of the Internal Revenue Bulletin on page 674.

35. Go to the IRS website and find the title for the following IRS Publications:
    a. Publication 5
    b. Publication 463
    c. Publication 936

36. For Reg §1.163-10T(c)(2):
    a. What does the "1" represent?
    b. What does the "163" represent?
    c. What does the "10T" represent?
    d. What does the "(c)" represent?
    e. What does the "(2)" represent?

    Locate the actual Regulation listed above. What is the title of the Regulation? What is the heading of the actual portion of the Regulation cited above?

37. Locate AOD 2011-006.
    a. What code section does the AOD interpret?
    b. What case does the AOD discuss?
    c. What is the recommendation of the AOD?

38. Determine whether each the following IRS Rulings is a Field Service Advice, Private Letter Ruling, Service Center Advice or Technical Memorandum.
    a. 201214021
    b. 200235031
    c. 200051044
    d. 200805009
    e. 201303008
39. Locate the IRS release at 2011-48 IRB 809.
    a. What type of release is it?
    b. What number was assigned to it?
    c. What topic does it deal with?

40. Locate IRS Notice 2008-39.
    a. What is the proper citation for the Notice?
    b. What issue does the notice address?

41. How many regulations have been issued for the following Code sections?
    a. 212
    b. 197
    c. 1502

Research Problems

42. Find the Revenue Procedure that provides the optional standard mileage rate for 2013 for the business use of an auto. What is the standard mileage rate? Provide a proper citation for the Revenue Procedure.

43. Locate a TAM to answer the question: Is a radio station license of "like kind" to a television station license? Provide a proper citation for the TAM and indicate its holding.

44. Locate a PLR to answer the question: Is racing fuel with 110 octane subject to the gasoline excise tax? Provide a proper citation for the PLR and indicate its holding.

45. Locate the 2012 Revenue Procedure that identifies the domestic tax areas where the IRS will not issue rulings or determination letters. Provide a proper citation for the Revenue Procedure. What are the four areas discussed in the Revenue Procedure? Provide a specific example of a tax issue identified under each of the four areas.

46. Locate a Revenue Ruling that answers the question: If an individual sells stock at a loss and causes his Roth IRA to purchase substantially identical stock within 30 days, is the loss on the sale of the stock disallowed? Provide a proper citation for the Revenue Ruling and indicate its holding.

47. Locate a Regulation that provides guidance on the definition of performance based compensation for purposes of the $1,000,000 compensation deduction limitation. Provide a proper citation for the Regulation.

48. Locate the two AODs involving the 1967 *Sidney Olson* Tax Court case. Provide a proper citation for each AOD. Why are there two AODs? Indicate the holding of each AOD.

49. Locate an IRS Publication that would provide guidance to an individual who became divorced during the year. What is the Publication number and title?

50. Locate Action on Decision 2012-002. What case is referenced in the AOD? Did the IRS issue an acquiesce or nonacquiesce in the case? Why is this AOD so unusual?

CHAPTER 3

Judicial Sources of Authority

Learning Objectives

1. Describe the relationship between the federal courts that decide tax cases.
2. Compare and contrast the entry level courts and understand when each court might be chosen to begin litigation.
3. Understand the proper citation for each court.
4. Prepare a court case brief.

¶3001 Introduction

The third branch of the government, the judiciary, also forms a source of tax authority through the many court cases involving tax matters. These tax cases may be tried in an initial court of record that hears only tax cases (e.g., the U.S. Tax Court), as well as courts that hear all types of civil and criminal cases (the U.S. District Court and the U.S. Court of Federal Claims). In addition, appeals of these lower-level cases are often heard by one of the 13 U.S. Circuit Courts of Appeal, and on occasion, by the U.S Supreme Court.

This chapter is devoted to a detailed examination of such judicial authorities. The discussion includes a description of each court, an explanation of the relative precedent value of each court, and guides for locating such authorities.

¶3003   The Court's Authority

.01   QUESTIONS OF LAW VS. QUESTIONS OF FACT

In assessing judicial authority, it is important to distinguish questions of law from questions of fact. The two concepts are distinguished as follows:

a. A **question of law** refers to a situation when an interpretation of the statute is unclear
b. A **question of fact** refers to a question as to how the law applies when a particular set of facts is unclear

In general, the more important court decisions tend to focus on questions of law. Many of these will be covered in Chapters 4 through 7, where the landmark court decisions are analyzed in detail. However, questions of how the law applies to a series of facts are also important, as many research questions are phrased in terms of this issue.

.03   LIMITS ON A COURT'S AUTHORITY

There are limits on a court's authority to interpret the tax law and/or apply the tax law to a particular set of facts. Two expressions of these limitations are:

a. *American Automobile Association.* "The validity of the long-established policy of the Court in deferring, where possible, to Congressional procedures in the tax field is clearly indicated in this case."[1]
b. *Eisner v. Macomber.* "And, as this court has so often said, the high prerogative of declaring an Act of Congress invalid, should never be exercised except in a clear case."[2]

These courts in effect are stating that their job is to interpret the law, and not to make the law. However, courts are not hesitant to overturn *interpretations* of that law. In some situations, court decisions have overturned certain interpretations of the Code as issued by the Treasury Department and the Internal Revenue Service. For example, in overturning controversial Treasury Regulations regarding the treatment of wraparound mortgages used in installment sales, the U.S. Tax Court noted the following:

Professional Equities.[3] "While we appreciate that Congress gave the Secretary wide discretion to regulate…we cannot approve an exercise of discretion to reach a result contrary to the basic objective of the statute."

.05   THE CONCEPT OF STARE DECISIS

Most courts follow a doctrine of *stare decisis* ("let the decision stand"), in that a court views its own prior decisions as precedents to be followed. Occasionally courts will revisit an issue and decide the case differently, perhaps because of changing times or revised thinking on an issue. But most of the time, courts tend to follow their own decisions as precedents. This is important information for a tax professional to know, as it may influence which court a taxpayer decides to use as a forum in connection with a disagreement with the IRS.

> **OBSERVATION**   A taxpayer may decide to avoid the U.S. Tax Court or the U.S. District Court if the Court of Appeals for the taxpayer's geographic location has ruled unfavorably on the issue. Instead, as explained below, they may choose to go to the U.S. Court of Federal Claims, which has its own appeals court (the Court of Appeals for the Federal Circuit).

[1]   *American Automobile Association*, SCt, 61-2 USTC ¶9517, 367 US 687.
[2]   *Eisner v. Macomber*, SCt, 1 USTC ¶32, 252 US 189, 40 SCt 189.
[3]   *Professional Equities*, 89 TC 15.

Settlement Opportunities with the IRS Prior to Going to Court

A taxpayer ends up going to court because they have been audited by the IRS and disagree with the additional tax assessed by the agent. But prior to going to court, there are opportunities to resolve the issue within the confines of the service. Chapter 9 discusses the audit process and describes settlement opportunities within the IRS. Usually the taxpayer will exhaust all possibilities of settling with the IRS before going to court due to the time and cost associated with taking a case to court.

Federal Court System

If a settlement is not reached, then the taxpayer's only recourse is to go to Court. The various routes a taxpayer may take in selecting an initial court and appealing a decision are illustrated below in **Figure 1**. Generally, the taxpayer may choose to go to one of three courts of original jurisdiction: The U.S. Tax Court (including a Small Cases division), the U.S. District Court, or the U.S. Court of Federal Claims. Each is described below.

Figure 1
Court Options for a Tax Case

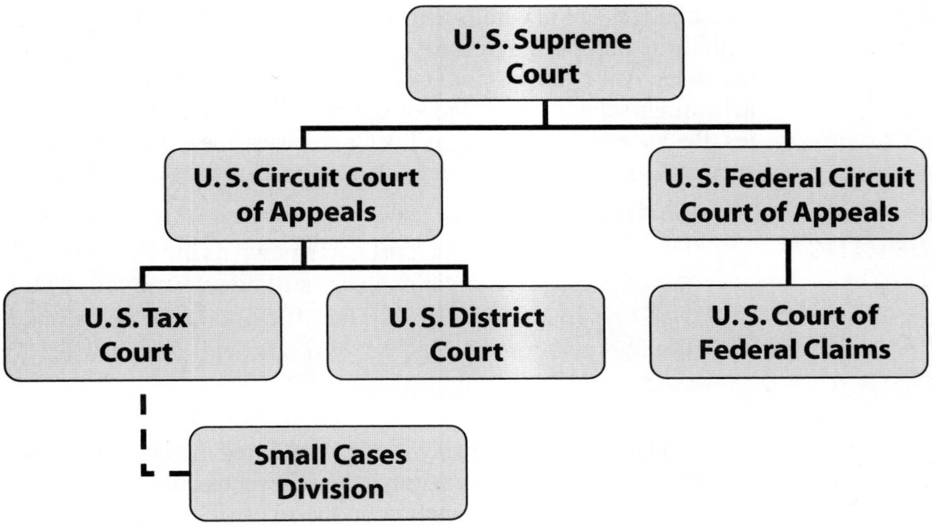

A taxpayer has three options for entering the court system: the U.S. Tax Court, the U.S. District Court or the U.S. Court of Federal Claims. Each trial court has different attributes and serves a different function within the Federal Judicial system. The trial courts appeal to 1 of 13 Courts of Appeals. The U.S. Tax Court and U.S. District Courts both appeal to 1 of the 12 geographical U.S. Circuit Courts of Appeals for the jurisdiction in which the taxpayer is located. The U.S. Court of Federal Claims appeals to the 13th Court of Appeals, the U.S. Federal Circuit Court of Appeals. A final appeal from the Circuit Court of Appeals may be available to the U.S. Supreme Court.

¶3005   The U.S. Tax Court

.01   THE SMALL CASES DIVISION OF THE TAX COURT

The U.S. Tax Court operates a Small Cases Division, which functions similar to a State Small Claims Court. The disputed deficiency (or overpayment) plus interest and penalties must not exceed $50,000. Legal representation is not required; taxpayers may represent themselves. The rules of evidence are relaxed and the hearing is informal; the judge is usually an experienced tax attorney appointed by the Tax Court. One disadvantage of this court is that no appeal is possible once the decision is rendered. The case decisions of the Small Cases Division are not published.

The appointed judge has the option of halting the proceeding and transferring the case to the regular U.S. Tax Court if it becomes apparent that important facts or issues of law would be better suited for the regular court. This does not happen very often.

OBSERVATION   A taxpayer with a deficiency of less than $50,000 still has the option of going to the regular Tax Court. That way, appeal options are still available to the taxpayer.

.03   THE REGULAR U.S. TAX COURT

A taxpayer must file a petition within 90-days from the mailing of the statutory notice of deficiency (discussed in Chapter 9) in order to have their case heard by the U.S. Tax Court. Taxpayers do not have to pay the deficiency to file in Tax Court; any amount due will be paid at the conclusion of the case. However, the interest clock is still running on the deficiency, so taxpayers may deposit the deficiency in escrow under special Tax Court procedures. Final settlement will be determined after the case concludes.

There are 19 Tax Court justices who are appointed by the President for 15-year terms. These judges are generally experienced tax attorneys with substantial litigation experience. Unlike the other original court options, the U.S. Tax Court is a national court that hears only tax cases. A jury trial is not possible; the case is generally heard by a single Tax Court judge at hearings scheduled around the country. The Tax Court hears cases in approximately 80 cities. Because of the backlog of Tax Court cases, the Chief Judge of the Tax Court may appoint special Associate Judges to try cases. Most cases are actually tried by the Associate Judges.

OBSERVATION   Prior to 1942, the Tax Court was known as the Board of Tax Appeals, and a number of these prior decisions may still be relevant law. The Board of Tax Appeals was first founded in 1924. The official cite for decisions of this court includes the abbreviation "BTA", while the official cite for decisions of the regular tax court includes the abbreviation "TC".

During the trial, the taxpayer is usually referred to as the "petitioner" and the IRS is normally called the "respondent." The taxpayer must be represented by a licensed attorney or an individual who passes a special examination on the rules of evidence for the Tax Court. Following the conclusion of the hearing, the Tax Court judge will draft a tentative opinion, and forward this opinion to the Chief Judge of the U.S. Tax Court in Washington, D.C. In most cases, the trial judge's decision is approved; however, the Chief Judge may designate the decision for review by the entire court. A decision reviewed by the entire court is referred to as an *en banc* **decision**.

Once a decision is made, the Chief Judge will designate the decision as either a *Regular decision* or a *Memorandum decision*. A **Regular decision** generally involves an important new or unusual point of law, and such a decision is published by the Tax Court through the Government Printing Office. There are approximately 60 to 70 regular decisions per year. A **Memorandum decision** typically involves either a straightforward application of existing law or an interpretation of facts, and these decisions are not published by the Court. There are approximately 500 to 600 Memorandum decisions each year. Although the United States government does not print these Memorandum decisions, private publishers such as CCH and RIA do publish these cases.

.05   APPEALS FROM THE U.S. TAX COURT

Although the Tax Court is a national court, appeals are made to 1 of the 12 geographically-situated U.S. Court of Appeals. In the case of a Tax Court decision, the appeal is to the geographic Circuit in which the taxpayer resides. The Circuit Court system is explained later in this chapter.

Under *Golsen*,[4] the Tax Court adopted a policy of following the Court of Appeals that has jurisdiction over the taxpayer. If that Circuit has not ruled on the issue, the Tax Court is free to decide the issue based on its own interpretation. Thus, Tax Court decisions may reach opposite conclusions because taxpayers reside in different Circuits. The Tax Court went on record in *Golsen*, however, as stating that as a matter of developing consistency among the courts, they would not as a rule reach opposite conclusions in different circuits on the same set of facts.

¶3007   The U.S. District Court

Taxpayers must pay the deficiency indicated on the statutory notice of deficiency and then file a claim for refund before the U.S. District Court will hear the case. The U.S. District Court is a federal court that hears all types of cases, not just tax cases. There are 94 geographical U.S. District Courts, spread among the 12 geographically-defined judicial circuits.

A map of the District Court system is provided in **Figure 2**. A District Court may cover a small geographic area (such as New York City) or an entire state. In some cases, a state has more than one District Court; for example, Virginia has an Eastern District and a Western District. The taxpayer will request a hearing before the District Court that has jurisdiction over the area where the taxpayer either lives or conducts business.

Figure 2
United States District Courts and Courts of Appeal

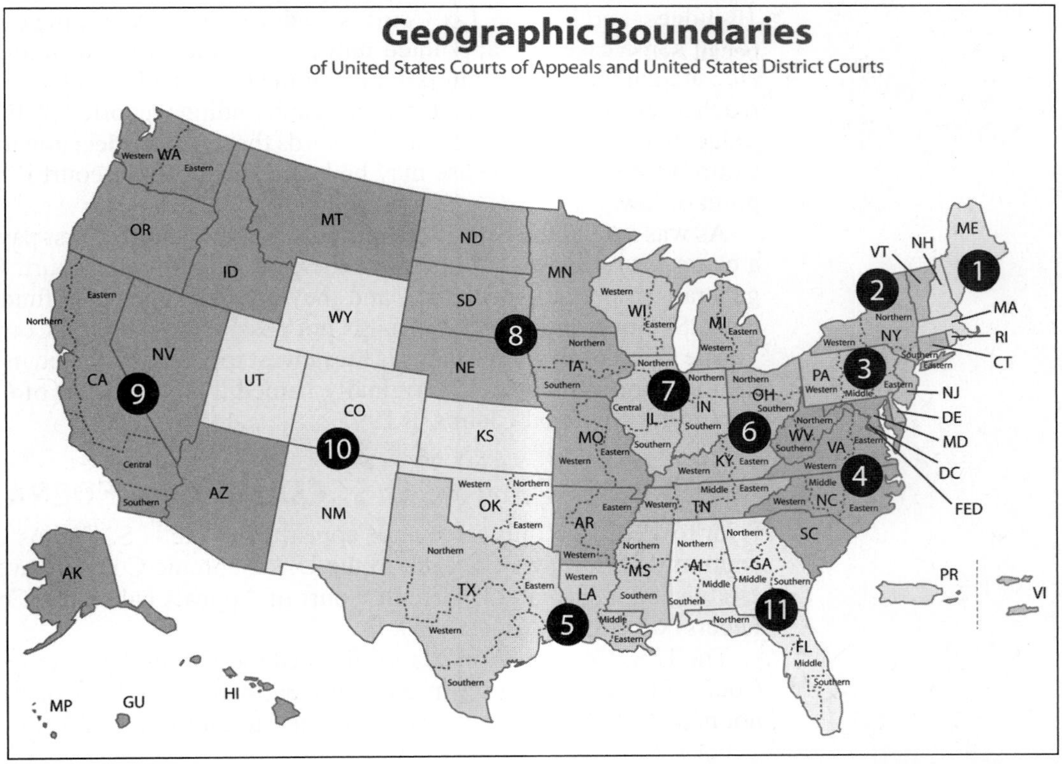

The U.S. District Court is the only court to offer a trial by jury; however, questions of law must be decided by the judge. A single judge presides over the case, and this court hears all types of civil and criminal cases. For that reason, the judge in the case is normally a generalist, and not a tax specialist. Since the judges are generalists, the decisions

---

[4]   *Golsen*, 54 TC 742.

across Districts Courts may vary considerably. Many of the decisions are well written and have important precedential value. However, other opinions are poorly conceived and are overturned on appeal. These opinions must be carefully reviewed to determine their precedential value before relying on them to solve a client's tax issue.

OBSERVATION   Since the District Court judge is usually not a tax specialist, he or she tends to rely more on Treasury interpretations than the judges on the U.S. Tax Court. For that reason, the taxpayer may choose the District Court route when there are published administrative pronouncements (e.g., revenue rulings, GCMs, etc.) that are favorable to his or her case. The District Court may also be chosen if the issue is one of fact and could find sympathy with a jury.

.01   U.S. DISTRICT COURT—APPEALS PROCEDURES

Appeals from the U.S. District Court are to the Circuit Court of Appeals in which the taxpayer resides. As discussed below, there are 12 geographically-based Circuit Courts of Appeal.

¶3009   The U.S. Court of Federal Claims

The U.S. Court of Federal Claims is a national court that hears all types of cases involving claims against the U.S. Government, not just tax cases. The Court is composed of 16 judges, and like the Tax Court, schedules trials around the country where one judge (or in some cases, an appointed judge) hears the case. Testimony, affidavits, evidence, etc., are gathered by Commissioners of the Court and reported to the judges. The judges reach a decision based on the evidence and findings reported by the Commissioners. This judge then drafts an opinion and forwards the tentative decision to the Chief Judge of the Court. Once again, the case may be heard by the entire court if it involves a significant point of law.

As was true of the U.S. District Court, a taxpayer must first pay the deficiency and file a claim for refund in order to have the case heard by this court. Judges in this court are generalists, not tax specialists, and they hear all types of refund cases brought against the U.S. Government. A jury trial is not possible in the U.S. Court of Federal Claims.

The Court of Federal Claims is the newest trial court, created in 1982 under the Federal Courts Improvement Act.[5] Originally named the U.S. Court of Claims, it was renamed the Court of Federal Claims in 1992.

.01   APPEALS FROM THE U.S. COURT OF FEDERAL CLAIMS

Prior to 1982, the only avenue of appeal from the U.S. Claims Court (the name of the court at that time) was directly to the U.S. Supreme Court. However, in 1982 Congress established a special 13th Circuit Court of Appeals called the Court of Appeals for the Federal Circuit.

The U.S. Court of Appeals for the Federal Circuit hears only appeals from the U.S. Court of Federal Claims. Since this is a national court, the Court of Federal Claims does not need to follow the decisions of other Circuit Courts of Appeal.

OBSERVATION   Since this Appeals Court has been in existence only since 1982, there are very few tax precedents on record in this court. For that reason, a taxpayer may choose the U.S. Court of Federal Claims as their court of original jurisdiction if that court has yet to rule on an issue similar to his or her issue.

---

[5] *Federal Courts Improvement Act*, P.L. 97-164.

¶3011   The Courts of Appeal

.01   LOCATING THE U.S. CIRCUIT COURTS OF APPEAL

The United States is divided into 12 geographical "circuits", with a U.S. Court of Appeals in each Circuit. For years there were only 10 geographic circuits, but eventually the migration to the Sun Belt caused Congress to split the 5th Circuit, which included Texas, Louisiana, Mississippi, Alabama and Florida. A new 11th Circuit was created, consisting of Florida, Georgia, and Alabama. Mississippi, Texas, and Louisiana remained in the 5th Circuit.

Subsequently, a 12th geographic Circuit Court was added in Washington, D.C. This court hears a number of important federal issues and is often called the "bullpen for future Supreme Court justices," as the Administration may make appointments to this court in order to observe someone's performance closely. Finally, as mentioned above, a 13th Circuit Court, known as the Court of Appeals for the Federal Circuit, was added in 1982 to hear appeals from the U.S. Court of Federal Claims only. See **Figure 2** for a map of the U.S. Courts of Appeal.

.03   OPERATION OF THE CIRCUIT COURTS OF APPEAL

Each Circuit Court has a panel of approximately 20 judges, and each case that is granted a hearing is assigned a panel of 3 judges. The Appeals Court typically accepts only cases that involve important points of tax law, as opposed to fact-based decisions. The Appeals Court will generally take one of three actions: (1) affirm the lower-court case, (2) reverse the lower-court case, or (3) remand the case back to the lower court with additional instructions.

Each Circuit Court follows a doctrine of *stare decisis*, in that the Court will always follow its own decisions as precedents; however, one Circuit Court is not required to follow another Circuit Court's decisions (but they may choose to do so, in the interests of promoting consistency in the judicial system). A Circuit Court is bound only to follow decisions of the U.S. Supreme Court.

OBSERVATION	Although the 5th and 11th Circuit Courts are independent, the 11th Circuit is still bound by all decisions of the 5th Circuit made prior to the split that formed the 11th Circuit in 1981. At that time, the 5th Circuit decisions were still controlling.

¶3013   The U.S. Supreme Court

.01   COMPOSITION OF THE COURT

Appeals from one of the U.S. Circuit Courts of Appeal are made to the U.S. Supreme Court, the final and ultimate court of appeal in the country. The Supreme Court is a national court headquartered in Washington, D.C. The Court has nine judges who are appointed by the President of the United States for life, with the consent of the Senate.

The Court hears very few tax cases during a term; typically, only 10–12 tax cases are heard in any one year. A *writ of certiorari* must be filed requesting a hearing by the Supreme Court, and at least four judges must approve the petition before a trial is granted. If the Court approves a petition, the certiorari is "granted"; if the Court does not approve the petition, the certiorari is "denied".

.03   THE COURT AND TAX CASES

The Supreme Court is more likely to grant a petition related to a tax case if either of two conditions are present. First, the Court may decide to hear a case where different Circuit Courts of Appeal have issued conflicting decisions on the issue. In the interest of providing uniform case law, the Court may decide to settle the issue.

A second circumstance in which the Court may grant certiorari is when the tax issue is of major significance to taxpayers and involves interpretation of existing law. For example, one of the last major tax cases considered by the Supreme Court was *Soliman*,[6] which involved the home office deduction. In an era of telecommuting where a large number of taxpayers worked out of their home, the Court decided that some resolution of the home office controversy was appropriate.

> **OBSERVATION**   A refusal by the Supreme Court to hear a case does not mean that the Court is affirming the lower-court ruling. Rather, it simply means that the Court does not consider the issue important or interesting enough to add to an already over-crowded calendar. Nonetheless, a decision that has not been granted certiorari is generally viewed as having more precedent value than one without, since this decision is likely to stand for a while.

¶3015 Locating and Citing Judicial Authority

.01   LOCATING JUDICIAL AUTHORITY—PRINT SERVICE REFERENCES

Figure 3

Type of Case	Official Reporter	Unofficial Reporters
Tax Court Regular	Tax Court Reports (T.C.) Board of Tax Appeals (BTA) for cases issued prior to 1942	CCH Tax Court Reporter RIA Tax Court Reports
Tax Court Memorandum	No official reporter	CCH Tax Court Reporter RIA Tax Court Reports
District Court	Federal Supplement Reporter (F. Supp.)	American Federal Tax Reports (AFTR)—published by RIA United States Tax Cases (USTC)—published by CCH
Claims Court	United States Court of Federal Claims Reporter (Fed. Cl.)—since 1992 Prior to 1992: United States Claims Court Reporter (Cl. Ct.)—1982-1992 Federal Reporter—1960-1982	American Federal Tax Reports (AFTR)—published by RIA United States Tax Cases (USTC)—published by CCH
Appellate Courts	Federal Reporter (F.; F.2d.; F.3d; F.4th)	American Federal Tax Reports (AFTR)—published by RIA United States Tax Cases (USTC)—published by CCH
Supreme Court	United States Reports (U.S.)	American Federal Tax Reports (AFTR)—published by RIA United States Tax Cases (USTC)—published by CCH

---

[6] *Soliman*, 93-1 USTC ¶50,014, 506 US 168.

Most court cases have both an "official reporter" (the original publication by the court, which is included in official case volumes that include all types of cases, other than the Tax Court) and an "unofficial reporter" (a separate reporter series by two tax publishers, CCH and RIA, that report relevant tax cases only). **Figure 3** summarizes the official and the unofficial reporters. The title of each reporter also includes the appropriate citation abbreviations used when citing a case (for example, the citation abbreviation for the Federal Supplement Reporter is "F. Supp.").

The "official reporter" for tax cases is either the Government Printing Office (for the Tax Court) or West Publishing (for most other courts). Also, two "unofficial reporters", the AFTR (by RIA) and the USTC (by CCH) include tax decisions from all courts other than the U.S. Tax Court. Thus, any particular court case from these courts will have three different citations: (1) an "official" citation with West Publishing Co., (2) a USTC cite for the CCH "unofficial" reporter, and (3) an "AFTR" cite for the RIA "unofficial" reporter.

OBSERVATION	"USTC" is an abbreviation for "United States Tax Cases" by CCH (Wolters Kluwer), and "AFTR" is an abbreviation for "American Federal Tax Reporter" by RIA (Thomson Reuters). See the discussion on case citations below for examples.

.03   LOCATING JUDICIAL AUTHORITY—ELECTRONIC RESOURCES

Finding a particular court case is much easier when it is done electronically. Most tax services on the Internet group cases into large databases and automatically locate a given citation from the appropriate court library.

More and more cases are being added for free access on the Internet. These sites include the following:

1. *http://lp.findlaw.com* (Findlaw Internet Legal Services site, contains Supreme Court and Circuit Court of Appeals cases)
2. *http://www.taxsites.com* (Follow the links for Federal tax law; Court Decisions; Free Services)

.05   CITING JUDICIAL AUTHORITY

The "citation" of a case usually includes the name of a case and relevant information to assist in locating the case. Generally, the cite will, at a minimum, consist of a series of numbers, followed by a series of letters, followed by another set of numbers such as: *111 XXXX 2222*, where "111" is the volume number of the case series, "XXXX" is the abbreviation of the case law series (e.g., F. Supp. for the Federal Supplement), and "2222" is the page number (or in some cases, the paragraph number) where the case is located. In addition, it is common to add a parenthetical expression to the cite disclosing the abbreviation of the relevant court (if not obvious from the citation) and the year of the case.

Generally, the form of the case name itself provides a clue as to the particular court involved in the decision. For example, consider the following three citations:

- *J.C. Johnson v. Commissioner* (indicates a Tax Court case)
- *J.C. Johnson v. Eisner* (an early Tax Court case, where Eisner was the Commissioner of Internal Revenue)
- *J.C. Johnson v. U.S.* (indicates a case in District Court or Claims Court, in that the taxpayer is suing for a refund of taxes already paid, as required by the court)

The official and unofficial court reporters, along with citation abbreviations, are summarized in Figure 3 above. Recall that for cases other than the U.S. Tax Court, the case will be published in an "official reporter" (usually West Publishing Co.) and also in the two "unofficial reporters" by CCH and RIA.

Tax Court Citation Examples

Tax Court Memorandum Decision

Nelson Bros Inc. TC Memo 1992-726 , RIA TC Memo ¶92726 (RIA citation)
Nelson Bros Inc. TC Memo 1992-726 , 64 CCH TCM 1594 (CCH citation)

Kraus, Dennis J. TC Memo 2003-10, RIA TC Memo ¶2003-010 (RIA citation)
Kraus, Dennis J. TC Memo 2003-10, 85 CCH TCM 750 (CCH citation)

Regular Tax Court Decision

Takahashi, Harry, 87 TC 126

District Court Decision

Flamingo Resort Inc v U.S., (1980, DC NV) 45 AFTR 2d 80-1487 (RIA citation)
Flamingo Resort Inc v U.S., (1980, DC NV) 485 F Supp 926 (Federal Supplement Reporter)
Flamingo Resort Inc v U.S., (1980, DC NV) 80-1 USTC ¶9312 (CCH citation) Note
that *DC NV* is the abbreviation for District Court, Nevada.

Court of Federal Claims Decision

Old U.S. Court of Claims citations:
Johnson, Marie v. U.S., (1986, Cl Ct) 58 AFTR 2d 86-5894 (RIA citation)
Johnson, Marie v. U.S., (1986, Cl Ct) 11 Cl Ct 17 (United States Claims Court Reporter)
Johnson, Marie v. U.S., (1986, Cl Ct) 86-2 USTC ¶9705 (CCH citation)
Note that *Cl Ct* is the abbreviation for Court of Claims.

Current Court of Federal Claims citations:

Purdey, William v. U.S., (1997, Ct Fed Cl) 80 AFTR 2d 97-7600 (RIA citation)
Purdey, William v. U.S., (1997, Ct Fed Cl) 39 Fed Cl 413 (United States Court of
Federal Claims Reporter)
Purdey, William v. U.S., (1997, Ct Fed Cl) 97-2 USTC ¶50894 (CCH citation)
Note that *Ct Fed Cl* is the abbreviation for Court of Federal Claims.

Circuit Court of Appeals Decisions

Decision of geographical Court of Appeals
U.S. v. Tuff, James H., (2006, CA9) 98 AFTR 2d 2006-7975 (RIA citation)
U.S. v. Tuff, James H., (2006, CA9) 469 F3d 1249 (Federal Reporter citation)
U.S. v. Tuff, James H., (2006, CA9) 2007-1 USTC ¶50103 (CCH citation)
Note that *CA9* is the abbreviation for the Court of Appeals, 9th Circuit.

Decision of Court of Appeals for Federal Circuit

Palahnuk, Jonathan v. U.S., (2007, CA Fed Cir) 99 AFTR 2d 2007-794 (RIA citation)
Palahnuk, Jonathan v. U.S., (2007, CA Fed Cir) 475 F3d 1380 (Federal Reporter citation)
Note that *CA Fed Cir* is the abbreviation for the Court of Appeals, Federal Circuit.

Supreme Court Decisions

Com. v. Soliman, Nader, (1993, S Ct) 71 AFTR 2d 93-463 (RIA citation)
Com. v. Soliman, Nader, (1993, S Ct) 506 US 168 (United States Reports citation)
Com. v. Soliman, Nader, (1993, S Ct) 93-1 USTC ¶50014 (CCH citation)
Note that *S Ct* is the abbreviation for Supreme Court.

.07   USING A CITATOR

When a court case appears to be relevant to a particular tax research question, it is extremely important to do a citation search on the case. A "Citator" lists any cases, rulings, or other authority that "cites" the case of interest. The level of detail in the cite depends on the particular Citator. Three popular Citators are the *CCH Citator*, the *RIA Citator*, and *Shephard's Citator*.

The *CCH Citator*, published by CCH, a Wolters Kluwer business, is included with the basic print or electronic subscription at no extra charge. This Citator lists cases or other authorities that "cite" the case of interest, but no other details are given. The *CCH Citator* is illustrated briefly in the discussion of the CCH Federal Tax Service in the Appendix to this chapter.

The *RIA Citator*, published by Thomson Reuters, was formerly known as the *Prentice-Hall Citator*. This Citator provides more details for each cited case, such as the issue(s) within the case being cited, and the relationship of the cited case to the case of interest (e.g., explained, distinguished, agreed on all fours, etc.)

The *Shephard's Citator* is included on the full-service LEXIS subscription and is also available in print as a separate service. This Citator is similar to the *RIA Citator*, in that more details as to issues and relationships between the cases are provided.

OBSERVATION   A common expression in the legal world is to "Shep" or "Shepardize" a case, meaning simply to check Shephard's citation for the particular case.

¶3017   Reading and Assessing Court Opinions

.01   SPECIAL ELEMENTS OF A CASE

Judicial decisions have their own terminology, and it is helpful to be familiar with some of the more common terms. Ten terms often mentioned when referring to court cases are:

1. *Majority Opinion.* The official published opinion and reasoning of the Court, generally written by one judge hearing the case.
2. *Concurring Opinions.* Opinions of one or more other judges in the case that while agreeing with the final decision of the majority, they would reach the same conclusion on alternative grounds.
3. *Dissenting Opinions.* Opinions of one or more judges in the case that disagree with the majority decision.
4. *En Banc Decision.* A decision rendered by all of the judges in a particular court.
5. *Petitioner (or Appellant).* The party filing suit (in an appeal, it is the party filing the appeal).
6. *Respondent.* The party being sued.
7. *Pro se.* Indicates that the taxpayer is representing himself or herself.
8. *Rule 155.* A notation sometimes found at the end of a Tax Court case that indicates that the Tax Court will leave the final determination of tax liability up to the taxpayer and the IRS.
9. *Dictum.* An observation or conclusion stated in the case, that while not crucial to the decision, may provide clues to future litigation (Example: "If the taxpayer had been in a trade or business…").
10. *Action on Decision.* A recommendation by the Office of the Chief Counsel of the IRS to the Department of Justice as to reaction to an adverse court decision.

.03   ASSESSING THE AUTHORITATIVE VALUE OF A CASE

One of the important tasks that a tax researcher faces is evaluating the authoritative value of a court decision. There are a few general guides that may aid in this process. In general, the higher the level of the Court, the more authoritative the value of the decision. Obviously, a U.S. Supreme Court decision trumps all others. En banc decisions are generally regarded as being more authoritative than regular decisions, especially in the U.S. Tax Court.

Courts of Appeal decisions that have had certiori denied tend to be viewed more authoritatively than those in which certiori was not sought. One Circuit Court of Appeal is not bound by decisions of another Circuit Court of Appeal, although they may choose to follow that Circuit's decision.

OBSERVATION   Decisions of the 2nd Circuit (that includes New York) and the 9th Circuit (that includes California) tend to be reviewed closely and treated with a high level of authority (because of the tremendous number of cases decided by those circuits).

U.S. Tax Court decisions are viewed generally as having more authority than U.S. District Court or U.S. Court of Federal Claims decisions. Furthermore, Tax Court regular decisions are viewed as being more authoritative than memorandum decisions. An en banc Tax Court decision is more authoritative than regular non-reviewed decisions. And finally, the precedential value of a decision increases as the number of judges participating in the majority opinion increases.

OBSERVATION   In a highly unusual result, in the case of *Carriage Square, Inc.*, the (then) 16 Tax Court judges were split as follows: 5 judges agreed with the majority opinion, 6 judges agreed with a concurring opinion, and 5 judges dissented to the result. Thus, 11 of the 16 judges did not agree with the majority decision![7]

.05   ACQUIESCENCE/NONACQUIESCENCE POLICY OF THE IRS

When the IRS loses a case, they will generally take one of three actions: acquiescence, nonacquiescence, or simply remain silent. When the IRS issues an acquiescence, they are indicating that they will abide by the adverse decision in regards to the same issue in the future. On the other hand, if the Service issues a nonacquiescence, they are indicating that they disagree with the result and may contest similar issues in the future. Finally, the Service may choose simply to do nothing, indicating that they may bide their time and contest the issue in another court (or circuit) in hopes of achieving victory in a different forum so that perhaps a higher court will overturn the original adverse decision.

Prior to 1990, the IRS would apply the acquiescence policy only to cases of the U.S. Tax Court; now the policy applies to all courts. The IRS will frequently issue their acquiescence or nonacquiescence in the form of a Revenue Ruling, or simply publish notice as an Action on Decision (AOD). AODs are initially published in the Internal Revenue Bulletin and then included in the Cumulative Bulletin. The AOD will include a brief review of the issue decided against the government, the relevant facts and a discussion of the IRS's reasoning for the acquiescence/nonacquiescence.

---

[7]   *Carriage Square, Inc.*, 69 TC 119.

¶3017.03

¶3019   Factors to Consider in Choosing a Court

.01   THE VALUE OF PRECEDENTS

Earlier the doctrine of **stare decisis** was discussed briefly. Translated literally, this expression means "let the decision stand." In other words, courts are hesitant to overturn their own decisions for fear of creating more ambiguity in the law. Therefore, any decisions of a court related to the issue at hand should be considered carefully for their value as a precedent.

In general, legal precedents are more likely to have been established in either the Appeals Courts or the U.S. Tax Court regular decisions, while factual precedents are more likely generated by the U.S. District Court, the Federal Court of Claims, or U.S. Tax Court memorandum decisions. It may prove easier to overcome a factual precedent because the actual facts of two cases are seldom the same, but legal precedents are another matter. Again, courts are hesitant to "rewrite" settled law.

What if the case involves a new issue, one not addressed previously by the courts? Most commentators suggest going to either the U.S. District Court or the Federal Court of Claims, as they may be more sympathetic to the taxpayer's position and a little more predictable than the U.S. Tax Court.

.03   OTHER FACTORS

A variety of other factors may come into play in choosing a court. For example, dollars may be an issue, and in this regard the U.S. Tax Court offers the only option of not paying until the case is heard. If the case appears to have technical merit, the U.S. Tax Court might also be the choice, since the judges are seasoned tax specialists. On the other hand, if the case is based largely on facts or a somewhat emotional appeal, then the trial by jury option with the U.S. District Court may be the better option. And if local knowledge is important to understanding the taxpayer's case, the U.S. District Court may once again be the best option.

The U.S. Tax Court may offer more opportunities for selecting representatives before the Court, as the Small Cases division does not require legal representation and the Tax Court allows individuals other than attorneys to try a case if they have passed a special Tax Court examination. The rules of evidence are also somewhat relaxed in the U.S. Tax Court. In addition, the Tax Court offers the advantage of less publicity, as it is a national court that hears only tax cases.

Briefing a Case

An important part of the research process is the ability to brief a case. When researching a tax issue, several cases may be relevant and it may be easy to confuse one case with the other. Briefing a case, that is, writing up a summary of the key elements of a case, is an indispensable part of tax research. A case brief should be limited to one page and consist of the following elements: (1) the case name and full legal citation at the top, (2) a summary of the facts of the case (1–2 paragraphs), (3) a listing of the key tax issues to be decided by the court, (4) the holding of the court on each issue, and (5) an analysis of the court's reasoning for its decision (1–2 paragraphs). A sample case brief is shown in **Figure 4**.

Figure 4—Sample Case Brief

Abraham Solkov
46 TC 190 (1969, Acq.)

Facts:
Ira Franken is a cantor of the Jewish faith. He is employed by a congregation on a full-time basis, and performs substantially all of the sacerdotal functions of the Jewish faith. Ira is unsure whether or not he can exclude from income the fair rental value of a home furnished to him by the congregation.

Issues:

Can a full-time cantor of the Jewish faith exclude from income the fair rental value of a home furnished to him by his congregation?

Conclusion:

Yes, the fair rental value of the home furnished by the congregation may be excluded from income.

Arguments and Authorities:

Code Sec. 107 states that "In the case of a minister of the gospel, gross income does not include (1) the rental value of a home furnished to him as part of his compensation, or (2) the rental allowance paid to him as part of his compensation, to the extent used by him to rent or provide a home." Reg. §1.107-1(a) provides specific examples of services that are considered to be duties of a minister of the gospel. These include the "performance of sacerdotal functions, the conduct of religious worship, and the administration and maintenance of religious organizations and their internal agencies."

The duties of a cantor of the Jewish faith were expressly addressed in this case. The Tax Court allowed the exclusion of the rental allowance for a full-time cantor who was formally installed by the congregation. The Court noted the dual ministry of the rabbi and the cantor, even though only rabbis are ordained. The Court concluded that a "cantor who has a bona fide commission and performs ministerial duties on a full-time basis" is a minister of the gospel within the meaning of Sec. 107 and is thus entitled to an exclusion of the fair rental value of a home furnished by the congregation.

¶3023   Summary

- The judicial branch provides interpretation of the Code through tax case decisions.
- Judicial decisions are the third primary source of tax law.
- The three initial trial courts are the U.S. Tax Court, the U.S. District Court and The U.S. Court of Federal Claims.
- A trial court decision (other than the small case division of the Tax Court) can be appealed to 1 of 13 Circuit Courts of Appeals.
- A few Court of Appeals decisions will be granted certiorari by the Supreme Court.
- Providing a proper citation for a court case is an important element of tax research.
- Court decisions are published by either the U.S. Government or private publishing companies and are readily available at various on-line sites.

Review Questions for Chapter 3

True or False

Indicate which of the following statements are true or false by circling the correct answer.

1. The 9th Circuit Court of Appeals must follow the opinion of the 2nd Circuit Court of   T   F
    Appeals if the 2nd Circuit has previously ruled on the same tax issue.

2. Only the IRS can file an appeal to the Supreme Court.   T   F

3. A jury trial is only available in the District Court.   T   F

4. Taxpayers must pay the assessed tax prior to filing a case with the Tax Court.   T   F

5. Appeals from the Court of Appeals for the Federal Circuit go to the Supreme Court,   T   F
    which decides which cases to hear.

6. The Circuit Court of Appeals has always had 11 geographical (numbered) circuits.   T   F

7. The U.S. Court of Federal Claims hears cases only in Washington, D.C.   T   F

8. The citation for *Boeing Company v. U.S.* is 537 U.S. 437. This means that the case ap-   T   F
    pears in Volume 537, page 437 of the United States Supreme Court Reports.

9. The citation for *Bush Brothers & Co.* is 73 TC 424. This indicates that the case was   T   F
    decided by the Tax Court in 1973.

10. The IRS will issue an acquiescence or nonacquiescence in all cases decided against   T   F
    the Commissioner.

Fill in the Blanks

Fill in each blank with the appropriate word or phrase that completes each sentence.

11. A(n) _____ enables tax researchers to locate authorities which have cited a particular case.
12. If the U.S. Supreme Court decides to hear an appeal in a tax case, the certiorari is _____.
13. The official published opinion and reasoning of the court is called the _____.
14. The _____ mandates that the Tax Court rule consistently with decision of the Circuit Court of Appeals for the circuit where the taxpayer resides or does business.
15. The _____ is the person who initially brings a lawsuit.
16. When the Tax Court reaches a decision without calculating the tax, the decision is said to be entered under _____.
17. The term _____ is used to indicate a decision of the whole court, rather than of one judge.
18. The U.S. Supreme Court has _____ justices.
19. A(n) _____ refers to a situation when an interpretation of the statute is unclear.
20. Most courts follow a doctrine of _____, in that a court views its own prior decisions as precedents to be followed.

Multiple Choice

Circle the best answer for each of the following questions.

21. In order to have a case heard in the small case division of the U.S. Tax Court require, the total amount of the dispute cannot exceed
    a. $5,000.
    b. $10,000.
    c. $50,000.
    d. $100,000.

22. A tax case *cannot* be appealed when initiated in the
    a.   U.S. Court of Federal Claims.
    b.   U.S. Tax Court.
    c.   U.S. Tax Court Small Case Division.
    d.   None of the above, tax cases can always be appealed.

23. Which of the following citations denotes a Tax Court regular decision?
    a.   85 AFTR 2d 2000-879
    b.   84 TCM 710 (2002)
    c.   121 TC 290 (2003)
    d.   cannot determine with the information provided

24. A jury trial is available in which of the following courts?
    a.   U.S. Court of Federal Claims.
    b.   U.S. District Court.
    c.   U.S. Tax Court
    d.   All of the above allow jury trials.

25. The IRS may acquiesce in which of the following court decisions?
    a.   U.S. District Court decisions.
    b.   U.S. Tax Court regular decisions.
    c.   Court of Appeals decisions.
    d.   U.S. Supreme Court decisions.
    e.   a, b and c

26. When the Tax Court follows the opinion of the Circuit Court of Appeals to which the case is appealable, the court is following
    a.   Rule 155.
    b.   the litigation consistency rule.
    c.   the Golsen rule.
    d.   the conformity rule.

27. Martha utilized the small case division of the Tax Court to hear her case. She disagrees with the judge's finding in her case. Which of the following options is available to Martha?
    a.   She can appeal the case to the U.S. Court of Appeals for her geographic circuit.
    b.   She can appeal her case to the Tax Court.
    c.   She can refile her case in either the District Court or Court of Federal Claims.
    d.   There is no appeal.

28. Given the following citation: *Williams, Lloyd E. Jr., 94 TC 464*, which of the following statements is true?
   a. The taxpayer, Lloyd Williams won the case because there is no reference to the IRS.
   b. The case appears on page 464 in Volume 94 of the official Tax Court of the United States Reports.
   c. This citation refers to a taxpayer conference between the IRS and the taxpayer.
   d. The case was decided in 1994.
   e. Both b and d are correct.

29. Tax Court memorandum decisions
   a. usually deal with factual variations of issues litigated previously.
   b. cannot be appealed.
   c. are not published.
   d. have no precedential value.

30. A taxpayer lives in an area where the 5th Circuit Court of Appeals has jurisdiction. The taxpayer is deciding which court of entry to use for his tax case. The following case history is available:
   Cases in favor of taxpayer: 1st, 3rd, and Federal Circuit Court of Appeals
   Cases against taxpayer: 5th, 7th, and 9th Circuit Court of Appeals

   Which court should the taxpayer file his case in?
   a. Tax Court
   b. District Court
   c. Court of Federal Claims
   d. 1st Circuit Court of Appeals

Review Problems

31. What are some of the factors to consider when deciding in which court to file a tax related claim?
32. Is it possible for the Tax Court to intentionally issue conflicting decisions? Explain.
33. What are the possible appeal advantages of having a case heard through the U.S. Court of Federal Claims?
34. If the U.S. District Court for Eastern Virginia, the Tax Court, and the 9th Circuit have all ruled on a particular issue, then what precedents have been set for which courts in the future?
35. What is the purpose of a Citator?
36. Discuss the differences and similarities between U.S. Tax Court regular and memorandum decisions.
37. Identify the circuit court of appeals for taxpayers living in each of the following states:
   a. Florida
   b. New York
   c. Arizona
   d. Oregon
   e. Michigan
38. By using only the citation information provided, determine which court(s) issued the decision(s).
   a. Ianniello, Matthew, (1992) 98 TC 165.
   b. Murillo, Francisco A., (1998) 75 CCH TCM 1564, affd (1998, CA2) 83 AFTR 2d 99-596.
   c. Wood, Roland v. U.S., (2002, DC FL) 2003-1 USTC ¶50193.
   d. McKinney, Herman v. U.S., (1976, DC TX) 38 AFTR 2d 76-6098, affd on other issue (1978, CA5) 574 F2d 1240, cert den (1979, S Ct) 439 US 1072.
   e. Wagner, Lawrence, (1934) 30 BTA 1099 .
   f. Com. v. Sullivan, Neil, (1958, S Ct) 58-1 USTC ¶9368, affg (1957, CA7) 57-1 USTC ¶9399 (1956) TC Memo 1956-5.

39. Compare and contrast the three entry level courts in the following areas:
    a. payment requirement
    b. availability of jury trial
    c. types of cases heard
    d. jurisdiction
    e. appeals court
40. Describe the Small Case Division of the Tax Court.

Research Problems

41. Locate a tax case that discusses the appropriate time for recognizing espionage payments. Provide the complete citation.
42. Locate a tax case that involves whether a neighbor of OJ Simpson can take a casualty loss deduction. Provide the complete citation.
43. Locate a tax case that involves the valuation of stock in the company that produces Korbel champagne. Provide the complete citation.
44. Locate a tax case involving a producer and promoter of the musical group New Kids on the Block. Provide the complete citation.
45. Locate a tax case involving the ex-wife of a member of the Eagles musical group regarding who should pay tax on royalty income. Provide the complete citation.
46. Locate a tax case involving tax deductions for a business selling medical marijuana. Provide the complete citation.
47. Locate the following cases and answer the questions (1) What year was the case decided and what tax year was involved? (2) What court heard the case? (3) What was the issue involved? (4) Did the taxpayer or the government prevail?
    a. 104 TC 140
    b. 117 TC 294 (answer questions 3 and 4 for Issue #3)
    c. 84 F. Supp. 2d 1043
    d. 349 F3d 102
    e. TC Memo 1997-498
    f. 668 F.3d 1008
48. Brief one of the following cases:
    a. Highway Farms, Inc., DC Iowa, 2002-1 USTC ¶50,281
    b. Robert J. Geary v. Commissioner, 235 F.3d 1207

CHAPTER 4

Tax Research—Locating and Assessing Tax Authority

Learning Objectives

1. Describe the various types of tax research.
2. Identify the steps in tax research.
3. Grasp the basics of communicating the results of tax research.
4. Understand how to use the CCH and RIA tax research services.

¶4001 Introduction

Tax research is a significant part of a tax advisor's practice and the foundation of a tax professional's career. Research is the basis for providing guidance to clients. A tax advisor must also understand that the consequences of wrong advice can be costly for both the client and the advisor. This chapter will help develop a process for research that can improve both research efficiency and effectiveness.

¶4003 Types of Tax Research

Most tax practitioners engage in three types of tax research: planning, compliance, and policy. **Planning research** (also know as before-the-event or open transaction research) is research performed before the client takes an action, before the facts are certain. This type of research allows the practitioner to clearly demonstrate the benefits of research by participating in the structuring of transactions and minimizing the associated taxes. The tax advisor's goal is to identify the optimal set of facts to achieve the client's desired business and tax outcomes. This type of research generally results from continued contact with the client throughout the year where the client shares thoughts and ideas about new directions for the company. Planning ideas can also develop during the compliance process by looking for areas where the client could save taxes.

Compliance research (also know as after-the-event or closed transaction research) is performed after the fact. This is probably the most common type of research because the issues are typically identified during the preparation of the tax return or during an audit. In this type of research, the transaction has already taken place, so there is less flexibility because the facts are already certain. The tax advisor's goal is to find the optimal solution based on the given facts.

Policy research includes analyzing different tax reform proposals being considered by Congress. It may also involve research to influence legislation for clients or to promote a tax position for the profession. Policy-type research may also be performed for education purposes. Professionals must learn new law in order to stay current and this often requires research into the legislative history, the Joint Committee's blue book, and IRS notices.

Given the complexity of the tax law, professionals need to know "how" to find the answers, rather than knowing all the answers. In the last 10 years, there have been over 20 major tax acts and a never-ending flow of rulings, cases, regulations, and other announcements. Since it is impossible to know all of the answers, it is important to learn how to efficiently find the answers. Practitioners must be willing to say, "I don't know, but I can find out."

¶4005   Steps in Tax Research

There are six identifiable steps in the research process.
1. Identify the facts
2. Determine the issues or questions
3. Search for authority
4. Analyze authority
5. Develop conclusions and recommendations
6. Communicate the results

.01   IDENTIFY THE FACTS

This is one of the most difficult steps in tax research because the facts must be obtained from the client. All the relevant facts must be elicited from the client in order for the professional to determine the issue and reach the correct conclusion. Many times, this is easier said than done. Once the facts are established, the advisor can then define the tax issues and locate the relevant authority.

The professional must learn to effectively interview clients in order to ascertain the relevant facts. The facts will include who, what, when, where and how. Important facts may initially be overlooked because the client does not provide the information, many times assuming that a detail is not important. For example, when property is sold, the fact that the purchaser is related to the seller may be overlooked, even though this is a critical fact. Professionals need to learn to be thorough in identifying and collecting facts during an initial client interview. If the general topic is known before the client meeting, do a little research ahead of time and develop a list of facts that need to be identified. Identifying the important facts will depend on the issues that need to be addressed. Remember that a change in the facts can and often will change the conclusion.

Example 4-1. What are the critical facts in the following transaction?

Jeff and Karen agreed to care for a troubled niece. She moved in on December 27, 2012, and lived with them for the entire year of 2013, except for time spent back at home to visit her parents.

What additional facts are needed?

Remember to elicit the facts from the client, not conclusions. For example, do not ask how many dependents the client has. Instead, discuss ages, full-time student status, gross income, etc. so that the number of dependents can be properly determined. Don't be afraid to ask "dumb" questions. It is less embarrassing to ask simple questions than to research an irrelevant issue.

Important Facts

As a beginning researcher it is difficult to determine what facts may be important. The following facts often impact a client's situation.

Type of business entity involved. The type of business entity may determine the tax treatment of a transaction. Always determine the form in which the business operates (partnership, corporation, sole proprietor, S corporation, etc.)

Worker status. Whether an individual is considered an employee or an independent contractor may impact the result.

Related parties. Tax treatment may differ for dealings between related parties compared to transactions with unrelated taxpayers. Ask questions about ownership percentages to determine whether taxpayers are related.

Taxpayer marginal rates, other gains/losses, and AMT situation. A transaction may impact the taxpayer's overall tax liability through its impact on phase-outs and AMT. The tax implications of gains/losses are impacted by other gain/loss transactions during the year and the character of the other transactions (passive, ordinary, capital).

Accounting methods. Does the taxpayer use cash or accrual basis? What inventory method is used?

Special tax status. Is the taxpayer in a business where special tax rules apply?

Taxpayer's location and location of transaction. The researcher should not just focus on federal tax issues. State or foreign tax issues may be relevant.

Timing of transaction. What is the taxpayer's time frame for completing the transaction? What is the taxpayer's motivation? Why is the taxpayer considering the transaction? What does the client want to accomplish? How flexible is the client?

.03   DETERMINE THE ISSUES OR QUESTIONS

This may be the hardest part of the research process. Experience, education and training are required to develop the skills needed to identify research issues. In some situations, the client will identify the issue. For example, the client may ask whether certain product research qualifies for the research credit. In other situations, the advisor will identify an issue from the information the client provided to prepare a tax return. For example, the client indicates a new home address. This may lead to questions regarding moving expenses, the deductibility of expenses associated with purchasing a home, or a gain/loss on the sale of the previous residence. In other situations, the client may mention the company's plans to begin distributing its product in Western Europe, and the tax practitioner must recognize the potential tax issues associated with foreign operations and bring them to the attention of the client.

Example 4-2. What are the potential tax issues in the following situation?

Faye and Hal's son graduated from high school in June. He started at State University in September. However, due to health issues, he withdrew from the university in early November. The university did not refund any of the $4,500 tuition and $3,500 room and board Faye and Hal had paid.

Tax issues frequently involve the following questions:
- Does the transaction generate taxable income? When must the income be recognized?
- What is the character of the income? (tax free, ordinary, capital gain)
- Does the transaction result in a tax deduction? What type of deduction is created? Are there any limits on the deductibility of the expense?
- What is property's basis?
- Is the transaction tax-free?
- Does the expenditure qualify for a credit?

Tax research generally involves multiple cycles through steps one through four. In many cases the researcher will identify new issues when evaluating authority. For example, if the Code requires that certain conditions are met before a deduction may be claimed, the researcher may have to obtain additional facts in order to complete the research. Few research projects progress from steps one through six without having to repeat earlier steps.

In order to identify all the tax issues involved, a researcher must usually consult the tax law. Experienced researchers are constantly thinking about new issues that might require investigation while reading the tax authority. Repeating research steps is a normal and necessary part of the tax research process.

.05   SEARCH FOR AUTHORITY

This step involves identifying the relevant authority that applies to the client's facts and circumstances and then ascertaining that the authority is still current. Tax authority can be classified as either primary or secondary authority. **Primary authority** includes original pronouncements that come from the statutory, administrative and judicial sources discussed in Chapters 1 through 3. **Secondary authority** includes unofficial sources of tax information that are helpful in clarifying complex tax issues. Examples of secondary authority are tax services (such as CCH's Standard Federal Income Tax Reporter, RIA's Federal Tax Coordinator, and BNA's Tax Management Portfolios), journals, textbooks, newsletters, and treatises.

As discussed in Chapter 1, statutory authority includes the Constitution, tax treaties, and the Internal Revenue Code. Administrative authority, discussed in Chapter 2, includes published rulings of the Treasury Department and the IRS such as Treasury Regulations, Revenue Rulings, Revenue Procedures, and other pronouncements. Judicial authority consists of decisions issued by the various courts discussed in Chapter 3.

Secondary authority can be very helpful to a researcher, especially when there is no primary authority directly on point or when the primary authority is not clear. When new legislation impacts a client and no regulations have been issued, secondary sources may help the researcher in developing logical conclusions. Tax treatises may be a good starting point for understanding a complicated issue and the footnotes may provide a basis for more detailed research. Tax journals include general publications as well as publications that focus on specialty areas such as state tax, international tax, estate tax, corporate tax and others. Exhibit 1 provides a listing of several tax journals and their publishers.

Exhibit 1
Selected Tax Journals

Title	*Publisher*
Corporate Taxation	Thomson
Estate Planning	Thomson
International Tax Journal	CCH
Journal of State Taxation	CCH
Journal of Tax Practice & Procedure	CCH
Journal of Taxation	Thomson
Practical Tax Strategies	Thomson
Tax Advisor	AICPA
Tax Notes	Tax Analysts
Taxes	CCH

.07   ANALYZE AUTHORITY

Locating the appropriate authority for a given tax issue only part of the process. Once a researcher has found relevant authority, the authority must be validated and then evaluated. It is important to validate authority because tax law is constantly changing. Case law is dynamic and cases may be appealed or overturned. The Code is amended by Congress at least once a year. Revenue Rulings and other administrative authority may be revoked or modified by subsequent pronouncements. Once the relevant authority is validated, then the researcher must evaluate the usefulness of the authority. A citator, as previously discussed in Chapter 3, can be very useful in validating IRS pronouncements and court decisions.

After locating relevant sources, the researcher should read through the information. The analysis should begin by reviewing the primary authority and discerning the weight afforded to each source. The research should then be evaluated in light of whether it provides precedence and legal authority.

In some situations, the researcher may encounter conflicting authority. When evaluating conflicting judicial authority, the advisor should determine the precedential value of the court decisions given the Circuit Court of Appeals that would have jurisdiction over the taxpayer's case. **Horizontal conflicts** involve courts at the same level, for example, two different trial courts, including two different district courts, the Tax Court and the Court of Federal Claims, or the Tax Court and a district court. **Vertical conflicts** involve courts at different levels, for example, a Circuit Court of Appeals and the Tax Court. When evaluating conflicting judicial authority, the researcher must keep in mind which court decisions are binding on other courts. For example, in many horizontal conflicts, the courts have equal authority and are not bound by the decision of the conflicting court. However, in vertical conflicts, the lower level court may be bound by the decision of a Circuit Court of Appeals. For example, the Eastern Virginia District Court is bound by a decision of the 4th Circuit Court of Appeals but not bound by a decision of the 5th Circuit Court of Appeals. The researcher must also keep in mind the *Golsen* rule, requiring that the Tax Court follow decisions in the Circuit to which the decision would be appealed. This provides consistency within circuits, but may result in inconsistency within the Tax Court as a whole.

A researcher must also evaluate the relevant authority in order to determine if **substantial authority** exists for purposes of avoiding the substantial understatement penalty under Code Sec. 6662. Code Sec. 6662 imposes a 20-percent penalty for the substantial understatement of an income tax liability, unless the understatement is due to the treatment of an item that is based on substantial authority or that was adequately disclosed. Under Reg. §1.6662-4(d), the substantial authority standard is defined as an objective standard involving an analysis of the law and application of the law to relevant facts. There is substantial authority for the tax treatment of an item only if the weight of the authorities supporting the treatment is substantial in relation to the weight of authorities supporting contrary treatment.

Under Notice 90-20,[1] and Reg §1.6662-4(d)(3)(iii), the following sources are considered authority for purposes of determining whether there is substantial authority for the tax treatment of an item:

- The Code
- Regulations, including proposed regulations that are not yet superseded
- Court cases
- Revenue rulings and procedures.
- Tax treaties, including IRS and other official explanations of such treaties.
- Congressional intent as reflected in committee reports, joint explanatory statements of managers included in conference committee reports, and floor statements made before enactment by one of a bill's managers.
- Private letter rulings, technical advice memoranda, actions on decisions, and general counsel memoranda after they have been released to the public and provided they are dated after Dec. 31, 1984.
- Internal Revenue Service information or press releases.
- Notices, announcements and other administrative pronouncements published by the IRS in the Internal Revenue Bulletin.
- General Explanations of tax legislation prepared by the Joint Committee on Taxation (i.e. "blue books").

When providing advice to a client, the tax advisor needs to make sure there is substantial authority for the tax position taken on a tax return or advise the client to disclose the issue.

.09   DEVELOP CONCLUSIONS AND RECOMMENDATIONS

In developing conclusions the researcher should review the client's facts and compare them with the located authorities. The researcher should then determine whether the client's facts are similar enough for the authority to be reasonably applied. In applying tax law to the client's facts, the researcher should be able to demonstrate in detail the relationship of the authority to the client's situation and to build a logical connection between the relevant authority and the facts.

In some cases, reaching a conclusion will be fairly easy once the law is identified. The researcher simply applies the law to the client's facts. At other times, the situation may prove more challenging. The researcher may find that the law is clear, but the facts are still uncertain; or the facts are clear but the law is uncertain; or the facts are clear but the law is incomplete. The researcher may be faced with conflicting statutes, a conflict between a statute and the legislative history, or conflicting interpretations of the law by the courts. In the more difficult situations, the tax advisor must use professional judgment in making recommendations based on the results of the research.

When conflicting authority exists, the tax advisor should inform the client of the options, the pros and cons of the alternatives, and the inherent risks in each position. After informing the client of the risks, the tax advisor should be prepared to make recommendations. In some cases a "best" option may be presented along with alternative recommendations. Ultimately, the client should make the final decision.

.11   COMMUNICATE THE RESULTS

The last step in the process is to communicate the results of the research. Written communication may include a memo to the file and a letter to the client. These communications usually include a summary of the facts, any assumptions that the researcher made, the issues addressed, the relevant authority, and the resulting recommendations.

[1]   Sec. V(A) (1990-1 CB 328).

¶4005.09

In communicating the research results, remember to write to the level of the reader. If the client is an unsophisticated taxpayer, do not include technical terminology or cites to authority. Write in specific but understandable terms. The research memo to the file will include the technical details and cites.

Exhibit 2 includes strategies for approaching the tax research process.

Exhibit 2

Strategy For Tax Research Assignments

Beginning researchers can significantly increase the quality of their work and reduce stress by developing an efficient strategy. The following steps are recommended.

Step 1: Establish the Facts and Determine the Issues
- Carefully read the entire assignment and make a first attempt at formulating questions.
- Develop a list of keywords to use.
- If you are not familiar with any aspect in the case, develop some background by reading about the topic in your textbook.
- Begin to develop a list of questions you will ask.

Step 2: Locate the Relevant Authorities
- Use the keywords and questions developed in Step 1 to search your research service. Start by selecting an editorial service in your database.
- Many hits will be irrelevant and not worth reading. If a large number of documents are located as hits, narrow the search by changing the keywords and/or target publications or using the advanced search techniques for proximity of words. If an acceptable number of documents are hits, read a few of the documents to see if they are on point.
- Try to find one or more Code Sections related to the questions. The editorial discussions allow you to identify the relevant Code Sections.
- Search for Regulations, other IRS pronouncements, and court cases that may be relevant. The annotations provide short summaries of IRS pronouncements and court cases in each area.
- Repeat the process for each keyword and issue.
- You need to develop your own intuition on when to stop searching. When repeated search attempts keep bringing you back to the same documents, then you are probably close to having a complete set of relevant authorities.

Step 3: Assess the Importance of the Authorities
- Always examine the relevant Code sections first. Often, you will want to save a quote from the Code to use in your file memo.
- Read relevant administrative authority, especially Regulations and Revenue Rulings. Where possible, read the full text of the Regulation or Ruling rather than relying on the editors' interpretation of them. Sometimes the editors' interpretations leave out some less frequently used parts of the IRS pronouncements that are crucial to an assignment.
- Read the CCH or RIA annotations about court decisions. Use your own judgment about whether or not to read the full text of a case. If undecided, read the headnote provided at the beginning of the case.
- If court decisions appear to be conflicting, read the headnotes to determine which decision should be applied in your case. If the decisions are inconsistent

between the Circuit Courts of Appeal, then follow the decision of the relevant Circuit Court for your client.

- If a particular court decision is vital to your conclusion, then use a citator to examine the case's history. This is usually done to make sure that the original decision was not overturned or modified by subsequent decisions. This is also a good way to identify other relevant cases.

Step 4: Reach Conclusions, Make Recommendations, and Communicate the Results

- Write a first draft of the research memo or client letter. Spell-check the document.
- Conduct additional research if needed. Read the assignment memo again and check that the memo follows the recommended format.
- Revise the content and style of the first draft. Spell-check the second draft. Reading the draft aloud may help you notice more errors. Note that spell check does not detect incorrectly used homonyms, such as to, too and two. Replace prepositional phrases with active verbs or adjectives to eliminate wordiness.

¶4007   The Research Memo

Good organization of written tax communications will improve the reader's understanding. Most tax communications should be structured to include the following elements:

1. Identify the question
2. Summarize the facts
3. Analyze relevant authority and discuss alternatives
4. Make conclusions and recommendations

.01   TAX RESEARCH MEMO STRUCTURE

This section discusses the components of the tax research memo and provides suggestions on what should be included in each section. Each firm and/or instructor will have his/her own preferences for a proper memo and may request a slightly different approach to the memo. A typical memo is divided into four sections: facts, issues, discussion and analysis, and conclusions. Exhibit 3 shows a sample research memo.

Fact Section. This section should summarize the important facts of the research case. Only include the relevant facts in a clear and concise manner.

Issue Section. Identify the issue(s) and state the issue(s) in the form of a question.

Discussion and Analysis Section. This section discusses the issue(s). Begin with the relevant code section(s). Identify the code section, paraphrase what it says and then discuss why it's important. Discussion of the relevant Treasury Regulations should follow. Identify the regulation, paraphrase the important sections and then address the importance of the regulation given the facts.

The discussion should continue by reviewing relevant Treasury pronouncements (Revenue Rulings, Revenue Procedures, Letter Rulings, etc.) and cases. Be sure to include a complete cite for each authority. Summarize the important facts of the pronouncement/case and then compare the facts of the pronouncement/case to the research facts. Discuss how the facts are similar or different. Explain how each ruling or case supports or weakens the client's position.

Documentation is a very important part of communicating tax research and all statements or opinions should be substantiated with supporting cites. Supporting cites should be to primary sources only except in rare or unusual situations.

Conclusion Section. Think of your conclusion as the "short" answer to your issue. The conclusion section is the place to provide tax advice, recommend action(s) for the client to take, or identify the need for additional information. There may not be a single "best" alternative to the client's issue so be sure to consider all applicable alternatives. Support your conclusion by referencing back to the authority you discussed in the discussion and analysis section.

Exhibit 3

Sample Tax Research Memo

To: File
From: Nina Wise
Re: Jonathan Jones

Facts

Jonathan Jones is considering selling land to McQuire, Inc. Jonathan purchased the 100 acres of land for $500,000 on March 17, 2006, as a long-term investment. The sellers, Mr. and Mrs. Karl Yoder, are not related to Jonathan. Jonathan has not made any improvements to the land since the date of purchase. During the last four years, he has neither purchased nor sold any other real estate. McQuire, Inc. is a closely held corporation with 1,000 shares of outstanding stock. The McQuire stock is owned by Jeffrey Jones, Jonathan's brother, Susan Smith, Jonathan's neice, and Zane Zimmerman, an unrelated individual. Jeffrey owns 400 shares, Susan owns 200 shares and Zane owns the remaining 400 shares.

Issue

Will Jonathan be entitled to deduct the loss on the sale of the land to McQuire?

Discussion and Analysis

Code Section 267(a) provides that a loss on the sale of property between related parties may not be deducted. Related parties are defined under Section 267(b) and include: members of a family as defined under Section 267(c)(4) and an individual and a corporation more than 50 percent in value of the outstanding stock of which is owned, directly or indirectly, by or for such individual.

Section 267(c) defines constructive ownership of stock as:

"(1)   Stock owned, directly or indirectly, by or for a corporation … shall be considered as being owned proportionately by or for its shareholders ….

(2)   An individual shall be considered as owning the stock owned, directly or indirectly, by or for his family;

(3)   individual owning … any stock in a corporation shall be considered as owning the stock owned, directly or indirectly, by or for his partner;

(4)   The family of an individual shall include only his brothers and sisters, spouse, ancestors and lineal descendants; and

(5)   Stock constructively owned by a person by reason of paragraph (1), shall, for the purpose of applying paragraph (1), (2) or (3), be treated as actually owned by such person, but stock constructively owned by a individual by reason of the application of paragraph (2) or (3) shall not be treated as owned by him for the purpose of again applying either of such paragraphs in order to make another the constructive owner of such stock."

Reg. §1.267(c)-1 further explains the rules regarding constructive ownership of stock. Under Reg. §1.267(c)-1(a)(3), an individual's constructive ownership under Code Sec. 267(c)(2) or (3), of stock owned by a family member is not to be considered actual ownership of such stock, and the individual's constructive ownership of the stock is not to be attributed to another member of his family.

The Regulation addresses the number of layers of constructive ownership of McQuire, Inc. that will be attributed to Jonathan. Since Jonathan does not directly own any stock in McQuire, Inc., only the direct ownership of the McQuire stock by Jeffrey, his brother, will be attributed to Jonathan. The ownership of stock by Jeffrey's daughter Susan will not be attributed to Jonathan. Jeffery's 40 percent direct ownership of McQuire, Inc. will be attributed to Jonathan. In order to be considered related parties under Section 267(b), Jonathan must own, either directly or indirectly, more than 50 percent in value of the outstanding stock of McQuire. Since Jonathan's attributed interest is only 40 percent, Jonathan and McQuire are not considered related parties.

Conclusion

Since Jonathan and McQuire, Inc. are not considered related parties under Code Sec. 267, Jonathan will be allowed to recognize the loss on the sale of property to McQuire. The loss will be a long-term capital loss under Code Sec.1222 since the property was held more than one year. As provided under Code Sec. 1211(b), the loss will be deductible in 2008 to offset capital gains plus $3,000.

¶4009   The Client Letter

Client letters will differ across tax advisors. This section briefly discusses two issues that should be considered to assure that the client letter is effective in communicating research findings and conclusions. These points will help reduce client confusion or dissatisfaction. Poor client communications can result in the client misinterpreting the research results and taking inappropriate steps or failing to act in a timely manner. Tax advisors who do not clearly communicate findings and conclusions to the client lose much of their effectiveness and increase their practice risk.

The first issue to consider is the level of tax sophistication of the client. The advisor's writing style should be tailored to each client. When a client does not have extensive tax knowledge, the letter should be written in laymen terms. The letter should not include technical terminology and usually omits detailed citations. For example, instead of stating, "Under Section 162(m), the corporation may deduct $1,000,000," the letter to an unsophisticated client may state, "The tax law allows a $1,000,000 deduction." The other end of the spectrum would be the letter to the Tax Director at a large corporate client. This individual has significant tax knowledge so the letter will include the detailed citations and discussion.

The second issue to consider is limitations to the advice provided in the letter. Tax advice should always be limited to the facts as stated and may also be limited to the tax law as it exists on a particular date. These limitations reduce the legal exposure of the advisor if the client has not provided complete and/or correct facts and if the law changes after the advice has been rendered.

All aspects of the letter must appear professional. Spelling or grammar errors, rambling sentences, lack of organization, and other distracting items suggest to the client that the research effort was also carelessly done. The negative impression of an unprofessional letter may result in the client arguing about the bill or deciding to look elsewhere for professional advice.

.01   LETTER FORMAT

The first paragraph should include a brief introduction to the reason the letter is being written and will introduce the need to review the facts presented in the second paragraph. Some advisors include a brief client pleasantry in the first paragraph.

The second paragraph should restate the facts and indicate that the findings, conclusions, and recommendations are based on the facts as stated. In some situations the letter may indicate the source of the facts (e.g., the Tax Director in a letter dated July 24). Including these statements reduces the potential legal liability if the facts are incorrect.

The following paragraphs should discuss the current tax law, the possible alternatives, and the recommended course of action. When there is a choice between alternatives, the letter should outline the potential risks of each alternative. Remember, the client makes the final choice. When the letter is lengthy, use headings to organize the letter and emphasize the main points.

Consider using bullet points to emphasize findings, steps the client should take, and relevant deadlines.

The final paragraph should express appreciation for the client selecting your firm to complete the tax research and indicate your willingness to assist with any future issues. The last sentence typically encourages the client to contact the advisor with questions. Exhibit 4 shows a sample client letter.

Exhibit 4

Sample Client Letter

September 27, 2008

Mr. Jonathan Jones
2331 Main Street
Jefferson, Virginia 21991

Dear Mr. Jones:

This letter is in response to your question regarding the tax consequences of a proposed sale of 100 acres of undeveloped land to McQuire, Inc. To ensure a complete understanding between us, I would like to review the facts of your case.

You purchased the 100 acres of land for $500,000 on March 17, 2006, as a long-term investment. The sellers, Mr. and Mrs. Karl Yoder, are unrelated to you. You have not made any improvements to the land since the date of purchase. During the last four years, you have neither purchased nor sold any other real estate. McQuire, Inc. is a closely held corporation with 1,000 shares of outstanding stock. The McQuire stock is owned by Jeffrey Jones, your brother, Susan Smith, his daughter, and Zane Zimmerman, an unrelated individual. Jeffrey owns 400 shares, Susan owns 200 shares and Zane owns the remaining 400 shares. The accuracy of my conclusions depends entirely on my understanding of these facts. If these facts are incomplete or incorrect, please notify me immediately.

If you sell the land to McQuire, Inc. for the proposed contract price of $400,000, you will realize a $100,000 loss. This loss equals the $400,000 cash you will receive at closing less your $500,000 investment in the land. You are allowed to report this loss on your individual tax return in the year of sale unless you and McQuire, Inc. are "related parties" within the meaning of the tax law. According to my research, you and McQuire, Inc. do not meet the definition of "related parties," even though your brother and neice own an aggregate 60 percent interest in McQuire, Inc. Therefore, you can report the $100,000 loss for tax purposes. Because you held the land for investment and owned it for more than one year, the loss will be classified as a long-term capital loss. You can deduct a long-term capital loss to the extent of your capital gains for the year. If your capital loss exceeds your capital gains, you can deduct $3,000 of the excess loss against other sources of income.

My conclusions are based on the facts above and the tax law as it existed on September 27, 2008.

Thank you for allowing my firm to advise you in this matter. If you have any questions about my conclusions, please do not hesitate to call. If you decide to sell the land, I would be glad to meet with you to develop a strategy to maximize your deduction of the projected $100,000 capital loss.

Sincerely,

Nina Wise
Manager

¶4011   Electronic Tax Services—An Introduction

Electronic services began to take hold about fifteen years ago when the major publishers (CCH and RIA) began offering their print services on CD-ROM. Prior to this time, several publishers had offered online (dialup) services, but they tended to be very expensive and inevitably involved technical problems. The primary players at the time were LEXIS-NEXIS, Westlaw, and PHINET (from the old Prentice-Hall Company).

A conversion to a web-based version of these products was slow, primarily because of the unreliability of using the Internet at the time. When these problems were minimized, publishers began to convert their materials to the Internet. Today most major tax services have an Internet presence.

¶4013   Print Services—Code-Based Versus Topic-Based

All major comprehensive tax services follow one of two major organizational patterns, either Code-based or topic based. A **Code-based service** is organized by Internal Revenue Code section, from Section 1 to the end. All information relevant to that particular Code section is in a single location; this includes Regulations, committee report extracts, editorial explanations, and extracts of relevant cases and rulings. The coverage for each Code section is more or less in the form of short snippets, and is arranged to find answers to tax questions easily and quickly.

A **topics-based service** is organized around logical tax topics, such as depreciation or partnerships, and not the Code. Thus, one topic may involve a number of different Code sections (e.g., partnerships). In contrast to a Code-based service, the coverage of the topic is in narrative form. Reading such a service is like reading a reference book; all relevant cases and rulings are discussed in the narrative and footnoted for reference. A topics-based service is designed for the tax professional who wants to learn more about a topic, in addition to just finding a simple answer to a question. The Code and Regulations tend to be grouped together in a separate section.

¶4015   The Current Players—An Historical Perspective

For many years, there were only two major players in the print tax research service market: Commerce Clearing House (now CCH, a part of Wolters Kluwer) and Prentice Hall (PH). Both were Code-based services and looked remarkably similar, from organizational pattern to content. A new player in the market arrived in the early 1980s: the Research Institute of America (RIA). RIA decided to take a topics-based approach with its major service, the Federal Tax Coordinator. A second player, Matthew Bender, also entered the tax service market with a topics-based approach.

The market was shaken up in the 1990s when RIA acquired Prentice Hall's tax service, thus enabling it to offer both a Code-based and a topic-based service. In response, CCH soon acquired Matthew Bender's service so that it could also offer a topic-based service. Thus, the two primary players left offer both types of services, and these may be summarized as follows:

Publisher	Code-based Service	Topics-based Service
CCH, a part of Wolters Kluwer	Standard Federal Tax Reporter	CCH Tax Research Consultant
Thomson Reuters/RIA	United States Tax Reporter	Federal Tax Coordinator 2nd

This section reviews the two primary online tax research services: CCH's IntelliConnect® and RIA's Checkpoint Network. Reviews of BNA's Tax Management Portfolios, CCH's Tax Research Consultant, and RIA's United States Tax Reporter are included in Appendix A.

As an introduction to these services, the following simple exercises demonstrate how to open the system, retrieve a particular Code section, display the complete organization of the Code, and examine the historical notes to the Code.

¶4017   Exercise 1: Going Directly to a Particular Code Section

Suppose you need to know: (1) which Subchapter of the Code contains Sec. 469, the statute describing the passive activity limitations; (2) who is treated as a "person" under Code Sec. 469(a)(2); and (3) when was Code Sec. 469(g) last amended. In this case, both services have similar features that allow you to easily find the answers to these questions. Here are the steps for each service.

.01   CCH INTELLICONNECT®

Question 1 (What Subchapter of the Code contains Sec. 469?):

1. Login to IntelliConnect and click on the Browse link on the left side of the screen.
2. Open the Federal Tax heading and click the + button beside Federal Tax Primary Sources to expand the list of Primary Sources.
3. Click in succession the appropriate expansion box link on each screen (based on the Code sections shown for each possibility) until you find the appropriate Subchapter containing Code Sec. 469

The answer is Subchapter E, Accounting Periods and Methods of Accounting, which includes Code Sections 441–483.

Question 2 (Who is treated as a person under Code Sec. 469(a)(2)?):

1. At the top of the page, click Citations.
2. Open the Federal Tax heading and click the + button beside Federal Tax Primary Sources to expand the list of Primary Sources.
3. Click on Current Internal Revenue Code. A box will open in the right hand screen.
4. In the box "IRC Code and History Sec.", enter 469 and click search.
5. Click on the first link (Enacted Law: Current IRC Sec 469).
6. Scroll down to Code Sec. 469(a)(2).

The answer is any individual, estate or trust, any closely-held C corporation, and any personal services corporation. (Note: in Step 4, you could have entered 469(a)(2) and you would have been taken directly to that Code paragraph.)

Question 3 (When was Code Sec. 469(g) last amended?):
1. Repeat Steps 1 – 3 above.
2. Click on the fifth link (IRC-HIST – Sec. 469(g) . . .).
3. Scroll through the history notes, searching for the bold-face references to amendments, to find the most recent amendment. The amendments are listed in reverse chronological order from the most recent backwards.

The answer is 1996, as part of P.L. 104-188.

.03   RIA'S CHECKPOINT

Question 1 (What Subchapter of the Code contains Sec. 469?):
1. Open RIA Checkpoint to the Main Search page.
2. Click the Table of Contents link at the top of the page.
3. Click Federal Library, then Federal Source Materials, then Code, Regulations, etc., then Internal Revenue Code, then Current Code.
4. Click in succession the appropriate link on each screen (based on the Code sections shown for each possibility) until you find the appropriate Subchapter containing Code Sec. 469.

The answer is Subchapter E, Accounting Periods and Methods of Accounting, which includes Code Sections 441-483.

Question 2 (Who is treated as a person under Code Sec. 469(a)(2)?):
1. Open RIA Checkpoint to the Main Search page.
2. On the left sidebar, under Find by Citation, click Code & Regulations.
3. In the first box for current code, enter 469 and click search.
4. Scroll down to Code Sec. 469(a)(2).

The answer is any individual, estate or trust, any closely-held C corporation, and any personal services corporation. (Note: in Step 3, you could have entered 469(a)(2) and you would have been taken directly to that Code paragraph.)

Question 3 (When was Code Sec. 469(g) last amended?):
1. Repeat Steps 1–3 above.
2. At the top of the page for Code Sec. 469, click the History button (Hist).
3. Click the Code Sec. 469 underlined link that appears on the left sidebar.
4. Scroll through the history notes, searching for the bold-face references to amendments, to find the most recent amendment that affected Code Sec. 469(g).

The answer is 1996, as part of P.L. 104-188.

.05   CCH INTELLICONNECT®'S STANDARD FEDERAL TAX RESEARCH SERVICE

CCH's tax research service, IntelliConnect, is a comprehensive database of documents related to tax. The service allows users to conduct research by browsing or searching. The core content library includes CCH's tax research materials organized into categories. The categories include Tax News, Journals and Newsletters, Federal Tax, State Tax, and Tools/Smart Charts. When the Federal Tax area is expanded, the categories include Editorial Content, such as the Master Tax Guide and Standard Federal Tax Reporter, Primary Sources, such as the code and regulations, and Tax Practice Tools.

The tax reporters, such as the Standard Federal Income Tax Reporter (SFITR), provide an interpretive description of current tax law, putting individual rules and legislation in the context of the entire body of tax law. The SFITR is a code-based service. As mentioned earlier, a Code-based service is organized by Internal Revenue Code section, from Section

1 to the end. All information relevant to that particular Code section is in a single location; this includes Regulations, committee report extracts, editorial explanations, and extracts of relevant cases and rulings. The coverage for each Code section is more or less in the form of short snippets, and is arranged to find answers to tax questions easily and quickly.

Performing a Simple Keyword Search With CCH's IntelliConnect® in the Federal Standard Income Tax Reporter

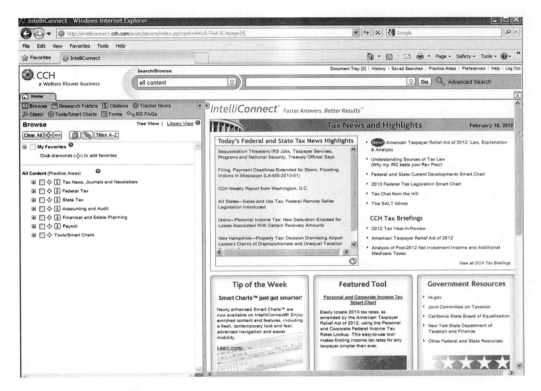

The Main Search Screen

Once you enter the IntelliConnect site, at the top of the window, directly below the Navigation Bar, is the search bar. The site's entire content can be searched by simply typing the search term in the Search Expression box. The results can be narrowed by using filters. The filters, which appear in the left pane, break down the results returned into smaller, more meaningful categories to allow the user to manage the results. To use the filters:

- Use the + and – icons to expand and collapse the filters.
- Click on a filter in the left pane and the results for that filter display in the right pane.

Another option in the top left corner of IntelliConnect is the Quick Bar. The Quick Bar contains a number of key functionalities that enable you to browse all the product content by drilling down through a menu tree on the left-hand side of the page. To browse the product content:

- Click Browse on the Quick Bar.
- The Browse Tree will appear in the left pane.

To locate the Standard Federal Income Tax Reporter by using the browse function
- Expand the Federal Tax category by clicking the +
- Expand the Federal Tax Editorial Content by clicking the +
- Choose the Standard Federal Income Tax Reporter. The expansion list shows the topics in Code order.

The white search box at the top of the screen is used to enter search terms.

The following discussion will highlight three methods for utilizing the Standard Federal Income Tax Reporter: a keyword search from the opening screen, using the browse function to search only in the SFITR, and a citation search.

Facts of the Sample Research Question

Sara Owens had owned all of the outstanding stock of Owens Consulting, a computer services corporation. During December 2010, she transferred 10,000 shares of the outstanding stock ($60,000 adjusted basis, $300,000 fair market value) to her son Al in exchange for an installment note which provided for 10 annual payments of $30,000 plus 10-percent interest on the unpaid balance, beginning on December 15, 2011. The terms of the purchase agreement included a clause stating that any principal and interest remaining due to the seller's death will be deemed "canceled and extinguished as though paid."

Sara Owens died on January 23, 2013, shortly after receiving the second $30,000 installment in December. She reported a capital gain of $24,000 ($30,000 × 80% gross profit ratio, i.e., $240,000 profit/$300,000 total contract price) on her 2011 and 2012 returns, as well as the interest income received. The fair market value of the note (with $240,000 to be collected) was estimated to be $200,000 at the time of Sara's death in January 2013. Are there any tax consequences for the estate income tax return for Sara Owens's estate?

¶4019   Formulating a Search Expression

There are certain general guidelines that must be kept in mind in formulating a search expression. First of all, select the most unique words related to your query and try them first. Words such as income and deduction just create noise and lead to a huge amount of documents retrieved. So try the most unique words first as a means of possibly delimiting the search. (Note: most search engines automatically check for plurals and possessives of words as well.)

Secondly, consider using search connectors to narrow your search. Most of us are familiar with most search connectors when using the Internet, but most tax services provide a few extra ones to help narrow the search even further. Exhibit 5 summarizes the Boolean connectors that may be used with both the CCH and RIA tax services.

Exhibit 5

Boolean Connectors (Work in both CCH and RIA Tax Services)

The BOOLEAN search method allows you to type search expressions using the Boolean connectors AND, OR, and NOT and the proximity connectors w/n, f/n, and p/n. These connectors indicate the relationship that two or more terms in the search expression must have in a document in order for the document to be selected. You simply type your terms using the connectors between your terms. Here is what each connector will retrieve:

AND—Placing the word AND between terms will retrieve documents that contain both of the terms. For example, gasoline and oil will retrieve documents that contain gasoline and oil.

OR—Placing the word OR between terms will retrieve documents that contain either or both of the terms. This is useful for entering synonyms or alternative terms like child or dependent. For example, gasoline or oil will retrieve documents that contain either term or both terms.

NOT—Placing the word NOT between terms will retrieve documents that contain the first terms only if the second term does not appear. This connector is useful when your keyword often appears in a context that is irrelevant to your research. For example, if you want to find documents concerning RICO litigation, the search expression RICO not Puerto will exclude documents in which RICO occurs as a part of Puerto Rico.

W/n—Placing w/n between terms will retrieve documents in which the first term appears within the specified number of words as the second term (where n equals the number of words between terms). For example, gasoline w/25 oil will retrieve documents that contain the words gasoline and oil when they appear within 25 words of each other. **Note:** The value of *n* cannot exceed 127 words.

F/n—Placing f/n between terms will retrieve documents in which the first term follows the second term by no more than *n* words. For example, credit f/2 foreign will retrieve documents containing *foreign n n credit*.

P/n—Placing p/n between terms will retrieve documents in which the first term precedes the second term by no more than *n* words. For example, foreign p/2 credit will retrieve documents containing *foreign n n credit*.

W/sen—Placing w/sen between terms will retrieve documents that contain the first terms within 20 words of the second terms. For example, gasoline station w/sen oil refinery will retrieve gasoline station within 20 words of oil refinery.

W/par—Placing w/par between terms will retrieve documents that contain the first terms within 80 words of the second terms. For example, gasoline station w/par oil refinery will retrieve gasoline station within 80 words of oil refinery.

*—Placing an * in a word holds the place of one character. For example, s****holder retrieves stockholder or shareholder.

!—Placing an ! at the end of a word holds the place of an infinite number of characters at the end of the word's root. For example, amort! retrieves amortize, amortization, and amortizing.

CCH offers a "Tax Thesaurus" option to look for synonyms that might improve the accuracy of the search. By selecting any of the alternatives, those selected will be added to the search list.

To apply the thesaurus to your search:
1.   Click the Advanced Search link. The "Advanced Search" box is displayed.
2.   Click in the checkbox next to Apply Thesaurus.
3.   Click the Apply Changes button to save your changes and close the "Advanced Search" box.
4.   Type your search term(s) in the "Search Expression" field.
5.   Click Go.

The search results are displayed on a new tab in the "Search Results" pane. In addition to returning results based on the search expression entered, IntelliConnect also returns results based on applying the online thesaurus.

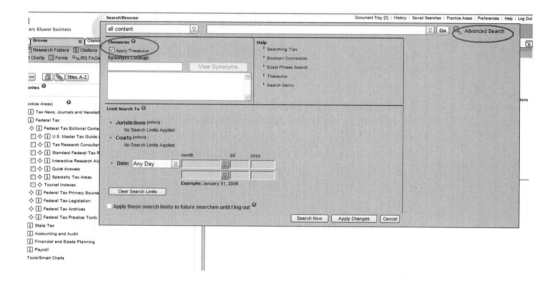

For purposes of this search, we will use just three words with the implied "and" connector. Type in the following search expression in the search box:

installment cancelled death

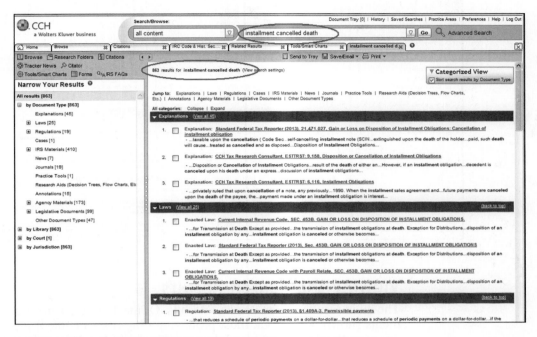

Selecting a Practice Area to Research

One of the advantages of a comprehensive tax service is that it provides "one-stop" shopping for all primary authorities. The editors of these services do a great job of condensing all relevant legislative, administrative, and judicial authorities, so it makes sense to search these secondary authorities first as a means of finding leads to relevant primary authority. A common practice with CCH is to select the Standard Federal Tax Reporter. Generally, you would not want to select both a tax service and primary authorities, such as court cases. A search of the services alone will pick up those cases.

Performing the Search and Narrowing the Search

After clicking the Search button (with all content selected), the results screen will appear as shown above. Note that a total of 863 documents were found. The results provide a few words around each key word hit to give you an idea of whether or not the document is relevant. To narrow the results to only those in the SFTR, click through the expansion list on the left side of the screen. Choose By Library, then Federal Tax, then Federal Tax Editorial Content, then 2013 Standard Federal Tax Reporter. By double clicking on SFTR, the results list in the right had box refreshes to include only the results found in the SFTR. The original 863 documents have been reduced to 48 documents.

If a search retrieves too many documents, you can refine the search term by adding other words or phrases. If you want to just search the documents retrieved with the initial search, change the content type from "all content" to "within results" and type your refined search expression in the search box and click GO.

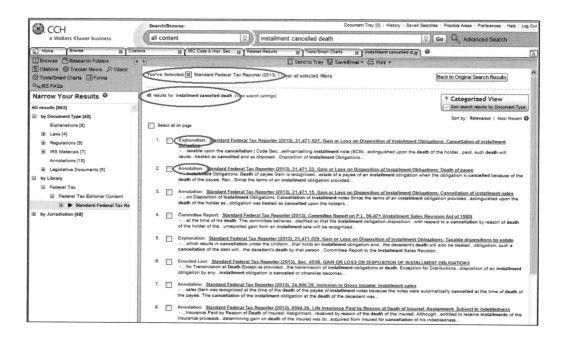

Viewing the Search Results

The main results screen displays 48 hits. Of the 48 documents listed, the first two documents shown below look most promising. The first document includes the designation "Explanation" and the second document includes the designation "Annotation."

> Explanation:
> Standard Federal Tax Reporter (2013), 21,471.027, Gain or Loss on Disposition of Installment Obligations: Cancellation of installment obligation
>
> Annotation:
> Standard Federal Tax Reporter (2013), 21,471.23, Gain or Loss on Disposition of Installment Obligations: Death of payee

Explanations provide editorial descriptions of the issue, links to the relevant code sections and very brief summaries of important cases in the area. Annotations provide abbreviated summaries of cases and rulings in the area. Most novice researchers will first review the Explanation document in order to gain an understanding of the issue and then move to the Annotation document to review the relevant cases and rulings.

When scrolling through the Explanations document, you will notice a brief discussion of the Robert Frane case. Click on the link for the case; this brings up the full text of the decision (note the use of the USTC citation to the CCH volumes). This is relevant to our facts, as it indicates that as a general rule the estate is taxed on the income when such a note is automatically cancelled at death.

After reviewing the case, click the "Citator" button in the Quick Bar at the top left hand side of the page. By copying and pasting the Frane case citation into the search box, the Citator provides a list of other cases that have "cited" this ruling. In some cases, a cited case or other authority may be closer to your set of facts, so always check the Citator. Note that the CCH Citator does not provide details of the relationship between the citing cases to the cited case.

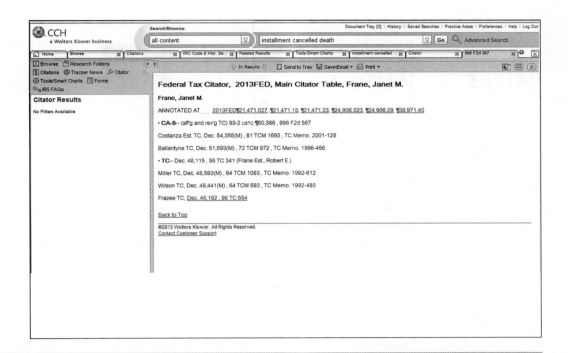

OBSERVATION

At this point, it looks like we have our answer. Since you will probably want a copy of the case and ruling for the file, each can be easily printed or saved on your computer using the options available in the gray box. Saving the document is especially helpful when portions of the case or ruling will be "clipped and pasted" into other memorandums, letters or other documents in the file.

Browse with the Standard Federal Income Tax Reporter

Sometimes it may be difficult to develop a set of key words or phrases to find the answer to a tax question. But if the topic is fairly narrowly defined, you may be able to "walk" your way to an answer by browsing. This technique simply involves selecting the "Browse" option on the main search screen and clicking successive filters until a result is (hopefully) found. In many respects, a Code-based service such as the SFITR makes it easier to browse, since the researcher generally knows what section (or at least "subpart") of the Code needs to be searched.

Example - Browse Search

Using the same facts as the earlier research question on self-cancelling installment notes, the first step is to browse through the filters until you choose the SFITR Explanations listing. Once the contents to the SFITR are on the screen, you will simply expand the best filters in succession that relate to the topic of cancellation of installment sales agreements. This will involve the following sequential "clicks":

1. Click on Accounting Methods and Periods (Sections 441-483)
2. Click on Taxable Year of Inclusion (Sections 451-460)
3. Click on Installment method
4. Click on Gain or Loss on Disposition of Installment Obligations (Section 453B)
5. Click on CCH Annotation, Gain or Loss on Disposition of Installment Obligations: Death of payee

Most researchers combine the browsing approach with a key word search. By filtering as far as possible, you will eliminate a lot of unnecessary documents in your search. When you have filtered as far as possible, simply enter key words or phrases in the search box and click GO. In the previous example, you may have gotten as far as Sec. 453B; by checking the Code Section and entering the search expression used earlier (installment cancelled death) in the search box.

¶4023 Performing a Citator Search with the Standard Federal Income Tax Reporter

.01 USING A CITATOR SEARCH

In researching a tax question, it may be that you have a citation to a possible piece of primary authority that may contain the answer to your question. In this situation, clicking on the "Citator" choice in the Quick Bar on the left side of the main search screen produces a template to take you directly to that authority. Simply choose the citation format for the particular authority that you are interested in, enter the citation, and click GO.

Once you locate the primary authority, you can then click on one of the tax service buttons at the top of the page (either FTC or ANNO), which will lead you back into the editorial discussion of the topic. This may help you find the answer to your tax question.

.03 EXAMPLE OF A CITATOR SEARCH

Once again, assume that we have the same research question as before involving the cancellation of an installment sale note at death. Assume that you had read a journal article earlier that mentioned the *Frane* case, and you would like to see if it is relevant to the case. Click on "Citator" in the Quick Bar, enter the citation for the *Frane* case (998 F2d 567), and click GO. The Citator results are listed in the bottom screen. By clicking on the links provided after "Annotated At" you can view the CCH Explanations that discuss the *Frane* case.

Appendix B provides a detailed review of how to use the CCH, RIA and Lexis/Nexis Citators.

¶4025 RIA Checkpoint on the Web

.01 PERFORMING A SIMPLE KEYWORD SEARCH WITH THE FEDERAL TAX COORDINATOR 2ND

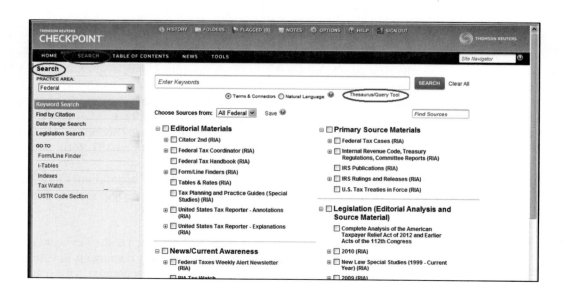

The Main Search Screen

As illustrated above, the complete service is organized by tabs, and the current tab selected is "Search". The display has two major components; the main display screen on the right, and a sidebar screen on the left shaded gray. Note also that the "Editorial Materials" (secondary authority) are separated from the Primary Source Materials (primary authority).

The Search screen literally lists the steps necessary to do a keyword search: (1) enter the key-word expression, (2) select the materials to be searched, and (3) click the search button. This process is reviewed in detail below.

The following discussion will highlight three search methods for utilizing the Federal Tax Coordinator 2nd: a keyword search, a menu-walk search, and a citation search. Each is illustrated using the same facts used above in the CCH service introduction.

.03   FORMULATING A SEARCH EXPRESSION

The same general guidelines discussed above regarding word choice apply to a search in the RIA service. The Boolean operators also work in the RIA service. The RIA service provides a few additional search operators that may be helpful. Exhibit 6 summarizes the connectors that may be used on Checkpoint and the USTR services:

Exhibit 6		
RIA Tax Service Search Operators		
To locate documents:	**Use:**	**Example:**
containing any of my keywords	OR, |	funding **OR** deficiency
containing at least one instance of each of my keywords	Space, &, AND	funding deficiency
that contain one keyword but exclude another	^, NOT	funding **NOT** deficiency
containing my *exact* phrase	" "	"funding deficiency"
containing variations of my keywords	* (asterisk)	deprecia*
disabling automatic retrieval of plurals and equivalencies	# (pound sign)	#damage (retrieves only damage, not damages)
containing single-character variations	? (question mark)	s????holder (retrieves stockholder, shareholder)
containing compound words	- (hyphen)	e-mail (retrieves e-mail e mail, email)

Note: The # character does not turn off the automatic retrieval of possessives (for example, customer's).
Because Checkpoint uses the characters * and / as search connectors, you cannot search for them as you would for other text or characters. If you include these characters in parentheses, they still function as search connectors.

To search for a word or phrase:	Use:	Example:
within n words of another (*in any order*)	/# (where # equals number)	"disclosure exception" **/7** negligence
within n words of another (*in exact order*)	pre/# (where # equals number)	"disclosure exception" **pre/7** negligence
within the same sentence (20 words) as another (*in any order*)	/s	"disclosure exception" **/s** negligence
within the same sentence (20 words) as another (*in exact order*)	pre/s	"disclosure exception" **pre/s** negligence
within one paragraph (50 words) as another (*in any order*)	/p	"disclosure exception" **/p** negligence

Finally, RIA offers a thesaurus link to look for synonyms that might improve the accuracy of your search. Click the Thesaurus link immediately above the Search button to activate this feature, click on the Thesaurus tab, and select any alternatives. Those selected will be added to the search list.

For purposes of this search, we will use just three words with the implied "and" connector. Type in the following search expression in the search box:

installment cancelled death

.05   SELECTING A PRACTICE AREA TO RESEARCH

Again, one of the advantages of a comprehensive tax service is that it provides "one-stop" shopping for all primary authorities. RIA offers two secondary sources that will lead you to primary authority. A common practice with RIA is to select both services by checking the Federal Tax Coordinator 2nd and the United States Tax Reporter Annotations. The results from the Coordinator are reviewed first.

Generally, you would not want to select both a tax service and primary authorities, such as court cases. A search of the services alone will pick up those cases. You may consider adding WG&L treatises, if included in the firm/school subscription, since these can provide a practical planning perspective. And for recent events, including the WG&L journals might be beneficial (searching these alone may provide up-to-date planning ideas and suggestions on recent law changes).

.07   PERFORMING THE SEARCH AND NARROWING THE SEARCH

After clicking the Search button, the results screen will appear as shown below. Note that a total of 11 documents were found. At this point, it is a good idea to check the "View hits only" box in the right corner of the screen. This limits any materials retrieved to the "document" found by the search engine (generally, one or two pages); otherwise, the entire volume is opened, and it is easy to become lost.

OBSERVATION   Sometimes you may discover that your answer appears to be "just beyond" the end of one of the documents you retrieved. In such a case, go back to the results screen and uncheck "View hits only"; this will open the entire volume to read. Or you can use the <Contents> arrows on the lower right of the screen, as explained below.

If the search retrieves too many documents, you can always refine the search term by adding other words or phrases. Click the "Search Within Results" option in the center of the Search Results line.

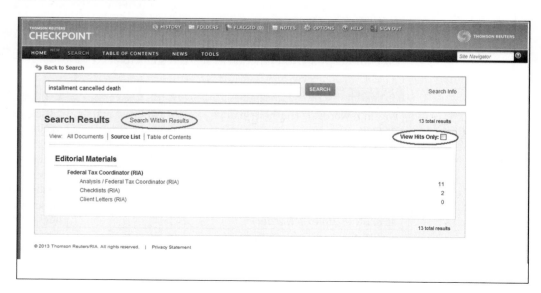

.09   VIEWING THE SEARCH RESULTS

The main results screen shown below discloses 11 hits. Click one of the sources to review the results; for example clicking the "Analysis – FTC" link will line up the 11 results (11 documents with hits) on the next screen. At this point, it is usually advisable to check the box "Display words around hits." This will display 25 words around the key words in a document to provide more information concerning the relevance of this document. Of the 11 documents listed, the third one (C-9528, Installment Obligations, Including Self-cancelling Notes) looks most promising. Click on this one now.

When scrolling through a document, note the three possible navigation options at the top right of the document. These work as follows:

\<Document\>	Clicking either arrow will take you to the next (or previous) document on the results list
\<Contents\>	Clicking either arrow will take you to the next document per the table of contents (an "open book," not just documents with hits)
\<Keyword\>	Clicking either arrow will take you to the next (or previous) occurrence of one of the search terms used in the search expression

When scrolling through this particular document, you will eventually come to a discussion of *Rev. Rul. 86-72* (footnote 26.7) and the *Frane* case (footnote 26.8). Both of these documents are relevant to our case. Click on the link for *Rev. Rul. 86-72*; this brings up the full text of the ruling. This is relevant to our case, as it indicates that as a general rule the estate is taxed on the income when such a note is automatically cancelled at death.

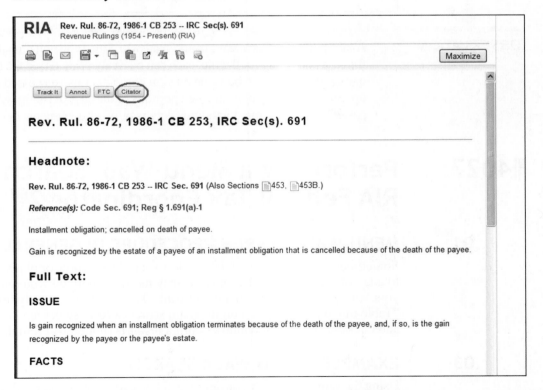

After reviewing the ruling, click the "Citator" button at the top of the document, and then click the link provided on the left sidebar. The citator, as explained below, provides a list of other cases that have "cited" this ruling. In some cases, a cited case or other authority may be closer to your set of facts, so always check the citator. Note that the RIA Citator tells you how the ruling was cited (i.e., favorably in all three cases).

Notice that on the upper center when the revenue ruling is in the viewer box, a link is provided to go "Back to results document." Do this, and now click on the link for the *Frane* case. Then click the citator button, and select the "Janet Frane" case from the list appearing on the left sidebar. The citator indicates that the Appeals court both affirmed and reversed the lower court decision, and the reversal related to the question of who pays tax on the gain. In this case, it is the estate, the same as in Revenue Ruling 86-72.

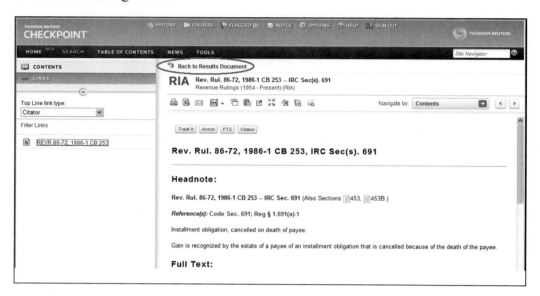

OBSERVATION   At this point, it looks like we have our answer. Since you will probably want a copy of the case and ruling for the file, each can be easily printed (see the discussion below) or exported to a file to be saved on your computer (also discussed below). The latter option is especially helpful when portions of the case or ruling will be "clipped and pasted" into other memorandums, letters or other documents in the file.

¶4027   Performing a Menu-Walk Search with the RIA Federal Tax Coordinator 2ⁿᵈ

.01   MENU-WALK SEARCH PROCEDURE IN GENERAL

Sometimes it may be difficult to develop a set of key words or phrases to find the answer to a tax question. But if the topic is fairly narrowly defined, you may be able to "walk" your way to an answer with a menu walk. This technique simply involves selecting the "Table of Contents" option on the main search screen, selecting the source(s) to search, and clicking successive windows until a result is (hopefully) found.

.03   EXAMPLE—MENU WALK SEARCH

Using the same facts as the earlier research question on self-cancelling installment notes, the first step is to click on the Table of Contents link at the top of the page. From the menu options given, select Federal Library, then Federal Editorial Materials, then Federal Tax Coordinator 2ⁿᵈ.

Once the contents to the Federal Tax Coordinator 2nd is on the screen, you will simply choose the best links in succession that relate to the topic of cancellation of installment sales agreements. This will involve the following sequential "clicks":
1. Click on the + sign at G-5990 Installment Sales, Repossessions, etc.
2. Click on the + sign at G-6450 Dispositions of Installment Obligations.
3. Click on the page icon at G-6462 Cancelled Obligations (icon indicates a document).
4. Scroll down to mention of the *Frane* case at footnote 26.8.

OBSERVATION When menu-walking in RIA, note the "+" signs before each entry. This indicates that there are subdivisions within that topic, and these are displayed by pressing the "+" sign. When a "–" sign or a printer symbol appears, there are no further subdivisions. Also, by pressing the minus sign, you began closing the lower subdivisions.

It is also possible to combine a menu walk search with a key word search. By menu walking as far as possible, you will eliminate a lot of unnecessary documents in your search. When you have walked as far as possible, simply click Search and enter key words or phrases in the search box. In the previous example, you may have gotten as far as G-5990; by checking G-5990 and entering the search expression used earlier (installment cancelled death) in the special search box at the bottom, only the documents in this section of the coordinator will be retrieved. A search at this point would retrieve only two documents; note that the main screen now displays the details of G-5990 (from G-6450 to G-6513), and the two documents containing the search expression are designated with red ones (G-6462 and G-6508). Both relate to the *Frane* case.

¶4029 Performing a Citation Search with the RIA Federal Tax Coordinator 2nd

.01 USING A CITATION SEARCH

In researching a tax question, it may be that you have a citation to a possible piece of primary authority that may contain the answer to your question. In this case, clicking on the "Find by Citation" choice on the left sidebar of the main search screen produces a template to take you directly to that authority. Simply choose the template for the particular authority that you are interested in, enter the citation, and click Search.

Once you locate the primary authority, you can then click on one of the tax service buttons at the top of the page (either FTC or ANNO), which will lead you back into the editorial discussion of the topic. This may help you find the answer to your tax question.

.03 EXAMPLE OF A CITATION SEARCH

Once again, assume that we have the same research question as before involving the cancellation of an installment sale note at death. Assume that you had read a journal article earlier that mentioned Rev. Rul. 86-72, and you would like to see if it is relevant to the case. Using the "Find by Citation" link on the left side of the page, choose the template for Tax Rulings, and enter 86-72. Once the ruling appears on screen, click on the FTC button at the top of the page, and then click the resulting link on the left sidebar to take you to the discussion in the Federal Tax Coordinator of that ruling. That in turn will lead you to your answer, the *Frane* case.

The same procedure could have been used if you had encountered a citation to the *Frane* case in your reading. By backing into the Federal Tax Coordinator, you may find passages in the discussion that will lead you to your answer. This is a major advantage of a topics-based service; the procedure does not work well in a Code-based service.

OBSERVATION   What if a colleague tells you that she heard that there was a recent Tax Court case that may relate to your tax question, and he remembers the name was Frane because that is her brother-in-law's name. How would you use this information? Open the cases library and do a search, including the words Frane, TC, installment, and death. This should lead you to the appropriate case, and from that point you can back into the services for additional discussion by clicking on the FTC or ANNO buttons.

¶4031   Summary

- The three types of tax research are planning, compliance, and policy.
- The tax research process involves six steps that may require the advisor to cycle through the various steps multiple times before completing the project.
- Communicating the results of tax research is an important last step in the process and includes a technical memo to the client's file and a letter to the client.
- Most tax research is done through on-line research services, requiring the advisor to develop efficient and effective keyword search skills.

Review Questions for Chapter 4

True or False

Indicate which of the following statements are true or false by circling the correct answer.

1. Tax planning only involves closed-fact situations.   T   F
2. Treasury Regulations are primary authority.   T   F
3. A Circuit Court of Appeals decision will always carry more weight than a Tax Court   T   F
    decision.
4. The first step in the research process is to identify the issues.   T   F
5. The last step in the research process is to make recommendations to the client.   T   F
6. Revenue Procedures, tax journals, and textbooks are all secondary sources of au-   T   F
    thority.
7. Since trial level courts do not establish precedent, a citator only includes appellate   T   F
    level cases.
8. Tax research in an open fact situation allows the tax advisor to be creative in struc-   T   F
    turing a transaction and its tax consequences.
9. A client letter should include references to the Code and specific cases so the client   T   F
    will know that the researcher has been thorough.
10. Substantial authority includes IRS announcements, Treasury Regulations, and the   T   F
    "Blue Book" explanation of legislation.

Fill in the Blanks

Fill in each blank with the appropriate word or phrase that completes each sentence.

11. Tax compliance research involves _____-fact situations.
12. CCH's *Standard Federal Income Tax Reporter*, IRS Publications, and Bittker and Eustice's *Federal Income Taxation of Corporations & Shareholders* are examples of _____ sources of authority.
13. The Internal Revenue Code, Revenue Rulings and a Tax Court decision are examples of _____ sources of authority.
14. In evaluating conflicting court cases, different decisions by the Court of Federal Claims and the Alabama District Court would be considered a(n) _____ conflict.
15. After the researcher has determined the issue(s), the next step in the research process is to

    _____.
16. Providing a client with guidance on how to structure a divorce settlement would be considered a tax _____ situation.
17. Using the Boolean operators, a researcher looking for casualty and loss within 10 words of each other would enter the search as _____.
18. Using the Boolean operators, a researcher looking for the exact phrase, "installment sale," would enter the search as _____.
19. After locating a relevant case, the researcher should use the _____ to determine if the IRS acquiesced in the case.
20. Analyzing tax legislation is an example of _____ research.

Multiple Choice

Circle the best answer for each of the following questions.

21. Why does a researcher use a citator?
    a. To determine whether a private letter ruling exists on the subject.
    b. To determine if an IRS Publication covers the research topic.
    c. To check on authorities issued subsequent to a court decision.
    d. None of the above.

22. Which of the following is not a primary source of authority?
    a. The Tax Advisor
    b. Treasury Regulations
    c. Revenue Rulings
    d. A 4th Circuit Court of Appeals decision

23. Which of the following is not a secondary source of authority?
    a. CCH's Standard Federal Income Tax Reporter
    b. RIA's Federal Tax Coordinator
    c. IRS's Revenue Procedure
    d. IRS's Instructions for forms
    e. All of the above are secondary sources.

24. Before a tax advisor can locate the appropriate authority, he/she must:
    a. Identify the facts
    b. Determine the issues or questions
    c. Read the Internal Revenue Code
    d. Use the citator
    e. Both a and b

25. Walter asked his tax advisor what assets he should use to make gifts to his grandchildren. The tax advisor's work is:
    a. A closed-fact situation
    b. A tax compliance situation
    c. A tax policy situation
    d. A tax planning situation
    e. An unknown-fact situation

26. Elizabeth started a new business during the year. When preparing her tax return, the advisor must determine which expenses are start-up expenses. The advisor's work is:
    a. A closed-fact situation
    b. A tax policy situation
    c. A tax planning situation
    d. An unknown-fact situation

27. Which of the following is not considered substantial authority under Code Sec. 6662?
    a. A proposed regulation
    b. A statement made by a Congressman on the floor before enactment of a tax bill
    c. A private letter ruling
    d. A discussion in the "blue book"
    e. All of the above are considered substantial authority

28. Which of the following facts would not be important in determining whether a child of a divorced parent meets the definition of a dependent?
    a. the age of the child
    b. where the child lived during the year
    c. the language in the divorce decree
    d. the mother remarried during the year
    e. all of the above are important

29. Molly leased a skybox at State University for the football season. She has deducted the cost of the skybox as a business expense. Which of the following facts is not important in determining if the skybox costs are deductible?
    a. the breakdown of the cost between the skybox lease and the football tickets
    b. whether the team won or lost the game
    c. how many games Molly attended
    d. who else used the skybox during each game
    e. all of the above are important facts

30. Which of the following would not usually be included in a letter to an individual client that is a doctor?
    a. a review of the facts
    b. a detailed review of the three relevant cases
    c. a statement that the research is based on current tax law
    d. appreciation for the client's business

Review Problems

31. Identify and explain the basic steps in tax research.

32. Identify and explain the different types of tax research.

33. What is a citator and why is it used by a researcher?

34. Indicate whether the following authorities are primary or secondary sources.
    a. Revenue Ruling
    b. Tax Court Memorandum decision
    c. Private Letter Ruling (PLR)
    d. Joint Committee on Taxation Report
    e. Tax Analysts Tax Notes Today
    f. Journal of Corporate Taxation
    g. IRS Publications

35. Bailey is a professor at Private University. Her son graduated from high school in June and began attending Private University in the fall. Because Bailey has been a professor at Private for more than five years, her son is allowed to attend at no cost. Identify the issue(s) in this case.

36. Paul Willard is a self-employed attorney. As a result of erroneous advice, one of Paul's clients incurred unnecessary costs of $20,000. Prior to legal action, Paul reimbursed this sum to his client. Although his malpractice insurance would have covered $15,000 of the $20,000, he chose not to file for reimbursement. Because he had two recent malpractice claims, Paul is convinced that another claim could cause him to be either uninsurable or insurable only at unaffordable rates. Identify the issue(s) in this case.

37. Harold, a recent college graduate, is planning to purchase a townhouse and then rent out two of the rooms to his old college roommates. Identify the issue(s) in this case.

38. Holly won a legal settlement against her employer for $50,000. The lawyer received the $50,000 on December 27, 2012. After deducting his 40 percent, the lawyer mailed a check for $30,000 to Holly on January 3, 2013. Identify the issue(s) in this case.

39. Using the Boolean operators, develop a search query for locating cases involving alternative minimum tax and stock options that would reduce the number of "hits".

40. Using Boolean operators, develop a search query for locating relevant authority about whether a caddy at the country club is an employee or independent contractor.

Research Cases

41. A client recently exchanged 200 ounces of gold bullion (adjusted basis, $60,000, fair market value $100,000) for 1,500 ounces of silver bullion (fair market value $100,000). Will this exchange qualify as a nontaxable like-kind exchange under Code Sec. 1031?

42. Brandy Corporation, a calendar-year, accrual-basis taxpayer, signed a contract on December 27, 2010, for the installation of a new central air conditioning unit. Because of various shipping delays, the unit was not installed until October 21, 2011, and was never used that year. The unit was first used on March 28, 2012. For purposes of determining MACRS recovery deductions, what year was the unit placed in service?

43. Anne White, a client, lives in Richmond has owned a second property in Wintergreen for three years. Each year, the taxpayer rents the property during the winter months (December through March) each year, and uses the property for personal reasons for the entire month of July each year. However, for two of those three years, her daughter Ellen lived in the property for those three months. For the remainder of the year, rentals are sporadic, usually totaling about 100 days. The taxpayer would now like to deduct interest paid on the mortgage on this property as interest on a second personal residence A colleague told you that you probably should check Sec. 280A(d) on vacation homes to see when (if at all) such a rental would be classified as a "residence."

44. Computer Geniuses, Inc. (CG) leases its employee computer experts to Cellular, Inc. under a contract where Cellular pays CG the wages of the employee, the employee's expenses plus a profit percentage. Since the employee typically travels to various Cellular sites, the employee incurs meals, hotel, and airfare expenses. The employee is reimbursed travel expenses under a "reimbursement or other expense allowance arrangement" within the meaning of Code Sec. 274(e)(3) between CG and the employee. CG sends Cellular a detailed monthly bill providing the employee's wages, a detailed account of reimbursable expenses, and the profit percentage. A copy of the employees travel expense substantiation is also included with the bill. Which company (CG or Cellular) is subject to the 50-percent disallowance of meals & entertainment expense?

45. Matthew sold 200 shares of Xerox stock on December 23, 2012. The stock had a basis of $4,000 and was sold for $2,100. When Matthew funds his IRA on January 3, 2013, he causes the IRA to purchase 400 shares of Xerox for $4,000. Can Matthew deduct the loss on the sale of the Xerox stock?

46. Provide the name of the tax cases at the following locations:

55 TCM 250	_____	7 AFTR2d 1438	_____
832 F2d 436	_____	62-1 USTC 9387	_____
26 BTA 1369	_____	9 TC 159	_____

47. Which court heard the case of *D. Jacobs*, 698 F.2d. 850? What was the Court's decision?

48. What tax issue do the *Melvin J. Cole*, *Dudley W. Gill*, and *Edward J. Holland* cases have in common? Do they all agree on the same issue? Explain.

Appendix A

REVIEWS OF BLOOMBERG BNA TAX MANAGEMENT PORTFOLIOS, CCH'S TAX RESEARCH CONSULTANT, AND RIA'S UNITED STATES TAX REPORTER

Researching a Tax Question with Bloomberg BNA

Introduction

The Bloomberg BNA on-line Tax and Accounting Center consists of the Tax Management U.S. Income Portfolios, the Code and Regulations, Treasury and IRS Pronouncements, and court cases. It also includes a number of new development sources including the Daily Tax Report, the Weekly Report, and BNA commentaries. Each of the 180 Tax Management Portfolios cover a specific tax topic and provide a single source for research, planning and implementation strategies on that topic.

The portfolios are organized by the following broad categories:
- Income Tax Accounting
- C Corporations
- Compensation Planning
- Corporate Returns and Computation of Tax
- Income, Deductions, Credits and Computation of Tax
- Natural Resources
- Other Pass-Through Entities
- Procedure and Administration
- Partnerships
- Real Estate

The following discussion uses the demonstration problem from the chapter to research a tax question using the BNA Tax Management Portfolios.

Key Word Search

Performing a key word search with BNA is very similar to using the RIA Federal Tax Coordinator. The example involving the self-canceling installment note is used to demonstrate this process.

Facts of the Sample Research Question

Sara Owens had owned all of the outstanding stock of Owens Consulting, a computer services corporation. During December, 2008, she transferred 10,000 shares of the outstanding stock ($60,000 adjusted basis, $300,000 fair market value) to her son Al in exchange for an installment note which provided for 10 annual payments of $30,000 plus 10-percent interest on the unpaid balance, beginning on December 15, 2009. The terms of the purchase agreement included a clause stating that any principal and interest remaining due to the seller's death will be deemed "canceled and extinguished as though paid."

Sara Owens died on January 23, 2010, shortly after receiving the second $30,000 installment in December. She reported a capital gain of $24,000 ($30,000 × 80% gross profit ratio, i.e., $240,000 profit/$300,000 total contract price) on her 2008 and 2009 returns, as well as the interest income received. The fair market value of the note (with $240,000 to be collected) was estimated to be $200,000 at the time of Sara's death in January 2010. Are there any tax consequences for the estate income tax return for Sara Owens' estate?

To Perform a Query Word Search using the BNA Tax Management Portfolio:

1. Log onto the BNA service from your computer and choose the Federal Tax tab at the top of the page.
2. Click on U.S. Income Portfolios (**Figure 1**).
3. Enter the following search expression: installment cancelled death (**Figure 2**) in the box at the top right corner of the screen. Click Search.
4. From the 20 hits, click the Real Estate link and then the link for Portfolio 565 – Installment Sales, followed by the link for Transactions generally resulting in taxable dispositions (**Figure 3**).
5. Scroll down the document until you reach the section Cancellation of Installment Obligation where the reference to the *Frane* case appears (screen appears as **Figure 4**).
6. To link to the *Frane* case, click on the link.
7. To link to Rev. Rul. 86-72, click on the link.

Figure 1: Main Screen – BNA Tax and Accounting Center

Figure 2: Search Screen

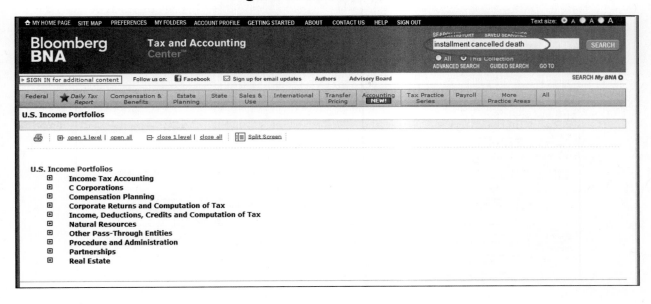

Figure 3: Search Results Screen

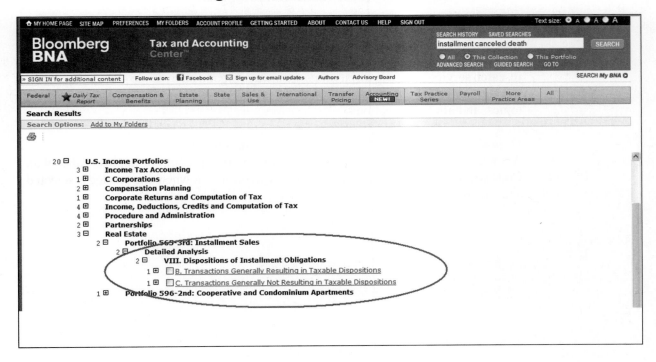

Figure 4: Analysis Section

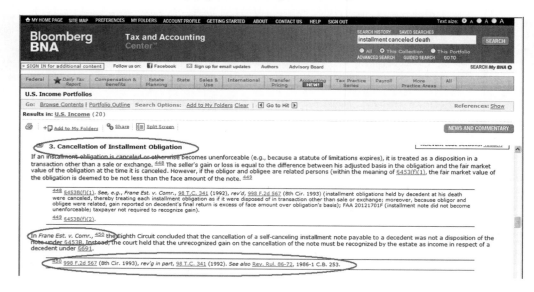

CCH Tax Research Consultant

Differentiating the Standard Federal Tax Reporter and the CCH Tax Research Consultant

As mentioned earlier, the Standard Federal Tax Reporter by CCH is a Code-based tax research service. As such, discussions are always organized by Code section. The *CCH Tax Research Consultant* is a topics-based service with coverage is organized around topics, and not Code sections.

Organization of the CCH Tax Research Consultant

As mentioned above, this service is organized around common topics, rather than Code sections. For example, a portion of the main screen when this service is selected appears as follows:

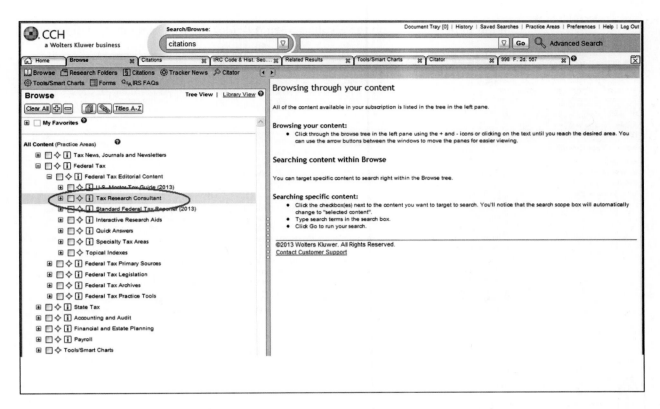

Each of the major topics have various subtopics. The text of the service is similar to the Federal Tax Coordinator, in that coverage is in narrative form with footnotes to primary authority. To perform a key word search, type the terms into the search box on the main screen. Using the installment debt cancellation example with the keywords "installment canceled death", the results are as follows:

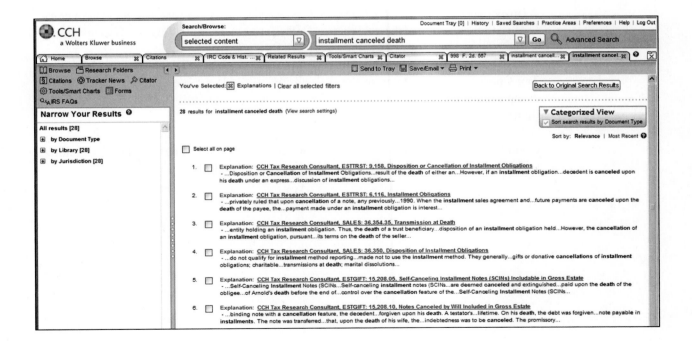

Linking to the 1st item on the results screen provides the following information:

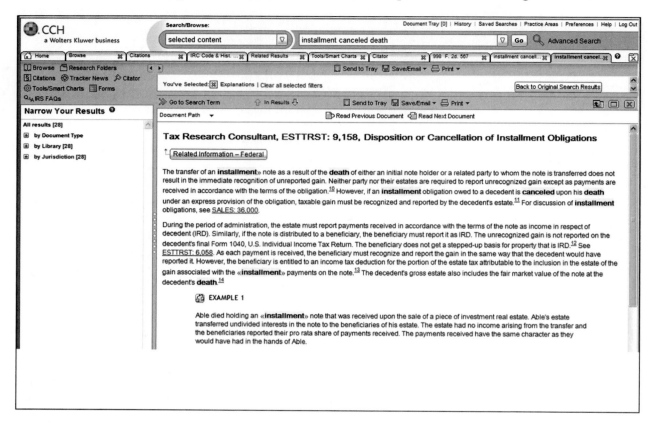

RIA Checkpoint USTR Annotations & Explanations

As mentioned earlier, RIA's *United States Tax Reporter* service is a code-based service including two of the features of the old Prentice-Hall print service: *Explanations and Annotations*.

A key-word search with the USTR is performed in a manner very similar to the Federal Tax Coordinator 2nd. Because the Annotations provide such exhaustive coverage of cases and rulings, a more precise search term may be used with the USTR tax service than with the Coordinator in some cases.

Continuing with the installment debt cancellation problem, the results of searching with the keywords 'installment cancelled death' are as follows:

Main Search Screen

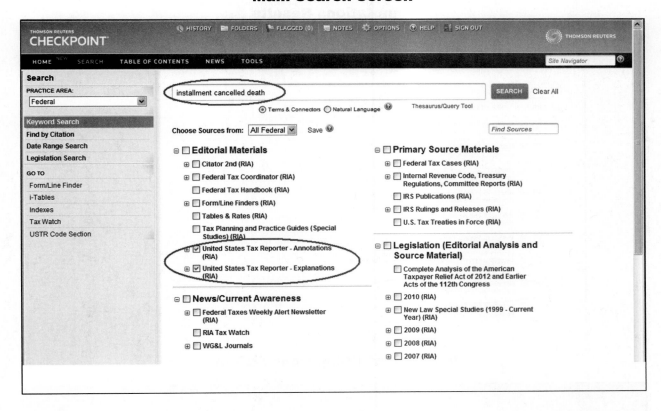

Results Screen

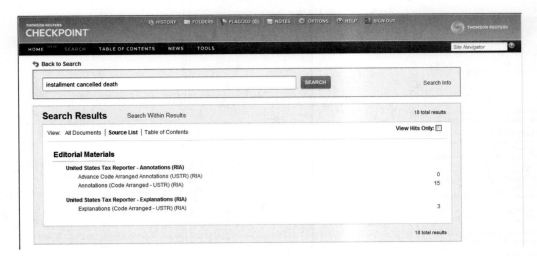

Annotations Results

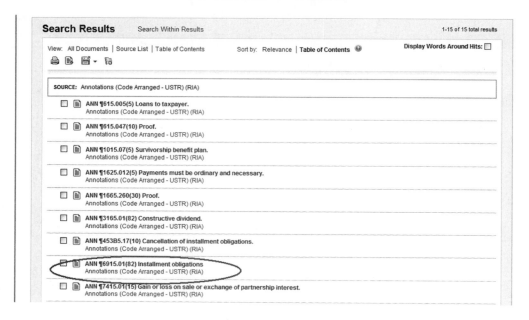

Installment Obligations Screen

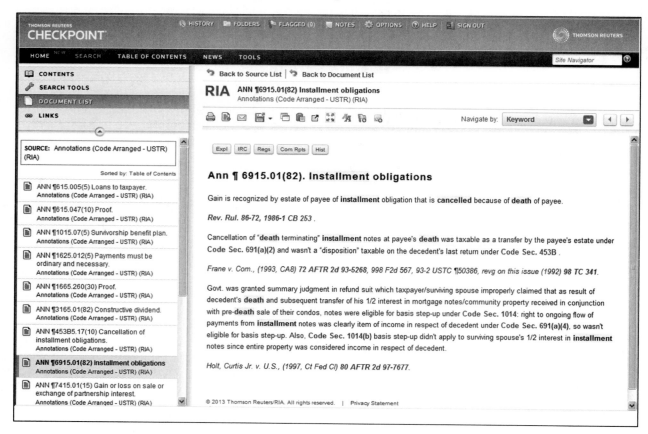

Appendix B
Using Tax Citators

The purpose of a citator is to track down a list of any tax authority that has "cited" a case or other authority of interest. This can be valuable information, as one of the cited authorities (usually a tax case) may be a better fit as an answer to your question. This would especially be the case when your research discloses a court case that is unfavorable to the position that you want to take. In that case, checking a citator may turn up a case that disagreed with the earlier case and thus provide some authority for your answer.

The following discussion highlights three basic citators offered by CCH, RIA, and Shephard's (available in Lexis and Westlaw). Each is illustrated using the same sample citations.

The CCH Citator

In the CCH print service, the citator is included automatically at no extra charge, and they have put the same citator online. This citator works well for unearthing all cases and other authority that cites an authority in question, but it does not indicate *how* the original case was cited: favorably, unfavorably, explained, agreed, etc.

The CCH Citator also does not indicate which issues are involved in the cite. When a taxpayer decides to take a case to court, they will often roll the dice and contest a number of issues since the legal expenses will probably be the same. So if a case has several issues, it is helpful to know which issue was being cited.

The CCH Citator may be illustrated by examining the citations for a U.S. Supreme Court case, *United Dominion Industries, Inc. v. U.S.* The headnote to the case (from the CCH USTC volume) is illustrated below, followed by the citator entry.

Note that there are two major parts of a citator entry for each level of judicial authority. First, the Judicial History of the *United Dominion* case is summarized, disclosing the results of any appeal (note that the U.S. Supreme Court reversed the Fourth Circuit's decision in the case). Secondly, the list of cases citing the *United Dominion* case is displayed.

Case Volume Syllabus (USTC):
US-SUP-CT, [2001-1 USTC ¶50,430], United Dominion Industries, Inc., Petitioner v. United States, Consolidated returns: Separate return limitation year: Carryback: Product liability losses.--, (June 04, 2001)
[2001-1 USTC ¶50,430] United Dominion Industries, Inc., Petitioner v. United States
Supreme Court of the United States, 00-157, 6/4/2001, Reversing and remanding a Court of Appeals decision, 2000-1 USTC ¶50,310

208 F3d 452.

On Writ of Certiorari to the United States Court of Appeals for the Fourth Circuit.
[*Code Sec. 1502*]

Consolidated returns: Separate return limitation year: Carryback: Product liability losses.--An affiliated group was entitled to include the product liability expenses (PLEs) of five group members in determining its product liability loss (PLL) for purposes of the 10-year carryback because the amount of the affiliated group's PLL was to be calculated on a consolidated, single-entity basis, not by determining PLLs separately for each company. Since the tax code and regulations that govern affiliated groups provide that net operating losses (NOLs) be calculated at the consolidated group level, PLLs must also be calculated at the group level. Comparable treatment of PLLs could only be achieved if the comparison of PLEs with consolidated NOLs (CNOLs) occurred at the consolidated level, after CNOLs had been determined. BACK REFERENCES: ¶33,168.831

Citator Entry – CCH:

Federal Tax Citator, 2013FED, Main Citator Table, United Dominion Industries, Inc.
United Dominion Industries, Inc.

ANNOTATED AT ... 2013FED ¶12,014.056, ¶33,168.05, ¶33,168.831
- **CA-4** -- (rem'g DC on remand) 2001-2 USTC ¶50,571, 259 F3d 193
- **SCt** -- (rev'g and rem'g CA) 2001-1 USTC ¶50,430, 532 US 822, 121 SCt 1934
  Boeing Co. SCt, 2003-1 USTC ¶50,273, 537 US 437, 123 SCt 1099
  South Beach Securities, Inc. CA-7, 2010-1 ustc ¶50,421, 606 F3d 366
  Xilinx, Inc. CA-9, 2009-1 USTC ¶50,405, 567 F3d 482
  Marek CA-1, 2008-2 USTC ¶50,676, 548 F3d 147
  Office Max, Inc. CA-6, 2005-2 USTC ¶70,246, 428 F3d 583
  Falconwood Corp. CA-FC, 2005-2 USTC ¶50,597, 422 F3d 1339
  Umbach CA-10, 2004-1 USTC ¶50,148, 357 F3d 1108
  Aeroquip-Vickers, Inc. CA-6, 2003-2 USTC ¶50,693, 347 F3d 173
  FedEx Corp. DC-TN, 2009-1 USTC ¶50,435
  Brunswick Corp. DC-IL, 2009-1 USTC ¶50,131
  Murphy DC-DC, 2007-2 USTC ¶50,531, 493 F3d 170
  Marvel Entertainment Group, Inc. DC-DE, 2002-1 USTC ¶50,302, 273 BR 58
  USA Choice Internet Service, LLC FedCl, 2006-2 USTC ¶70,262, 73 FedCl 780
  America Online, Inc. FedCl, 2005-1 USTC ¶70,238
  Young TC, Dec. 57,726(M), 97 TCM 1101, TC Memo 2009-24
  PSB Holdings, Inc. TC, Dec. 57,159, 129 TC 131
  State Farm Mutual Automobile Ins. Co. TC, Dec. 54,966 , 119 TC 342
  Specking TC, Dec. 54,470, 117 TC 95
  Let. Rul. 200323002, January 31, 2003
  T.D. 9089, IRB 2003-43, 906; 2003-2 CB 906
- **CA-4** -- (rev'g and rem'g DC) 2000-1 USTC ¶50,310, 208 F3d 452
  Intermet Corp. CA-6, 2000-1 USTC ¶50,382, 209 F3d 901
- **DC-NC** -- 98-2 USTC ¶50,527
  Intermet TC, Dec. 52,979, 111 TC 294

The RIA Citator

The RIA Citator displays more information than the CCH service by (1) providing information about how the case of interest was cited and (2) which issue is involved in the cite. Issues are numbered in the headnote of each case included in the AFTR tax volumes. The citator may also be searched by the name of the taxpayer involved in the case; if it is a unique name, use only the last name to avoid missing the relevant case. The RIA Citator may be illustrated by once again examining the citations for a U.S. Supreme Court case, *United Dominion Industries, Inc. v. U.S.* The headnote to the case is illustrated below, followed by the citator entry. Note that in the citator entry, the manner in which the cited case relates to the case in question is given (cited favorably, questioned, etc.) as well as the issue number when a specific issue is being cited. In this particular case, there is only one issue listed in the case volume (net operating loss carrybacks), although two of the citations refer to Issue 1.

Case Volume Syllabus (AFTR):

UNITED DOMINION INDUSTRIES, INC., PETITIONER v. UNITED STATES.

Case Information:

Code Sec (s):	172; 1502
Court Name:	U.S. Supreme Court,
Docket No.:	Docket No. 00-157,
Date Decided:	06/04/2001.
Prior History:	Court of Appeals, (2000, CA4) _85 AFTR 2d 2000-1512, _208 F3d 452, _2000-1 USTC ¶50310, reversing and remanding (1998, DC NC) _82 AFTR 2d 98-5037, _98-2 USTC ¶50527, reversed and remanded.
Tax Year(s):	Years 1973, 1974, 1975, 1976, 1983, 1984, 1985, 1986.
Disposition:	Decision for Taxpayer.
Cites:	87 AFTR 2d 2001-2377, 532 US 822.

HEADNOTE

1. Consolidated returns—product liability losses (PLLs)—NOL carrybacks— separate return year to consolidated return year. Consolidated group was entitled to calculate carry back PLLs on consolidated/"single entity" basis rather than as aggregate of each group member's separate PLL: pursuant to IRC and regs' "comparable treatment" purpose and regs' explicit, exclusive definition of NOL as *consolidated* NOL, PLL's underlying product liability expense (PLE)/loss comparison had to be made at consolidated level in 1st instance. And, govt.'s reliance on separate taxable income (STI) as functional surrogate for members' separate NOLs was based on erroneous interpretation of STI; Reg. §1.1502-79's separate NOL provision applied only in separate return year carryback context; and govt. didn't show separate member approach otherwise comported with comparable treatment purpose. Also, double deduction argument was rejected; Reg. §1.1502-12's failure to specifically provide for PLE blending didn't necessarily prohibit same; and govt. could address tax avoidance concerns, which were also implicated by separate member approach, via Code Sec. 269 or by amending consolidated return regs.

Reference(s): ¶ 1725.04(6) ; ¶ 15,025.09(20) Code Sec. 172 ; Code Sec. 1502

Citator Entry, RIA:

UNITED DOMINION INDUSTRIES INC v. U.S., 87 AFTR 2d 2001-2377, 532 US 822, 121 S Ct 1934, 2001-1 USTC ¶50,430 (US, 6/4/2001)

Judicial History

Reversing & remanding: United Dominion Industries Inc. v. U.S., 85 AFTR 2d 2000-1512, 208 F3d 452 *(CA4, 3/24/2000)*

Later proceeding at: United Dominion Industries Inc v. U.S., 88 AFTR 2d 2001-5323 *(CA4, 8/1/2001) on rem*

Same case or ruling: United Dominion Industries Inc v. U.S., 82 AFTR 2d 98-5037 *(DC NC, 6/19/1998)*

Cited In

Cited in dissent: Boeing Co. & Consolidated Subsidiaries, The v. U.S., 91 AFTR 2d 2003-1098 , 537 US 457, 123 S Ct 1112 *(US, 3/4/2003) [See 87 AFTR 2d 2001-2384, 532 US 839]*

Cited favorably: Umbach, Eric N. v. Com., 92 AFTR 2d 2003-7330 , 357 F3d 1112, 83 Fed Appx 278 *(CA10, 12/11/2003) [See 87 AFTR 2d 2001-2383, 532 US 836]*

Cited favorably: Falconwood Corporation, The v. U.S., 96 AFTR 2d 2005-5987, 422 F3d 1351 *(CA Fed Cir, 9/2/2005) [See 87 AFTR 2d 2001-2378, 532 US 826]*

Cited favorably: OfficeMax, Inc. v. U.S., 96 AFTR 2d 2005-6834, 428 F3d 594 *(CA6, 11/2/2005) [See 87 AFTR 2d 2001-2384, 532 US 839, concurring op.]*

Cases reconciled: Murphy, Marrita v. IRS, 100 AFTR 2d 2007-5081, 493 F3d 179 *(CA Dist Col, 7/3/2007) [See 87 AFTR 2d 2001-2384, 532 US 839 and n.1, concurring and dissenting ops.]*

Cited generally: America Online, Inc. v. U.S., 95 AFTR 2d 2005-1700, 64 Fed Cl 576 *(Ct Fed Cl, 3/30/2005) [See 87 AFTR 2d 2001-2384, 2001-2385, 532 US 838, 839, concurring and dissenting ops.]*

Cited favorably: USA Choice Internet Service, LLC v. U.S., 98 AFTR 2d 2006-7824, 73 Fed Cl 789 *(Ct Fed Cl, 11/15/2006) [See 87 AFTR 2d 2001-2384, 532 US 838, 839 and n.1]*

Cited favorably: State Farm Mutual Automobile Insurance Co. & Subs., <u>119 TC 354</u>, 119 TCR 208 *(12/19/2002) [See 87 AFTR 2d 2001-2384, 532 US 838]*

Cited favorably: Coram Healthcare Corp., In re, <u>94 AFTR 2d 2004-6281</u> *(Bktcy Ct DE, 10/5/2004) [See 87 AFTR 2d 2001-2382–2001-2383, 532 US 834-835]*

Cited favorably: PSB Holdings, Inc, 129 TC No. 15, <u>129 TCR 85</u> *(11/1/2007) [See 87 AFTR 2d 2001-2383, 532 US 836-837]*

Cited favorably: Specking, Joseph D., et al, <u>117 TC 111</u>, 117 TCR 66 *(8/28/2001) [See 87 AFTR 2d 2001-2383, 121 S Ct 1942-1943]*

Cited favorably: Smith, L. Ben & Carol, 2006 <u>RIA TC Memo 2006-393</u> *(3/23/2006) [See 87 AFTR 2d 2001-2383, 532 US 836-837, cited at 117 TC 111]*

Cited generally 1: Aeroquip-Vickers Inc & Subsidiaries v. Com., <u>92 AFTR 2d 2003-6571</u>, 347 F3d 193 *(CA6, 10/20/2003)*

Cases reconciled 1: Temple-Inland Inc. & Subsidiaries v. U.S., <u>96 AFTR 2d 2005-7009</u> *(Ct Fed Cl, 11/8/2005)*

Cited favorably 1: T.D. 9089, 2003-2 CB 907, 909

Shephard's Citator

Shephard's Citator is the most comprehensive citator available today. This citator is included with the Lexis and Westlaw online research services, and is organized somewhat similarly to the RIA Citator in that issues are delineated in the case notes and referenced in the citator, along with the relationship between the two cases. A common expression in law practice is to "Shep" a case, meaning to use the Shephard's citator.

Shephard's Citator may be illustrated by once again examining the citations for a U.S. Supreme Court case, *United Dominion Industries v. U.S.* The headnote to the case is illustrated below, followed by a portion of the citator entry.

Case Volume Syllabus:

CASE SUMMARY

PROCEDURAL POSTURE: Petitioner's predecessor in interest, the parent corporation of an affiliated group of corporations, sued respondent United States, seeking refunds of taxes based on the carry back of product liability losses. The district court ruled in favor of petitioner, but the United States Court of Appeals for the Fourth Circuit reversed. Petitioner corporation's petition for writ of certiorari was granted.

OVERVIEW: Petitioner's predecessor in interest was the parent of an affiliated group of corporations that properly elected to file consolidated tax returns. The parent reported a consolidated net operating loss (CNOL) that exceeded the aggregate of its 26 individual members' product liability expenses (PLEs). Five companies reported a positive separate taxable income (STI). The parent followed a "single-entity" approach to calculate its consolidated product liability loss (PLL). However, the Government argued for a "separate-member" approach, contending that PLEs incurred by an affiliate with positive STI could not contribute to a PLL eligible for 10-year carryback. In the tax refund action, the appellate court ruled in favor of the Government, determining that determining PLL separately for each group member was correct. On certiorari review, the court reversed the judgment. By expressly and exclusively defining net operating loss as CNOL, the regulations supported the position that group members' PLEs should be aggregated and the affiliated group's PLL determined on a consolidated, single-entity basis.

OUTCOME: Judgment was reversed because petitioner's "single-entity" approach to calculating its consolidated product liability loss was correct.

CORE TERMS: consolidated, product liability, consolidated returns, affiliated group, group member, single-entity, carryback, affiliate's, operating loss, calculating, calculation, separate return, separate-member, affiliated, taxable income, tax years, consolidated group, individual members', omission, refund, entity, capital gains, separately, computing, several items, comparable, aggregate, ambiguity, consolidated net operating loss, charitable-contribution

LexisNexis® Headnotes Hide Headnotes

Tax Law > Federal Income Tax Computation > Deductions for Losses > Net Operating Loss (IRC secs. 172, 382) > Affiliated Corporations
Tax Law > Federal Income Tax Computation > Deductions for Losses > Net Operating Loss (IRC secs. 172, 382) > Elections
Tax Law > Federal Taxpayer Groups > General Overview

HN1

Under § 172(b)(1)(I) of the Internal Revenue Code of 1954, 26 U.S.C.S. § 172(b)(1)(I), a taxpayer may carry back its "product liability loss" up to 10 years in order to offset prior years' income. Regarding the method for calculating the product liability loss of an affiliated group of corporations electing to file a consolidated federal income tax return, the group's product liability loss must be figured on a consolidated basis in the first instance, and not by aggregating product liability losses separately determined company by company.

Editor Note: Twelve additional headnotes are omitted due to length.

Citator Entry:

United Dominion Indus. v. United States, 532 U.S. 822, 121 S. Ct. 1934, 150 L. Ed. 2d 45, 2001 U.S. LEXIS 4124, 69 U.S.L.W. 4413, 2001 Cal. Daily Op. Service 4524, 2001 D.A.R. 5553, 2001-1 U.S. Tax Cas. (CCH) P50430 (2001)

SHEPARD'S SUMMARY

Unrestricted Shepard's Summary	
Subsequent appellate history contains possible negative analysis.	
Citing References:	
Cautionary Analyses:	Distinguished (3)
Positive Analyses:	Followed (3)
Neutral Analyses:	Dissenting Op. (5), Explained (3)
Other Sources:	Law Reviews (46), Statutes (7), Treatises (29), Court Documents (58)
LexisNexis Headnotes:	HN1 (6), HN2 (4), HN4 (4), HN5 (2), HN6 (4), HN7 (2), HN8 (6), HN9 (6), HN10 (1), HN11 (1), HN12 (4)

PRIOR HISTORY (7 citing references)

1.	*Amtel, Inc. v. United States*, 31 Fed. Cl. 598, 1994 U.S. Claims LEXIS 139, 74 A.F.T.R.2d (RIA) 5448, 94 TNT 150-11, 94-2 U.S. Tax Cas. (CCH) ¶50,391 (1994)
2.	Affirmed without opinion by: *Amtel, Inc. v. United States*, 59 F.3d 181, 1995 U.S. App. LEXIS 22873 (Fed. Cir. 1995)
3.	Reported in full at: *Amtel, Inc. v. United States*, 1995 U.S. App. LEXIS 15361, 76 A.F.T.R.2d (RIA) 5168, 95 TNT 132-6, 95-2 U.S. Tax Cas. (CCH) ¶50,402 (Fed. Cir. 1995)
4.	Related proceeding at: *United Dominion Indus. v. United States*, 1998 U.S. Dist. LEXIS 9950, 82 A.F.T.R.2d (RIA) 5037, 98-2 U.S. Tax Cas. (CCH) ¶50,527 (W.D.N.C. 1998)
5.	Reversed by, Remanded by: *United Dominion Indus. v. United States*, 208 F.3d 452, 2000 U.S. App. LEXIS 4853, 85 A.F.T.R.2d (RIA) 1512, 2000-1 U.S. Tax Cas. (CCH) ¶50,310 (4th Cir. N.C. 2000)
6.	Writ of certiorari granted: *United Dominion Indus. v. United States*, 531 U.S. 1009, 121 S. Ct. 562, 148 L. Ed. 2d 482, 2000 U.S. LEXIS 7695, 69 U.S.L.W. 3363, 2000 Cal. Daily Op. Service 9525 (2000)
7.	Motion granted by: *United Dominion Indus. v. United States*, 531 U.S. 1049, 121 S. Ct. 652, 148 L. Ed. 2d 556, 2000 U.S. LEXIS 8306, 69 U.S.L.W. 3397 (2000)
8.	Reversed by, Remanded by (CITATION YOU ENTERED): *United Dominion Indus. v. United States*, 532 U.S. 822, 121 S. Ct. 1934, 150 L. Ed. 2d 45, 2001 U.S. LEXIS 4124, 69 U.S.L.W. 4413, 2001 Cal. Daily Op. Service 4524, 2001 D.A.R. 5553, 2001-1 U.S. Tax Cas. (CCH) ¶50,430 (2001)

SUBSEQUENT APPELLATE HISTORY (1 citing reference)

CITING DECISIONS (58 citing decisions)

U.S. SUPREME COURT

9.	Cited by: Mayo Found. for Med. Educ. & Research v. United States, 131 S. Ct. 704, 178 L. Ed. 2d 588, 2011 U.S. LEXIS 609, 79 U.S.L.W. 4015, 22 Fla. L. Weekly Fed. S 743, 107 A.F.T.R.2d (RIA) 341, Unemployment Ins. Rep. (CCH) ¶14691C, 160 Lab. Cas. (CCH) ¶35,864, 2011-1 U.S. Tax Cas. (CCH) ¶50,143 (U.S. 2011) 131 S. Ct. 704 p.712 178 L. Ed. 2d 588 p.598

10.	Cited in Dissenting Opinion at: *Boeing Co. v. United States*, 537 U.S. 437, 123 S. Ct. 1099, 155 L. Ed. 2d 17, 2003 U.S. LEXIS 1947, 71 U.S.L.W. 4131, 16 Fla. L. Weekly Fed. S 118, 2003 Cal. Daily Op. Service 1887, 91 A.F.T.R.2d (RIA) 1088, 2003-1 U.S. Tax Cas. (CCH) ¶50,273 (2003)
11.	Cited by: *Barnhart v. Peabody Coal Co.*, 537 U.S. 149, 123 S. Ct. 748, 154 L. Ed. 2d 653, 2003 U.S. LEXIS 752, 71 U.S.L.W. 4041, 16 Fla. L. Weekly Fed. S 35, 2003 Cal. Daily Op. Service 419, 2003 D.A.R. 501, 29 Employee Benefits Cas. (BNA) 2089 (2003)
12.	Cited by: *Chevron U.S.A. Inc. v. Echazabal*, 536 U.S. 73, 122 S. Ct. 2045, 153 L. Ed. 2d 82, 2002 U.S. LEXIS 4202, 70 U.S.L.W. 4516, 15 Fla. L. Weekly Fed. S 344, 67 Cal. Comp. Cas. (MB) 781, 2002 Cal. Daily Op. Service 5023, 2002 D.A.R. 6379, 10 Accom. Disabilities Dec. (CCH) ¶10,056, 13 Am. Disabilities Cas. (BNA) 97 (2002)

3RD CIRCUIT—COURT OF APPEALS

13.	Cited by: *Harvard Secured Creditors Liquidation Trust v. IRS (In re Harvard Indus.)*, 568 F.3d 444, 2009 U.S. App. LEXIS 13009, 103 A.F.T.R.2d (RIA) 2701, 47 Employee Benefits Cas. (BNA) 1270 (3d Cir. N.J. 2009) LexisNexis Headnotes HN2, HN6 *568 F.3d 444 p.446*

3RD CIRCUIT—U.S. DISTRICT COURTS

14.	Cited by: *Marvel Entm't Group, Inc. v. Mafco Holdings, Inc. (In re Marvel Entm't Group, Inc.)*, 273 B.R. 58, 2002 U.S. Dist. LEXIS 2033, 89 A.F.T.R.2d (RIA) 916, 2002-1 U.S. Tax Cas. (CCH) ¶50,302 (D. Del. 2002) **LexisNexis Headnotes HN1, HN8, HN12**

4TH CIRCUIT—COURT OF APPEALS

15.	Cited by: *United Dominion Indus. v. United States*, 259 F.3d 193, 2001 U.S. App. LEXIS 17126, 88 A.F.T.R.2d (RIA) 5323, 2001-2 U.S. Tax Cas. (CCH) ¶50,571 (4th Cir. 2001)

6TH CIRCUIT—COURT OF APPEALS

16.	Cited by: *Knochelmann v. Comm'r*, 455 Fed. Appx. 536, 2011 U.S. App. LEXIS 18253, 108 A.F.T.R.2d (RIA) 6011, 2011-2 U.S. Tax Cas. (CCH) ¶50,605 (6th Cir. 2011) 455 Fed. Appx. 536 p.539
17.	Cited by: *Officemax, Inc. v. United States*, 428 F.3d 583, 2005 U.S. App. LEXIS 23635, 2005 FED App. 435P (6th Cir.), 96 A.F.T.R.2d (RIA) 6824, 2005-2 U.S. Tax Cas. (CCH) ¶70,246 (6th Cir. Ohio 2005)
18.	Cited by: *Sidney Coal Co. v. SSA*, 427 F.3d 336, 2005 U.S. App. LEXIS 22438, 2005 FED App. 418P (6th Cir.), 36 Employee Benefits Cas. (BNA) 1045 (6th Cir. Ky. 2005)
19.	Cited in Dissenting Opinion at: *Aeroquip-Vickers, Inc. v. Comm'r*, 347 F.3d 173, 2003 U.S. App. LEXIS 21111, 2003 FED App. 370P (6th Cir.), 92 A.F.T.R.2d (RIA) 6555, 2003-2 U.S. Tax Cas. (CCH) ¶50,693 (6th Cir. 2003) **LexisNexis Headnotes HN1, HN4, HN8**

9TH CIRCUIT—COURT OF APPEALS

20.	Cited in Dissenting Opinion at: *Abreu-Reyes v. INS*, 292 F.3d 1029, 2002 U.S. App. LEXIS 10973, 2002 Cal. Daily Op. Service 5053, 2002 D.A.R. 6423 (9th Cir. Cal. 2002)

10TH CIRCUIT—COURT OF APPEALS

21.	Cited by: *Umbach v. Comm'r*, 357 F.3d 1108, 83 Fed. Appx. 274, 2003 U.S. App. LEXIS 24936, 92 A.F.T.R.2d (RIA) 7327 (10th Cir. 2003)

D.C. CIRCUIT—COURT OF APPEALS

22.	Cited by: *Murphy v. IRS*, 377 U.S. App. D.C. 197, 493 F.3d 170, 2007 U.S. App. LEXIS 15816, 100 A.F.T.R.2d (RIA) 5075, 2007-2 U.S. Tax Cas. (CCH) ¶50,531 (2007)

FEDERAL CIRCUIT—COURT OF APPEALS

23.	Cited by: *Falconwood Corp. v. United States*, 422 F.3d 1339, 2005 U.S. App. LEXIS 19054, 96 A.F.T.R.2d (RIA) 5977, 2005-2 U.S. Tax Cas. (CCH) P50597 (Fed. Cir. 2005) **LexisNexis Headnotes HN5, HN9**

FEDERAL CLAIMS COURT

24.	Cited by: *USA Choice Internet Serv., LLC v. United States*, 73 Fed. Cl. 780, 2006 U.S. Claims LEXIS 344, 98 A.F.T.R.2d (RIA) 7815, 2006-2 U.S. Tax Cas. (CCH) P70262 (2006)
25.	Cited by: *Viacom, Inc. v. United States*, 70 Fed. Cl. 649, 2006 U.S. Claims LEXIS 122, 38 Employee Benefits Cas. (BNA) 2353 (2006)
26.	Distinguished by: *Temple-Inland Inc. v. United States*, 68 Fed. Cl. 561, 2005 U.S. Claims LEXIS 333, 96 A.F.T.R.2d (RIA) 7000, 2006-1 U.S. Tax Cas. (CCH) P50119 (2005) **LexisNexis Headnotes HN9**
27.	Cited by: *Am. Online, Inc. v. United States*, 64 Fed. Cl. 571, 2005 U.S. Claims LEXIS 86, 95 A.F.T.R.2d (RIA) 1697 (2005) **LexisNexis Headnotes HN1**

U.S. TAX COURT

28.	Cited by: *PSB Holdings, Inc. v. Comm'r*, 129 T.C. 131, 2007 U.S. Tax Ct. LEXIS 35, 129 T.C. No. 15 (2007)
29.	Cited by: *Smith v. Comm'r*, T.C. Memo 2006-51, 2006 Tax Ct. Memo LEXIS 53, 91 T.C.M. (CCH) 909 (T.C. 2006) **LexisNLexis Headnotes HN12**
30.	Followed by: *State Farm Mut. Auto. Ins. Co. v. Comm'r*, 119 T.C. 342, 2002 U.S. Tax Ct. LEXIS 58, 119 T.C. No. 21 (2002) **LexisNexis Headnotes HN1, HN4, HN8, HN12**
31.	Cited by: *Specking v. Comm'r*, 117 T.C. 95, 2001 U.S. Tax Ct. LEXIS 40, 117 T.C. No. 9 (2001) **LexisNexis Headnotes HN12**

IRS AGENCY MATERIALS

32.	Followed by, Explained by: *Chief Couns. Adv. Mem. 200714017*, IRS CCA 200714017, 2006 IRS CCA LEXIS 85 (I.R.S. 2006)
33.	Cited by: *PLR 200447037*, PLR 200447037, 2004 PLR LEXIS 1157 (I.R.S. 2004)
34.	Cited by: *T.D. 9089*, 2003-2 C.B. 906, 2003 IRB LEXIS 1860, 2003-43 I.R.B. 906, T.D. 9089 (2003)
35.	Distinguished by: *PLR 200323002*, PLR 200323002, 2003 PLR LEXIS 238 (I.R.S. 2003)
36.	Cited by: *Chief Couns. Adv. Mem.*, IRS CCA 200323002, 2003 IRS CCA LEXIS 15 (I.R.S. 2003)
37.	Cited by: *Chief Couns. Adv. Mem.*, IRS CCA 200305019, 2002 IRS CCA LEXIS 140 (I.R.S. 2002)
38.	Cited by: *PLR 200305020*, PLR 200305020, 2002 PLR LEXIS 1671 (I.R.S. 2002)
39.	Cited by: *Gen. Litig. Bull. 200205047*, GLB 200205047, 2001 GLB LEXIS 13 (I.R.S. 2001)
40.	Cited by: *Chief Couns. Adv. Mem.*, IRS CCA 200149008, 2001 IRS CCA LEXIS 216 (I.R.S. 2001)

GEORGIA COURT OF APPEALS

41.	Cited by: *Ga. Dep't of Revenue v. Ga. Chemistry Council, Inc.*, 270 Ga. App. 615, 607 S.E.2d 207, 2004 Ga. App. LEXIS 1543, 2004 Fulton County D. Rep. 3787 (2004) **LexisNexis Headnotes HN2, HN4, HN6, HN8, HN9**

MASSACHUSETTS SUPREME JUDICIAL COURT

42.	Cited by: *FMR Corp. v. Comm'r of Revenue*, 441 Mass. 810, 809 N.E.2d 498, 2004 Mass. LEXIS 294 (2004) **LexisNexis Headnotes HN7, HN9, HN10, HN11**

CHAPTER 5

Landmark Judicial Decisions—Income

Learning Objectives

1. Describe the objectives of taxation.
2. Summarize the considerations used in measuring taxable income, the role that accounting methods play in income recognition and the concepts that override accounting methods elections.
3. Summarize the landmark cases that define the realization concept, windfall gains, accounting methods and assignment of income issues.

¶5001 Introduction

The recognition of income is a complex topic encompassing a variety of income recognition and realization concepts. While the 16th amendment to the Constitution gave the Congress the power to "tax income from whatever source derived" no guidance was given on what constitutes income. As a result taxpayers have used the courts to dispute assertions by the IRS that a sum of money or other tangible or intangible asset received by a taxpayer rightfully should be considered income rather than a non-taxable transfer of wealth from one person to another. Once it has been determined that a "benefit" has been received and constitutes taxable income, the next step is to determine "when" i.e. in which tax year, should this income be reported. Again taxpayers have turned to the courts in their disputes with the income as to when income should be recognized. This chapter explores the answers to these questions by analyzing key court cases that have been decided over the years on various aspects of income recognition. In many cases, the decisions reached in these cases have later been codified in the Internal Revenue Code.

In some instances when the courts decided against the IRS, Congress later added various code sections to "override" these court decisions for subsequent taxpayers with similar or identical issues. As we progress through this chapter we will explore how income is measured and analyze the basic income recognition concepts that have been developed by the courts.

For all of its importance, the concept of "income" is never really defined in the Code. The closest that Congress comes to defining income is found in Code Sec. 61, reprinted below:

Code Sec. 61

a. General definition.

Except as otherwise provided in this subtitle, gross income means all income from whatever source derived, including (but not limited to) the following items:

1. Compensation for services, including fees, commissions, fringe benefits, and similar items;
2. Gross income derived from business;
3. Gains derived from dealings in property;
4. Interest;
5. Rents;
6. Royalties;
7. Dividends;
8. Alimony and separate maintenance payments;
9. Annuities;
10. Income from life insurance and endowment contracts;
11. Pensions;
12. Income from discharge of indebtedness;
13. Distributive share of partnership gross income;
14. Income in respect of a decedent; and
15. Income from interest in an estate or trust.

b. Cross references.

For items specifically included in gross income, see Part II (Sec. 71 and following). For items specifically excluded from gross income, see Part III (Sec. 101 and following).

Several points are worth noting in examining Code Sec. 61. First, the phrase "except as otherwise provided" clearly suggests that any doubt about a particular item of income is resolved in favor of including that item in gross income. The exceptions to the general inclusion rule must be found in this subtitle, meaning that an item of income is presumed to be taxable unless it is specifically exempted within Subtitle A (Income Taxes) of the Code.

These statutory exceptions are collectively identified as exclusions, and are enumerated in Code Secs. 101–140 (Part III of Subchapter B, Computation of Taxable Income). For example, lottery winnings are taxable because there is no statutory provision allowing exclusion for such an item. On the other hand, interest income from a city of Chicago bond is not generally taxable because Code Sec. 103 provides exclusion for interest on state and local bonds (with limited exceptions discussed later in the course).

Note also that the phrase "from whatever sources derived" indicates that income can come in many forms and from many different sources. For example, a corporation that finds buried treasure on its property must generally report the fair market value of the treasure as gross income, since the treasure is a clear accession to wealth and there is no statutory exclusion for such income. Also note that, although Code Sec. 61 lists 15 common sources of income, the phrase "including, but not limited to" indicates that this list is not all-inclusive.

The purpose of this chapter is to review the landmark court decisions involving the concept on income. A discussion of these cases is preceded by a brief review of the tax notion of income and the factors that have shaped that definition.

¶5003 Objectives of Taxation—The Macro View

There are many influences that motivate Congress when defining "income" as part of our tax law. Before examining concepts unique to the definition of income itself, it may be beneficial to review briefly the diverse objectives that Congress may have in mind in enacting, modifying, or repealing the tax law.

.01   RAISE REVENUE

One can never lose sight of the fact that the primary purpose of our tax laws is to raise revenue. Former Chief Justice of the Supreme Court Oliver Wendell Holmes was quoted as saying "Taxes are what we pay for a civilized society." Without these voluntary yet compulsory transfers to the federal government, there would be no interstate highway system, social security program, or federal immunization programs. Although members of Congress are often quick to cite other reasons for a tax increase, usually the reason is simply to raise revenue necessary to keep the government functioning.

.03   STIMULATE THE ECONOMY

Tax policy has often been used as a method of stimulating the economy. When the economy is sluggish, a tax cut will inject additional dollars into the system, which in turn increases demand. This increased demand causes businesses to hire more workers, who in turn will now also demand more goods and services, and another cycle of spending and hiring commences. Recall that Keynes's theory suggested that for $X dollars injected into the economy, the national income would go up by a multiple equal to $1/(1 - MPC)$, where MPC represents the consumers' average marginal propensity to consume. For example, if consumers spend an average of $.80 on consumption from every $1.00 they earn, the "multiplier" is 5, or $1/(1 - .80)$. This, if an additional $1 million is injected into the economy, national income would be predicted to increase by $5 million.

Keynes's multiplier effect has been validated by several infusions of additional cash in the economy, notably the many public works programs started during the depression. The mulitiplier effect is equally applicable to a tax cut; for example, in 1963 tax rates were cut by one third, and yet total tax collections for the next couple of years actually increased. And tax cuts have the advantage of offering an immediate stimulus (more cash in the economy) by quickly cutting withholding rates and estimated tax requirements.

OBSERVATION   A good example of a tax cut to stimulate the economy was the 2% rate reduction to the payroll tax withheld from employees' wages in 2011 and 2012. This temporary tax cut provided an economic stimulus of ap-proximately $120 billion per year by increasing take home pay between $700-$1,800 per year for most of the 160 million workers in the US.

OBSERVATION   Well, if tax cuts work that well, why don't we just cut taxes all the time? The answer should be obvious; the stimulus is only temporary, and you are left with a lower tax rate structure that will eventually produce less revenue. The real battleground with tax cut proposals is the dueling projections of the *elasticity* of the cut, that is, how long will the beneficial effects last before they "turn around" and begin hemorrhaging revenue.

.05   REGULATE DEMAND

Tax policy has also been used as a tool for dampening demand if an economy heats up too quickly. If demand begins to outstrip supply from a stimulus in the economy, prices will go up and inflation becomes a problem. To regulate this demand, taxes can be raised immediately through changes in the withholding and estimated tax requirements. As people have less money to spend, they demand less goods and services and prices decrease.

OBSERVATION   A good example of how tax policy can regulate demand occurred in 1965. A combination of the 1963 tax cuts and an escalating conflict in Vietnam created strong inflationary pressures. Congress reacted by enacting a temporary 10 percent surtax on individuals, that is, after a taxpayer had computed his or her tax liability, they increased it 10 percent. This greatly dampened demand and reduced the inflationary pressure on prices. Of course, that was 1965; can you imagine what would happen to a politician these days who proposed such a 10 percent surtax?

.07   ENCOURAGE GROWTH

Some tax proposals are geared towards promoting the long-term growth of the economy by encouraging spending on durable goods rather than consumption items. For example, the accelerated depreciation provisions came about in World War II as a means of encouraging businesses to invest in durable machinery to aid the war effort. Now this provision is used to encourage businesses to invest in more plant capacity to produce more goods (the supply side theory of growth). And economic evidence disclosed that the investment tax credit provisions that were effective for the 25-year period ending in 1965 helped stimulate investment in new machinery and equipment.

.09   ACHIEVE CERTAIN SOCIAL GOALS

Tax policy has always been an instrument of social change by encouraging certain types of social change and behaviors and discouraging others. For example, the tax law has been used to encourage investments in affordable low-income housing and rehabilitation of historical structures. Special tax breaks have also been enacted to encourage such diverse activities as adoption and the purchase of electric vehicles. Furthermore, additional tax deductions are available for blind taxpayers and taxpayers age 65 or older.

OBSERVATION   One of the more interesting attempts by Congress to influence behavior is the earned income tax credit. This tax provision works much like the negative income tax idea proposed long ago by Milton Friedman, whereby every taxpayer is guaranteed a basic subsidy by the government. As the taxpayer begins to earn income, the subsidy actually *increases*, eventually decreasing as the taxpayer earns above the poverty line. The earned income credit is not a true negative income tax, in that there is no "payment" unless the taxpayer has earned income. It is interesting to note that various tax reform proposals emphasizing a "flat tax" would do away with the earned income tax credit; even though no tax would be owed if income was $30,000 or less under most of these proposals, that amounts to a tax *increase* for individuals who otherwise qualified for the earned income credit.

.11   ACHIEVE CERTAIN POLITICAL OBJECTIVES

A list of Congressional motivations for tax change would be incomplete without including political objectives. The tax law has been used to bestow various favors on constituents, some needed and some not. Sometimes this happens with tax laws that adversely affect certain taxpayers, who are provided a softer landing through various transition rules.

OBSERVATION   As part of the 1986 Act, Congress repealed a special ESOP tax credit provision, but exempted from the repeal all taxpayers meeting the following conditions listed in Code Sec. 1171 of the Act:

SECTION 1171. — The amendments made by section 1171 shall not apply in the case of a tax credit employee stock ownership plan if:

(1)   such plan was favorably approved on September 23, 1983, by employees, and
(2)   not later than January 11, 1984, the employer of such employees was 100 percent owned by such plan.
   (b) SUBTITLE NOT TO APPLY TO CERTAIN NEWSPAPER. --The amendments made by this subtitle shall not apply to any daily newspaper --

(1)   which was first published on December 17, 1855, and which began publication under its current name in 1954, and
(2)   which is published in a constitutional home rule city (within the meaning of section 143(d)(3)(C) of the Internal Revenue Code of 1986) which has a population of less than 2,500,000.

Query: Wouldn't it have just been easier to say *"Houston Chronicle"* instead of "certain newspaper"?

OBSERVATION   On October 1, 2008 the IRS issued Notice 2008-83 waiving the Sec. 382 ownership change rules limiting the deductibility of built-in losses and net operating loss carry forwards for banks. On October 3, 2008, Wells Fargo announced that it was acquiring Wachovia Bank Corporation which had substantial losses incurred in the financial crisis of 2008. Without this waiver, Wells Fargo's would not have been able to use the majority of Wachovia's loss carry forwards. Was the issuance of the notice a coincidence? As one commentator noted, the notice was a "huge gift to the financial institutions."[1]

In some cases, a proposed tax change may have political, economic, and social considerations. For example, in the early 1970s, Chrysler Corporation was in deep financial trouble, and they asked Congress to allow them to "cash out" their net operating loss carryovers, rather than waiting until profitable years returned (if ever). In the end, Congress decided to guarantee several loans for Chrysler rather than grant this special tax provision. But Chrysler is part of an important segment of the economy, and having it go under would have serious social implications as well through high unemployment. So it is difficult to classify that proposal as being primarily political in nature.

---

[1]   Sheppard, Lee, Technical Objections to the Bailout, Part 2, 121 Tax Notes 359 (Oct 27, 2008).

¶5005   Considerations in Measuring Taxable Income

Economists, accountants, and tax authorities have their own definitions of income. To the economist, income generally includes both realized and unrealized increases in wealth; in this regard, income is more or less a measure of the increase or decrease in the net worth of an individual or a business. Thus, this measure would include such items as an increase in value of land on which a business is located, even though that increase has not been realized through a market transaction.

The accountants' concept of income is much closer to the definition used for federal income tax purposes, in that accounting income generally includes only those increases and decreases in wealth that are realized in a verifiable market transaction. Thus, an increase in the value of company land would be ignored until such land was sold or exchanged in a transaction where the gain is realized and could be objectively measured.

And yet, there are still significant differences between financial accounting income and taxable income, which are discussed in Chapter 17. Some of these differences may be explained by certain considerations assumed in defining taxable income; these are described below.

.01   WHEREWITHAL TO PAY PRINCIPLE

The **wherewithal-to-pay** concept is based on the premise that a tax should be imposed when a taxpayer is best able to pay and the government is best able to collect. This concept is a central tenet in much of the Code, and the application of this principle overrides any financial accounting or basis election of the taxpayer. Two simple examples illustrate how this concept is applied both to the detriment of the taxpayer and to the benefit of the taxpayer.

Example 5-1. Jen Corporation owns a shopping center. One of the tenants prepaid three years rent in advance. Although such rent would be reported only as earned over the three-year period for financial accounting purposes, the entire amount is taxed immediately in the year of receipt. Why? Because the taxpayer is best able to pay the tax this year (when the cash is available), and this is also the best time for the IRS to collect the tax.

Example 5-2. Brown Company's business warehouse was destroyed by a fire during the current year. Brown's adjusted (cost) basis in the warehouse was $200,000, and Brown had insured the warehouse for its $500,000 fair market value. When Brown receives the $500,000 insurance proceeds, it will normally report a $300,000 taxable gain. However, if Brown reinvests the entire $500,000 (or more) in a new warehouse within two years, Code Sec. 1033 of the Code permits Brown to defer any gain in the year of receipt (through a basis adjustment described later) because Brown has no wherewithal-to-pay tax after purchasing the new warehouse. If Brown spends only $430,000 for a new warehouse, then Brown will have to report a $70,000 gain, because this portion of the insurance proceeds not reinvested represents a wherewithal-to-pay tax.

.03   OBJECTIVITY IN DEFINING INCOME

As mentioned earlier, the financial accounting concept of income is much closer to the taxable income concept because both generally require that an amount of income be realized in a verifiable market transaction before being recognized. However, the realization concept is applied more strictly in determining taxable income. For example, price level adjustments are ignored for tax purposes because any inflationary or deflationary effects have not been realized in a verifiable market transaction. The IRS would have an impossible audit task if the accounting records veer away from their historical roots.

.05 EQUITY AND UNIFORMITY

In a perfect world, every tax statute would be equitable and uniform in terms of how all taxpayers are affected by a particular provision. In the real world, this is seldom the case. Two principles that are often applied in assessing the fairness and uniformity of a particular tax provision are the notions of horizontal equity and vertical equity.

The principle of **horizontal equity** states that equal incomes should pay equal taxes. While this is a worthy goal, the tax laws do not always adhere to this principle. For example, A, B, and C each have $100,000 of taxable income but they will pay vastly different taxes because A's income is from a salary, B's income is from a long-term capital gain, and C's income is from City of Dayton municipal bonds.

The principle of **vertical equity** states that higher incomes should pay higher taxes. This principle is the backbone of the progressive rate structure of the federal income tax laws; as income increases, the proportion of that income paid in taxes should also increase. But this principle is also not always followed in our tax laws; for example, during 2012, a taxpayer with $200,000 salary was in the 33-percent tax bracket. But if this taxpayer also incurred a $100,000 long-term capital gain, he or she paid only a 15-percent rate on such gain, even though income was increasing.

.07 EASE AND CONSISTENCY OF ADMINISTRATION

Congress's attempt to provide for an efficient and effective tax administration also influences the definition of taxable income. This occurs most often on the expense side, where financial accounting permits a more liberal use of estimates. For example, an estimate of total warranty expenses to be incurred in future years is usually accrued in the year of sale for financial accounting purposes, since this permits a better matching of income and expense. However, Congress realizes that permitting such estimates for income tax purposes would create an administrative nightmare for IRS auditors who would be forced to judge the reliability of such estimates. Therefore, for tax purposes, warranty expenses generally are not deductible until actually incurred when they can be objectively measured.

.09 SPECIFIC SOCIAL, ECONOMIC, AND SOCIAL GOALS

Finally, one cannot ignore that the federal tax law is often used as an instrument of economic and social policy. Tax provisions that reflect these goals often have no counterpart in financial accounting. For example, the concept of percentage depletion has no financial accounting counterpart, because such a recovery method is not based on cost. Nonetheless, Congress believed that such a recovery method makes economic sense in that it helps the country to remain energy independent.

Also, life insurance proceeds on a company officer that are received by a corporation are generally not taxable, although such proceeds would be included in financial accounting income. Although the proceeds represent an accession to wealth, Congress felt that social considerations dictate that such proceeds should be exempt from taxation.

¶5007 Income Recognition and Accounting Methods

Often, the tax year in which an item of income is reportable (or an item of expense is deductible) depends on the taxpayer's "method of accounting." The statutory requirements for accounting methods are contained in Code Sec. 446. Some of the details regarding these methods are discussed later in the session on accounting methods and records (Chapter 8). The following discussion provides an overview of the two common overall methods of accounting permitted by Code Sec. 446: the cash method and the accrual method.

.01   THE CASH METHOD

Under the **cash method**, income is generally reported when it is received and expenses when they are paid; however, there are a number of modifications and exceptions to these general rules. For example, a cash-basis taxpayer who receives income in the form of property or services must report the value of the property or services as income in the year received under the cash equivalent doctrine, discussed later in this section. Other exceptions and overriding principles are also discussed next and in Chapter 6.

A particularly troublesome area in applying the cash-basis rules to income is when a taxpayer receives a promissory note. For example, is the fact that a note is negotiable or that it has an ascertainable fair market value enough to require recognition under the cash basis? In the leading case involving such notes, the Court of Appeals for the 5th Circuit stated that such facts are not necessarily determinative for tax purposes. According to the Court, recognition should be required only if:

> "a promise to pay of a solvent obligor is unconditional and unassignable, not subject to set-offs, and is of a kind that is frequently transferred to lenders or investors at a discount not substantially greater than the generally prevailing premium for the use of money, such promise is the equivalent of cash and taxable in like manner as cash would have been taxable had it been received by the taxpayer rather than the obligation."[2]

.03   THE ACCRUAL METHOD

Under the **accrual method**, income is generally reported when it is earned (even though not received), and expenses are reported when they are incurred (even though not yet paid). This tax reporting method is very close to the accrual method used for financial accounting reporting purposes, although some differences do exist. Under the accrual method, it is the right to receive income, and not the receipt of the income itself, that determines when the income is reported.

With accrual accounting, Reg. §1.451-1(a) states that income is generally recognized in the year that (1) all the events have occurred that fix the taxpayer's right to receive the income and (2) the amount can be determined with reasonable accuracy. Although this two-pronged test is generally used to determine the point of income recognition for accrual-basis taxpayers, it is not always determinative. As discussed later, special rules may cause the receipt of certain deposits and prepayments by accrual-basis taxpayers to be taxable under cash-basis principles.

.05   HYBRID METHODS OF ACCOUNTING

Code Sec. 446(c)(4) specifically permits a taxpayer to use a **hybrid method** of accounting, where two or more permissible methods are combined into one method. For example, Myron Company in the previous two examples could use the accrual method for reporting gross income from inventory sales (as required by the Regulations) and then use the cash basis for reporting other expenses not related to the inventories. This permits companies like Myron to keep relatively simple accounting records (perhaps a checking account) and then make the simple gross profit conversions at the end of the tax year.

¶5009   Concepts Overriding Accounting Method Elections

The basic requirements for the cash and accrual methods are subject to several modifications for certain principles developed by Congress, the IRS, and courts over the years. In most cases, these principles override any cash-basis or accrual-basis designation. These

---

[2] See Cowden, CA-5, 61-1 USTC ¶9382, 289 F2d 20.

principles include the cash equivalent doctrine, the constructive receipt doctrine, the claim of right doctrine, and the inventories requirement. Each is discussed in the following sections.

.01   CASH EQUIVALENT DOCTRINE

As mentioned earlier, income can take many forms. For example, income may be received in the form of cash, property, or services. In order to prevent cash-basis taxpayers from arranging to receive non-cash property or services in return for services rendered, the **cash equivalent** concept has been developed over the years. Thus, a cash-basis taxpayer who receives property or services as payment must report the fair market value of such property or services as income. This doctrine is equally applicable to an exchange of services between two taxpayers.

OBSERVATION   In recent years, a number of "barter clubs" have emerged to facilitate barter exchanges of property or services between two parties who must both realize gross income. The club generally facilitates the exchange by providing a directory of members who offer various services or products. Frequently, the barter club will provide credit units to members who provide goods or services to other members. These credit units can then be used to buy goods or services from other members of the club or may be sold to other members of the club. Generally, the club charges a cash commission on all barter purchases. Because of tax avoidance potential of such clubs, the IRS has initiated a special "Barter Exchange Project" for auditing the returns of both the exchanges and their members. In addition, various reporting and withholding requirements have been established as a means of identifying such clubs. The IRS and the courts have also taken an aggressive stance as to how and when income should be reported by the club and its members. For example, the IRS contends that a member who receives credit units in return for services or goods provided must report the fair market value of the goods or services provided at the time the credit units are received.[3]

Also consider the phenomenal rise of eBay, which was founded in 1995. eBay has built an online person-to-person trading community on the Internet where buyers and sellers are brought together in a manner where sellers are permitted to list items for sale and buyers can bid on items of interest in a fully automated way. Browsing and bidding on items is free of charge, with eBay collecting listing fees and a fee equal to a percentage of the final sales price. Query: Since eBay simply brings together the seller and the buyer who finish the transaction independently of eBay, is there a requirement for eBay to report the transaction to the IRS? If there is no third party reporting, how many "sellers" of items on eBay are reporting the profits from these transactions on their tax returns?

.03   CONSTRUCTIVE RECEIPT DOCTRINE

The **constructive receipt** doctrine is another vehicle for preventing cash-basis taxpayers from avoiding recognition of income by delaying receipt. In general, income must be reported immediately when it can be reduced to the taxpayer's possession; a taxpayer may not delay recognition by avoiding receipt of the income. This doctrine is described more fully in Reg. §1.451-2(b) as follows:

"Income, although not actually reduced to a taxpayer's possession, is constructively received by him in the taxable year during which it is credited to his account, set apart for him, or otherwise made available so that he may draw

---

[3]   See Rev. Rul. 80-52, 1980-1 CB 100.

upon it at any time, or so that he could have drawn upon it during the taxable year if notice of intention to withdraw had been given. However, income is not constructively received if the taxpayer's control of its receipt is subject to substantial limitations or restrictions."

Under this doctrine, a taxpayer is taxed on interest income as it is earned, even though the taxpayer chooses not to withdraw the interest during the year. On the other hand, a damage deposit received by a lessor is generally not taxed at receipt, since there is a legal obligation to repay the deposit if no damage exists at the end of the rental period.

.05   CLAIM OF RIGHT DOCTRINE

The **claim-of-right** doctrine is a judicially-based concept that holds that an amount is includible in income at the latest when it is received, provided that the taxpayer has an unrestricted right to the funds. This is so even if the amounts are received in error or the right to such income is contested and subsequent events require repayment. This doctrine reflects the basic principle that each tax year stands on its own. For example, this provision has been used to tax an embezzler on embezzlement proceeds in the year they are embezzled, even though the taxpayer eventually had to repay the funds when caught by the authorities.[4]

This doctrine is generally traced to the U.S. Supreme Court decision in *North American Oil Consolidated v. Burnet,*[5] where the taxpayer and the U.S. government were in litigation over income generated by certain oil fields. The government sued for possession of the land in 1916 and was successful in having a court-appointed receiver take over the land and hold all income. In 1917, a district court ruled in favor of the taxpayer and had the receiver turn over all income to the taxpayer. The government appealed, but the lower court decision was affirmed by the circuit court in 1920 and a subsequent appeal to the U.S. Supreme Court was denied in 1922. The question in the *North American Oil Consolidated* case was when should the taxpayer report the income: 1916, 1917, 1920, or 1922? The court ruled that the income was reportable in 1917, the first year that the taxpayer had a claim of right over the income and had in fact received the income.

This completes a review of the basic concepts involved in the determination of "income" under the Internal Revenue Code. The following cases are focused on interpretations of those basic concepts, and in some cases the decision extends those concepts. You should read each case thoroughly before continuing your reading in this Chapter. An abstract summarizing the basic facts of each case is provided in the discussion.

¶5011   Landmark Income Cases— The Realization Concept

.01   TAXABILITY OF A STOCK DIVIDEND

Eisner (Commissioner) v. Macomber[6]

Facts of the Case: On January 1, 1916, the Standard Oil Company of California, a corporation of that State, out of an authorized capital stock of $100,000,000, had shares of stock outstanding, par value $100 each, amounting in round figures to $50,000,000. In addition, it had surplus and undivided profits invested in plant, property, and business and required for the purposes of the corporation, amounting to about $45,000,000, of which about $20,000,000

---

4   *See James*, SCt, 61-1 USTC ¶9449, 366 US 213, 81 SCt 1052.
5   *North American Oil Consolidated*, SCt, 3 USTC ¶943, 286 US 417.
6   *Macomber*, SCt, 1 USTC ¶32,252 US 189, 40 SCt 189.

had been earned prior to March 1, 1913, the balance thereafter. In January 1916 in order to readjust the capitalization, the board of directors decided to issue additional shares sufficient to constitute a stock dividend of 50 percent of the outstanding stock, and to transfer from surplus account to capital stock account an amount equivalent to such issue. Appropriate resolutions were adopted, an amount equivalent to the par value of the proposed new stock was transferred accordingly, and the new stock duly issued against it and divided among the stockholders.

Defendant in error, being the owner of 2,200 shares of the old stock, received certificates for 1,100 additional shares, of which 18.07 percent, or 198.77 shares, par value $19,877, were treated as representing surplus earned between March 1, 1913, and January 1, 1916. She was called upon to pay, and did pay under protest, a tax imposed under the Revenue Act of 1916, based upon a supposed income of $19,877 because of the new shares; and an appeal to the Commissioner of Internal Revenue having been disallowed, she brought action against the Collector to recover the tax. In her complaint she alleged the above facts, and contended that in imposing such a tax the Revenue Act of 1916 violated Art. I, sec. 2, cl. 3, and Art. I, see. 9, cl. 4, of the Constitution of the United States, requiring direct taxes to be apportioned according to population, and that the stock dividend was not income within the meaning of the Sixteenth Amendment.

Note: Affirmed a District Court decision

In essence, this case asks a simple question: should a true proportionate stock dividend be taxed as gross income? In other words, did the shareholder realize income because of the distribution of additional stock? The IRS contended that the taxpayer did recognize income, because the transaction was no different than if the taxpayer had been paid a cash dividend and then turned around and bought more stock. And, of course, the Service noted that the *Revenue Act of 1916* specifically stated that a stock dividend should be taxable as income. On the other hand, the taxpayer contended that stock ownership is ownership in a "common fund of assets," and that interest did not change as a result of the stock dividend.

The U.S. Supreme Court sided with the taxpayer, noting that the asset and the income are "inseparable" in this case. In this respect, the Court quoted the famous "fruit and tree" analogy of capital and income, with the capital "being likened to the tree or the land" and the income "to the fruit or the crop." The court stated that the dividend was nothing more than a "book adjustment", and that it was impossible to sever the income from the property. This concept of *severability* would become central to a number of cases decided after this one.

The Court also noted the lack of a wherewithal to pay on behalf of the taxpayer. This was stated as follows:

> "Yet, without selling, the shareholder, unless possessed of other resources, has not the wherewithal to pay an income tax upon the dividend stock. Nothing could more clearly show that to tax a stock dividend is to tax a capital increase, and not income, than this demonstration that in the nature of things it requires conversion of capital in order to pay the tax."

In dissenting to this decision, Justice Holmes noted that the two methods of paying dividends (cash or additional stock) are just a matter of management choice, and that if the dividend had been paid in bonds or preferred stock it would have been taxable. He further noted that realization is not required for income recognition in other parts of the tax law; for example, partners in a partnership are taxed on their shares of income even though such income may not be distributed. Additionally, income from foreign corporations must be reported when earned, even though not distributed. In short, Justice Holmes stated that it should be a "clear case" to invalidate an act of Congress.

OBSERVATION

The decision in this case was eagerly awaited for by the financial community, and the first reporter out the Court door got it wrong; he thought that the court had ruled the dividend to be taxable. As a result, the stock market went down for a while until the correct decision was noted. Question: Did the reporter really get it wrong, or had he shorted a few stocks earlier in the day?

In struggling with the definition of income (and consulting dictionaries!), the Supreme Court referred to two earlier decisions of the Court that defined income as "gain derived from capital, from labor, or from both combined, provided that it be understood to include profit gained through a sale or conversion of capital assets."[7] This was the first time that the Court was specifically on record as supporting the argument that income includes gain from the sale of assets, as well as income earned on such assets. This paved the way for Congress to start taxing such transactions as part of the 1921 Act.

Some commentators agreed with Justice Holmes in contending that the Court went too far in overturning a statute that many perceived as fair and equitable. Henry Simons, in his landmark treatise *Personal Income Taxation (1938)* stated this argument in the following manner:

"Actually, an utterly trivial issue was made the occasion for injecting into our fundamental law a mass of rhetorical confusion which no orderly mind can contemplate respectfully, and for giving constitutional status to naïve and ridiculous notions about the nature of income and the rationale for income taxes."[8]

The concept of severability arose twenty years later in the *Helvering v. Bruun* case, discussed next. This time, the Court addressed the issue in an entirely different context.

.03   TAXABILITY OF LEASEHOLD IMPROVEMENTS TO THE LESSOR

Helvering (Commissioner) v. Bruun[9]

Facts of the Case: On July 1, 1915, the respondent, as owner, leased a lot of land and the building thereon for a term of ninety-nine years. The lease provided that the lessee might, at any time, upon giving bond to secure rentals accruing in the two ensuing years, remove or [tear down and build] on the land, provided that no building should be removed or torn down after the lease became forfeited, or during the last three and one-half years of the term. The lessee was to surrender the land, upon termination of the lease, with all buildings and improvements thereon.

In 1929 the tenant demolished and removed the existing building and constructed a new one which had a useful life of not more than fifty years. July 1, 1933, the lease was cancelled for default in payment of rent and taxes and the respondent regained possession of the land and building. The parties stipulated "that as at said date, July 1, 1933, the building which had been erected upon said premises by the lessee had a fair market value of $64,245.68 and that the unamortized cost of the old building, which was removed from the premises in 1929 to make way for the new building, was $12,811.43, thus leaving a net fair market value as at July 1, 1933, of $51,434.25, for the aforesaid new building erected upon the premises by the lessee." On the basis of these facts, the petitioner determined that in 1933 the respondent realized a net gain of $51,434.25.

Note: Reversing the 8th Circuit Court of Appeals, which had affirmed a BTA opinion

---

[7]   *Macomber,* SCt, 1 USTC ¶32.

[8]   Henry Simons, Personal Income Taxation, The Definition of Income as a Problem of Fiscal Policy (Chicago: University of Chicago Press, 1938).

[9]   *Bruun,* SCt, 40-1 USTC ¶9337, 309 US 461, 60 SCt 631.

¶5011.03

The issue in this case was a fairly simple one: does a lessor recognize income from the receipt of a leasehold improvement made by the lessee during the lease, if such improvement reverts to the lessor at the end of the lease? The IRS contended that there was a clear enhancement in value of the asset, and such enhancement should be reported as income. Not surprisingly, the taxpayer used the *Macomber* decision to argue that the improvement was *inseverable* from the property, and that gain should be recognized only when the underlying property was sold (i.e., when the lessor had a wherewithal to pay).

Interestingly, in 1917 the IRS had issued a ruling stating that income should be reported in such a situation at the termination of a lease, but the 9th Circuit subsequently said that income should be recognized when the improvement was completed. (This decision did not bother the IRS at all, and they amended the Regulations to follow this decision, further stating that the lessor could depreciate the improvement.) But in 1935 the 2nd Circuit ruled that such improvements were nontaxable, and the conflicting decisions led the Supreme Court to agree to hear the case.

Perhaps stung by previous criticism of their *Macomber* decision, the Court reconsidered the idea of severability and noted that the *Macomber* argument was not relevant to this case. Specifically, the Court noted that the idea of severability was used as a descriptor in *Macomber* only to show that "*in the case of a stock dividend, the stockholder's interest in the corporate assets after receipt of the dividend was the same as and inseverable from that which he owned before the dividend was declared.*" In ruling for the taxpayer, the Court noted that every gain need not be realized in cash to be taxable; otherwise, cash would be avoided and a barter system might develop to circumvent the tax laws. There was a clear increase in the taxpayer's wealth, and this increase did not have to be severed to measure such increase for tax purposes.

OBSERVATION

In the case facts, the Court mentions that the lease was terminated due to the lessee's default on rent and taxes. The Court did not address this issue, but it could be argued that some of the value of the improvement should be applied to that default, which meant that the income would be reported as a substitute for rental income in any case. Obviously, the amount involved was nowhere near the value of the improvement, and since the Court ruled that the improvement was taxable anyway, the issue was moot.

In response to this decision, some lessors began to either extend the lease period and/or reduce rental payments in hopes of enticing lessees to renew their leases. This would delay the recognition of income on the improvement. Because of these potential problems and concerns about wherewithal-to-pay issues, Congress enacted Code Sec. 109 in 1954, which excludes the value of such improvements from income. However, the basis in the improvements is $0, so that in effect the gain is merely postponed until the property is eventually sold by the lessor. And of course, any improvements made in lieu of paying rent would be taxed as rent, and this would in turn establish a depreciable basis in the improvement for the lessor.

The wherewithal-to-pay logic of this decision has been tested in several later cases. One such case, *Thomas C. Davis*,[10] is discussed in Chapter 7.

---

[10] *Davis*, SCt, 62-2 USTC ¶9509, 370 US 65, 82 SCt 1190.

.05   GIFTS VS. COMPENSATION

Old Colony Trust Company v. Commissioner[11]

Facts of the Case: William M. Wood was president of the American Woolen Company during the years 1918, 1919 and 1920. In 1918 he received as salary and commissions from the company $978,725, which he included in his federal income tax return for 1918. In 1919 he received as salary and commissions from the company $548,132.27, which he included in his return for 1919. On August 3, 1916, the American Woolen Company had adopted the following resolution, which was in effect in 1919 and 1920:

"Voted: That this company pay any and all income taxes, State and Federal, that may hereafter become due and payable upon the salaries of all the officers of the company, including the president, William M. Wood; the comptroller, Parry C. Wiggin; the auditor, George R. Lawton; and the following members of the staff, to wit: Frank H. Carpenter, Edwin L. Heath, Samuel R. Haines, and William M. Lasbury, to the end that said persons and officers shall receive their salaries or other compensation in full without deduction on account of income taxes, State or Federal, which taxes are to be paid out of the treasury of this corporation."

This resolution was amended on March 25, 1918, as follows:

"Voted: That, referring to the vote passed by this board on August 3, 1916, in reference to income taxes, State and Federal, payable upon the salaries or compensation of the officers and certain employees of this company, the method of computing said taxes shall be as follows, viz: 'The difference between what the total amount of his tax would be, including his income from all sources, and the amount of his tax when computed upon his income excluding such compensation or salaries paid by this company.'"

Pursuant to these resolutions, the American Woolen Company paid to the collector of internal revenue M. Wood's federal income and surtaxes due to salary and commissions paid him by the company, as follows:

Taxes for 1918 paid in 1919 .... $681,169.88
Taxes for 1919 paid in 1920 ....   351,179.27

The decision of the Board of Tax Appeals here sought to be reviewed was that the income taxes of $681,169.88 and $351,179.27 paid by the American Woolen Company for Mr. Wood were additional income to him for the years 1919 and 1920.

Note: Affirming the 1st Circuit Court of Appeals, which had upheld a BTA decision

---

The question in this case was a fairly simple one: should a company officer be taxed on the payment made by his employer to pay the federal and state income tax due on his salary. In other words, the corporation paid not only the salary but the federal and state income tax due (computed on a marginal tax basis) on that salary as well. The IRS argument was straight-forward: the payment represented additional

---

[11] *Old Colony Trust Company*, SCt, 1 USTC ¶408, 279 US 716, 49 SCt 499.

compensation to the employee, even though it was not directly received by the employee. The taxpayer tried several defenses, including (1) the payment was a gift, (2) it was not received by the taxpayer anyway, and (3) to tax the amount would be to pay an illegal tax on another tax.

The Supreme Court ruled that the payment was taxable compensation received in consideration of services performed. (The Court also pointed out the absurdity of the "tax on tax" argument.) Although this decision may seem to be an easy one in hindsight, this case is cited in hundreds of cases that followed because of three basic principles established by the Court in this case (as illustrated by the excerpts below):

1. The form of payment makes no difference *("The form of the payment is expressly declared to make no difference.")*
2. Discharge of an obligation by a third party is the same as receipt *("The discharge by a third person of an obligation to him is equivalent to receipt by the person taxed.")*
3. A voluntary payment does not make the payment a gift *("The payment for services, even though entirely voluntary, was nevertheless compensation within the statute.")*

The principles established in this case have been applied to a variety of cases. For example, if a former spouse pays both the alimony and the income tax due on the alimony, both amounts are taxable to the recipient. And lessors must include as income the lessee's payment of such items as taxes and mortgages.

.07 THE REALIZATION CONCEPT—ADDITIONAL CASES

A. Tucker v. Commissioner.[12] In this case, a teacher in New York state engaged in an illegal strike, and under the Taylor Act, was penalized one day's pay for each day on strike. This strike penalty was withheld from the paycheck of the teacher. The Tax Court ruled that the amount withheld as a penalty was income, because it extinguished an obligation owed to the state; furthermore, since the payment was classified as a penalty, it was not deductible. In *Rev. Rul. 76-130*, the IRS also applied this principle to the garnishment of wages.[13]

Commissioner v. R. J. Kowalski.[14] In this case, amounts advanced to a New Jersey state trooper as a meal allowance were held to be taxable. The taxpayer contended that the payments met the Code Sec. 119 conditions for exclusion, in that they were (1) for the convenience of the employer and (2) furnished on the business premises ("the road"). The Court ruled that such amounts were taxable because the taxpayer had complete dominion over the funds (he was not required to spend the amounts at all), Code Sec. 119 does not cover cash allowances, and the payments represented a clear accession to wealth over which the taxpayer had total control.

Bingler (District Director) v. Johnson.[15] In this case, engineers with an atomic power laboratory received "scholarship" payments from a two-phase Westinghouse doctoral program offer. They performed regular job duties while completing the coursework (with eight hours a week release time), and they received a leave of absence to work on their dissertation. During this time, they receive 70–90 percent of their regular pay (based on prior salary), kept their fringe benefits, and agreed to stay with Westinghouse for two years after completion. Westinghouse deducted the payments as "indirect labor." The Supreme Court ruled that the arrangement was "bargained compensation", and the exclusion provisions for scholarships were never intended to exclude payments that were for the benefit of the grantor.

---

[12] *Tucker,* 69 TC 675 (1978).
[13] Rev. Rul. 76-130, 1976-1 CB 15.
[14] *Kowalski,* SCt, 77-2 USTC ¶9748, 434 US 77, 98 SCt 315.
[15] *Johnson,* SCt, 69-1 USTC ¶9348, 394 US 741, 89 SCt 1439.

¶5013 Landmark Income Cases—Windfall Gains

.01 TAXABILITY OF DAMAGES

Commissioner v. Glenshaw Glass Company[16]

Facts of the Case: The Glenshaw Glass Company, a Pennsylvania corporation, manufactures glass bottles and containers. It was engaged in protracted litigation with the Hartford-Empire Company, which manufactures machinery of a character used by Glenshaw. Among the claims advanced by Glenshaw were demands for exemplary damages for fraud and treble damages for injury to its business by reason of Hartford's violation of the federal antitrust laws. In December, 1947, the parties concluded a settlement of all pending litigation, by which Hartford paid Glenshaw approximately $800,000. Through a method of allocation which was approved by the Tax Court, 18 T. C. 860, 870-872 [CCH Dec. 19,146], and which is no longer in issue, it was ultimately determined that, of the total settlement, $324,529.94 represented payment of punitive damages for fraud and antitrust violations. Glenshaw did not report this portion of the settlement as income for the tax year involved. The Commissioner determined a deficiency claiming as taxable the entire sum less only deductible legal fees. As previously noted, the Tax Court and the Court of Appeals upheld the taxpayer.

Commissioner v. William Goldman Theatres, Inc. William Goldman Theatres, Inc., a Delaware corporation operating motion picture houses in Pennsylvania, sued Loew's, Inc., alleging a violation of the federal antitrust laws and seeking treble damages. After a holding that a violation had occurred, *William Goldman Theatres, Inc. v. Loew's, Inc.,* 150 Fed. (2d) 738, the case was remanded to the trial court for a determination of damages. It was found that Goldman had suffered a loss of profits equal to $125,000 and was entitled to treble damages in the sum of $375,000. *William Goldman Theatres, Inc. v. Loew's, Inc.,* 69 Fed. Supp. 103, aff'd, 164 Fed. (2d) 1021, cert. denied, 334 U. S. 811. Goldman reported only $125,000 of the recovery as gross income and claimed that the $250,000 balance constituted punitive damages and as such was not taxable. The Tax Court agreed, 19 T. C. 637 [CCH Dec. 19,401], and the Court of Appeals, hearing this with the *Glenshaw* case, affirmed. 211 Fed. (2d) 928 [54-1 USTC ¶9328].

It is conceded by the respondents that there is no constitutional barrier to the imposition of a tax on punitive damages. Our question is one of statutory construction: are these payments comprehended by §22(a)?

Note: Reversing the 3rd Circuit Court of Appeals

This case involves a question regarding the taxability of punitive damages paid under a lawsuit involving violations of the federal antitrust laws. The IRS simply argued that such damages are taxable because they are a clear accession to wealth and are not excludable, and that Congress intended for Code Sec. 61 to exert the full taxing power of the Constitution. The taxpayer in the case essentially used the *legislative reenactment* defense, noting that the U.S. Tax Court had recently ruled that such damages were nontaxable and that Congress's failure to mention such damages when they revisited Code Sec. 22 (now Code Sec. 61) after this ruling meant that they were "content" with this decision. In other words,

---

[16] *Glenshaw Glass Company*, SCt, 55-1 USTC ¶9308, 348 US 426, 75 SCt 473.

by not acting to counteract the Tax Court decision, Congress was in effect "legislatively reenacting" current law that does not specifically state that such payments are taxable.

The Court agreed with the IRS, noting that Code Sec. 22 (now Code Sec. 61) was designed to "exert the full measure of the taxing power" of the government. In referencing several cases, the Court stated that a liberal construction of the statute was necessary, and that everything is taxed unless exempted by Congress. The Court also noted that there is no question that the original damages are taxable (the original violation, or one-third of the total; the punitive damages were the other two thirds). Finally, the Court noted that *Macomber* is not applicable to this case since there was no accession to wealth in that case.

The Court also specifically addressed the legislative reenactment issue. The Court noted that such a defense is "an unreliable indicium at best." They also noted that the IRS had nonacquiescenced to the Tax Court decision and had consistently held since then that such damages were taxable.

OBSERVATION In essence, this decision is based on the Code Sec. 61 principle that all income is taxable unless specifically exempted by the courts. But what about other damage awards? Interestingly, prior case law had conflicting decisions on gender, sex, and race discrimination awards; the first two were taxable, and the latter was not. The different verdicts were due to the fact that in each case, the Courts examined the underlying wording of the antidiscrimination statute involved, and the Civil Rights Act was the only one that mentioned "tort" remedies. Because of these inconsistent decisions, Congress decided to tax *all* damages as part of the 1996 Act; the only exceptions are those based on personal physical injury or sickness, and for punitive damages, only those based on a civil action related to wrongful death.

.03   GIFT VS. COMPENSATION

Commissioner v. M. Duberstein[17]

Facts of the Case: No. 376, *Commissioner v. Duberstein.* The taxpayer, Duberstein, was president of the Duberstein Iron & Metal Company, a corporation with headquarters in Dayton, Ohio. For some years the taxpayer's company had done business with Mohawk Metal Corporation, whose headquarters were in New York City. The president of Mohawk was one Berman. The taxpayer and Berman had generally used the telephone to transact their companies' business with each other, which consisted of buying and selling metals. The taxpayer testified, without elaboration, that he knew Berman "personally" and had known him for about seven years. From time to time in their telephone conversations, Berman would ask Duberstein whether the latter knew of potential customers for some of Mohawk's products in which Duberstein's company itself was not interested. Duberstein provided the names of potential customers for these items.

One day in 1951 Berman telephoned Duberstein and said that the information Duberstein had given him had proved so helpful that he wanted to give the latter a present. Duberstein stated that Berman owed him nothing. Berman said that he had a Cadillac as a gift for Duberstein, and that the latter should send to New York for it; Berman insisted that Duberstein accept the car, and the latter finally did so, protesting however that he had not intended to be compensated for the information. At the time Duberstein already had a Cadillac and an Oldsmobile, and felt that he did not need another car. Duberstein testified that he did not think Berman would have sent him the Cadillac if he had not furnished him with information

---

[17] *Duberstein,* SCt, 60-2 USTC ¶9515, 363 US 278, 80 SCt 1190.

about the customers. It appeared that Mohawk later deducted the value of the Cadillac as a business expense on its corporate income tax return. Duberstein did not include the value of the Cadillac in gross income for 1951, deeming it a gift.

No. 546, *Stanton v. United States.* The taxpayer Stanton had been for approximately 10 years in the employ of Trinity Church in New York City. He was comptroller of the Church corporation, and president of a corporation, Trinity Operating Company, the church set up as a fully owned subsidiary to manage its real estate holdings, which were more extensive than simply the church property. His salary by the end of his employment there in 1942 amounted to $22,500 a year. Effective November 30, 1942, he resigned from both positions to go into business for himself. The Operating Company's directors, who seem to have included the rector and vestrymen of the church, passed the following resolution upon his resignation: "Be it Resolved that in appreciation of the services rendered by Mr. Stanton … a gratuity is hereby awarded to him of Twenty Thousand Dollars, payable to him in equal installments of Two Thousand Dollars at the end of each and every month commencing with the month of December, 1942; provided that, with the discontinuance of his services, the Corporation of Trinity Church is released from all rights and claims to pension and retirement benefits not already accrued up to November 30, 1942."

The Operating Company's action was later explained by one of its directors as based on the fact that, "Mr. Stanton was liked by all of the Vestry personally. He had a pleasing personality. He had come in when Trinity's affairs were in a difficult situation. He did a splendid piece of work, we felt. Besides that… he was liked by all of the members of the Vestry personally." And by another: "[W]e were all unanimous in wishing to make Mr. Stanton a gift. Mr. Stanton had loyally and faithfully served Trinity in a very difficult time. We though[t] of him in the highest regard. We understood that he was going in business for himself. We felt that he was entitled to that evidence of good will." On the other hand, there was a suggestion of some ill-feeling between Stanton and the directors, arising out of the recent termination of the services of one Watkins, the Operating Company's treasurer, whose departure was evidently attended by some acrimony. At a special board meeting on October 28, 1942, Stanton had intervened on Watkins' side and asked reconsideration of the matter. The minutes reflect that "resentment was expressed as to the 'presumptuous' suggestion that the action of the Board, taken after long deliberation, should be changed."

Note: Reversing the 6th Circuit Court of Appeals in Duberstein, and vacating and remanding the decision of the 2nd Circuit Court of Appeals in Stanton

This case actually involves the consolidation of two cases that involve the same tax issue: what is an excludable "gift" for federal tax purposes? In *Duberstein*, a supplier (Mohawk Metal) gave the taxpayer a Cadillac in appreciation for referrals to potential customers in the industry. In *Stanton*, a controller of a church operating company resigned after the firing of the Treasurer, and the operating company's Board of Directors passed a resolution granting Stanton $20,000 "in appreciation of the services rendered by Mr. Stanton."

In both situations, the IRS contended that a gift should be viewed as a transfer for personal reasons, that the gift definition for gift tax purposes is not controlling, and that the lack of an obligation does not make a transfer a gift; in short, the "maxims of experience" indicate that the transfers were at heart business related (the cost of the Cadillac was deducted) and should be viewed as compensation. The taxpayers in both situations responded that there was a lack of an obligation, the transfers represented a "detached generosity", and that the transferor in both cases intended the transfers to be nontaxable gifts. The Supreme Court granted certiori because of a conflict among the circuits and at the urging of the government to provide clarification to such determinations.

The Court struggled with this decision, and tried to look for guidance by examining the definition of a gift used in prior decisions, such as *LoBue* (" a detached and disinterested generosity")[18] and *Robertson* ("out of affection, respect, admiration, charity, or like impulses").[19] In the end, the Court agreed with the Government's argument of applying the "maxims of experience", and that in the end it is a question of fact in each case. In *Duberstein*, the Court concluded that the transfer was "at bottom compensation," either for past or future services. However, in *Stanton*, the Court vacated the decision and remanded the case to the lower courts to reveal the facts, stating that the sparse facts used in the original case were insufficient for a decision.

In reaching its decision, the Court noted that their conclusion "may not satisfy an academic desire for tidiness, symmetry and precision in the area," but if Congress fears more fact-based litigation, then Congress could provide more explicitness in the law by delineating the factors that are controlling in gift situations. In a strongly worded dissent, Justice Frankfurter noted that greater explicitness was possible in arriving at a decision, and that the Court was "yielding responsibility to juries."

On remand, the District Court in retrying the *Stanton* case determined that the transfer was a gift, and this decision was upheld on appeal. The *Duberstein* case has sometimes been referred to derisively as a "Gentlemen, you can't do that" decision, in that many commentators believed the Court had a chance to clarify the treatment of such transfers but chose not to do so. Both cases bring up a broader issue: can a corporation ever make a "gift" to an employee? Certainly not, if they deduct it like Mohawk did (recall that gift deductions are limited to $25 per donee per year). The Code now provides exclusions for a variety of fringe benefits offered to employees that at one time may have been considered "gifts"; examples include courtesy discounts, *de minimis* Christmas gifts, free access to company athletic facilities, and free flights for airline employees. But unanswered questions remain: for example, if an employer offered $1,000 to any employee who quit smoking, would that be a gift or compensation?

OBSERVATION   What about voluntary employer payments to the surviving family members of deceased employees—would this be a nontaxable gift? At one time the Code granted a $5,000 exclusion for such payments just to reduce the volume of such cases in the courts system. However, as part of the broadening of the tax base to finance the 1986 tax cuts, Congress repealed this provision. So we are back to the gift issue once again, and if the employer did not deduct the payment, the family members are free to once again try to convince the IRS that the transfer was a "detached generosity."

.05   WINDFALL GAINS—ADDITIONAL CASES

J.W. Banks II.[20] Two successful litigants, one who based an action on employment discrimination, and the other who alleged wrongful discharge, were required to include in gross income the total amount of their respective settlement funds, including the amounts paid to their attorneys pursuant to contingent-fee agreements. The Supreme Court applied the anticipatory assignment of income doctrine, which precludes an individual from excluding an economic gain from income by assigning the gain in advance to another person. The Supreme Court looked to who maintained control over the income-generating asset and reasoned that in a litigation matter the income-generating asset is the cause of action based on the plaintiff's legal injury and control rests with the plaintiff.

[18] *LoBue,* SCt, 56-2 USTC ¶9607, 351 US 243.
[19] *Robertson*, SCt, 52-1 USTC ¶0343, 343 US 711.
[20] *Banks II*, SCt, 2005-1 USTC ¶50,155, 543 US 426, 125 SCt 826.

U.S. v. Kirby Lumber Company.[21] In this case, the taxpayer repurchased some of its own bonds at less than par and did not report any gain on the transaction. The Service argued that the Regulations indicate that such a repurchase would generate taxable gain, and that the taxpayer had realized a clear accession to income (previously encumbered assets were now set free). The Court agreed with the IRS, noting that the Code Sec. 61 definition of income includes income from all sources not otherwise excluded. The Court also relied on a net worth test, noting that the net worth of the company had gone up (liabilities decreased more than the decrease in assets).

Eugene C. James v. U.S.[22] In this case, the taxpayer was a union official who embezzled in excess of $738,000 over a three-year period. Earlier court decisions on such thefts were mixed, with one court ruling that extortion proceeds were taxable (*Rudkin*)[23] and another court ruling that embezzlement proceeds were not taxable (*Wilcox*).[24] The latter decision was based on the theory that the taxpayer had no claim of right over the money and had an obligation to repay the money. The Supreme Court concluded that the taxpayer had actual command over the money and should be taxed on the amount when embezzled.

OBSERVATION   Even though the Court in *James* taxed the amounts when embezzled, the Union would not be entitled to a deduction until the theft was actually discovered, which was years later.

¶5015   Landmark Income Cases— Accounting Methods

.01   PREPAID ASSOCIATION DUES

American Automobile Association v. U.S.[25]

Facts of the Case: The Association is a national automobile club organized as a nonstock membership corporation with its principal office in Washington, D.C. It provides a variety of services to the members of affiliated local automobile clubs and those of ten clubs which [the] taxpayer itself directly operates as divisions, but such services are rendered solely upon a member's demand. Its income is derived primarily from dues paid one year in advance by members of the clubs. Memberships may commence or be renewed in any month of the year. For many years, the association has employed an accrual method of accounting and the calendar year as its taxable year. It is admitted that for its purposes the method used is in accord with generally accepted commercial accounting principles. The membership dues, as received, were deposited in the Association's bank accounts without restriction as to their use for any of its corporate purposes.

However, for the Association's own accounting purposes the dues were treated in its books as income received ratably over the 12-month membership period. The portions thereof ratably attributable to membership months occurring beyond the year of receipt, *i.e.,* in a second calendar year, were reflected in the Association's books at the close of the first year as unearned or deferred

---

[21]   *Kirby Lumber Company*, SCt, 2 USTC ¶814, 284 US 1, 52 SCt 4.
[22]   *James*, SCt, 61-1 USTC ¶9449, 366 US 213, 81 SCt 1052.
[23]   *Rudkin*, SCt, 52-1 USTC ¶9260, 343 US 130.
[24]   *Wilcox*, SCt, 46-1 USTC ¶9188, 327 US 404.
[25]   *American Automobile Association*, SCt, 61-2 USTC ¶9517, 367 US 687.

income. Certain operating expenses were chargeable as prepaid membership cost and deducted ratably over the same periods of time as those over which dues were recognized as income.

Note: Affirming the Court of Claims

This case is the middle case in what is often referred to as the "trilogy" of cases involving prepayments of income: the *Automobile Club of Michigan* case, the *American Automobile Association (AAA)* case, and the *Schlude* case. All are interesting cases because the taxpayer in all three cases follow generally accepted accounting principles (GAAP) in reporting the prepayments of income only as they were "earned." In fact, the AICPA joined in some of these cases by supporting the taxpayers involved.

As a general rule, the tax treatment of advance payments is governed by the wherewithal-to-pay and claim-of-right concepts. When the taxpayer receives the advance payment under an unrestricted claim of right, this is the point in time when the taxpayer is best able to pay the tax and the IRS is best able to collect the tax. As a result, most advance payments of income are taxed immediately upon receipt. Over the years, Congress and the IRS have carved out a number of special exceptions to the treatment of selected advance payments for goods and services, but absent such a special provision, the general rule applies of taxing such advances immediately.

In the *AAA* case, the taxpayer reported prepaid membership receipts on an accrual basis, over the life of the membership. The dues were normally paid one year in advance, and the AAA prorated based on the statistical correlation to when the services were provided by the AAA (i.e., when the costs were incurred, which in turn was based on when the members demanded the services). The taxpayer contended that this followed GAAP and was a logical way to follow the "matching principle," whereby the income is matched to the expenses generating such income. The IRS also argued that there were no restrictions on the use of such funds, and that the Supreme Court had ruled that such prepayments received by the Automobile Club of Michigan were taxed immediately.

In a 5-4 decision, the Supreme Court sided with the IRS, noting that the taxpayer at all times had access to the funds, and that recognition of income cannot depend on averages. The Court implied that the taxpayer did not know when the services would be demanded, and therefore a statistical estimate was only that—a guess. The Court also noted that Congress had extended a deferral provision to publishers for their prepaid subscriptions,[26] and had not chosen to do so for such membership organizations as the AAA. As to the argument that the taxpayer was following GAAP, the Court responded in the following manner:

> *"This is only to say that in performing the function of business accounting the method employed by the Association 'is in accord with generally accepted commercial accounting principles and practices.' It is not to hold that for income tax purposes it so clearly reflects income as to be binding on the Treasury."*

Some of the arguments used by the IRS and the Court are somewhat dubious. First, in arguing that the *Automobile Club of Michigan* was controlling in this case, the IRS ignored the obvious facts that the statistical methods used by the AAA were much better; apparently, the records of the Michigan club were a big mess. Secondly, the IRS argued that in 1954 Congress had repealed two provisions of the Code (Secs. 452 and 462) that permitted proper accruals of income and expenses. But the fact is Congress repealed these before they went into effect, because the projected revenue loss would have been too great. Congress had in fact enacted the provisions to *minimize book and tax differences*, and it was a bit of sleight of hand to argue that now Congress repealed them because they were "wrong."

---

[26] Code Sec. 455.

OBSERVATION	When the AAA lost this case, they did like many taxpayers—don't get mad, get even! The AAA immediately began lobbying Congress to provide them the same deferral provision that was available to publishers, and Congress eventually relented by enacting Code Sec. 456. As a result, the AAA may now defer prepaid dues over the period of membership.

.03   PREPAYMENTS FOR SERVICES

Schlude v. Commissioner[27]

Facts of the Case: Taxpayers, husband and wife, formed a partnership to operate ballroom dancing studios (collectively referred to as "studio") pursuant to Arthur Murray, Inc., franchise agreements. Dancing lessons were offered under either of two basic contracts. The cash plan contract required the student to pay the entire down payment in cash at the time the contract was executed with the balance due in installments thereafter. The deferred payment contract required only a portion of the down payment to be paid in cash. The remainder of the down payment was due in stated installments and the balance of the contract price was to be paid as designated in a negotiable note signed at the time the contract was executed.

Both types of contracts provided that (1) the student should pay tuition for lessons in a certain amount, (2) the student should not be relieved of his obligation to pay the tuition, (3) no refunds would be made and (4) the contract was noncancelable. The contracts prescribed a specific number of lesson hours ranging from five to 1,200 hours and some contracts provided lifetime courses entitling the student additionally to two hours of lessons per month plus two parties a year for life. Although the contracts designated the period during which the lessons had to be taken, there was no schedule of specific dates, which were arranged from time to time as lessons were given. Cash payments received directly from students and amounts received when the negotiable notes were discounted at the bank or fully paid were deposited in the studio's general bank account without segregation from its other funds. The franchise agreements required the studio to pay to Arthur Murray, Inc., on a weekly basis, 10% of these cash receipts as royalty and 5% of the receipts in escrow, the latter to continue until a $20,000 indemnity fund was accumulated. Similarly, sales commissions for lessons sold were paid at the time the sales receipts were deposited in the studio's general bank account.

The studio, since its inception in 1946, has kept its books and reported income for tax purposes on an accrual system of accounting. In addition to the books, individual student record cards were maintained showing the number of hours taught. The terms of the contract in substance operated as follows: when a contract was entered into, a "deferred income" account was credited for the total contract price. At the close of each fiscal period, the student record cards were analyzed and the total number of taught hours was multiplied by the designated rate per hour of each contract. The resulting sum was deducted from the deferred income account and reported as earned income on the financial statements and the income tax return. In addition, if there had been no activity in a contract for over a year, or if a course were reduced in amount, an entry would be made canceling the untaught portion of the contract, removing that amount from the deferred income account, and recognizing gain to the extent that the deferred income exceeded the balance due on the contract, *i.e.,* the amounts received in advance. The amounts representing lessons taught and the gains from cancellations constituted the

---

[27] *Schlude*, SCt, 63-1 USTC ¶9284, 372 US 128, 83 SCt 601.

chief sources of the partnership's gross income. The balance of the deferred income account would be carried forward into the next fiscal year to be increased or decreased in accordance with the number of new contracts, lessons taught and cancellations recognized. Deductions were also reported on the accrual basis except that the royalty payments and the sales commissions were deducted when paid irrespective of the period in which the related receipts were taken into income. Three certified public accountants testified that in their opinion the accounting system employed truly reflected net income in accordance with commercial accrual accounting standards.

Note: Affirming and reversing in part the 8th Circuit Court of Appeals

The *Schlude* case also involved a prepayment of income, in this case the prepayment for dance lessons at an Arthur Murray dance studio franchise that the taxpayers owned. The taxpayers used the accrual method of accounting, and sold lessons for a specific number of hours within either a fixed period of time or within a lifetime. The lessons were either sold under a *cash plan* (a cash down payment plus installment notes) or a *deferred payment plan* (a down payment, some installment notes, and a balance due in a negotiable note). Most of the negotiable notes were discounted at the bank. At the end of the year, the taxpayers examined the individual "dance cards" related to the prepayments to determine how much income had been earned from each customer during the year. Once again, the taxpayer argued that their accounting method followed GAAP, and the AICPA agreed and filed an amicus brief on the taxpayer's behalf. The IRS initially contended that the taxpayer should include in income all advances and the face amount of any notes and contracts.

The case has an interesting history. The taxpayer won in the Tax Court, but the IRS won the appeal in the 8th Circuit Court of Appeals. The case reached the Supreme Court shortly after the *AAA* decision. Because of that decision, the Supreme Court remanded the decision back to the 8th Circuit Court, which now found for the IRS, and the Supreme Court granted certiorari this time to see if the Service was exceeding the scope of the *AAA* decision. This time around, the IRS retreated somewhat by not taxing immediately any future payments for which services had not been performed and such payments were not represented by a negotiable note.

In a 5-4 decision, the Supreme Court decided for the Service, noting that the decision was squarely controlled by the *AAA* decision. The taxpayer had argued that unlike the *AAA* case where statistical methods were used to estimate income recognition, their "punched cards" provided an accurate calculation of exactly how much services revenue was earned each year. But once again the Court noted the fundamental weakness of the AAA's defense, which also existed for *Schulde*; they did not know *when* their services would be demanded. The only real taxpayer defense left at this point was the repealed Code Sec. 452 that would have allowed such deferrals. And in response, the Court noted that Congress had enacted specific exceptions for publishers (Code Sec. 455) and membership organizations (Code Sec. 456), and that this indicated that Congress had chosen to deal with this problem by enacting "precise provisions of narrow applicability." The Court's explanation in the decision then offers an often-quoted phrase: "Consequently, as in the *American Automobile Association* case, we invoke the long-established policy of the Court in deferring, where possible, to Congressional procedures in the tax field."

In voicing his dissent, Justice Stewart noted that the repeal of Code Sec. 452 was a red herring, in that the repeal was solely for revenue concerns, and that the legislative intent of the original enactment of the provisions had been completely ignored. In a stinging indictment of the decision, Justice Stewart concluded by noting the following:

"It seems to me that this decision, the third of a trilogy of cases purportedly decided on their own peculiar facts, in truth completes the mutilation of a basic element of the accrual method of reporting income—a method which has been explicitly approved by Congress for almost half of a century."

OBSERVATION	Note that the common thread running through the trilogy is the fact that the taxpayer could not determine *when* a customer would demand the service, so that any attempt to match income and expenses would be a fruitless exercise. Thus, a seasonal business such as King's Dominion, if their tax year ends in the middle of their busy season when open, would have to report prepaid season passes as income when received because they do not know when the customer will demand their services.

OBSERVATION	In 1971, the IRS issued *Rev. Proc. 71-21*,[28] which allowed accrual-basis service providers to defer prepayments over the period of time that the services will be performed, provided that the services would be completely performed by the end of the following tax year. If the services could not be performed by the end of the following tax year, they were taxed immediately. The Service modified this procedure in 2004 by issuing *Rev. Proc. 2004-34*,[29] which allows qualifying taxpayers to defer advance payments to the next succeeding taxable year to the extent they are *also deferred for financial reporting purposes*. However, in no event will this revenue procedure allow deferral to a taxable year later than the next succeeding taxable year. This would permit deferral even if the advance payments are not included in gross receipts for financial reporting purposes by, or the income is not earned through performance by, the end of the next succeeding taxable year. However, in no event will this revenue procedure allow deferral to a taxable year later than the next succeeding taxable year.

.05 ACCEPTABLE ACCOUNTING METHODS

Ansley-Sheppard Burgess Co. v. Commissioner[30]

Facts of the Case: At the time the petition was filed in the instant case, petitioner maintained its principal office in Savannah, Georgia. Petitioner was incorporated in the State of Georgia on January 3, 1980. Petitioner's stock is equally owned by three individuals: Tim F. Ansley, J.E. Sheppard, and W.D. Burgess. Petitioner is a subchapter C corporation engaged in the construction business. In addition to performing construction projects using its own personnel, petitioner is frequently responsible for hiring and monitoring subcontractors for various construction projects. The majority of the construction projects petitioner has performed were completed within 6 to 9 months, with its longest project lasting 1-1/2 years.

Petitioner is a calendar year taxpayer and has always maintained its books and records, and reported its income for Federal tax purposes, on the cash receipts and disbursements method of accounting (the cash method). Petitioner does not maintain an inventory. Petitioner's bonding company and banks, however, require petitioner to maintain financial statements using the percentage of completion method of accounting. Petitioner uses the services of a certified public accountant to prepare financial statements reporting its income on the percentage of completion method. Petitioner then submits the financial statements to its bonding company and banks.

During May of 1993, respondent mailed petitioner a notice of deficiency in which respondent determined, inter alia, that petitioner's use of the cash method did

---

[28] Rev. Proc. 71-21, 1971-2 CB 549.
[29] Rev. Proc. 2004-34, IRB 2004-22, 991.
[30] *Ansley-Sheppard Burgess Co.*, 104 TC 367 (1995).

not clearly reflect its income. In the notice of deficiency, respondent determined that the percentage of completion method clearly reflected petitioner's income and required petitioner to use such method to compute its taxable income. The notice of deficiency designates petitioner's taxable year 1990 as the first year of the accounting change. Respondent's use of the percentage of completion method results in a decrease of $9,503 to petitioner's taxable income for its taxable year 1990, before any section 481 adjustment. A section 481 cumulative adjustment, however, increases petitioner's taxable income in the amount of $55,053 for its taxable years 1980 through 1989. The parties stipulated that if petitioner had computed its taxable income using the percentage of completion method since its incorporation, petitioner would have included an additional $6,117 in net income per year. The parties also stipulated that for all relevant years in issue, petitioner qualifies as a corporation with not more than $5 million in gross receipts for purposes of section 448(b)(3). The average annual gross receipts for petitioner's taxable years 1987, 1988, and 1989 was $2,394,510.60.

Note: original case in Tax Court

In this case, a taxpayer in the construction business used the cash method of accounting, which the IRS challenged. The taxpayer used the cash method for book and tax purposes, but used the percentage of completion method for financial statements furnished to the bonding company. The taxpayer maintained that it was allowed to use the cash method because it qualified for (1) the small business exception from the completed-contract method requirement for contractors of Code Sec. 460 (less than $10 million gross receipts), (2) the exception to the accrual basis method requirements for C corporations under Code Sec. 448 (less than $5 million gross receipts), and (3) the exception to the accrual basis for inventories because the company did not maintain inventories.

The IRS argued that the taxpayer should use the percentage of completion method for tax purposes because it "more clearly reflects income," a condition of Sec. 442(b) over which the IRS was given broad discretion to make such determinations by Congress. Specifically, the IRS argued that the taxpayer's method of accounting did not produce an *identity of results* with the Service's proposed method. The IRS was basing its argument on its victory in *American Fletcher Corp.*,[31] where the Court of Appeals sustained the IRS position that the taxpayer's method of accounting (the cash method) did not produce a *"substantial identity of results"* with the method selected by the Commissioner (the accrual method). The taxpayer in the case used various estimates in applying the cash basis, and the Court believed that an accurate determination was not possible with this method.

In this case the Tax Court had problems with the Service's identity of results method, especially when the taxpayer did not appear to maintain inventories. The Court noted that the "clearly reflect" standard should be decided on a case-by-case basis, and that the IRS victories since the *American Fletcher* decision had been cases involving the inventory requirement of Reg. §1.446-1(c)(2)(i). This regulation requires the accrual method of accounting for gross profit computations when inventories are a "component of income." Referring to an earlier decision in *Molson*,[32] the Tax Court reiterated that the IRS cannot force a taxpayer to change from one method of accounting that "clearly reflects" income to another method that "clearly reflects" income. And since the parties had stipulated that the taxpayer did not maintain inventories, the taxpayer met the Code Sec. 460 and Code Sec. 448 exceptions, and had consistently used the cash method, the Court ruled for the taxpayer.

This decision was a major victory for taxpayers in that it dampened the Service's enthusiasm for using the "identity of results" method as a litmus test for determining if a taxpayer's method of accounting clearly reflected income. In effect, this decision limited

---

[31] *American Fletcher Corporation*, CA-7, 87-2 USTC ¶9603, 832 F2d 436.
[32] *Molson*, 85 TC 485 (1985).

the application of this test to cases that involved inventories. The court specifically noted that the IRS is abusing its discretion when requiring a taxpayer to switch to *another* acceptable method of accounting that the Service likes better.

OBSERVATION	The Service continues to use the identity of results test when inventory questions arise. However, a string of taxpayer victories convinced the Service that a few small business exceptions to the inventory requirement would be in the best interests of tax administration. As a result, the Service issued two administrative exceptions to the inventories requirement. These are *Rev. Proc. 2001-1*,[33] (an exception for any taxpayers with $1 million or less of average gross receipts) and *Rev. Proc. 2002-28* [34] (an exception permitting the use of the cash basis for certain non-service taxpayers with $10 million or less of average gross receipts).

.07   ACCOUNTING METHODS—ADDITIONAL CASES

U.S. v. Lewis.[35] In this case, a taxpayer received a bonus of $22,000 in error in 1944, and had to return $11,000 of the total to his employer in 1946. The Supreme Court ruled that the taxpayer could not simply file an amended return and recalculate the 1944 tax, since the taxpayer had an unrestricted claim of right over the funds at the end of 1944 and each tax year stands on its own. The Court noted that the taxpayer would be entitled to take a deduction on his 1946 return when the funds were returned. (*Note*: current Code Sec. 1341 may provide some tax relief in this regard by allowing a credit in 1946 for the marginal tax paid erroneously in 1944; this would avoid inequities if the taxpayer was in a higher tax bracket in 1944.)

Commissioner v. Indianapolis Power and Light.[36] In this case, the utility required new customers to make cash deposits prior to receiving service, and such deposits were eventually returned or credited to future bills once the taxpayer had proven his or her credit worthiness. The tax question to be answered was whether the deposits were in effect security deposits or advance payments for services. After examining the facts of the case, the Court ruled for the taxpayer, noting that (1) the intent was to treat the amounts as deposits, (2) such amounts were in segregated accounts that paid interest, and (3) there was a strong possibility that the money would be returned to the customers.

Artnell v. Commissioner.[37] This case involved the season ticket sales for the Chicago White Sox baseball team. The team's tax year was a fiscal year ending during the season, and the taxpayer deferred that portion of the season ticket sales that related to the following year. Citing the "trilogy" of cases on prepayments mentioned earlier, the IRS argued that the payments should be taxed immediately. However, the Court accepted the taxpayer's method of accounting for the prepayments, because unlike the "trilogy" of prepayment cases, the taxpayer knew exactly *when* the services would be performed, per the fixed baseball season schedule.

¶5017   Assignment of Income Issues

The *assignment of income* is an expression often used to describe an attempt by a taxpayer to have income earned by the taxpayer paid to another taxpayer so that it will be taxed to the latter. Generally, income from services must be reported by the taxpayer who performed the services, and such income cannot be assigned to another taxpayer. On the other hand, income from property is generally taxed to the owner of the property.

---

[33] Rev. Proc 2001-1, IRS Announcement 2002-45, 2002-1 CB 833.
[34] Rev. Proc. 2002-28, 2002-18 IRB 815.
[35] *Lewis*, SCt, 51-1 USTC ¶9211, 340 US 590, 71 SCt 522.
[36] *Indianapolis Power and Light*, 493 US 203 (1990).
[37] *Artnell Company*, CA-7, 68-2 USTC ¶9593, 400 F2d 981.

Example 5-3. Martha White, a CPA, establishes an accounting partnership with her 13-year old son Seth, and splits the profits 50/50. This partnership will not be recognized for tax purposes because Martha is the only partner performing the services, and all of the services income will be taxed to her.

Example 5-4. Martha White transfers $500,000 of cash and property to a trust in 15-year old daughter Mary's name. Assuming that the transfer is irrevocable, the income from the trust will be taxed to her daughter Mary.

Example 5-5. Assume the same facts as the previous example, except that $5,000 of the income from the trust each year is used to provide for Mary's education. This $5,000 will be taxed to Martha, since she has a legal obligation to provide for the support of her minor child. In effect, Martha is being relieved of her own financial obligation.

OBSERVATION

In the above example, if Mary was younger than 19 years of age, or younger than 25 and a full-time student, a portion of the income from the trust would be taxed at her mother's marginal income tax rate under the allocable parental tax rules. In 1986, Congress took three actions to limit the abilities of parents to shift income-producing assets to their children by (1) limiting the standard deduction for a dependent, (2) eliminating a personal exemption deduction for someone being claimed as a dependent by someone else, and (3) instituting the allocable parental tax. Tax planning issues related to the allocable parental tax are discussed in Chapter 11.

In determining who must report an amount of income, it is important to determine who has earned the income. In this respect, the classic quote regarding the assignment of income doctrine was by Justice Holmes of the U.S. Supreme Court in the case of *Lucas v. Earl*, where Justice Holmes noted that such an attempt is an arrangement by which *"the fruits are attributed to a different tree from that on which they grew"*. In other words, once an amount of income "ripens" for a taxpayer, it cannot be assigned to a different tree. Two cases illustrate the application of these principles.

.01   LUCAS (COMMISSIONER) V. EARLE[38]

In this case, an attorney set up a law partnership with his wife under a valid California contract of joint tenancy and split the earnings 50/50. At the time there was no option to file a married-filing jointly tax return, so this saved taxes on the two individual tax returns. The Court noted that the taxpayer was "...then only party to the contracts by which the salary and fees were earned," and ruled that the "fruit" cannot be assigned to a different "tree."

OBSERVATION

What if Ms. Earle had worked during the years that Mr. Earle was in law school and had paid his education costs. Would Mr. Earle have grounds for assigning some of the income to her as repayment for her working years? In one case, the court allowed Randy Hundley, a catcher with the Chicago Cubs, to assign a portion of his signing bonus earnings (a whooping $11,000!) to his dad who had coached him for many hours and taught him the finer points of the game. The two had entered into a contingency contract whereby Mr. Hundley senior would receive 50 percent of any signing bonus as compensation for teaching services and representing his son.[39]

[38] *Guy C. Earl*, SCt, 2 USTC ¶496, 281 US 111, 50 SCt 241.
[39] *See Cecil R. Hundley, Jr.*, 48 TC 339 (1967).

.03   *HELVERING (COMMISSIONER) V. HORST*[40]

This case also involved an assignment of income, this time between father and son. The taxpayer made a gift of detachable coupon bonds to his son shortly before the due dates of the coupons. Interest was paid to the owner of the bonds. The Court ruled that the taxpayer should be taxed on the interest income, and not his son, since he enjoyed the "fruition of the economic gain." The court noted that the taxpayer received the same satisfaction as if he had spent the money himself, and noted in a famous quote that *"the power to dispose of income is equivalent to ownership."* Naturally, the Court referred to the "fruit and tree" analogy as well.

OBSERVATION   The key to determining who is taxed on the income is to determine who retains ownership of the underlying property. For bonds, interest accrues on a daily basis, while dividends become income only once declared.

¶5019   Summary

- The objectives of taxation are to raise revenue, stimulate the economy, encourage growth and achieve social and political goals.
- The considerations used in measuring taxable income include the wherewithal to pay concept, and the ease and consistency in administering the tax laws.
- Accounting methods include the cash, accrual, and hybrid methods.
- Certain concepts overriding the basic accounting method concepts include the constructive receipt and claim of right doctrines.
- Landmark cases further refine what is meant by the realization concept, windfall gains, accounting methods and assignment of income.

---

[40]   Horst, SCt, 40-2 USTC ¶9787, 311 US 112, 61 SCt 144.

Review Questions for Chapter 5

True or False
Indicate which of the following statements are true or false by circling the correct answer.

1. The list of 15 items of income in Code Sec. 61 is not all-inclusive; other items that are not listed may also be treated as gross income. T F

2. Mudslides in Mary Allen's neighborhood have led to an estimated $30,000 decrease in the value of her undamaged home. This $30,000 may be reported as a loss on Mary's income tax return. T F

3. The objectivity principle states that gains and losses should be recognized as soon as increases or decreases in value can reasonably be estimated through valid market quotes. T F

4. Vertical equity requires that taxpayers with equal incomes should pay equal taxes. T F

5. Under the cash method, income is always recognized only when actual cash is received. T F

6. The logic of the "severability" argument in *Eisner v. Macomber* was also accepted by the Supreme Court as controlling in the *Helvering v. Brunn* decision. T F

7. A strike penalty withheld from an employee's paycheck is not taxable, since the payment will be deductible. T F

8. Lawsuit damages received that compensate for lost income are taxable, but any treble damages associated with the amount are not taxable. T F

9. As a general rule, the tax law is bound by generally accepted accounting principles (GAAP) unless a compelling reason exists for an exception. T F

10. The IRS can force a taxpayer to change from one acceptable accounting method to another acceptable accounting method. T F

Fill in the Blanks
Fill in each blank with the appropriate word or phrase that completes each sentence.

11. An item of income that is statutorily exempted from taxation is referred to as a(n) _____.

12. The _____ principle states that an amount of income should be taxed when the taxpayer is best able to pay the tax and the government is best able to collect the tax.

13. _____ equity states that larger incomes should pay relatively larger taxes.

14. Using the accrual basis for sales of merchandise and the cash basis for other items of income and expense is an example of a(n) _____ accounting method.

15. Prepaid rents are taxable but damage deposits are not; this is an example of the _____ principle.

16. In the "fruit and tree" analogy cited by the Supreme Court in discussing stock dividends in *Eisner v. Ma-Comber*, the fruit represents _____ and the tree represents _____.

17. The _____ principle states that income should be reported by the taxpayer who earns it, and not someone else who eventually receives the income.

18. The tax law may be used to regulate demand and thus reduce inflationary pressures by simply _____ taxes.

19. The installment sales provisions, that permit a taxpayer to recognize income only as payments are received, is a beneficial example of the _____ principle.

20. Taxing long-term capital gains at a preferential tax rate violates the _____ equity principle.

Multiple Choice

Circle the best answer for each of the following questions.

21. Which of the following is not generally considered to be an objective of Congress in defining income:
    a.   encourage growth
    b.   stimulate demand
    c.   raise revenue
    d.   all of the above are stated objectives

22. The tax treatment of warranty expenses is best explained by the:
    a.   wherewithal to pay principle
    b.   objectivity principle
    c.   political principle
    d.   ease and consistency of administration principle

23. A negotiable note will be treated as the equivalent of cash if:
    a.   the promise to pay is of a solvent obligor
    b.   the promise is unconditional and unassignable
    c.   the discount for transfers in not substantially greater than prevailing rates
    d.   all of the above

24. Under the accrual method, income is recognized in the year that:
    a.   all events have occurred to fix the taxpayer's right to receive the income
    b.   the amount can be estimated with reasonable accuracy
    c.   economic performance has occurred
    d.   (a) and (b) only

25. Tim Allen, a plumber, joins a barter club for services. Tim signs an agreement to provide 50 hours of plumbing services on demand of any other member, and at that time Tim received 50 hourly "tickets" that can be redeemed at any time for services provided by other members. For federal tax purposes:
    a.   Tim will never recognize income from the barter tickets
    b.   Tim will recognize income as soon as he receives the tickets
    c.   Tim will recognize income only as he performs services for other members
    d.   Tim will recognize income only as he uses the tickets received

26. Sue Aka received a $5,000 bonus in error in 2012, and had to repay the amount in 2013. For tax purposes, Sue must:
    a.   refile her 2012 return, omitting the $5,000
    b.   include the $5,000 in 2012, and deduct that amount in 2013
    c.   include the amount in 2012, and take a credit in 2013 for the additional tax paid in 2012
    d.   either (b) or (c)

27. The principal contribution of the *Old Colony Trust Co.* case in regards to gift vs. compensation issues is the principle that:
    a.   discharge of an obligation by a third part is the same as receipt
    b.   a voluntary payment does not make the payment a gift
    c.   the form of a payment makes no difference
    d.   all of the above

28. In the *American Automobile Association* case, the Supreme Court described the relationship between the Internal Revenue Code (tax law) and generally accepted accounting principles (GAA)) as follows:
    a. GAAP rules trump tax rules and must be followed in tax issues
    b. the tax law is not constrained by GAAP, as each has different purposes
    c. the earlier enacted rule (tax or GAAP) is controlling
    d. none of the above

29. Currently, an accrual-basis services provider may defer a prepayment for services for tax purposes if:
    a. the services will be performed by the end of the next tax year
    b. the same reporting method is also used for financial accounting purposes
    c. the payment is only in property, and not cash
    d. (a) and (b)

30. Which of the following taxpayers would most likely be able to defer a portion of prepaid income received during the tax year, assuming that the taxpayer's tax year ends before all services will be performed?
    a. the owner of a summer amusement park
    b. the owner of a professional basketball team
    c. a bank that charges a nonrefundable fee for credit cards of customers
    d. all of the above would qualify for deferral

Review Problems

31. Code Sec. 61, in defining gross income, uses the expression "Except as otherwise provided in this subtitle." Explain how this expression relates to the notion of exclusions.
32. Explain the wherewithal-to-pay concept, and how this concept sometimes overrides the financial accounting treatment of a particular item.
33. Explain the "fruit and tree" analogy as it relates to income and the assignment of income doctrine.
34. "A lessor who obtains an improvement on leased property at the end of the lease may postpone, but not eliminate gain related to that improvement." Do you agree? Explain.
35. Describe the concept of severability and its importance in the *Eisner v. Macomber* and *Helvering v. Brunn* cases.
36. Graham, Inc., owns a residential apartment complex consisting of 20 apartments. During 2012 Graham received the following amounts in connection with the rental:
    * $184,000 cash from rents, of which $13,000 represents late payments of 2011 rents and $15,500 represents prepayments of 2013 rents;
    * $12,500 prepayments of rent for the last month of new leases entered into in 2012;
    * $8,200 of damage deposits on new rental leases (refundable if no damage exists at the end of the lease);
    * $1,600 forfeited deposits on leases expiring in 2012 (Graham expects to spend this amount in the near future on deductible repair expenses.);
    * $830 value of a painting given to Graham by a tenant in lieu of two months rent; and
    * $1,040 value of a greenhouse room addition to an apartment left by a tenant at the end of the lease (as a condition for constructing the greenhouse, Graham agreed to reduce the rent $100 for each of the six months remaining on the lease).

    How much must Graham, Inc., report as gross rental income on its 2012 tax return assuming that Graham uses (a) the cash basis and (b) the accrual basis?
37. Under Ace Corporation's dividend reinvestment plan, a shareholder may elect to receive the quarterly dividend in cash or additional shares of Ace common stock. Will the dividend be taxable if (1) the shareholder elects the cash, or (2) if the shareholder elects the stock? Explain.
38. Explain the significant contributions of the *Old Colony Trust* decision that taxed a company officer on the payment of his income tax liability by the corporation.
39. Mason Corporation sues Republic Company for patent infringement, and is awarded $6,000,000 of damages and an additional $12,000,000 of punitive damages. How much, if any, of these payments is taxable to Mason? Should Republic Company be able to deduct any of these amounts? Explain.

40. In the *Duberstein* case, the accounting records of Mohawk Corporation played a role in the decision to tax Duberstein on the value of the new Cadillac received from Mohawk. Explain why the accounting records were important in this regard.

41. What was the fatal flaw in the arguments of the taxpayers for deferring advance payments based on statistical evidence in the advance payment triology of cases (*Auto Club of Michigan, American Automobile Association,* and *Shlude*)?

42. "The IRS can force a taxpayer to change from one acceptable method of accounting to another acceptable method of accounting if the taxpayer's method does not produce an 'identity of results' with the IRS method." Do you agree? Explain.

Research Questions

43. Due to increased air traffic, the U.S. government awarded two new airport slots (airplane takeoff and landing rights) to Denver during the current year. Because such rights are very valuable, the government awarded the slots by lottery to give all carriers an equal chance of winning. CheapAir, Inc., won the slots, and was immediately offered $50,000 by a competing airline for the slots. Does CheapAir recognize gross income for federal tax purposes as a result of winning this lottery? Explain.

44. In 2012, Teague Co., a regular C corporation, deducted a $45,000 payment as a business expense deduction. In 2013, after Teague Co. had converted to an S corporation, the company recovered $20,000 of the deduction. Will the shareholders of Teague Co. (the owners of the S corporation) be required to report any taxable income due to the operation of the tax benefit rule (i.e., income to the extent that the former C corporation benefited from the initial deduction)? Explain.

45. Sara Waters, a shareholder in Wicket Corporation, leased a building to Wicket at an annual rental of $60,000. A fair and reasonable annual rent for the building has been determined to be only $48,000. Will the additional $12,000 of rent be taxed as rental income or as dividend income? Explain.

46. Mary Sue, owner of The Gadget Store, began selling a wide range of her kitchen gadgets on eBay. Since these on-line transactions are conducted on the internet between her and the bidder, she has decided not to include these sales in her gross income. Is Mary Sue correct? Explain. You should comment on the possible ways the IRS could reconstruct her income from her eBay transactions. (You may want to refer to the IRS Cash Intensive Businesses Audit Techniques Guide at: http://www.irs.gov/Businesses/Small-Businesses-&-Self-Employed/Cash-Intensive-Businesses-Audit-Techniques-Guide—Chapter-4)

Planning Questions

47. The Qwik-Pass CPA Review Co., charges $10,000 for its review classes, and offers a "money-back" guarantee, if the student does not pass on the first try. The company collected $500,000 from students in its first class, which was held from July through October of 2012. Since the grades of the students on the November exam will not be known until January 2013, the owner of Qwik-Pass intends to not recognize any income until the number of students who actually passed is known, so that he can report income and refunds in the same year. What is your advice to the client?

48. Nanson Co., a calendar-year taxpayer, received a check for $180,000 in payment for services rendered as a commissioned sales agent near the end of 2012. In 2013, the customer discovered that the commission was incorrectly computed on the sale, and Nanson refunded $30,000 of the $180,000 to the customer. Nanson was in the 35-percent tax bracket in 2012, but is in the 25-percent marginal tax bracket in 2013. Since Nanson was taxed on the full $180,000 in 2012 under the claim of right doctrine, he may deduct the $30,000 in 2013, but this will not "make him whole." Are there any tax elections that Nanson may make to deal with this problem? Explain.

Compliance Question

49. Discuss the special filing requirements for electing to defer services income under Rev. Proc. 2004-34.

CHAPTER 6

Landmark Judicial Decisions—Deductions

Learning Objectives

1. Describe the four positive and the four negative criteria for a deduction.
2. Differentiate the deductibility of expenses under (1) the cash method and (2) the accrual method.
3. Describe the "economic performance" rules for deducting prepayments.
4. Summarize the major conclusions of the courts in deciding the following cases involving testing the deduction criteria: *Gilmore* (divorce costs), *Welch v. Helvering* (voluntary repayments), and *Tank Truck Rentals* (illegal payments).
5. Summarize the major conclusions of the courts in determining the following cases differentiating business vs. personal expenses: *Flowers* (travel costs) and *Whipple* (bad debts).
6. Summarize the major conclusions of the courts in determining the following cases involving methods of accounting: *Boylston Markets* (prepaid expenses), *Dixie Pine Products* (accrual of contested liabilities), *Indopco* (merger fees), and *General Dynamics* (self-insurance costs).

¶6001 Introduction

The income tax is computed by multiplying taxable income by one or more tax rates. Taxable income is computed by subtracting **deductions** from gross income. In Chapter 5, it was mentioned that *everything* received is considered to be income unless specifically excluded under the Code. And yet we will find in this chapter that *nothing* is deductible unless authorized by the Code or the Regulations.

In contrast, financial accounting net income is generally defined as the difference between properly matched revenues and expenses for some time period, typically one year. Are all "properly matched expenses" also "deductions" for tax purposes? The answer is no. While most financial accounting expenses are deductible for tax purposes, some are not. For example, federal income tax is an expense for financial accounting purposes, but it is not deductible for tax purposes. Other differences in financial accounting expenses and tax deductions are due to timing, notably depreciation.

The purpose of this chapter is to provide a review of the basic tax principles applicable to deductions, and to examine the landmark court cases that have tested the bounds of these deduction principles. Generally, a deduction must meet eight specific criteria under the Code (four positive and four negative), and also comply with three fundamental Code requirements. Each of these conditions is discussed in the following sections of this chapter.

¶6003   The Four Positive Criteria of a Deduction

To be deductible, expenses must either be specifically authorized by a Code section or satisfy eight general criteria. Four of these criteria are stated in a positive fashion, in that each condition must be present for an item to be deductible. The four positive criteria are:

1. Incurred in a permissible activity
2. Ordinary
3. Necessary
4. Reasonable in amount

.01   INCURRED IN A PERMISSIBLE ACTIVITY

To deduct any item, the taxpayer must be able to point to some provision of the Internal Revenue Code that authorizes the deduction.[1] It is not necessary that the statute list the specific item by name, but the item must clearly fall under one of the provisions of the law. In this regard, a mere reading of the Code may not reveal whether or not an item is deductible, since new Treasury Regulations, Revenue Rulings, and court decisions continuously update interpretations of the statutes. Knowledge of these interpretations constitutes the real stock in trade of the tax practitioner.

In general, expenses and losses are deductible only if they fit within the framework of three Code provisions. An item is deductible only under the general umbrella of Code Sec. 162 (trade or business expenses), Code Sec. 212 (income-producing activity expenses), or under specific-item provisions of the Code related to personal expenditures. In addition, **losses** are deductible under the same three rationales, i.e., trade or business, income-producing, or specific-item personal losses; however the authority for deducting such losses is Code Sec. 165, as explained below.

Code Secs. 162 and 212 provide a broad grant of authority for deductions related to either a trade or business (Code Sec. 162) or the production of income (Code Sec. 212). Since a purely personal expenditure does not fit either of these categories, such an item is deductible only if a specific Code provision authorizes the deduction. Examples include alimony, certain residential interest, state and local taxes, contributions, and medical expenses.

Deductions for an individual are further grouped into two broad categories: **deductions "for adjusted gross income (AGI)"** and **deductions "from adjusted gross income."** Deductions for AGI are listed in Code Sec. 62 and are composed mainly of business-related expenditures, although over the years Congress has added some personal expenditures, such as alimony and payments to individual retirement accounts, to the "for AGI" category. A net capital loss is also a deduction "for AGI," subject to a $3,000 annual limitation.

---

[1]   See *New Colonial Ice Co.*, SCt, 4 USTC ¶1292, 292 US 435, 54 S.Ct. 788.

The authority for deductions may be viewed within the context of the following diagram:

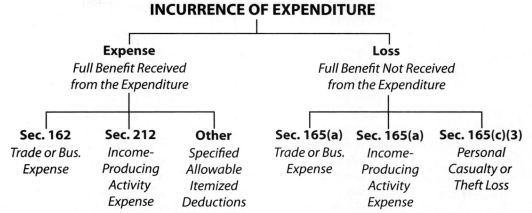

Code Sec. 162 Business Deductions. The broadest provision that pertains to deductions—and, incidentally, the provision that comes closest to approximating the expense concept in accounting—is Code Sec. 162(a), which reads in part as follows:

Abstract—Code Sec. 162(a):

a.   In general, there shall be allowed as a deduction all the ordinary and necessary expenses paid or incurred during the taxable year in carrying on any **trade or business**, including:

1.   a reasonable allowance for salaries or other compensation for personal services actually rendered;

2.   traveling expenses (including amounts expended for meals and lodging other than amounts which are lavish or extravagant under the circumstances) while away from home in the pursuit of a trade or business; and

3.   rentals or other payments required to be made as a condition to the continued use or possession, for purposes of the trade or business, of property to which the taxpayer has not taken or is not taking title or in which he has no equity.

Although the general words of Code Sec. 162 may suggest to the unsuspecting taxpayer (or student) that virtually every "business expense" is deductible, an investigation of the interpretations given these words by tax administrators and courts would not support such a conclusion. While the term trade or business is commonly used in tax law, there is no singular definition. The intention to make a profit is necessary, but the actual recognition of a profit is not necessary.

On the other hand, the intention to make a profit is not a sufficient condition. Many transactions and business ventures are profit-oriented, but they are not deemed to constitute a trade or business for tax purposes. Rather, there must be some ongoing personal effort of an entrepreneurial nature before any income-producing activity can be said to constitute a trade or business. The Supreme Court has adopted an **"all events" test** for determining the existence of a trade or business. Such activities must be pursued "in good faith and with regularity."[2]

What if an activity is (1) an ongoing personal effort of an entrepreneurial nature and (2) pursued in good faith and with regularity, yet the primary motive for the activity is personal enjoyment rather than making a profit? Such an activity is classified as a hobby

---

[2]   *See Groetzinger*, SCt, 87-1 USTC ¶9191, 480 US 23, 107 SCt 980.

for tax purposes, not a trade or business. The "hobby" classification results because the primary motive is not a profit motive. While net income from a hobby is taxed just like net income from a trade or business, net losses from a hobby are not deductible and provide no tax benefit.

For **hobby** activities, the taxpayer is protected by a presumptive rule. If the activity is profitable for at least three out of five years (seven years for racehorse activities), then the activity is presumed to be a business rather than a hobby. As a business, years in which the activity's deductions exceed the activity's gross income generate tax losses that can reduce other income of the taxpayer. If the presumptive rule is met, the burden of proof is on the IRS to demonstrate that the taxpayer's primary intent is personal enjoyment rather than to make a profit. In virtually all other confrontations with the IRS, the burden of proof is on the taxpayer to prove his or her innocence.

Code Sec. 212 Production of Income Deductions. As already explained, many business-oriented activities do not qualify as a trade or business for tax purposes because no ongoing personal effort of an entrepreneurial nature is involved. Until the Revenue Act of 1942, deductions for expenses related to these income-producing activities were frequently denied because they did not qualify as a trade or business. For example, in 1941 the U.S. Supreme Court found that expenses incurred by a wealthy taxpayer to maintain an office for the purpose of managing his securities and real estate were not those of a trade or business and were therefore nondeductible personal expenses.[3]

Following this decision, Congress enacted the first two paragraphs of the present Code Sec. 212. The third paragraph, relating to deduction of expenses incurred in connection with the determination of taxes, was incorporated later by the Revenue Act of 1954. Code Sec. 212 reads as follows:

Abstract – Code Sec. 212:

Expenses for production of income. In the case of an individual, there shall be allowed as a deduction all the ordinary and necessary expenses paid or incurred during the taxable year:
1. for the production or collection of income;
2. for the management, conservation, or maintenance of property held for the production of income; or
3. in connection with the determination, collection, or refund of any tax.

The effect of this section is to make many income-related expenses deductible even though they are not incurred in a trade or business. For example, an expense attributable to the renting of a single property is not deductible under Code Sec. 162 because such limited rental activity normally does not constitute a trade or business. Nevertheless, Code Sec. 212 authorizes such a deduction.

The Regulations help delineate the meaning of "production of income." Reg. §1.212-1(b) states in part:

"The term 'income' for the purpose of Sec. 212 includes not merely income of the taxable year but also income which the taxpayer has realized in a prior taxable year or may realize in subsequent taxable years; and is not confined to recurring income but applies as well to gains from the disposition of property. For example, ordinary and necessary expenses paid or incurred in the management, conservation, or maintenance of a building devoted to rental purposes are deductible, notwithstanding that there is actually no income therefrom in the taxable year, and regardless of the manner in which or the purpose for which the property in question was acquired."

---
[3] *See Higgins,* SCt, 41-1 USTC ¶9233, 312 US 212, 61 SCt 475.

Code Sec. 212 is the primary authority for the deduction of such expenses as safety deposit box rental and investment counsel fees that relate to investments in securities that produce taxable income. Many other expenses associated with property or an activity intended to produce income also become deductible under Code Sec. 212. In determining whether any expense is deductible, the major consideration is whether it is related to an activity entered into with the hope of making a profit or is merely engaged in for pleasure or personal reasons.

Statutory Personal Deductions. Code Sec. 262(a) states "Except as otherwise expressly provided in this chapter, no deduction shall be allowed for personal, living, or family expenses". In light of Code Sec. 262 and other rules, all expenses can be categorized as either (a) directly related to a trade or business, (b) related to a profit-making venture that is not a trade or business, or (c) incurred without any intention of profit. The last category consists of purely personal expenses.

Such expenses are disallowed as deductions unless some section of the law specifically provides for their deductibility. The difficulty in everyday tax practice, of course, comes in fitting actual expenses into the proper category. Purely personal deductions that are specifically allowed by the Code include such items as medical expenses, charitable contributions, mortgage interest, and property taxes.

Losses. The same three-way classification of expenses (trade or business, income-producing, or personal statutory deductions) also applies for losses. However, the authority for deducting such losses is contained in only one Code section: Sec. 165. Generally, Code Sec. 165(a) provides a deduction for any losses incurred; however, Code Sec. 165(c) limits the loss deduction for individuals to those (1) incurred in a trade or business,[4] (2) those incurred in an income-producing activity,[5] or those personal losses resulting from a qualifying casualty or theft.[6]

OBSERVATION	In essence, Code Sec. 165(c)(3) disallows all personal losses unless such losses *"arise from fire, storm, shipwreck, or other casualty, or from theft."* Code Sec. 165(h) also specifies two special floors that apply to such personal casualty or theft losses: a $100 floor per casualty or theft, and a 10 percent of adjusted gross income floor on the total net loss for the year. A loss on the sale or exchange of a purely personal asset, such as a residence or an automobile, is not deductible. On the other hand, a loss on the sale of a stock investment is deductible; even though the stock is a personal asset, it is held for income-producing purposes.

.03 ORDINARY

An expense need not be incurred frequently by the taxpayer in order to be ordinary. The essence of the **ordinary** criterion seems to be that the expense would be acceptable or commonplace among other taxpayers who find themselves in comparable circumstances. In the usual meaning of the term, the "comparable circumstances" may indeed be extraordinary. See the *Welch* decision, discussed below.

.05 NECESSARY

To be **necessary** an expense must be capable of making a contribution to a trade or business. Fortunately for the taxpayer, the courts and tax administrators do not insist that necessity be determined in retrospect; it is sufficient if the expense appeared to be appropriate and helpful at the time it was incurred. The "prudent person" test is applied; if, in the same circumstances, a prudent person would have incurred the expense in the expectation that it would be helpful in the taxpayer's business, it will likely be deemed "necessary."

---

[4] Code Sec. 165(c)(1)
[5] Code Sec. 165(c)(2).
[6] Code Sec. 165(c)(3).

.07   REASONABLE

Finally, even an ordinary and necessary expense incurred in a trade or business or in connection with the production of income must be **reasonable** in amount before it can be deducted for tax purposes. Technically, this requirement is stated in Code Sec. 162(a)(1) only in relation to compensation, but the courts have found that the element of reasonableness is inherent in the phrase "ordinary and necessary."[7]

As a practical matter, the reasonableness criterion is typically at issue in the case of compensation of related taxpayers. For example, a corporation may attempt to pay its sole stockholder-executive (or his or her children) an unreasonably large salary, interest, or rental payment. If allowed, these expenses could be used to disguise payments that in reality are dividends. Dividends are not deductible by the corporation, but salary, interest, and rental payments are deductible. Therefore, the IRS often screens compensation and other transactions between related parties to determine their reasonableness. Reasonable compensation is the amount that would ordinarily be paid for like services by like enterprises under like circumstances. Thus, every case of reasonable compensation must stand on its own facts and circumstances.

OBSERVATION   The portions of Code Secs. 162 and 212, quoted earlier in this module, include the words "*paid or incurred during the taxable year*" in specifying which deductions are allowable. A cash-basis taxpayer ordinarily deducts expenses only when paid, whereas the accrual-basis taxpayer is entitled to take a deduction as soon as there is a fixed and determinable liability incurred by the taxpayer. Reg. §1.461-1(a) further explains how to determine the year in which a deduction is to be taken by a cash-basis taxpayer. Questions are frequently raised about prepayment of expenses. These issues are discussed below.

¶6005   The Four Negative Criteria of a Deduction

In addition to meeting the four positive criteria, a deduction must also satisfy four negative criteria. In other words, none of these four conditions may apply if the expenditure is to be deductible. The four negative criteria are:

1. Capital expenditures
2. Personal expenditures
3. Related to tax-exempt income
4. Contrary to public policy

.01   CAPITAL EXPENDITURES

Code Sec. 263 states that amounts incurred for incidental repairs and maintenance of property are generally currently deductible and are not treated as **capital expenditures**. Those expenditures which merely keep an asset at its present condition are expensed. Generally, the financial accounting rules used for solving the capitalization or expense riddle also apply for tax purposes.

In financial accounting, capital expenditures are not expensed in the period they are paid. Likewise, capital outlays are not deductible for tax purposes in the year they are incurred. For both financial accounting and tax accounting, depreciation, depletion, or amortization deductions are utilized for certain types of capital expenditures.

Code Sec. 263(a) provides the following general rule for capital expenditures:

---

[7]   *See Dunn and McCarthy, Inc.*, CA-2, 43-2 USTC ¶9688, 139 F2d 242.

Abstract – Code Sec. 263(a):

No deduction shall be allowed for:
1. any amount paid out for new buildings or for permanent improvements or betterments made to increase the value of any property or estate. [or]
2. any amount expended in restoring property or in making good the exhaustion thereof for which an allowance is or has been made.

Example 6-1. T Company spent $15,000 to overhaul a drill press and $1,000 to lubricate a punch machine. The $15,000 expenditure would be capitalized, but the $1,000 expenditure would be expensed.

Contrary to the general rule of Code Sec. 263(a) quoted above, other parts of Code Sec. 263 provide exceptions (i.e., immediate deductions) for a limited set of specific expenses such as certain mining expenses, research and experimentation, and certain farming expenses. Another exception is provided by Code Sec. 179, which allows small businesses to immediately expense limited amounts of the cost of depreciable tangible personal property (e.g., computers, equipment, furniture, fixtures, machinery) purchased during the year and used in business. And since the *Indopco* decision (discussed below) and the recent regulations, the issue of capitalization has achieved even more importance.

.03 PERSONAL EXPENDITURES

As mentioned earlier, Code Sec. 262(a) provides a blanket disallowance against the deduction of personal expenditures by stating "Except as otherwise expressly provided in this chapter, no deduction shall be allowed for personal, living, or family expenses". Such expenses are disallowed as deductions unless some section of the law specifically provides for their deductibility. For some expenditures, such as groceries, the application of the rule is obvious; for others, such as legal fees,[8] the application is less clear.

.05 EXPENDITURES IN VIOLATION OF PUBLIC POLICY

Code Sec. 162 specifies several types of expenditures that are nondeductible because they are linked to activities which are against public policy.[9] Nondeductible items include:
- Fines or penalties for violation of law.
- Illegal payments such as bribes and kickbacks.
- Any kickback, rebate, or bribe under Medicare or Medicaid.
- A portion (usually two thirds) of treble damages paid under antitrust laws in criminal proceedings.

Kickbacks, bribes, and similar payments are deductible if they are not in violation of the law, and if they are ordinary and necessary. Thus, payments to officials of foreign governments are not deductible if such payments would be a violation of U.S. laws such as the Foreign Corrupt Practices Act of 1977.

OBSERVATION What about lobbying expenses? Code Sec. 162(e) disallows certain lobbying expenses. No deduction is allowed for activities that are intended to influence legislation, public opinion, or political elections at the national level. Code Sec. 276 disallows deductions for advertising in a political convention program and admission to any political dinner or political program if any of the proceeds will be used by a political party or candidate.

---

[8] *See* the *Gilmore* case below.
[9] The *Tank Truck Rentals* case, discussed below, was an impetus for this statute.

In contrast, a taxpayer can deduct expenses in connection with influencing legislation at the local level if the legislation is of direct interest to the taxpayer's business. A *de minimis* rule under Code Sec. 162(e)(5)(b) provides for deductions up to $2,000 per year for in-house expenditures directed at influencing any legislation (national or regional), but no deduction is allowed for payments to lobbyists or lobbying organizations.

.07 EXPENDITURES ASSOCIATED WITH TAX-EXEMPT INCOME

Code Sec. 265 disallows a deduction for any interest or other expense paid or incurred in connection with tax-exempt income. This provision prevents taxpayers with high marginal tax rates from using arbitrage to earn tax-exempt income. In general, an arbitrage is a transaction which is profitable but requires no net personal funds or significant personal effort. In the case of tax-exempt income, an arbitrage would be accomplished if an investor profits from obtaining a loan on which the interest is deductible and invests the loan proceeds in a tax-exempt investment.

OBSERVATION

The concept of arbitrage may be illustrated with a simple example. Assume a taxpayer in the 40-percent tax bracket borrows $1 million at 8 percent and invests the entire amount in municipal bonds that pay 6 percent tax-exempt interest. The interest income for the year is $60,000 and is not taxable. The interest expense on the loan is $80,000. Yet, since the interest is deductible, its after-tax cost to the investor is only $48,000 [$80,000 interest cost less tax savings from deducting the interest (40 percent of $80,000, or $32,000)]. Thus, the investor's after-tax arbitrage profit is $12,000 ($60,000 tax-exempt interest income less $48,000 after-tax interest cost). Code Sec. 265 prevents this arbitrage from being successful by disallowing the $80,000 interest deduction.

¶6007 Accounting for Expenses Under the Cash Method

Code Sec. 461 states that deductions are allowed for the taxable year "which is the proper taxable year under the method of accounting used in computing taxable income." As mentioned earlier, most business taxpayers are unable to use the cash method of accounting due to their size and/or the "clear reflection of income" standard. Therefore, most of the following discussion is devoted to the accrual method of reporting expense deductions. But first, a few comments on the use of the cash method are appropriate.

.01 CASH-BASIS RULES FOR DEDUCTIBILITY

Reg. §1.461-1(a)(1) states the following: "Under the cash receipts and disbursements method of accounting, amounts representing allowable deductions shall, as a general rule, be taken into account for the taxable year in which paid." This is the general rule; however, the same Regulation continues by stating the following:

> "Further, a taxpayer using this method may also be entitled to certain deductions in the computation of taxable income which do not involve cash disbursements during the taxable year, such as the deductions for depreciation, depletion, and losses under Sec. 167, 611, and 165, respectively."

Thus, the deductions allowed to **cash-basis** taxpayers include some items that do not involve an outlay of cash.

Note that as a general rule, the Regulations required that a payment must actually be made; there is no doctrine of constructive payment equivalent to the doctrine of constructive receipt, which was discussed in Chapter 5. However, a deduction may be allowed for payment with a noncash asset, such as property or services. Payments by check are considered to be payment at the time of delivery, even though actual receipt or deposit by the recipient may occur at a later point in time. When payments are made by mail, the usual rule is that mailing constitutes payment because the postal system is deemed to be the agent of the addressee as well as the mailer, but there are conflicting decisions on this point.

.03 DEDUCTIBILITY OF PREPAYMENTS BY CASH-BASIS TAXPAYERS

Questions are frequently raised about the deductibility of prepaid expenses. Reg. §1.461-1(a) notes that "If an expenditure results in the creation of an asset having a useful life which extends substantially beyond the close of the taxable year, such an expenditure may not be deductible, or may be deductible only in part, for the taxable year in which made." Ordinarily, a prepayment such as the purchase of supplies can be deducted in the year of payment even if the supplies are not completely used until the following year. There are conflicting decisions over the proper period for deduction of prepaid rent and insurance by cash-basis taxpayers. As a generalization, however, it can be said that such prepayments must be allocated over the period for which payment was made if to do otherwise would result in a material distortion of income.

In *Rev. Rul. 79-229*,[10] the IRS proposed a three-part test for determining the deductibility of a prepayment: (1) the payment must not be a deposit (deposits are not generally deductible until the goods are received), (2) the prepayment must meet the ordinary and necessary requirements for a deductible business expense, and (3) a current deduction must not cause a material distortion of income. Over the years, a one-year rule developed as an informal line of demarcation between a deductible and a capitalizable prepayment.[11] And this approach was adopted in recently released Regulations discussed below.

¶6009 Accounting for Expenses Under the Accrual Method

Normally, an **accrual-basis** taxpayer is entitled to a deduction under Code Sec. 461 only when (1) all events have occurred that determine that a liability exists (the liability becomes "fixed"), (2) the amount can be determined with reasonable accuracy, and (3) "*economic performance*" has occurred. The first two requirements mirror the conditions for recognition of income by an accrual-basis taxpayer, and many of the same concepts apply. For example, a condition precedent will usually deny a deduction until the condition occurs (for example, deducting attorney fees that will not be determined until a final judgment is rendered), while a condition subsequent will not usually serve to deny the deduction (for example, a payment may be refunded upon the occurrence of a relatively rare event). Also, the same arguments regarding reasonable accuracy are equally applicable for estimating accrual-basis deductions.

The third prong of the tests for deductibility, economic performance, was added to the Code in 1984 and has caused much controversy and consternation among taxpayers and tax professionals. Much of the following discussion is devoted to an examination of this requirement. But first it is necessary to review the importance of the all events test in deciding the proper year of deductibility.

.01 THE ALL EVENTS TEST FOR ACCRUAL-BASIS DEDUCTIONS

There are many timing differences between deductions on the tax return and those that are generally accepted in financial accounting. Many of these exist because there is no fixed liability (a requirement of the all events test), even though an expense may be estimated with reasonable accuracy for financial accounting purposes. A good example is the timing difference resulting from a deduction in the financial reports for estimated costs of guaran-

---

[10] Rev. Rul. 79-229, 1979-2 CB 210.
[11] *See* the discussion of *Zaninovich*, CA-9, 80-1 USTC ¶9342, 616 F2d 429.

tees and warranties at the time the related product or service is sold. These costs cannot be deducted on the tax return until the service under the warranty is actually rendered, because the event that fixes the liability (e.g., the equipment failure) has not yet occurred. Thus, for tax purposes, warranty costs are deductible only as actually incurred.[12] The landmark case for the all events test is the *General Dynamics* case, discussed below.

.03 THE ECONOMIC PERFORMANCE REQUIREMENT

Code Sec. 461(h) was added to the Code in 1984 as a third prong on the tests for deductibility for accrual-basis taxpayers. Code Sec. 461(h)(1) notes that "For purposes of this title, in determining whether an amount has been incurred with respect to any item during any taxable year, the all events test shall not be treated as met any earlier than when **economic performance** with respect to such item occurs."

This provision was added to the Code because of a perceived large gap of time between payment and performance for certain liabilities. For example, in *Ford Motor Co.,* the taxpayer was required to pay out tort claims totaling over $24 million over a period of time as long as 58 years.[13] Ford purchased an annuity contract for $4 million to fund these settlements and deducted the $4 million on its financial accounting records.

However, for tax purposes, Ford deducted the entire $24 million under the theory that the all events test had been met (the fact that a liability was fixed and determinable with reasonable accuracy). Although the IRS won the case on the basis that Ford's deduction did not clearly reflect income (the case involved tax years prior to the enactment of the economic performance requirement), other taxpayers had won on similar issues. Such cases as this one convinced Congress to enact the economic performance requirement, which, as discussed later, would in the Ford case delay the deduction until each payment is made from the annuity to the plaintiffs.

¶6011 Economic Performance: When Does It Occur?

Congress deemed the concept of "economic performance" to be a more feasible solution to the potential time lag between payment and performance than a present value approach. Obviously it becomes important to determine exactly when economic performance occurs. Code Sec. 461(h) and accompanying regulations establish when economic performance occurs in four basic situations: (1) services or property provided to the taxpayer; (2) use of property provided to the taxpayer, (3) property or services provided by the taxpayer, and (4) certain designated "payment" liabilities. Each is discussed briefly in the following pages.

.01 SERVICES OR PROPERTY PROVIDED TO THE TAXPAYER

Code Sec. 461(h)(2)(A) provides that if property or services are provided "to" the taxpayer, economic performance occurs as the property or services are provided to the taxpayer. Thus, a taxpayer who prepays a janitorial service $10,400 for a year's worth of cleaning services (performed every Saturday) may deduct 1/52 of the total, or $200 for each week that such services are received. Amounts allocable to any services not received by the end of the taxpayer's year must be deferred until the services are delivered.

Reg. §1.461-4(d)(6)(ii) provides an exception to this general rule by stating that economic performance is deemed to occur at the date of payment if the taxpayer reasonably expects the property or services to be provided within 3½ months after the payment is made. Thus, a calendar-year, accrual-basis taxpayer who pays $3,000 for three months of janitorial services beginning in December can deduct the entire payment, even though two months of the services will be received in the next tax year. In such cases, the accelerated deduction may justify the prepayment.

---

[12] *See* TAM 7742002.
[13] *Ford Motor Company*, 102 TC 87 (1994).

.03   USE OF PROPERTY PROVIDED TO THE TAXPAYER

If property is provided to a taxpayer for use, economic performance occurs as the taxpayer uses such property. The Regulations provide that such economic performance occurs ratably over the period of time the taxpayer uses the property; however, if the charge for the property is based on usage or income from the property, economic performance occurs as such usage occurs (or as such income is generated). In some cases, the usage of the property may have both fixed and variable elements.

Example 6-2. Zill Corporation, an accrual-basis corporation, leases a copier for one year by prepaying $12,000. The lease contract also requires Zill to pay an additional charge of $.03 for each copy made in excess of 10,000 copies during a month. Economic performance with reference to the $12,000 base charge occurs ratably over the 12 months, or $1,000 per month. For any additional charges incurred under the contract, economic performance occurs as such excess usage occurs.

.05   SERVICES OR PROPERTY PROVIDED BY THE TAXPAYER

If services or property are to be provided by the taxpayer, Code Sec. 461(h)(2)(B) provides that economic performance occurs as the taxpayer provides such property or services. In Reg. §1.461-4(d)(4)(i), the IRS has indicated that such performance should be measured as the taxpayer incurs costs in connection with the taxpayer's obligation to provide such services. This requirement seems to make sense, since the taxpayer is actually deducting the costs and not the liability to perform.

.07   PAYMENT LIABILITIES

Code Sec. 461(h)(2)(C) provides that for liabilities related to tort liabilities and workers compensation laws, economic performance occurs as the payments are made to such persons. The rationale for this "payment liabilities" requirement is that the only objective way to ensure that economic performance has occurred with respect to such liabilities is to require actual payment.[14]

Reg. §1.461-4 added several other categories of liabilities to this payment requirement: they include any liabilities arising under (1) a breach of contract or violation of law, (2) rebates and refunds, (3) jackpots, prizes, and awards, (4) insurance, warranty, or service contracts, and (5) taxes (other than creditable foreign taxes). The Regulations also consign any other type of liability not covered by Code Sec. 461(h) or the regulations to the "payment" category, where economic performance does not occur until payment is actually made. The normal cash-basis principles discussed earlier are used in determining when a "payment" has been made.

.09   THE RECURRING ITEM EXCEPTION

Code Sec. 461(h)(3) provides a limited **recurring item exception** to the economic performance requirement for certain liabilities. Under this exception, a liability is treated as being incurred during the taxable year in question if (1) the all events test is met as of the end of the year, (2) economic performance occurs before the earlier of the due date of the return (including extensions) or the 15th day of the 9th month following the close of the tax year, (3) the item is recurring in nature, and (4) the liability is either not material or the accrual in the current year results in a better matching of income and expenses.

Note that the extended due date of a corporate return would also be 8½ months following the close of the tax year. This exception does not apply to liabilities related to workers compensation laws, tort claims, breach of contract, or violations of the law. The recurring item exception is a method of accounting and must be elected and adopted by the taxpayer.

---

[14] Note that the *Ford Motor Co.* case described earlier would be covered by this requirement, and Ford would deduct the tort liability only as payments were made to the actual plaintiffs and not to an insurance company for the annuity to fund such payments.

This concludes a brief review of the criteria for deducting an expenditure. The following discussion examines the landmark court decisions that test these criteria.

¶6013　Landmark Deduction Cases— Testing the Criteria

.01　BUSINESS OR INCOME-PRODUCING JUSTIFICATIONS FOR DEDUCTIONS FOR DIVORCE COSTS

U.S. vs. D. Gilmore[15]

Facts of the Case: In 1955 the California Supreme Court confirmed the award to the respondent taxpayer of a decree of absolute divorce, without alimony, against his wife Dixie Gilmore. 45 Cal. 2d 142, 287 P. 2d 769. The case before us involves the deductibility for federal income tax purposes of that part of the husband's legal expense incurred in such proceedings as is attributable to his successful resistance of his wife's claims to certain of his assets asserted by her to be community property under California law. At the time of the divorce proceedings, instituted by the wife but in which the husband also cross-claimed for divorce, respondent's property consisted primarily of controlling stock interests in three corporations, each of which was a franchised General Motors automobile dealer. As president and principal managing officer of the three corporations, he received salaries from them aggregating about $66,800 annually, and in recent years his total annual dividends had averaged about $83,000. His total annual income derived from the corporations was thus approximately $150,000. His income from other sources was negligible.

As found by the Court of Claims the husband's overriding concern in the divorce litigation was to protect these assets against the claims of his wife. Those claims had two aspects: *first,* that the earnings accumulated and retained by these three corporations during the Gilmores' marriage (representing an aggregate increase in corporate net worth of some $600,000) were the product of respondent's personal services, and not the result of accretion in capital values, thus rendering respondent's stockholdings in the enterprises *pro tanto* community property under California law; *second,* that to the extent that such stockholdings were community property, the wife, allegedly the innocent party in the divorce proceeding, was entitled under California law to more than a one-half interest in such property. The respondent wished to defeat those claims for two important reasons. *First,* the loss of his controlling stock interests, particularly in the event of their transfer in substantial part to his hostile wife, might well cost him the loss of his corporate positions, his principal means of livelihood. *Second,* there was also danger that if he were found guilty of his wife's sensational and reputation-damaging charges of marital infidelity, General Motors Corporation might find it expedient to exercise its right to cancel these dealer franchises. The end result of this bitterly fought divorce case was a complete victory for the husband. He, not the wife, was granted a divorce on his cross-claim; the wife's community property claims were denied in their entirety; and she was held entitled to no alimony. 45 Cal. 2d 142, 287 P. 2d 769. Respondent's legal expenses in connection with this litigation amounted to $32,537.15 in 1953 and $8,074.21 in 1954—a total of $40,611.36 for the two taxable years in question.

Note: Reversed a decision of the Claims Court

[15] *Gilmore,* SCt, 63-1 USTC ¶9285, 372 US 39.

This case tests the criterion of nondeductibility of personal expenses. The taxpayer attempted to deduct legal expenses related to a divorce because he claimed that he was protecting business assets (controlling interests in three auto dealerships) from the claims of his ex-wife, and if he lost the case he would probably lose his job (due to his ex-wife assuming control of the dealerships) and General Motors might cancel his dealership because of his tarnished reputation if marital infidelity accusations were upheld. So in essence, the taxpayer was maintaining that he was defending his stockholdings and thus could deduct the legal expenses as "conservation of income-producing property" under Code Sec. 212. The IRS contended that the legal expenditures were personal in nature due to the fact that the origin of the expenses was a personal relationship (e.g., the marriage). The Claims Court had allowed 20 percent of the expenditures as deductions, concluding that the overriding concern of the taxpayer in the divorce was the protection of the assets related to the dealership.

In considering this case, the Supreme Court noted in a review of the history of Code Sec. 212 that Congress appears to have set the same stringent standards for deductibility under Code Sec. 212 that they have for deductions under Code Sec. 162. After much wrangling with the definition of an expense, the Supreme Court accepted the IRS argument that the origin of the expense, and not its consequences, determines the deductibility of the expenditure. Specifically, the IRS contended that the origin of the claims was the question of community property, a personal issue. The Supreme Court noted the fallacy of basing deductions on the consequences of an expenditure with the following example:

> "If two taxpayers are each sued for an automobile accident while driving for pleasure, deductibility of their litigation costs would turn on the mere circumstance of the character of the assets each happened to possess, that is, whether the judgments against them stood to be satisfied out of income or non-income-producing property. We should be slow to attribute to Congress a purpose producing such unequal treatment among taxpayers, resting on no rational foundation."[16]

OBSERVATION

This decision is sometimes referred to as the "*but for*" decision, in that one line from this case is quoted in countless subsequent questions regarding business vs. personal expenditures: *"For no such property could have existed **but for** [emphasis supplied] the marital relationship."*

The Court also addressed the earlier result in *Baer v. Commissioner,* where the Claims Court allowed a deduction for the legal costs because the taxpayer was "relatively unconcerned" about the divorce itself, but was very concerned about losing his livelihood.[17] Once again, the Court referred to the "consequences only" theory as being insufficient to justify a deduction. And yet the Court's decision in this case does not square with *Howard,* where an Army officer was permitted to deduct legal costs associated with a court-martial hearing for failure to pay alimony.[18]

OBSERVATION

Although Gilmore was not permitted to deduct the legal expenses, he was subsequently able to capitalize them as part of the cost basis of the underlying stock. This was because the expenditure was primarily to defend the title to the property.

---

[16] *Id.*
[17] *Baer,* CA-8, 52-1 USTC ¶9310, 196 F2d 646. The Claims Court had cited this decision as precedent in the *Gilmore* case.
[18] *Howard,* CA-9, 53-1 USTC ¶9213, 202 F2d 28.

.03   THE ORDINARY REQUIREMENT FOR VOLUNTARY REPAYMENTS

Welch v. Helvering[19]

Facts of the Case: The question to be determined is whether payments by a taxpayer, who is in business as a commission agent, are allowable deductions in the computation of his income if made to the creditors of a bankrupt corporation in an endeavor to strengthen his own standing and credit. In 1922 petitioner was the secretary of the E. L. Welch Company, a Minnesota corporation, engaged in the grain business. The company was adjudged an involuntary bankrupt, and had a discharge from its debts. Thereafter the petitioner made a contract with the Kellogg Company to purchase grain for it on a commission. In order to re-establish his relations with customers whom he had known when acting for the Welch Company and to solidify his credit and standing, he decided to pay the debts of the Welch business so far as he was able.

In fulfillment of that resolve, he made payments of substantial amounts during five successive years. In 1924, the commissions were $18,028.20; the payments $3,975.97; in 1925, the commissions $31,377.07; the payments $11,968.20; in 1926, the commissions $20,925.25, the payments $12,815.72; in 1927, the commissions $22,119.61, the payments $7,379.72; and in 1928, the commissions $26,177.56, the payments $11,068.25. The Commissioner ruled that these payments were not deductible from income as ordinary and necessary expenses, but were rather in the nature of capital expenditures, an outlay for the development of reputation and good will.

Note: Reversed and remanded a decision of the Court of Claims

This case is testing the criteria of capitalization and the ordinary and necessary requirements for an expenditure designed to restore the taxpayer's business reputation. In this case, the taxpayer voluntarily repaid debts that he was relieved of through bankruptcy proceedings. The purpose of the repayments was to reestablish his reputation with former customers in his new job as a commissioned grain purchase agent. The IRS contended that such expenditures were capital expenditures, an outlay related to personal goodwill and reputation. The taxpayer contended that they were ordinary and necessary business expenses that were required for the taxpayer to derive a livelihood as a commissioned agent.

In deciding this case, the Supreme Court noted that the expenditures were "appropriate and helpful" to Welch's business, and therefore met the necessary requirement. However, the Court noted that the ordinary requirement refers to common and accepted means of doing business, and although an ordinary expense need not be habitual, it cannot be erratic either. Based on this reasoning, the Court ruled that it is not an ordinary practice for a taxpayer to pay the debts of others, and that such payments were for reputation and learning that are more akin to capital assets. Thus, the expenditure represented a capitalizable asset, and not a deductible expense.

This decision is interesting, because the expenditure, while necessary, was not deemed ordinary. It is interesting that the courts usually accept a taxpayer's definition of "necessary," in that hindsight by the Court is always 20/20, but the Court will not accept the taxpayer's definition of "ordinary." The Court certainly did not provide a beacon for future cases on this issue when it stated the following:

> *"Here, indeed, as so often in other branches of the law, the decisive distinctions are those of degree and not of kind. One struggles in vain for any verbal formula that will supply a ready touchstone. The standard set up by the statute is not a rule of law: it is rather a way of life. Life in all its fullness must supply the answer to the riddle."*[20]

---

[19] *Welch*, SCt, 3 ustc ¶1164, 290 US 111, 54 SCt 8.
[20] *Id.*

OBSERVATION   In an interesting decision with parallels to the *Welch* case, the President of a corporation was having financial problems and employees of the company pooled funds to loan the President. Reflecting his gratitude for the gesture, the President promptly took the funds to the racetrack and lost every penny. The company's Board of Directors decided to repay the employees, and the company deducted the repayments on its tax return. The Court allowed the deduction, rationalizing that the payments retained existing goodwill and did not create new goodwill. (*Query: Wasn't* Gilmore *doing exactly the same thing?*) The Court also noted that it was "an outlay that many corporations would make under similar circumstances."[21]

.05   THE NECESSARY REQUIREMENT AND ILLEGAL ACTIVITIES

Tank Truck Rentals v. Commissioner[22]

Facts of the Case: Petitioner, a Pennsylvania corporation, owns a fleet of tank trucks which it leases, with drivers, to motor carriers for transportation of bulk liquids. The lessees operate the trucks throughout Pennsylvania and the surrounding States of New Jersey, Ohio, Delaware, West Virginia, and Maryland, with nearly all the shipments originating or terminating in Pennsylvania. In 1951, the tax year in question, each of these States imposed maximum weight limits for motor vehicles operating on its highways. Pennsylvania restricted truckers to 45,000 pounds, however, while the other States through which petitioner operated allowed maximum weights approximating 60,000 pounds. It is uncontested that trucking operations were so hindered by this situation that neither petitioner nor other bulk liquid truckers could operate profitably and also observe the Pennsylvania law. Petitioner's equipment consisted largely of 4,500 to 5,000 gallon tanks, and the industry rate structure generally was predicated on fully loaded use of equipment of that capacity. Yet only one of the commonly carried liquids weighed little enough that a fully loaded truck could satisfy the Pennsylvania statute. Operation of partially loaded trucks, however, not only would have created safety hazards, but also would have been economically impossible for any carrier so long as the rest of the industry continued capacity loading. And the industry as a whole could not operate on a partial load basis without driving shippers to competing forms of transportation. The only other alternative, use of smaller tanks, also was commercially impracticable, not only because of initial replacement costs but even more so because of reduced revenue and increased operating expense, since the rates charged were based on the number of gallons transported per mile.

Confronted by this dilemma, the industry deliberately operated its trucks overweight in Pennsylvania in the hope, and at the calculated risk, of escaping the notice of the state and local police. This conduct also constituted willful violations in New Jersey, for reciprocity provisions of the New Jersey statute subjected trucks registered in Pennsylvania to Pennsylvania weight restrictions while traveling in New Jersey. In the remainder of the States in which petitioner operated, it suffered overweight fines for several unintentional violations, such as those caused by temperature changes in transit. During the tax year 1951, petitioner paid a total of $41,060.84 in fines and costs for 718 willful and 28 innocent violations. Deduction of that amount in petitioner's 1951 tax return was disallowed by the Commissioner.

Note: Upheld the U.S. Tax Court and the 3rd Circuit Court of Appeals

---

21   *See Dunn & McCarthy, Inc.*, CA-2, 43-2 USTC ¶9688, 139 F2d 242.
22   *Tank Truck Rentals, Inc.*, SCt, 58-1 USTC ¶9366, 356 US 30, 78 SCt 507.

In this case, once again the taxpayer is testing the bounds of the ordinary and necessary requirements vs. payments that frustrate public policy. The facts are relatively straightforward: the taxpayer, a trucking company, deliberately violated the Pennsylvania weight limits (and through a reciprocal agreement, those of New Jersey as well) because it was not economically feasible (and to a degree more dangerous) for the company to comply. The taxpayer deducted $41,060 in fines (for 718 willful and 28 innocent violations), contending that the fines met all the conditions of an "ordinary and necessary" business expense. The IRS countered that these were illegal payments that would subsidize noncompliance by violating state policy, which surely could not be an ordinary and necessary expense.

The case is an interesting one, because the taxpayer made an impressive case for ordinary and necessary business treatment. It was not economically feasible for any one in the industry to operate at less than full capacity, and was dangerous to do so as well. Furthermore, the taxpayer could not economically justify using smaller trucks. Add to this the fact that Pennsylvania set their weight limits at what many considered to be unreasonably low levels: 45,000 pounds versus 60,000 pounds of other states. But the IRS argument of subsidizing noncompliance seemed to sway the Supreme Court, who noted that the fines were punitive and not merely tolls, and that an expenditure cannot be necessary if it violates the law. The Court also ruled that the same logic would apply to the "innocent" fines as well.

Congress subsequently responded to this case by codifying the nondeductibility of fines, bribes, kickbacks and penalties in Code Sec. 162(f). A fine under the statute must either involve a violation of law or lead to the loss of a professional license. Thus, a contractor who pays a kickback to a local official may be able to deduct the expenditure if there is no local law prohibiting such payments. On the other hand, a physician making payments for referrals under Medicare could not deduct such payments because such a practice could lead to the loss of his or her medical license.

OBSERVATION   These provisions do not solve all the questions involving public policy. The courts have consistently held that expenses are deductible even if the income matched to the expenses is from an illegal activity. For example, the expenses incurred by a gambler are deductible for tax purposes even if the gambler operates his or her business in a state that prohibits gambling. Yet, this rule can be viewed as equitable because the illegal income is fully taxable. And just because the expenses of an illegal business are deductible, the owner of the business is still subject to penalties prescribed by federal and state authorities. In contrast, with regard to trafficking illegal drugs, Code Sec. 280E prohibits the deduction of any expenses (although cases have allowed deductions for the "*cost of goods sold*," which are not treated as expenses).

.07   TESTING THE CRITERIA—ADDITIONAL CASES AND RULINGS

American Bemberg Corporation v. Commissioner.[23] In this case, a taxpayer incurred significant costs for drilling, grouting, and filling in cavities to stop cave-ins of soil near their manufacturing facility. The taxpayer expensed the amounts, contending that such expenditures were repairs that did not cure the underlying geological defect. The IRS argued that such amounts should be capitalized, primarily due to the size of the expenditures. The U.S. Tax Court agreed with the taxpayer, noting that "repairs" do not always have to be inexpensive year to year mendings.

---

[23] *American Bemberg Corporation*, 10 TC 361 (1948).

OBSERVATION	The IRS recently reissued proposed regulations under Code Secs. 263 and 263A that deal with the treatment of amounts paid to acquire, produce, or improve tangible property. These rules provide a de minimis expensing rule and a safe harbor for deducting routine maintenance costs. The rules include an optional simplified repair allowance method. If finally approved, these regulations will lessen many of the controversies between taxpayers and the IRS regarding capitalization issues. Other aspects of these regulations are discussed below.

Rev. Rul. 63-232.[24] In this ruling, the IRS used a scientific study to examine the "suddenness" of termite damage and thus determine if such damage qualified as a casualty or theft loss (allowed only for "sudden" events, per Code Sec.165(c)). The government study disclosed that the period of time from first infestation to actual damage is usually three to eight years, leading the IRS to conclude in this ruling that such damage does not meet the "sudden" requirement of the Code.

Patel v. Commissioner.[25] This decision more or less puts to bed an interesting tax avoidance scheme that was first allowed by the Court in *Scharf v. Commissioner, T.C.M. 1973-265*. In that case, an individual bought a prime piece of real estate with a "tear down" structure on it, i.e., a house they intended to demolish. Rather than paying a construction company to tear down the house, the taxpayers donated the house to the local fire department (to set ablaze!) for use in their drills, taking a charitable deduction for the estimated value of the property. The planning technique was first curtailed early in 2011 in *Rolfs v. Commissioner, 138 T.C. 33*, where the court ruled that the value of the home did not exceed the $10,000 estimated value of the "free demolition," and therefore there was no excess to deduct. In effect, the Court stated that the value of the house should take into account its "imminent demise." Then, the death knell was added in *Patel*, where the Court ruled that the contribution deduction was not allowed because it was a contribution of a partial interest (house, but no land), and Sec. 170 denies a deduction for charitable gifts of partial interests.

¶6015 Landmark Deduction Cases—Business v. Personal

.01 TRAVEL EXPENSES

Commissioner v. J.N. Flowers[26]

Facts of the Case: The taxpayer, a lawyer, has resided with his family in Jackson, Mississippi, since 1903. There he has paid taxes, voted, schooled his children and established social and religious connections. He built a house in Jackson nearly thirty years ago and at all times has maintained it for himself and his family. He has been connected with several law firms in Jackson, one of which he formed and which has borne his name since 1922. In 1906 the taxpayer began to represent the predecessor of the Gulf, Mobile & Ohio Railroad, his present employer. He acted as trial counsel for the railroad throughout Mississippi. From 1918 until 1927 he acted as special counsel for the railroad in Mississippi. He was elected general solicitor in 1927 and continued to be elected to that position each year until 1930, when he was elected general counsel. Thereafter he was annually elected general counsel until September 1940 when the properties of the predecessor company and another railroad were merged and he was elected vice president and general counsel of the newly formed Gulf, Mobile & Ohio Railroad.

---

[24] Rev. Rul. 63-232, 1963-2 CB 97.
[25] 138 T.C. 23 (2012).
[26] *Flowers*, SCt, 46-1 USTC ¶9127, 326 US 465, 66 SCt 250.

The main office of the Gulf, Mobile & Ohio Railroad is in Mobile, Alabama, as was also the main office of its predecessor. When offered the position of general solicitor in 1927, the taxpayer was unwilling to accept it if it required him to move from Jackson to Mobile. He had established himself in Jackson both professionally and personally and was not desirous of moving away. As a result, an arrangement was made between him and the railroad whereby he could accept the position and continue to reside in Jackson on condition that he pay his traveling expenses between Mobile and Jackson and pay his living expenses in both places. This arrangement permitted the taxpayer to determine for himself the amount of time he would spend in each of the two cities and was in effect during 1939 and 1940, the taxable years in question.

The railroad company provided an office for the taxpayer in Mobile but not in Jackson. When he worked in Jackson his law firm provided him with office space, although he no longer participated in the firm's business or shared in its profits. He used his own office furniture and fixtures at this office. The railroad, however, furnished telephone service and a typewriter and desk for his secretary. It also paid the secretary's expenses while in Jackson. Most of the legal business of the railroad was centered in or conducted from Jackson, but this business was handled by local counsel for the railroad. The taxpayer's participation was advisory only and was no different from his participation in the railroad's legal business in other areas.

The taxpayer's principal post of business was at the main office in Mobile. However, during the taxable years of 1939 and 1940, he devoted nearly all of his time to matters relating to the merger of the railroads. Since it was left to him where he would do his work, he spent most of his time in Jackson during this period. In connection with the merger, one of the companies was involved in certain litigation in the federal court in Jackson and the taxpayer participated in that litigation.

During 1939 he spent 203 days in Jackson and 66 in Mobile, making 33 trips between the two cities. During 1940 he spent 168 days in Jackson and 102 in Mobile, making 40 trips between the two cities. The railroad paid all of his traveling expenses when he went on business trips to points other than Jackson or Mobile. But it paid none of his expenses in traveling between these two points or while he was at either of them. The taxpayer deducted $900 in his 1939 income tax return and $1,620 in his 1940 return as traveling expenses incurred in making trips from Jackson to Mobile and as expenditures for meals and hotel accommodations while in Mobile. The Commissioner disallowed the deductions.

Note: Reversing the 5th Circuit Court of Appeals, which had reversed the U.S. Tax Court

This case examines the question of business versus personal expenditures within the context of the travel expense provisions of the Code. The taxpayer was hired as the General Solicitor of a railroad company, and though the position was located in Mobile, Alabama, the taxpayer continued to live in Jackson, Mississippi, where he had his own law practice and had developed strong business and personal ties. He deducted the expenses for 73 trips between the two locations for the two years in question, but was able to spend the majority of his time in Jackson while working on merger matters of the railroad.

The taxpayer contended that his **tax home** was in Jackson (defined as his "abode"), and that he was traveling on business to Mobile and thus should be able to deduct the expenses associated with such travel while "away from home." The IRS contended that his tax home was in Mobile (his "post of duty"), and such expenses were thus personal and nondeductible. Code Sec. 23(a)(1)(A) of the Code (now Code Sec. 162(a)(2)) allows a deduction for "traveling expenses, including amounts expended for meals and lodging other than amounts which are lavish or extravagant under the circumstances while away from home in the pursuit of a trade or business." Because of the wording of the statute, this decision was eagerly awaited by the business community, as everyone hoped that the Supreme Court would finally answer the question of what Congress meant by the word "home" in the expression "**away from home** on business." The Tax Court had essentially said that Flowers' home was in Mobile (the "post of duty"), and the 5th Circuit Court of Appeals had said that his home was in Jackson (his "abode").

Unfortunately, the Supreme Court did not tackle this problem directly. The Court noted that three conditions were necessary to justify a travel deduction: (1) the expense is reasonable and necessary, (2) the expense is incurred while "away from home", and (3) the expense is incurred in pursuit of business. In ruling for the Service, the Court noted that the "pursuit of business" test was failed because the railroad gained nothing from the arrangement, and it was for the taxpayer's personal satisfaction that the trips were made.

Justice Rutledge dissented to the decision, noting that the taxpayer had kept his law business in Jackson, the bulk of his work was done there, and under common law his "home" was in Jackson. He also agreed with the 5th Circuit Court that if Congress had meant "business headquarters" for home, it would have said "business headquarters." But one of the factors that no doubt influenced the court was the fact that the taxpayer practiced little law in Jackson for anyone other than the railroad for those two years. If the law practice in Jackson had been substantial, the Court would have probably allowed the deduction.

The IRS continues to view one's tax home as being his or her principal "post of duty." And in some cases, the Service has ruled that a taxpayer has no home, where the taxpayer lived on the road and the "post of duty" was each job site and the taxpayer had not otherwise established residency.

OBSERVATION

In *Rev. Rul. 73-529*,[27] the IRS specified the criteria it will apply in determining a taxpayer's "home." And in an interesting case with many tax twists, the U.S. Tax Court ruled in *C.W. Walker*, that a taxpayer could deduct the commuting expenses while in travel status even though the taxpayer did not qualify for the home office deduction under the *Soliman* decision (discussed below).[28] In *Rev. Rul. 94-47*,[29] the IRS announced that it would not follow this decision.

.03   BUSINESS VS. NONBUSINESS BAD DEBTS

Whipple v. Commissioner[30]

Facts of the Case: Prior to 1941, petitioner was a construction superintendent and an estimator for a lumber company but during that year and over the next several ones he was instrumental in forming and was a member of a series of partnerships engaged in the construction or construction supply business. In 1949 and 1950 he was an original incorporator of seven corporations some of which were successors to the partnerships and in 1951 he sold his interest in the corporations along with his equity in five others in the rental and construction business, the profit on the sales being reported as long-term capital gains. In 1951 and 1952 he formed eight new corporations, one of which was Mission Orange Bottling Co. of Lubbock, Inc., bought the stock of a corporation known as Mason Root Beer and acquired an interest in a related vending machine business. From 1951 to 1953 he also bought and sold land, acquired and disposed of a restaurant and participated in several oil ventures.

On April 25, 1951, petitioner secured a franchise from Mission Dry Corporation entitling him to produce, bottle, distribute and sell Mission beverages in various

---

[27]   Rev. Rul. 73-529, 1973-2 CB 37.
[28]   *Walker*, 101 TC 537 (1994).
[29]   Rev. Rul. 94-47, IRB 1994-29, 6.
[30]   *Whipple*, SCt, 63-1 USTC ¶9466, 373 US 193, 83 SCt 1168.

counties in Texas. Two days later he purchased the assets of a sole proprietorship in the bottling business and conducted that business pursuant to his franchise as a sole proprietorship. On July 1, 1951, though retaining the franchise in his own name, he sold the bottling equipment to Mission Orange Bottling Co. of Lubbock, Inc., a corporation organized by petitioner as mentioned, of which he owned approximately 80% of the shares outstanding. In 1952 he purchased land in Lubbock and erected a bottling plant thereon at a cost of $43,601 and then leased the plant to Mission Orange for a 10-year term at a prescribed rental. Depreciation was taken on the new bottling plant on petitioner's individual tax returns for 1952 and 1953.

Petitioner made sizable cash advances to Mission Orange in 1952 and 1953, and on December 1, 1953, the balance due him, including $25,502.50 still owing from his sale of the bottling assets to the corporation in July 1951, totaled $79,489.76. On December 15, 1953, petitioner advanced to Mission Orange an additional $48,000 to pay general creditors and on the same day received a transfer of the assets of the corporation with a book value of $70,414.66. The net amount owing to petitioner ultimately totaled was $56,975.10, which debt became worthless in 1953 and is in issue here. During 1951, 1952 and 1953 Mission Orange made no payments of interest, rent or salary to petitioner although he did receive such income from some of his other corporations. Petitioner deducted the $56,975.10 debt due from Mission Orange as a business bad debt in computing his 1953 taxable income. The Commissioner, claiming the debt was a nonbusiness bad debt, assessed deficiencies.

Note: Vacating and remanding decision of the 5ᵗʰ Circuit Court of Appeals, that had previously upheld the U.S. Tax Court

---

This case deals with the characterization of loans from an individual with controlling interests in several businesses. Mission Orange, a corporation in which he had an 80-percent interest, failed to repay several loans related to a bottling plant that it had leased from the taxpayer (who had built the bottling facility). The taxpayer deducted the losses as business bad debts, contending that earlier cases had made similar classifications once a business relationship had been established. The IRS argued that the "business" relationship should be construed narrowly, and that a person's status as an investor is insufficient to establish such a relationship.

The U.S. Tax Court construed such definition narrowly, ruling against the taxpayer because he was not in the trade or business of promoting, financing, or bottling—all activities that would, in the Court's definition, satisfy such a high standard. The 5ᵗʰ Circuit Court of Appeals upheld the Tax Court's decision. The Supreme Court seemed to accept this line of reasoning, noting that when Congress added Sec. 212 to the Code and also limited the deductibility of nonbusiness bad debts (treating these as short-term capital losses), they had "broadened Sec. 23(a) to reach income-producing activities not amounting to a trade or business and conversely narrowed Sec. 23(k) to exclude bad debts arising from these same sources." The Court also stated the following:

> "When the only return is that of an investor, the taxpayer has not satisfied his burden of demonstrating that he is engaged in a trade or business since investing is not a trade or business and the return to the taxpayer, though substantially the product of his services, legally arises not from his own trade or business but from that of the corporation."[31]

In the end, however, the Supreme Court decided that the Tax Court and the 5ᵗʰ Circuit Court had overlooked one key possibility, and as a result remanded the case back to the Tax Court. Specifically, the Court noted that *"While the Tax Court and the Court of Appeals dealt separately with assertions relating to other phases of the petitioner's case, we do not find that either court disposed of the possibility that the loan to Mission Orange, a tenant of petitioner, was incurred in petitioner's business of being a landlord."*[32]

---

[31] *Id.*
[32] *Id.*

<table>
<tr><td>

OBSERVATION

</td><td>

There is no further court record of this case after the Supreme Court decision, so the case was probably settled prior to being heard once again by the U.S. Tax Court. It is interesting to note that had Mission Orange been operated as a sole proprietorship, and not a corporation, a business bad debt would most likely have been allowed.

</td></tr>
</table>

Cases subsequent to the *Whipple* decision did not apply quite as stringent of a business requirement to such investor loans. For example, in *U.S. v. Generes,* the Supreme Court noted that a *dominant* business motive, and not merely a *significant* one, must be present for a business bad debt deduction when a taxpayer, a shareholder/employee, loaned money to his corporate employer as a means of protecting his salary.[33] This "catastrophic effect" type of test was applied in similar cases following the *Generes* decision.

.05   BUSINESS VS. PERSONAL—ADDITIONAL CASES AND RULINGS

Commissioner v. Soliman.[34] In this case, the taxpayer was an anesthesiologist who spent 30 to 35 hours each week at three different hospital facilities. Because none of the hospitals provided office space to the taxpayer, he took a home office deduction under Code Sec. 280A on his return, arguing that such an office was needed for billing, retaining records, and reading medical journals. The IRS contended that, following a string of earlier cases, the "focal point" of his business was the hospitals and therefore that was where his "office" should be. The Supreme Court agreed with the IRS, effectively overturning a line of pro-taxpayer decisions in the U.S. Tax Court that had gotten away from the focal point test. Justice Stephens dissented to the case, noting that their decision creates confusion regarding a clause in Code Sec. 280A (home office deduction allowed if a principal place of business *or* a place to meet clients or customers), since the decision seems to say that both conditions are required.

<table>
<tr><td>

OBSERVATION

</td><td>

The *Soliman* decision was viewed by many as an improper interpretation of Code Sec. 280A, in part due to the logic of Justice Stephens and especially in light of the computer and information revolution where many taxpayers can work efficiently at home. In 1997 Congress responded to pressures to overturn the *Soliman* decision by adding the following sentence to Code Sec. 280A(c)(1):

"For purposes of subparagraph (A), the term 'principal place of business' includes a place of business which is used by the taxpayer for the administrative or management activities of any trade or business of the taxpayer if there is no other fixed location of such trade or business where the taxpayer conducts substantial administrative or management activities of such trade or business."

</td></tr>
</table>

Michael J. Knight.[35] Individuals deduct certain income-producing expenses, such as investment advisory fees, as miscellaneous itemized deductions subject to a two-percent-of-AGI floor. For income tax purposes, trusts and estates are basically subject to the same tax rules, with an exception to the two-percent floor in Code Sec. 67(e) for expenditures "which would not have been incurred if the property were not held in such trust or estate." The meaning of these 14 words was a mystery for over 20 years, resulting in a three-way split among the Circuit Courts. In *Knight*, the Supreme Court interpreted this provision: "costs incurred by trusts that escape the two-percent floor are those that would not 'commonly' or 'customarily' be incurred by individuals." In effect, such costs are fully deductible only if the expenses are unique to the administration of a trust.

---

[33] *Generes*, SCt, 72-1 USTC ¶9259, 405 US 93, 92 SCt 827.
[34] *Soliman*, 506 US 168.
[35] *Michael J. Knight*, SCt, 2008-1 USTC ¶50,132, 128 SCt 782.

¶6017 Landmark Deduction Cases— Methods of Accounting

.01 DEDUCTIBILITY OF PREPAID EXPENSES

Commissioner v. Boylston Market Association[36]

Facts of the Case: The taxpayer in the course of its business, which is the management of real estate owned by it, purchased from time to time fire and other insurance policies covering periods of three or more years. It keeps its books and makes its returns on a cash receipts and disbursements basis. The taxpayer has since 1915 deducted each year as insurance expenses the amount of insurance premiums applicable to carrying insurance for that year regardless of the year in which the premium was actually paid. This method was required by the Treasury Department prior to 1938 by *G. C. M. 13148,* XIII-1 Cum. Bull. 67 (1934).

Prior to January 1, 1936, the taxpayer had prepaid insurance premiums in the amount of $6,690.75 and during that year it paid premiums in an amount of $1,082.77. The amount of insurance premiums prorated by the taxpayer in 1936 was $4,421.76. Prior to January 1, 1938, it had prepaid insurance premiums in the amount of $6,148.42 and during that year paid premiums in the amount of $890.47. The taxpayer took a deduction of $3,284.25, which was the amount prorated for the year 1938. The Commissioner in his notice of deficiency for the year 1936 allowed only $1,082.77 and for the year 1938 only $890.47, being the amounts actually paid in those years, on the basis that deductions for insurance expense of a taxpayer on the cash receipts and disbursements basis is limited to premiums paid during the taxable year.

Note: 1st Circuit Court of Appeals decision, affirming the Board of Tax Appeals

---

This case involved a simple question of whether a cash-basis company could accrue insurance expenses as they were incurred, rather than when the premiums were paid in cash. Interestingly, the IRS argued that the cash basis should be used for such payments, citing an earlier decision by the 1st Circuit in *Welch v. Dubois.*[37] The taxpayer argued that the accrual method provides a clearer reflection of income and conforms to accepted accounting practices.

The Board of Tax Appeals subsequently failed to follow the *Welch v. Dubois* decision in a later case, and the 1st Circuit decided to reexamine the issue. This time, the Court decided that such payments should be treated no differently than advance rentals or payment of bonuses, and thus prorated over their useful life. In this regard, the Court noted that "To permit the taxpayer to take a full deduction in the year of payment would distort his income." The court also noted that prepaid insurance for a three-year period, such as in this case, is easily allocated and such prorating is needed because the life of the asset extends beyond the taxable year. The Court also noted the following:

> *"The line to be drawn between capital expenditures and ordinary and necessary business expenses is not always an easy one, but we are satisfied that in treating prepaid insurance as a capital expense we are obtaining some degree of consistency in these matters."*[38]

The decision in this case led the IRS to draft Reg. §1.461-1(a)(1), which requires any prepaid cost to be allocated if the asset has a life extending *substantially beyond* the close of the tax year. Since that time, the cash method has been opposed by the IRS on numerous occasions as not "clearly reflecting income."

---

[36] *Boylston Market Association*, CA-1, 42-2 USTC ¶9820, 131 F2d 966.
[37] *Welch v. DeBlois*, CA-1, 38-1 USTC ¶9118, 94 F2d 842.
[38] *Id.*

OBSERVATION

In *Zaninovich*, the Court allowed a taxpayer to deduct a rent prepayment for 11 months, if it was treated consistently each year.[39] This has led to the *"Zaninovich rule,"* which allows deduction for prepayments of one year or less for such items as insurance and rent, provided that they are treated consistently each year. The IRS nonacquiesced to this decision. Is there an equivalent "Zaninovich rule" for accrual basis taxpayers? The IRS said no in *U.S. Freightways,* and the Tax Court agreed, noting that deducting a prepayment of insurance and licenses even for one year or less is inconsistent with the accrual method (when the expense was *incurred*). However, the 7th Circuit Court of Appeals reversed this decision on appeal, specifically noting that the taxpayer's method of accounting has nothing to do with the **one-year rule**.[40] The one-year rule has subsequently been endorsed by the IRS in new capitalization regulations, discussed below.

.03   DEDUCTIBILITY OF ACCRUED CONTESTED STATE TAX PAYMENTS

Dixie Pine Products Company v. Commissioner[41]

Facts of the Case: In 1936 the Mississippi taxing authorities declared that a solvent used by petitioner in its business was gasoline within the meaning of a state law defining gasoline and laying a tax upon its receipt and use. Accordingly a tax was assessed against the petitioner with respect to the receipt and use of the solvent in 1936. Petitioner paid the tax, and, in the same year, brought suit against the Motor Vehicle Commissioner of Mississippi alleging that the solvent was not within the comprehension of the state law and that the Commissioner should be temporarily and permanently enjoined from future collections of tax in respect of it. The Commissioner's demurrer to the complaint was sustained but, on appeal, the Supreme Court of Mississippi decided that, on the pleadings, the solvent was not within the definition of gasoline contained in the state statute. After this decision petitioner denied that it owed, and ceased and refused to pay, any gasoline tax on solvent used by it.

In December 1937, on advice of counsel, petitioner (which kept its books and filed its federal income tax returns on the accrual basis) made book entries accruing gasoline tax assessed by the Motor Vehicle Commissioner in 1937. The actual accrual entries were made sometime between January 1 and March 15, 1938, as of December 31, 1937, in the amount of approximately $21,000, and petitioner deducted this amount from income in making its 1937 federal income tax return, although the sum had not been, and never was, paid. In December 1938 petitioner and the Attorney General of Mississippi filed an agreed statement of facts in the state court suit, and, in the same month, the trial judge entered a final decree perpetually enjoining the Motor Vehicle Commissioner from assessing gasoline tax on the solvent used by petitioner. This decree was subsequently affirmed by the Supreme Court of Mississippi. In its 1938 federal income tax return petitioner, by way of compensating entry, included the sum of $21,000 as income and as a recovery, in view of the Mississippi trial court's decree of December 1938. The sole question is whether the Commissioner was right in disallowing the deduction for the tax year 1937.

Note: Affirming the 5th Circuit Court of Appeals, which had affirmed the Board of Tax Appeals

[39] *Zaninovich*, CA-9, 80-1 USTC ¶9342, 616 F2d 429.
[40] *U.S. Freightways*, CA-7, 270 F3d 1137.
[41] *Dixie Pine Products*, SCt, 44-1 USTC ¶9127, 320 US 516, 64 SCt 364.

This case essentially represents an application of the all events test to an accrual of a tax on gasoline that theoretically was owed by the taxpayer but in fact was being currently contested in the courts. The accrual was made in 1937, and a decision was rendered for the taxpayer in 1938, thus negating the requirement to pay the tax. As a result, the taxpayer included the amount in 1938 income to compensate for the 1937 accrual of a deduction. The IRS contended that the item should have never been accrued, as the "event" that would fix the liability was the taxpayer's loss in court. The taxpayer contended that the accrual was proper accounting and clearly reflected income, and that the event that "fixed the liability" was the state demanding payment.

The Supreme Court ruled for the IRS, noting that "all the events must occur in that year which fix the amount and the fact of the taxpayer's liability for items of indebtedness deducted though not paid; and this cannot be the case where the liability is contingent and is contested by the taxpayer." The Court went on to note that the taxpayer should have waited for adjudication of the issue by the courts, in effect establishing this as a *condition precedent* to a deduction.

OBSERVATION   If the taxpayer had actually paid the tax under protest, it would have been deductible that year. As a general rule, **contested liabilities** are not deductible, since the contest establishes a "condition precedent" to deductibility. However, Code Sec. 461(f) provides a mechanism whereby a taxpayer who contests a liability can obtain a current deduction by transferring money or other property in satisfaction of the liability. The transfer must be to either the other party who is asserting the liability or to an independent third-party trustee. Other requirements for such arrangements are described in Reg. §1.461-2. Code Sec. 461(h), the economic performance requirement, and 461(f), the special provision for contested liabilities, are two special statutory provisions that override the normal accrual-basis rules used for financial accounting purposes. In a sense, these rules "trump" the all events test.

This was one of the earliest decisions involving the all events test. A more recent test is examined below in the *General Dynamics* case.

.05   DEDUCTIBILITY OF FRIENDLY MERGER FEES

Indopco v. Commissioner[42]

Facts of the Case: Petitioner Indopco, Inc., formerly named National Starch and Chemical Corporation and hereinafter referred to as National Starch, is a Delaware corporation that manufactures and sells adhesives, starches, and specialty chemical products. In October 1977, representatives of Unilever United States, Inc., also a Delaware corporation (Unilever), expressed interest in acquiring National Starch, which was one of its suppliers, through a friendly transaction. National Starch at the time had outstanding over 6,563,000 common shares held by approximately 3,700 shareholders. The stock was listed on the New York Stock Exchange. Frank and Anna Greenwall were the corporation's largest shareholders and owned approximately 14.5% of the common. The Greenwalls, getting along in years and concerned about their estate plans, indicated that they would transfer their shares to Unilever only if a transaction tax-free for them could be arranged.

Lawyers representing both sides devised a "reverse subsidiary cash merger" that they felt would satisfy the Greenwalls' concerns. Two new entities would be created--National Starch and Chemical Holding Corp. (Holding), a subsidiary

---

[42] *Indopco*, SCt, 92-1 USTC ¶50,113, 503 US 79, 112 SCt 1039.

of Unilever, and NSC Merger, Inc., a subsidiary of Holding that would have only a transitory existence. In an exchange specifically designed to be tax-free under §351 of the Internal Revenue Code, 26 U.S.C. §351 , Holding would exchange one share of its nonvoting preferred stock for each share of National Starch common that it received from National Starch shareholders. Any National Starch common that was not so exchanged would be converted into cash in a merger of NSC Merger, Inc., into National Starch.

In November 1977, National Starch's directors were formally advised of Unilever's interest and the proposed transaction. At that time, Debevoise, Plimpton, Lyons & Gates, National Starch's counsel, told the directors that under Delaware law they had a fiduciary duty to ensure that the proposed transaction would be fair to the shareholders. National Starch thereupon engaged the investment banking firm of Morgan Stanley & Co., Inc., to evaluate its shares, to render a fairness opinion, and generally to assist in the event of the emergence of a hostile tender offer. Although Unilever originally had suggested a price between $65 and $70 per share, negotiations resulted in a final offer of $73.50 per share, a figure Morgan Stanley found to be fair. Following approval by National Starch's board and the issuance of a favorable private ruling from the Internal Revenue Service that the transaction would be tax-free under §351 for those National Starch shareholders who exchanged their stock for Holding preferred, the transaction was consummated in August 1978.

Morgan Stanley charged National Starch a fee of $2,200,000, along with $7,586 for out-of-pocket expenses and $18,000 for legal fees. The Debevoise firm charged National Starch $490,000, along with $15,069 for out-of-pocket expenses. National Starch also incurred expenses aggregating $150,962 for miscellaneous items—such as accounting, printing, proxy solicitation, and Securities and Exchange Commission fees—in connection with the transaction. No issue is raised as to the propriety or reasonableness of these charges. On its federal income tax return for its short taxable year ended August 15, 1978, National Starch claimed a deduction for the $2,225,586 paid to Morgan Stanley, but did not deduct the $505,069 paid to Debevoise or the other expenses. Upon audit, the Commissioner of Internal Revenue disallowed the claimed deduction and issued a notice of deficiency. Petitioner sought redetermination in the United States Tax Court, asserting, however, not only the right to deduct the investment banking fees and expenses but, as well, the legal and miscellaneous expenses incurred.

Note: Affirming the 3rd Court of Appeals, which had affirmed the U.S. Tax Court

On its 1978 federal income tax return, Indopco, Inc., claimed a deduction for certain investment banking fees and expenses that it incurred during a friendly acquisition in which it was transformed from a publicly held, freestanding corporation into a wholly owned subsidiary. After the IRS disallowed the deduction, Indopco, Inc., took its claim to the Tax Court, claiming that the expenses were ordinary and necessary costs that did not create a "separate and distinct asset." The Tax Court ruled that because long-term benefits accrued to Indopco from the acquisition, the expenditures were capital in nature and not deductible under Code Sec. 162(a). The Court of Appeals affirmed, rejecting Indopco's argument that, because the expenses did not "create or enhance...a separate and distinct additional asset," they were deductible.

The Supreme Court held that deductions are exceptions to the norm of capitalization and are allowed only if there is clear provision for them in the Code and the taxpayer has met the burden of showing a right to the deduction. The Court noted that the creation of a separate and distinct asset may be a sufficient condition for classification as a capital expenditure, but it is not a prerequisite to such classification. Although the presence of an incidental future benefit may not warrant capitalization, a taxpayer's realization of benefits beyond the year in which the expenditure is incurred is important in determining whether the appropriate tax treatment is an immediate deduction or capitalization.

OBSERVATION   The U.S. Supreme Court also used the *Indopco* decision to clarify their earlier decision in *Lincoln Savings and Loan Association*. In the *Lincoln* case, the Court had stated that any expenditure that serves to "create or enhance a separate and distinct asset" should be capitalized under Code Sec. 263.[43] The taxpayer in *Indopco* argued that since the investment banking fees did not create such an asset, the expenditure could be deducted as an expense. However, the Supreme Court noted that their earlier decision in *Lincoln* in no way implied that only expenditures that create such a separate and distinct asset need to be capitalized. In *Wells Fargo & Co. v. Commissioner*, the 8th Circuit Court in ruling that the costs of expanding an existing business are deductible, noted that *Indopco* did not represent that all costs resulting in a future benefit beyond one tax year should be capitalized.[44]

The transaction in the *Indopco* case produced significant benefits to Indopco extending beyond the tax year in question. Thus, related expenses were capitalizable. Two key capitalization criteria were identified in *Indopco, Inc.* The creation of a separate and distinct asset may be a sufficient, but is not a necessary, condition to classification as a capital expenditure. Also, a taxpayer's realization of benefits beyond the year the expenditure is incurred is important in determining whether the appropriate tax treatment is a capitalization or current deduction. Yet, the mere presence of an incidental future benefit may not warrant capitalization. This is because many period expenses have effect beyond the tax year (e.g., repairs).

An interesting application of the *Indopco* decision is the tax treatment of environmental cleanup activities, such as toxic waste cleanups. This has been a long-standing area of disagreement between taxpayers and the IRS. In general, taxpayers have attempted to deduct environmental cleanup costs as ordinary and necessary business expenses. On the other hand, the IRS has argued that such costs are more in the nature of nondeductible capital expenditures. They have used the Supreme Court's *Indopco, Inc.* decision for support. For example, in Technical Advice Memorandum (TAM) 9240004, the IRS ruled that the costs of removing and replacing asbestos insulation in certain manufacturing equipment should be capitalized as improvements or betterments to the property under Code Sec. 263. In addition to reducing or eliminating the human health risks posed by the presence of asbestos, the expenditures increased the value of the taxpayer's equipment and made the taxpayer's property more marketable.

Similarly, in TAM 9315004, the Service ruled that the costs of an environmental cleanup of PCB contamination are also improvements or betterments under Code Sec. 263. In this TAM, the Service specifically noted that "costs of the environmental cleanup activities are capital expenditures. The extensive modifications to the taxpayer's property under the cleanup operation constitute replacement and betterments…the rehabilitation will benefit the taxpayer's property for the duration of the useful life of the system."

The IRS positions in the two TAMs created much controversy, and in 1994 the IRS agreed to reconsider the treatment of various environmental remediation activities. One of the first taxpayer-friendly rulings as a result of this process is Rev. Rul. 94-38.[45] In this ruling, the Service permitted current deductions for an accrual-basis corporation for ongoing soil remediation and groundwater treatment costs incurred because of hazardous waste discharged as part of its manufacturing process. The Service noted that the expenditures did not increase the value of the property in comparison to its value before contamination. However, the cost of any tangible groundwater treatment facilities would be capitalized, since they have an extended useful life.

---

[43] *Lincoln Savings and Loan Association*, 403 US 45.
[44] *Wells Fargo and Co.*, CA-8, 2000-2 USTC ¶50,697, 224 F3d 874.
[45] Rev. Rul 94-38, 1994-1 CB 35.

¶6017.05

OBSERVATION

In a more recent case, an S corporation was not entitled to deduct, as ordinary business expenses, environmental remediation costs incurred subsequent to the purchase of contaminated commercial properties that were previously operated as gas stations.[46] The properties were contaminated *prior* to the taxpayer's purchase; thus, its expenditures did not restore the properties to their condition at the time of purchase. Moreover, the Court noted that the taxpayer did not contaminate the properties through its normal business operations, and its expenditures increased the value of the properties.

With all the controversy concerning capitalization issues following the *Indopco* decision, the IRS initiated a regulations project on capitalization in general. This resulted in a set of new regulations issued in 2008 and then reissued in 2011 which are summarized below in the additional notes.

.07   **MEDICAL REIMBURSEMENT PLANS AND THE ALL-EVENTS TEST**

U.S. v. General Dynamics Corp.[47]

Facts of the Case: General Dynamics uses the accrual method of accounting for federal tax purposes; its fiscal year is the same as the calendar year. From 1962 until October 1, 1972, General Dynamics purchased group medical insurance for its employees and their qualified dependents from two private insurance carriers. Beginning in October, 1972, General Dynamics became a self-insurer with regard to its medical care plans. Instead of continuing to purchase insurance from outside carriers, it undertook to pay medical claims out of its own funds, while continuing to employ private carriers to administer the medical care plans. To receive reimbursement of expenses for covered medical services, respondent's employees submit claims forms to employee benefits personnel, who verify that the treated persons were eligible under the applicable plan as of the time of treatment. Eligible claims are then forwarded to the plan's administrators. Claims processors review the claims and approve for payment those expenses that are covered under the plan.

Because the processing of claims takes time, and because employees do not always file their claims immediately, there is a delay between the provision of medical services and payment by General Dynamics. To account for this time lag, General Dynamics established reserve accounts to reflect its liability for medical care received, but still not paid for, as of December 31, 1972. It estimated the amount of those reserves with the assistance of its former insurance carriers. Originally, General Dynamics did not deduct any portion of this reserve in computing its tax for 1972. In 1977, however, after the IRS began an audit of its 1972 tax return, General Dynamics filed an amended return, claiming it was entitled to deduct its reserve as an accrued expense, and seeking a refund. The IRS disallowed the deduction, and General Dynamics sought relief in the Claims Court.

Note: Reversing the Claims Court

This case clarifies the concept of the all events test as it applies to accruals for estimated expenses. In this case, the IRS denied an accrual for estimated payments under the company's self-insurance program, noting that the "event" that fixes the fact of a liability was when the claims were received by the company and approved for payment. The company claimed that the "event" that fixed the liability was when the employee incurred the medical expense; therefore, they were justified in estimating the outstanding

---

[46]   *United Dairy Farmers, Inc.*, CA-6, 2001-2 USTC ¶50,680.
[47]   *General Dynamics Corp.*, SCt, 87-1 USTC ¶9280, 481 US 239, 107 SCt 1732.

(but unfiled) claims at the end of the year, as long as the accrual was reasonably estimated.

The Supreme Court ruled that General Dynamics could not deduct the accrued but unpaid claims because it failed the all events test. Specifically, the Court ruled that the filing of the claim by the employee, and not the receipt of medical services by the employee, was the event that fixes the fact of the liability. In effect, the filing of the claim was viewed by the court as a significant condition precedent to the recognition of the deduction. Obviously, the taxpayer argued that the possibility that employees would not file a claim was extremely remote and should not be a factor. Nonetheless, the Court considered such filing more than a mere technicality, and not just a "ministerial duty."

One of the cases that the taxpayer relied on in its defense was *Hughes Properties*, where the Supreme Court had approved of a casino's method of accruing a progressive jackpot on its slot machines.[48] In essence, the Court ruled that every pull of the lever increased the liability, since it was all but certain that the jackpot would eventually be paid (who would choose not to file this claim if they won the jackpot?) The Court distinguished this decision because there were no further conditions precedent to payment other than the pulls of the slot machine handle. (Interesting note: the IRS agreed that a pull of the handle fixed the fact of the liability—but it had to be the winning pull!)

Judge O'Connor dissented in the *General Dynamics* decision, arguing that she saw no essential differences in facts from the *Hughes* decision. Judge O'Connor noted that the company was required to pay under the medical reimbursement plan even if the company were bankrupt or even if they had fired the employee. She also lamented the fact that this decision further drives a wedge between financial accounting and tax accounting.

OBSERVATION   An interesting application of the all events test is to the issue of cooperative advertising arrangements. In such an arrangement, a wholesaler agrees to reimburse a retailer for local advertising that mentions both the wholesaler's product and the retail dealer's location. Typically, the dealer had to fill out a reimbursement form and submit it, along with a copy of the ad, to the wholesaler for reimbursement. The question arose as to when the all events test is met for the wholesaler to accrue a liability for estimated payments to dealers. Initially, the IRS contended in TAM 9416004 that the liability was fixed only when the claim was submitted; however, in Rev. Rul. 98-39, the Service ruled that the accrual was permitted as soon as the advertising was run. This result better squared with PLR 9143083, which concluded that the wholesaler had income as soon as the ad was placed, and that submitting and reviewing the claim was just a "ministerial act."

.09   METHODS OF ACCOUNTING—ADDITIONAL CASES

A. E. Staley v. Commissioner.[49] Unlike the *General Dynamics* case, which involved a friendly takeover, the legal and accounting costs incurred in this case related to a hostile takeover. In this case, the Court ruled that such expenditures were deductible, noting that no long-run benefits were promised. However, the Court noted that if any of the costs facilitated the merger, they should be capitalized.

Ohio Collieries, Inc. v. Commissioner.[50] Perhaps more than any other event, this case convinced the IRS of the necessity of asking Congress to legislate some type of economic performance requirement in the Code. In this case, an accrual-basis coal company deducted the estimated reclamation costs required under state law once a strip-mining operation was completed. The estimated reclamation costs include such things as refilling, grading, resoiling, and planting mining areas. The Tax Court allowed the taxpayer to deduct such estimates because the estimated costs met the all events test, even though actual payment of such reclamation costs would in some cases occur

---

[48] *Hughes Properties*, SCt, 476 US 593.
[49] *A.E. Staley Manufacturing Company*, CA-7, 97-2 USTC ¶50,521, 119 F3d 482.
[50] *Ohio River Collieries*, 77 TC 1369 (1981).

years after mining operations had been completed. The IRS believed that this decision had stretched the "all events" test much too far and that taxpayers would now feel free to accrue and deduct expenditures that would not actually be paid until several years in the future. One solution to the problem would be to apply present value concepts to the accrual, but in the end, Congress favored the economic performance test as a final hurdle for deductibility of accrued expenses.

T.D. 9564. At the end of 2011, the IRS issued proposed and temporary regulations on the capitalization issue (T.D. 9564). These regulations replaced a 2008 set of temporary regulations that proved so controversial that they were eventually withdrawn. Figure 2 provides a summary of these regulations and examples adapted from the regulations. These regulations are likely to be finalized in 2013, and would be effective beginning in 2014.

As noted in Figure 2, the regulations rely on the concept of a "unit of property" as the basis for determining whether or not costs are capitalized or deducted. For property other than buildings, a single unit of property includes all components that are *functionally interdependent*, i.e., each component depends on the placing in service of another component. This test is based more or less on the decision in *FedEx Corporation, 412 F3d 617 (CA-6, 2005), affirming 291 F.Supp. 2d 699 (W.D. Tennessee, 2003)* where the court determined that an engine is a functionally interdependent part of a fully-assembled aircraft, and therefore treated periodic scheduled "heavy maintenance" on such engines (removing, cleaning, and testing the engine) as deductible repair expenses. The court noted that "Although new engines and APUs were separately manufactured and sold separately from new airframes, the engines and APUs were designed to be compatible with certain airframes, were acquired at the same time as those airframes, and were delivered to FedEx as part of the completely assembled aircraft or as spares to fit the specific airframe type being acquired." Thus, when using the cost of the aircraft as a point of reference (instead of the cost of a replacement engine), the *heavy maintenance costs* were considered much more reasonable. Similar logic had prevailed in the case of tugboat engines in *Ingram Industries, T.C. Memo 2000-323.*

OBSERVATION
In the discussion of capitalization of amounts paid to facilitate certain capital transactions, the Service noted that capitalization is required only for those costs that are either "inherently facilitative" or related to activities taking place after a "bright line" date. These tests replace the "but for" assumption used in cases related to the *Indopco* decision (i.e., the cost would not have been incurred "but for" the purpose of acquisition). The phrase *"inherently facilitative"* refers to such costs as investigating and pursuing the transaction, determining the value of the target, structuring the transaction, or seeking tax advice. The *"bright-line date"* is the earlier of (1) the date of a signed letter of intent or other written communication or (2) the date material items of the transaction are approved by the Board of Directors. Costs incurred after this date are presumed to be capitalizable expenditures.

Figure 1:

Summary – Capitalization Regulations of T.D. 9564
(Interpreting Secs. 162(a), 168, and 263)

1. **Unit of Property Standard** – The appropriate basis for determining whether or not costs should be expensed or capitalized is a "unit of property," where all components of that property are functionally interdependent (i.e., the hard drive and the motherboard are all components of a single unit of property, a computer, but a computer and an printer are separate units of property). Two exceptions to the general rule are for (1) components of plant property that perform a discrete or major function or operation within the functional equipment (i.e., the electrical system), and (2) a component that uses a different MACRS class or recovery method.

Example 6-3. A trucking company segregates the cost of tires from the total cost of a tractor-trailer, and recovers their cost over a shorter MACRS period. The tires are separate units of property.

2. *Routine Maintenance Activities* – The cost of routine maintenance activities (i.e., inspection, cleaning, testing, and replacement of parts with comparable parts) may be expensed, if at the time the property is placed in service, the taxpayer expects to perform the activity more than once during the *MACRS class life* of the unit of property. This safe harbor rule does not apply to (1) buildings or their structural components, or (2) the replacement of a component if the adjusted basis of the old component had been included in the loss on the sale or exchange, or loss from casualty of that component. (Note – this does not mean that the expenditure must be capitalized, as further investigation may reveal that the expenditure did not result in a betterment, restoration, or new or better use.)

Example 6-4. A trucking company sells its used tires (treated as a separate component) to a junkyard at a loss at the end of their useful life. The cost of the replacement tires does not fit within the safe harbor described above, and thus cannot be treated as routine maintenance.

3. *Materials and Supplies* – Materials and supplies are defined as tangible property that is used or consumed in the taxpayer's operations, is not inventory, and is (1) a component used to maintain or improve a unit of property, (2) fuel, lubricants, water, etc., (3) property having a life of less than 12 months, (4) property costing less than $100 per unit, or (5) other items identified in future regulations. The materials and supplies may be either *incidental* (those for which no inventory or record of consumption is kept, which usually means currently deductible) or *nonincidental* (all others, which are generally deductible only when used in operations). The three possible tax treatments are (a) deduct when acquired under the de minimis rules described below, (b) deduct in the year used, or (c) capitalize and depreciate.

Example 6-5. Ace Construction does not keep a record or an inventory of nails, screws, and bolts used on the job. The cost of these items is deductible when purchased.

4. *De Minimis Rules* – Special *de minimis* rules apply for the costs of acquiring or producing a unit of property, or to repair or improve existing tangible property (other than land or inventory). To qualify, the taxpayer must have (1) a written accounting procedure (in place at the beginning of the year) for expensing property costing less than a specified amount, (2) an "applicable financial statement" (audited, regulatory, or SEC submission), and (3) expensed the property in the same manner in the financial statement. If these requirements are met, the taxpayer is allowed a current deduction of property, materials and supplies less than or equal to the larger of (a) *0.1% of gross receipts* for the year disclosed on the tax return, or (b) *2% of total depreciation or amortization deducted on the financial statements.* Note – if the expenditures are larger than the *de minimis* amount, the taxpayer MUST elect to capitalize the excess; otherwise, *none* qualify for the *de minimis* rule.

Example 6-6. Tee Corporation has $60,000,000 gross receipts for tax purposes and $1,800,000 book depreciation in 2013. The maximum amount deductible as repairs or maintenance under the *de minimis* rule is $60,000 ($60,000,000 × .001), since this exceeds 2% of book depreciation, or $36,000. If Tee has $77,000 of costs qualifying for the *de minimis* amount in 2013, they must elect to capitalize $17,000 of such costs; otherwise, none of the amounts will be deductible under the *de minimis* safe harbor.

5. *Betterments, Restorations, and Adaptations* – The regulations define three types of expenditures that must be capitalized: betterments, restorations, and adaptations to a new or different use:

Betterment – The term includes (1) amelioration of a material defect that existed prior to the acquisition of property or arose in the production of the property, (2) a material addition to the unit of property, such as expansion or enlargement, or (3) a material increase in capacity, productivity, strength, efficiency, quality or output of the property. For example, the replacement of wood shingles with asphalt shingles that are better quality with a longer warranty would be treated a betterment.

Restoration – A restoration includes the replacement of a component where the taxpayer deducted a loss on the component, used the basis of the component in a gain or loss computation or a casualty loss computation, returning a unit to a functioning state when the unit had deteriorated to the point of no longer functioning, rebuilding a unit to like-new condition at the end of its class life, or replacing a major component or substantial structure of a unit of property. In the latter case, a facts and circumstances approach is used to determine if the replacement is "major" or "substantial."

New or Different Use – A "new or different use" is a use that is not consistent with the taxpayer's intended ordinary use of the unit of property at the time the taxpayer originally placed the property in service. For example, a tobacco farming operation rehabilitating several warehouses and modifying them to serve as curing rooms for tobacco would have to capitalize the conversion costs.

6. *Dispositions of Structural Components* – Taxpayers using "general asset accounts" (i.e., grouping all assets acquired during the year that use the same depreciation method, MACRS life, and acquisition-year assumption into a single account) may recognize losses on the sale, abandonment, or retirement of structural components by using any reasonable allocation method to determine the cost and adjusted basis of such component.

¶6019 Summary

- The four positive criteria of a deduction require that the expenditure be (1) incurred in a permissible activity, (2) ordinary, (3) necessary, and (4) reasonable in amount.
- The four negative criteria of a deduction require that the expenditure not be (1) a capital expenditure, (2) a personal expenditure, (3) related to tax-exempt income, or (4) contrary to public policy.
- A cash-basis taxpayer generally may take a deduction only if the expenditure in question has been incurred ("used up") and is paid.
- An accrual-basis taxpayer may take a deduction only if (1) all events have occurred to fix the fact of the liability, (2) the liability is reasonably estimable, and (3) economic performance has occurred.

- Economic performance occurs in one of four situations: (1) goods or services provided *to* the taxpayer, (2) property is used by the taxpayer, (3) goods or services are provided *by* the taxpayer, and (4) the expenditure is classified as a payment liability.
- The major court decisions in testing the deduction criteria include:
  - *Gilmore* (divorce costs are inherently personal in origin, and thus are nondeductible).
  - *Welch v. Helvering* (voluntary repayments of cancelled debts fail the "ordinary" test for deductibility).
  - *Tank Truck Rentals* (illegal payments that frustrate public policy are not deductible).
- The major court decisions differentiating business vs. personal expenses include:
  - *Flowers* (transportation costs between the taxpayer's abode and his or her post of duty fail the "pursuit of business" test for deduction).
  - *Whipple* (investor status does not by itself justify business bad debt status for a loan from a shareholder to a corporation).
- The major court decisions involving methods of accounting for deductions include:
  - *Boylston Markets* (prepaid expenses are allocable over the period of usage).
  - *Dixie Pine Products* (accrual for contested liabilities that are not paid are not deductible under final court adjudication).
  - *Indopco* (legal and accounting fees incurred in a friendly merger are capitalizable, as future benefits are expected to be realized).
  - *General Dynamics* (accruals for expected expenditures under a self-insurance plan fail the all events test and are not deductible).

Review Questions for Chapter 6

True or False

Indicate which of the following statements are true or false by circling the correct answer.

1. An expenditure is not deductible unless it is specifically authorized by the Code or Regulations.   T   F

2. An intention to make a profit is sufficient condition for an activity to be classified as a trade or business under Code Sec. 162.   T   F

3. Purely personal expenditures are deductible only if they are specifically provided in the Code as deductions.   T   F

4. A rebate paid by an accrual-basis manufacturer to a retail dealer is deductible as soon as the manufacturer receives notification from the sales department that a sale has been made.   T   F

5. Legal expenses incurred in a divorce are generally deductible.   T   F

6. In the *Tank Truck Rentals* case, the Court allowed the taxpayer to deduct those fines that were unintentionally incurred.   T   F

7. Any expenses incurred in an illegal activity other than trafficking illegal drugs are generally deductible.   T   F

8. In *Flowers v. Commissioner*, the IRS finally resolved the controversy over the definition of a taxpayer's "home" for tax purposes.   T   F

9. The *Zaninovich* rule allows a cash-basis taxpayer to deduct certain prepayments of up to one year if the expenditure is treated consistently from year to year.   T   F

10. Contested liabilities are never deductible.   T   F

Fill in the Blanks

Fill in each blank with the appropriate word or phrase that completes each sentence.

11. The two "umbrella" provisions that allow numerous items as deductions under the Internal Revenue Code are Code Secs. 162 and _____.

12. When a cost has expired and the full benefit was not received from the expenditure, such a cost is categorized as a(n) _____.

13. An activity is presumed to be a hobby unless a profit is shown from the activity in at least _____ of the preceding five years.

14. An expenditure that would be acceptable or commonplace among other taxpayers who find themselves in comparable circumstances is said to be _____.

15. A prepayment for services is deductible when paid by an accrual-basis taxpayer near year-end if the services will be provided within _____ months of the payment.

16. The *Gilmore* decision on the deductibility of divorce costs concluded that the _____ or the expense determines the ultimate deductibility of such costs.

17. In the *Welch v. Helvering* case, the Court determined that the voluntary payments made by Welch to his former business associates, while probably being necessary, were not _____.

18. As a general rule, the Internal Revenue Service regards a taxpayer's "home" for tax purposes as being the location where the taxpayer _____.

19. In the *Whipple* case, the Supreme Court remanded the case back to the lower courts for a determination as to whether or not the taxpayer could take a business bad debt deduction in his capacity as a _____.

20. In the *Hughes Properties* case involving a casino, the Supreme Court _____ (did, did not) view the payment of a progressive jackpot as a mere ministerial event.

Multiple Choice

Circle the best answer for each of the following questions.

21. To be deductible under Code Sec. 162, an expenditure must be:
    a. ordinary
    b. necessary
    c. reasonable in amount
    d. all of the above

22. Which of the following expenditures is not deductible under Code Sec. 212?
    a. $80 safety deposit box rental used to store securities held as an investment
    b. $2,400 alimony paid to a former spouse during the year
    c. $200 fee for preparation of a U.S. federal gift tax return
    d. all of the above are deductible under Code Sec. 212

23. Which of the following items would be deductible?
    a. a $400 payment to a county supervisor for a driveway to taxpayer's business (no county statute for bribes)
    b. a $200 speeding ticket
    c. a $300 interest charge on the underpayment of federal income tax
    d. none of the above are deductible

24. Mason Adams, a cash-basis, calendar-year taxpayer, borrows $10,000 on a 90-day, six-percent note on November 1, 2013. The $10,000 principal and $150 interest for the three months is repaid on February 1, 2014. On Mason's 2013 tax return, he may deduct interest expense of:
    a. $0
    b. $50
    c. $100
    d. $150

25. Which of the following is not a condition for the "recurring item exception" to apply?
    a. the all events test has been met
    b. the amount is reasonably estimable
    c. economic performance occurs no later than 3½ months after the end of the year of payment
    d. all of the above are conditions for the recurring item exception rule

26. In the *Dixie Pine Products* case, the central issue on state tax payments involved:
    a. an accrual of a tax by the taxpayer that had not yet been paid due to litigation
    b. a payment of a tax by the taxpayer that had not yet been accrued due to litigation
    c. the deductibility of a state tax payment on the federal return in any year
    d. none of the above

27. The key new finding in the *Indopco* case by the U.S. Supreme Court was that:
    a. some intangible costs may have to be capitalized
    b. merger banking fees may be deductible, but merger accounting costs are not
    c. a separate and distinct asset does not have to be created in order for an intangible to be capitalized.
    d. the costs of fighting off a hostile takeover are generally never deductible

28. The IRS has made clear that the costs of soil remediation for an environmental hazard:
    a. are never deductible
    b. are generally always deductible
    c. are capitalizable and depreciable
    d. none of the above

29. In the *General Dynamics* case, the event that fixed the fact of a liability was:
    a. the actual incurrence of medical expenses by the employee
    b. a precise estimate of the claim amounts to be filed by year-end
    c. the filing of a claim for reimbursement of medical expenses by the employee
    d. the offer in writing of a company reimbursement plan

30. In order for the recurring item exception rules to apply, deducting the expenditure in question early must be justified by the fact that:
    a. the item is immaterial
    b. the current deduction results in a better matching of income
    c. either (a) or (b)
    d. both (a) and (b)

Review Problems

DRT Company is a manufacturer of gasoline-powered go-karts and other power products. DRT is a calendar-year, accrual-basis taxpayer. DRT generally files their tax return by the extended due date (8½ months following the close of the tax year). In late December, representatives of DRT ask for your assistance in determining the appropriate deduction for the current year for 10 different items described in the chart below. DRT is willing to elect the recurring item exception for any item listed, and all amounts are assumed to be material. In addition, DRT also has two specific questions regarding the reporting of intangibles related to (1) the acquisition of a business during the year and (2) the disposition of two intangibles from an acquisition six years ago. Information for these two questions is provided the last two sections of the chart shown below.

Questionable Item	Proposed Deduction by DRT
31. On November 1 of the current year, DRT paid rent for 10 months in advance for a utility warehouse (a total of $48,000). In addition, DRT paid a $5,000 damage deposit on the property, refundable at the end of the lease if no damage exists. Assume that the amount is material.	$53,000
32. In relaying the information on the rental agreement in (1) above, a Vice President at DRT asks if the result would be different if DRT used the cash method of accounting. DRT is considering the acquisition of a services provider that uses the cash method, and they are curious as to how certain items would be handled under a system. Answer for the cash method, based on the facts in (1).	$53,000

33. DRT rents crate-making machinery from Arrow Rentals. On October 1 of the current year, DRT prepaid a basic two-year rental fee of $360,000. In addition, the lease provides that if DRT produces more than 200,000 crates, an extra rental charge of $60,000 is immediately due, along with a variable charge of $3 for each crate made in excess of 200,000 under the lease. As of the end of the current year, DRT has produced 85,000 crates, and they estimate that the total crates produced under the lease will be approximately 240,000 (with 100,000 of those being produced next year).	$360,000
34. Auditors from the State Tax Commission recently informed DRT that a solvent furnished with their products sold was subject to a special fuel tax under state law. The tax computed on current-year sales is $260,000. DRT paid the $260,000 to the tax Commission on December 15 under protest, and file the necessary paperwork to contest the tax. The case is to be heard in April of next year. Attorneys for DRT estimate their chances of winning at approximately 40 percent.	$260,000
35. DRT provides a full six-month warranty for all go-karts sold. Using statistical estimates that have proven fairly reliable in the past, DRT estimates that the warranty expense related to current-year sales is $580,000. As of December 31 of the current year, DRT had incurred $470,000 of actual expenses (parts and labor) related to current-year sales; the remaining warranty work for current-year sales is expected to occur uniformly over the first six months of the next year. DRT accrued the $580,000 as the current-year warranty expense on their financial accounting records.	$580,000
36. For the first time, during the current year DRT offered a $75 rebate to retail customers on sales of their top-of-the-line go-kart. The rebate offer covers purchases up to the end of the current year, and customers must submit the rebate form with proof of purchase no later than January 31 of next year. Rebates will be mailed to customers in March of next year. DRT has received requests for $340,000 in rebates by the end of the current year, and their sales records indicate that total rebate coupons outstanding (and not received) at the end of the current year total an additional $100,000. DRT plans to continue to offer the rebate program each fall in the future.	$440,000
37. On December 22, DRT purchased $30,000 of postage from the U.S. Postal Service. DRT expects to use the entire amount by March 1 of next year.	$30,000
38. During the spring of the current year, DRT leased 100 acres of land to construct a sunken racetrack for purposes of demonstrating their products to potential buyers. The lease agreement required DRT to reclaim the land when the lease expired in November, returning the land to its original condition. DRT estimates that this work will cost $560,000. As of the end of the current year, DRT had spent $130,000 on the reclamation project.	$560,000

39. DRT has requested assistance in classifying three expenditures that are potentially subject to capitalization. The questionable items are:
  a. a $430,000 expenditure to remove a poisonous lead chemical from the basement of the factory building (the problem was discovered when architects were drafting plans for a complete factory renovation of $6,000,000, due to begin in February of next year)
  b. a $560,000 expenditure to excavate contaminated soil and backfill with uncontaminated soil at the factory location; DRT discovered the contamination during the current year that was caused by a chemical leak of the former owner of the plant
  c. a $210,000 expenditure for a new advertising campaign designed to attract new customers from the over-30 market
	$1,200,000

40. As part of a court-supervised $2,400,000 settlement related to a personal injury lawsuit concerning an explosion at the test track, DRT contributed $300,000 to qualified settlement fund for the victims. DRT is legally required to contribute the same amount in each of the next seven years. As of the end of the current year, the $300,000 had not yet been distributed from the fund to the victims. (Hint: see Reg §1.468B.)	$2,400,000

41. DRT acquired the assets of Maybe Company on September 1 of the current year, and placed these assets in service in their own business on November 1 of the current year. DRT would like to know the appropriate Code Sec. 197 deduction for the year on these assets. DRT believes that the following assets (with assumed values displayed) would be capitalizable as Code Sec. 197 assets:
  • State and local manufacturing permits $300,000
  • Covenant not to compete for 10 years   450,000
  • Specialized computer design programs for a new style go-kart drafted and coded by the prior owner 150,000
	60,000

42. DRT acquired the assets of Rudder Company exactly six years ago. One of the Code Sec. 197 intangibles acquired in the purchase was a patent for $1,500,000. During the current year, DRT sold the patent for $820,000. This is the only Code Sec. 197 intangible sold from the original acquisition. What is DRT's deductible loss on the sale of the patent? (Hint: see Reg. §1.197-2(g).)	$780,000

43. Would the *Hughes Property* and *General Dynamics* cases likely be decided in the same manner if such cases followed the enactment of the economic performance rules? Explain.
44. Do the loss deduction rules generally follow the same statutory pattern as the expense deduction rules in the Code? Explain.
45. Did the *Flowers* decision resolve the issue of the definition of a "tax home"? Explain.
46. "An expense may never be deducted before it is incurred, even for a cash-basis taxpayer." Do you agree with this statement? Explain.
47. Is it possible for a shareholder/employee to take a business bad debt deduction on a loan to the corporation in which the shareholder/employee owns stock? Explain.
48. Tech Company, an accrual-basis computer manufacturer, began offering a one-year warranty on their computers sold in 2013. As of December 31, 2013, they have paid out $45,000 in expenses honoring warranties, and they estimate that the remaining warranty claims yet to be filed on the 2013 sales are $16,000. In 2014, the actual amount of remaining claims from 2013 sales that were filed in 2014 turned out to be $16,012, all of which were completely repaired within the first four months of the year. May Tech deduct the $16,000, in addition to the $45,000 amount, in 2013 by electing to use the recurring item exception?

Research Problems

49. A cash-basis taxpayer paid an estimated state intangible property tax. The tax was paid early, and the state law did not have any provision for such prepayments. May the taxpayer deduct the estimated payment as taxes on her federal income tax return, assuming that the state accepts payment? Explain.

50. Anne White, a client who lives in Richmond, has owned a second property in Wintergreen for three years. Each year, the taxpayer rents the property during the winter months (December through March), and uses the property for personal reasons for the entire month of July. However, for two of those three years, her daughter Ellen lived in the property for those three months, paying less than fair rental. For the remainder of the year, rentals are sporadic, usually totaling about 100 days. The taxpayer would now like to deduct interest paid on the mortgage on this property as interest on a second personal residence. A colleague told you that you probably should check Code Sec. 280A(d) on vacation homes to see when (if at all) such a rental would be classified as a "residence." Check this Code section, and follow links to find an answer to the client's question.

Planning Problems

51. Mary Allen, an accrual-basis calendar-year taxpayer, owns and operates a department store in Raleigh, North Carolina. In December 2013 Mary contracts with Ace Bladers to remove snow from her parking lot during the winter season. The charge for this service is $4,000 (come snow or sunshine), and Mary receives the bill on December 27, 2013. What advice would you give Mary?

Compliance Problems

52. If a company decides to use the recurring item exception to the economic performance rules, must they request permission to do so from the IRS? In other words, is the recurring item exception a "method of accounting"? Explain.

CHAPTER 7

Landmark Judicial Decisions—Property Transactions

Learning Objectives

Upon completion of this chapter you will:
1. Understand the definition of a capital asset.
2. Understand the capital gain and loss netting process for individuals and corporations.
3. Understand the Code Sec. 1231 tax treatment of dispositions of business use assets.
4. Understand the Code Sec. 1245 and 1250 ordinary income depreciation recapture provisions.
5. Understand how to defer recognition of gains and losses on Code Sec. 1031 like-kind exchanges and Code Sec. 1033 involuntary conversions.

¶7001 Introduction

The courts have played a major role in shaping the tax law with regard to the sale or exchange of properties. For all of its importance, the term "capital asset" is never really defined in the Internal Revenue Code. Instead the Code merely lists properties that are *never* treated as capital assets. These exceptions (discussed below) are generally based on the theory that none of the items are entitled to capital gains treatment.

This chapter reviews the major judicial decisions that have influenced the reporting of gains and losses from the sale or exchange of property. This discussion is preceded by a review of the capital asset definition, the capital gain and loss netting procedures for individuals and corporations, and the Code Sec. 1231 netting procedure for sales and exchanges of properties used in a trade or business.

¶7003   The Capital Asset Definition

Code Sec. 1221 (**Figure 1**) defines (in a negative fashion) a **capital asset**. Several observations are relevant in examining this Code section. First, this provision applies "within this subtitle," which refers to Subtitle A of the Internal Revenue Code, Income Taxes.[1] Second, the items listed in Code Sec. 1221 are not automatically relegated to ordinary income or loss treatment. For example, Code Sec. 1231 operates to treat certain net gains on the sale or exchange of business properties as capital gain, even though these properties are not capital assets. By the same token, property *not* listed in Code Sec. 1221 are not automatically granted capital asset status, even though Reg. §1.1221-1(a) states that the term "*includes all classes of property not specifically excluded by Sec. 1221.*" Several of these properties are discussed in the cases below.

Although the Code does not provide a straight-forward definition of a capital asset, Congress has provided a number of statutory inclusions for this treatment. For example, Code Sec. 166(d)(1)(B) states that a nonbusiness bad debt is reported as a short-term capital loss. Other statutory inclusions are discussed in this chapter.

Many of the cases discussed in this chapter involve the definitional problem of a capital asset, it may prove worthwhile to examine each of the exceptions to capital gains treatment and to provide the rationale for each exception.

.01   CODE SEC. 1221(a)(1)—INVENTORY AND SIMILAR PROPERTIES HELD PRIMARILY FOR RESALE

In enacting Code Sec. 1221(a)(1), Congress wanted to distinguish business properties from investment properties. The courts generally view gains from inventory-type properties as primarily attributable to the taxpayer's personal efforts, and taxable the same as personal services income. Of course, the problem is determining if a property is "held primarily for resale." For example, are demo autos held by a car dealer inventory? Generally, the answer is yes!

Figure 1

Code Sec. 1221. Capital asset defined.

(a)   In general, for purposes of this subtitle, the term "capital asset" means property held by the taxpayer (whether or not connected with his trade or business), but does not include—

    (1)   stock in trade of the taxpayer or other property of a kind which would properly be included in the inventory of the taxpayer if on hand at the close of the taxable year, or property held by the taxpayer primarily for sale to customers in the ordinary course of his trade or business;

    (2)   property, used in his trade or business, of a character which is subject to the allowance for depreciation provided in section 167, or real property used in his trade or business;

    (3)   a copyright, a literary, musical, or artistic composition, a letter or memorandum, or similar property, held by—

       (A)   a taxpayer whose personal efforts created such property,

       (B)   in the case of a letter, memorandum, or similar property, a taxpayer for whom such property was prepared or produced, or

---

[1]   Code Secs. 1–1563.

(C)   a taxpayer in whose hands the basis of such property is determined (other than by reason of Sec. 1022), for purposes of determining gain from a sale or exchange, in whole or part by reference to the basis of such property in the hands of a taxpayer described in paragraph (A) or (B);

(4)   accounts or notes receivable acquired in the ordinary course of trade or business for services rendered or from the sale of property described in paragraph (1);

(5)   a publication of the United States government (including the Congressional Record) which is received from the United States Government or any agency thereof, other than by purchase at the price at which it is offered for sale to the public, and which is held by—

(A)   a taxpayer who so received such publication, or

(B)   a taxpayer in whose hands the basis of such publication is determined, for purposes of determining gain from a sale or exchange, in whole or in part by reference to the basis of such publication in the hands of a taxpayer described in subparagraph (A).

(6)   any commodities derivative financial instrument held by a commodities derivatives dealer, unless—

(A)   it is established to the satisfaction of the Secretary that such instrument has no connection with the activities of such dealer as a dealer, and

(B)   such instrument is clearly identified in such dealer's records as being described in subparagraph (A) before the close of the day on which it was acquired, originated, or entered into (or such time as the Secretary may prescribe regulations);

(7)   any hedging transaction which is clearly identified as such before the close of the day on which it was acquired, originated, or entered into (or such other time as the Secretary may prescribe regulations); or

(8)   supplies of a type regularly used or consumed by the taxpayer in the ordinary course of a trade or business of the taxpayer.

.03   CODE SEC. 1221(a)(2)—PROPERTIES USED PRODUCTIVELY IN A TRADE OR BUSINESS

Code Sec. 1221(a)(2) was enacted in 1938 to exempt business properties from the capital asset definition so that taxpayers selling an asset at a loss during the depression could report the loss as an ordinary loss. By 1942 taxpayers became concerned about the ordinary *gains* on sales, since many taxpayers were selling assets at a gain to the government (often involuntarily) to support the war effort. Congress responded by enacting Code Sec. 117(n), the forerunner of Code Sec. 1231, which allows taxpayers the best of both tax worlds on these properties: a net gain on the sale is taxed as a long-term capital gain, and a net loss is deductible as an ordinary loss. This netting process is discussed later in this chapter.

The phrase "property used in a trade or business" has created some definitional problems. The Code Sec. 1221(a)(2) definition virtually mirrors the Code Sec. 1231 definition of business property. The phrase "used" has been interpreted liberally by the courts; for example: lots sold by the taxpayer were not used in any trade or business and were not held primarily for sale to customers in the regular ordinary course of business. The loss sustained on the sale was, therefore, a capital loss.[2] However, in a similar case the court held that the question of whether certain property subdivided and sold by the taxpayer

[2] *Jay Burns*, 14 TCM 544, TC Memo 1955-147.

was property held for sale to customers in the ordinary course of business was a question of fact, and that gains from the sale were reportable as ordinary income.[3]

.05 CODE SEC. 1221(a)(3)—COPYRIGHTS AND OTHER ARTISTIC COMPOSITIONS

As noted earlier, copyrights and other artistic compositions are automatically excluded from capital gains treatment, primarily because they are the result of the taxpayer's personal efforts and are equivalent to inventory. The ordinary income taint also applies to a carryover basis recipient, and in the case of letters, memoranda, and similar property, also to the person for whom the property was produced. These restrictions were designed to prevent a charitable deduction based upon the fair market value of what is in essence "ordinary income" property.

> **OBSERVATION** Although copyrights are excluded from the capital asset definition, patents are not. Congress excluded copyrights after a court had ruled that Dwight Eisenhower was an "amateur writer" and thus could report copyright royalties from his book *Crusade in Europe* as capital gains. At the same time, they did not include patents because they wanted to retain an incentive for inventive activity in the Code. Thus the expression, it is better to "invent rather than create."

.07 CODE SEC. 1221(a)(4)—ORDINARY ACCOUNTS AND NOTES RECEIVABLES

The Code Sec. 1221(a)(4) exception to capital asset treatment, added in 1954, ensures that both gains and losses from the sale or exchange of ordinary business accounts and notes receivables will be reported as ordinary income. For a cash-basis taxpayer, the basis in receivables is generally zero, and selling the receivable results in the same character of income as collecting the receivable. For an accrual-basis taxpayer, the basis in the receivable is the amount reported as income at the time of sale. Thus, if a lesser amount is collected on the sale or the exchange of the receivable (which would ordinarily be the case), Code Sec. 1221(a)(4) guarantees an ordinary loss deduction to the taxpayer.

.09 CODE SEC. 1221(a)(5)—PUBLICATIONS OF THE U.S. GOVERNMENT ISSUED AT A DISCOUNT

Code Sec. 1221(a)(5) prohibits capital asset treatment for any publication of the U.S. government that was not acquired from the U.S. government at the purchase price normally offered to the public. The same treatment applies to a carryover basis recipient. As was true with Code Sec. 1221(a)(3), the principal purpose of this provision (enacted in 1976) is to limit the deductibility of "ordinary income" properties under Code Sec. 170. Thus, a government employee who receives publications free of charge will not be able to deduct their fair market value when they are donated to a charity since their tax basis is zero.

.11 CODE SEC. 1221(a)(6)—COMMODITIES DERIVATIVE FINANCIAL INSTRUMENTS

Code Sec. 1221(a)(6) prohibits capital asset treatment for certain commodities derivative financial instruments held by a commodities derivatives dealer. Congress felt that such transactions were "integrally related" to the ordinary course of the trade or business of commodities derivatives dealers, unless clearly not related to the activities of a dealer.

---

[3] *Peebles*, CA-4, 57-2 USTC ¶10,032, 249 F2d 92.

.13   CODE SEC. 1221(a)(7)—HEDGING TRANSACTIONS

Code Sec. 1221(a)(7) denies capital asset treatment to any "hedging" transaction that is clearly identified as of the close of the day it was acquired, originated, or entered into. As discussed later in this chapter, a hedging transaction is one entered into to manage risk of (1) price changes or currency fluctuations with respect to ordinary property held by the taxpayer or (2) interest rate or price changes or currency fluctuations related to borrowings by the taxpayer. The statute also provides the Treasury the flexibility of adding other categories of qualifying hedges per the regulations.

.15   CODE SEC. 1221(a)(8)—SUPPLIES USED IN A TRADE OR BUSINESS

Code Sec. 1221(a)(8) codifies a 1997 regulation that treats supplies used by a taxpayer in the ordinary course of business as not qualifying for capital asset treatment. In effect, this confirms that supplies deductible by a business should be treated as ordinary income rather than as capital assets.

OBSERVATION   If the properties listed in Code Sec. 1221 never qualify as capital assets, then exactly what *does* qualify as a capital asset? Generally, any asset owned by an individual for personal or investment purposes is a capital asset. This includes items such as an individual's personal residence, automobile, land, and stock or bond investments. However, many assets have both capital and noncapital characteristics, and the Congress, the IRS, and the courts have found it necessary to provide some rather arbitrary distinctions. Certain assets such as collectibles, Code Sec. 1202 stock, and "unrecaptured Sec. 1250 gain, are taxed at different rates even though they meet the definition of a "capital asset."

¶7005   The Capital Gain and Loss Netting Process for Individuals

In order to report a transaction as a capital gain or loss, there must be a "*sale or exchange.*" Although this term is not defined in the Code, the Supreme Court has stated that such terms should be given their "ordinary, everyday meaning."[4] As a practical matter, a sale involves a transfer of property for money and possibly other property or services, and an exchange involves a reciprocal transfer of property. Examples of transactions not treated as sales or exchanges include: collections on a note receivable and abandonment of property.

.01   NETTING CAPITAL GAINS AND LOSSES

The capital gain and loss netting process of individuals was significantly complicated by many changes made to the way capital gains and losses are taxed. In order to simplify the discussion, initially assume that the only capital transactions of an individual are either regular short-term capital gains and losses (capital assets held one year or less) or long-term capital gains and losses (capital assets held more than 12 months) that qualify for the preferential capital gains tax rate. The first step is to understand the tax consequences of four possible results, assuming there is only one capital transaction:

1. ***Short-term Capital Gain.*** Gain is fully taxable at ordinary income rates.
2. ***Short-term Capital Loss.*** Loss may offset up to $3,000 of ordinary (noncapital gains income); any excess loss is carried forward indefinitely as a short-term loss.
3. ***Long-term Capital Gain.*** Gain is fully taxable; however, the taxpayer will never pay a rate of tax exceeding 20 percent on the net gain (0 percent if the taxpayer is

---

[4]   *Crane,* SCt, 47-1 ustc ¶9217, 331 US 1, 67 SCt 1047.

in the 10- or 15-percent ordinary income tax bracket and 15-percent if the taxpayer is in the 25-, 28-, 33-, or 35-percent bracket).

4. *Long-term Capital Loss.* Loss may offset up to $3,000 of ordinary (noncapital gains income); any excess loss is carried forward indefinitely as a long-term loss. (*Note:* If both short- and long-term losses are present in a year, only $3,000 in total may offset ordinary income, with the short-term losses being used first.)

Once the four basic results are understood, the netting process for several capital transactions incurred during a year is a simple three-step process. First, the short-term gains and losses (on properties held one year or less) are netted to determine a net short-term result. Second, the long-term gains and losses are netted to determine a net long-term result. And finally, the signs of the two results are compared. If the signs are the *same* (both are gains or both are losses), each result enters income separately under the four rules listed above; if the signs are *different* (one is a gain and one is a loss), they are combined and the net difference enters income under the four rules listed above.

The capital gain and loss netting rules are illustrated in Table 1. In each year, the capital gains and losses are listed before the carryovers. Note that net capital gains are included in gross income, and that net capital losses are deductions from adjusted gross income. Also note that capital loss carryovers retain their short-term or long-term character in the next taxable year.

Table 1 — Examples of Individual Capital Gain and Loss Netting					
	2009	2010	2011	2012	2013
Current-Year Capital Transactions (Before c/o):					
ST Gain	$16,000	$18,000	$ 3,000	$ 2,000	$ 9,000
ST Loss	(18,000)	(26,000)	(2,000)	(6,000)	(1,000)
ST Carryover			(4,000)		(1,000)
Net St	(2,000)	(8,000)	(3,000)	(4,000)	7,000
LT Gain	24,000	2,000	8,000	4,000	8,000
LT Loss	(12,000)	(1,000)	(2,000)	(8,000)	(6,000)
LT Carryover					(4,000)
Net LT	12,000	1,000	6,000	(4,000)	(2,000)
Net Result:	10,000*	(3,000)	3,000*	(3,000)	5,000
Capital Loss Carryover:					
ST	0	(4,000)	0	(1,000)	0
LT	0	0	0	(4,000)	0
* Qualifies for the preferential capital gains rate					

.03   NETTING CAPITAL GAINS AND LOSSES WITH 25- AND 28-PERCENT RATE GAINS AND LOSSES

Congress complicated capital gains reporting by providing multiple tax rates for capital gains in legislation enacted between 1997-2003. Because of multiple rates for capital gains, a number of questions arose as to the proper netting for transactions. The netting process follows the steps summarized in diagram form in Figure 2, which assumes the taxpayer is eligible for a long term capital gains tax rate of 15%. (Note: some taxpayers may qualify for a 0% long term capital gains tax rate, or may be taxed at a higher 20% tax rate for long term capital gains. The 0%, 15%, or 20% long term capital gains tax rate depends upon the taxpayer's regular marginal tax rate.) In each step, the taxpayer receives the optimum use of capital losses (offsetting 28-percent gain first, then 25-percent, then 15-percent). Also note that any long-term capital loss carryover is auto-matically a 28-percent loss in the carryover year.

OBSERVATION

- *15 percent.* **The rate applicable to long-term capital gains (those assets held longer than 12 mo**nths). Note: if the taxpayer is in the 10- or 15-percent tax bracket, the rate is 0 percent; if the taxpayer is in the 39.6% marginal tax rate, the rate is 20%.
- *25 percent.* A special rate applicable to "unrecaptured Sec. 1250 gain" on realty.
- *28 percent.* This rate applies to "collectibles," e.g., stamps, artwork, gold, antiques, etc. and 50 percent of the gain on the sale of Qualified Small Business Stock (QSBS).[5] The QSBS must have been acquired from a corporation whose aggregate gross assets did not exceed $50 million on the date the stock was issued, held for more than five years and the 50-percent exclusion is applied to the greater of $10 million or 10 times the adjusted basis in the stock. Thus, the effective tax rate on the gain from the sale of QSBS is 14 percent (28% × 50%).

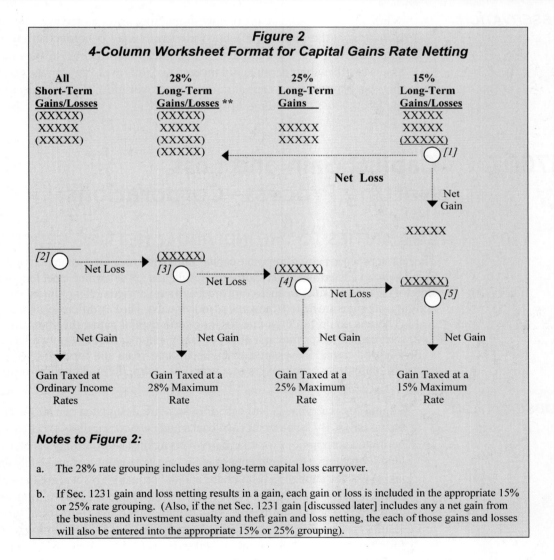

Figure 2
4-Column Worksheet Format for Capital Gains Rate Netting

Notes to Figure 2:

a. The 28% rate grouping includes any long-term capital loss carryover.

b. If Sec. 1231 gain and loss netting results in a gain, each gain or loss is included in the appropriate 15% or 25% rate grouping. (Also, if the net Sec. 1231 gain [discussed later] includes any a net gain from the business and investment casualty and theft gain and loss netting, the each of those gains and losses will also be entered into the appropriate 15% or 25% grouping).

---

[5]   Code Sec. 1202.

.05 MEDICARE TAX ON NET INVESTMENT INCOME

For tax years after 2012, The Affordable Care Act imposes a 3.8% Medicare tax on "net investment income" of individuals who have modified Adjusted Gross Income of $200,000, if single, or $250,000, if married filing a joint return. Modified Adjusted Gross income equals adjusted gross income, plus any income excluded under Sec. 911 (foreign income). Net investment income includes dividend and capital gain income. The amount of the tax is equal to 3.8% of the lesser of an individual's net investment income or the excess of modified adjusted gross income over the threshold amount.

Example 7-1: Mr. G, single, has modified adjusted gross income of $220,000 which includes capital gain income of $50,000. His Medicare tax on net investment income is only $760 [($220,000 - $200,000) x 3.8%].

OBSERVATION While the new Medicare tax on investment income is scored as a "revenue raiser," it may have the opposite effect. Individuals may postpone selling investment assets to avoid the Medicare tax on net investment income, or they may sell loss assets to offset their capital gain income and thus avoid paying the tax, or perhaps they may spread their capital gain income over multiple tax years to stay under the $200,000/$250,000 modified AGI limits.

¶7007 Capital Gain and Loss Netting Process—Corporations

.01 SIMILARITIES TO THE INDIVIDUAL NETTING PROCESS

The first steps when netting corporate capital gains and losses for corporations are the same as for individuals: (1) determine a net short-term result, and (2) determine a net long-term result. The signs of these two results are then compared, and similar signs enter ordinary income separately and opposite signs are netted (the same as individuals). The key differences for corporations are:
1. There is no preferential rate for long-term capital gains; the gains are fully taxable.
2. Net capital losses may not offset ordinary income; they can only offset capital gains.
3. Unused capital losses are carried back three years and forward five years, then lost.
4. All capital loss carryovers of a corporation are defined as short-term in nature.

OBSERVATION Capital loss carrybacks and carryforwards are designated as short-term to benefit the taxpayer. By labeling all carrybacks and carryforwards as short-term, Congress permitted corporations to offset carryovers against short-term gains first, thus taxing long-term gains at the preferential rate for long-term gains. Unfortunately for corporate taxpayers, the capital gains tax rates and the ordinary tax rates are the same.

Example of netting process. Corporation X had a $14,000 long-term capital gain and a $5,000 short-term capital loss. Since the short-term and long-term results are opposite signs, they are netted, and the $9,000 net long-term gain is fully taxable (no preferential capital gains rate exists for corporations).

Example of netting process. Corporation X had a $14,000 long-term capital loss and a $5,000 short-term capital gain. Since the short-term and long-term results are opposite signs, they are netted, and the $9,000 net long-term loss may not offset ordinary income. It is carried back to the third preceding tax year as a short-term capital loss. If there were no capital gains in any of the three preceding tax years, the $9,000 loss could be carried forward to the next tax year and could be used to offset up to $9,000 of net long-term gains reported in that year. To receive the tax benefit of a capital loss carryback the corporation must file an amended return.

¶7009 The Special Case of Code Sec. 1231 Properties

.01 BACKGROUND

As mentioned earlier, the definition of capital assets in Code Sec. 1221 expressly excludes depreciable property and real property used in a trade or business. During the Depression, business taxpayers asked Congress to exclude these assets from the capital asset definition so that losses on the sale or exchange of these properties could be reported as ordinary losses. Such treatment would be favorable to a taxpayer selling an asset at a loss, since capital loss limitations would not apply. A complementary ordinary income treatment accorded to gains on property, however, could be detrimental to business taxpayers by discouraging disposition of unproductive assets and acquisition of newer, more productive properties. During World War II, many businesses were sold assets to the government at a profit. Once again taxpayers successfully lobbied Congress to provide favorable tax treatment on the gain side as well. Thus, Code Sec. 1231 and its predecessors were enacted partly to encourage greater mobility of capital in the economy by granting long-term capital gains treatment to net Code Sec. 1231 gains.

In effect, Code Sec. 1231 was designed to provide the taxpayer with the *best of both tax worlds*: long-term capital asset treatment for "net Sec. 1231 gains," and ordinary loss deductions for "net Sec. 1231 losses." Its significance regarding the taxation of the disposition of business property was lessened tax rate cuts of the Tax Reform Act of 1986, and then increased when higher ordinary income rates were enacted by the Taxpayer Relief Act of 1997. Generally, net capital gain of an individual taxpayer can be taxed at a rate as low as 15 percent, as opposed to 35 percent for ordinary income (recall that corporations receive no preferential capital gains tax rate). Further, net Code Sec. 1231 gains may be offset by both individual and corporate taxpayers by capital losses that otherwise might be limited, and net Code Sec. 1231 losses may be deducted without limits.

.03 CODE SEC. 1231 PROPERTIES DEFINED

In order to understand more fully the desirable results that may arise under Code Sec. 1231 it is necessary to consider the definition of properties, the netting procedures that result in net Code Sec. 1231 gain or loss, and the potential impact of depreciation recapture. Each concept is discussed below. Figure 3 reproduces subsection (a)(1)–(3) of Code Sec. 1231. In general, 1231 includes two basic types of property transactions:

1. Recognized gains and losses from the sale or exchange of property used in a business and held on a long-term basis; and
2. Recognized gains and losses from the involuntary conversion of property and also capital assets used in a trade or business and income-producing activities. Both types of properties must be held on a long-term basis.

Figure 3 — Code Sec. 1231(a)(1)-(3)

(a) General Rule. –

    (1) Gains exceed losses. – If –

        (A) the section 1231 gains for any taxable year, exceed

        (B) the section 1231 losses for such taxable year,

        such gains and losses shall be treated as long-term capital gains or long-term capital losses, as the case may be.

    (2) Gains do not exceed losses. – If –

        (A) the section 1231 gains for any taxable year, do not exceed the section 1231 losses for such taxable year,

        such gains and losses shall not be treated as long-term capital gains or long-term capital losses, as the case may be.

    (3) Section 1231 Gains and Losses. – For purposes of this subsection –

        (A) Section 1231 Gain. – The term "section 1231 gain" means –

            (i) any recognized gain on the sale or exchange of property used in the trade or business, and

            (ii) any recognized gain from the compulsory or involuntary conversion (as a result of destruction in whole or in part, theft or seizure, or an exercise of the power of requisition or condemnation or the threat or imminence thereof) into other property or money or –

                (I) property used in the trade or business, or

                (II) any capital asset which is held for more than 1 year and is held in connection with a trade or business or a transaction entered into for profit.

        (B) Section 1231 Loss. – The term "section 1231 loss" means any recognized loss from a sale or exchange or conversion described in subparagraph (A).

The holding period requirement conforms to the long-term definition of capital assets in Code Sec. 1222. Thus, property must be held longer than one year to qualify as Code Sec. 1231 assets. (However, as discussed earlier, for individual taxpayers, the Code Sec. 1231 gain is further broken into 15-, 25-, and 28-percent categories depending on actual holding period and special recaptures.) Several points should be noted in reference to these transactions that are covered by the Code Sec. 1231 definition.

First, only *recognized* gains and losses are included in the Code Sec. 1231 definition. Any gains or losses deferred through the operation of the nontaxable exchange provisions are not included in the Code Sec. 1231 netting.

Second, Code Sec. 1231 encompasses **involuntary conversions** of business and income-producing properties. An involuntary conversion is defined in the same manner as Code Sec. 1033, e.g., the destruction, theft, seizure, condemnation, or the threat of condemnation of these two types of properties. Thus, the term involuntary conversion refers to a broader class of transactions than those covered by the casualty and theft rules. Such a distinction is important because of (1) the special casualty and theft netting procedure described below and (2) the prohibition against deducting a loss on the condemnation of a purely personal property, such as a residence.

Third, the Code Sec. 1231 provisions apply only to properties with a long-term holding period. Gains and losses on the sale, exchange, or involuntary conversion of business properties held one year or less will always be ordinary gains and losses, since these properties are not covered by the definition of Code Sec. 1231 assets or capital assets.

Fourth, Code Sec. 1231 includes gains and losses from the involuntary conversion of business assets (or capital assets used in a business or income-producing activity) but *not* the gains and losses on the involuntary conversion of personal assets. As discussed below, personal casualties and thefts have been subject to a special nettings process since 1983.

Finally, it should be noted that Code Sec. 1231 does not provide the authority for loss deductions. This authority is granted by Code Sec. 165, which permits a deduction for trade or business losses, income-producing losses, and casualty or theft losses. Furthermore, Code Sec. 1231 does not alter the basic requirement that casualty or theft losses on nonbusiness and non-income-producing capital assets must be deducted *from* adjusted gross income by individuals.

Code Sec. 1231 was first made applicable to involuntary conversions, because many businesses in the shipping industry were required to sell ships to the government during World War II. Sales and exchanges were later added to Code Sec. 1231 definition.

The tax treatment offered by Code Sec. 1231 is available only for properties used in a trade or business (unless a capital asset used in a business or an income-producing activity is involuntarily converted). Shortly after the enactment of the forerunner of Code Sec. 1231, it was not surprising to find political pressures by various groups to have their business transactions covered by the definition of "property used in a trade or business." As a result, the Code Sec. 1231(b) definition of qualifying trade or business property has been modified over the years to accommodate a variety of transactions.

In general, depreciable or real property such as machinery, equipment, buildings, and land may qualify as "property used in a trade or business"; however, inventory and other property held primarily for sale to customers does not qualify. Copyrights, literary or artistic computations, and government publications acquired at a discount are also specifically excluded from Code Sec. 1231 treatment.

However, Congress has added five special properties to the Code Sec. 1231 definition, even though such properties would normally be better characterized as "used" or "held for sale" in a trade or business. These properties are the cutting of timber, the mining of coal, the mining of domestic iron ore, the sale of livestock, and the sale of unharvested crops.

.05 THE CODE SEC. 1231 GAIN AND LOSS NETTING PROCESS

A taxpayer totals all of the Code Sec. 1231 gains and losses incurred during the year. If the net result is a *gain*, the gain is reported as a long-term capital gain (to be combined with other capital gains and losses). On the other hand, if the net result is a *loss*, the net loss is reported as an ordinary loss (not subject to any capital loss limitation). Thus, the taxpayer receives the best of both tax worlds for either net gains or net losses.

As if the netting process for individual taxpayers was not hard enough, it is possible to have Code Sec. 1231 gain subject to two different tax rates: 15 percent (properties not subject to 25-percent rate recapture) and 25 percent (properties subject to a special recapture rule). Since neither collectibles nor Code Sec. 1202 stock fit the definition of Code Sec. 1231 property, it is not possible for Code Sec. 1231 assets taxed at the 28-percent rate.

When combined with special netting rules for personal and business casualty and theft gains and losses, the complete property transaction process can be summarized using a five-column worksheet to determine the final netting result for property transactions. There are columns for Personal Casualty and Thefts, Business and Investment Casualties and Thefts, Code Sec. 1231 Gains and Losses, Capital Gains and Losses, and Ordinary Income. **Figure 4** illustrates the general format. Note that in each case the columns are totaled and net gains are transferred to the next column on the right while net losses are transferred to the Ordinary column on the far right. Thus, the taxpayer has the "best of both tax worlds" treatment when it comes to netting personal and business casualty and theft gains and losses. A comprehensive spreadsheet illustrating the four-column worksheet for capital gains rate netting and the five-column worksheet for netting property transactions is included in the Appendix.

Prior to 1983, all casualties and thefts (both business and personal) were grouped together in a single netting, with a net gain treated as a Code Sec. 1231 gain and a net loss treated as a Code Sec. 1231 loss. (This best of both worlds netting was instituted in 1969 so that a taxpayer with a large casualty or theft loss that the taxpayer had no control over would not be penalized by having to offset it against a large Code Sec. 1231 gain that would otherwise qualify for favorable capital gains rate.) However, when Congress instituted the overall 10 percent of adjusted gross income floor for personal casualty and thefts, a circular computation problem was created: the net casualty and theft loss deduction was dependent upon AGI, but to determine AGI, the net casualty and theft laws are required. To solve the problem, the Congress transferred personal casualties and thefts to yet another "best of both worlds" netting, as illustrated in **Figure 4**.

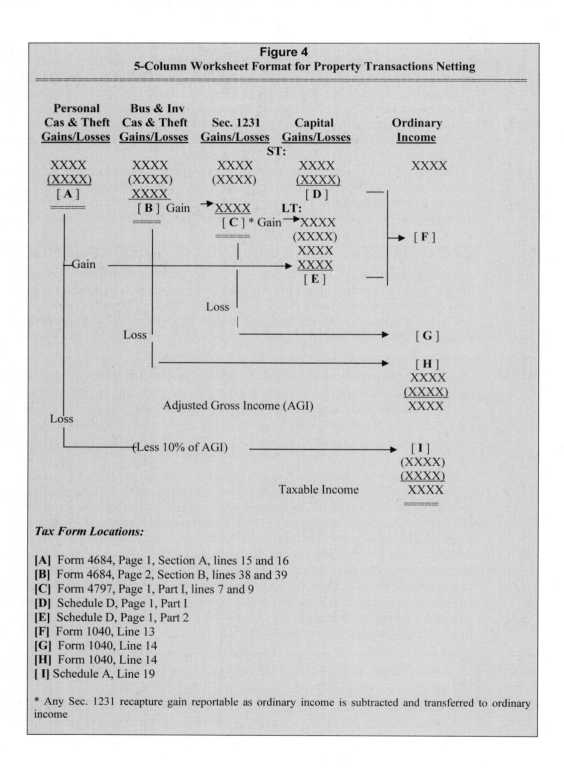

Figure 4
5-Column Worksheet Format for Property Transactions Netting

Tax Form Locations:

[A] Form 4684, Page 1, Section A, lines 15 and 16
[B] Form 4684, Page 2, Section B, lines 38 and 39
[C] Form 4797, Page 1, Part I, lines 7 and 9
[D] Schedule D, Page 1, Part I
[E] Schedule D, Page 1, Part 2
[F] Form 1040, Line 13
[G] Form 1040, Line 14
[H] Form 1040, Line 14
[I] Schedule A, Line 19

* Any Sec. 1231 recapture gain reportable as ordinary income is subtracted and transferred to ordinary income

In applying the five-column format, note that (1) any personal casualty or theft loss is reduced by the $100 floor prior to entering the amount, (2) if personal casualties and thefts net to a loss, it is necessary to determine AGI before the first column can be closed, (3) and depreciation recapture or Code Sec. 1231 recapture (described below) will be entered in the ordinary column. Also, if a property meets the Code Sec. 1231 definition except that it was not held longer than 12 months, any gain or loss on that asset is reported as ordinary income or loss (recall that properties used in a trade or business are excluded from the capital asset definition under Code Sec. 1221).

.07 DEPRECIATION RECAPTURE UNDER CODE SECS. 1245 AND 1250

By the early 1960s, it was discovered that some taxpayers were using accelerated depreciation to generate large ordinary depreciation deductions and then selling the property and paying tax at the lower capital gains tax rates. Taxpayers were in effect exchanging ordinary depreciation deductions (which lowered basis) for larger gains taxed as capital gains under Code Sec. 1231. Legislation was enacted to take away the benefits of possible capital gain on the later sale by converting some or all of the gain into ordinary income through "depreciation recapture," as described below.

Code Sec. 1245 Recapture. Code Sec. 1245 property has three characteristics: it is (1) depreciable **personalty**, (2) held on a long-term basis, and (3) sold at a gain. If all conditions are present, gain on the sale of property is ordinary income to the extent of total depreciation taken on the asset since 1961. If the gain exceeds this ordinary income "recapture", the excess gain is Code Sec. 1231 gain (note that the definition of Code Sec. 1245 property fits within the broader definition of Code Sec. 1231 property, this property is also a Code Sec. 1231 asset). If the property is sold at a loss, the loss is a Code Sec. 1231 loss.

Code Sec. 1250 Recapture. Code Sec. 1250 property has four characteristics: it is (1) depreciable realty, (2) held on a long-term basis, (3) sold at a gain, and (4) is property on which "excess depreciation" (accelerated depreciation in excess of straight-line) has been taken. There is ordinary income to the extent of any "excess depreciation" taken. However, on the sale of *nonresidential ACRS realty*, the Code Sec. 1245 recapture rules apply (e.g., total depreciation recapture, not just excess). Note that if straight-line depreciation is used, there is no Code Sec. 1250 recapture since there is no excess depreciation.

OBSERVATION

There is yet another recapture provided for certain net Code Sec. 1231 losses. Code Sec. 1231(c) states that if the Code Sec. 1231 netting results in a net gain, the gain must be reported as ordinary income to the extent of any unrecaptured Code Sec. 1231 net losses from the previous five years. This rule is designed to prevent taxpayers from bunching Code Sec. 1231 losses into one year and Code Sec. 1231 gains into different years so that the best of both tax worlds is achieved in each year. In applying the recapture for individual taxpayers, it is assumed that the recapture first comes from any 28-percent Code Sec. 1231 gain, then any 25-percent Code Sec. 1231 gain, and finally from any 15-percent Code Sec. 1231 gain. Once again, the best possible result is given to the taxpayer.

Code Sec. 291 Recapture. Code Sec. 291 was enacted in 1982 to reduce the tax benefit of accelerated depreciation on business realty owned by a corporation. When the 1986 act repealed accelerated depreciation for buildings, Code Sec. 291 was not repealed and continues to apply to realty owned by corporations. It requires that a portion of the realized gain be treated as ordinary income as if Code Sec. 1245 applied. The recapture is limited to 20 percent of the accumulated depreciation.

OBSERVATION   Since ordinary income and capital gains are taxed at the same rate for corporations, the main impact of Code Sec. 291 is to reduce the amount of capital gain income available to utilize capital loss carry forwards.

Example 7-2. C Corporation sold a building for $1,000,000. The purchase price was $600,000 and accumulated depreciation was $300,000. The realized gain is $700,000, and $60,000 ($300,000 × 20%) is treated as ordinary income and the remaining gain of $640,000 is treated as a Code Sec. 1231 gain. If the corporation had a $700,000 unused capital loss carry forward, it would only be able to use $640,000 of the loss carry forward.

¶7011   Nontaxable Exchanges of Property

There are two special provisions for deferring gain on the exchange or replacement of certain properties: Code Sec. 1031 like-kind exchanges and Code Sec. 1033 involuntary conversion.

.01   CODE SEC. 1031 LIKE-KIND EXCHANGES

Code Sec. 1031 applies to any exchange of property that is either used in a trade or business or held for the production of income for similar property in either category; a taxpayer may switch categories (business for investment or vice versa). However, swaps of personalty for realty are not allowed. Also, the provisions do not apply to exchanges of inventory, purely personal assets, stocks and securities, and partnership interests. If the exchange is covered by Code Sec. 1031, its application is mandatory.

The final tax result of a Code Sec. 1031 exchange depends on whether or not boot is involved in the exchange. **Boot** refers to nonqualifying property, such as cash. The basic rules for nonrecognition of a realized accounting gain are as follows:
- *Solely like-kind exchange.* No gain or loss is recognized, and the adjusted basis of the new property equals the adjusted basis of the old property.
- *Monetary (cash or cash equivalent) boot given.* No gain or loss is recognized.
- *Nonmonetary boot given.* Gain or loss is recognized on the boot given to the extent its fair market value differs from its adjusted basis, but only if gain or loss would have been recognized on a sale of the boot for its fair market value.
- *Monetary or nonmonetary boot received.* Loss is never recognized, but gain is recognized to the extent of the lesser of the realized (accounting) gain or the fair market value of the boot received.
- *Liabilities transferred in the exchange.* Liabilities transferred in the exchange are treated as boot received (if assumed by the other party in the transaction) or boot given (if assumed by the taxpayer in the transaction). If both parties are transferring liabilities, they are netted to determine if there was net boot given or net boot received.

The adjusted basis of the replacement property received in a qualifying Code Sec. 1031 exchange is its fair market value reduced by the gain not recognized (i.e., "postponed gain") or increased by the loss not recognized (i.e., "postponed loss"). The postponed gain or loss is the difference between the accounting gain or loss and the taxable gain or loss. The replacement property also includes the holding period of the old property, in other words the holding period is "tacked on."

.03   CODE SEC. 1033 ELECTIONS TO DEFER GAIN ON INVOLUNTARY CONVERSIONS

Code Sec. 1033 provides an election whereby *gain* (but not loss) recognized on the involuntary conversion of property is limited to that portion of the insurance or condemnation proceeds not reinvested in *qualifying replacement property* within a *qualified replacement period.* This rule is a direct reflection of the wherewithal to pay principle.

An involuntary conversion includes casualties or other destruction, theft, condemnations of property, and threats of condemnation of property. A net gain occurs when the insurance (or condemnation) proceeds exceed the adjusted basis of the property destroyed. Qualifying replacement property generally serves the same function as the converted property. The qualified replacement period is generally two years from the end of the tax year in which gain is first recognized from the involuntary conversion. For example, if a calendar year taxpayer's business warehouse is destroyed by fire on 12/22/10, and the taxpayer receives an insurance check on 1/4/11, the taxpayer has until 12/31/13 to acquire replacement property. The adjusted basis of the new replacement property is its cost less the gain postponed by electing Code Sec. 1033. As was true with like-kind exchanges, the holding period of the old property is "tacked on" to the holding period of the new property.

¶7013 Landmark Property Cases—The Capital Asset Definition

As mentioned earlier, Code Sec. 1221 cannot be viewed as an escape valve from capital gain or loss treatment. Over the years the courts and the IRS have wrestled with a number of gray areas concerning the applicability of capital gain or loss treatment. Many of these relate to the use of properties in a trade or business, and many can be traced to the landmark decision in *Corn Products*.

.01 INVENTORY SUBSTITUTES

Corn Products Refining Company[6]

Facts of the Case: Petitioner is a nationally known manufacturer of products made from grain corn. It manufactures starch, syrup, sugar, and their byproducts, feeds and oil. Its average yearly grind of raw corn during the period 1937 through 1942 varied from thirty-five to sixty million bushels. Most of its products were sold under contracts requiring shipment in thirty days at a set price or at market price on the date of delivery, whichever was lower. It permitted cancellation of such contracts, but from experience it could calculate with some accuracy future orders that would remain firm. While it also sold to a few customers on long-term contracts involving substantial orders, these had little effect on the transactions here involved.

In 1934 and again in 1936 droughts in the corn belt caused a sharp increase in the price of spot corn. With a storage capacity of only 2,300,000 bushels of corn, a bare three weeks' supply, Corn Products found it was unable to buy at a price which would permit its refined corn sugar, cerelose, to compete successfully with cane and beet sugar. To avoid a recurrence of this situation, petitioner, in 1937, began to establish a long position in corn futures "as a part of its corn buying program" and "as the most economical method of obtaining an adequate supply of raw corn" without entailing the expenditure of large sums for additional storage facilities. At harvest time each year it would buy futures when the price appeared favorable. It would take delivery on such contracts as it found necessary to its manufacturing operations and sell the remainder in early summer if no shortage was imminent. If shortages appeared, however, it sold futures only as it bought spot corn for grinding. In this manner it reached a balanced position with reference to any increase in spot corn prices. It made no effort to protect itself against a decline in prices.

---

[6] *Corn Products Refining Company*, SCt, 55-2 USTC ¶9746, 350 US 46, 76 SCt 20.

In 1940 it netted a profit of $680,587.39 in corn futures, but in 1942 it suffered a loss of $109,969.38. In computing its tax liability Corn Products reported these figures as ordinary profit and loss from its manufacturing operations for the respective years. It now contends that its futures were "capital assets" under §117 and gains and losses should have been treated as arising from the sale of a capital-asset. In support of this position it claims that its futures trading were separate and apart from its manufacturing operations and that in its futures trans-actions it was acting as a "legitimate capitalist." *United States v. New York Coffee & Sugar Exchange,* 263 U. S. 611, 619. It denies that its futures transactions were "hedges" or "speculative" dealings as covered by the ruling of *General Counsel Memorandum* 17322, XV-2 Cum. Bull. 151 [1936 CCH ¶6610], and claims that it is in truth "the forgotten man" of that administrative interpretation.

Note: Upholding the Tax Court and the 2nd Circuit Court of Appeals

---

In *Corn Products Refining Co.,* the taxpayer manufactured products made from corn. Usually, shipments of product would be made within 30 days of an order. Occasionally, the taxpayer purchased commodity futures as a long position against droughts, price increases, and storage problems. These were bought as needed and either exercised as needed or sometimes sold for a profit. The taxpayer initially reported the gain as ordinary income, and then amended the return to report capital gain. The taxpayer contended that the futures were not hedges, and that the company was merely acting as a "legitimate capitalist." The IRS contended that the corn futures were an "integral part of the day to day business" of the company in insuring a steady inventory supply. The Tax Court and Court of Appeals agreed with the government that the corn futures were an "integral part of the taxpayer's business," in that the futures assured a ready supply of corn and thus offered protection against future price increases.

The Supreme Court upheld the lower courts' determination that the gains should be reported as ordinary income. The Court noted that the company officers testified that the purchases reflected good management planning and were an attempt to "protect a part of manufacturing costs." The Court indicated that the essential purpose of the futures purchases was to protect and preserve the underlying business, and that such "hedging" activity was reportable as ordinary income under the 1934 Code. In its decision, the Court noted that "This Court has always construed narrowly the term 'capital assets' in Sec. 117 [now Code Sec. 1221]." The Court also distinguished profits and losses from business operations in the following manner:

> But the capital asset provision of Sec. 117 must not be so broadly applied as to defeat rather than further the purpose of Congress.... Congress intended that profits and losses arising from the every day operation of a business be considered as ordinary income or loss rather than capital gain or loss. The preferential treatment provided by Sec. 117 applies to transactions in property which are not the normal source of business operations.... Since this section is an exception from the normal tax requirements of the Internal Revenue Code, the definition of a capital asset must be narrowly applied and its exclusions interpreted broadly.

The *Corn Products* decision represented a major victory for the government, in that the concept of capital asset status was dramatically narrowed for properties used in a trade or business. This decision led to other government victories for gains on the sale of properties that were "integral parts" of the taxpayer's trade or business. For example, in *Hollywood Baseball Association,*[7] a minor league baseball team sold contracts of its professional players to major-league teams. The Court of Appeals ruled that the purpose of the minor league team was to hold, develop, and sell such contracts to the parent team, and the gain was ordinary. The Court noted that "*if transactions are everyday, there is no excessive tax burden at ordinary rates.*"

---

[7]   *Hollywood Baseball Association,* CA-9, 70-1 USTC ¶9251, 423 F2d 494.

In the *Hollywood* case, the Court held that the team was carrying on two businesses: fielding a team and selling the player contracts. The team had treated the player contracts as depreciable business properties. The Court's decision was widely interpreted as dramatically narrowing the scope of Code Sec. 1231, the "best of both tax worlds" treatment for properties used in a trade or business. The government won a number of similar cases based on the principle established in *Corn Products*.

The *Corn Products* decision soon proved to be a double-edged sword for the government, in that the same logic should apply to similar "Corn Products" properties sold at a loss. Because of the breadth of the *Corn Products* decision, taxpayers were reporting ordinary losses for a variety of properties where the "every day operation of a business" standard was highly questionable. For example, in *Booth Newspapers, Inc.*,[8] a newspaper owned stock in a paper mill that was originally acquired to insure a steady source of paper. When the taxpayer sold the stock, the Court of Claims ruled that the loss was ordinary, citing *Corn Products*. Similarly, in *Steadman*,[9] a taxpayer was granted ordinary loss treatment on the sale of stock that he had originally purchased for the purpose of insuring that he would be retained as counsel for the issuing company.

Faced with a growing problem of *Corn Products*-type cases on the loss side, the government formed a new strategy by examining each case for a potential investment motive in such transactions. If the government could successfully contend that there was a "substantial investment motive" in acquiring the property in question, then the property might be viewed as a capital asset. This was especially true in cases where stock in another company was the property in question.

The government's first victory in the "mixed motive" cases occurred in *Dearborne Co.*,[10] where a furniture manufacturer purchased stock in a company producing lumber and furniture parts. In deciding that the loss on the sale was a capital loss, the Court of Claims noted that the taxpayer had both a business motive and a "substantial" investment motive in acquiring the investment. However, the existence of such an investment motive worked against the government in *Agway*,[11] where the court ruled that a gain on the sale was capital, stating that "*Corn Products will be applied in this court to purchases of company stock to obtain a source of supply, only if there is no substantial investment intent.*" Once again, a government victory turned into a double-edged sword, this time on the gain side of such transactions. The government's most significant victory in the "mixed motive" case was the *W.W. Windle* case, discussed later.

In the *Arkansas Best* case, the taxpayer, a holding company, had purchased additional shares of stock in a bank (in which it already owned stock) in order to prevent the bank's failure. The taxpayer claimed that the purchases, made at a time in which Arkansas Best was trying to divest all of the stock because of the Bank Holding Company Act, were a means of protecting the company's reputation. The taxpayer contended that the loss on the sale of the shares should be reported as ordinary loss, since the company had a dominant business motive on the additional purchases of stock. The IRS argued that the taxpayer initially viewed this as a profitable investment, and that was their primary motive in acquiring the stock.

.03 NARROWING THE CAPITAL ASSET DEFINITION

Arkansas Best Corporation[12]

Facts of the Case: Arkansas Best is a diversified holding company. In 1968 it acquired approximately 65% of the stock of the National Bank of Commerce

---

8 *Booth Newspapers, Inc.*, CtCls, 62-2 USTC ¶9530, 303 F2d 916, 157 CtCls 886.
9 *Steadman*, CA-6, 70-1 USTC ¶9328, 424 F2d 1.
10 *Dearborn Company*, CtCls, 71-1 USTC ¶9478, 444 F2d 1145.
11 *Agway, Inc.*, CtCls, 75-2 ustc ¶9777, 524 F2d 1194, 207 CtCls 682.
12 *Arkansas Best Corp.*, SCt, 88-1 USTC ¶9210, 485 US 212, 108 SCt 971.

(Bank) in Dallas, Texas. Between 1969 and 1974, Arkansas Best more than tripled the number of shares it owned in the Bank, although its percentage interest in the Bank remained relatively stable. These acquisitions were prompted principally by the Bank's need for added capital. Until 1972, the Bank appeared to be prosperous and growing, and the added capital was necessary to accommodate this growth. As the Dallas real estate market declined, however, so too did the financial health of the Bank, which had a heavy concentration of loans in the local real estate industry. In 1972, federal examiners classified the Bank as a problem bank. The infusion of capital after 1972 was prompted by the loan portfolio problems of the bank.

Petitioner sold the bulk of its Bank stock on June 30, 1975, leaving it with only a 14.7% stake in the Bank. On its federal income tax return for 1975, petitioner claimed a deduction for an ordinary loss of $9,995,688 resulting from the sale of the stock. The Commissioner of Internal Revenue disallowed the deduction, finding that the loss from the sale of stock was a capital loss, rather than an ordinary loss, and that it therefore was subject to the capital loss limitations in the Internal Revenue Code.

Arkansas Best challenged the Commissioner's determination in the United States Tax Court. The Tax Court, relying on cases interpreting *Corn Products Refining Co. v. Commissioner* [55-2 USTC ¶9746], 350 U.S. 46 (1955), held that stock purchased with a substantial investment purpose is a capital asset which, when sold, gives rise to a capital gain or loss, whereas stock purchased and held for a business purpose, without any substantial investment motive, is an ordinary asset whose sale gives rise to ordinary gains or losses. See [CCH Dec. 41,581] 83 T.C. 640, 653-654 (1984).

Note: Upholding the 8th Circuit Court of Appeals, which had reversed the Tax Court

The Tax Court treated the additional share purchases as ordinary income properties under *the Corn Products* doctrine. However, the Court of Appeals for the 8th Circuit ruled that the loss on the sale of the additional shares should be reported as a capital loss, citing a restrictive reading of Code Sec. 1221.

The Supreme Court affirmed the 8th Circuit decision, noting that the phrase "whether or not connected with his trade or business" in Code Sec. 1221 effectively *prohibits* consideration of motive in such determinations: "*The broad definition of the term 'capital asset' explicitly makes irrelevant any consideration of the property's connection with the taxpayer's business, whereas the petitioner's rule would make this factor dispositive.*" The Court noted that the Code Sec. 1221 list of exceptions is an exclusive one, and that Congress never intended for the courts to add another one through the *Corn Products* doctrine.

In addressing the relevance of the *Corn Products* decision to this case, the Supreme Court noted the following:

> *We conclude that Corn Products is properly interpreted as standing for the narrow proposition that hedging transactions that are an integral part of a business' inventory-purchase system fall within the inventory exclusion of Sec. 1221. Arkansas Best, which is not a dealer in securities, has never suggested that the Bank stock falls within the inventory exclusion. Corn Products thus has no application to this case.*

Thus, the *Arkansas Best* decision greatly limited the scope of the *Corn Products* doctrine, which had been the central focus of over 30 years of litigation. The Court in *Arkansas Best* essentially referred to the *Corn Products* case as a hedging case related to a surrogate for inventories, and noted that this "doctrine" had been greatly abused over the years.

Several cases have cited the *Arkansas Best* case as a precedent in questioning ordinary loss treatment on the sale of financial institution stock[13] and foreign currency contracts.[14] And, in an interesting twist, in *Azar Nut Co.,*[15] the taxpayer was denied ordinary loss treatment on the sale of a residence originally purchased for an employee as part of the employment contract. Although the Court noted the Tax Court stated that the original purchase was connected with a business purpose, the motive of the taxpayer in originally purchasing the residence was not relevant, and the residence was not "used" in the taxpayer's business.

Do these decisions mean that, for all practical purposes, the "*Corn Products* doctrine" is dead? Not necessarily, as a later Claims Court decision indicates. In *Circle K Corporation,*[16] a gas retailer was allowed an ordinary loss deduction on the sale of stock in an oil and gas company. The taxpayer had acquired the stock as a means of obtaining access to raw material, and the Court used the "source of supply" principle of *Corn Products* to justify ordinary loss treatment. The Court specifically noted that the Supreme Court in *Arkansas Best* had continued to uphold such treatment for hedging transactions. The applicability of the *Arkansas Best* case was further narrowed by the Tax Court in the case of *Federal National Mortgage Association* discussed later.

Code Sec. 1221(a)(1) lists three possible characteristics of these properties: (1) stock in trade, (2) other property of a kind includible in inventory at the end of the year, and (3) property held primarily for sale to customers in the ordinary course of business. Although the courts have interpreted the third characteristic ("primarily for sale") as being a prerequisite for the first two, neither the Code nor the Code Sec. 1221 regulations address the meaning of this phrase. However, this phrase was the focal point of the 1966 Supreme Court case below.

In *Malat v. Riddell*, the taxpayer was part of a joint venture that purchased land with the intention of either selling the land or developing it as rental property, depending on which action appeared to be more profitable. The venture soon encountered financial problems and sold some of the interior lots, reporting the gain as ordinary income. After considering developing the remaining lots, the group sold the remaining lots and reported the gain as capital gain. The IRS argued that under the "dual purpose" theory, the property was held primarily for business due to a *substantial* business motive. The taxpayer argued that the last properties sold were investment properties and should be treated differently from the first properties sold.

.05   DEFINING "PRIMARILY FOR SALE"

William Malat[17]

Facts of the Case: Petitioner was a participant in a joint venture which acquired a 45-acre parcel of land, the intended use for which is somewhat in dispute. Petitioner contends that the venture's intention was to develop and operate an apartment project on the land; the respondent's position is that there was a "dual purpose" of developing the property for rental purposes or selling, whichever proved to be the more profitable. In any event, difficulties in obtaining the necessary financing were encountered, and the interior lots of the tract were subdivided and sold. The profit from those sales was reported and taxed as ordinary income.

The joint ventures continued to explore the possibility of commercially developing the remaining exterior parcels. Additional frustrations in the form of

---

[13] *See Olson*, 58 TCM 393, TC Memo 1989-564.

[14] *See Barnes Group, Inc.*, CA-2, 89-1 USTC ¶9262, 872 F2d 528.

[15] *Azar Nut Co.*, CA-5, 91-1 USTC ¶50,257, 931 F2d 314.

[16] *Circle K Corp.*, 43 TCM 1524, TC Memo 1982-298.

[17] *Malat v. Riddell*, SCt, 66-1 USTC ¶9317, 383 US 569, 86 SCt 1030.

zoning restrictions were encountered. These difficulties persuaded petitioner and another of the joint ventures of the desirability of terminating the venture; accordingly, they sold out their interests in the remaining property. Petitioner contends that he is entitled to treat the profits from this last sale as capital gains; the respondent takes the position that this was "property held by the taxpayer primarily for sale to customers in the ordinary course of his trade or business," and thus subject to taxation as ordinary income.

Note: Remanding 9th Circuit Court of Appeals and U.S. District Court

___

The District Court and the Court of Appeals ruled for the government, noting that the taxpayer could not prove that the lots were *not* held "primarily for sale" to customers. However, the Supreme Court remanded the case back to the lower courts, with instructions as to how to interpret the word "primarily":

> *"The respondent urges upon us a construction of "primarily" as meaning that a purpose may be "primary" if it is a 'substantial' one. . . As we have often said, "the words of statutes — including revenue acts — should be interpreted where possible in their ordinary everyday senses. . . We hold that, as used in Sec. 1221(1), 'primarily' means 'of first importance' or 'principally.'*

OBSERVATION   The Court in effect substituted "principal" for "substantial" in defining "primarily" on remand. Upon remand, the lower court (not surprisingly) held that the land was not held "primarily" for sale to customers.

Although the Malat case involved a dual purpose of investment or sale when the property was acquired, the 7th Circuit Court of Appeals stated that the result is not only applicable in a dual motive situation. In *Scheuber*,[18] the Court held that *Malat* principles apply where property is acquired with the singular purpose of selling it at sometime in the future.

.07   THE CAPITAL ASSET DEFINITION—ADDITIONAL CASES

***W.W. Windle v. Commissioner.*[19]** In this case, the taxpayer had acquired shares of stock in a bankrupt customer, and contended that the loss on the eventual sales should be reported as an ordinary loss. However, the Tax Court ruled that the taxpayer need only have a "substantial" investment motive in acquiring the securities to convert the loss to a capital loss, noting that:

> *"We are ultimately persuaded to hold that stock purchased with a substantial investment purpose is a capital asset even if there is a more substantial business motive for the purchase. There are two basic reasons for this holding. In the first place, to expand the statutory exceptions to 'capital assets' into mixed-motive cases will be greatly to enlarge the far more limited category of noncapital assets which would otherwise exist.... Secondly, in the last analysis, Congress has decided what is a capital asset, and there must be limits to the liberties we can take with the statutory language."*

The Court in *Windle* also differentiated this case from the *Corn Products* decision, noting that "*[a]s we move from inventory-related corn futures to a more traditional form of capital asset, such as stock, we should be more reluctant to be innovative in further broadening the domain of subjective analysis and unpredictability.*" Thus, by being allowed to show only a "secondary" investment motive, the government greatly curtailed the applicability of the *Corn Products* decision to losses, particularly those on stock investments.

___

18   *Scheuber*, CA-7, 67-1 USTC ¶9219, 371 F2d 996.
19   *Windle*, CA-1, 77-1 USTC ¶9203, 550 F2d 43.

FNMA.[20] In this case, the taxpayer (FNMA) held certain interest rate risk hedges related to the issuance of certain debentures and the acquisition of certain mortgages. The court ruled that FNMA could rely on *Arkansas Best* to obtain ordinary gain or loss treatment upon disposing of the hedges, since FNMA's mortgages were in effect *notes receivable* that are specifically excluded from capital asset treatment under Code Sec. 1221(a)(4), as noted above. The Tax Court concluded that the hedging transactions were in effect surrogates for the notes receivable. In a key finding, the Court also noted that although the *Arkansas Best* case limited the application of the *Corn Products* doctrine to inventory-type properties, the Supreme Court did *not* preclude ordinary gain or loss treatment for sales or exchanges of assets that were integrally related to *other* exceptions to Code Sec. 1221.

Reg. §1.1221-27. The decision in *Federal National Mortgage Association* somewhat blunted the zeal of the IRS in applying the *Arkansas Best* rationale to various types of "hedging" transactions, and in 1994 the IRS issued regulations that exempted certain business hedges from capital asset treatment. A "hedging transaction" is defined as one that a taxpayer enters into in the normal course of its trade or business primarily (1) to reduce the risk of price changes or currency fluctuations with respect to ordinary income property held or to be held by the taxpayer, or (2) to reduce the risk of interest rate or price changes or currency fluctuations with respect to borrowings or ordinary obligations incurred or to be incurred. As long as hedging transactions meet the specific conditions of Reg. §1.1221-2, any gain or loss upon disposition of the hedge would be ordinary gain or loss.

Under the regulations, taxpayers must immediately and unambiguously identify a transaction as a hedge on the day that the transaction is entered into. Once a transaction is identified as a hedge, any gain on a future disposition is automatically classified as ordinary income, even if one or more of the conditions for hedging treatment is not met.

OBSERVATION As part of the Tax Relief Extension Act of 1999 Congress broadened the Code Sec. 1221 listing of assets not qualifying for capital asset treatment. These three classes, discussed earlier in this chapter, were for commodities derivative financial instruments of a dealer in commodities,[21] hedging transactions,[22] and supplies consumed in a business.[23] These statutory additions basically codified the language of the 1994 regulations, including the same-day identification requirement for hedges. There was one exception, however: the regulations requirement that such assets "reduce risk" was changed to "manage risk." In effect, Congress somewhat loosened the risk requirements for these three types of assets.

¶7015 Landmark Property Cases— The Realization Principle

Generally, the IRS and the Courts insist that the fair market value of the property *received* in an exchange be used to measure the amount realized, since this amount will also serve as the basis of the property received. If the properties involved in the exchange do not have equal fair market values, then this approach assures that "good" or "bad" deals do not affect the initial determination of the basis of property received. In a few instances, a Court has expressed a preference for using the fair market value of the property *given up*, where the good or bad deal should be recognized immediately.[24]

Occasionally, the IRS and the Courts recognize that the value of certain properties received cannot be determined with a reasonable degree of certainty. In such cases, the value of the property given up is used as a surrogate for the value of the property received, since in an

---

[20] *Federal National Mortgage Association*, 100 TC 541.
[21] Code Sec. 1221(a)(6).
[22] Code Sec. 1221(a)(7).
[23] Code Sec. 1221(a)(8).
[24] *Budd International Corp.*, CA-3, 44-2 ustc ¶9425, 143 F2d 784.

arm's-length transaction, the two should be approximately equal. One of the leading cases that applied this rule was the present case, *Thomas C. Davis*.

.01   MEASURING THE AMOUNT REALIZED

U.S. vs. Thomas C. Davis[25]

Facts of the Case: These cases involve the tax consequences of a transfer of appreciated property by Thomas Crawley Davis to his former wife pursuant to a property settlement agreement executed prior to divorce, as well as the deductibility of his payment of her legal expenses in connection therewith. The Court of Claims upset the Commissioner's determination that there was taxable gain on the transfer but upheld his ruling that the fees paid the wife's attorney were not deductible [61-1 USTC ¶9276]. 287 F. 2d 168. We granted certiorari on a conflict in the Courts of Appeals and the Court of Claims on the taxability of such transfers. 368 U. S. 813. We have decided that the taxpayer did have a taxable gain on the transfer and that the wife's attorney's fees were not deductible.

In 1954 the taxpayer and his then wife made a voluntary property settlement and separation agreement calling for support payments to the wife and minor child in addition to the transfer of certain personal property to the wife. Under Delaware law all the property transferred was that of the taxpayer, subject to certain statutory marital rights of the wife including a right of intestate succession and a right upon divorce to a share of the husband's property. Specifically as a "division in settlement of their property" the taxpayer agreed to transfer to his wife, *inter alia,* 1,000 shares of stock in E. I. du Pont de Nemours & Co. Mrs. Davis agreed to accept this division "in full settlement and satisfaction of any and all claims and rights against the husband whatsoever (including but not by way of limitation, dower and all rights under the laws of testacy and intestacy)." Pursuant to the above agreement which had been incorporated into the divorce decree, one-half of this stock was delivered in the tax year involved, 1955, and the balance thereafter. Davis' cost basis for the 1955 transfer was $74,775.37, and the fair market value of the 500 shares there transferred was $82,250. The taxpayer also agreed orally to pay the wife's legal expenses, and in 1955 he made payments to the wife's attorney, including $2,500 for services concerning tax matters relative to the property settlement.

Note: Upholding the 6th Circuit Court of Appeals, which had reversed the Board of Tax Appeals

---

In this case, the taxpayer voluntarily transferred 1,000 shares of DuPont stock to his former spouse as a property settlement. The transfer was in return for "*full settlement of all claims arising in the marital relationship.*" Davis had a cost basis of approximately $74,000 in the shares, and they were worth $82,000 at the time of the transfer. The taxpayer contended that the taxpayer had no wherewithal to pay after the transfer, and that the "claims arising from the marital relationship could not be valued anyway. The IRS contended that the transaction was no different than if Davis had first sold the stock and transferred the cash to his former spouse, and that an equivalence of value can be presumed in an **arm's length** transaction between what is received and what is given up in a transaction.

In the original hearing before the Board of Tax Appeals, the Court decided that it was not possible to measure the value of the property received by Davis (the release of all marital claims), and the transaction was treated as a nontaxable division of property.

---

[25] *Thomas C. Davis*, SCt, 62-2 USTC ¶9509, 370 US 65, 82 SCt 1190.

However, on appeal the 6th Circuit stated that an equivalence of value can be assumed between the stock and the release of marital rights, and the value of the stock should be used as the amount realized for purposes of determining the gain reportable by Davis.

The Supreme Court affirmed the Court of Appeals decision, noting that it was better *"to make a rough approximation of the gain realized thereby than to ignore altogether its tax consequences."* Once again, the emphasis was on the arm's-length nature of the transaction: *"It must be assumed, we think, that the parties acted at arm's length and that they judged the marital rights to be equal in value to the property for which they were exchanged. There was no evidence to the contrary here."*

OBSERVATION	The tax result in *Davis* was reversed as part of the 1984 Act. However, this case is still important for establishing the principal of using the value of the property surrendered as the amount realized in cases where the value of the property received couldn't be estimated. For example, the severing of a joint tenancy between nonspouses would be taxed in a manner similar to *Davis*.

The phrase "fair market value of the property (other than money) received" in Code Sec. 1001(b) was first added to the Code in 1924. Prior to this time, the reference to fair market value was phrased as follows: "on an exchange of property, real, personal, or mixed, for any other such property, no gain or loss shall be recognized unless the property received in exchange has a readily realizable fair market value."[26] The IRS has vigorously interpreted the 1924 change as indicating that value can be determined in almost any case for tax purposes.

One of the first tests of the IRS approach was the present case, *Burnet v. Logan.* In this case, the taxpayer, Edith Logan, and a group of shareholders sold their closely-held stock, which had as its principal asset stock in a second corporation with a valuable iron mine. The stock was sold in 1916 for $2.2 million plus $.60 for each ton of ore extracted from the mine. In the year in question (1916), Ms. Logan's total share received was less than her basis in the stock.

.03 CONTINGENT SALES PRICES

Edith Logan[27]

Facts of the Case: Prior to March, 1913, and until March 11, 1916, respondent, Mrs. Logan, owned 250 of the 4,000 capital shares issued by the Andrews & Hitchcock Iron Company. It held 12% of the stock of the Mahoning Ore & Steel Company, an operating concern. In 1895 the latter corporation procured a lease for 97 years upon the "Mahoning" mine and since then has regularly taken large, but varying, quantities of iron ore--in 1913, 1,515,428 tons; in 1914, 1,212,287 tons; in 1915, 2,311,940 tons; in 1919, 1,217,167 tons; in 1921, 303,020 tons; in 1923, 3,029,865 tons. The lease contract did not require production of either maximum or minimum tonnage or any definite payments. Through an agreement of stockholders (steel manufacturers) the Mahoning Company is obligated to apportion extracted ore among them according to their holdings.

On March 11, 1916, the owners of all the shares in Andrews & Hitchcock Company sold them to Youngstown Sheet & Tube Company, when thus acquired, among other things, 12% of the Mahoning Company's stock and the right to receive the same percentage of ore thereafter taken from the leased mine. For the shares so acquired the Youngstown Company paid the holders $2,200,000 in money and agreed to pay annually thereafter for

---

[26] Code Sec. 202(c), 42 Stat. 230.
[27] *Edith Logan*, SCt, 2 USTC ¶736, 283 US 404, 51 SCt 550.

distribution among them 60 cents for each ton of ore apportioned to it. Of this cash Mrs. Logan received 250/4000ths—$137,500; and she became entitled to the same fraction of any annual payment thereafter made by the purchaser under the terms of sale. Mrs. Logan's mother had long owned 1,100 shares of the Andrews & Hitchcock Company. She died in 1917, leaving to the daughter one-half of her interest in payments thereafter made by the Youngstown Company. This bequest was appraised for federal estate tax purposes at $277,164.50.

During 1917, 1918, 1919 and 1920 the Youngstown Company paid large sums under the agreement. Out of these respondent received on account of her 250 shares $9,900.00 in 1917, $11,250.00 in 1918, $8,995.50 in 1919, $5,444.30 in 1920--$35,589.80. By reason of the interest from her mother's estate she received $19,790.10 in 1919, and $11,977.49 in 1920.

Reports of income for 1918, 1919 and 1920 were made by Mrs. Logan upon the basis of cash receipts and disbursements. They included no part of what she had obtained from annual payments by the Youngstown Company. She maintains that until the total amount actually received by her from the sale of her shares equals their value on March 1, 1913, no taxable income will arise from the transaction. Also that until she actually receives by reason of the right bequeathed to her a sum equal to its appraised value, there will be no taxable income there from.

On March 1, 1913, the value of the 250 shares then held by Mrs. Logan *exceeded* $173,089.80--the total of all sums actually received by her prior to 1921 from their sale ($137,500.00 cash in 1916 plus four annual payments amounting to $35,589.80). That value also exceeded original cost of the shares. The amount received on the interest devised by her mother was less than its valuation for estate taxation; also less than the value when acquired by Mrs. Logan.

The Commissioner ruled that the obligation of the Youngstown Company to pay 60 cents per ton had a fair market value of $1,942,111.46 on March 11, 1916; that this value should be treated as so much cash and the sale of the stock regarded as a closed transaction with no profit in 1916. He also used this valuation as the basis for apportioning subsequent annual receipts between income and return of capital. His calculations, based upon estimates and assumptions, are too intricate for brief statement. He made deficiency assessments according to the view just stated and the Board of Tax Appeals approved the result.

Note: Affirming 2nd Circuit Court of Appeals, which had reversed the Board of Tax Appeals

The IRS insisted that the buyer's promise to pay could be estimated by assuming that the estimated ore reserves would be extracted evenly over the mine's estimated life, and that the net present value of these expected payments should be treated as the "amount realized" in the year of sale (resulting in a **closed transaction**). The taxpayer contended that neither the value of the interest received (royalty) nor the value of the interest given up (the closely-held stock) could be determined, and therefore the taxpayer should be permitted to use a cost-recovery method (an **open transaction**, where nothing is taxed until the taxpayer recovers her basis).

The Supreme Court decided for the taxpayer, stating that the right to a future share of profits has no ascertainable value:

¶7015.03

"The consideration for the sale was $2,200,000.00 in cash and the promise of future money payments wholly contingent upon facts and circumstances not possible to foretell with anything like fair certainty. The promise was in no proper sense equivalent to cash. It had no ascertainable fair market value. The transaction was not a closed one. Respondent might never recoup her capital investment from payments only conditionally promised."

Taxpayer Logan was permitted to use a cost recovery basis; no gain was recognized until total collections under the contract exceeded her adjusted basis. This procedure has become known as the **open transaction doctrine**, since the lack of an ascertainable value of the property received means that the transaction cannot be closed. In somewhat of a rebuke to the accuracy of the government's approach, the Court noted that "*As annual payments on account of extracted ore come in they can be readily apportioned first as return of capital and later as profit. The liability for income tax ultimately can be fairly determined without resort to mere estimates, assumptions, and speculation.*"

OBSERVATION   Two points are worth noting about the *Logan* case. First, one key finding in the case was that the stock of the closely-held corporation could not be valued. If a reasonable value for the stock had been determined, then the Court would likely have assumed that in an arm's length transaction, the value of the cash payment plus the promise to pay would equal the value of the stock. In that case, the value of the stock would have been substituted as the "amount realized," and gain could have been measured in the year of sale. Secondly, the tax year in question was 1916, *before* a preference for capital gains was included in the tax law. If Ms. Logan had also qualified for capital gains, the tax stakes would have been even higher, and this may have influenced the result.

In order to understand the *Tufts* decision, it is necessary to refer to an earlier case that is discussed later in this section, the *Crane* case. In *Crane*,[28] the taxpayer inherited an apartment building and lot valued for estate tax purposes at $255,000. The property was subject to a $255,000 nonrecourse debt, and over $7,000 of interest was in default at the time the property was inherited. Ms. Crane agreed to continue to rent the property and remit all net rentals to the mortgagee. She did this for seven years, during which time the interest in default increased to approximately $15,800. Under a threat of foreclosure, the taxpayer sold the property for $3,000, less $500 selling expenses.

Ms. Crane reported the transaction as a $1,250 long-term capital gain ($2,500 net gain less a 50-percent long-term capital gains exclusion). The taxpayer contended that she had no "equity" in the building, and thus no basis. The IRS contended that the mortgage should be included in both the amount realized and the original basis of the property, and after allocations and allowable depreciation, the taxpayer would have a small loss on the land and $24,000 ordinary income due to recapture on the building.

.05   LIABILITY ASSUMPTION AS PART OF THE AMOUNT REALIZED

Commissioner v. John F. Tufts[29]

Facts of the Case: Section 752(d) of the Internal Revenue Code of 1954 (IRC) provides that liabilities incurred in the sale or exchange of a partnership interest are to be treated "in the same manner as liabilities in connection with the sale or exchange of property not associated with partnerships." Under §1001(a) of the IRC, the gain or loss from a sale or other disposition of property is defined as the difference between

---

[28]   *Crane*, SCt, 47-1 USTC ¶9217, 331 US 1, 67 SCt 1047.
[29]   *John F. Tufts*, SCt, 83-1 USTC ¶9328, 461 US 300, 103 SCt 1826.

"the amount realized" on the disposition and the property's adjusted basis. Section 1001(b) defines the "amount realized" as "the sum of any money received plus the fair market value of the property (other than money) received." A general partnership formed by respondents in 1970 to construct an apartment complex entered into a $1,851,500 nonrecourse mortgage loan with a savings association. The complex was completed in 1971. Due to the partners' capital contributions to the partnership and income tax deductions for their allocable shares of ordinary losses and depreciation, the partnership's claimed adjusted basis in the property in 1972 was $1,455,740.

Because of an unanticipated reduction in rental income, the partnership was unable to make the payments due on the mortgage. Each partner thereupon sold his interest to a third party, who assumed the mortgage. The fair market value on the date of transfer did not exceed $1,400,000. Each partner reported the sale on his income tax return and indicated a partnership loss of $55,740. The Commissioner of Internal Revenue, however, determined that the sale resulted in a partnership gain of approximately $400,000 on the theory that the partnership had realized the full amount of the nonrecourse obligation. The United States Tax Court upheld the deficiencies, but the Court of Appeals reversed.

Note: Reversing the 5th Circuit Court of Appeals, which had reversed the Tax Court

The Supreme Court agreeing with the IRS in reaching its decision, noting that "*we could not accept petitioner's contention that the $2,500.00 net cash was all she realized on the sale except on the absurdity that she sold a quarter-of-a-million dollar property for roughly one percent of its value, and took a 99 percent loss.*" The Court was persuaded that the transfer of the nonrecourse mortgage created a benefit as real as having a personal debt assumed by another person. The Court also stressed the need for "symmetry" in computing the adjusted basis and the amount realized.

One of the interesting facts in the case was that the value of the building essentially equaled the amount of the nonrecourse debt, so the seller (Ms. Crane) did have some incentive to hold the building or to sell it. But what if the value of the building was substantially less than the amount of the nonrecourse debt: would the seller realize a benefit equal to the debt assumed when the property was sold? After all, the taxpayer could just walk away from the property and leave the creditor with just the property, so wouldn't the value of the property be more accurate as the "amount realized"? The Supreme Court did not address this issue in Crane, but did note the following in the infamous footnote 37 of the case:

> "*Obviously, if the value of the property is less than the amount of the mortgage, a mortgagor who is not personally liable cannot realize a benefit equal to the mortgage. Consequently, a different problem might be encountered where a mortgagor abandoned the property or transferred it subject to the mortgage without receiving boot (i.e., cash or other property). That is not this case.*"

This "different problem" was encountered in the *Tufts* case. In *Tufts*, a general partnership in an apartment complex was formed with a $1,850,000 nonrecourse loan. By 1972, the basis of the property after losses and depreciation was $1,455,000, even though the face amount of the note remained at $1,850,000. At this time, each partner should transfer his or her interest to an unrelated party for $250 plus the transfer of the nonrecourse note. The value of the property at the date of transfer was estimated to be $1,400,000. The partners reported a $55,000 loss on the transfer ($1,400,000 amount realized less $1,455,000 adjusted basis), assuming that the debt forgiveness should be limited to the fair market value of the property.

The Commissioner contended that the taxpayers realized a $395,000 gain ($1,850,000 amount realized less $1,455,000 adjusted basis), relying on the *Crane* decision as a basis for including the full face value of the mortgage in the amount realized. The taxpayer argued that the full face value of the note could not be realized, as implied by the Court in footnote 37 of the *Crane* case.

The Tax Court originally ruled for the Commissioner, but the 5th Circuit Court of Appeals reversed this decision and ruled for the taxpayers. The Supreme Court in turn reversed the Court of Appeals decision, noting that the partnership had not suffered a real economic loss and had realized the full amount of the mortgage. The Court also stated that asymmetrical treatment between the basis and the amount realized was not possible; since the partnership had based their deductions on the $1,850,000 mortgage included in basis, the same amount must be included in the amount realized on the transfer.

In deciding this case, the Supreme Court realized that they had to deal with footnote 37 of the *Crane* case. In that decision the Court had implied that if the fair market value of the property was *less* than the mortgage, a mortgagor cannot "realize a benefit equal to the mortgage." Once again, the Court relied on the argument of "symmetry" to justify their decision:

> *Crane ultimately does not rest on its limited theory of economic benefit; instead, we read Crane to have approved the Commissioner's decision to treat a nonrecourse mortgage in this context as a true loan. This approval underlies* Crane's *holdings that the amount of the nonrecourse liability is to be included in calculating both the basis and the amount realized on disposition. That the amount of the loan exceeds the fair market value of the property thus becomes irrelevant.*

OBSERVATION

The IRS can attack the transfer of nonrecourse liabilities from two angles: the amount realized or the adjusted basis of the property. For example, using the facts of *Tufts*, two possible methods of computing a $395,000 gain on the transaction are:

	Amount Realized Approach	Basis Adjustment Approach
Amount Realized.	$ 1,850,000	$ 1,400,000
Adjusted Basis	(1,455,000)	(1,005,000)*
Realized Gain	$ 395,000	$ 395,000

* $1,455,000 basis less $450,000 excess of nonrecourse debt over the fair market value of the property.

The IRS used the "amount realized" approach in the *Tufts* case in determining the $395,000 gain. However, they easily could have accepted the taxpayers' argument that it was impossible for them to realize more than the fair market value of the property on the release of the debt. In that case, they could use the earlier victories in basis decisions and other precedents to justify reducing the taxpayers' adjusted basis by the amount that the taxpayer has no economic incentive to pay (e.g., the excess above the fair market value of the property).[30] Under either approach, the result is the same: a $395,000 realized gain.

A credit sale is defined as a sale where part of the consideration passing to the seller is a claim against the purchaser. Assuming that the installment sales rules of Code Sec. 453 do not apply, the value of the claim against the purchaser must generally be included in the amount realized. However, the total dollars includible in the amount realized depends on whether the seller reports on the cash or accrual basis.

If the seller is on the *cash basis,* Reg. §1.1001-1(a) requires that the fair market value of the obligation be included in the amount realized in the year of sale. In effect, the government views the promise to pay as "other property" under Code Sec. 1001, to be valued at its fair market value.

---

[30] For example, *see Pleasant Summit Land Corporation*, CA-3, 88-2 USTC ¶9601, 863 F2d 263, and *Regents Park Partners*, 63 TCM 3131, TCM 1992-336.

On the other hand, if the taxpayer is on the accrual basis, the IRS has consistently treated the obligation as "money received," and not "property (other than money)." As a result, the face value of the obligation must be included in the amount realized of the seller. In Rev. Rul. 79-292,[31] the IRS stated that "treating a note received as property under Code Sec. 1001(b) of the Code and valuing it at its fair market value is inconsistent with the well-established principle that an accrual method taxpayer includes in income amounts which it has a right to receive." In effect, the Service is arguing that the taxpayer's method of accounting (accrual basis) overrides the cash-basis treatment implied in Code Sec. 1001(b).

This difference in treatment creates a number of practical problems. For example, the illustrations for cash-basis taxpayers in *Reg. §1.1001-1* indicate that the other party in the exchange, the buyer, will include the *face value* of the obligation in his or her tax basis, even though a cash-basis seller may include a smaller amount in the amount realized because the fair market value of the obligation is less than its face value. Thus, a disconformity between the two parties is created.

It is interesting to note that the Tax Court has objected to the differing approaches to cash-basis and accrual-basis taxpayers. Specifically, the Tax Court recognized the difficulties in valuing such obligations, and was concerned that if the cash-basis seller were a service provider, income would not be taxed until the cash was received. The Court has also been concerned about the seller's wherewithal to pay tax; in some cases, the seller may have to sell the obligation at a steep discount just to be able to pay the tax on the gain reportable in the year of sale.

The Tax Court's approach in these cases has been to focus more on the "cash" side of Code Sec. 1001(b), rather than the "other property" side. Specifically, if the Court believes that the obligation is not the equivalent of cash and cannot be immediately valued, they have tended to allow the taxpayer to use a cost recovery (open transaction) method for the payments. In this case, no payments are taxable until the taxpayer's basis is recovered. This was essentially the taxpayer's argument in the *Warren Jones* case, that the note received in the transaction was not the "equivalent of cash." The IRS contended that Code Sec. 1001 requires the "fair market value of property other than money" be included in the amount realized, and that the taxpayer should have simply elected the installment method to avoid this problem.

.07   DEFERRED PAYMENT CONTRACTS

Warren Jones Paving v. Commissioner[32]

Facts of the Case: On May 27, 1968, the taxpayer, a family-held corporation chartered by the State of Washington, entered into a real estate contract for the sale of one of its Seattle apartment buildings, the Wallingford Court Apartments, to Bernard and Jo Ann Storey for $153,000. When the sale closed on June 15, 1968, the Storeys paid $20,000 in cash and took possession of the apartments. The Storeys were then obligated by the contract to pay the taxpayer $1,000 per month, plus 8 percent interest on the declining balance, for a period of fifteen years. The balance due at the end of fifteen years is to be payable in a lump sum. The contract was the only evidence of the Storeys' indebtedness, since no notes or other such instruments passed between the parties. Upon receipt of the full purchase price, the taxpayer is obligated by the contract to deed the Wallingford Apartments to the Storeys.

The Tax Court found, as facts, that the transaction between the taxpayer and the Storeys was a completed sale in the taxable year ending on October 31, 1968, and that in that year, the Storeys were solvent obligors. The court

---

[31] Rev. Rul. 79-292, 1979-2 CB 287.
[32] *Warren Jones Company*, CA-9, 75-2 USTC ¶9732, 524 F2d 788.

also found that real estate contracts such as those between the taxpayer and the Storeys were regularly bought and sold in the Seattle area. The court concluded, from the testimony before it, that in the taxable year of sale, the taxpayer could have sold its contract, which had a face value of $133,000, to a savings and loan association or a similar institutional buyer for approximately $117,980. The court found, however, that in accordance with prevailing business practices, any potential buyer for the contract would likely have required the taxpayer to deposit $41,000 of the proceeds from the sale of the contract in a savings account, assigned to the buyer, for the purpose of securing the first $41,000 of the Storeys' payments. Consequently, the court found that in the taxable year of sale, the contract had a fair market value of only $76,980 (the contract's selling price minus the amount deposited in the assigned savings account).

On the sale's closing date, the taxpayer had an adjusted basis of $61,913 in the Wallingford Apartments. In determining the amount it had realized from the sale, the taxpayer added only the $20,000 down payment and the portion of the $4,000 in monthly payments it had received that was allocable to principal. Consequently, on its federal income tax return for the taxable year ending October 31, 1968, the taxpayer reported no gain from the apartment sale. The taxpayer's return explained that the corporation reported on the cash basis and that under the Tax Court's holding in *Nina J. Ennis* [CCH Dec. 18,543], 17 T. C. 465 (1951), it was not required to report gain on the sale until it had recovered its basis. The return also stated, however, that in the event the taxpayer was required to report gain in the taxable year of the sale, it elected to do so on the installment basis (I. R. C. §453).

The Commissioner disagreed with the taxpayer's assertion that it had realized no gain on the sale, but he conceded that the sale qualified as an installment sale. Consequently, the Commissioner recalculated the taxpayer's gain in accordance with section 453 and notified the taxpayer that it had recognized an additional $12,098 in long term capital gain. The taxpayer then petitioned the Tax Court for a redetermination of its liability.

Note: Reversing the Tax Court

In this case at the lower court level, the Tax Court ruled for the taxpayer. The Court noted that *"The fundamental difficulty in these deferred payment cases is that to treat every evidence of indebtedness in the hands of a cash basis taxpayer as the equivalent of cash to the extent of fair market value obliterates the fundamental difference between the cash and accrual methods as to the treatment of receivables."*

The Tax Court's decision in *Warren Jones* was appealed to the 9th Circuit by the government, which won a reversal of the Tax Court ruling. In its decision, the Appeals Court noted that the installment method was available for any hardships caused by the differing tax treatments for cash- and accrual-basis taxpayers. Despite this setback, the Tax Court has continued to apply the "equivalence of cash" test to credit sales. Thus, cash-basis taxpayers that opt out of the installment method have their best chance for success in the Tax Court.

OBSERVATION   Although the examples given thus far appear to create a hardship for the cash-basis seller, in some cases they may actually create a tax benefit. Specifically, if the fair market value of the obligation is *less* than the adjusted basis of the property, a loss may be reported in the year of sale.

.09   **THE REALIZATION PRINCIPLE—ADDITIONAL CASES**

Pleasant Summit Land Corporation v. Commissioner.[33] In this case, the Tax Court determined that the price (mostly nonrecourse debt) paid by a partnership for an apartment complex greatly exceeded its fair market value, and no bona fide debt existed for tax purposes. However, on appeal the 3rd Circuit determined that it was appropriate to disallow only that portion of the nonrecourse debt *in excess* of the fair market value of the property, and to treat the remaining nonrecourse debt as bona fide debt to the extent that it does not exceed such value. The court reasoned that if the taxpayer defaulted, the creditor would probably be willing to accept payment equal to the fair market value of the property since nothing more would be gained by foreclosure. In effect, the taxpayer would probably have the "option" of retaining the property by paying an amount equal to its fair market value to the creditor.

Walter M. Hort v. Commissioner.[34] In this case, a lessor received a payment from the lessee to terminate a lease before the expiration date. Taxpayer Hort contended that he had "sold" his rights to future rents for a lump sum at a loss, in that he received $140,000 for the right to rents with a present value of approximately $165,500. The Supreme Court held that Hort should recognize $140,000 of ordinary income, in that the payment was merely a substitute for a portion of the rents that would have been taxed as ordinary income if received. The court also noted that the taxpayer never reported any of the rent as income and had no grounds for claiming a "basis" in the foregone rents.

¶7017 Landmark Property Cases— Nontaxable Exchanges

The original Code Sec. 1031 provisions were generally interpreted as requiring a simultaneous transfer of property in order to qualify for like-kind treatment. Reg. §1.1002-1(d) refers to a *"reciprocal transfer of property, as distinguished from a transfer of money."* Initial rulings by the IRS as far back as 1922 generally required a simultaneous passage of title for both properties. However, such a requirement generally conflicted with other sections of the Code, such as the liberal exchange provisions of Code Secs. 351 and 1036.

The courts have generally been far less restrictive in interpreting the timing of the exchange. In a major decision that generally negated the "simultaneous exchange" standard, the 9th Circuit in *Starker v. U.S.* extended Code Sec. 1031 treatment to a deferred exchange. In *Starker*, the taxpayer conveyed 1,800 acres of timberland for a promise from the other party to the exchange (Crown Corporation) to deliver like-kind property at a future date.

.01   **DEFERRED EXCHANGES**

T. J. Starker v. U.S.[35]

Facts of the Case. On April 1, 1967, T. J. Starker and his son and daughter-in-law, Bruce and Elizabeth Starker, entered into a "land exchange agreement" with Crown Zellerbach Corporation (Crown). The agreement provided that the three Starkers would convey to Crown all their interests in 1,843 acres of timberland in Columbia County, Oregon. In consideration for this transfer, Crown agreed to acquire and deed over to the Starkers other real property in Washington and Oregon. Crown agreed to provide the Starkers suitable real property within five years or pay any outstanding balance in cash. As part of the contract, Crown agreed to add to the Starkers' credit each year a "growth factor", equal to six percent of the outstanding balance.

---

[33] *Pleasant Summit Land Corporation*, CA-3, 88-2 USTC ¶9601, 863 F2d 263.
[34] *Walter M. Hort*, SCt, 41-1 USTC ¶9354, 313 US 28, 61 SCt 757.
[35] *T. J. Starker*, CA-9, 79-2 USTC ¶9541, 602 F2d. 1341.

On May 31, 1967, the Starkers deeded their timberland to Crown. Crown entered "exchange value credits" in its books: for T. J. Starker's interest, a credit of $1,502,500; and for Bruce and Elizabeth's interest, a credit of $73,000. Within four months, Bruce and Elizabeth found three suitable parcels, and Crown purchased and conveyed them pursuant to the contract. No "growth factor" was added because a year had not expired, and no cash was transferred to Bruce and Elizabeth because the agreed value of the property they received was $73,000, the same as their credit. Closing the transaction with T. J. Starker, whose credit balance was larger, took longer. Beginning in July 1967 and continuing through May 1969, Crown purchased 12 parcels selected by T. J. Starker. Of these 12, Crown purchased 9 from third parties, and then conveyed them to T. J. Starker. Two more of the 12 (the Timian and Bi-Mart properties) were transferred to Crown by third parties, and then conveyed by Crown at T. J. Starker's direction to his daughter, Jean Roth. The twelfth parcel (the Booth Property) involved a third party's contract to purchase. Crown purchased that contract right and reassigned it to T. J. Starker.

The first of the transfers from Crown T. J. Starker or his daughter was on September 5, 1967; the twelfth and last was on May 21, 1969. By 1969, T. J. Starker's credit balance had increased from $1,502,500 to $1,577,387.91, by means of the 6 per cent "growth factor". The land transferred by Crown to T. J. Starker and Roth was valued by the parties at exactly $1,577,387.91. Therefore, no cash was paid to T. J. Starker, and his balance was reduced to zero.

In their income tax returns for 1967, the three Starkers all reported no gain on the transactions, although their bases in the properties they relinquished were smaller than the market value of the properties they received. They claimed that the transactions were entitled to nonrecognition treatment under section 1031 of the Internal Revenue Code (I. R. C. §1031. The Internal Revenue Service disagreed, and assessed deficiencies of $35,248.41 against Bruce and Elizabeth Starker and $300,930.31 plus interest against T. J. Starker. The Starkers paid the deficiencies, filed claims for refunds, and when those claims were denied, filed two actions for refunds in the United States District Court in Oregon.

Note: Affirming and reversing in part the U.S. District Court

---

Crown deposited $1.5 million in escrow while they attempted to locate properties which were acceptable to Starker. The escrow agreement provided for a six-percent interest growth factor during the search. Eventually, twelve properties were located and transferred to Stark.

The IRS contended that the transaction did not meet the *form* of the law, in that the exchange was not simultaneous. The taxpayer contended that the transaction met the *substance* of the law, because in the end an exchange was completed and the taxpayer never had constructive receipt over the amount in escrow.

The 9th Circuit decided that the transaction was a qualified Code Sec. 1031 exchange because it involved similar "bundles" of properties and that taxpayer Stark preferred replacement properties to cash at all times. The IRS initially agreed with the *Starker* decision in a 1979 letter ruling, and then disagreed with the decision in a 1980 letter ruling.

Congress responded to an IRS request to end this controversy by enacting Code Sec. 1031(a)(3) in 1984 (**Figure 5**), which limits the time that may elapse between reciprocal transfers of property. This statutory requirement is reproduced in the following extract.

Figure 5

Code Sec. 1031(a)(3). Requirement that property be identified and that exchange be completed not more than 180 days after transfer of exchanged property. For purposes of this subsection, any property received by the taxpayer shall be treated as property which is not like-kind property if—

    (A)   such property is not identified as property to be received in the exchange on or before the day which is 45 days after the date on which the taxpayer transfers the property relinquished in the exchange, or

    (B)   such property is received after the earlier of—

        (i)   the day which is 180 days after the date on which the taxpayer transfers the property relinquished in the exchange, or

        (ii)   the due date (determined with regard to extension) for the transferor's return of the tax imposed by this chapter for the taxable year in which the transfer of the relinquished property occurs.

In summary, a deferred exchange qualifies under Code Sec. 1031 only if the taxpayer meets the 45-day "identification period" and the 180-day "exchange period." Note that the identification period is actually only 44 days ("before the day"). Also note that the due date of the return includes any extensions of time to file the return. For calendar-year taxpayers, an exchange occurring prior to October 17th is subject to the 180-day limit (unless an extension is granted to the taxpayer). Both the 45-day and 180-day periods begin on the date of the *first* transfer of properties, if multiple properties are involved. The IRS later issued detailed regulations interpreting the operation of the new time limits.

In order to qualify under Code Sec. 1033, the replacement property must generally be purchased property that is "similar or related in use." The "similar or related in service or use" requirement has been litigated a number of times in regards to rental properties. Initially, the IRS contended that the actual end uses of the properties should be the same (i.e., the properties perform the same function). On the other hand, owner-lessors have contended that the relevant use is by the owner, and a simple replacement of rental property with other rental property would meet this requirement.

The owner-lessor argument eventually prevailed in a number of cases. The leading case in this area was *Liant Records, Inc.* In this case, the taxpayers owned an office building rented to commercial tenants. Upon receiving condemnation proceeds for the building, they invested in residential rental property. The IRS argued that the replacement properties were *not similar or related in use*, noting that one was commercial property and the other was residential property. The taxpayer argued that there is a difference for owner/lessor properties, in that both perform the same basic function: to provide rental income.

.03   OWNER-LESSOR PROPERTIES

Liant Record, Inc. v. Commissioner[36]

Facts of the Case. The sole question presented is whether the proceeds from the condemnation of an office building were reinvested in property which was "similar or related in service or use" within the meaning of §1033 of the Internal Revenue Code of 1954 when the taxpayers purchased three apartment buildings. The Tax Court held that they were not, since the tenants of the office building used the property for a different purpose than the tenants of the apartment buildings. We reverse and remand.

---

[36] *Liant Record, Inc.*, CA-2, 62-1 USTC ¶9494, 303 F2d 326.

The taxpayers and Norman Einstein owned a 25-story, steel-frame office building located at 1819 Broadway, Manhattan, New York. The building, which had been erected about 1913, was, on November 17, 1953, rented to 82 commercial tenants, including accountants, attorneys, real estate firms, a doctor, a dentist, and a bank, all of whom used it exclusively to conduct business. On November 17, 1953 the City of New York instituted condemnation proceedings against the taxpayers' office building and acquired title on the same date. Each of the taxpayers received payments in settlement for the condemned property during 1954 and 1955 which substantially exceeded their respective tax bases in the property.

Between July 12, 1955 and November 1, 1956 the taxpayers acquired three pieces of real estate each containing an apartment building. Each taxpayer's contribution to the total purchase prices of the three parcels exceeded his share of the proceeds from the condemnation. 3 The 9-story building located at 55 West 11th Street, New York City, contained 77 apartments used for residential purposes and 6 commercial tenants. The 6-story brick building at 400 East 80th Street, New York City, contained 47 residential apartments and 4 stores. The 11-story, steel-frame building located at 35 East 84th Street, New York City, contained 40 residential apartments and 6 commercial tenants. The taxpayers held the properties for rental income and did not occupy any of the properties.

The taxpayers, contending that their gain on the involuntary conversion was nontaxable under §1033 of the Internal Revenue Code of 1954, did not report any income from the disposition of the condemned office building. The Commissioner, on the other hand, took the view that the three apartment buildings were not "similar or related in service or use" to the condemned office building, and that therefore the taxpayers should have reported an aggregate capital gain on their 1955 income tax returns of $427,012.61. Consequently, the Commissioner asserted an aggregate deficiency of $107,716.51 against the taxpayers.

Note: Reversing the U.S. Tax Court

In deciding for the taxpayer, the Appeals Court ruled that it was the relationship between the taxpayer and the property, rather than the end users (the lessees), that determines Code Sec. 1033 applicability. This led to widespread adoption of the owner/lessor tests for reinvestment under Code Sec. 1033.

OBSERVATION   The IRS eventually issued *Rev. Rul. 67-237*,[37] which specified four factors to be considered in determining if a conversion of owner-lessor properties qualifies under Code Sec. 1033. The factors are: (1) nature of risks associated with the property, (2) level of management required, (3) services required, and (4) relationship of the taxpayer with other parties. Particular emphasis has been placed by the courts on the level of services provided by the owner-lessor.

¶7019   Summary

- The taxation of the disposition of assets is complex and depends not only on the type of taxpayer disposing of the asset, but also the type of the asset being disposed of.
- With proper tax planning, the individual taxpayer can maximize the gains taxed at the current favorable long term capital gains rate of 15 percent.

---

[37] Rev. Rul. 67-237, 1967-2 CB 167.

- While corporate taxpayers do not have preferential tax rates when disposing of capital assets, proper tax planning is a must in order to utilize any capital loss carryforwards within the carryforward period.
- The ordinary income depreciation recapture mitigates to some extent the accelerated depreciation allowed on business-use assets.
- Much of the authority for recognition of capital gains and losses is the result of judicial decisions that have in some cases favored the taxpayer and in others favored the IRS.
- The taxpayer should consult with a tax advisor before a business or capital asset is disposed of in order to minimize the current and future tax liability.

Review Questions for Chapter 7

True or False

Indicate which of the following statements are true or false by circling the correct answer.

1. The Code provides a clear definition of a capital asset.   T   F

2. Copyrights and other artistic compositions are automatically excluded from
    capital gains treatment.   T   F

3. Net short-term capital gains are fully taxable at ordinary income tax rates.   T   F

4. Individual taxpayers with capital loss carry forwards must first offset 28-percent
    gains before offsetting 15-percent gains.   T   F

5. There is no preferential rate for long-term capital gains for corporate taxpayers.   T   F

6. A net capital loss of a corporation is deductible up to the $3,000 annual capital loss limit.   T   F

7. Code Sec. 1231 was designed to provide ordinary tax treatment for capital gains and
    capital loss tax treatment for ordinary losses.   T   F

8. Code Sec. 1245 recapture applies to depreciable realty acquired after 1961.   T   F

9. Code Sec. 1031 applies to an exchange of property used in a trade or business or held
    for the production of income, provided the properties are similar.   T   F

10. In *Corn Products Refining Co.*, the Supreme Court upheld the lower court's determina-
    tion that gain from the sale of commodity futures should be taxed as ordinary income.   T   F

Fill in the Blanks

11. In enacting Code Sec. 1221(a)(1), Congress wanted to distinguish _____ properties from
    _____ properties.

12. The phrase "_____" has created definitional problems under both Code Sec. 1221
    and Code Sec. 1231.

13. Code Sec. 1221(a)(2) specifically excludes "_____" from the definition
    of a capital asset.

14. The __-percent capital gains tax rate applies to "unrecaptured Sec. 1250 gain."

15. Code Sec. 1231 applies only to assets that have been held more than ____ year(s).

16. Code Sec. 1245 depreciation recapture does not apply to property that was sold at a _____.

17. Code Sec. 291 recapture does not apply to _____ taxpayers.

18. Involuntary conversions include: casualty and theft losses, and _____ of property.

19. The *Corn Products* decision stands for the narrow proposition that _____ that are an
    integral part of a business inventory-purchase system fall within the inventory exclusion of Code Sec. 1221.

20. In the *Tufts* decision, the Supreme Court held that the value of the real estate was equal to the amount of
    the _____ debt on the property.

Multiple Choice:

Circle the best answer for each of the following questions.

21. Cynthia has wage income of $100,000 and the following capital gains and losses: $3,000 STCL, $3,000 28-percent gain, $2,000 25-percent gain, and $6,000 15-percent gain. Her net capital gain is:
    a. $2,000 @25% and $6,000 @15%
    b. $2,000 @28% and $6,000 @15%
    c. $3,000 @28%, $2,000 @25%, and $3,000 @15%
    d. $1,000 @25% and $7,000 @15%

22. Henry has wage income of $100,000 and the following capital gains and losses: $14,000 short-term capital loss, $6,000 28-percent gain, and $7,000 15-percent gain. Henry has a:
    a. $1,000 capital loss deduction.
    b. $3,000 capital loss deduction.
    c. $1,000 net capital gain.
    d. $6,000 net capital gain.

23. Cybil Company acquired a new machine on January 15. It sold the machine 10 months later incurring a $10,000 loss on the disposition. What is the nature of the loss?
    a.   A capital loss
    b.   An ordinary loss.
    c.   A nonseparately stated inventory loss
    d.   A Code Sec. 1231 loss

24. Cybil Company has a net Code Sec. 1231 gain of $45,000 in the current year. In the previous tax year it had a $22,000 net Code Sec. 1231 loss. For the current tax year Cybil's net Code Sec. 1231 gain is:
    a. $23,000 long-term capital gain and $22,000 ordinary loss.
    b. $45,000 ordinary gain.
    c. $23,000 long-term capital gain and $22,000 ordinary gain.
    d. $45,000 capital gain.

25. Cybil Company sold the following assets in the current tax year:

Asset	Holding Period	Sales Price	Adjusted Basis
Office Equipment	six years	$1,100	$0
Automobile	eight months	$1,200	$2,000
ABC Stock (capital asset)	two years	$3,200	$1,800

   What is the net capital gain and net ordinary income?
    a. $1,700 LTCG.
    b. $600 LTCG and $300 ordinary gain.
    c. $1,400 LTCG and $300 ordinary gain.
    d. $2,500 LTCG and $800 ordinary loss.

26. April Corporation sold the following asset on December 1 of the current year. What is the net Code Sec. 1231 gain and net Code Sec. 1245 recapture?

Asset	Holding Period	Sales Price	Cost	Accum. Depr.
Equipment	three years	$27,000	$30,000	$9,000

    a.   Code Sec. 1245 recapture of $6,000.
    b.   Code Sec. 1231 gain of $3,000 and $3,000 Code Sec. 1245 recapture.
    c.   Code Sec. 1231 gain of $6,000.
    d.   Code Sec. 1231 gain of $6,000 and $3,000 Code Sec. 1245 recapture.

27. Blue Company sold the following asset on October of the current year. What is the net Code Sec. 1231 gain or loss and net Code Sec. 1245 recapture?

Asset	Holding Period	Sales Price	Cost	Accum. Depr.
Equipment	three years	$55,000	$49,000	$34,800

   a. $6,000 Code Sec. 1231 gain, $34,800 Code Sec. 1245 recapture gain
   b. $0 Code Sec. 1231 gain, $40,400 Code Sec. 1245 recapture gain
   c. $6,000 Code Sec. 1231 gain, $40,400 Code Sec. 1245 recapture gain.
   d. $14,200 Code Sec. 1231 loss, $40,400 Code Sec. 1245 recapture gain,.

28. Blue Company's machine was destroyed in a fire in Feb 1 of the current year. What is the net Code Sec. 1231 gain or loss, net Code Sec. 1245 recapture, and/or casualty loss?

Asset	Holding Period	Insurance Proceeds	Cost	Accum. Depr.
Machine	four years	$10,000	$49,000	$34,800

   a. $10,000 Code Sec. 1231 loss.
   b. $10,000 Code Sec. 1245 recapture gain.
   c. $4,200 casualty loss.
   d. $4,200 Code Sec. 1231 loss.

29. Blue Company's machine was destroyed in a fire in Feb 1 of the current year. What is the net Code Sec. 1231 gain or loss, net Code Sec. 1245 recapture, and/or casualty loss assuming the machine was not replaced?

Asset	Holding Period	Insurance Proceeds	Cost	Accum. Depr.
Machine	four years	$30,000	$49,000	$34,800

   a. $4,200 ordinary loss.
   b. $15,800 Code Sec. 1245 recapture gain.
   c. $14,200 Code Sec. 1245 recapture gain.
   d. $30,000 Code Sec. 1231 gain.

30. Purple Corporation sold a commercial building on May 1 of the current year. What is the Code Sec. 291 gain from the disposition of this building?

Asset	Holding Period	Sales Price	Cost	Accum. Depr.
Building	11 years	$322,000	$400,000	$104,000

   a. $104,000.
   b. $26,000.
   c. $20,800
   d. $5,200

31. Grey Corporation exchanged a business use machine with an adjusted basis of $22,000 and a fair market value of $30,000 for a similar use machine with a fair market value of $28,000 and $2,000 cash. What is the recognized gain?
   a. $0.
   b. $2,000.
   c. $6,000.
   d. $8,000.

32. Mary Sue exchanged a rental house at the beach with an adjusted basis of $225,000 and a fair market value of $200,000 for a rental house in the mountains with a fair market value of $180,000 and cash of $20,000. What is her recognized gain or loss?
   a. $0.
   b. $20,000.
   c. ($20,000).
   d. ($25,000).

33. BiLo Corporation exchanged a warehouse for an office building. The adjusted basis of the warehouse is $600,000 and the fair market value of the office building is $350,000. BiLo also received cash of $150,000. The recognized gain or loss and the basis of the office building are:
    a. $0 and $350,000.
    b. $0 and $450,000.
    c.   ($150,000) and $300,000.
    d.   ($200,000) and $350,000.

34. BiLo Corporation exchanged a rental building with an adjusted basis of $520,000, for investment land with a fair market value of $700,000. BiLo Corporation also received cash of $100,000. The recognized gain or loss and the basis of the investment land are:
    a. $0 and $420,000.
    b. $100,000 and $420,000.
    c. $100,000 and $520,000.
    d. $280,000 and $700,000.

35. Brighton Corporation exchanged an apartment building with an adjusted basis of $47,000 and a fair market value of $90,000 and boot (Green, Inc. stock) with an adjusted basis of $8,000 and a fair market value of $5,000 for similar rental property with a fair market value of $95,000. What is the recognized gain or loss?
    a. $0.
    b. $40,000.
    c. $43,000.
    d.   ($3,000).

36. Paulene's adjusted basis in farm land is $525,000 and there is a $390,000 mortgage on the land. She exchanges the land for an office building with a fair market value of $450,000. What is Paulene's recognized gain or loss on the exchange assuming she is relieved of the mortgage on the land?
    a. $0.
    b. $315,000.
    c. $390,000.
    d. $840,000.

37. Black Corporation and White Corporation exchange real estate in a like-kind exchange. Black's property is subject to a $40,000 mortgage and has a basis of $75,000. Black receives real estate with a fair market value of $72,000 and White assumes the mortgage. What is the recognized gain and adjusted basis for the real estate received?
    a. $0; $75,000.
    b. $37,000; $72,000.
    c. $37,000; $75,000.
    d. $40,000; $115,000.

38. An office building with an adjusted basis of $320,000 was destroyed by fire on December 3 of the current year. On January 21 of the subsequent year the owner received $450,000 from the insurance company. A replacement office building was purchased on March 15 for $410,000. What is the Code Sec. 1033 recognized gain?
    a. $0 and $320,000.
    b. $0 and $410,000.
    c. $40,000 and $320,000.
    d. $130,000 and 410,000.

39 Naomi Corporation's office building with an adjusted basis of $625,000 and a fair market value of $885,000 is condemned on December 3 of the current year. A condemnation award of $850,000 was paid on May 1 of the subsequent tax year. The corporation builds a replacement new office building at a cost of $830,000 which is placed in service one year later. What is the recognized gain on receipt of the condemnation award and the basis for the new office building?
   a. $0; $605,000.
   b. $20,000; $830,000.
   c. $20,000; $625,000.
   d. $225,000; $830,000.

40. A factory building destroyed by a hurricane has an adjusted basis of $400,000 and an appraised value of $425,000. The insurance proceeds of $390,000 were used to construct a replacement building with a total cost of $450,000. The recognized gain or loss and basis of the new factory building is:
   a. $0 and $450,000.
   b. $0 and $460,000.
   c. ($10,000) and $440,000.
   d. ($10,000) and $450,000.

Problems

41. A cash-basis taxpayer paid an estimated state intangible property tax. The tax was paid early, and the state law did not have any provision for such prepayments. May the taxpayer deduct the estimated payment as taxes on her federal income tax return, assuming that the state accepts payment? Explain.

42. Brandy Corporation, a calendar-year, accrual-basis taxpayer, signed a contract on December 27, 2010, for the installation of a new central air conditioning unit. Because of various shipping delays, the unit was not installed until October 21, 2011, and was never used that year. The unit was first used on March 28, 2012. For purposes of determining MACRS recovery deductions, what year was the unit placed in service?

43. R formed New Corporation, a Qualifying Small Business Corporation by contributing cash of $20,000 for 100 percent of the stock. Seven years later, R sold her stock for $1,000,000.
   a. Compute her tax liability on the gain assuming: she treats the stock as qualified small business stock under Code Sec. 1202, or she treats the gain as a long-term capital gain eligible for 15-percent capital gain treatment.
   b. How would your answer change if she is subject to a 20-percent capital gains tax?

Research Problems:

44. *Facts.* Big Times Communication, Inc. decided to move its headquarters from Newark, NJ to Durham, NC. In order to entice its key employees to make the move the corporation offered a home-buying plan to assist employees in the sale of their personal residences in NJ. Under the plan, the company would make up to six monthly mortgage payments of up to $2,000 per month while the home was listed for sale. If at the end of six months the house was still on the market, the company would purchase the home for its appraised fair market value. During the current year, the company purchased the home of its district manager for $585,000, its appraised value. The company paid cash of $185,000 and assumed the first mortgage on the residence of $400,000. While the home was on the market, the company reimbursed the manager $12,000 (6 months × $2,000) towards the mortgage payments. The company has an offer to sell the home for $500,000. The corporate controller would like your advice regarding the deductibility of the potential $85,000 ($500,000 – $585,000) loss on the sale of the residence, the deductibility of the six mortgage payments made before the residence was purchased and the deductibility of the mortgage payments after the residence was acquired from the manager.

45. **Facts.** The Deerfield Corporation is owned by John Hunter. John also owns 100 percent of the stock of Elkton Corporation. Elkton lost a contract that it had with the U.S. government which was the primary source of income to Elkton. Deerfield made an advance to Elkton of $500,000 to cover its cash flow problem. The advance had no fixed maturity date and interest payments were contingent upon the future profitability of Deerfield. 18 months after making the advance, Deerfield determined that Elkton would never be able to repay the advance and claimed a business bad debt of $500,000 on its corporate tax return. The IRS is currently auditing Deerfield Corporation and has proposed to disallow the bad debt. Write a memo to John discussing whether Deerfield can successfully protest the disallowance of the bad debt.

46. **Facts.** Jim Brown is a dairy farmer in Wisconsin. He has a herd of 200 cows and sells milk to the local farm cooperative. Jim is also a computer whiz and spends two to four hours per day, five days per week trading cattle futures. During the year, he engaged in 300 hedge transactions regarding cattle futures. Due to an unforeseen increase in the supply of dairy cattle, Jim's hedging transactions proved to be unprofitable and he sustained a loss of $50,000 for the year. Since Jim is actively involved in the dairy business, he deducted the hedging losses as an ordinary and necessary business expense on his Schedule F, Farm income, on his form 1040. The loss reduced his net farm income to less than $400, so he paid no self-employment tax when he filed his tax return.

    The IRS is auditing Jim's tax return and proposes to increase Jim's net income from farming by $50,000 and to allow him instead a $3,000 short term capital loss. Jim has asked you to represent him in his dispute with the IRS. What advice would you give Jim?

47. **Facts.** Sam Sullivan won the Arkansas lottery which is payable in 20 annual installments of $100,000 each. Four years later, Sam's various business ventures proved to be unsuccessful and he was faced with the prospect of losing his personal residence to foreclosure. While surfing the Internet he found a company that purchases lottery annuities for 60 percent of their face value. Same contacted the firm and is ready to "sign up" to receive a cash payment of $960,000 ($100,000 × 16 × 60%). However, he is unsure of the tax treatment of receiving a lump sum payment in exchange for his annuity. His Uncle Louie has recommended that Sam take the lump sum payment since by "selling" his annuity he would be entitled to long term capital gain treatment resulting in the proceeds being taxed at 15 percent.

    Required. Write a memo to Sam outlining the proper tax treatment of the sale of the future lottery payments.

48. **Facts.** Property owned by Ellwood Inc., was condemned by the City of Denver so that the city could build a new middle school on the property. The property was used to sell and repair autos and consisted of a sales office, a display lot, and an auto repair shop. The fair market value of the property was set at $1,000,000. Upon receipt of the cash, the corporation invested the proceeds in a strip retail shopping center. Will the replacement property qualify for like exchange treatment under Code Sec. 1033?

49. **Facts.** Ted Tumble purchased a 5,000 acre ranch in Montana. He tried unsuccessfully for 15 years to raise buffalo and to sell buffalo meat to a chain of health food stores. He offered the ranch for sale, but was unable to find a suitable buyer because of the size of the property. He decided to market the property in 50 parcels, each approximately 100 acres, to hunting enthusiasts as private game reserves. He advertised in magazines read by hunters and outdoor enthusiasts. During the current year, he was able to sell 10 parcels at a net profit of $400,000. Ted would like your advice regarding the proper tax treatment of this gain.

50. **Facts.** Bobby Corporation is a real estate developer. It acquired a 50 acre tract of citrus grove near Orlando, FL with the intention of developing a retirement golfing community. The land was leased back to the seller who continued to grow and harvest citrus. Bobby Corporation purchased the land for $1,500,000 and immediately secured a $1,400,000 mortgage on the property. Two years after purchasing the property, the corporation abandoned its plans to develop the retirement community. Also, in that year a severe frost damaged most of the citrus trees and the lessor of the land was unable to make the lease payments to Bobby Corporation which had been using these payments to service the

debt on the property. On December 1 of the current year, the bank foreclosed on the loan and Bobby Corporation surrendered title to the Bank. At the date of foreclosure the property had a fair market value of $1,000,000 and the outstanding balance on the mortgage was $1,250,000. Bobby Corporation claimed an ordinary loss deduction on its tax return of $500,000 ($1,000,000 – $1,500,000) believing that there was no sale or exchange of the land.

Discuss the proper tax treatment of this transaction assuming:
(a) the mortgage is a recourse debt and the corporation was required to pay the bank $250,000 upon foreclosure.
(b) the mortgage is a nonrecourse debt and the corporation was not obligated to make any payment to the bank upon foreclosure.

51. ***Comprehensive Tax Return Problem.*** Prepare Schedules A, D, and Form 4797 of the Form 1040 using the following information.

Facts: John is single with no dependents.			
Wage Income (income tax withheld, $20,000)			$ 100,000
Unreimbursed Moving Expense, distance from old residence to new employer 875 miles, distance from new residence to new employer, 35 miles			$ 5,840
Itemized Deductions ($3,500 state income tax, $6,000 cash contribution to qualifying charity)			$ 9,500
Property Transactions:	Sales Price (Insurance Proceeds)	Adjusted Basis	Gain (Loss)
Personal Theft Loss, auto, purchased 1/1/2007, stolen 6/1/2012, cost $25,000, FMV at date of theft $18,000, no insurance, less $100 floor.	$0	$18,000	$17,900
Business Theft Loss, laptop computer purchased 1/1/2009, stolen 6/1/2012, cost $2,000, accumulated depreciation $650, Insurance proceeds based upon FMV at date of theft $1,800	$1,800	$1,350	$450
Section 1231 loss @15%, undeveloped land purchased 1/2/2007, sold 8/1/2012	$2,500	$3,900	-$1,400
Section 1231 gain @ 15%, undeveloped land purchased 1/1/2001, sold 8/1/2012	$36,000	$20,400	$15,600
Section 1231 gain @ 25%, warehouse purchased 1/1/2001 for $19,000, accumulated straight line depreciation $8,000.	$19,000	$11,000	$8,000
Short term capital loss, sale of ABC stock purchased 2/2/2012, sold 9/8/2012	$5,000	$6,000	-$1,000
Long term capital loss @ 15%, XYZ stock purchased 5/5/2008, sold 10/10/2012	$3,000	$4,500	-$1,500
Long term capital gain @ 28%, gold purchased 2/6/2006, sold 11/11/2012	$10,000	$5,000	$5,000

Internet Problem:

52. Using the fact pattern from problem 48, use your favorite web browser to locate three companies who purchase lottery annuity payments. Write a one-paragraph summary describing the promotional material found on each web site. Do you think that Sam will actually be able to sell his lottery annuity payments for the amount suggested in problem 48?

53. Use your favorite web browser to find the top marginal tax rates on dividend, capital gain, and ordinary income from 1973 to 2013. Also locate a summary of the American Taxpayer Relief Act of 2012 which increased the top marginal tax rates on individual and the maximum tax rate on long term capital gain income. How do you think these changes will affect the likelihood that corporations will pay dividends to their shareholders? How do you think these changes will affect the realization of long term capital gains by taxpayers affected by the higher tax rate on capital gains?

CHAPTER 8

Landmark Judicial Decisions—Accounting Records, Accounting Methods and Income Allocations

Learning Objectives

1. Explain the importance of two U.S. Supreme Court cases related to accounting records: the *Arthur Young* case (tax accrual workpapers) and the *Marion L. Holland* case (indirect methods of estimating income).

2. Summarize the principle conclusions of the courts in the following cases related to accounting methods: the *Thor Power Tool* case (writedowns for obsolete inventory) and the *Hillsboro Bank/Bliss Dairy* case (the tax benefit rule).

3. Explain the conclusions and underlying reasoning of the courts in the following cases related to income allocations: the *American College of Physicians* case (journal advertising and the unrelated business income tax), the *Allied Signal* case (unitary principle of apportioning income for state tax purposes), the *Bausch and Lomb* case (international transfer pricing and royalty issues), and the *Barclays Bank/Colgate Palmolive* case (unitary principle as applied to world-wide income).

¶8001　Introduction

This chapter reviews the landmark judicial decisions as they relate to accounting records, accounting methods, and income allocation methods. None of these topics fit well in the last three chapters (cases relating to income, deductions, and property transactions), so this chapter in some respects is a catchall for other important Supreme Court decisions in taxation.

The following discussion provides some background on the cases under each topic, and highlights the major tax issues covered by each of these important decisions. This brief review of each topic is followed by a comprehensive analysis of the major decisions, as well as brief summaries of other cases and authority of note. You should read the brief background notes and case headnote first, read the full text of each case next, and then, and only then, review the analysis of the case.

¶8003　Accounting Records Cases

In Chapter 9, a number of administrative and ethical issues regarding taxpayer representation are introduced. One of the hot topics in this area is the right of the IRS to subpoena the tax accrual workpapers during an audit. The genesis of this problem goes back to the landmark *Arthur Young* case, the first case discussed below.

The second case included in this grouping examines a different issue related to accounting records. Specifically, can the IRS use an indirect method of reconstructing income as a "first shot" in the audit of a taxpayer, rather than starting with a detailed examination of the taxpayer's books and records? The *Holland* case addresses this issue.

.01　IRS ACCESS TO TAXPAYER RECORDS—THE *ARTHUR YOUNG* CASE

Background

Code Sec. 7602(a) authorizes access for the IRS to any books and records of the taxpayer that are relevant to a tax inquiry. The specific provision is worded as follows:

Abstract—Code Sec. 7602(a)

SEC. 7602. EXAMINATION OF BOOKS AND WITNESSES.

7602(a) AUTHORITY TO SUMMON, ETC. — For the purpose of ascertaining the correctness of any return, making a return where none has been made, determining the liability of any person for any internal revenue tax or the liability at law or in equity of any transferee or fiduciary of any person in respect of any internal revenue tax, or collecting any such liability, the Secretary is authorized –

  (1) To examine any books, papers, records, or other data which may be relevant or material to such inquiry;

  (2) To summon the person liable for tax or required to perform the act, or any officer or employee of such person, or any person having possession, custody, or care of books of account containing entries relating to the business of the person liable for tax or required to perform the act, or any other person the Secretary may deem proper, to appear before the Secretary at a time and place named in the summons and to produce such books, papers, records, or other data, and to give such testimony, under oath, as may be relevant or material to such inquiry; and

  (3) To take such testimony of the person concerned, under oath, as may be relevant or material to such inquiry.

This provision grants access to the IRS to books and records for purposes of "ascertaining the correctness of any return," among other things. But is this a carte blanche grant of authority, or are there limits as to what the IRS can request? That is the tax issue involved in the first case we will discuss, the *Arthur Young* case.

In addition to addressing the accounting records issue, this case also goes much deeper by examining the question of confidentiality between a taxpayer and his or her representative as to tax matters. The legal profession has long had privileged communications between client and attorney, and this case addresses the same issue between taxpayer and tax advisor. As discussed below, this case as well as others led to a limited privilege for tax professionals and clients in the Code that is subject to all kinds of qualifiers, especially in light of recent developments described later in this chapter.

U.S. v. Arthur Young & Co.[1]

Facts of the Case: Respondent certified public accountant firm, as the independent auditor for respondent corporation, was responsible for reviewing the corporation's financial statements as required by the federal securities laws. In the course of reviewing these statements, the accounting firm verified the corporation's statement of its contingent tax liabilities, and, in so doing, prepared tax accrual workpapers relating to the evaluation of the corporation's reserves for such liabilities. When a routine audit by the Internal Revenue Service (IRS) to determine the corporation's income tax liability for certain years revealed that the corporation had made questionable payments from a "special disbursement account," the IRS instituted a criminal investigation of the corporation's tax returns.

In that process, the IRS, pursuant to §7602 of the Internal Revenue Code of 1954—which authorizes the Secretary of the Treasury to summon and "examine any books, papers, records, or other data which may be relevant or material" to a particular tax inquiry—issued a summons to the accounting firm requiring it to make available to the IRS all of its files relating to the corporation, including its tax accrual workpapers. When the corporation instructed the accounting firm not to comply with the summons, the IRS commenced an enforcement action in Federal District Court, which, upon finding that the tax accrual workpapers were relevant to the IRS investigation within the meaning of §7602 and refusing to recognize an accountant-client privilege that would protect the workpapers, ordered the summons enforced. The Court of Appeals affirmed in part and reversed in part.

While agreeing that the workpapers were relevant to the IRS investigation, the court held that the public interest in promoting full disclosure to public accountants, and in turn ensuring the integrity of the securities markets, required protection under a work-product immunity doctrine for the work that independent auditors perform for publicly owned corporations. Accordingly, because it found that the IRS had not made a sufficient showing of need to overcome the immunity and was not seeking to prove fraud on the corporation's part, the court refused to enforce the summons insofar as it sought the tax accrual workpapers.

Note: Affirming and Reversing in part the 2nd Circuit Court of Appeals

---

Analysis

As mentioned in the introduction, Code Sec. 7602(a) authorizes the IRS to seek any books and records of the taxpayer that are relevant to a tax inquiry. In this case, the IRS sought access to the tax accrual workpapers of the CPA firm that related to verifying

---

[1] *Arthur Young & Co.*, SCt 84-1 USTC ¶9305, 465 US 805, 104 SCt 1495.

the company's reserve for contingent tax liabilities. Fearing that this would provide the IRS with a "roadmap" to all kinds of adjustments for questionable items, the taxpayers instructed the CPA firm not to comply. The IRS sought relief in the courts, and the U.S. District Court sided with the IRS, and the 2nd Circuit Court of Appeals agreed with the logic of the District Court but nonetheless ruled for the taxpayer because they believed that the public interest and integrity of the securities market demanded protection for the accountant's work. The Supreme Court agreed to hear the case because of the muddled decision of the 2nd Circuit (relevant but no access granted) and an earlier decision of the 10th Circuit that said the papers were not relevant unless used with the return preparation.

In essence, the 2nd Circuit decision carved out a **work product immunity** doctrine for a taxpayer and his or her accountant. And this was the taxpayer's argument: to allow the IRS access would violate privileged communications between the taxpayer and the accountant, particularly since such documents were not related directly to the preparation of the return (a condition imposed by the 10th Circuit). In particular, the taxpayer feared that the IRS would be provided a roadmap to the "thought processes" of the accountants and the taxpayer in assessing the likelihood of having positions sustained on various tax issues. The IRS argued that Code Sec. 7602 provides the Service access to any records that will "shed light" on the preparation of the return.

In two earlier cases, the Supreme Court had upheld a summons for other types of records[2] and had denied the existence of privileged communication between accountant and client.[3] So in this sense, it probably came as no surprise that the Supreme Court sided with the IRS in this case, ruling that such accrual workpapers are relevant in "throwing light on" the preparation of the return. The Court also noted that the government needs extensive information-gathering authority, and to rule otherwise the Court would need "unambiguous directions" from Congress.

One of the arguments used by the taxpayer in this case was one used by the 2nd Circuit Court, which had argued that providing access to the tax accrual workpapers would have a "chilling effect" on the relationships between taxpayers and their accountants. In other words, clients would be less likely to share information with their accountants if they feared that such information may eventually end up in the IRS's hands. Taken to the extreme, this might mean that the CPA firm would have to issue a qualified opinion because the client might "clam up" on important issues. The Supreme Court stated that this concern was misplaced, since the Securities and Exchange Commission can force disclosure of such information in any event.

OBSERVATION   What the IRS won in the courts would be all for naught if they lost the victory in new legislation by Congress. Fearing this possibility, the IRS revised the *Internal Revenue Manual* in an attempt to reassure taxpayers and their representatives that they would not overstep their bounds after this decision. Specifically, the IRS stated that they would seek such workpapers only in unusual circumstances, the papers would be used as a collateral source only, and any request for access must be approved by the Chief of the Examination Division.

The decision in the *Arthur Young* case led the American Institute of Certified Public Accountants to become more politically active. One of the first successes of this lobbying effort was the passage of Code Sec. 7525 as part of the 1998 Act. This statute reads as follows:

---

2   *See Powell*, SCt, 64-2 ustc ¶9858, 379 US 48, 85 SCt 248.
3   *See Couch*, SCt, 73-1 ustc ¶9159, 409 US 322, 93 SCt 611.

SEC. 7525. CONFIDENTIALITY PRIVILEGES RELATING TO TAXPAYER COMMUNICATIONS

(a) Uniform Application to Taxpayer Communications with Federally Authorized Practitioners. —

    (1) GENERAL RULE. — With respect to tax advice, the same common law protections of confidentiality which apply to a communication between a taxpayer and an attorney shall also apply to a communication between a taxpayer and any federally authorized tax practitioner to the extent the communication would be considered a privileged communication if it were between a taxpayer and an attorney.

    (2) LIMITATIONS. — Paragraph (1) may only be asserted in –

        (A) any noncriminal tax matter before the Internal Revenue Service; and

        (B) any noncriminal tax proceeding in Federal court brought by or against the United States

    (3) DEFINITIONS. —For purposes of this subsection –

        (A) FEDERALLY AUTHORIZED TAX PRACTITIONER. —The term "federally authorized tax practitioner" means any individual who is authorized under Federal law to practice before the Internal Revenue Service if such practice is subject to Federal regulation under section 330 of title 31, United States Code.

        (B) TAX ADVICE. —The term "tax advice" means advice given by an individual with respect to a matter which is within the scope of the individual's authority to practice described in subparagraph (A).

(b) SECTION NOT TO APPLY TO COMMUNICATIONS REGARDING TAX SHELTERS. —The privilege under subsection (a) shall not apply to any written communication which is –

    (1) between a federally authorized tax practitioner and –

        (A) any person,

        (B) any director, officer, employee, agent, or representative of the person, or

        (C) any other person holding a capital or profits interest in the person, and

    (2) in connection with the promotion of the direct or indirect participation of the person in any tax shelter (as defined in section 6662(d)(2)(C)(ii)).

This victory by the AICPA may not be quite all it seems to be. For example, this statute does not modify common-law attorney-client privilege in any manner, other than to extend the privilege to certain business professionals. However, this privilege is extended solely for the purposes of receiving the *advice* of tax professionals, and not in other capacities, such as the preparation of the tax return. Most commentators have concluded that the confidentiality offered by Code Sec. 7525 will not generally apply to (1) the preparation of tax returns, (2) the preparation of tax accrual workpapers, or (3) the provision of business or accounting advice.

Recent developments seem to buttress the IRS arguments for access to the tax accrual workpapers. For example, Schedule M-3 is a newly required tax form for reconciling book-tax income of large corporations, partnerships, S corporations, and life insurance companies. This three-page form requires substantially disclosing details on many income and expense items, and conceivably the IRS may request the workpapers to support some of these numbers. And then there are some troubling implications of the *Textron* case, which is summarized below under other developments.

.03   IRS INDIRECT METHODS OF ESTIMATING INCOME— THE *HOLLAND* CASE

Background

Although there is no question that the IRS can gain access to some records, what if the taxpayer does not have any records? There have been a few incidents where taxpayers had mysterious "fires" or other accidents that destroy their records right before the audit. What can the IRS do in this case? Over the years, the Service has developed a few sophisticated indirect methods of estimating a taxpayer's income. And the courts have allowed such methods because the IRS has no other choice in such instances.

But what if the IRS starts using the indirect methods to "test" the accuracy of a taxpayer's books and records? Is that carrying the use of the indirect method too far, in terms of fairness to the taxpayer, especially when the taxpayer offers a complete set of records for the agent to examine? That was the question addressed in the *Holland* case that is discussed below.

Marion L. Holland v. U.S.[4]

Facts of the Case: Petitioners, husband and wife, stand convicted under §145 of the Internal Revenue Code of an attempt to evade and defeat their income taxes for the year 1948. The prosecution [54-1 USTC ¶9177] was based on the net worth method of proof, also in issue in three companion cases and a number of other decisions here from the Courts of Appeals of nine circuits. During the past two decades this Court has been asked to review an increasing number of criminal cases in which proof of tax evasion rested on this theory. We have denied certiorari because the cases involved only questions of evidence and, in isolation, presented no important questions of law. In 1943 the Court did have occasion to pass upon an application of the net worth theory where the taxpayer had no records. *United States v. Johnson,* 319 U. S. 503 [43-1 USTC ¶9470]. [*Use of Net Worth Method in Proving Tax Evasion*]

In recent years, however, tax-evasion convictions obtained under the net worth theory have come here with increasing frequency and left impressions beyond those of the previously unrelated petitions. We concluded that the method involved something more than the ordinary use of circumstantial evidence in the usual criminal case. Its bearing, therefore, on the safeguards traditionally provided in the administration of criminal justice called for a consideration of the entire theory. At our last Term a number of cases arising from the Courts of Appeals brought to our attention the serious doubts of those courts regarding the implications of the net worth method. Accordingly, we granted certiorari in these four cases and have held others to await their decision.

Note: Affirming the 10th Circuit Court of Appeals

Analysis

This case asks the question of whether or not the IRS had gone too far in applying its indirect methods of determining taxable income in an audit of individual taxpayers. Traditionally, such a tool was merely used to corroborate unreported income, or to substitute

---

[4] *Holland,* SCt, 54-2 USTC ¶9714, 348 US 121, 75 SCt 127.

for the lack of accounting records furnished by the taxpayer. Specifically, the Court was concerned that the net worth method had evolved *"from the final volley to the first shot in the Government's battle for revenue, and its use in the ordinary income-bracket cases greatly increases the chances for error."*

In this case, the lower courts and the 10th Circuit Court of Appeals found the taxpayer guilty of tax fraud. The taxpayer had reported only $10,000 of income, while the IRS estimated such income as $32,000 using the net worth method. The taxpayers contended that the IRS had refused to examine their records, and that they had also refused to track down leads that the taxpayers furnished as reasons for the discrepancy in reported income (primarily, the classic **cash horde defense**: the excess spending was from a stash in the mattress from past years). The IRS contended that they did not have to track down every lead for other sources of income, and that the taxpayer could not disprove the net worth method.

OBSERVATION

The **net worth method** essentially compares a taxpayer's net worth based on comparative balance sheets using historical costs at the beginning and end of a tax year, and then adds all consumption expenditures for the year (which, of course, would not be reflected in the ending net worth figure). A taxpayer is given a chance to explain where the money came from to create a discrepancy between reported income and estimated income with the net worth method. A common defense of taxpayers is that they had the money "buried away" from previous years and tapped into those funds during the current year.

The Supreme Court had previously approved the use of the net worth method when a taxpayer had no records.[5] In this particular case, the IRS presented strong circumstantial evidence to support their net worth computations that indicated that taxable income had been substantially underreported. During the year in question, the taxpayer had purchased a hotel, bar, and restaurant (the *Holland House*), and had also bought and sold a few stocks. The IRS also demonstrated that the taxpayer's business was the likely source of that unreported income.

Based on this showing, the Supreme Court ruled for the IRS. They noted that "reasonable doubt" does not mean that the IRS must follow every taxpayer lead as to a likely source of income, and that the IRS does not have to accept the taxpayer's books as being correct. The Court noted that the Service must be free to go around the records, and that *the IRS is auditing the taxpayer, and not his or her books and records.* The Court noted that the taxpayer's business appeared fully capable of being the source of the unexplained income, and that the taxpayer had willfully established a *"clear and consistent pattern of underreporting."*

OBSERVATION

Another favorite indirect method used by the IRS to estimate underreported income is the **cash flow analysis**, sometimes referred to as the *Tennessee T-Account Method*. In this method, the Service basically tries to tie down all sources and uses of cash, both taxable and nontaxable. The Service uses numbers off the tax return whenever possible, and is especially careful in tying down the beginning and ending cash balances. For example, the cash analysis may appear as follows:

---

[5] *See Johnson*, SCt, 43-1 USTC ¶9470, 319 US 503, 63 SCt 1233.

Cash T-Account Analysis			
Beginning cash balance	$ 22,000	Ending cash balance	$ 26,000
Sales (cash-basis) *	146,000	Purchases (cash basis) *	102,000
Salary *	80,000	Bus. Expenses (cash basis)	98,000
Interest income *	20,000	Itemized deductions (cash) *	34,000
Loan proceeds	64,000	Loan repayments	45,000
Inheritance	24,000	Personal expenses (cash)	212,000
Lottery winnings *	15,000	Vacation expenses (cash)	58,000
Total Sources of Cash	$371,000		
Discrepancy	204,000		
	$575,000	Total Uses of Cash	$575,000
* Taken directly from tax return			

OBSERVATION

In this case, the IRS would assume that the $204,000 discrepancy is unreported gross receipts, overstated deducted expenses, or a combination of both. The taxpayer would then be given an opportunity to explain the discrepancy. Sometimes there may be a perfectly innocent explanation for an income discrepancy, and yet the taxpayer may withhold the information from his or her representative and actually make things worse. For example, a large gift or inheritance in cash might explain the difference, but the client will not tell his or her representative for fear that such amounts are taxable.

.05   ACCOUNTING RECORDS—OTHER CASES OF NOTE

BDO Seidman.[6] In this case, the appellate court found that the district court, in *BDO Seidman*,[7] properly denied a motion to intervene by several clients of an accounting firm that was under investigation for the marketing of abusive tax shelters. The clients sought to prevent the disclosure of certain documents revealing their identities as individuals who participated in the tax shelters promoted by the accounting firm. They claimed that such documents were privileged under Code Sec. 7525. However, the individuals failed to establish that the mere identification of themselves as clients would disclose some actual confidential communication. Moreover, their participation in potentially abusive tax shelters was information ordinarily subject to full disclosure under federal tax law. Accordingly, because they could not demonstrate a colorable claim of privilege, the district court's determination was sustained.

OBSERVATION

As part of the American Jobs Creation Act of 2004, Congress amended Code Sec. 7525(b) to specifically state that the federally authorized tax practitioner privilege does not apply to any communications related to a tax shelter. Note the revised wording in the abstract printed above. Prior to this amendment, the rule applied only to communications regarding corporate tax shelters. This change is in direct response to decisions such as the *BDO Seidman* case discussed above.

Richard A. Frederick.[8] In this case, the Circuit Court ruled that an attorney hired to prepare returns for a married couple and their corporation could not assert the attorney-client or work product privilege as a ground for refusing to comply with IRS summonses seeking information transmitted to him by the taxpayers or created by him in connection

---

6   *BDO Seidman*, CA-7, 2003-2 USTC ¶50,582, 337 F3d 802.
7   *BDO Seidman*, DC Ill., 2003-1 USTC ¶50,255.
8   *Frederick*, CA-7, 99-1 USTC ¶50,465, 182 F3d 496.

with return preparation. Code Sec. 7525, which extends the attorney-client privilege to federally authorized tax practitioners, did not protect the attorney's work product in the present case. That provision shelters communications between taxpayers and nonlawyers authorized to practice before the IRS only to the extent that a communication would be deemed privileged if it were between a taxpayer and an attorney.

U.S. v. Textron.[9] In this case, the U.S. District Court of Rhode Island ruled that the tax accrual workpapers of the taxpayer were protected by the work-product privilege. The IRS had requested all of the workpapers of a subsidiary (TFC) that the IRS considered to be a tax shelter at the time (sale-in, lease-out transactions, or SILOs), before the listed transactions requirement. But the IRS also requested the workpapers of Textron, the parent company, contending that the workpapers were not protected by privilege since the information was of the type disclosed to the Securities and Exchange Commission. Furthermore, the information had been disclosed to the outside auditors, which the IRS contended was a waiver of confidentiality. The District Court ruled for Textron, noting that the workpapers were protected by the work-product doctrine since they contained legal analysis and opinions in anticipation of litigation.

In a most unwelcome surprise to practicing tax professionals, the First Circuit Court reversed the District Court in an *en banc* decision (see *Textron, Inc., CA-1, 2009-2 USTC ¶50,574*). In doing so, the Court muddied the water even further by seemingly creating a new standard for privilege. Specifically, the Court contended that the phase "prepared in anticipation of litigation or for trial" in Rule 26(b)(3) of the Federal Rules of Evidence 501 does not mean prepared for some purpose other than litigation. Rather, it means that the work is done in advance *for* litigation. This interpretation is at odds with the decision of the Second Circuit in *M. Aldman, 134 F3d 1194 (CA-2, 1998)*, where the Court noted that "Nowhere does Rule 26(b)(3) state that a document must have been prepared to *aid in* the conduct of litigation in order to constitute work product, much less *primarily or exclusively* in litigation. Preparing a document 'in anticipation' of litigation is sufficient."

On May 24, 2010, the Supreme Court decided not to review the Textron case by denying a writ of certiorari (Supreme Court Docket No. 09-750). Although this refusal to grant certiori ". . . imports no expression of opinion upon the merits of the case" (*United States v. Carver, 260 U.S. 482, 490 (1923)*), it nonetheless allows the First Circuit's decision to stand.

OBSERVATION
There are many troubling issues raised by the *Textron* decisions. First, the Court did not accept the argument that the tax accrual workpapers were not protected by attorney-client or accountant-client privilege, since they had been disclosed to outside auditors. Secondly, this decision is clearly out of the mainstream with similar cases, in that this decision raises the bar to require that the workpapers be prepared in advance for litigation, not just in anticipation of litigation.

Interestingly, in its formal appeal of the lower-court decision, the IRS raised a somewhat novel argument: the IRS needed to see the taxpayer's workpapers because the documentation with the tax return was so overwhelming! Apparently, the agents had little patience with sorting through a 4,000-page tax return, including attachments.

¶8005   Special Accounting Method Cases

Several cases discussed in Chapters 4 and 5 touched on the issue of accounting methods for income and expenses. Two other accounting methods cases that do not fit into these

---

[9]   *Textron*, DC R.I., 2007-2 USTC ¶50,605.

categories are discussed in this chapter. One case (*Thor Power Tool*) involves an inventory question within the context of **generally accepted accounting principles (GAAP)**, and the other (*Hillsboro Bank/Bliss Dairy*) involves the judicially-developed concept of the tax benefit rule.

.01 TAX INVENTORY METHODS AND GAAP—THE *THOR POWER TOOL* CASE

Background

The relationship between GAAP and tax reporting was an important concept in several of the cases discussed in previous chapters, including both income issues (e.g., *American Automobile Association*[10] and *Schlude*[11]) and deduction issues (e.g., *General Dynamics*[12] and *Boylston Markets*[13]). In this chapter, an inventory issue forms the basis of the landmark decision in *Thor Power Tool*. Specifically, does GAAP trump the tax regulations in the treatment of excess or obsolete inventories? This case highlights the differing objectives of financial reporting and tax reporting, and raises some interesting nontax issues as well.

Thor Power Tool v. Commissioner[14]

Facts of the Case: Taxpayer is a Delaware corporation with principal place of business in Illinois. It manufactures hand-held power tools, parts and accessories, and rubber products. At its various plants and service branches, Thor maintains inventories of raw materials, work-in-process, finished parts and accessories, and completed tools. At all times relevant, Thor has used, both for financial accounting and for income tax purposes, the "lower of cost or market" method of valuing inventories. App. 23-24. See Treas. Reg. §1.471-2(c), 26 CFR §1.471-2(c) (1978).

Thor's tools typically contain from 50 to 200 parts, each of which taxpayer stocks to meet demand for replacements. Because of the difficulty, at the time of manufacture, of predicting the future demand for various parts, taxpayer produced liberal quantities of each part to avoid subsequent production runs. Additional runs entail costly retooling and result in delays in filling orders.

In 1960, Thor instituted a procedure for writing down the inventory value of replacement parts and accessories for tool models it no longer produced. It created an inventory contra account and credited that account with 10% of each part's cost for each year since production of the parent model had ceased. 64 T. C., at 156-157; App. 24. The effect of the procedure was to amortize the cost of these parts over a 10-year period. For the first nine months of 1964, this produced a write-down of $22,090. 64 T. C., at 157; App. 24.

In late 1964, new management took control and promptly concluded that Thor's inventory in general was overvalued. After "a physical inventory taken at all locations" of the tool and rubber divisions, *id.,* at 52, management wrote off approximately $2.75 million of obsolete parts, damaged or defective tools, demonstration of sales samples, and similar items. *Id.,* at 52-53. The Commissioner allowed this writeoff because Thor scrapped most of the articles shortly after their removal from the 1964 closing inventory. Management also wrote

---

[10] *American Automobile Association*, SCt, 61-2 USTC ¶9517, 367 US 687.
[11] *Schlude*, SCt, 63-1 USTC ¶9284, 372 US 128, 83 SCt 601.
[12] *General Dynamics*, SCt, 87-1 USTC ¶9280, 481 US 239, 107 SCt 1732.
[13] *Boylston Market Association*, CA-1, 42-2 USTC ¶9820, 131 F2d 966.
[14] *Thor Power Tool*, SCt, 79-1 USTC ¶9139, 439 US 522, 99 SCt 773.

down $245,000 of parts stocked for three unsuccessful products. *Id.,* at 56. The Commissioner allowed this write-down, too, since Thor sold these items at reduced prices shortly after the close of 1964. *Id.,* at 62.

This left some 44,000 assorted items, the status of which is the inventory issue here. Management concluded that many of these articles, mostly spare parts, were "excess" inventory, that is, that they were held in excess of any reasonably foreseeable future demand. It was decided that this inventory should be written down to its "net realizable value," which, in most cases, was scrap value. 64 T. C., at 160-161; Brief for Petitioner 9; Tr. of Oral Arg. 11.

Two methods were used to ascertain the quantity of excess inventory. Where accurate data were available, Thor forecast future demand for each item on the basis of actual 1964 usage, that is, actual sales for tools and service parts, and actual usage for raw materials, work-in-process, and production parts. Management assumed that future demand for each item would be the same as it was in 1964. Thor then applied the following aging schedule: the quantity of each item corresponding to less than one year's estimated demand was kept at cost; the quantity of each item in excess of two years' estimated demand was written off entirely; and the quantity of each item corresponding to from one to two years' estimated demand was written down by 50% or 75%. App. 26. Thor presented no statistical evidence to rationalize these percentages or this time frame. In the Tax Court, Thor's president justified the formula by citing general business experience, and opined that it was "somewhat in between" possible alternative solutions.[5] The first method yielded a total write-down of $744,030. 64 TC 160.

At two plants where 1964 data were inadequate to permit forecasts of future demand, Thor used its second method for valuing inventories. At these plants, the company employed flat percentage write-downs of 5%, 10%, and 50% for various types of inventory.[6] Thor presented no sales or other data to support these percentages. Its president observed that "this is not a precise way of doing it," but said that the company "felt some adjustment of this nature was in order, and these figures represented our best estimate of was required to reduce the inventory to net realizable value." App. 67. This second method yielded a total write-down of $160,832. 64 T. C., at 160.

Although Thor wrote down all its "excess" inventory at once, it did not immediately scrap the articles or sell them at reduced prices, as it had done with the $3 million of obsolete and damaged inventory, the write-down of which the Commissioner permitted. Rather, Thor retained the "excess" items physically in inventory and continued to sell them at original prices. *Id.,* at 160-161. The company found that, owing to the peculiar nature of the articles involved,[7] price reductions were of no avail in moving this "excess" inventory. As time went on, however, Thor gradually disposed of some of these items as scrap; the record is unclear as to when these dispositions took place.

Thor credited this sum to its inventory contra account, thereby decreasing closing inventory, increasing cost of goods sold, and decreasing taxable income for the year by that amount. The company contended that, by writing down excess inventory to scrap value, and by thus carrying all inventory at "net realizable value," it had reduced its inventory to "market" in accord with its "lower of cost or market" method of accounting. On audit, the Commissioner disallowed the write-down in its entirety, asserting that it did not serve clearly to reflect Thor's 1964 income for tax purposes.

Note: Affirming 7th Circuit Court of Appeals

Analysis

This case represents yet another chapter in the controversy of GAAP versus tax accounting. In the *Thor Power Tool Co*. case, a new management team ordered additional writedowns of excess inventories of spare parts based on an aging schedule. This practice conformed to a basic generally accepted accounting principle that inventories should be written down to their net realizable values. Both the taxpayer and the IRS relied on the following wording of Code Sec. 471(a) to bolster their case:

Abstract

Sec. 471(a) – General Rule.—Whenever in the opinion of the Secretary the use of inventories is necessary in order to clearly reflect the income of any taxpayer, inventories shall be taken by such taxpayer on such basis as the Secretary may prescribe as conforming as nearly as may be to the best accounting practice in the trade or business and as most clearly reflecting the income.

In this case, the taxpayer was relying on the phrase *best accounting practice in the trade or business* to justify their writedown procedure, and the IRS was relying on the phrase *clearly reflecting the income* to deny the use of that procedure. The real problem for the taxpayer was that their procedure, though accepted throughout the industry as a "best practice" for financial accounting purposes, did not comply with the Code Sec. 471 regulations. Specifically, Reg. §1.471-2(c) requires that inventory items written down must be offered for sale at a *bona fide selling price* within 30 days of the ending inventory date. Only then would a writedown to a bona fide selling price *clearly reflect income*. This rule also meant that items that were completely written off must have been scrapped.

The taxpayer argued that their writedowns were in conformity to GAAP, in that the cost of the goods was written down to estimated net realizable values. The IRS contended that such writedowns do not clearly reflect income, since they were not based on bona fide selling prices as established by the 30-day requirement in the regulations (or, in the case of complete writedowns, the items were scrapped).

In essence, this case boiled down to a question of whether the regulation in question was a valid interpretation of the Code's reference to a bona fide selling price. In the end, the Supreme Court accepted the IRS argument that the regulation is a valid interpretation of Congressional intent, and that GAAP is not controlling in this instance. In this regard, the Court offered the following often-quoted explanation:

> "The primary goal of financial accounting is to provide useful information to management, shareholders, creditors, and others properly interested; the major responsibility of the accountant is to protect these parties from being misled. The primary goal of the income tax system, in contrast, is the equitable collection of revenue; the major responsibility of the Internal Revenue Service is to protect the public fisc."

Finally, the Court also noted that financial accounting is not under the same constraints as tax accounting. Specifically, the Court stated that *"Financial accounting, in short is hospitable to estimates, probabilities, and reasonable certainties; the tax law, with its mandate to preserve the revenue, can give no quarter to uncertainty."*

OBSERVATION The *Thor Power Tool* decision has affected the operations of a number of businesses. For example, in recent years the time interval for a book to go from hard cover to paper back and then to discounted hard cover has been drastically reduced. Years ago one could seldom buy the hardcover book at a deep discount, since publishers wanted to sell as many at full price as possible, and then go to paperback. But all of those excess hard cover copies could not be written off unless offered for sale at the writedown prices, and bookstores gobbled them up and sold them for deeply discounted prices once the paperback edition had more or less run its course.

OBSERVATION	One taxpayer's misery may provide a golden opportunity for another taxpayer. After this decision, a business sprang up that offered to "buy" a taxpayer's excess inventories so that the writedowns could be taken; however, the purchaser guaranteed the seller access to the items if needed (of course, access would be at market prices, and not writedown prices). For example, a company with excess spare parts normally selling for $395 each might write them down to $39.50 each, and justify this writedown by actually selling them to the "warehouse" purchaser. As part of the sales contract, the seller could repurchase the parts at $395 each if they were ever needed. The IRS challenged this arrangement in *Paccar,*[15] and the Tax Court and the 9th Circuit Court agreed with the IRS that the arrangement was nothing more than the seller renting space from the warehouse purchaser. Thus, the writedowns were denied.

.03 **THE TAX BENEFIT RULE—THE *HILLSBORO BANK/BLISS DAIRY CO.* CASES**

Background

The second accounting methods case discussed in this chapter is the *Hillsboro National Bank/Bliss Dairy Co.* decision, which addresses the **tax benefit rule**. In general, the tax benefit rule requires inclusion in income of any amount that was erroneously deducted in a prior year, but only to the extent that the deduction generated a tax benefit in that year. This rule is the reason, for example, that a taxpayer must include a state income tax refund in taxable income in the year received, but only if the taxpayer itemized in the prior year (i.e., benefited from a tax deduction). The same logic applies to unexpected reimbursement of a medical expense that was deducted in the previous tax year.

But the issues in the *Hillsboro Bank/Bliss Dairy* cases (two cases combined into one at the Supreme Court level) are far from being this simple in applying the tax benefit rule. The cases are all the more interesting because the tax benefit is a largely judicially-defined concept; little is said about this doctrine in the Code, other than Code Sec. 111(a), which states the following:

Abstract

Sec. 111(a) Deductions.—*Gross income does not include income attributable to the recovery during the taxable year of any amount deducted in any prior taxable year to the extent such amount did not reduce the amount of tax imposed by this chapter.*

Hillsboro National Bank/Bliss Dairy v. Commissioner[16]

Facts of the Case: Until 1970, Illinois imposed a property tax on shares of stock held in incorporated banks, but in 1970 the Illinois Constitution was amended to prohibit such taxes. The Illinois courts thereafter held that the amendment violated the Federal Constitution, but, pending disposition of the case in this Court, Illinois enacted a statute providing for collection of the disputed taxes and placement of the receipts in escrow. Petitioner Bank in No. 81-485 paid

---

[15] *Paccar,* CA-9, 88-1 USTC ¶9380, 849 F2d 393.
[16] *Hillsboro National Bank,* SCt, 83-1 USTC ¶9229, 460 US 370, 103 SCt 1134.

the taxes for its shareholders in 1972, taking the deduction for the amount of the taxes pursuant to §164(e) of the Internal Revenue Code of 1954 (IRC), which grants a corporation a deduction for taxes imposed on its shareholders but paid by the corporation and denies the shareholders any deduction for the tax. The authorities placed the receipts in escrow. After this Court upheld the constitutional amendment, the amounts in escrow were refunded to the shareholders. When petitioner, on its federal income tax return for 1973, recognized no income from this sequence of events, the Commissioner of Internal Revenue assessed a deficiency against petitioner, requiring it to include as income the amount paid its shareholders from the escrow. Petitioner then sought a redetermination in the Tax Court, which held that the refund of the taxes was includible in petitioner's income. The Court of Appeals affirmed.

In No. 81-930, respondent corporation, which operated a dairy, in the taxable year ending June 30, 1973, deducted the full cost of the cattle feed purchased for use in its operations as permitted by §162 of the IRC, but a substantial portion of the feed was still on hand at the end of the taxable year. Two days into the next taxable year, respondent adopted a plan of liquidation and distributed its assets, including the cattle feed, to its shareholders. Relying on §336 of the IRC, which [then] shields a corporation from the recognition of gain on the distribution of property to its shareholders on liquidation, respondent reported no income on the transaction. The Commissioner challenged respondent's treatment of the transaction, asserting that it should have included as income the value of the feed distributed to its shareholders, and therefore increased respondent's income by $60,000. Respondent paid the resulting assessment and sued for a refund in Federal District Court, which rendered a judgment in respondent's favor. The Court of Appeals affirmed.

Note: Reversed, and Reversed and Remanded 7th Circuit Court of Appeals

Analysis

As mentioned earlier, this case actually represents two cases that address the application of the tax benefit rule. In the *Hillsboro National Bank* case, the taxpayer under Illinois law paid a property tax on shares held by their shareholders and deducted the amount under Code Sec. 164(e), which is allowed if the bank is not reimbursed by the shareholders. After a 1970 law change, Hillsboro refunded the tax directly to the shareholders from an escrow account set up by the bank in anticipation of the repeal of the tax, although the amount was deducted by the bank. The IRS contended that the refunded amount should be included in Hillsboro's taxable income under the tax benefit rule, due to the deduction in the prior year. The taxpayer contended that they had no "recovery," since such amounts were refunded directly to the shareholders.

In the *Bliss Dairy* case, a cash-basis, closely-held farm corporation that operated a dairy had deducted the full cost of cattle feed during a tax year as permitted to qualified farmers under Code Sec. 162. Approximately $60,000 of this feed was still on hand at the end of the tax year, and the corporation liquidated two days later tax-free under then Code Sec. 333. The feed was then distributed tax-free to the shareholders under Code Sec. 336, as permitted at the time; this provision was subsequently repealed. The shareholders continued to operate the business in an unincorporated form after this time, eventually using the feed and deducting such amounts (according to the basis rules of Code Sec. 333). The IRS contended that the tax benefit rule applied to the $60,000 amount previously deducted, and once again the taxpayer contended that there had been no "recovery" and therefore the tax benefit rule should not apply.

In both of these cases, the taxpayers were arguing that for the tax benefit rule to apply, there must be an actual "recovery," such as in the case of state income tax refunds, repayment of bad debts previously written off, or medical expense reimbursements. The IRS contended that a recovery is not necessary for the rule to apply, and cited the situation where an accrued expense might never have been paid.

OBSERVATION   Recall that the *Dixie Pine Products*[17] case discussed in Chapter 6 involved an accrual of tax expense for a gasoline tax that was never paid. In that case, the Court ruled that the tax benefit rule applied even though there was no amount to "recover." This was the argument being put forth by the Service in this case.

The Supreme Court agreed with the Service that a recovery is not necessary for the tax benefit rule to apply, in that each situation needs to be decided on a case by case basis. The Court also noted the need for *"rough transactional parity"* in such cases. Rather than relying on the recovery aspect of such transactions, the Supreme Court concluded that the proper test is whether or not there was an *inconsistent event* subsequent to the deduction, citing cases such as *Barnett v. Commissioner*, where the following statement was made:

> *"[When] some event occurs which is inconsistent with a deduction taken in a prior year, adjustment may have to be made by reporting a balancing item in income for the year in which the change occurs."*[18]

Using the logic of an "inconsistent event," the Court reached different conclusions in the two cases. In *Hillsboro Bank*, the Court ruled that there was no inconsistent event, in that the taxpayer bank never received the money, i.e., the change was merely a *"change in funds in the hands of state."* On the other hand, the Court ruled in *Bliss Dairy* that there was an inconsistent event, in that the feed distributed to the shareholders could be converted to a different (nonbusiness) use. This case was remanded back to the court to determine the appropriate amount of income recognition.

Judge Blackmun, in an acerbic dissent to the *Bliss Dairy* decision, questioned why the Court would develop such a complicated solution to a relatively simple problem. In his view, when the issue involves consecutive years, the taxpayer should simply file an amended return for the first year in question and leave everything else alone. He noted that this is the same result obtained when the IRS audits a taxpayer, in that the Service is "amending" the prior-year return. Justice Blackmun concluded by observing the following:

> *"I realize that my position is simplistic, but I doubt if the judge-made tax benefit rule really was intended, at its origin, to be regarded as applicable in simple situations of the kind presented in these successive-tax-year cases. So often a judge-made rule, understandably conceived, ultimately is used to carry us further than it should."*

OBSERVATION   There are a couple of important tax issues related to these cases that were not addressed by the court. First of all, would the shareholders of Hillsboro bank be taxed on the refunds? More than likely, they would, since the payment appears to be in essence a constructive dividend. Secondly, what basis if any would the Bliss shareholders have in the leftover feed? Since they were being taxed on its value, this would be the established basis in the feed. If such feed was used in their continuing unincorporated business, it presumably could be deducted again.

.05   ACCOUNTING METHODS—OTHER CASES OF NOTE

***Dominion Resources, Inc. v. U.S.*[19]** The taxpayer, Dominion Resources, Inc. (DRI), was subject to regulated rates, including those used to project current and future tax liabilities. The rates charged by DRI were based in part on accruals of tax expenses expected in the future when timing differences on its books would reverse for tax purposes. In 1986, Congress reduced the maximum corporate rate from 46 percent to 34 percent, and the regulatory agencies required DRI to refund approximately $10 million as a one-time payment to customers to compensate for what in effect were overcharges based on the expected future tax liabilities. The refund

---
[17] *Dixie Pine Products*, SCt, 44-1 USTC ¶9127, 320 US 516, 64 SCt 364.
[18] *Barnett*, 39 BTA 864.
[19] *Dominion Resources*, CA-4, 2000-2 USTC ¶50,633, 219 F3d 539.

went to customers in the year paid (1991), rather than the customers who had been subject to excess charges in earlier years. The $10 million payment reduced DRI's 1991 tax liability by $3.4 million (at a 34-percent rate), but DRI invoked Code Sec. 1341 to grant a deduction for an additional $1.2 million since the income had been taxed in earlier years at a 46-percent rate. (Code Sec. 1341 permits a taxpayer to take a credit in a repayment year for the additional tax paid in the earlier year if the tax benefit rule applies, so that the taxpayer is not penalized if tax rates are different in the two years in question). The IRS contended that DRI did not meet the requirements to invoke Code Sec. 1341 (i.e., an unrestricted right to the funds when received in the earlier years, determined to be in error in a later year, and the adjustment exceeds $3,000). In ruling for DRI, the Circuit Court noted that DRI had apparently met all of the requirements of Code Sec. 1341, and that Congress had intended for that statute to cover a broad range of cases.

OBSERVATION

Code Sec. 1341 is usually invoked by individual taxpayers who mistakenly receive income in one year and have to repay it in a later year (such as the *Lewis* case discussed in Chapter 5). For example, what if a taxpayer received $10,000 income erroneously in 2012 when in a 35-percent tax bracket, and had to pay it back in 2013 when in a 15-percent bracket? Because the claim of right doctrine would require the taxpayer to report the $10,000 in 2012, the taxpayer would normally take a $10,000 deduction in 2013. However, since the amount exceeds $3,000, the taxpayer may elect under Code Sec. 1341 to take a credit of $3,500 on the 2013 return, an amount equal to the additional tax paid in 2012, so that he or she is not penalized by changing tax rates. The court in the *DRI* case decided that Code Sec. 1341 could apply to that case as well.

Hallmark Cards.[20] In this case, the greeting card company changed its policy of shipping Valentine's day cards in October of each year to shipping the cards in December. However, title did not pass to the buyer until January 1 of the next tax year (as opposed to the time of the shipment, as used earlier). Thus, Hallmark deferred recognition of income on the cards until the following year. The IRS contended that this was a change of accounting method, and as such, the taxpayer must seek permission from the IRS to make such a change (as required by Code Sec. 446). The Tax Court ruled that the change in reporting Valentine card sales resulted from a *change in underlying facts,* and not a change of accounting method (the passage of title was more than a ministerial act). Therefore, permission from the IRS was not required to make the change.

OBSERVATION

In general, the IRS is hostile to a request to change an accounting method, and taxpayers have discovered the change in underlying facts technique as a method around the Code requirement to request IRS permission. This can produce some interesting results. In *Decision, Inc.*, a calendar-year taxpayer changed the date of shipping employment directories from November to January. Since this was the taxpayer's only source of income, a large net operating loss was created for the year of change (the income was shifted forward a year) and the taxpayer received a huge tax refund![21]

Dayton Hudson Company and Subsidiaries v. Commissioner.[22] In this case, the taxpayer, a publicly held corporation primarily engaged in retailing, used an estimate of shrinkage not verified by year-end physical count in computing its year-end inventory. The IRS argued that the use of such estimate is prohibited by Reg. §1471-2(d). Thus, the IRS argued that the taxpayer's use of such estimate caused its accounting method, as a matter of law, to fail to clearly reflect income. The taxpayer objected to the IRS's motion on the ground that the regulation does not prohibit the estimate at issue, and

[20] *Hallmark Cards*, 90 TC 26.
[21] *Decision, Inc.*, 47 TC 58.
[22] *Dayton Hudson*, 101 TC 462.

¶8005.05

that whether its accounting method clearly reflects income therefore is a question of fact. The Tax Court held that the regulation does not prohibit the use of a shrinkage estimate in computing year-end inventory. Accordingly, the taxpayer's estimate did not, as a matter of law, cause its accounting method to fail to clearly reflect income. The court also noted, however, whether Dayton Hudson's accounting method, including the use of the shrinkage estimate at issue, clearly reflects income is a question of fact over which there is a genuine controversy.

OBSERVATION

In response to the *Dayton-Hudson* decision, Congress enacted Code Sec. 471(b) in 1998. Following the enactment of this provision, a business is not required to actually take a year-end inventory in order to determine if any inventory shrinkage has occurred. Prior to this time, other courts had also ruled that taxpayers' methods of accounting for shrinkage without physical inventories were permissible because the methods conformed to the best accounting practices in the industry and clearly reflected income. The House Committee Report for P.L. 105-34 stated *"it was inappropriate to require a physical count of a taxpayer's entire inventory to be taken exactly at year-end, provided that physical counts are taken on a regular and consistent basis."* Thus, the deduction for the estimated shrinkage may only be claimed if the business (1) normally takes a physical count of its inventories at each business location on a regular and consistent basis, and (2) makes proper adjustments to its inventories and to its estimating methods to the extent its estimates are more or less than the actual shrinkage.

¶8007 Income Allocation Method Cases

Thus far the gross income cases analyzed in this text has been confined to more or less narrow questions defining gross income and determining when such income should be recognized for tax purposes. But there are a lot of interesting questions regarding the allocation of income in various manners, and four of these questions are examined in this chapter. These four major cases involve unrelated business income of a tax-exempt entity, state and local income allocation issues, international income allocation issues, and finally a case that combines both state and worldwide income issues.

These four cases not only address very important tax issues, but they also offer excellent tutorials on four different aspects of tax law. In explaining their reasoning, the Court in each case initially provides a comprehensive yet succinct description of the prevailing law applicable to each transaction. In many respects, reading these cases will teach you more about nonprofits, international transfer pricing, and the state and local unitary principle than you will ever glean from a textbook.

.01 UNRELATED BUSINESS INCOME OF TAX-EXEMPT ENTITIES— THE *AMERICAN COLLEGE OF PHYSICIANS* CASE

Background

In order to prevent tax-exempt entities from having an unfair competitive advantage to their for-profit counterparts, Congress instituted an **unrelated business income tax (UBIT)** in Code Sec. 512 that would tax such entities on any profits not related to their tax-exempt purpose. Therefore, a college bookstore that sells furniture to students is likely to be subject to the UBIT. But what about a professional medical journal that accepts paid advertising to keep its readers abreast of current medical products? Is that "related to the tax-exempt function" of the medical society, or is it unrelated business income? That was the question addressed in the *American College of Physicians* case.

U.S. v. American College of Physicians[23]

Facts of the Case: Respondent, the American College of Physicians, is an organization exempt from taxation under §501(c)(3) of the Internal Revenue Code. The purposes of the College, as stated in its articles of incorporation, are to maintain high standards in medical education and medical practice; to encourage research, especially in clinical medicine; and to foster measures for the prevention of disease and for the improvement of public health. App.16a. The principal facts were stipulated at trial. In furtherance of its exempt purposes, respondent publishes The Annals of Internal Medicine (Annals), a highly regarded monthly medical journal containing scholarly articles relevant to the practice of internal medicine.

Each issue of Annals contains advertisements for pharmaceuticals, medical supplies, and equipment useful in the practice of internal medicine, as well as notices of positions available in that field. Respondent has a longstanding policy of accepting only advertisements containing information about the use of medical products, and screens proffered advertisements for accuracy and relevance to internal medicine. The advertisements are clustered in two groups, one at the front and one at the back of each issue.

In 1975, Annals produced gross advertising income of $1,376,322. After expenses and deductible losses were subtracted, there remained a net income of $153,388. Respondent reported this figure as taxable income and paid taxes on it in the amount of $55,965. Respondent then filed a timely claim with the Internal Revenue Service for refund of these taxes, and when the Government demurred, filed suit in the United States Claims Court.

Note: Reversing Court of Appeals for the Federal Circuit

Analysis

This case involves the simple issue of whether or not the advertising accepted for its journal by the American College of Physicians (ACP), a Code Sec. 501(c)(3) organization, is substantially related to their tax-exempt function, and thus not subject to taxation under the Code Sec. 512 UBIT (unrelated business income tax) rules. The paid ads were for such items as pharmaceuticals, medical equipment, medical supplies, and job openings. The ACP contended that they had a long-standing policy of accepting only ads relevant to the use of medical products and/or providing timely medical information, and that such ads were screened for accuracy.

Based on this policy, the taxpayer contended that the ads were substantially related to their tax-exempt purpose of *"maintaining high medical standards, encouraging research, fostering the prevention of disease, and improving public health."* The taxpayer insisted that the key test of relevancy was to look at what was provided to the reader of the journal. The IRS on the other hand contended that any connection of the ads to the organization's educational purpose was purely coincidental, that contracts were entered into through an ad agency, and the primary requirement for an ad seemed to be the ability of the client to pay.

In analyzing the case, the Supreme Court contended that in order to qualify for exemption, the activities of the organization must (1) be a trade or business that is (2) carried on (i.e., regularly performed) and is (3) substantially related to the tax-exempt function. The IRS contended that the activities of the ACP could never meet the third test, as its advertising was driven by demand (similar in scope to Example 7 of Reg §1.512-1). The Supreme Court agreed with the Service, noting that the law was "clearly antagonistic" towards such activities and that the ads did not contribute importantly to the educational purposes of the organization.

[23] *American College of Physicians*, SCt, 86-1 ustc ¶9339, 475 US 834, 106 SCt 1591.

¶8007.01

OBSERVATION	The taxpayer's "educational value" arguments were undercut by the fact that the same ad would often run several times during the year. Naturally, this caused the Court to ask how much marginal value does the reader obtain by seeing the ad a third or fourth time?

.03   THE UNITARY METHOD OF ALLOCATING STATE AND LOCAL INCOME—THE *ALLIED SIGNAL* CASE

Background

For years most states have operated under a "unitary theory" of taxation when attempting to tax companies that do business in their state as well as many other states. Under the unitary theory, a company's income is treated as being generated by one unitary business, and rather than try to isolate intra-state activity state by state, the income is apportioned among all the states with activity. Generally, this allocation is performed using a three-factor formula (total payroll, property, and sales of one state as a percentage of the sum of the same three factors for all states the company operates in) times the total income earned by the company.

But occasionally some states want it all and will attempt to tax certain transactions in their entirety as belonging solely to their state. This was the issue in the *Allied Signal* case, where the state of New Jersey attempted to tax the entire gain recognized by the taxpayer on the sale of a stock investment. This case zeroes in on the heart of the unitary principle and helps explain why it has been around for so long.

Allied Signal v. Director-Division of Taxation[24]

Facts of the Case: Petitioner, Allied-Signal, Inc., is the successor-in-interest to the Bendix Corporation (Bendix). The present dispute concerns Bendix's corporate business tax liability to the State of New Jersey for the fiscal year ending September 30, 1981. Although three items of income were contested earlier, the controversy in this Court involves only one item: the gain of $211.5 million realized by Bendix on the sale of its 20.6% stock interest in ASARCO Inc. (ASARCO). The case was submitted below on stipulated facts, and we begin with a summary.

During the times in question, Bendix was a Delaware corporation with its commercial domicile and headquarters in Michigan. Bendix conducted business in all 50 States and 22 foreign countries. Having started business in 1929 as a manufacturer of aviation and automotive parts, from 1970 through 1981, Bendix was organized in four major operating groups: autos; aerospace/electronics; industrial/energy; and forest products. *Id.,* at 154-155. Each operating group was under separate management, but the chief executive of each group reported to the chairman and chief executive officer of Bendix. *Id.,* at 155. In this period Bendix's primary operations in New Jersey were the development and manufacture of aerospace products. *Id.,* at 161.

ASARCO is a New Jersey corporation with its principal offices in New York. It is one of the world's leading producers of nonferrous metals, treating ore taken from its own mines and ore it obtains from others. *Id.,* at 163-164. From December 1977 through November 1978, Bendix acquired 20.6% of ASARCO's stock by purchases on the open market. *Id.,* at 165. In the first half of 1981, Bendix sold its stock back to ASARCO, generating a gain of $211.5 million. *Id.,* at 172. The issue before us is whether New Jersey can tax an apportionable part of this income.

---

[24] *Allied Signal v. Director, Division of Taxation,* SCt, 504 US 768, 112 SCt 2251.

Our determination of the question whether the business can be called "unitary," see *infra*, at ____- ____, is all but controlled by the terms of a stipulation between the taxpayer and the State. They stipulated: "During the period that Bendix held its investment in ASARCO, Bendix and ASARCO were unrelated business enterprises each of whose activities had nothing to do with the other." *Id.,* at 169. Furthermore, "[p]rior to and after its investment in ASARCO, no business or activity of Bendix (in New Jersey or otherwise), either directly or indirectly (other than the investment itself), was involved in the nonferrous metal production business or any other business or activity (in New Jersey or otherwise) in which ASARCO was involved. On its part, ASARCO had no business or activity (in New Jersey or otherwise) which, directly or indirectly, was involved in any of the businesses or activities (in New Jersey or otherwise) in which Bendix was involved. None of ASARCO's activities, businesses or income (in New Jersey or otherwise) were related to or connected with Bendix's activities, business or income (in New Jersey or otherwise)." *Id.,* at 164-165.

The stipulation gives the following examples of the independence of the businesses:

"There were no common management, officers, or employees of Bendix and Asarco. There was no use by Bendix of Asarco's corporate plant, offices or facilities and no use by Asarco of Bendix's corporate plant, offices or facilities. There was no rent or lease of any property by Bendix from Asarco and no rent or lease of any property by Asarco from Bendix. Bendix and Asarco were each responsible for providing their own legal services, contracting services, tax services, finance services and insurance. Bendix and Asarco had separate personnel and hiring policies…and separate pension and employee benefit plans. Bendix did not lend monies to Asarco and Asarco did not lend monies to Bendix. There were no joint borrowings by Bendix and Asarco. Bendix did not guaranty any of Asarco's debt and Asarco did not guaranty any of Bendix's debt. Asarco had no representative on Bendix's Board of Directors. Bendix did not pledge its Asarco stock. As far as can be determined there were no sales of product by Asarco itself to Bendix or by Bendix to Asarco. There were certain sales of product in the ordinary course of business by Asarco subsidiaries to Bendix but these sales were minute compared to Asarco's total sales…. These open market sales were at arms length prices and did not come about due to the Bendix investment in Asarco. There were no transfers of employees between Bendix and Asarco." *Id.,* at 169-171.

While Bendix held its ASARCO stock, ASARCO agreed to recommend that two seats on the 14-member ASARCO Board of Directors be filled by Bendix representatives. The seats were filled by Bendix chief executive officer W.M. Agee and a Bendix outside director. *Id.,* at 168. Nonetheless, "Bendix did not exert any control over ASARCO." *Ibid.* After respondent assessed Bendix for taxes on an apportioned amount which included in the base the gain realized upon Bendix's disposition of its ASARCO stock, Bendix sued for a refund in New Jersey Tax Court. The case was decided based upon the stipulated record we have described, and the Tax Court held that the assessment was proper. *Bendix Corp. v. Taxation Div. Director,* 10 N.J. Tax 46 (1988). The Appellate Division affirmed, *Bendix Corp. v. Director, Div. of Taxation,* 237 N.J. Super. 328, 568 A.2d 59 (1989), and so, in turn, did the New Jersey Supreme Court. *Bendix Corp. v. Director, Div. of Taxation,* 125 N.J. 20, 592 A.2d 536 (1991).

The New Jersey Supreme Court held it was constitutional to consider the gain realized from the sale of the ASARCO stock as earned in Bendix's unitary business, drawing from our decision in *Container Corp. of America v. Franchise Tax Bd.,*

463 U. S. 159, 166 (1983), the principle that "the context for determining whether a unitary business exists has, as an overriding consideration, the exchange or transfer of value, which may be evidenced by functional integration, centralization of management, and economies of scale." 125 N.J., at 34, 592 A.2d, at 543-544. The New Jersey Supreme Court went on to state: "The tests for determining a unitary business are not controlled, however, by the relationship between the taxpayer recipient and the affiliate generator of the income that becomes the subject of State tax." *Id.*, at 35, 592 A.2d, at 544. Based upon Bendix documents setting out corporate strategy, the court found that the acquisition and sale of ASARCO "went well beyond...passive investments in business enterprises," *id.*, at 36, 592 A.2d, at 544, and Bendix "essentially had a business function of corporate acquisitions and divestitures that was an integral operational activity." *Ibid.* As support for its conclusion that the proceeds from the sale of the ASARCO stock were attributable to a unitary business, the New Jersey Supreme Court relied in part on the fact that Bendix intended to use those proceeds in what later proved to be an unsuccessful bid to acquire Martin Marietta, a company whose aerospace business, it was hoped, would complement Bendix's aerospace/electronics business. *Id.*, at 36, 592 A.2d, at 545.

Note: Reversed and Remanding New Jersey Supreme Court

Analysis

The U.S. Supreme Court granted certiorari to this case because the New Jersey courts were in effect seeking to overturn the **unitary principle** of taxation for income generated in a state. As mentioned earlier, under this principle, a business engaged in multi-state activities is viewed as one unitary business unit, and each state should tax only a portion of the company's total income based on the proportion of value created in that state. Generally, that proportion was based on the three-factor test using payroll, property, and sales figures for the state in question as compared to the total figures for all states that the company did business in. For example, if the three-factor computation indicated that 20 percent of a company's payroll-property-sales totals were in New Jersey, then New Jersey had the right to tax 20 percent of the multi-state income.

But to be apportionable, the income had to have some rational relationship between the taxing state and the intrastate business in order to create a **nexus** of activity. And that was the question addressed in *Allied Signal*, where the taxpayer (then Bendix Corporation, a Delaware-based company) had bought a 20-percent interest in ASARCO, a New Jersey Corporation that was a leading producer of nonferrous metals. Bendix was involved in four lines of business, including an aerospace business in New Jersey. When Bendix sold the stock investment for a $211.5 million gain, the state of New Jersey taxed Bendix on an apportioned amount. This decision was (surprise, surprise!) upheld by the New Jersey Tax Court, the New Jersey Appeals Court, and the New Jersey Supreme Court.

The taxpayer contended that none of the income should be apportionable to New Jersey, since there was no business relationship between ASARCO and Bendix. They were unrelated businesses and had no common workers, services, or expenses. The only minimal relationship was that due to the size of the investment, ASARCO agreed to allocate 2 of the 14 Board seats to Bendix. The State of New Jersey pointed out that Bendix did have an aerospace investment in New Jersey, which could be related to the metals produced by ASARCO, and that the proceeds of the stock sale were used to invest in Martin-Marietta, an aerospace company. The state also contended that Bendix regularly engaged in corporate acquisitions and divestitures, and that such pursuits could be considered regular business activities of the taxpayer.

One of the cases cited by the State of New Jersey was the *Container Corporation of America* case (discussed below), where the Supreme Court had concluded that a "flow of value" may be enough to establish nexus with a state. However, the Supreme Court relied more on other cases that required more than a minimal connection between the company and the state in order to establish nexus. The Court overturned the state decisions and ruled for the taxpayer, noting that the state decisions ignored the court's experience with the unitary method, that such decisions would overturn numerous state codes, and that there was simply no operational relationship between the two companies.

Interestingly, the State of New Jersey attempted to cite *Corn Products* as a precedent for investment activities that serve an operational business function, but this was not a very persuasive argument. Justice O'Connor dissented to the decision, noting that the Court had not given enough weight to the relationship between the subsequent acquisition of Martin-Marietta stock and the aerospace interests of the taxpayer.

OBSERVATION	One of the leading cases that addressed the nexus issue between companies and a state was *Quill Corporation v. North Dakota*.[25] In that case, the Supreme Court ruled that "substantial nexus" must be established before a state may impose a use tax on a company, and that solicitation of mail orders alone without outlets or sales representatives may not establish this relationship. This decision upheld an earlier decision in *National Bellas Hess v. Department of Revenue*, where the question of nexus arose in connection with catalog mail orders from the state.[26] In that case, the Court established that three ads run in the state indicated that the taxpayer solicited customers regularly, and nexus may be established to collect tax on the deliveries of merchandise.

It is interesting to note that New Jersey was recently involved in another nexus case, this time involving a telecommuting employee (*Telebright Corporation, Inc. v. Director, Division of Taxation*). In this case, an employee worked as a software developer for Telebright, a Maryland-based company. The employee relocated to New Jersey due to a spouse's job change, and Telebright allowed the employee to telecommute on a full-time basis. The employee developed and wrote software code on a laptop computer from her home in New Jersey and uploaded it to Telebright's computer in Maryland. The employee began and ended her day by checking in electronically with her employer, and regularly received assignments electronically as well. The New Jersey Superior Court found that Telebright was subject to New Jersey's corporate business tax because (1) the company was doing business in New Jersey. (2) the employee's daily presence in the state for Telebright's business purposes established nexus, and (3) the corporation enjoyed the benefits of the state's labor market. A similar result was reached in *Warwick McKinley Inc., California State Board of Equalization, Case No. 489090.*

.05   TRANSFER PRICING FOR INTERNATIONAL TRANSACTIONS—*THE BAUSCH & LOMB* CASE

Background

In a bid to attract international business, many countries have offered tax holidays and/or low tax rates to U.S. companies as a reward for locating in their country. When these countries offer tax rates significantly lower than the United States, there is a temptation for the U.S. company to manipulate transactions so that more income is taxed at the foreign country's rate and less at the U.S. rate. This can be accomplished by (1) shifting most of the income to the foreign country by charging the U.S. location a high transfer price for goods or (2) paying a small royalty to the U.S. company for rights and property that generate large incomes in the lower-taxed foreign country. Both of these techniques were the focus of the *Bausch & Lomb* case, and once again the case offers an excellent tutorial on the tax stakes involved in transfer pricing and royalty issues.

---

[25] *Quill Corporation v. North Dakota*, SCt, 504 US 298, 112 SCt 1904.
[26] *National Bellas Hess v. Department of Revenue*, SCt, 386 US 753, 87 SCt 1389.

Bausch & Lomb, Inc. v. Commissioner[27]

Facts of the Case: In 1978, B&L was a major participant in the soft contact lens industry, controlling upwards of 50.6 percent of the United States market. Between 1978 and 1980, B&L prepared long range forecasts that predicted increasing demand for soft contact lenses in international markets, particularly in Europe. In 1978, B&L began to investigate the possibility of an overseas manufacturing facility to complement its existing plant in Rochester, New York. Responding to various incentives offered by the Industrial Development Authority of the Republic of Ireland ("IDA"), including a tax holiday on all export profits through 1990, B&L determined to establish a manufacturing facility in Waterford, Ireland. The Tax Court found as fact that [B&L] had sound business reasons for the establishment of B&L Ireland. [B&L] had reason to believe that manufacturing capacity at its Rochester facility was inadequate to meet expected increases in soft contact lens demand. [B&L] determined that it was prudent to establish additional manufacturing capacity overseas in order to minimize regulatory delays, establish an alternative supply source to the Rochester facility, and to have a facility capable of more efficiently servicing the increasingly important European markets. Ireland was determined to be the location at which these objectives could be realized most cost effectively due to the incentives offered by the Republic of Ireland to induce the location of manufacturing facilities within the Republic. Since a non-Irish company could not receive [IDA-sponsored] financing, there were sound business reasons for incorporating an Irish manufacturing facility rather than merely operating the facility as a division of B&L. [CCH Dec. 45,547], 92 T.C. at 582-83.

Accordingly, B&L Ireland was incorporated on February 1, 1980, and B&L, B&L Ireland, and the IDA entered into an agreement on or about February 10, 1981, that specified the incentives to be provided for the venture by the IDA and the reciprocal commitments undertaken by B&L and B&L Ireland. B&L Ireland agreed, inter alia, not to enter into any royalty commitments, except that B&L Ireland could pay royalties to B&L or any subsidiaries in an amount not to exceed five percent of B&L Ireland's annual net sales.

Among the reasons for B&L's success was its manufacturing expertise. In the early 1960s, a Czechoslovakian chemist developed the "spin cast" method of manufacturing soft contact lenses, a process that uses centrifugal force by injecting a mixture into a spinning mold. As a result of a number of licensing agreements and lawsuits, B&L obtained nonexclusive rights to use the patents secured on the first spin cast machines. B&L acquired two spin cast machines from the inventor and, between 1966 and 1981, made several significant process modifications that increased the yield of usable lenses to a commercially acceptable level. Through 1982, B&L was the only manufacturer in the United States using the cost effective spin cast method. Thus, B&L was able to produce lenses at a cost of $1.50 each, which was far below its competitors' costs. During 1981 and 1982, for example, a competitor of B&L had per unit costs of over $4.00 using a cast molding process, and over $6.00 using a lathing process.

In January 1981 B&L granted B&L Ireland a nonexclusive license to manufacture lenses using B&L's spin cast technology. In addition, the

---

[27] *Bausch & Lomb*, CA-2, 91-1 USTC ¶50,244, 933 F2d 1084.

license agreement entitled B&L Ireland to any improvements resulting from B&L's ongoing research and development in the manufacture of contact lenses, and permitted B&L Ireland to sell soft contact lenses anywhere under B&L's trademarks. In exchange, B&L was to receive a royalty of five percent of the subsidiary's net contact lens sales. The agreement was terminable upon the written notice of either party.

B&L Ireland began manufacturing lenses in March 1981. It performed all processing, packaging, inspecting and labeling at its Waterford facility, with the exception of some insignificant expiration date labeling on a limited number of lenses done in Rochester in 1981. Thus, when lenses left Ireland, they were ready for sale to optical practitioners and chains. B&L Ireland's unit sales were 1,116,000 and 3,694,000 lenses for the years 1981 and 1982, respectively. B&L was under no contractual obligation to purchase any lenses from B&L Ireland, but sixty-one percent of B&L Ireland's total sales in 1981 and fifty-six percent in 1982 were to B&L for resale in the United States. The balance of B&L Ireland's sales were to overseas affiliates of B&L. Throughout that two year period, the intercompany transfer price was $7.50 per lens. The purchasers also paid the duty and freight charges, which in the case of B&L were $0.62 per lens.

The Commissioner's proposed deficiency sought to "reflect an arm's length consideration for the use of [B&L's] intangible assets by B&L Ireland" by limiting B&L Ireland to "a net profit before taxes of 20 percent of sales." The notice of deficiency, invoking section 482, accordingly reallocated from B&L Ireland to B&L taxable income in the amounts of $2,778,000 and $19,793,750 for the years 1980 and 1981, respectively, with an offsetting elimination of the royalty income that B&L Ireland had reported for those years, resulting in a net reallocation of $2,359,331 for 1981 and $18,425,750 for 1982. In response to B&L's petition to the Tax Court for redetermination of the deficiencies, the Commissioner further contended that the reallocation was necessary "because of the lack of arms-length pricing between" B&L and its subsidiary.

Note: Affirming U.S. Tax Court

Analysis

This case highlights two of the major issues of international taxation, namely transfer pricing and royalty arrangements. In this case, Bausch and Lomb (B&L) established an Irish Subsidiary (B&LI) to process, package and label contact lenses with their new "spin cast" method. Ireland offered B&L a tax holiday on exports through 1990 to locate in that country. B&L was the only company offering the spin cast method, and they were able to produce lenses for about $1.50 each, while the costs for other producers was around $6.00 each. B&L and B&LI entered into an agreement that B&LI would pay B&L a five-percent royalty (based on sales price) for use of the spin cast method, and that the transfer price of the finished goods from BL&I to B&L would be $7.50 each. During 1981 and 1982, approximately 55 to 60 percent of B&LI's sales were to B&L.

The IRS challenged the royalty and transfer price arrangements, contending that (1) payments for the use of B&L's intangibles were undervalued and (2) the transfer price was set too high. Both arrangements enabled B&L to shift income to lower-taxed Ireland by lowering profits in the United States due to low royalties and high cost of goods sold (the latter reflected in the transfer price). The IRS challenged this arrangement under Code Sec. 482, which states the following:

SEC. 482. ALLOCATION OF INCOME AND DEDUCTIONS AMONG TAXPAYERS.

In any case of two or more organizations, trades, or businesses (whether or not incorporated, whether or not organized in the United States, and whether or not affiliated) owned or controlled directly or indirectly by the same interests, the Secretary may distribute, apportion, or allocate gross income, deductions, credits, or allowances between or among such organizations, trades, or businesses, if he determines that such distribution, apportionment, or allocation is necessary in order to prevent evasion of taxes or clearly to reflect the income of any of such organizations, trades, or businesses. In the case of any transfer (or license) of intangible property (within the meaning of Sec. 936(h)(3)(B)), the income with respect to such transfer or license shall be commensurate with the income attributable to the intangible.

Specifically, the IRS contended that there was a lack of arm's length pricing in setting the royalty arrangement, and that a proper arrangement would limit B&LI's pre-tax profit to 20 percent of sales. And secondly, the IRS asked why B&L should pay $7.50 per lens when the product was being produced for only $1.50 each, especially when B&LI should be viewed as little more than a "contract manufacturer"? The taxpayer contended that B&LI did bear the risks in the transactions, in that B&L did not have to purchase from them, and all other manufacturers charged more than $7.50 per lens.

One of the key factors applied in this case was Reg. §1.482-2(e), which states that such royalty arrangements and transfer prices should be established at an arm's length price, defined as *"the price that an unrelated party would have paid under the same circumstances for the property involved in the controlled sale."* The U.S. Tax Court examined the royalty and transfer price issues separately. First, the Court accepted the transfer price, noting that the transfer price was comparable to the prices of four other companies in the industry, and that this negates the contract manufacturer argument. Secondly, the Court ruled that, based on expert testimony, the royalty rate should be set at 20 percent of B&LI's net sales (the equivalent of approximately 50 percent of B&LI's profits on the sales), and a reallocation was made.

On appeal, the 2nd Circuit Court started with a basic premise, summarized by the Court as follows: *"[The Commissioner] is indifferent as to whether the royalty is increased or the transfer price is decreased as long as the result is that B&L Ireland receives only its cost of production and a reasonable markup."* On Appeal, the IRS argued that B&L would have terminated the agreement and negotiated new terms if dealing with an independent licensee. Nonetheless, after considering the quality and quantity of evidence unearthed by the Tax Court, the Circuit Court upheld the lower court decision.

OBSERVATION Transfer pricing continues to be a major issue in international taxation. Various whitepapers and proposed regulations have been drafted to deal with the issue, and there is discussion of an "Advanced Pricing Agreement Program," where the parties involved would send data to the IRS, propose a transfer pricing mechanism, and if accepted by the IRS the parties could in effect be provided a safe harbor. One post-1986 change made that makes a lot of sense is the simple requirement that the inventory cost assigned to imported items cannot exceed the value declared for customs.

.07 THE UNITARY METHOD AND WORLD-WIDE INCOME—THE *BARCLAYS BANK/COLGATE PALMOLIVE* CASES

Background

The *Barclays Bank/Colgate Palmolive* cases (once again, two cases combined into one by the Supreme Court) addresses a different issue related to the unitary method. Specifically, if a foreign company operates in a state, should the income allocated with the unitary method be only the income earned within the United States, or should it be the world-wide income of the foreign company? For many years, most states accepted the idea of only using domestic income, but California decided to up the ante by using the worldwide income of such foreign companies. This led to the *Barclays Bank/Colgate Palmolive* case, where the Supreme Court tackled some rather thorny constitutional issues. And this case also led to the infamous **water's edge election**.

Barclays Bank, PLC v. Franchise Tax Board of CA[28]

Facts of the Case: The first of these consolidated cases, No. 92-1384, is a tax refund suit brought by two members of the Barclays Group, a multinational banking enterprise. Based in the United Kingdom, the Barclays Group includes more than 220 corporations doing business in some 60 nations. The two refund-seeking members of the Barclays corporate family did business in California and were therefore subject to California's franchise tax. Barclays Bank of California (Barcal), one of the two taxpayers, was a California banking corporation wholly owned by Barclays Bank International Limited (BBI), the second taxpayer. BBI, a United Kingdom corporation, did business in the United Kingdom and in more than 33 other nations and territories.

In computing its California franchise tax based on 1977 income, Barcal reported only the income from its own operations. BBI reported income on the assumption that it participated in a unitary business composed of itself and its subsidiaries, but not its parent corporation and the parent's other subsidiaries. After auditing BBI's and Barcal's 1977 income year franchise tax returns, the Tax Board, respondent here, determined that both were part of a worldwide unitary business, the Barclays Group. Ultimately, the Board assessed additional tax liability of $1,678 for BBI and $152,420 for Barcal.

Barcal and BBI paid the assessments and sued for refunds. They prevailed in California's lower courts, but were unsuccessful in California's Supreme Court. The California Supreme Court held that the tax did not impair the Federal Government's ability to "speak with one voice" in regulating foreign commerce, see *Japan Line, Ltd. v. County of Los Angeles,* 441 U.S., at 449, and therefore did not violate the Commerce Clause. Having so concluded, the California Supreme Court remanded the case to the Court of Appeal for further development of Barclays' claim that the compliance burden on foreign-based multinationals imposed by California's tax violated both the Due Process Clause and the non-discrimination requirement of the Commerce Clause. *Barclay's Bank Int'l, Ltd. v. Franchise Tax Bd.,* 2 Cal. 4th 708, 829 P.2d 279, cert. denied, 506 U.S. ___ (1992). On remand, the Court of Appeal decided the compliance burden issues against Barclays, 10 Cal. App. 4th 1742, 14 Cal. Rptr. 2d 537 (3d Dist. 1992), and the California Supreme Court denied further review. The case is therefore before us on writ of certiorari to the California Court of Appeal. 510 U.S. ___ (1993). Barclays has conceded, for purposes of this litigation, that the entire Barclays Group formed a worldwide unitary business in 1977.

The petitioner in No. 93-1839, Colgate-Palmolive Co., is a Delaware corporation headquartered in New York. Colgate and its subsidiaries doing business in the United States engaged principally in the manufacture and distribution of household and personal hygiene products. In addition, Colgate owned some 75 corporations that operated entirely outside the United States; these foreign subsidiaries also engaged primarily in the

---

[28] *Barclays Bank PLC v. Franchise Tax Board of California*, SCt, 512 US 298.

manufacture and distribution of household and personal hygiene products. When Colgate filed California franchise tax returns based on 1970-1973 income, it reported the income earned from its foreign operations on a separate accounting basis. Essentially, Colgate maintained that the Constitution compelled California to limit the reach of its unitary principle to the United States' water's edge. See *supra,* at 6. The Tax Board determined that Colgate's taxes should be computed on the basis of worldwide combined reporting, and assessed a 4-year deficiency of $604,765. Colgate paid the tax and sued for a refund.

Colgate prevailed in the California Superior Court, which found that the Federal Government had condemned worldwide combined reporting as impermissibly intrusive upon the Nation's ability uniformly to regulate foreign commercial relations. No. 319715 (Super. Ct. Sacramento County, Apr. 19, 1989) (reprinted in App. to Pet. for Cert. in No. 92-1839, pp. 88a-102a). The Court of Appeal reversed, concluding that evidence of the federal Executive's opposition to the tax was insufficient. 4 Cal. App. 4th 1681, 1700-1712, 284 Cal. Rptr. 780, 792-800 (3d Dist. 1991). The California Supreme Court returned the case to the Court of Appeal with instructions "to vacate its decision and to refile the opinion after modification in light of "that Court's decision in *Barclays.* __ Cal. 4th __, 831 P.2d 798 (1992)." In its second decision, the Court of Appeal again ruled against Colgate. 13 Cal. Rptr. 2d 761 (3d Dist. 1992). The California Supreme Court denied further review, and the case is before us on writ of certiorari to the Court of Appeal. 510 U.S. __ (1993). Like Barclays, Colgate concedes, for purposes of this litigation, that during the years in question, its business, worldwide, was unitary.

Note: Affirming California Court of Appeals

Analysis

This case involves the unitary principle as applied on an international basis. Barclay's Bank Group, a United Kingdom group of 220 corporations worldwide, did business in California and reported as unitary income subject to apportionment only that income earned by BARCAL (a California-based bank) and BBI (an international UK company), as well as the subsidiaries of these two companies. The State of California contended that the worldwide income of the much larger Barclay's Group should be subject to apportionment. In a second case, Colgate-Palmolive, which owned 75 corporations operating in foreign companies, reported only income earned in domestic operations as subject to apportionment.

In both cases, the taxpayers contended that the unitary principle applied on to the *"water's edge"* (within the United States), in that foreign operations were not related to the business transacted in California. The taxpayers also noted that traditionally foreign operations were subject to separate accounting for federal income tax purposes, which *"treats each corporate entity discretely for the purpose of determining income tax liability."*

The State of California contended that the *worldwide* income of both companies should be subject to apportionment. Thus, the three-factor formula would be applied based on payroll, property and sales as a percentage of the worldwide total for the three factors, and multiplied times the worldwide income of the controlling parent. The California Supreme Court upheld this decision, and the U.S. Supreme Court agreed to hear the case due to concerns regarding possible constitutional issues involved.

At the outset, the U.S. Supreme Court noted that in *Container Corp. of America v. Franchise Tax Board*, the Court had upheld the California worldwide computation as it related to a *domestic-based multinational corporation*, but that they had *not* ruled on the scheme as applied to domestic corporations with foreign parents or to foreign corporations with foreign parents or foreign subsidiaries.[29] The Court then framed its decision based on an analysis of the following six factors that had been established in earlier cases that would prohibit such a taxation scheme because the tax:

- Applies to an activity lacking substantial nexus with the state[30]
- Is not fairly apportioned[31]
- Discriminates against interstate commerce[32]
- Is not fairly related to services provided by the state[33]
- Enhances the risk of multiple taxation[34]
- Restricts the federal government's capacity to speak with one voice when regulating commerce with foreign governments[35]

The first four factors were identified in *Complete Auto* as being hurdles to survive the Commerce Clause of the Constitution. The Court concluded that California's scheme easily met the three of the first four criteria; nexus was established, neither party stated that the apportionment method was unfair, and there was no question that the taxpayers were afforded services in the form of "protection, opportunities and benefits" by the state for which the state can demand a return. As to the discrimination factor, the Court determined that the compliance burden did not discriminate against interstate commerce (e.g., the additional reporting costs due to California's scheme could be approximated).

This still leaves the final two factors that the Court felt deserved additional scrutiny when a state seeks to tax foreign commerce. As to the risk of multiple taxation, the Court conceded that this is possible, in that Barclays has more of its operations outside the United States than U.S. domestic multinational corporations and thus has more income taxed by foreign countries. However, the Court also noted that the same problems of double taxation exist with "separate accounting." The Court noted that to disallow California's scheme would, as the Court noted in *Container Corporation*, *"require California to give up one allocation method that sometimes results in double taxation in favor of another allocation method that also sometimes results in double taxation."*

As to the last factor, restricting the federal government's ability to speak with one voice in international trade, the Court found no *"specific indications of Congressional intent"* to preempt California's tax scheme. In concluding that California's taxation worldwide reporting scheme was constitutional, the Court stated the following: *"we leave it to Congress—whose voice, in this area, is the Nation's—to evaluate whether the national interest is best served by tax uniformity, or state autonomy."*

The State of California's victory was short-lived, as Barclays and other corporations spoke with their feet and began relocating into states with more favorable unitary schemes. Faced with a drastic loss of international business, in 1988 California instituted a "water's edge election," whereby such companies could elect to have the unitary method apply only to domestic operations. California was one of the last states to institute such an election.

OBSERVATION	The 1988 legislation by the State of California instituted a complicated domestic disclosure sheet and reporting system that involved a high reporting fee. Five years later, the state was facing retaliation threats from the United Kingdom, federal pressures, and a weak economy. As a result, the state removed the fee and simplified the disclosure reporting system in 1993.

---

[29] *Container Corporation of America v. California Franchise Tax Board*, SCt, 463 US 159, 103 SCt 2933.
[30] *Complete Auto Transit, Inc. v. Brady*, SCt, 430 US 274, 97 SCt 1076.
[31] *Id.*
[32] *Id.*
[33] *Id.*
[34] *Container Corporation of America*, 463 US 159.
[35] *Japan Line v. County of Los Angeles*, SCt, 441 US 434, 99 SCt 1813.

.09 INCOME ALLOCATIONS—OTHER CASES OF NOTE

Container Corp. of America v. Franchise Tax Bd.[36] In this case, the taxpayer manufactured paperboard packaging. The State of California decided to tax income the taxpayer received from its wholly-owned and mostly-owned foreign subsidiaries. Although the subsidiaries were in the same line of business as Container Corporation, they were given a fair degree of autonomy. They purchased only one percent of their materials from the parent, and personnel transfers from parent to subsidiaries were rare. However, Container Corporation guaranteed much of the debt of the subsidiaries, provided advice and consultations regarding manufacturing and other issues, and assisted in the procurement of equipment. Based on these factors, the U.S. Supreme Court concluded that a "flow of value" occurred between the parent and the subsidiaries (even though there was not a "flow of goods"), and this was enough to establish nexus. The Court also applied the three key tests for a unitary business developed in *F.W. Woolworth v. Taxation and Revenue Department of New Mexico*: (1) functional integration, (2) centralized management, and (3) economies of scale.[37]

Disabled American Veterans v. U.S.[38] In this case, the Claims Court ruled that a qualified exempt organization realized unrelated business taxable income on a portion of premiums it sent to donors in connection with its semi-annual solicitation of funds. Those premiums that were provided for a contribution that was substantially in excess of the premium's retail value were not subject to the tax. However, those premiums offered for a contribution not greatly in excess of their retail value resulted in unrelated business taxable income equal to the retail value of the premiums involved since they were offered in a competitive and commercial manner. Receipts from the rental of names from the organization's list of donors were business taxable income and were not excludable from unrelated business taxable income under Code Sec. 512(b)(2) as passive income. Neither the premium solicitation nor the rental of the mailing list were related to the exempt purposes of the organization since no causal relationship existed between these activities and the organization's exempt activities other than the need for funds to pay for the latter.

California Proposition 39 (11/6/2012). Once again, California emerges on the forefront of the unitary taxation issue. On November 6, 2012, the voters of California approved Proposition 39, which had three major components: (1) require out-of-state businesses to calculate their California tax liability based solely on the percentage of their sales in California, (2) repeal an existing law that gives businesses an option to choose a tax liability formula that provides favorable tax treatment for businesses with property and payroll outside California, and (3) use the projected $550 million additional revenue to fund projects dedicated to clean energy and and energy efficiency. In essence, the normal "three-factor" test was reduced to one factor: sales. This was a welcomed change for companies like Qualcomm, which has large investments in employees and communications plant and equipment in California, and not so welcomed by companies like Microsoft, which has most of its employees, plant and equipment in Redmond, Washington.

¶8009 Summary

- The major court decisions relating to accounting records include:
  - *Arthur Young* (the IRS has the right to examine tax accrual workpapers, which may shed light on the preparation of the return).
  - *Marion L. Holland* (the IRS may reconstruct the taxpayer's income with an indirect method of estimating income, even if the taxpayer has accounting records).

---

[36] *Container Corporation of America*, 463 US 159.
[37] *F.W. Woolworth v. Taxation and Revenue Department of New Mexico*, SCt, 458 US 354, 102 SCt 3128.
[38] *Disabled American Veterans*, CtCls, 81-1 USTC ¶9443, 650 F2d 1158.

- The major court decisions related to accounting methods include:
  - *Thor Power Tool* (regulations specifying conditions for the writedown of obsolete inventories were upheld, even though contrary to generally accepted accounting principles).
  - *Hillsboro Bank/Bliss Dairy* (the proper application of the tax benefit rule is based on the presence of an inconsistent event subsequent to the deduction in question).
- The major court decisions related to income allocations include:
  - *American College of Physicians* (advertising revenue from a professional medical journal was taxable since it was unrelated to the business activity of the organization).
  - *Allied Signal* (gain on the sale of a stock investment was not subject to taxation in New Jersey, since nexus with the state was not established).
  - *Bausch and Lomb* (the transfer price between a U.S. corporation and its Irish subsidiary was deemed sufficient, but the royalty payment from the subsidiary to the parent for use of its technology was too low).
  - *Barclays Bank/Colgate Palmolive* (California did not violate the commerce and due process clauses of the Constitution when it applied the unitary theory based on world-wide company incomes).

Review Questions for Chapter 8

True or False

Indicate which of the following statements are true or false by circling the correct answer.

1. A tax-exempt astronomy association that sells telescopes could possibly be subject to federal income taxes.   T   F

2. The *Barclays Bank* case involved an attempt by the State of California to tax a foreign corporation on that portion of its income generated in the United States.   T   F

3. One of the arguments used by the IRS in the *Arthur Young* case was that providing access to the workpapers would have a "chilling effect" on the relationships between taxpayers and their accountants.   T   F

4. Prior to the *Holland* case, the IRS was never permitted to use an indirect method of estimating the taxable income of a taxpayer.   T   F

5. The Court of Appeals decision in the *Textron* case effectively shields tax accrual workpapers from an IRS subpoena.   T   F

6. In the *Hillsboro National Bank/Bliss Dairy* case, the U.S. Supreme Court stated that the tax benefit rule applied to *Bliss Dairy* (distributions of feed) but did not apply to *Hillsboro National Bank* (refunds of taxes paid by bank).   T   F

7. In the *Allied Signal* case, the Supreme Court determined that there was no substantial business relationship between the parent (Bendix Corporation) and the subsidiary (ASARCO).   T   F

8. In the *Barclay's Bank* case, the California Franchise Tax Board attempted to apply the three-factor unitary formula to the world-wide income of the taxpayer, rather than domestic income.   T   F

9. In the *American College of Physicians* case, the Supreme Court determined that the organization's advertising revenue was subject to the unrelated business income tax.   T   F

10. In the *Thor Power Tool* decision, the Supreme Court accepted the taxpayer's method of writing down obsolete inventory because the method used was consistent with generally accepted accounting principles (GAAP).   T   F

Fill in the Blanks

Fill in each blank with the appropriate word or phrase that completes each sentence.

11. The requirement that a state income tax refund be included in the subsequent year's gross income if the taxpayer itemized deductions in the prior year is an example of the _____ rule.

12. If a company does business in a state and benefits from the use of the state's resources, it is generally assumed that the company has established _____ with the state.

13. An election available in California to a foreign company that will effectively limit state tax levies only on the income earned within the United States is termed the _____ election.

14. In a key phrase of the justification for their decision in the *Arthur Young* case, the Supreme Court noted that providing IRS access to the tax accrual workpapers will _____ on the preparation of the return.

15. One of the implied conclusions of the Supreme Court in the *Holland* Case (relating to indirect methods of reporting income) is that the IRS is auditing the _____ and not his or her _____.

16. In the *Thor Power* case, the Supreme Court found as reasonable a regulation that requires any writedowns in the cost of excess inventories to be allowable only if the taxpayer actually offers such inventory for sale within _____ days of the inventory date.

17. In order for the tax benefit rule to apply to a transaction, the Supreme Court in the *Hillsboro Bank/Bliss Dairy* case ruled that there must be a(n) _____ event.

18. Under the _____ principle, a state should tax only a portion of a company's total multi-state income based on the proportion of value created in that state.

19. In the *Textron* Court of Appeals decision, the Court decided for the government because the workpapers were not prepared specifically for _____.

20. In the *Holland* decision, the Supreme Court indicated that the IRS _____ (does, does not) have to follow every lead offered by the taxpayer as to the source of unreported income.

Multiple Choice

Circle the best answer for each of the following questions.

21. Code Sec. 7602 grants the IRS the power to examine any books, papers, records, or other data that may be relevant to:
    a. ascertaining the correctness of any return
    b. making a return where none has been made
    c. determining the liability of any person for any internal revenue tax
    d. any of the above

22. Under the unitary theory, a company operating in multiple states will generally allocate its income among the states according to a three-factor formula. Which of the following is not one of those three factors?
    a. sales
    b. payroll
    c. capital stock outstanding
    d. property

23. The *Bausch and Lomb* case focused on which of the following relationships between the domestic corporation and its foreign subsidiary?
    a. royalty arrangement on property
    b. foreign tax credits
    c. transfer prices of goods
    d. (a) and (c)

24. Under the IRS policy of self-restraint in requesting a taxpayer's workpapers during an audit, the IRS would request such documents only in unusual circumstances, and any request must be approved by the:
    a. Commissioner of the IRS
    b. District Director of the IRS
    c. Chief of the Examination Division
    d. None of the above

25. Which of the following factors was cited by the Supreme Court in ruling against the taxpayer in the *American College of Physicians* case, which dealt with the taxability of journal advertising revenue of the tax-exempt taxpayer?
    a. the gross receipts from the advertising exceeded $100,000
    b. a number of ads were repeated several times during the year
    c. the taxpayer did little screening of the ads for determining any educational value
    d. (b) and (c)

26. In the *Bausch and Lomb* case, the IRS was concerned that the parent corporation was avoiding taxes by:
    a. establishing too small of a royalty and too large of a transfer price with a subsidiary
    b. establishing too large of a royalty and too small of a transfer price with a subsidiary
    c. establishing too small of a royalty and a transfer price with a subsidiary
    d. establishing too large of a royalty and a transfer price

27. The Code Sec. 7525 privilege between taxpayers and their authorized tax practitioners is most likely to apply to documents related to which of the following?
    a. preparation of tax returns
    b. tax advice
    c. preparation of tax accrual workpapers
    d. provision of business or accounting advice

28. In the *Holland* decision, the Supreme Court indicated that the IRS could use an indirect method of estimating income when:
    a. the taxpayer's records were missing
    b. as a first "check" on the general accuracy of a taxpayer's records
    c. either (a) or (b)
    d. neither (a) nor (b)

29. A taxpayer reports $8,500 medical expenses on Schedule A; however, only $1,000 is deductible after applying the 7.5-percent of adjusted gross income floor. As a result, the taxpayer's itemized deductions exceeded her allowable standard deduction by $1,250. If the taxpayer unexpectedly receives $1,800 reimbursement on the medical expenses in the next taxable year, the taxpayer must report income in that year of:
    a. $0
    b. $1,000
    c. $1,250
    d. $1,800

30. When comparing the *Thor Power Tool* case with the *Ford Motor Company* case (discussed in Chapter 6), it can be stated that the IRS argued that generally accepted accounting principles (GAAP) are:
    a. good in *Thor Power Tool* and bad in *Ford Motor Company*
    b. bad in *Thor Power Tool* and good in *Ford Motor Company*
    c. good in both *Thor Power Tool* and *Ford Motor Company*
    d. bad in both *Thor Power Tool* and *Ford Motor Company*

Review Problems

31. Although the issue of contention in *Thor Power Tool* had to do with deductions for inventory writedowns, at its core the case has much in common with the trilogy of cases related to advance payments of income discussed in Chapter 5 (e.g., the *Auto Club of Michigan*, the *American Automobile Association*, and the *Schlude* cases). Explain.

32. Describe the IRS policy of self-restraint in seeking access to a taxpayer's workpapers, and how recent events may have the potential to "loosen" that policy.

33. Code Sec. 7525 was enacted in 1998 to provide some confidentiality privilege on communications between the taxpayer and his or her federally authorized practitioners. Explain how this provision applies to documents related to (1) tax return preparation and (2) tax advice.

34. Money Mint produces dated collector plates each year. Historically, most of their sales of the plates occur in the first three months of the year, and so Money has a policy of writing down the cost of each year's plates unsold after three months to 20 percent of cost (their estimated net realizable value). Will the IRS likely accept this writedown? What if Money also wrote off the entire cost of the excess plates after six months?

35. In order to apply the tax benefit rule, must there be a "recovery," e.g., a refund of an item previously deducted? Explain.
36. The Tax Court just ruled on an inventory method, and their decision runs contrary to IRS regulatory advice. Mecan Company changes their inventory method to conform to the Tax Court decision, stating that this is not an accounting change but a change in the underlying facts (a new major source of authority). Do you agree? Explain.
37. Explain the unitary principle as it relates to the taxation of a company's income from multi-state operations. Did the Supreme Court's decision in the *Allied Signal* case uphold this principle, or overturn it? Explain.
38. In the *Bausch & Lomb* case, the Supreme Court was examining the economic substance of two arrangements between the U.S. parent and an Irish subsidiary: a royalty arrangement and a transfer pricing policy. Explain how these two factors may be abused by taxpayers in an attempt to lower total income taxes paid.
39. Describe how the Franchise Tax Board of California modified the traditional three-factor formula of the unitary theory in attempting to tax Barclay's Bank. Was this modification upheld in the *Barclays Bank* decision by the Supreme Court, and what happened in the aftermath of the decision?
40. Was the decision in *Hillsboro National Bank/Bliss Dairy* (regarding the tax benefit method) consistent with the decision in *Dixie Pine Products*, discussed in Chapter 6? Explain.

Research Problems

41. A company wishes to change the MACRS class life on equipment it uses in distribution activities from seven to five years. Must the company request permission from the IRS to do so? Explain.
42. A social club that was classified as being tax exempt under Code Sec. 501(c)(7) had taxable unrelated business income derived from dividends on investments. Can the social club claim the dividends received deduction allowed by Code Sec. 243 against this income? Explain.
43. ABC Bank Company collected insurance proceeds to compensate for an employee's embezzlement of funds. The bank had never reported the embezzled amounts as income, and had not taken a loss deduction. Should the company report this amount as income, and does the tax benefit rule apply in this case? Explain.

Planning Problems

44. Grape Corporation is audited every year, and in preparation for this year's audit, Grape's tax advisor CPA firm discovers that Grape has been using an incorrect method of computing inventories for 20 years. It is more likely to be discovered in this year's audit, since the product line was discontinued. When the potential adjustment was computed, the CPA determined that Cost of Goods Sold had been overstated by a total of $400,000. What are Grape's options at this point? Explain. (Hint: refer to Rev. Proc. 97-27 and Rev. Proc. 2009-39.)
45. Hannah Idaho, a sole proprietor, is required to change her accounting method for inventories following an IRS audit of their 2013 tax return. Hannah had been using the incorrect method for the past five years, and the proposed Code Sec. 481 involuntary adjustment of $40,000 is composed of the following amounts:

Year	Positive (Negative)	Hannah's Marginal Tax Rate Adjustment
2009	($ 2,000)	35%
2010	$ 5,000	35%
2011	$ 8,000	15%
2012	$14,000	28%
2013	$15,000	28%
Total	$40,000	

How should Hannah handle the reporting of this adjustment? Explain. (Hint: refer to Code Sec. 481(b)(1) and (b)(2)).

Compliance Problems

46. A company wishes to change their accounting method for reporting research and experimentation expenses from immediate deduction to five-year amortization. What steps must the company take to accomplish this change? (Hint: Read about change of accounting method and Form 3115 on the CCH Tax Research network.)

47. On a Schedule M-3, will the book-tax difference for the amortization of goodwill be reported in the "temporary difference" or "permanent difference" columns of the schedule? Explain. (Hint: read the Instructions for Form 1120, Schedule M-3.)

CHAPTER 9

Tax Practice—Procedures, Administration and Sanctions

Learning Objectives

1. Understand the organizational structure of the IRS.
2. Learn how returns are chosen for audit and the administrative procedures associated with an audit.
3. Differentiate between the various taxpayer and tax return preparer penalties.
4. Examine the ethical standards that guide tax practitioners.

¶9001 Introduction

This chapter provides an overview of the IRS's role in tax enforcement and collection including tax return audits, tax-related penalties for both taxpayers and tax return preparers. Standards for tax practitioners as provided in Circular 230 and the AICPA's Statements of Standards for Tax Services are also covered.

¶9003 Role and Structure of the Internal Revenue Service

The Internal Revenue Service (IRS) is the largest of the Department of Treasury's bureaus. In FY 2011, the IRS collected more than $2.4 trillion in revenue and processed more than 234 million tax returns.

.01   STATUTORY AUTHORITY

Congress authorized the Secretary of the Treasury to supervise the administration and enforcement of the Internal Revenue Code.

Section 7801: Authority of Department of the Treasury.

(a) (1) In general.
Except as otherwise expressly provided by law, the administration and enforcement of this title shall be performed by or under the supervision of the Secretary of the Treasury.

The IRS was organized under the Treasury Department to carry out the administration and enforcement of the internal revenue laws. To carry out this duty, Congress granted very broad authority to the Secretary to "examine any books, papers, records, or other data which may be relevant" to determining the correctness of any tax return, or the tax liability of any person.

The IRS's mission is to:

> "Provide America's taxpayers top-quality service by helping them understand and meet their tax responsibilities and by applying the tax law with integrity and fairness to all."[1]

.03   STRUCTURE OF THE IRS

The IRS is headed by the Commissioner, an office created under Code Sec. 7803. The Commissioner is appointed by the President, with the consent of the Senate. The IRS Oversight Board recommends candidates to the President. However, the President is not required to nominate the Oversight Board candidate. The Commissioner is initially appointed to a five-year term and may be reappointed for additional five-year terms. The Commissioner serves at the pleasure of the President and may be removed at the will of the President.

Six specialized units report directly to the Commissioner's office. In addition, two Deputy Commissioner's report directly to the Commissioner and oversee the four primary operating divisions and IRS support functions. **Figure 1** shows the organization chart detailing the structure of the IRS.

.05   IRS OPERATING DIVISIONS

The IRS is organized into four operating divisions that are responsible for the major customer segments:

1. Wage & Investment, which serves taxpayers with wage and investment income only;
2. Small Business/Self-Employed, which serves taxpayers who are fully or partially self-employed individuals and small businesses;
3. Large & Mid-Size Businesses, which serves corporations with assets greater than $10 million; and
4. Tax Exempt & Government Entities, which serves employee plans, exempt organizations, and government entities.

Within each of these divisions, personnel perform audit examinations, collections, and appeals for the particular taxpayers that the division serves.

.07   IRS OVERSIGHT BOARD

The IRS Oversight Board was created in the IRS Restructuring and Reform Act of 1998 by enacting Code Sec. 7802. It is made up of nine members; seven members appointed by the President and confirmed by the Senate plus the Secretary of the Treasury and the IRS Commissioner. One member must be a representative of the IRS employees.

---

[1] IRS Strategic Plan, 2005–2009 available on the IRS website at *http://www.irs.gov/pub/irs-utl/strategic_plan_05-09.pdf*.

¶9003.01

The Board acts much like a corporate board of directors. It provides long-term guidance and direction to the IRS, utilizing the private-sector experience and expertise of its members. It reviews and approves the IRS strategic plan and budget requests, reviews the evaluation and compensation of senior IRS employees, and evaluates the IRS performance reports.

Figure 1
IRS Organization Chart

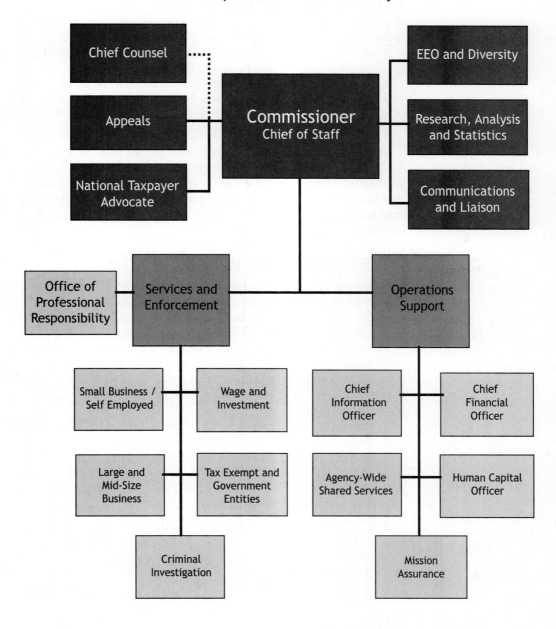

INTERNAL REVENUE SERVICE
Department of the Treasury

Source: *http://www.irs.gov/pub/irs-utl/irsorgchart.pdf*

¶9003.07

¶9005   Taxpayer Rights

.01   TAXPAYER ADVOCATE SERVICE

The Taxpayer Advocate Service was established under the *1996 Taxpayer Bill of Rights 2,* replacing the Office of the Taxpayer Ombudsman. The Taxpayer Advocate Service is an independent organization within the IRS whose employees assist taxpayers who are experiencing economic harm, who are seeking help in resolving tax problems that have not been resolved through normal channels, or who believe that an IRS system or procedure is not working as it should.

The Taxpayer Advocate Service is led by the National Taxpayer Advocate (NTA). The NTA is appointed by the Treasury Secretary, after consultation with the Commissioner and the Oversight Board. The NTA reports directly to the Commissioner, but operates independently from the IRS.

Code Sec. 7803 outlines the NTA's responsibilities. Specifically, the advocate is charged with the following duties:

- Assist taxpayers in resolving problems with the IRS;
- Identify areas in which taxpayers have problems when dealing with the IRS;
- Propose changes to IRS administrative practices to mitigate future problems; and
- Identify possible changes to the law in order to mitigate future problems.

Each year, the NTA must submit two reports to Congress. The first report, due June 30, outlines the objectives of the Office of the National Taxpayer Advocate for the year and includes statistical information and a full and substantial analysis. The second report, due December 31, identifies initiatives taken to improve taxpayer service and the IRS response to taxpayer problems. This report includes summaries of at least 20 of the most serious problems encountered by taxpayers when dealing with the IRS.

.03   TAXPAYER BILL OF RIGHTS

In response to complaints about overzealous IRS employees, the first *Taxpayer Bill of Rights* was passed by Congress as part of the *Technical and Miscellaneous Revenue Act of 1988.* Additional taxpayer protections were added under the *1996 Taxpayer Bill of Rights 2* and by the *1998 IRS Restructuring Act.*

Both the taxpayer and the IRS benefit when the taxpayer understands his/her rights early in the dispute resolution process. Therefore, the IRS must prepare and distribute a statement of rights and procedures to all taxpayers contacted in connection with the determination or collection of any tax. The statement must provide in simple and non-technical language:

- the rights of a taxpayer and the obligations of the IRS during an examination,
- the procedure by which a taxpayer may appeal an adverse decision of the IRS (including administrative and judicial appeals),
- the procedures for filing refund claims and taxpayer complaints, and
- the procedures the IRS may use in enforcing the tax laws (including assessment, levy and enforcement of liens).

The IRS provides this information through various publications, including Publication 1, *Your Rights as a Taxpayer;* Publication 5, *Appeal Rights and Preparation of Protests for Unagreed Cases*; Publication 556, *Examination of Returns, Appeal Rights and Claims for Refund*; Publication 594, *The IRS Collection Process;* and Publication 1660, *Collection Appeal Rights.*

.05   TAXPAYER INTERVIEWS

Code Sec. 7521 provides the procedures that must be followed during taxpayer interviews. The taxpayer has the right to make an audio recording of any in-person interview with an IRS employee, as long as he/she provides the IRS with 10 days advance notice. The IRS also has the right to record the interview with the same 10 days advance notice requirement. In addition, the taxpayer has the right to be represented during an interview by an authorized representative. Finally, the taxpayer may suspend the interview at any time in order to consult with a representative.

¶9007 Selecting a Return for Audit

The primary objective of examining returns is to promote voluntary compliance. To achieve this objective, the IRS uses a classification system to determine which returns should be examined. The IRS attempts to select tax returns for audit that have the highest probability of error.

IRS Publication 1, *Your Rights as a Taxpayer,* outlines the audit selection process. Returns are selected in one of two ways. First, computer programs identify returns that may have errors. These may be simply math errors or "matching" errors where the information reported on the return does not agree to the amounts reported by third parties on information returns such as Forms 1099, W-2, and K-1. Additionally, the computer programs select returns for examination based upon studies of past examinations or issues identified by compliance projects. Second, the IRS relies upon information from outside sources, including newspapers, public records, and individuals.

IRS campuses (formerly called service centers) process over 200 million tax returns each year. Regional campuses are located in Andover, MA; Atlanta, GA; Austin, TX; Cincinnati, OH; Fresno, CA; Holtsville, AL; Kansas City, MO; Memphis, TN; Ogden, UT; and Philadelphia, PA. As tax returns are filed, they are checked for mathematical correctness and then classified and selected for examination by either computer or manual identification. Returns classified for audit by the computer may then be screened by an IRS employee to identify audit issues and set the scope of the examination, or to determine that the returns do not warrant examination.

The methods used to identify returns for audit include:
- the Discriminant Function System (DIF);
- matching returns with information documents (or, where no return is filed, examining documents from third parties to determine that a return should have been filed);
- examining large corporate returns under the large case and Coordinated Examination Program;
- selecting returns involving issues or transactions with other taxpayers, such as business partners and investors, whose returns were selected for audit;
- identifying returns in connection with district office local compliance projects dealing with areas such as return preparers or specific market segments;
- identifying returns under IRS audit selection criteria for tax shelters;
- screening returns of exempt organizations for high-interest audit areas; and
- the Frivolous Return Program.

.01 DISCRIMINANT FUNCTION SYSTEM

The **Discriminant Function (DIF)** system is a mathematical program used for identifying and selecting returns for examination. Mathematical formulas identify returns by assigning weights to certain return characteristics. The weights are then added together to produce a score for each return. Returns are then ranked in numerical sequence from the highest to lowest score. Generally, the higher the score, the greater the likelihood of a significant change on examination. The DIF mathematical formulas are kept confidential and examination departments are only provided the list of returns with high DIF scores, not the actual scores.

.03 DOCUMENT MATCHING, MATH ERROR, AND SUBSTITUTE RETURN PROGRAMS

The Document Matching program matches income, deductions, and credits reported on the tax return with the wage and information return data reported by employers, banks, credit unions, partnerships and S corporations on Forms W-2, 1099 and K-1.

The Math Error program identifies mathematical errors and mismatches of taxpayer information that would result in a tax change. A reviewer validates items including social security numbers, the child tax credit, the earned income tax credit, and tax calculations. In 2011, the IRS mailed approximately 6 million math error notices addressing approximately 8 million math errors (a notice may cover more than one math error).

The Automated Substitute Return program uses information returns and historical filing information to look for people who have not filed income tax returns and to create a tax return for them. It then tries to locate the taxpayer to give them a chance to file their return voluntarily.

.05 IRS COMPLIANCE RESEARCH

The IRS uses information from its compliance studies to determine the audit selection formulas. In September 2002, the IRS began a new compliance study titled the National Research Program (NRP). Under the NRP, the IRS reviewed 46,000 individual returns for 2001, completing the study in 2006. The IRS announced a second NRP study to examine approximately 13,000 randomly selected 2006 individual returns. The information obtained from these studies will be used to update compliance estimates and develop more efficient methods for identifying returns for examination.

Prior to the NRP, the previous tax compliance research program, called the Taxpayer Compliance Measurement Program (TCMP) was performed in 1988. Every line item was audited on returns selected for TCMP examinations, making the exams highly intrusive and extremely costly to both the IRS and the taxpayer.

.07 FRIVOLOUS RETURN PROGRAM

Some taxpayers attempt to reduce their federal income tax liability by filing a return that reports no income and no tax liability (a "zero return") even though they have taxable income. There is no authority under U.S. law that permits a taxpayer with taxable income to avoid income tax by filing a zero return. The claim that filing a zero return will allow a taxpayer to avoid income tax liability, or permit a refund of taxes withheld, is frivolous. These returns are processed through the Frivolous Return Program. Under this program, the IRS confirms whether taxpayers who take frivolous positions have filed all of their required tax returns, computes the correct amount of tax and interest due, and determines whether civil or criminal penalties should apply. The IRS also determines whether civil or criminal penalties should apply to return preparers, promoters, and others who assist taxpayers in taking frivolous positions.

.09 OTHER SELECTION METHODS

The Internal Revenue Manual contains additional guidelines for identifying returns for examination including:

Claims for Refund or Credit. Upon receipt of a claim for refund, the IRS screens the original return to determine whether the return should be examined before issuing the refund.

Nonresident Alien Returns. Most Form 1040 NRs are examined by the Compliance Director.

Section 338 Elections. When a Section 338 election is made, the returns of all involved taxpayers are evaluated for possible examination.

Related Returns. An examination of the tax return of a related taxpayer may be required to determine if the tax return under audit is filed correctly. For example, if an individual's return includes income from a partnership, the partnership may also need to be examined.

Multi-Year Examination. An audit may be expanded to include prior or subsequent years if an adjustment to one year's return should also be made on another year's return.

Miscellaneous Triggering Factors. The filing of certain forms with a tax return will likely result in the return being auditing. These forms include Form 8283 (Non-Cash Charitable Contributions), Form 8082 (Notice of Inconsistent Treatment), and Form 8275 (Disclosure Statement for Positions Lacking Substantial Authority).

The examination function is carried out within the four operating divisions: Wage and Investment, Small Business/Self Employed, Large and Mid-Size Businesses, and Tax-Exempt and Government Entities.

.11 CHANCES OF AUDIT

The IRS examined nearly 1.6 million individual income tax returns in FY 2011 representing slightly more than one percent of all returns filed, more than double the number examined in FY 2000. Individual returns with positive income of $1 million or more stand the greatest chance of being audited (12.5%), followed by individual returns with business income of $100,000 to $200,000 (4.3%). Approximately 70 percent of the audits were correspondence audits, with the remaining 30 percent representing office and field audits.

The individuals' chances of being audited by the IRS are greater under the following circumstances:

- large amounts of itemized deductions that exceed IRS targets.
- own or work in a business that receives cash and/or tips in the ordinary course of business.
- business expenses are large in comparison to income.
- claim an office-in-home deduction.
- a prior IRS audit resulted in a tax deficiency.
- complex transactions or investment/business expenses on the return.
- rental expenses on the return.
- a shareholder or partner in an audited corporation or partnership.
- large cash contributions in comparison to reported income.

Examinations of business tax returns (corporations, S corporations, and partnerships) grew to approximately 62,900 in 2011. Large corporations are more likely to be audited. The IRS audited over 63 percent of corporations reporting greater than $5 billion in assets during 2011. Almost 97 percent of corporate audits were office and field audit, with the remaining 3 percent representing correspondence audits.

¶9009 Types of IRS Examinations

There are three main types of audits performed by the Internal Revenue Service: the correspondence audit, the office audit, and the field audit. The type of audit is determined by the audit potential of the return, the nature of the potential error, and the type of taxpayer.

A **correspondence audit** is conducted by either mail or telephone. These audits generally involve only one or two items on a return. The IRS generally sends a letter to the taxpayer questioning a single tax issue, such as charitable contributions, medical expenses or other itemized deductions. The letter will request additional information and ask the taxpayer to submit supporting documentation to the IRS. Supporting documentation may include receipts, cancelled checks, correspondence, etc. The IRS reviews the submitted documents and determines the necessary adjustments to the return, if any. The taxpayer is again notified by letter of any proposed changes and the resulting tax and interest.

An **office audit** is conducted in a local IRS office. These audits are more complex, usually involving issues that will require some analysis or judgment on the part of the examiner. The returns selected for office audit are generally individual returns that may or may not have a small amount of business income. The returns usually involve common items such as dependency exemptions, travel and entertainment expenses, casualty losses, income from rents and royalties, and income from partnerships and trusts. Once a return is selected for an office audit, the taxpayer will receive a letter in the mail (called an appointment letter) informing him/her of the audit and requesting the taxpayer to bring in documentation supporting the items on the tax return that are being questioned.

The taxpayer's goal should be to complete the audit in one meeting with the IRS. This is best accomplished by bringing to the appointment all supporting documents that have been requested. The taxpayer will be presented with any proposed changes at the end of the audit.

A **field audit** is used mostly for business returns and larger, more complex individual returns and is conducted at the taxpayer's place of business or home. The revenue agents that perform field audits are the most experienced auditors. These audits usually involve tax issues that require a review of the taxpayer's books and records. The taxpayer may request that the audit be moved to the office of the taxpayer's representative (attorney or accountant). The agent will review the entire financial operations of the taxpayer, including the taxpayer's history, the system of internal controls, the location of business assets, and accounting methods. The audit will also include an examination of relevant business agreements or documents, a reconciliation of book income to taxable income, the testing of gross receipts, and verification of expense deductions. The agent will review officers' compensation and related party transactions. Like all other audits, the IRS will present the taxpayer with any proposed changes to the tax return at the end of the audit.

¶9011 Working with an Auditor

Taxpayers receiving an audit notice from the IRS should consider the following suggestions:

- ***Don't ignore the notice.*** Taxpayers usually have thirty (30) days to respond to the audit notice. If they don't respond the IRS has the right to automatically adjust their tax liability.
- ***Read the notice carefully.*** The notice will tell the taxpayer which year and which items in that return are being questioned as well as what the IRS would like the taxpayer to bring to the audit. Often just one or two items are being questioned and it is a simple matter to collect the necessary records to substantiate those items.
- ***Consider asking a representative to attend the audit.*** If the taxpayer is uncomfortable dealing with the audit, seek a professional to represent him/her at the audit.
- ***Bring only what is requested to the audit.*** Bring only the documents that deal with the scope of the audit. If the taxpayer takes additional documents, he/she runs the risk of having the audit expanded to other areas. As a rule, auditors don't go beyond what was requested.
- ***Be organized.*** The taxpayer should review the return being audited and organize the records. If records are missing, locate them prior to the audit. Be thoroughly prepared—if the records clearly substantiate the items claimed on the return, the agent won't waste time conducting a more in-depth audit.
- ***Be polite.*** Be professional and courteous (and expect the same treatment in return). The taxpayer should ask to speak to the auditor's supervisor if the agent is treating him/her unfairly.
- ***Tell the truth.*** Deliberately lying during an audit is a criminal offence. If the taxpayer doesn't know the answer to a question, just say you don't know.
- ***Only bring copies of documents to the IRS.*** Occasionally the IRS misplaces paperwork. Bring photocopies to an audit and leave the originals at home.
- ***Stay on point.*** The taxpayer should not volunteer any information that hasn't been requested or the auditor may turn his/her attention to other aspects of the tax return.
- ***Know your rights as a taxpayer.*** The taxpayer should read IRS Publication 1 (Taxpayers' Bill of Rights) before the audit. In general, it may be preferable to agree to the assessment at the conclusion of the audit but an appeals process (discussed later in the chapter) is available when the taxpayer disagrees with the audit report.

¶9013   Possible Audit Outcomes

There are four possible outcomes to an audit:

1. *No change.* The auditor proposes no change in the taxpayer's tax liability. The taxpayer will be officially notified that the return is accepted as filed.
2. *Agreed.* The auditor proposes adjustments to the taxpayer's return and the taxpayer agrees to the adjustments. The taxpayer will sign Form 870, Waiver of Restrictions on Assessment and Collection of Deficiency in Tax. By signing Form 870, the taxpayer waives the right to a notice of deficiency, allowing the IRS to immediately assess the tax.
3. *Unagreed.* The auditor proposes adjustments to the taxpayer's return and the taxpayer does not agree to the adjustments. The IRS will issue a 30-day letter including a copy of the audit report and advise the taxpayer of his/her rights to appeal.
4. *Partially Agreed.* The auditor proposes adjustments to the taxpayer's return and the taxpayer agrees to some of the adjustments, but not to others. The IRS will issue a 30-day letter including a copy of the audit report and advise the taxpayer of his/her rights to an appeal.

.01   30-DAY LETTER

In general, a **30-Day Letter** is issued in unagreed and partially agreed cases. The 30-Day Letter requests the taxpayer to either sign and return Form 870, a waiver of restrictions on assessment, if the taxpayer agrees with the findings, or exercise his/her appeal rights. If the taxpayer fails to respond within 30 days, the case is processed based on the proposed adjustments and a 90-Day Letter is issued.

A 30-Day Letter allows the taxpayer 30 days to request a meeting with an appeals officer. If requested by the taxpayer, the IRS will generally grant an extension of time to file the appeal request. The method for requesting an appeal depends upon the amount and the type of case. When the total proposed tax and penalties exceeds $25,000 for any taxable period, the taxpayer must submit a formal written protest. A formal written protest must also be filed in all partnership and S corporation cases.

While there is no official IRS form for a formal written protest, the IRS will reject a protest if it fails to include the following:

- A statement that the taxpayer wants to appeal the examiner's findings to the Appeals office;
- The taxpayer's name and address and daytime telephone number;
- A copy of the letter showing the proposed changes and findings being protested or the date and symbols from the letter;
- The tax periods or years involved;
- An itemized schedule of the adjustments with which the taxpayer does not agree;
- A statement of facts supporting the taxpayer's position on any contested factual issue;
- A statement outlining the law or other authority, if any, upon which the taxpayer is relying;
- A declaration under penalties of perjury attesting the statement of facts is true and accurate. This may be done by adding the following signed declaration to the protest document:

> *"Under penalties of perjury, I declare that I have examined the statement of facts stated in this protest, including any accompanying documents and, to the best of my knowledge and belief, they are true, correct, and complete."*

When the total tax and penalties amount is $25,000 or less, the taxpayer may request an appeal using the small case procedures. This requires the taxpayer to submit a letter setting forth the changes that the taxpayer does not agree with and the reasons for disagreement.

.03   APPEALS PROCESS

Dispute resolution is handled by the Appeals Division in the IRS. Its mission is "to resolve tax controversies, without litigation, on a basis which is fair and impartial to both the

Government and the taxpayer and in a manner that will enhance voluntary compliance and public confidence in the integrity and efficiency" of the IRS. The Appeals Division tries to accomplish this by considering taxpayer appeals, holding conferences, and negotiating settlements. This is usually the last administrative opportunity for both the taxpayer and the IRS to resolve a dispute without litigation.

The Appeals Officer assigned to a case has the responsibility of applying the tax laws reasonably and impartially in an effort to achieve settlement with the taxpayer. The Appeals Officer is authorized to enter into settlement with a taxpayer based on the perceived hazards of litigation. Almost 70 percent of cases taken to Appeals are resolved there.

If after consideration of the case by Appeals, a satisfactory settlement cannot be reached and there is a tax deficiency, Appeals will prepare and issue a statutory notice of deficiency (i.e., a 90-Day Letter).

.05 90-DAY LETTER

The **90-Day Letter** is the statutory notice of deficiency. The letter offers the taxpayer the option of filing a protest in Tax Court within the 90 days before making any payment or signing the waiver form. Signing and returning the waiver permits the IRS to assess the deficiency. If the taxpayer does not sign and return the waiver or file a petition with the Tax Court, then the IRS will assess and bill the taxpayer for the deficiency after 90 days from the date of the letter (150 days if the letter is addressed to a taxpayer outside the United States).

.07 STATUTORY AGREEMENTS

Two types of agreements may be used to resolve tax disputes: closing agreements and offers in compromise.

Closing Agreements

Code Sec. 7121 authorizes the IRS to enter into binding agreements with taxpayers, referred to as **closing agreements**. Closing agreements finally and conclusively settle a tax issue between the IRS and a taxpayer unless there is a showing of fraud or malfeasance, or misrepresentation of a material fact.

The purpose of closing agreements is to (1) enable the taxpayer and the government to settle finally and completely all controversies with respect to the tax liability for any previous taxable period, (2) to protect the taxpayer against the reopening of a matter at a later date, and (3) to prevent the filing of additional claims for refund or the institution of suit for the same purpose by the taxpayer.

The IRS has the discretion to decide whether to sign a closing agreement and is generally reluctant to enter into closing agreements. Since a closing agreement binds the IRS, the IRS often subjects the agreement to more rigorous processing and review than a private letter ruling. As a matter of policy, the IRS will enter a closing agreement only if:

- There appears to be an advantage in having the case "permanently and conclusively closed"; or
- "Good and sufficient reasons" are shown by the taxpayer for entering into a closing agreement and it is determined that the United States will suffer no disadvantages by entering into the agreement.

Offers in Compromise

Code Sec. 7122 allows the IRS to compromise civil and criminal tax liabilities before the case is referred to the Department of Justice. An **offer in compromise** is a procedure for settling unpaid tax accounts for less than the full amount of the assessed balance due. The offer in compromise is made by the taxpayer and may cover all taxes, interest and penalties owed. Once an offer in compromise is accepted by the IRS, a contract exists whereby the taxpayer must comply with all the terms of the offer in compromise in exchange for the IRS's agreement to reduce the tax liability owed.

The IRS may accept an offer in compromise for one of the following reasons:
- *Doubt as to liability.* Doubt exists that the assessed tax is correct.
- *Doubt as to collectability.* Doubt exists that the taxpayer could ever pay the full amount of tax owed.
- *Effective Tax Administration.* There is no doubt the tax is correct and could be collected but an exceptional circumstance exists that allows the IRS to consider the taxpayer's offer. To be eligible for a compromise on this basis, the taxpayer must demonstrate that collection of the tax would create an economic hardship or would be unfair and inequitable.

Effective July 16, 2006, the operation of the offer in compromise program and its role in the IRS collection process was changed. Under the new law:
- Taxpayers submitting lump-sum offers must make a 20-percent nonrefundable, up-front payment to the IRS;
- Taxpayers submitting a periodic-payment offer must make a nonrefundable, up-front payment, plus any other proposed payments that may be due, while the IRS is evaluating the offer; and
- An offer in compromise application is deemed accepted if the IRS fails to act upon it within two years.

Requests are submitted using Form 656, Offer in Compromise and must include certain taxpayer financial information. When submitting Form 656, taxpayers must send an application fee of $150 unless they qualify for the low-income exemption[2] or are filing a doubt-as-to-liability offer.[3]

¶9015   Interest

Code Sec. 6601 imposes interest on underpayments of tax. An underpayment arises when the taxpayer fails to pay any tax on or before the last date prescribed for payment. It makes no difference whether the failure to pay is due to the payment of less than the amount of the tax due on a return, an understatement of the liability on the return, or a failure to file a return.

Interest, compounded daily, is charged on any unpaid tax from the due date of the tax return until the date of tax payment. Interest accrues from the original due date of the tax return, even if the taxpayer properly filed for an extension of time to file the return. Interest is also charged on the penalties imposed for failure to file a return as well as other penalties imposed for negligence, fraud, etc.

Example 9-1. Zeta Corporation requested an extension of time to file from March 15, 2013, until September 15, 2013. Zeta Corporation filed its return on July 23, 2013. The return showed a net tax due of $22,000. Zeta paid the tax on July 23. Zeta will owe interest on the $22,000 from March 15 to July 23, 2013.

For taxpayers other than corporations, the overpayment and underpayment rate is the federal short-term rate plus three percent. **Table 1** includes the interest rates from 2005 through 2012. In the case of a corporation, the underpayment rate is the federal short-term rate plus three percent and the overpayment rate is the federal short-term rate plus two

---

2 If a taxpayer certifies that his/her total monthly household income is at or below levels based on the IRS Low Income Guidelines, then the fee will be waived. For example, a taxpayer residing in one of the 48 contiguous states with a family unit size of four will be exempt from the fee if the total household income is less than $4,167. The low income guidelines are published in the IRS Offer in Compromise booklet, Form 656.

3 "Doubt-as-to-liability" means that a legitimate doubt exists that the taxpayer owes part or all of the assessed tax liability.

percent. The rate for large corporate underpayments is the federal short-term rate plus five percent. The rate is determined quarterly.

When refunds are paid within 45 days after the return was filed, the IRS pays the refunds without interest.

Interest terminates on the date the tax is paid (the date the IRS receives the payment). If, however, the IRS issues a notice and demand for the underpayment and the taxpayer makes payment within 21 calendar days (10 business days if the amount for which such notice and demand is made equals or exceeds $100,000) after the date of the notice, interest terminates on the date of the notice. Generally the notice and demand is made after the end of the 90-day period following the issuance of the 90-day letter.

Example 9-2. Shirley's 2010 tax return was audited by the IRS. Shirley originally filed her return on March 21, 2011. At the completion of the audit, she agreed to pay a $1,000 tax deficiency. The IRS issued a notice and demand for payment on November 20, 2013. The interest amount included on the notice was calculated on the $1,000 tax deficiency from April 15, 2011, until November 20, 2013. As long as Shirley pays the tax and interest assessed by December 11 (21 days after the date of the IRS notice), she will not pay interest for the period November 21 through December 11.

Table 1 Tax Deficiency Interest Rates from 2005 to 2010 (Federal Short-Term Rate Plus 3%)		
From	To	Interest Rate
10/01/11	03/31/13	3%
04/01/11	09/30/11	4%
01/01/11	03/31/11	3%
04/01/09	12/31/10	4%
1/1/09	3/31/09	5%
10/1/08	12/31/08	6%
7/1/08	9/30/08	5%
4/1/08	6/30/08	6%
1/1/08	3/31/08	7%
7/1/06	12/31/07	8%
10/1/05	6/30/06	7%

¶9017 Statute of Limitations

Generally, all taxes must be assessed within three years after the date the return was filed.[4] If a return is filed prior to the due date, the return is considered filed on the due date.

Example 9-3. Larry Landes files his Form 1040 on February 7, 2013. The three-year statute of limitations expires on April 15, 2016.

In certain cases the assessment period is extended to six years and in other situations the assessment period remains open indefinitely. The assessment period is extended to six years for tax returns that omit from gross income more than 25 percent of the reported gross income. For individuals, gross income includes all sources of taxable income such

[4] Code Sec. 6501.

as salaries, dividends, and interest. In applying this test, capital gains and losses aren't netted; only capital gains are taken into account. In the case of a trade or business, gross income is the total of amounts received or accrued from the sale of goods or services before reduction by cost of goods sold or cost of services. Omitted amounts do not include amounts that have been adequately disclosed in the return.

Example 9-4. Richard Thatcher reported a $120,000 salary, $40,000 in dividends, $10,000 in interest and a net capital gain of $20,000 ($70,000 in gains less $50,000 in losses) on his 2013 tax return. He failed to report the $50,000 of income he won on a game show. The assessment period remains at three years because Richard's omitted income is less than 25 percent of his gross income (25% × $240,000 = $60,000). His gross income of $240,000 includes his $120,000 salary, $40,000 in dividends, $10,000 in interest and capital gains of $70,000.

Example 9-5. Zeta Corporation's 2008 tax return as filed shows the following:

Gross sales	$1,000,000
Cost of goods sold	600,000
Gross profit	400,000
Expenses	100,000
Taxable income	$ 300,000

Zeta omitted $300,000 of cash sales from the return. The limitation on Zeta's 2008 return would be extended to six years because the omission exceeds 25 percent of gross income ($300,000 > 25% of $1,000,000).

Under Code Sec. 6501, the assessment period is open indefinitely where a taxpayer:
- fails to file a required return,
- files a false or fraudulent return with the intent to evade tax, or
- willfully attempts in any manner to defeat and evade taxes.

A 90-day letter suspends the assessment period. The assessment period stops running on the date the IRS mails the 90-day letter, and resumes 60 days after: (1) the 90-day period ends (150 days if the letter is addressed to a person outside the United States) if no petition is filed, or (2) the Tax Court's decision becomes final.

¶9019 Penalties

The Internal Revenue Code contains a number of penalties that may be applied to both taxpayers and tax professionals for certain actions. In some cases the penalties applicable to a taxpayer will not apply if he or she has **"substantial authority"** for the position taken on the tax return. In addition, tax return preparers may be subject to penalties for taking an "unreasonable position" on a return. The IRS uses a "more likely than not" standard for determining unreasonable positions. **Figure 2** reviews the different levels of certainty regarding the likelihood that a taxpayer's position would be sustained if challenged by the IRS.

Figure 2

Reasonable Basis for a Position: Standards of Certainty

The professional literature and guidance from the IRS (primarily through Circular 230) provide for different levels of certainty regarding the likelihood that a taxpayer's position on a particular item would be sustained if challenged by the IRS. Certain levels are required to avoid the imposition of a penalty, and other levels are required for taking a position on a return, with a higher level generally required for not disclosing that position on the return.

These levels may be summarized as follows, with the likelihood of success (expressed as a percentage) increasing as one moves from the left to the right:

Frivolous Position	Reasonable Basis	Realistic Possibility	Substantial Authority	More Likely Than Not
0%_____	?%_____	33.3%_____	?%_____	50%_____

Frivolous. A "patently improper" position than is not sustainable, even if disclosed on the return. Such a position should never be taken on a return. (Earlier publications of the American Bar Association suggest that this level of certainty should be five percent or less.)

Reasonable Basis. If this standard is met, a taxpayer will not be subject to an understatement penalty if the position is adequately disclosed on the return. (There is no guidance as to what percentage possibility for success that this basis should cover.)

Realistic Possibility. If this standard is met, a tax preparer may take a particular position on a return and sign the return. If the standard is not met but the taxpayer's position is "not frivolous," the preparer may still sign the return if the position is disclosed adequately and a Form 8275 is filed. (The regulations, Circular 230, and the Statements on Responsibilities in Tax Practice establish the minimum "odds" for this position as being one out of three or greater.)

Substantial Authority. The Code Sec. 6662 accuracy penalty related to a substantial understatement will not apply if this level of certainty is reached, and the position need not be disclosed on the return. If only a "reasonable basis" standard is met, the position must be disclosed on the return. (There is no guidance as to what percentage possibility for success that this basis should cover, other than it is greater than a "realistic possibility" and less than "more likely than not.")

More Likely than Not. Tax shelters, reportable transactions, and listed transactions, as defined in the Code, must meet this standard before taking a position on a return. Regulations define this probability as being greater than 50 percent.

¶9021   Civil Penalties Applicable to Taxpayers

In order to encourage taxpayers to timely file and pay their taxes, the Code includes a number of taxpayer penalties. **Table 2** below summarizes the major penalties that may apply to taxpayers.

Table 2	
Selected Penalty Provisions Applicable to Taxpayers	
Action of Taxpayer	**Penalty**
a. Failure to file a return by the due date (including legal extensions) [§6651(a)(1)]	5 percent of tax liability for each month the return is late (25 percent maximum); 15 percent per month with 75 percent maximum if fraud is involved
b. Failure to pay a tax liability by the due date for payment [§6651(a)(2)]	.5 percent per month for each month (or portion) that the payment is late. This penalty can offset any failure to file penalty.
c. Failure by individual to pay estimated income tax [§6654]	The underpayment rate times the underpayment amount for the period of the underpayment.
d. Failure by corporation to pay estimated income tax [§6655]	The underpayment rate times the underpayment amount for the period of the underpayment
e. Substantial understatement of tax liability (defined as exceeding the greater of $5,000 [$10,000 corp.] or 10% of the correct liability), certain valuations, or listed and reportable transactions [§6662]	20 percent of the understatement amount, unless "substantial authority" exists for the position taken on the tax return
f. Filing a "frivolous return" (one that does not have enough information to determine the tax liability or one that on its face is clearly incorrect) [§6702]	$500 (includes any return filed for the purpose of delaying or interfering with the administration of tax laws)
g. Negligence or intentional disregard of rules or regulations related to the income tax [§6662(a)]	20 percent of the underpayment of the portion of tax liability attributable to negligence
h. Underpayment due to fraud [§6663(a)]	75 percent of the underpayment due to fraud (criminal penalties of fines up to $100,000 and imprisonment of up to one year may be assessed in lieu of the civil penalty)

.01 FAILURE TO FILE AND FAILURE TO PAY PENALTIES

The failure to file and failure to pay penalties were enacted to ensure the timely filing of tax returns and the prompt payment of the tax liability. Code Sec. 6651 imposes a *failure to file penalty* if a return is not filed on or before its due date, unless such failure is due to reasonable cause and not willful neglect. The penalty applies to all income tax returns of an individual, a corporation, and a trust or estate. The failure to file penalty is 5 percent per month (or fraction thereof) of the net tax due. The maximum penalty for failure to file is 25 percent. If a taxpayer filed an extension, the extended due date is used to determine the failure to file penalty. When the failure to file is considered fraudulent, the penalty rate increases to 15 percent per month, up to a maximum penalty of 75 percent.

In some cases, a minimum amount is assessed. If the taxpayer does not file a return within 60 days of the due date, including extensions, the penalty will not be less than the smaller of (1) $100 or (2) 100 percent of the tax due on the return. Taxpayers who do not owe tax with the filing of their return are not subject to the failure-to-file penalty.

Example 9-6. Paul Payton did not file his return on April 15 but he did request an extension of time to file until October 15. Paul enjoyed an extended vacation in the fall and didn't bother to file his return until December 20. Paul owed $300 when he filed his return and paid that amount on December 20. Paul's failure to file penalty would be $45 under the normal calculation (5% × 3 months × $300). However, because the return is more than 60 days late, the minimum penalty of $100 is assessed (the smaller of $100 or the $300 tax due on the return).

If the failure to file is due to reasonable cause, the penalty is not imposed. The reasonable cause exception is explained in Reg. §301.6651-1(c), which provides:

"If the taxpayer exercised ordinary business care and prudence and was nevertheless unable to file the return within the prescribed time, then the delay is due to a reasonable cause."

The following explanations may justify reasonable cause: the return was mailed on time, but to the wrong IRS office; death or serious illness of the taxpayer or close family member; fire, casualty or natural disaster that destroyed tax records or prevented compliance in some way; or reliance on a competent tax advisor.

The *failure to pay penalty* is assessed on a taxpayer who fails to pay the tax shown on a return on or before the date prescribed for payment. The penalty is 0.5 percent per month (or fraction thereof) that the tax remains unpaid, up to a maximum penalty of 25 percent. The penalty is based on the net tax due at the beginning of the month. Similar to the failure to file penalty, the IRS may waive the failure to pay penalty if the taxpayer shows reasonable cause.

An extension of time to file a return does not extend the payment date. Taxpayers who request an extension without paying 100 percent of their tax liability may be assessed the failure to pay penalty. The Regulations provide an exemption from the failure to pay penalty if the additional tax due when the return is filed does not exceed 10 percent of the tax owed for the year.

Example 9-7. Joe Jeffries files an extension for his individual tax return. When he files his return on August 12, his total tax is $10,000. Joe paid in $4,500 through withholdings, made $3,500 of estimated tax payments and paid in $500 with the extension request. Joe's tax return shows a balance due of $500, which he pays on August 12. Joe is exempt from the failure to pay penalty since his balance due ($500) does not exceed 10 percent of his total tax (10% × $10,000 = $1,000).

If Joe's tax liability had been $11,000, he would have owed $1,500 when he filed the return and a failure-to-pay penalty of $30 (0.5% × 4 months × $1,500).

Even if a taxpayer cannot pay the tax due, he/she should timely file the return in order to avoid the failure-to-file penalty. The taxpayer will still be liable for the failure to pay penalty, but it is a much smaller penalty than the failure-to-file penalty (5 percent per month compared to 0.5 percent per month).

In many instances, a taxpayer will be subject to both the failure-to-file and the failure-to pay penalties. In a month when the taxpayer is subject to both penalties, the five percent per month failure to file penalty is reduced by the failure to pay penalty, resulting in the two penalties combined totaling five percent.

Example 9-8. Debbie Dillon decided not to file her return on April 15 because she couldn't pay the $5,000 tax she owed. She did not request an extension, did not have reasonable cause for filing late, but did not commit fraud. Debbie filed her return on June 7, paying the full amount due at that time. Because Debbie did not request an extension and paid the $5,000 tax due when she filed her return on June 7, she will be assessed both the failure to file penalty and the failure to pay penalty as follows:

Failure to pay	0.5% × 2 months × $5,000		$ 50
Failure to file	5% × 2 months × $5,000	$500	
Less: Failure to pay penalty for 2 months		(50)	450
Total penalties			$500

Remember that (1) the penalty is assessed for each month or portion thereof and (2) the failure to pay penalty reduces the failure to file penalty in months when both penalties are assessed.

Example 9-9. Assume instead that Debbie filed the return on June 7 but could not pay the tax until September 21. The penalties are as follows:

Failure to pay	0.5% × 6 months × $5,000		$150
Failure to file	5% × 2 months × $5,000	$500	
Less: Failure to pay penalty for 2 months		(50)	450
Total penalties			$600

.03 UNDERPAYMENT OF ESTIMATED TAX

Both individuals and corporations are subject to a penalty for the underpayment of estimated taxes. Where payments of tax, either through withholding or by making estimated tax payments during the year, don't equal the amount required, a penalty is imposed unless the taxpayer meets one of the exceptions. The penalty for underpayment of an estimated tax installment equals the amount of underpayment for the period of underpayment times the applicable rate. The penalty is calculated separately for each installment due date.

Individual Underpayment Penalty

Individuals may owe the penalty if they do not pay in at least the smaller of:
a. 90 percent of the tax shown on the current year return, or
b. 100 percent of the tax shown on the prior year return (110 percent if the AGI on the prior year return exceeded $150,000 or $75,000 for married filing separately).

The tax amount includes the regular tax, plus the alternative minimum tax, less any tax credits, plus self-employment tax, and any other additional taxes. The amount subject to the penalty is the total tax that should have been paid during the quarter (based on a. and b. above) less the sum of the estimated tax actually paid during the quarter plus the withholdings attributable to the quarter. Unless the taxpayer proves otherwise, taxes withheld are deemed to be withheld equally throughout the year. The underpayment penalty ends on the date the underpayment is actually paid or the due date for the return (April 15 for individuals).

Example 9-10. Jerry Jenkins incurs a regular tax liability of $22,000 and self-employment tax of $4,000 in the current year. His total tax liability last year for both income and self-employment taxes was $16,000. His AGI last year did not exceed $150,000. Jerry had $8,000 of taxes withheld from his current year salary. Jerry's should make estimated tax payments for the current year as calculated below:

Lesser of: 90% of current year's tax (90% × $26,000 = $23,400) or		
100% of prior year's $20,000 liability	$ 20,000
Minus: Tax withheld from salary	6,000
Estimated tax payments required to avoid penalty	$ 14,000
Quarterly payment amount	$ 3,500

Jerry made estimated payments of $2,500 on April 15, June 15, September 15, and January 15. Assume an underpayment rate of eight percent for the entire period. Jerry files his return on April 10 of next year and pays the $10,000 balance due ($26,000 – $6,000 withholding – $10,000 estimated taxes). Jerry's underpayment penalty is calculated as follows:

	Quarter			
	1st	2nd	3rd	4th
Req. Tax Pay ($20,000/4)	$5,000	$5,000	$5,000	$5,000
Less: Withholding Estimated payment	(1,500) (2,500)	(1,500) (2,500)	(1,500) (2,500)	(1,500) (2,500)
Underpayment	$1,000	$1,000	$1,000	$1,000
# of days until April 10*	359	298	206	84
Penalty at 8%	$79	$65	$45	$18

* The underpayment penalty ends on the date the underpayment is actually paid or the due date for the return (April 15 for individuals).

The total penalty equals $207 ($79 + $65 + $45 + $18).

If an individual's income varies during the year, he or she may be able to reduce the amount of one or more required estimated payments by using the annualized income method. For more information on this method, see the instructions to Form 2210, Underpayment of Estimated Tax by Individuals, Estates and Trusts.

Exceptions to the Penalty

The penalty for the underpayment of estimated tax will not be imposed if:

a. the total tax shown on the return for the current year, reduced by withholdings, is less than $1,000, or

b. the taxpayer had no tax liability for the preceding year.

Corporate Underpayment Penalty

A corporation may be subject to the underpayment penalty unless the amount paid in is at least the smaller of:

a. 100 percent of the tax shown on the current year return, or

b. 100 percent of the tax shown on the prior year return (however, a large corporation can only base its first quarter estimated payment on the prior year's tax).

A corporation may not use the prior year return method if the prior year was less than a 12-month period, or if the corporate return for the prior year did not show a liability for tax. Therefore, if a corporation's tax return shows $0 tax liability for the prior tax year, the corporation can not use the prior year method.

Example 9-11. Alpha Corporation incurred a net operating loss in 2012 and filed a tax return showing a $0 tax liability. In 2013, Alpha's tax return showed a $2,000 tax liability. Since Alpha's 2012 tax return did not show a tax liability, Alpha cannot use the prior year tax method for determining its estimated tax payments for 2013.

Large corporations may only use the prior year method for determining the first quarter estimated tax payment. The remaining estimated payments must be determined based on current year tax. A large corporation is defined as a corporation that had taxable income of $1,000,000 or more during any of the three tax years immediately preceding the current tax year. If a large corporation pays a reduced amount in its first estimated payment as a result of the prior year method, the reduction must be recaptured by increasing the amount of the second estimated payment by the amount of the reduction.

Example 9-12. Beta Corporation reported $2,000,000 of taxable income in 2012, resulting in a $680,000 tax liability. Beta's 2013 taxable income is $2,500,000 with a resulting tax liability of $850,000. Beta can use the $680,000 tax liability from 2012 to determine its first quarter 2013 estimated payment, resulting in a first quarter payment of $170,000 ($680,000/4). Beta's second quarter estimate must be based on its 2013 income, resulting in a quarterly payment of $212,500 ($850,000/4). In addition to paying the second quarter amount, Beta must also recapture the reduction in the first quarter payment of $42,500 ($212,500 under the current year method − $170,000 paid using prior year method). Thus, Beta's total second quarter payment is $255,000. Beta's third and fourth quarter payments will be based on the current year method, resulting in third and fourth quarter payments of $212,500 each.

A corporation may also use an adjusted seasonal installment method or an annualized income method for determining its estimated payments. These methods are described in the instructions to Form 2220, Underpayment of Estimated Tax by Corporations.

.05   ACCURACY RELATED PENALTIES

A 20-percent accuracy-related penalty applies to underpayments attributable to negligence or disregard of rules or regulations, substantial understatement of income tax, and substantial valuation overstatement. Because an accuracy-related penalty attaches when there has been an underpayment of the tax that is *required* to be shown on the return, the penalty can apply even if the taxpayer's return as originally filed shows no tax liability, but, as a result of IRS audit or court proceedings, a tax liability is later determined.

Negligence Penalty

The 20-percent accuracy-related penalty will apply when the IRS determines that the taxpayer has an underpayment of tax as a result of negligence or disregard of rules or regulations. The penalty applies only to that portion of the underpayment resulting from negligence. Interest is also charged on the negligence penalty. The negligence penalty will not be assessed for any portion of an underpayment if the taxpayer had reasonable cause for the position and acted in good faith.

"Negligence" includes any failure to make a reasonable attempt to comply with the provisions of the Code or to exercise ordinary and reasonable care in the preparation of a tax return. Reg. §1.6662-3 provides that negligence includes any failure to keep adequate books and records or to substantiate items properly. The negligence penalty may be applied where a taxpayer fails to make a reasonable attempt to ascertain the correctness of a deduction, credit or exclusion which would seem to be "too good to be true" under the circumstances. "Disregard" includes any careless, reckless, or intentional disregard of the Code, temporary or final regulations, and revenue rulings or IRS notices published in the Internal Revenue Bulletin.

Example 9-13. Upon completion of the audit of Sally Sanders's tax return, the IRS assesses a $5,000 deficiency, of which $3,000 is attributable to negligence. Sally agrees to the additional tax of $5,000. The negligence penalty equals $600 (20% × $3,000).

Substantial Understatement Penalty

The 20-percent accuracy related penalty is also applied to an underpayment of tax caused by a "substantial understatement" of the tax liability. However, to the extent the understatement is due to the treatment of an item that is based on substantial authority or that was adequately disclosed, the penalty is not imposed. The definition of substantial authority is included in the Circular 230 discussion later in the chapter.

An understatement of tax is "substantial" if the understatement exceeds the greater of:
a. 10 percent of the tax required to be shown on the return for that year, or
b. $5,000 ($10,000 for corporations).

Example 9-14. Harry Hoffman's return was audited by the IRS and he agreed to a $7,500 deficiency, increasing his tax liability from $32,500 to $40,000. Harry did not make any disclosure regarding the items resulting in the deficiency and he did not have substantial authority for the tax treatment of those items. Therefore, Harry's understatement is $7,500. The understatement is substantial because it exceeds both 10 percent of his tax ($10\% \times \$40,000 = \$4,000$) and the $5,000 minimum. His substantial understatement penalty is $1,500 ($20\% \times \$7,500$).

In addition, for corporate taxpayers an understatement of tax will be considered substantial if the amount exceeds $10 million. Congress believes that an understatement of more than $10 million is substantial in and of itself, regardless of the proportion it represents of the taxpayer's total tax liability.

Substantial Valuation Overstatement

A valuation overstatement penalty applies when an asset value has been overstated on a return. A substantial valuation misstatement exists if the value or adjusted basis of any property claimed on a return is 150 percent or more of the correct value or adjusted basis. The penalty does not apply unless the portion of the underpayment attributable to the valuation misstatement exceeds $5,000 ($10,000 for corporations). This penalty is most often assessed for the overstatement of noncash charitable contributions.

Example 9-15. Wanda, a single taxpayer in the 33-percent marginal tax rate, claimed a charitable contribution deduction of $100,000 for a painting. In an audit by the IRS, the painting was valued at $60,000. The substantial valuation misstatement penalty of 20 percent will apply since the value of the painting was overstated by > 150% ($100,000/$60,000 = 167%). The penalty amount equals $2,640 ($40,000 overvaluation $\times$ 33% marginal rate $\times$ 20% penalty).

Example 9-16. Martha, a single taxpayer in the 28-percent marginal tax rate, claimed a charitable contribution deduction of $25,000 for a painting. In an audit by the IRS, the painting was valued at $14,000. The value of the painting was overstated by 179% ($25,000/$14,000). However, the 20-percent penalty will not be assessed because the underpayment attributable to the overstatement is less than $5,000 ($11,000 $\times$ 28% = $3,080).

The 20-percent accuracy related penalty for a substantial valuation misstatement increases to a 40-percent penalty for the portion of an underpayment attributable to *gross* valuation misstatements. A gross valuation misstatement exists when the value or adjusted basis claimed is 200 percent or more of the correct value or adjusted basis. Where a value or adjusted basis is claimed on a return for any property that has a correct value or adjusted basis of zero, the claimed value or adjusted basis is considered to be 200 percent or more of the correct amount.

Example 9-17. Harold, a single taxpayer in the 33-percent marginal tax rate, claimed a charitable contribution deduction of $200,000 for a painting. In an audit by the IRS, the painting was valued at $50,000. The gross overvaluation penalty of 40 percent will apply since the value of the painting was overstated by > 200% ($200,000/$50,000 = 400%). The penalty amount equals $20,000 ($150,000 overvaluation $\times$ 33% marginal rate $\times$ 40% penalty).

¶9023 Criminal Penalties Applicable to Taxpayers

Compliance with the tax laws relies heavily on the self-assessment of tax. When individuals and corporations make deliberate decisions to not comply with the law, they face the possibility of criminal investigation which could result in prosecution and possible jail time.

The primary criminal statutes applicable to taxpayers are summarized in **Table 3**.

Table 3 Criminal Penalty Statutes Applicable to Taxpayers	
Section	**Provisions**
Code Sec. 7201—Attempt to evade or defeat tax	Any person who willfully attempts to evade or defeat any tax—a felony punishable by a fine of up to $100,000 (for individuals) and/or imprisonment not to exceed five years.
Code Sec. 7202—Willful failure to collect or pay over tax	Any person required to collect, account for, and pay over any tax who willfully fails to collect and pay over such tax—a felony punishable by a fine of up to $250,000 and/or imprisonment not to exceed five years.
Code Sec. 7203—Willful failure to file return, supply information, or pay tax	Any person required to pay any estimated tax or tax, or required to make a return, keep any records, or supply any information, who willfully fails to pay such tax, make such return, keep such records, or supply such information—a misdemeanor punishable by a fine of up to $100,000 and/or imprisonment not to exceed one year.
Code Sec. 7206 (1)—Fraud and false statements	Any person who willfully makes and subscribes any return, statement, or other document under penalties of perjury, which he does not believe to be true and correct—a felony punishable by a fine of up to $250,000 and/or imprisonment not to exceed three years.
Code Sec. 7207—Fraudulent returns, statements, or other documents	Any person who willfully files a false or fraudulent document—a misdemeanor punishable by a fine of up to $100,000 and/or imprisonment not to exceed one year

Taxpayers can be convicted on more than one criminal statute, increasing the potential fine and length of prison time. Criminal and civil statutes are not mutually exclusive. Therefore, a taxpayer can be acquitted under the criminal statutes and still be liable for civil penalties.

OBSERVATION

Celebrities Convicted Under Criminal Tax Statutes

Richard Hatch, the original *Survivor* winner, was found guilty by a jury in January 2006 on two counts of tax evasion and one count of filing a false corporate tax return. Hatch failed to report the $1 million Survivor prize money, income from celebrity appearances and co-hosting a radio show and rental income on his 2000 tax return. He was sentenced to 51 months in jail. Hatch's conviction was upheld on appeal in February 2008.

In February 2008 actor Wesley Snipes was found guilty on three misdemeanor charges for failing to file income tax returns. He was acquitted on felony charges of conspiracy to defraud the IRS and presenting a fraudulent claim for payment to the IRS. Snipes began serving a three year sentence in December 2010.

Information about criminal tax cases can be found on the U.S. Department of Justice, Tax Division's website at *http://www.usdoj.gov/tax/*.

¶9025   Penalties Applicable to Tax Return Preparers

In response to growing abusive tax return practices, Congress began to regulate the actions of tax return preparers. Persons who prepare tax returns or refund claims for compensation may be subject to penalties for not complying with the practice regulation rules, for engaging in improper practices, or for criminal misconduct. Since 2007 there has been a flurry of legislative activity to regulate paid return preparers to better combat non-compliance.

.01   DEFINITION OF TAX RETURN PREPARER

A **tax return preparer** is defined as any person who prepares for compensation or employs or engages another to prepare, all or a substantial portion of any tax return or refund claim. In order to be subject to the return preparer sanctions, a person must prepare a return for compensation. Therefore, a person who prepares a return for free is not considered a tax return preparer.

A person is not considered a tax return preparer merely because he/she:

a.   furnishes typing, reproducing, or other clerical assistance,

b.   prepares a return or refund claim for his/her employer (or of an officer or employee of the employer),

c.   prepares as a fiduciary a return or refund claim,

d.   prepares a claim for refund for a taxpayer during the course of an IRS audit or appeal,

e.   provides general tax advice to a taxpayer,

f.   is an employee of the IRS performing job related duties, or

g.   provides tax assistance under an IRS sponsored program such as the Volunteer Income Tax Assistance program or a qualified Low-Income Taxpayer Clinic.

A tax return preparer includes a person who prepares a "substantial portion" of a tax return. Someone who provides advice on how to treat a transaction or prepares an estate plan may also be subject to tax preparer penalties. Under Revenue Procedure 2009-11[5] the IRS provided final guidance regarding the interpretation of substantial portion. The Rev. Proc. defines substantial portion to mean "a schedule, entry, or other portion of a tax return or claim for refund that, if adjusted or disallowed, could result in a deficiency determination...that the preparer knows or reasonably should know is a significant portion of the tax liability reported on the tax return." Therefore, determining whether a person has prepared a substantial portion of a tax return will depend on the relative size of the deficiency attributable to the schedule, entry, or other portion.

---

[5]   Rev. Proc. 2009-11, 2009-3 IRB 313, 12/15/2008.

¶9027 Civil Penalties Applicable to Preparers

Table 4 below summarizes the major civil penalties that may apply to tax return preparers.

Table 4 Selected Penalty Provisions Applicable to Tax Return Preparers	
Action of Preparer	**Penalty**
a. Disclosure or use of information from a tax return by a preparer [§7431]	$1,000 (or damages caused, if larger) and/or imprisonment for up to one year
b. Failure to furnish a copy of the tax return to the taxpayer [§6695(a)]	$50 per failure (unless due to "reasonable cause"), $25,000 maximum
c. Failure to sign the return as an income tax preparer [§6695(b)]	$50 per failure (unless due to "reasonable cause"), $25,000 maximum
d. Failure to furnish identifying number on prepared returns [§6695(c)]	$50 per failure, $25,000 maximum
e. Failure to retain a copy of each return prepared (or a list of such returns) [§6695(d)]	$50 per failure, $25,000 maximum
f. Negotiation or endorsement of a check in respect to taxes that is issuable to a taxpayer [§6695(f)]	$500 for each such check
g. Failure to be diligent in determining eligibility for the earned income credit [§6695(g)]	$100 for each failure
h. Understatement of tax liability due to an unreasonable position (there is no substantial authority for the position) [§6694(a)(2)(A)]	Greater of: $1,000 or 50 percent of the income derived (or to be derived) by the tax return preparer for preparing the return or claim
i. Willful attempt to understate tax liability or reckless or intentional disregard of rules or regulations [§6694(b)]	Greater of: $5,000 or 50 percent of the income derived (or to be derived) by the tax return preparer for preparing the return or claim $1,000 for each return
j. Aiding and abetting an understatement of tax liability on a tax return [§6701]	$1,000 for each return
k. Willful preparation of a return in which material items are known to be incorrect [[§7206]	$250,000 fine and/or imprisonment for up to three years (this is a criminal penalty, not a civil penalty)

.01 PREPARER DISCLOSURE PENALTIES

Unless reasonable cause is shown, five different penalties may apply to tax return preparers who do not comply with the practice regulation rules:

1. $50 for each failure to furnish a completed copy of each return prepared to the taxpayer.
2. $50 for each failure to retain a copy of the return, or alternatively, a list of all prepared returns and taxpayer identification numbers,
3. $50 for each failure to include the preparer's tax identification number on the return,
4. $50 for each failure to sign a return, and
5. $50 for failure to retain and make available a record of employed preparers plus $50 for each item that is omitted from that record.

For each of the above items, the maximum penalty is $25,000 per year.

Example 9-18. Assume Flash Tax LLP has 50 tax return preparation offices throughout the United States. The offices prepare a total of 10,000 tax returns during the year. The company does not require its office to maintain a copy of the tax returns it prepares or a list of returns prepared. When the IRS audited Flash Tax, the auditors only found copies of 2,000 returns. The IRS assessed the maximum $25,000 penalty for failure to retain copies of returns (the lesser of $50 × 8,000 returns = $400,000 or $25,000).

.03   PREPARER CONDUCT PENALTIES

The Code includes a variety of penalties that may be imposed when a preparer engages in improper practices. Those penalties include:

1. understatement of tax liability due to an unreasonable position,
2. willful understatement of tax liability or intentional disregard for the rules
3. endorsing or negotiating a refund check,
4. disclosure or use of tax return information by the preparer, and
5. failure to comply with due diligence requirements in determining eligibility for the earned income tax credit.

Understatement Due to an Unreasonable Position

The Small Business and Work Opportunity Tax Act of 2007 increased the penalty amount and changed the standard for avoiding penalties with regard to tax return positions. Under the new law, a tax return preparer who prepares a return or refund claim on which an understatement of tax liability is due to an unreasonable position must pay a penalty equal to the greater of:

- $1,000 or
- 50 percent of the income derived (or to be derived) for preparing the return with respect to the position(s) taken on the return that gave rise to the understatement.[6]

A tax return position is considered unreasonable if:

1. the return preparer knew, or reasonably should have known, of the position,
2. there was not a reasonable belief that the position lacks substantial authority, and
3. the position was not disclosed in the return.

OBSERVATION

Section 506 of the Tax Extenders and Alternative Minimum Tax Relief Act of 2008 amended the standards that must be met by preparers to avoid a Sec. 6694(a) penalty to a "substantial authority for an undisclosed position." The act also provides that tax shelter and reportable transaction positions are considered unreasonable unless it is reasonable to believe that the position would more likely than not be sustained on its merits.

Tax return positions that are adequately disclosed in the return are not subject to the penalty. In addition, no penalty will be imposed if there is reasonable cause for the understatement and the tax return preparer acted in good faith.

The 2007 Act expanded the return preparer penalty to cover all tax return preparers, not just income tax return preparers. Preparers of many information returns will not be subject to the new penalty provision unless they willfully understate tax or act in reckless or intentional disregard of the law.

Regulations §1.6694–1 thru –4

In December 2008 the IRS finalized the regulations on the preparer penalties under Code Sec. 6694. The Regulations implement the changes to Code Sec. 6694 made in May 2007. Some highlights of the Regulations include:

---

[6] Prop. Reg. §1.6694-1(f).

- The previous "one preparer per firm" rule is being replaced by a position-by-position analysis. The new approach will focus the penalty toward the parties responsible for a position leading to a return understatement.

- The IRS limited the penalty calculation based on "income derived for preparing the return" to the income received "with respect to the position taken on the return."

- Preparers are still allowed a good-faith reliance on information provided by others. However, preparers should make a reasonable inquiry when information appears to be incorrect or incomplete.

The Regulations apply only to returns filed and advice given after December 31, 2008.

Willful Understatement

The 2007 Tax Act also increased the penalty amount for any part of a tax liability understatement that is due to "willful or reckless conduct." The penalty is the greater of:
- $5,000 or
- 50 percent of the income derived (or to be derived) for preparing the return or claim.

Willful or reckless conduct is defined as conduct by the preparer which is:
1. a willful attempt to understate the tax liability on the return or claim, or
2. a reckless or intentional disregard of rules or regulations.

The willful understatement penalty is reduced by the unreasonable position penalty.

Endorsing or Negotiating a Refund Check

Any preparer who endorses or negotiates an income tax refund check issued to another person will be subject to a $500 per check penalty.

Disclosure or Use of Taxpayer Information by Preparer

Under Code Sec. 6713, a penalty is imposed for improper disclosure or use of information obtained in preparing an income tax return. The penalty applies to any person engaged in the business of preparing tax returns or providing services in connection with preparation of income tax returns, or to any person who for compensation prepares an income tax return for another person. The penalty is imposed if that person discloses information for any purpose other than to prepare or assist in preparing the return.

The penalty is $250 for each improper disclosure or use, up to $10,000 maximum per year. The final Regulations under Code Sec. 7216 (effective after December 31, 2008) provide that the penalty provisions will not apply to any disclosure of information if the disclosure is made pursuant to any of the following documents:
1. The order of any court of record,
2. A subpoena issued by a federal or state grand jury,
3. A subpoena issued by Congress,
4. An administrative order, demand, summons or subpoena that is issued in the performance of its duties by (i) any federal agency, or (ii) a state agency or commission charged with the licensing, registration, or regulation of preparers.
5. A written request from a professional association ethics committee or board investigating the ethical conduct of the preparer, or
6. A written request from the Public Company Accounting Oversight Board in connection with an inspection or investigation under sections 104 or 105 of the Sarbanes-Oxley Act.

Earned Income Credit Due Diligence

A preparer who fails to comply with the due diligence requirements imposed under Reg. §1.6695-2 with respect to determining the eligibility for, or the amount of, an earned income tax credit will be subject to a special preparer penalty. The penalty is $100 for each failure.

¶9027.03

¶9029   Criminal Penalties Applicable to Preparers

Tax return preparer fraud generally involves the preparation and filing of false income tax returns by preparers who claim inflated personal or business expenses, false deductions, unallowable credits or excessive exemptions on returns completed for their clients or fictitious taxpayers. Preparers may also manipulate income figures to fraudulently obtain tax credits, such as the earned income tax credit.

Table 5 summarizes the statutes most frequently used to prosecute preparers.

Table 5 Tax Preparer Criminal Statutes	
Title & Section	**Provisions**
Code Sec. 7201—Attempt to evade or defeat tax	Any person who willfully attempts to evade or defeat any tax—a felony punishable by a fine of up to $100,000 (for individuals) and/or imprisonment not to exceed five years.
Code Sec. 7206 (1)—Fraud and false statements	Any person who willfully makes and subscribes any return, statement, or other document under penalties of perjury, which he does not believe to be true and correct—a felony punishable by a fine of up to $250,000 and/or imprisonment not to exceed three years.
Code Sec. 7206 (2)—Fraud and false statements	Any person who willfully aids or assists in, or procures, counsels, or advises the preparation or presentation under the IRC of a return, affidavit, claim, or other document, which is fraudulent or is false as to any material matter—a felony punishable by a fine of up to $250,000 and/or imprisonment not to exceed three years.
Code Sec. 7207—Fraudulent returns, statements, or other Documents	Any person who willfully files a false or fraudulent document—a misdemeanor punishable by a fine of up to $100,000 and/or imprisonment not to exceed one year
Code Sec. 7212—Attempts to interfere with administration of the Internal Revenue Laws	Anyone who corruptly or by force or threats of force (including any threatening letter or communication) endeavors to intimidate or impede any employee of the United States acting in an official capacity—a felony punishable by a fine of up to $5,000 and/or imprisonment not to exceed three years.

Most tax return preparers are prosecuted under the criminal statutes for aiding and assisting in the preparation of a false tax return under Code Sec. 7206(2). Return preparers can be convicted under more than one criminal statute, increasing the potential fine and length of prison time. Criminal and civil statutes are not mutually exclusive. Therefore, a return preparer can be acquitted under the criminal statutes and still be liable for civil penalties.

OBSERVATION

Selected Tax Return Preparer Cases

In February 2007 Jonathan Marshall Sr. of Austin, Texas, was sentenced to 18 years in prison for preparing fraudulent tax returns for clients. The jury found that from 2000 to 2005, Marsh falsified dependents and business income and losses on client tax returns in order to obtain larger tax refunds. The majority of the returns involved falsely qualifying clients for the Earned Income Credit.

In January 2012, Howard Levine was sentenced to 37 months in prison for aiding in the preparation of false income tax returns for clients. Levine admitted to preparing no fewer than 56 false income tax returns that contained fictitious deductions, business expenses and corporate losses.

Information on additional tax return preparer cases can be found on the IRS Criminal Enforcement website at *http://www.irs.gov/compliance/enforcement/index.html.*

¶9031 Reportable Transactions

Congress and the IRS have aggressively pursued abusive tax shelters resulting in disclosure requirements that impact both the taxpayer and tax return preparers. Reg. §1.6011-4 outlines the disclosure requirements for "reportable transactions." A reportable transaction must be disclosed on Form 8886 which is attached to the tax return in each year that the tax return reflects tax consequences related to the transaction. In the first year the taxpayer participates in the transaction, a copy of Form 8886 must also be filed with the IRS Office of Tax Shelter Analysis.

Under Reg. §1.6011-4(b) issued in July 2007, reportable transactions include:
- listed transactions (a transaction that the IRS has determined to be a tax avoidance transaction),
- confidential transactions (a transaction offered under conditions of confidentiality for a fee),
- transactions with contractual protection (a transaction where the taxpayer has the right to a full or partial refund of fees if all or part of the intended tax consequences are not sustained),
- loss transactions (a transaction where the taxpayer reports a substantial loss under Section 165), and
- transactions of interest (a transaction identified by the IRS).

For additional information about reportable transactions see the instructions to Form 8886 on the IRS website.

Code Sec. 6707A sets forth the penalties for failure to comply with the disclosure requirements of Reg. §1.6011-4. The penalties are:
- $10,000 for each reportable transaction and $100,000 for each listed transaction not properly disclosed by a natural person.
- $50,000 for each reportable transaction and $200,000 for each listed transaction not properly disclosed by a corporation.

The substantial understatement penalties discussed earlier may also apply to the listed and reportable transactions. The 20-percent penalty will apply if the transaction results in a substantial understatement and was adequately disclosed. If the transaction was not adequately disclosed, then the penalty increases to 30 percent.

The *American Jobs Creation Act of 2004* added a requirement that a "material advisor" (a person who provides material aid, assistance, or advice on a reportable transaction) must file Form 8918 describing the transaction and any potential tax benefits expected to result from the transaction. For additional information regarding material advisors see the instructions for Form 8918 available on the IRS website.

¶9033 Administrative Constraints: Circular 230

Treasury Department Circular 230, *Regulations Governing the Practice of Attorneys, Certified Public Accountants, Enrolled Agents, Enrolled Actuaries, and Appraisers Before the Internal Revenue Service*, is a collection of regulations governing practice before the IRS. As such, this set of regulations affects the largest group of tax professionals. The following discussion highlights the key provisions of Circular 230 (as revised in August 2011), with special emphasis on those sections geared toward providing "best practices" that may avoid potential ethical problems.

.01 SUBPART A—RULES GOVERNING AUTHORITY TO PRACTICE

- *Definition of Practice.* Practice before the IRS is defined as "*all matters connected with a presentation to the Internal Revenue Service or any of its officers or employees relating to a taxpayer's rights, privileges, or liabilities under laws or regulations administered by the Internal Revenue Service. Such presentations include, but are not limited to preparing and filing documents, corresponding and communicating with the Internal Revenue Service, and representing a client at conferences, hearings, and meetings.*"

- *Who May Practice.* Certain professionals are automatically granted the right to practice before the IRS. These include attorneys, certified public accountants, enrolled agents, enrolled actuaries and enrolled retirement plan agents (although the latter two groups are limited to representation with respect to only certain issues, mostly related to the pension and deferred compensation provisions of the Coded). The right to practice is also granted to certain former employees of the IRS.
- T.D. 9501 introduced a new category of practitioners: registered tax return preparers. Under T.D. 9501 all individuals who for compensation prepare tax returns or refund claims filed after December 31, 2010, must obtain and use a valid preparer tax identification number (PTIN). Practice as a registered tax return preparer is limited to preparing and signing tax returns and claims for refund, and other documents for submission to the IRS and representation before the IRS with regard to an examination of such returns, claims and other documents.

In January 2013, the United States District Court for the District of Columbia struck down the IRS's registered tax return preparer program and enjoined it from enforcing the regulations (Loving, No. 12-385 (D.D.C. 1/18/13)). As a result of the ruling, tax return preparers covered by this program are not currently required to register with the IRS, to complete competency testing or secure continuing education. The IRS closed the PTIN system in February 2013. The system will remain closed while the courts consider the IRS's appeal of the decision.

- *Limited Practice Rules.* Circular 230 provides special rules regarding limited practice. First, individuals may appear on their own behalf before the IRS. Secondly, an individual who is not enrolled to practice may in limited circumstances represent a related or associated taxpayer before the IRS. This group of eligible representatives includes family members, employees, general partner, corporate officer, trustee, or governmental officer. In addition, an individual who prepares and signs a return, or who just prepares the return, may represent the taxpayer, but only for that tax return and period in question and only before the examination division of the IRS.

.03   SUBPART B—DUTIES AND RESTRICTIONS RELATING TO PRACTICE BEFORE THE IRS

- *Information Requests From the IRS.* Circular 230 requires practitioners to submit promptly any records or information in any manner before the IRS unless the practitioner believes in good faith and on reasonable grounds that the records or information are privileged. Reasonable inquiries must be made if the records are not immediately available. Practitioners are also required to furnish information to the Director of Practice (and possibly testify) when requested to do so regarding information on possible violations of the regulations, unless once again the practitioner believes in good faith and on reasonable grounds that the records or information are privileged.
- *Knowledge of Client Omission.* If a practitioner knows that a client has not complied with the revenue laws or has made an error in or omission from any return, document, or other paper related to the revenue laws, he or she must advise the client promptly of this fact. The practitioner must also advise the client of the consequences under the law related to such noncompliance, error, or omission.
- *Due Diligence Requirements.* A practitioner must exercise due diligence in all matters related to the IRS, including return and document preparation, determining the correctness of oral and written representations to both the Treasury and the clients. The practitioner may rely on the work product of another person, provided the practitioner used reasonable care in engaging, supervising, training, and evaluating the person. However, the practitioner may not knowingly accept assistance from any person under disbarment or suspension from practice before the IRS, or accept assistance from former government employees subject to special restrictions (see below).

ETHICAL QUESTION Susan Beale prepared the federal income tax return of Abby Kaufman last year. This return included $121,000 of dividend income on Intel stock. This year, Abby is not reporting any dividend income in the preliminary information furnished to Susan. Susan knows that Intel did not suspend dividend payments this year. What are Susan's ethical obligations at this point in time?

All ethical guidance stresses the need to do due diligence, and to make additional inquiries when other documentation is insufficient. Susan should follow up with Abby and ask about the lack of dividend income on the return. Even if Abby no longer owns the stock, its disposition may have resulted in capital gain or some other form of recognition. Susan should not sign the return until the issue is resolved.

- *Fees.* A practitioner may not charge an unconscionable fee for representing a client before the IRS. In addition, a practitioner may not charge a contingent fee for preparing an original tax return or for any advice rendered in connection with a position taken on such return. A contingent fee may be charged for services rendered in connection with the IRS examination of, or challenge to, (1) an original tax return, or (2) an amended return or claim for refund or credit filed within 120 days of the taxpayer receiving a written notice of the examination, or a written challenge to the original tax return. The final regulations also permit the use of contingent fees for interest and penalty reviews and for services rendered in connection with any judicial proceeding arising under the Internal Revenue Code.

- *Return of Client's Records.* At the request of a client, a practitioner must return any and all records of the client that are necessary for the client to comply with his or her federal tax obligations. The term "records of the client" is defined very broadly to include any documents or written or electronic materials provided to the practitioner by a client or third party, as well as documents provided to the client by the practitioner. A dispute over fees generally does not allow the preparer to retain records. However, if state law allows record retention in the case of a fee dispute, then the preparer is only required to return the records that must be attached to the taxpayer's return and allow the client to review and copy other records.

- *Solicitation.* Practitioners may not use any form of public communication or private solicitation that contains false, fraudulent, or coercive claims, or misleading or deceptive statements or claims. The practitioner may not use such terms as "certified", or make any implication of an employer/employee relationship with the IRS. Acceptable descriptions are "enrolled to represent taxpayers before the IRS," "enrolled to practice before the IRS," and "admitted to practice before the IRS." Any lawful solicitation made must clearly identify the solicitation as such, and identify the source of the information used in choosing the recipient (if applicable).

- *Fee Information.* A practitioner may publish the availability of a fee schedule, and publish information on (1) fixed fees for routine services, (2) hourly rates, (3) range of fees for particular services, and (4) fee charged for an initial consultation. If costs may be incurred in connection with the fee, a statement disclosing whether clients will be responsible must be included. A practitioner may charge no more than the published rates for at least 30 days from the last date rates were published.

- *Negotiation of Checks.* A practitioner who prepares returns may not endorse or otherwise negotiate any check issued to a client by the government in respect of a federal tax liability.

- *Best Practices for Tax Advisors.* Tax advisors should provide clients with the highest quality representation concerning federal tax issues by adhering to best practices. These best practices include (1) communicating clearly with the client regarding terms of the engagement, (2) establishing the facts, relating the applicable law, and arriving at a conclusion supported by the law and the facts, and (4) advising the client of the import of the conclusions reached (e.g., avoiding penalties, etc.). Tax advisors with responsibility for overseeing a firm's practice of providing advice should insure that all firm procedures are consistent with best practices.

¶9033.03

.05   STANDARDS FOR ADVISING WITH RESPECT TO TAX RETURN POSITIONS AND FOR PREPARING OR SIGNING RETURNS

Section 10.34(a) of Circular 230 closely mirrors the tax return preparer penalty provisions under Sec. 6694. Under Section 10.34(a)(1) a practitioner may not recklessly, willfully, or through gross incompetence sign a tax return or refund claim, advise a client to take a position on a claim for refund or a tax return, or prepare a portion of a return or refund claim that the practitioner knows or reasonably should have known contains a tax return position that lacks a reasonable basis. Such tax return position, advice, or preparation may not involve an unreasonable position, as described in Sec. 6694(a)(2), related regulations, or other published guidance.

An "unreasonable position" for purposes Section 10.34 has the same meaning as used in Code Section 6694 (a)(2) and related guidance. Under Section 6694 (a)(2), a position is considered unreasonable unless there is or was substantial authority for the position. Substantial authority is addressed in Section 6662. Under Reg. §1.6662-3 "reasonable basis" means a return position is reasonably based on one or more of the authorities set forth in Reg. §1.6662-4(d)(3)(iii) (taking into account the relevance and persuasiveness of the authorities, and subsequent developments). The authorities under Reg. §1.6662-4(d)(3)(iii) are listed in **Table 6**.

Additionally, Section 10.34(a)(l) states that a willful attempt by any practitioner to understate tax liability or one that involves a reckless or intentional disregard of rules or regulations described in Sec. 6694(b)(2) violates Section 10.34(a). Responding to practitioner concerns that a violation of Section 6694 would automatically result in a violation of Section 10.34, the IRS has indicated that they will make an independent determination regarding the Section 10.34 violation. The Section specifically provides that a pattern of conduct is a factor that will be taken into account in determining whether a practitioner has acted recklessly, willfully, or through gross incompetence. A violation of Section 10.34 may lead to the practitioner being censured, suspended, or disbarred.

Table 6
Substantial Authority as Defined in Reg. §1.6662-4(d)(3)(i)

1. The Internal Revenue Code and other statutes
2. Regulations (final, temporary, and proposed)
3. Court cases
4. Tax treaties
5. Statements of Congressional intent, including:
   - House Ways and Means Committee Reports
   - Senate Finance Committee Reports
   - Joint Conference Committee Reports
   - Congressional Record
   - Joint Committee on Taxation Report (the "Blue Book")
6. Administrative pronouncements, including:
   - Revenue Rulings
   - Revenue Procedures
   - Private Letter Rulings (PLRs)
   - Technical Advice Memoranda (TAMs)
   - Actions on Decisions (AODs)
   - General Counsel Memoranda (GCMs)
   - Notices, Press Releases, and similar documents

Covered Opinions: In September 2012 the IRS released proposed regulations that would eliminate the complex rules in Circular 230 governing covered opinions. The proposed regulations would expand the requirements for written advice under Circular 230, Section 10.37

as a replacement for the current covered opinion rules. Proposed Section 10.37 will require practitioners to base all written advice on reasonable factual and legal assumptions, exercise reasonable reliance, and consider all relevant facts that the practitioner knows or should know.

Current Circular 230, Section 10.35, contains detailed rules for tax opinions that constitute "covered opinions." Covered opinions include written advice concerning:
1. A listed transaction;
2. A transaction with the principal purpose of tax avoidance or evasion; or
3. A transaction with a significant purpose of tax avoidance or evasion, if the advice is a reliance opinion, marketed opinion, subject to conditions of confidentiality, or subject to a contractual protection.

Section 10.35 requires practitioners to comply with extensive requirements when providing written advice that constitutes a written opinion. In the preamble to the proposed regulations, the IRS concedes that the current covered opinion rules have "produced some unintended consequences and should be reconsidered." The IRS specifically refers to the prominent disclaimer stating that the opinion cannot be relied on for penalty protection used by many practitioners in an attempt to exempt their advice from the covered opinion rules. The IRS has concluded that the rules are overbroad, are difficult to apply, and do not necessarily produce higher-quality tax advice.

Requirements for Other Written Advice. Under current Section 10.37, if advice is not a covered opinion, a practitioner must follow a more relaxed set of requirements. However, the practitioner must still (1) not base the advice on unreasonable factual or legal assumptions, not rely on unreasonable representations and statements of the taxpayer and others, must consider all relevant facts, and must ignore the possibility of IRS audit. The taxpayer may rely on the taxpayer's statements and facts without verification, absent any indication that such information is incomplete, inconsistent, or misleading. All circumstances, including the scope of the engagement and specificity of the advice sought by the client will be considered in determining whether a practitioner has failed to comply with these rules. Proposed changes to this section will require practitioners to base all written advice on reasonable factual and legal assumptions, exercise reasonable reliance, and consider all relevant facts that the practitioner knows or should know.

.07   SUBPART C—SANCTIONS FOR VIOLATIONS OF THE REGULATIONS

- ***Sanctions.*** The Secretary of the Treasury, after notice and an opportunity for a proceeding, may censure (public reprimand), suspend, or disbar any practitioner from practice before the IRS if the practitioner is shown to be incompetent or disreputable, fails to comply with any regulation, or willfully and knowingly misleads or threatens a client or prospective client with intent to defraud. The same general rules apply to appraisers.

  The Secretary may also impose a monetary penalty against a practitioner if the practitioner is shown to be incompetent or disreputable, fails to comply with Circular 230 regulations, or knowingly misleads or threatens a client or prospective client with intent to defraud. The monetary penalty may be imposed in addition to any other sanction, and a monetary penalty may be imposed on the practitioner's employer, firm, or other entity that knew or should have known of the practitioner's conduct.

- ***Incompetent and Disreputable Conduct.*** Such conduct is defined to include convictions for criminal offense under the federal tax laws, for dishonesty or breach of trust, or any felony rendering the practitioner unfit to practice before the IRS. Such conduct also includes the giving of false or misleading information or testimony; using false representations to solicit employment; failure to make a federal tax return; willfully assisting, counseling, or encouraging a client to violate any federal tax law; misappropriation of client funds; bribes or coercion of IRS employees; disbarment or suspension of professional license; the willful failure to sign a tax return prepared by a practitioner; and any unauthorized disclosure of tax return information by the practitioner. Finally, the term includes providing false opinions due to a pattern of reckless conduct or gross incompetence.

- *Receipt of Information Concerning Practitioner.* IRS officers and employees, as well as any other persons, who have reason to believe that a practitioner has violated the Circular 230 regulations will make a written report (or oral report by other persons) to the Director of Practice (or to any IRS employee, in the case of other persons). The Director of Practice must destroy such reports as soon as permissible under the applicable records control schedule.

.09   ## SUBPART D—RULES APPLICABLE TO DISCIPLINARY PROCEEDINGS

- *Institution of Proceeding.* If the Director of Practice determines that a practitioner has violated any laws and regulations under Circular 230, he or she may reprimand the taxpayer or institute a proceeding for censure, suspension, or disbarment of the practitioner.
- *Effects of Disbarment, Suspension or Censure.* The effects of the decision are:
  - *Disbarment.* Respondent is not permitted to practice before the IRS until authorized to do so by the Director of Practice (see reinstatement below).
  - *Suspension.* Respondent is not permitted to practice before the IRS during the period of suspension; after the suspension, the Director of Practice may impose additional conditions.
  - *Censure.* Respondent is still able to practice before the IRS, but the Director of Practice may impose additional conditions.

The Director of Practice may entertain a petition for reinstatement from any practitioner or appraiser disbarred from practice before the IRS after the expiration of five years following such disbarment or disqualification.

¶9035   Statements of Standards for Tax Services

In addition to Circular 230, tax return preparers who are certified public accountants are subject to the AICPA Code of Professional Conduct and Statements on Standards for Tax Services, and State Board of Accountancy Regulations. In 2000, the AICPA adopted eight Statements on Standards for Tax Services (SSTS) as enforceable standards for AICPA members. Revised standards were issued in November 2009 and became effective on January 1, 2010. With the combining of SSTS Nos. 6 and 7, there are now seven standards. These standards are intended to supplement the AICPA Code of Conduct and Circular 230.

A brief summary of the seven standards and two interpretations of the standards follows:

SSTS No. 1, Tax Return Positions. This statement provides standards for members when recommending tax return positions and preparing or signing tax returns (including amended returns, claims for refund and information returns) filed with any taxing authority. The standards recognize members' responsibilities to both taxpayers and to the tax system. SSTS No. 1 requires a member to determine and comply with the applicable taxing authorities' tax return reporting standards. If there are no written standards, a member should not recommend a tax return position or prepare or sign a tax return taking a position unless the member has a good-faith belief that the position has at least a realistic possibility of being sustained. A member should not sign or prepare a return containing a position that does not meet this standard, unless there is a reasonable basis for the position and it is properly disclosed.

Interpretation No. 1-1, "Realistic Possibility Standard," of SSTS No. 1.
Interpretation No. 1 explains various aspects of the realistic possibility standard
including examples of when the realistic possibility standard has or has not been
met. For purposes of SSTS No. 1, acceptable authorities include sources of tax
analysis and reference tools used by tax preparers and advisors, as well as articles in
recognized professional publications and well-reasoned treatises. Members should
also consider the type of authority; whether the taxpayer's particular facts and circumstances can be distinguished from those covered by the court case, regulation,
or other authority; and whether the authority critically analyzes the issue or merely
states a conclusion.

Interpretation No. 1-2, "Tax Planning" of SSTS No. 1. This Interpretation offers
additional guidance to members when providing services in connection with tax
planning. The Interpretation clarifies how the Standards apply across the spectrum
of tax planning, including those situations involving tax shelters.

SSTS No. 2, Answers to Questions on Returns. This statement provides guidance
regarding whether a member should sign a tax return if one or more questions on
the return have not been answered. SSTS No. 2 requires that members "make a reasonable effort" to obtain the information necessary to provide appropriate answers
to all questions on a tax return before signing as a preparer. If information is not
"readily available and the answer is not significant in terms of taxable income or
loss or the tax liability shown on the return," omitting an answer to a question may
be reasonable and require no explanation. Another acceptable reason for omitting
an answer may be that the information requested is voluminous, in which case the
preparer should provide a statement that the information will be furnished upon
examination. SSTS No. 2 reminds members not to omit answers simply because
they may be disadvantageous to the taxpayer and to consider whether omitted information will cause the return to be "deemed incomplete" or may result in penalties.

SSTS No. 3, Certain Procedural Aspects of Preparing Returns. This statement
outlines members' obligation to examine or verify supporting data or to consider
information related to another taxpayer when preparing a tax return. Although a
member may in good faith rely upon information provided by the taxpayer or a third
party without independent verification, the member should not ignore the implication
of information furnished to or known by the member. This may include information
from another taxpayer's return, if the information is relevant and necessary.

The Standard expects members to be aware of their obligation to exercise
due diligence. For example, a member should make reasonable inquiries if the
information appears to be incorrect, incomplete, or inconsistent and encourage the
taxpayer to provide the necessary underlying documentation. Whenever possible,
the member should refer to the taxpayer's returns for at least one previous year.

SSTS No. 4, Use of Estimates. This statement provides guidance for the use of taxpayer estimates. In preparing or signing a tax return, the member may use a taxpayer's
estimates unless prohibited by statute or rule. The member may also use estimates if
it is impracticable to obtain exact data and the estimated amounts are reasonable.

***SSTS No. 5, Departure From a Position Previously Concluded in an Administra-
tive Proceeding or Court Decision.*** This statement applies when members recommend positions that depart from those determined in an administrative proceeding
or court decision concerning the taxpayer's prior return. When an administrative
proceeding or court decision results in a determination based on a specific tax
treatment on a prior tax return, a member should usually recommend the same
treatment for subsequent years. SSTS No. 5 identifies several circumstances that

may justify departure from a prior position. For example, departure is justified 1) when supporting documentation becomes available or subsequent rulings are more favorable to the taxpayer's current position; or 2) where the taxpayer yielded for settlement purposes or did not appeal an adverse decision, even if the questioned tax return position met the standards in SSTS No. 1.

SSTS No. 6, Knowledge of Error: Return Preparation and Administrative Proceedings. This statement addresses the standards when a member becomes aware of an error in a taxpayer's previously filed tax return, an error in a return that is the subject of an administrative proceeding, or of a taxpayer's failure to file a required return. If a member becomes aware of an error, the member should inform the taxpayer promptly, advise the taxpayer of the potential consequences of the error, and recommend the necessary corrective measures. Consistent with the AICPA Code of Professional Conduct, members are not obligated to inform the taxing authority of the error and, in fact, may not do so without the taxpayer's permission unless required by law. Although the statement prohibits disclosure to the taxing authority without the taxpayer's permission, it suggests that members request permission to disclose the error before the administrative proceeding is concluded, to avoid any perception of bad faith based on "misleading information." Ultimately, the taxpayer must decide whether to correct or disclose the error to the taxing authority. If the taxpayer does not correct or disclose an error, SSTS No. 6 advises the member to consider withdrawing from any continued relationship.

SSTS No. 7, Form and Content of Advice to Taxpayers. This statement sets the standards for members providing advice to taxpayers. A member should use professional judgment to ensure that tax advice provided to a taxpayer reflects competence and appropriately serves the taxpayer's needs. The statement states that members providing tax advice to a taxpayer should assume that the advice will affect how the matters or transactions considered would be reported or disclosed on the taxpayer's return. Although the advice does not have to be provided in any standard format; members should exercise professional judgment in deciding on what form advice should take. The Statement also examines the circumstances in which a member has a responsibility to communicate with a taxpayer when subsequent developments affect advice previously provided.

¶9037   Summary

- In order to provide appropriate advice, a tax professional must be knowledgeable of how the IRS is structured and how it operates.
- Not only are tax underpayments subject to interest, but both the taxpayer and the tax return preparer may also be subject to civil and/or criminal penalties.
- Individuals who practice before the IRS are subject to the rules of conduct provided in Circular 230. Tax professionals who are CPAs are also subject to the AICPA Statements on Standards for Tax Services.

Review Questions for Chapter 9

True or False
Indicate which of the following statements are true or false by circling the correct answer.

1. The IRS Oversight Board hires the Commissioner, after approval by the President. T F
2. The Taxpayer Advocate Service will provide a representative to attend the initial office audit meeting between the taxpayer and the IRS. T F
3. The document matching program would identify a taxpayer who failed to report a Microsoft dividend payment on his tax return. T F
4. If the taxpayer does not file a protest within 30 days of the date of the 30-day letter, the IRS will issue a 90-day letter. T F
5. A taxpayer has 30 days to file a petition with the Tax Court following the date of the Statutory Notice of Deficiency. T F
6. A taxpayer who fails to file his return and fails to pay his tax is subject to a combined 5.5-percent monthly penalty on the underpayment. T F
7. Less than one percent of all tax returns filed for the year are audited by the IRS. T F
8. The statute of limitations on a return that is never filed is extended to six years. T F
9. A taxpayer is always allowed to bring an audio tape recorder to an IRS audit meeting, even if the agent is not given prior notice. T F
10. The interest rate is the same for individuals owing tax to the IRS or being paid interest on a refund from the IRS. T F

Fill in the Blanks
Fill in each blank with the appropriate word or phrase that completes each sentence.

11. Wanda owns and operates a technology repair shop "One Day Repairs." She reported $3 million in revenues on her Schedule C last year. The IRS's _____ operating division would be responsible for Wanda's return.
12. The primary objective of examining returns is to _____.
13. Suzanne Sanders's tax return includes charitable contributions equal to 15 percent of her AGI. Her return was selected for audit and the auditor only wants to verify the charitable contributions. Suzanne will most likely be subject to a(n) _____ audit.
14. Hansel Hamilton goes to her IRS office audit with a shoebox full of receipts. When the auditor asks her to support a deduction, Hansel spends at least 10 minutes sifting through her shoebox looking for the receipt. Hansel did not follow the IRS audit suggestion to _____.
15. When the total proposed tax, penalties, overassessment or claimed refund exceeds _____ for any taxable period, the taxpayer must submit a formal written protest.
16. Walter Watson prepared 30 tax returns this year that he did not sign. The penalty for failure to sign a return is $_____ per return.
17. Martin Manning was convicted of tax evasion. He faces a possible prison term not to exceed _____ years.
18. Jessica Johnson filed a proper request for extension of her individual tax return. Jessica filed her return in July and paid the $2,000 owed at that time. The IRS will likely assess the _____ penalty.
19. William Weber was assessed a $10,000 deficiency increasing his total tax from $35,000 to $45,000. William will likely be assessed the _____ penalty.

20. An individual who takes the position that the U.S. tax system is a voluntary system, therefore he/she does not have to pay income tax would be considered to have taken a(n) _____ position.

Multiple Choice

Circle the best answer for each of the following questions.

21. Which of the following is *not* a function of the IRS Oversight Board?
    a. provides long-term guidance and direction to the IRS
    b. evaluates IRS performance reports
    c. prepares the IRS's budget request to Congress
    d. reviews the compensation of the Commissioner
    e. All of the above are functions of the Oversight Board

22. A taxpayer will receive a 30-day letter:
    a. if the taxpayer is 30 days late filing his/her tax return
    b. after filing a protest to appeals
    c. only if the taxpayer does not sign Form 870
    d. to notify him that his return was selected for audit

23. If a taxpayer files a proper request for extension:
    a. the taxpayer has until the extended due date to pay the tax without interest
    b. the taxpayer has 90 days following the original due date to pay estimated taxes without penalty
    c. the taxpayer must still pay the tax by the original due date
    d. the statute of limitations time period begins on the original due date of the return

24. Jeremiah Weaver owns a restaurant and reported $50,000 of gross receipts from the restaurant on his 2008 tax return. The return was filed on April 3, 2009. Jeremiah accidently failed to report $75,000 of additional cash receipts. The statute of limitations for this return will expire on:
    a. April 3, 2012
    b. April 15, 2012
    c. April 3, 2015
    d. April 15, 2015
    e. There is no expiration date for the statue of limitations in this case

25. Danielle Davidson prepares a tax return for Mickey Matthews. Mickey's return includes a deduction that is contrary to an extant Revenue Ruling. Because of a recent court decision in another circuit that is favorable to the deduction, Danielle believes that there is a 60-percent chance that she would prevail if Mickey's return was audited. Danielle did not disclose the position on Mickey's return. What potential preparer penalties would Danielle face if Mickey's return is audited?
    a. No preparer penalties would be assessed regardless of whether the position was upheld in court.
    b. Danielle would be subject to the Understatement Due to an Unreasonable Position penalty if Mickey loses in court.
    c. Danielle would be subject to the Understatement Due to an Unreasonable Position penalty if Mickey wins or loses in court.
    d. Danielle would be subject to the Willful Understatement penalty if Mickey loses in court because a preparer cannot take a position contrary to a Revenue Ruling.

26. Which of the following individuals is *not* considered a tax return preparer?
    a.   Amy provides general advice about itemizing deductions to a client for compensation.
    b.   Jason provides tax advice for compensation on the sale of small business stock involving a $200,000 gain on a tax return reporting taxable income of $250,000.
    c.   Larry prepares for compensation the Schedule C for a taxpayer. The Schedule C income represents 80 percent of the total income reported on the return.
    d.   Holly prepares for compensation the estate tax return of her uncle.

27. Heather Lam filed an extension request for her 2011 tax return on April 3, 2012. The request extended Heather's time to file the return until October 15, 2012. Heather eventually filed her return on November 20, 2012, and paid the $3,000 due at that time. For what period of time will Heather be subject to interest on the $3,000 tax due?
    a.   April 3–November 20, 2012
    b.   April 15–November 20, 2012
    c.   October 15–November 20, 2012
    d.   Heather will not be subject to interest as long as she has reasonable cause for paying her tax after the due date.

28. Heather Lam filed an extension request for her 2011 tax return on April 3, 2012. The request extended Heather's time to file the return until October 15, 2012. Heather eventually filed her return on November 20, 2012, and paid the $3,000 due at that time.
    b.   Heather will be subject to the failure to file penalty for one month and the failure to pay penalty for six months.
    c.   Heather will be subject to the failure to file penalty for two months and the failure to pay penalty for two months.
    d.   Heather will be subject to the failure to file penalty for seven months and the failure to pay penalty for seven months.
    e.   Heather will be subject to the failure to file penalty for two months and the failure to pay penalty for seven months.

29. The rules of Circular 230 allow a tax preparer to:
    a. Take a position on a tax return that is contrary to a decision of the U.S. Supreme Court
    b. Charge a $5,000 fee to prepare a Form 1040EZ
    c. Purposely delay the tax audit process
    d. Advertise their services on the Internet
    e. None of the above

30. A tax preparer is in violation of Circular 230 if he or she:
    a.   Discusses the content of a client's tax return with a friend
    b.   Does not sign the tax return that is prepared as a favor for a relative
    c.   Files a tax return that includes a math error
    d.   All of the above

Review Problems

31. For each independent situation, indicate which section, if any, the practitioner has violated under Circular 230.

    a. The practitioner found an error on a client's prior year return. The practitioner advised the client of the consequences of the error but did not report the error to the IRS.

    b. The practitioner reviews a new client's prior year return and notes a number of areas where it appears the new client did not take all the deductions she would be entitled to. The practitioner proposes a contingent fee structure based on a percentage of the tax savings from any new deductions the practitioner identifies. This fee structure would apply to the current year return and an amended return for the prior year.

    c. In a local advertisement, the practitioner includes a statement that his initial consultation fee is $50 and he charges between $100 and $500 for a Form 1040 including a Schedule A for itemized deductions.

    d. A client's prior return preparer was suspended from practice before the IRS. The prior preparer completed the client's Schedule C. The new practitioner uses the Schedule C as completed by the prior preparer in finishing the client's current tax return.

32. The IRS selected Edward's 2012 tax return for audit with respect to employee business expenses. Edward has just met with a revenue agent who contends that Edward owes $1,500 of additional taxes. Discuss briefly the procedural alternatives available to Edward.

33. Helen's income tax liability for 2011 was $24,000. Her self-employment tax was $4,000. Helen projects that her income tax for 2012 will be $34,000 and her self-employment tax will be $6,000. Helen will have $4,000 of income tax withholdings in 2012. Helen makes estimated payments of $3,000 on April 15, 2012; $5,000 on June 8, 2012; $5,000 on September 15, 2012; and $4,000 on January 3, 2013. Helen files her return and pays the tax due on March 21, 2012. Compute Helen's estimated tax underpayment for each quarter (if any) and indicate the time period for the underpayment penalty for each payment.

34. Gamma Corporation estimates that its 2012 taxable income will be $800,000. Thus, it is subject to a flat 34-percent income tax rate and incurs a $272,000 liability. For each of the following independent cases, compute Gamma's minimum quarterly estimated tax payments that will avoid an underpayment penalty.

    a. Gamma's 2011 tax return showed taxable income of $600,000 and a tax liability of $204,000.

    b. Gamma's 2011 tax return showed a tax loss of ($200,000). The loss was carried back to 2009 and Gamma received a tax refund of $68,000.

    c. Gamma's 2011 tax return showed taxable income of $600,000 and a tax liability of $204,000. Gamma's 2010 tax return showed taxable income of $3,000,000 and a tax liability of $1,020,000.

35. The actor Wesley Snipes was indicted in 2006 for not filing tax returns for the years 1999 through 2004 and filing refund claims for approximately $12 million for 1996 and 1997, claiming that only income from foreign sources was subject to tax. What potential civil and/or criminal penalties might be assessed against either Mr. Snipes or his tax return preparer?

36. Simon is single and self-employed, reporting $400,000 of receipts from his business. His Schedule C includes significant entertainment expenses and an office-in-home deduction. During the year, he gave a $50,000 contribution to his undergraduate university for them to name a scholarship after him. Harold is married and files jointly with his wife. They claim six additional dependents, four children under the age of 15, Harold's father and his wife's mother. Their return includes salary income of $400,000, significant itemized deductions for mortgage interest and real estate taxes, and a $30,000 loss from raising cattle. Which return is more likely to be selected for audit? Which type of audit would the taxpayer most likely be subject to? Explain.

37. Sigma Corporation, a long time client, believes that the services they provide meet the definition of a production activity under Code Sec. 199, thereby qualifying the company for a domestic production deduction. A proposed Regulation suggests that the business does not meet the definition under Code Sec. 199, but the IRC is unclear. The committee reports do not provide any additional insights. The company definitely wants to take the deduction, even if it's an aggressive position. What recommendations would you make to the client based on varying levels of certainty that you might have about the ability to sustain the deduction upon audit?

Web-Based Research Problems

38. Locate the AICPA Statements of Standards for Tax Services (SSTS) through the internet. Review The Statement on Standards for Tax Services No. 1, Tax Return Positions. What standard does it require a member to use to recommend a tax return position and in preparing or signing a tax return? How does a tax advisor meet this standard? How is this standard the same or different from Circular 230 and the Internal Revenue Code preparer penalties?

39. Locate the Ethics and Independence Rules Concerning Independence, Tax Services, and Contingent Fees on the Public Company Accounting Oversight Board's (PCAOB) website. What types of tax services can be provided to an audit client? What tax services cannot be provided by the outside auditing firm? What involvement does the audit committee have in overseeing tax services provided by the outside auditing firm?

40. Locate the most recent Annual Report to Congress by the National Taxpayer Advocate. What are the 20 most serious problems identified in the report?

CHAPTER **10**

Tax Communications Between the Client, Tax Preparer and the IRS

Learning Objectives:

In this chapter you will learn:
1. About the importance of recordkeeping and which documents a taxpayer should keep and how long these records should be retained.
2. What records a business taxpayer should keep, including supporting documents and books and records.
3. What are the "Best Practices" for tax return preparers and advisors.
4. About electronic workpapers and electronic filing of tax returns.

¶10,001   Introduction

The basis for communication between the taxpayer, the tax return preparer and the IRS is an adequate set of books and records. An issue related to whether books and records are adequate to satisfy record-keeping requirements is what items can be considered to be part of a taxpayer's books and records. Numerous cases and rulings provide for the admissibility of a wide variety of business records into evidence in federal court proceedings. Balance sheets and profit and loss statements constitute part of a taxpayer's books and records.[1] Accountants' worksheets or workpapers maintained for reconciling book depreciation with tax depreciation also constitute part of a taxpayer's books and records

---

[1]   *Stonegate of Blacksburg, Inc.*, 33 TCM 956, TC Memo. 1974-213.

when they are permanent, are maintained with regular books and reconcile differences.[2] In today's electronic environment it is possible to communicate with clients using electronic workpapers and to electronically file tax returns. Gone are the days when tax returns were prepared by hand and massive folders containing workpapers were maintained for each client. Today's "paperless" environment raises a host of issues regarding document retention and security of confidential information transmitted in electronic format. But even in an electronic environment, "Best Practices" must start with identifying and retaining the appropriate documents.

¶10,003   Why Keep Records?

There are many reasons to keep good records. Any person subject to income tax, or required to file an information return concerning income, must keep permanent accounts or records, including inventories, that are sufficient to establish that person's gross income, deductions, credits or other information required by the return.[3] Failure to keep adequate records allows the IRS to recompute a taxpayer's income according to the net worth method.[4] Books and records must be kept available for inspection by the IRS and retained as long as their contents are material to the administration of any internal revenue law.[5]

The following discussion is based upon record keeping requirements explained in IRS publication 552, Recordkeeping for Individuals, and IRS publication 583, Starting a Business and Keeping Records, and should be viewed as the minimum standard for good recordkeeping. A taxpayer must be able to provide the tax return preparer with timely and accurate tax information in order to comply with tax law reporting. Good records enable the taxpayer to:

- Identify sources of income, including money or property received from the performance of services or sales of goods. In addition, nonbusiness sources of income, such as dividends, interest, and capital gains must be accounted for and reported separately. Occasionally, the taxpayer may also receive nontaxable income, such as tax-exempt interest income.
- Keep track of expenses. By recording expenses in a timely fashion, deductions will not be omitted when computing taxable income. You can use your records to identify expenses for which you can claim a deduction. This will help you determine if you can itemize deductions on your tax return.
- Keep track of the basis of property. It is important to keep records that show the basis of property, including the original cost or other basis and any improvements made.
- Prepare tax returns. Good records help you to file a timely and accurate tax return.
- Support items reported on tax returns. Should your tax return be audited by the IRS you may be asked to explain the items reported. Good records will help you explain any item and arrive at the correct tax with a minimum of effort. If you do not have records, you may have to spend time getting statements and receipts from various sources. If you cannot produce the correct documents, you may have to pay additional taxes and be subject to penalties.

¶10,005   Recordkeeping for Individuals

You are not required to keep your records in a particular way. However, they should be kept in a manner that allows you and the IRS to determine your correct tax. Use a checkbook to keep a record of income and expenses. Record amounts, sources of deposits, and types of expenses. Keep documents such as receipts and sales slips that can help prove a deduction. Records should be kept in an orderly fashion and in a safe place. Keep them

---

[2]   Rev. Rul. 58-601, 1958-2 CB 81.

[3]   Reg. §1.6001-1(a).

[4]   *P. Mazzoni*, CA-3, 71-2 USTC ¶9764, 451 F2d 197.

[5]   Reg. §1.6001-1(e).

by year and type of income or expense. One method is to keep all records related to a particular item in a designated envelope.

Computerized records. Computer software packages can be used for recordkeeping. These packages are relatively easy to use and require little knowledge of bookkeeping and accounting. If you use a computerized system, you must be able to produce legible records of the information needed to determine your correct tax liability. In addition to your computerized records, you must keep proof of payment, receipts, and other documents to prove the amounts shown on your tax return.

Copies of tax returns. Keep copies of your tax returns as part of your tax records. They can help you prepare future tax returns, and you will need them if you file an amended return. Copies of your returns and other records can be helpful to your survivor or the executor or administrator of your estate. If necessary, you can request a copy of a return and all attachments (including Form W-2) from the IRS by using Form 4506, Request for Copy of Tax Return.

Basic Records. Basic records are documents that prove your income and expenses. If you own a home or investments, your basic records should contain documents related to those items. Table 1 lists documents you should keep as basic records.

Table 1. Records to Keep

FOR items concerning your:	KEEP as basic records:
Income	• Form(s) W-2 • Form(s) 1099 • Bank statements • Brokerage statements • Form(s) K-1
Expenses	• Sales slips Invoices • Receipts • Canceled checks or other proof of payment
Home	• Closing statements • Purchase and sales invoices • Proof of payment • Insurance records
Investments	• Brokerage statements • Mutual fund statements • Form(s) 1099 • Form(s) 2439
Legal Documents	• Birth certificates—eligibility for additional standard deduction amounts, dependency exemption issues, special provisions (e.g., credit for child and dependent care expenses, Kiddie Tax, child tax credit) • Real estate closing statements—sale price, basis, and expense of sale issues for both the buyer and seller • Divorce/separation agreements and decrees—filing status, alimony, and support issues • Leases—deduction and capitalized lease issues • Insurance policies • Contracts • Buy-sell agreements • Lawsuit decrees and settlement documents • Wills • Deed of gift and gift tax returns

Income. Basic records prove the amounts you report as taxable or non-taxable income on your tax return. If you receive a Form W-2, keep Copy C until you begin receiving social security benefits. This will help protect your benefits in case there is a question about your work record or earnings in a particular year and can be used to validate the information shown on your annual Social Security Statement.

Expenses. Basic records prove the expenses for which you claim a deduction (or credit) on your tax return. Deductions may include alimony, charitable contributions, mortgage interest, and real estate taxes. You may also have child care expenses for which you can claim a credit.

Personal Residence. Basic records are used to determine the basis or adjusted basis of your home and are used when the home is sold to determine if you have a gain or loss or to compute depreciation if you use part of your home for business or rental purposes. The records should show the purchase price, settlement or closing costs, and the cost of any improvements. You should also keep any information pertaining to casualty losses deducted and insurance reimbursements for casualty losses.

Investments. Basic records should enable you to determine your basis in an investment and whether you have a gain or loss when you sell it. Investments include stocks, bonds, and mutual funds. Your records should show the purchase price; sales price; and commissions and information pertaining to reinvested dividends, stock splits and dividends, load charges, and original issue discount (OID).

Proof of Payment. Keep these records to support certain amounts shown on your tax return. Proof of payment alone is not proof that the item claimed on your return is allowable. You should also keep other documents that will help prove that the item is allowable. Generally, you prove payment with a cash receipt, financial account statement, credit card statement, canceled check, or substitute check. If you make payments in cash, you should get a dated and signed receipt showing the amount and the reason for the payment. If you make payments by electronic funds transfer you may be able to prove payment with an account statement.

Account statements. You may be able to prove payment with a legible financial account statement prepared by your bank or other financial institution. These statements are accepted as proof of payment if they show the items reflected in Table 2.

Table 2. Proof of Payment

IF payment is by:	THEN the statement must show the:
Cash	• Amount • Payee's name • Transaction date
Check	• Check number • Amount • Payee's name • Date the check amount was posted to the account by the financial institution
Debit or credit card	• Amount charged • Payee's name • Transaction date
Electronic funds transfer	• Amount transferred • Payee's name • Date the transfer was posted to the account by the financial institution
Payroll deduction	• Amount • Payee code • Transaction date

Paycheck statements. You may have deductible expenses withheld from your paycheck, such as union dues or medical insurance premiums. Keep your year-end or final pay statements as proof of payment of these expenses.

.01   RECORDS FOR SPECIFIC ITEMS

Alimony. If you receive or pay alimony, keep a copy of your written separation agreement or the divorce, separate maintenance, or support decree. If you pay alimony, you will also need to know your former spouse's social security number.

Business Use of Your Home. You may be able to deduct certain expenses connected with the business use of your home. Keep records that show the part of your home that you use for business and the expenses related to that use.

Casualty and Theft Losses. To deduct a casualty or theft loss, you must be able to prove that you had a casualty or theft and be able to support the amount you claim.

- For a casualty loss, your records should show the type of casualty (car accident, fire, storm, etc.), when it occurred, that the loss was a direct result of the casualty, and that you were the owner of the property.
- For a theft loss, your records should show when you discovered your property was missing, that your property was stolen, and that you were the owner of the property.

Child Care Credit. Record the name, address, and taxpayer identification number for all persons or organizations that provide care for your child or dependent in your records. You can use Form W-10, Dependent Care Provider's Identification and Certification, or various other sources to get the information from the care provider.

Contributions. The kinds of records you must keep for charitable contributions depend on the amount of the contribution and whether the contribution is in cash.

- Contributions from which you benefit.   Generally, if you make a charitable contribution that is more than $75 and is partly for goods or services, the organization must give you a written statement indicating the portion of the contribution that is tax deductible.
- *Cash.*   Cash contributions include those paid by cash, check, credit card, or payroll deduction. For each cash contribution, you must keep one of the following:
  - A canceled check or other proof of payment,
  - A receipt from the organization showing the name of the organization, the amount, and date of the contribution, or
  - Other reliable written records that are reasonable under the circumstances and that include the name of the organization, the amount, and the date of the contribution; and
  - A written acknowledgment of your contribution from the organization.
- *Out-of-pocket expenses.*   Keep records of out-of-pocket expenses when you perform services for a charitable organization. If you use your car when doing volunteer work, record the name of the organization and the unreimbursed gas and oil expenses directly related to the volunteer work in a diary. If you do not want to keep records of your actual expenses, you can keep a log of the miles you drove your car for the charitable purpose and use the current standard mileage rate. Also keep records of parking fees, tolls, taxi fares, and bus fares.
- *Property.* For each contribution of property, keep:
  - A receipt from the organization showing:
    - The name of the organization,
    - The date and location of the contribution, and
    - A reasonably detailed description of the property;
  - A letter or other written communication from the organization containing the above information;
  - Reliable written records for each item of donated property including the:
    - Fair market value of the property at the time of the contribution,
    - Cost or other basis of the property, and
    - Terms of any conditions attached to the contribution.

Education Expenses. If you have the records to prove your expenses, you may be entitled to claim certain tax benefits for your education expenses. You may qualify to exclude from income items such as a qualified scholarship, interest on U.S. savings bonds, or reimbursement from your employer. You may also qualify for certain credits or deductions.

Exemptions. If you are claiming an exemption for a person under a multiple support agreement, get a signed statement from all other eligible individuals who could have claimed the exemption and keep these statements in your records.

Gambling Winnings and Losses. Keep an accurate diary of your winnings and losses including the:

- Date and type of gambling activity,
- Name and address or location of the gambling establishment,
- Names of other persons present with you at the gambling establishment, and
- Amount you won or lost.

Health Savings Account (HSA) and Medical Savings Account (MSA). For each qualified medical expense you deduct or pay with a distribution from your HSA or MSA, you must keep a record of the name and address of each person you paid and the amount and date of the payment.

Individual Retirement Arrangements (IRAs). Keep copies of the following forms and records until all distributions are made from your IRA(s).

- Form 5498, IRA Contribution Information, or similar statement received for each year showing contributions you made, distributions you received, and the value of your IRA(s).
- Form 1099-R, Distribution From Pensions, Annuities, Retirement or Profit-Sharing Plans, IRAs, Insurance Contracts, etc., received for each year you received a distribution.
- Form 8606, Nondeductible IRAs, for each year you made a nondeductible contribution to your IRA or received distributions from an IRA if you ever made nondeductible contributions.

Medical and Dental Expenses. In addition to records you keep of regular medical expenses, keep records on transportation expenses that are primarily for and essential to medical care. Record gas and oil expenses directly related to that transportation. If you do not want to keep records of your actual expenses, you can keep a log of the miles you drive your car for medical purposes and use the standard mileage rate. You should also keep records of any parking fees, tolls, taxi fares, and bus fares.

Mortgage Interest. If you paid mortgage interest of $600 or more, keep Form 1098, Mortgage Interest Statement, and your mortgage statement and loan information in your records.

Moving Expenses. Keep a record of qualified moving expenses relating to transportation of you, your family, and your household goods that are not reimbursed to your new place of employment.

Pensions and Annuities. Use the worksheet in your tax return instructions to figure the taxable part of your pension or annuity. Keep a copy of the completed worksheet until you fully recover your contributions.

Taxes. Form(s) W-2 and Form(s) 1099-R show state income tax withheld from your wages and pensions. Keep a copy of these forms to prove the amount of state withholding. If you made estimated state income tax payments, keep a copy of the form or your check(s).

- Keep copies of your state income tax returns. If you received a refund of state income taxes, the state may send you Form 1099-G, Certain Government Payments.
- Keep mortgage statements, tax assessments, or other documents as records of the real estate and personal property taxes you paid.
- If you deducted actual state and local general sales taxes instead of using the optional state sales tax tables, keep your actual receipts showing general sales taxes paid.

Tips. Keep a daily record to accurately report tip income. Use Form 4070A, Employee's Daily Record of Tips, which is found in Publication 1244, Employee's Daily Record of Tips and Report to Employer, to record your tips.

.03   RECORD RETENTION PERIOD

Keep records as long as they may be needed for the administration of any provision of the Internal Revenue Code. Generally, this means you must keep records that support items shown on your return until the period of limitations for that return runs out. The period of limitations is the period of time in which you can amend your return to claim a credit or refund or the IRS can assess additional tax. Table 3 contains the periods of limitations applicable to income tax returns. Unless otherwise stated, the years refer to the period beginning after the return was filed. Returns filed before the due date are treated as being filed on the due date.

Table 3. Period of Limitations

IF you:	THEN the period is:
1. Owe additional tax and (2), (3), and (4) do not apply to you	Three years
2. Do not report income that you should and it is more than 25 percent of the gross income shown on your return	Six years
3. File a fraudulent return	No limit
4. Do not file a return	No limit
5. File a claim for credit or refund after you filed your return	Later of three years or two years after tax was paid.
6. File a claim for a loss from worthless securities	seven years

Property. Keep records relating to property until the period of limitations expires for the year in which you dispose of the property in a taxable disposition. Keep these records to figure your basis for computing gain or loss when you sell or otherwise dispose of the property. Generally, if you received property in a nontaxable exchange, your basis in that property is the same as the basis of the property you gave up. Keep the records on the old property, as well as the new property, until the period of limitations expires for the year in which you dispose of the new property in a taxable disposition.

Keeping records for nontax purposes. When your records are no longer needed for tax purposes, do not discard them until you determine if they should be kept longer for other purposes. Your insurance company or creditors may require that certain records be kept for a longer period.

¶10,007   Recordkeeping for Businesses

Every business must keep records. Good records will help you:

- Monitor the progress of your business. Good records monitor the progress of your business. Records can show whether your business is improving, which items are selling, or what changes you need to make. Good records increase the likelihood of business success.
- Prepare your financial statements. You need good records to prepare accurate financial statements, including income (profit and loss) statements and balance sheets. These statements can help you when dealing with your bank or creditors and in managing your business.
- Identify source of receipts. Money or property can be received from many sources. Good records identify the source of these receipts and enable you to separate business from nonbusiness receipts and taxable from nontaxable income.
- Keep track of deductible expenses. Expenses may be overlooked when preparing your tax return unless you record them in a timely manner.
- Prepare your tax returns. Good records help you to prepare your tax return and support the income, expenses, and credits reported. Generally, these are the same records you use to monitor your business and prepare your financial statements.

- Support items reported on tax returns. If the IRS examines any of your tax returns, you may be asked to explain the items reported. A complete set of records will speed up the examination.

Except in a few cases, the law does not require any specific kind of records. You can choose any recordkeeping system suited to your business that clearly shows your income and expenses. The business you are in affects the type of records you need to keep for federal tax purposes. Set up your recordkeeping system using an accounting method that clearly shows your income for your tax year. If you are in more than one business, you should keep a complete and separate set of records for each business. A corporation should keep minutes of board of directors' meetings.

A recordkeeping system should include a summary of all business transactions. This summary is ordinarily made in your books (for example, accounting journals and ledgers). Your books must show your gross income, as well as your deductions and credits. For most small businesses, the business checkbook (discussed later) is the main recordkeeping source.

.01   SUPPORTING DOCUMENTS

Purchases, sales, payroll, and other transactions you have in your business generate supporting documents. Supporting documents include sales slips, paid bills, invoices, receipts, deposit slips, and canceled checks. These documents contain information you need to record in your books. It is important to keep these documents because they support the entries in your books and on your tax return. Keep them in an orderly fashion and in a safe place. For instance, organize them by year and type of income or expense.

Gross receipts. Gross receipts are the income you receive from your business. Keep the following supporting documents showing the amount and source of gross receipts.

- Cash register tapes.
- Bank deposit slips.
- Receipt books.
- Invoices.
- Credit card charge slips.
- Forms 1099-MISC.

Purchases. Purchases are the items you buy and resell to customers. If you are a manufacturer or producer, this includes the cost of all raw materials or parts purchased for manufacture into finished products. These records will help you determine the value of your inventory at the end of the year. Keep the following supporting documents showing the amount paid and that the amount was for purchases.

- Canceled checks.
- Cash register tape receipts.
- Credit card sales slips.
- Invoices.

Expenses. Expenses are costs incurred, other than purchases, to carry on your business. Keep the following supporting documents showing the amount paid and that the amount was for a business expense.

- Canceled checks.
- Cash register tapes.
- Account statements.
- Credit card sales slips.
- Invoices.
- Petty cash slips for small cash payments.

A petty cash fund is used to make payments without having to write checks for small amounts. Each time a payment is made, make out a petty cash slip and attach it to your receipt as proof of payment.

Travel, transportation, entertainment, and gift expenses. Specific recordkeeping rules apply to these expenses requiring the taxpayer to document the amount, time, place and business purpose of each expenditure. Failure to retain proper documentation for these expenses may result in their disallowance. Expenditures for meals and entertainment may be subject to partial disallowance.

Employment taxes. There are specific employment tax records you must keep. These are discussed in Publication 15, Circular E, Employer's Tax Guide.

Assets. Assets are the property, such as machinery and furniture you own and use in your business. Keep the following supporting documents to verify certain information about your business assets and to compute annual depreciation deductions and the gain or loss when the assets are sold.

- Purchase and sales invoices.
- Real estate closing statements.
- Canceled checks.
- When and how you acquired the asset.
- Purchase price.
- Cost of any improvements.
- Code Sec. 179 deduction taken.
- Deductions taken for depreciation.
- Deductions taken for casualty losses, such as losses resulting from fires or storms.
- How you used the asset.
- When and how you disposed of the asset.
- Selling price.
- Expenses of sale.

If you do not have a canceled check, you may be able to prove payment with certain financial account statements prepared by financial institutions. These include account statements prepared for the financial institution by a third party. Refer to Table 2 for items acceptable as Proof of Payment. Proof of payment of an amount, by itself, does not establish you are entitled to a tax deduction. Keep other documents, such as credit card sales slips and invoices, to show that you also incurred the cost.

There are many helpful IRS publications that offer examples of the types of records that should be kept for various income and expense items. A list of these publications is found in Table 4.

Table 4. IRS Publications

The following IRS publications provide additional information about documents that you should keep for tax purposes:

- 463, Travel, Entertainment, Gift and Car Expenses
- 501, Exemptions, Standard Deduction, and Filing Information
- 502, Medical and Dental Expenses
- 503, Child and Dependent Care Expenses
- 504, Divorced or Separated Individuals
- 521, Moving Expenses
- 523, Selling Your Home
- 524, Credit for the Elderly or the Disabled
- 526, Charitable Contributions
- 529, Miscellaneous Deductions
- 531, Reporting Tip Income
- 538, Methods for Valuing Inventory
- 547, Casualties, Disasters, and Thefts
- 550, Investment Income and Expenses
- 564, Mutual Fund Distributions

- 575, Pension and Annuity Income
- 584, Casualty, Disaster, and Theft Loss Workbook (Personal-Use Property)
- 587, Business Use of Your Home
- 590, Individual Retirement Arrangements (IRAs)
- 936, Home Mortgage Interest Deduction
- 946, Code Sec. 179 Deduction and the Special Depreciation Allowance
- 969, Health Savings Accounts and Other Tax-Favored Health Plans
- 970, Tax Benefits for Education.
- 3207, a CD for small businesses. or any taxpayer about to start a business

.03   RECORDING BUSINESS TRANSACTIONS

Business transactions are ordinarily summarized in books called journals and ledgers.
- A journal is a book where you record each business transaction shown on your supporting documents. You may have to keep separate journals for transactions that occur frequently.
- A ledger is a book that contains the totals from all of your journals. It is organized into different accounts.

Whether you keep journals and ledgers and how you keep them depends on the type of business you are in. For example, a recordkeeping system for a small business might include the following items:
- Business checkbook
- Daily summary of cash receipts
- Monthly summary of cash receipts
- Check disbursements journal
- Depreciation worksheet
- Employee compensation record

The system used to record business transactions will be more effective if you follow good recordkeeping practices. For example, record expenses when they occur, and identify the source of recorded receipts. Generally, it is best to record transactions on a daily basis.

Business checkbook. One of the first things you should do when you start a business is open a business checking account. Keep your business account separate from your personal checking account. The business checkbook is your basic source of information for recording your business expenses. You should deposit all daily receipts in your business checking account. You should check your account for errors by reconciling it. Use a checkbook that allows enough space to identify the source of deposits as business income, personal funds, or loans. Note on the deposit slip the source of the deposit and keep copies of all slips. Make all payments by check to document business expenses. Write checks payable to yourself only when making withdrawals from your business for personal use. Avoid writing checks payable to cash. If you must write a check for cash to pay a business expense, include the receipt for the cash payment in your records. If you cannot get a receipt for a cash payment, you should make an adequate explanation in your records at the time of payment. Use the business account for business purposes only. Indicate the source of deposits and the type of expense in the checkbook.

Reconciling the checking account. When you receive your bank statement, make sure the statement, your checkbook, and your books agree. The statement balance may not agree with the balance in your checkbook and books if the statement:
- Includes bank charges you did not enter in your books and subtract from your checkbook balance, or
- Does not include deposits made after the statement date or checks that did not clear your account before the statement date.

By reconciling your checking account, you will:
- Verify how much money you have in the account,
- Make sure that your checkbook and books reflect all bank charges and the correct balance in the checking account, and
- Correct any errors in your bank statement, checkbook, and books.

Reconcile your checking account each month. Begin with the balance shown in your checkbook at the end of the previous month and then add the total cash deposited during the month and subtract the total cash disbursements. The result should agree with your checkbook balance at the end of the month. If the result does not agree, you may have made an error in recording a check or deposit. You can find the error by:

1. Adding the amounts on your check stubs and comparing that total with the total in the "amount of check" column in your check disbursements journal. If the totals do not agree, check the individual amounts to see if an error was made in your check stub record or in the related entry in your check disbursements journal.
2. Adding the deposit amounts in your checkbook. Compare that total with the monthly total in your cash receipt book, if you have one. If the totals do not agree, check the individual amounts to find any errors.

When your checkbook balance agrees with the balance figured from the journal entries, you may begin reconciling your checkbook with the bank statement. Many banks print a reconciliation worksheet on the back of the statement. To reconcile your account, follow these steps.

1. Compare the deposits listed on the bank statement with the deposits shown in your checkbook. Note all differences in the dollar amounts.
2. Compare each canceled check, including both check number and dollar amount, with the entry in your checkbook. Note all differences in the dollar amounts. Mark the check number in the checkbook as having cleared the bank. After accounting for all checks returned by the bank, those not marked in your checkbook are your outstanding checks.
3. Prepare a bank reconciliation. One is illustrated later under *Sample Record System.*
4. Update your checkbook and journals for items shown on the reconciliation as not recorded (such as service charges) or recorded incorrectly.

The adjusted bank statement balance should now equal your adjusted checkbook balance. If you still have differences, repeat the previous steps to find the errors.

.05   BOOKKEEPING SYSTEM

A single-entry system of bookkeeping is the simplest to maintain, but is not suitable for most businesses. A double-entry system is usually preferable because it has built-in checks and balances to assure accuracy and control.

Single-entry. A single-entry system is based on the income statement (profit or loss statement). It can be a simple and practical system if you are starting a small business. The system records the flow of income and expenses through the use of:

1. A daily summary of cash receipts, and
2. Monthly summaries of cash receipts and disbursements.

Double-entry. A double-entry bookkeeping system uses journals and ledgers. Transactions are first entered in a journal and then posted to ledger accounts. These accounts show income, expenses, assets (property a business owns), liabilities (debts of a business), and net worth (excess of assets over liabilities). The income and expense accounts are closed at the end of each tax year. Asset, liability, and net worth accounts remain open on a permanent basis. The double-entry system is self-balancing because every transaction is recorded as a debit entry in one account and as a credit entry in another. Under this system, the total debits must equal the total credits after the journal entries are posted to the ledger accounts. If the amounts do not balance, the error is found and corrected. An example of a journal entry exhibiting a payment of rent in October is:

Date	Description of Entry	Debit	Credit
Oct. 5	Rent expense	300.00	
	Cash		300.00

Computerized Accounting Systems. Computer software packages can be purchased in many retail stores or from on-line vendors. These packages are very helpful and relatively easy to use; they require very little knowledge of bookkeeping and accounting. If you use a computerized system, you must be able to produce sufficient legible records to support and verify entries made on your return and determine your correct tax liability. To meet this qualification, Rev. Proc. 98-25,[6] requires that the machine-sensible records must reconcile with your books and return. These records must provide enough detail to identify the underlying source documents. You must also keep all machine-sensible records and a complete description of the computerized portion of your recordkeeping system. This documentation must be sufficiently detailed to show all of the following items.

- Functions being performed as the data flows through the system.
- Controls used to ensure accurate and reliable processing.
- Controls used to prevent the unauthorized addition, alteration, or deletion of retained records.
- Charts of accounts and detailed account descriptions.

Electronic Storage System. Records maintained in an electronic storage system are accepted for recordkeeping purposes if the system complies with Rev. Proc. 97-22.[7] An electronic storage system is one that either images hardcopy (paper) books and records or transfers computerized books and records to an electronic storage media, such as an optical disk.

How Long To Keep Records. You must keep records as long as they may be needed for the administration of any provision of the Internal Revenue Code. Generally, this means you must keep records that support an item of income or deduction on a return until the period of limitations for that return runs out. Refer to Table 3 for the period of limitations discussed earlier. Keep copies of your filed tax returns. They help in preparing future tax returns and making computations if you file an amended return.

Employment taxes. If you have employees, keep all employment tax records for at least four years after the date the tax becomes due or is paid, whichever is later.

Assets. Keep records relating to property until the period of limitations expires for the year in which you dispose of the property in a taxable disposition. You must keep these records to figure any depreciation, amortization, or depletion deduction, and to figure your basis for computing gain or loss when you sell or otherwise dispose of the property. Generally, if you received property in a nontaxable exchange, your basis in that property is the same as the basis of the property you gave up, increased by any money you paid. Keep the records on the old property, as well as on the new property, until the period of limitations expires for the year in which you dispose of the new property in a taxable disposition.

¶10,009   Sample Recordkeeping System

The following seven worksheets illustrate a single-entry system used by Patrick Evans, the sole proprietor of an auto body repair shop. Patrick has one part-time employee, uses the cash method of accounting and purchases parts only as they are used. The following sample records should not be viewed as a recommendation of how to keep your records, but only to illustrate the business records that should be maintained.

---

[6]   Rev. Proc. 98-25, 1998-1 CB 689.
[7]   Rev. Proc. 97-22, 1997-1, CB 652.

1. Daily Summary of Cash Receipts	Year:	2012
	Month:	April
	Day:	3
Cash sales:	$263.60	
Sales tax:	$4.20	
TOTAL RECEIPTS:		$267.80
Cash on hand		
Cash in register (including unspent petty cash)		
Coins:	$23.75	
Bills:	$143.00	
Checks:	$134.05	
TOTAL CASH IN REGISTER:		$300.80
Add: Petty cash slips:	$17.00	
TOTAL CASH:		$317.80
Less: Change and petty cash		
Petty cash slips:	$17.00	
Coins and bills (unspent petty cash):	$33.00	
TOTAL CHANGE AND PETTY CASH FUND:		$50.00
TOTAL CASH RECEIPTS:		$267.80

2. Monthly Summary of Cash Receipts			Year:	2012
			Month:	April
Day	Net Sales	Sales Tax	Daily Receipts	Deposit
1	$133.30	$2.13	$135.43	
2	$188.59	$2.85	$191.44	$326.87
3	$263.60	$4.20	$267.80	
4	$212.00	$3.39	$215.39	
5	$194.40	$3.10	$197.50	$680.69
7	$222.40	$3.54	$225.94	
8	$231.15	$3.68	$234.83	
9	$137.50	$2.13	$139.63	$600.40
10	$187.90	$2.99	$190.89	
11	$207.56	$3.31	$210.87	$401.76
12	$128.95	$2.05	$131.00	
14	$231.40	$3.77	$235.17	
15	$201.28	$3.21	$204.49	
16	$88.01	$1.40	$89.41	$660.07
17	$210.95	$3.36	$214.31	
18	$221.80	$3.53	$225.33	$439.64
19	$225.15	$3.59	$228.74	
21	$221.93	$3.52	$225.45	
22	$133.53	$2.13	$135.66	$589.85
23	$130.84	$2.08	$132.92	
24	$216.37	$3.45	$219.82	$352.74
25	$220.05	$3.50	$223.55	
26	$197.80	$3.15	$200.95	
28	$272.49	$4.34	$276.83	$701.33
29	$150.64	$2.40	$153.04	
30	$224.05	$3.56	$227.61	$380.65
Total	$5,053.64	$80.36	$5,134.00	$5,134.00

3. Check Disbursements Journal Year: 2012 Month: April

Day	Paid To	Check #	Amount	Materials	Gross Payroll	Federal Withholding Tax	FICA-Social Security	FICA-Medicare	State Withholding Tax	Employer's FICA Tax	Electric	Interest	Rent	Telephone	Truck/Auto	Drawing Account	Other Accounts	
3	Dale Advertising	74	$85.00														Advertising	$85.00
4	City Treasurer	75	$35.00														License	$35.00
4	Auto Parts, Inc.	76	$203.00	$203.00														
4	John E. Marks	77	$214.11		$260.00	$(20.00)	$(16.12)	$(3.77)	$(6.00)									
6	Henry Brown	78	$250.00													$250.00		
6	Ace Office Supplies	79	$36.00														Office Supplies	$36.00
6	Joe's Service Station	80	$74.50	$29.50											$45.00			
6	ABC Auto Paint	81	$137.50	$137.50														
7	Henry Brown	82	$225.00													$225.00		
14	Telephone Co.	83	$27.00											$27.00				
15	National Bank (Tax Deposit)	84	$119.56			$40.00	$32.24	$7.54		$39.78								
18	National Bank	85	$90.09									$18.09					Loan	$72.00
18	Auto Parts, Inc.	86	$472.00	$472.00														
18	Henry Brown	87	$275.00													$275.00		
18	John E. Marks	88	$214.11		$260.00	$(20.00)	$(16.12)	$(3.77)	$(6.00)									
21	Electric Co.	89	$175.30								$175.30							
21	M.B. Ignition	90	$66.70	$66.70														
21	Baker's Fender Co.	91	$9.80	$9.80														
21	Petty Cash	92	$17.00	$15.00													Postage	$2.00
21	Henry Brown	93	$225.00													$225.00		
25	Baker's Fender Co.	94	$150.00	$150.00														
25	Enterprise Properties	95	$300.00										$300.00					
25	State Treasurer	96	$12.00						$12.00									
25	State Treasurer	97	$65.00														Sales Tax	$65.00
	Subtotal		$3,478.67	$1,083.50	$520.00	$-	$-	$-	$-	$39.78	$175.30	$18.09	$300.00	$27.00	$45.00	$975.00		$295.00
	Bank service charge		$10.00															$10.00
	Totals		$3,488.67	$1,083.50	$520.00	$-	$-	$-	$-	$39.78	$175.30	$18.09	$300.00	$27.00	$45.00	$975.00		$305.00

4. Bank Reconciliation	Year:	2012
	Month:	April
Balance per bank statement		$1,458.12
Add: Deposits not credited:		
28	$701.33	
31	$516.08	
Total Deposits not credited:		$1,217.41
Subtotal		$2,675.53
Less: Outstanding checks:		
90	$66.70	
91	$9.80	
94	$150.00	
95	$300.00	
Total Outstanding Checks		$526.50
Adjusted balance per bank statement		$2,149.03
Balance per checkbook		$2,153.03
Add:		
Error on deposit on the 8th		$6.00
Subtract:		$2,159.03
Bank service charge		$(10.00)
Adjusted balance per checkbook		$2,149.03
Difference: Bank to Book		$-

5. Employee Compensation Record	Year:	2012				
	Month:	April				
Name:	John Marks					
Address:	1 Elm St. Anywhere, NJ, 07101					
Phone	555-6075					
Social Security #	567-00-8901					
Date of Birth	12/21/1969					
# of Exemptions	1/Single					
Deductions						
Pay Period Ending	Bi-Weekly Salary	Social Security	Medicare	Federal Income Tax	State Income Tax	Net Pay
4/2/2012	$260.00	$16.12	$3.77	$20.00	$6.00	$214.11
4/16/2012	$260.00	$16.12	$3.77	$20.00	$6.00	$214.11
Total for Month	$520.00	$32.24	$7.54	$40.00	$12.00	$428.22

6. Depreciation Worksheet Assets purchased in 2010:	Date placed in Service	Cost	Depreciation Method	Recovery Period	Rate	Deduction
Used Equipment	1-Jan	$3,000	200% DB/ HY	7	14.29%	$428.70
Used Pickup Truck	1-Feb	$8,000	200% DB/ HY	5	20.00%	$1,600.00
Used Tow truck	1-Mar	$30,000	200% DB/ HY	5	20.00%	$6,000.00
Used Engine Hoist	1-Mar	$4,000	200% DB/ HY	7	14.29%	$571.60
Total		$45,000				$8,600.30

7. Annual Summary		
Cash Receipts		$60,644
Expenses:		
Materials	$13,002	
Gross Payroll	$6,240	
Employer's FICA Tax	$477	
Electric	$2,104	
Interest	$1,217	
Rent	$3,600	
Telephone	$324	
Tow-Truck	$1,390	
Miscellaneous	$2,256	
Total Cash Expenses		$30,610
Pick-up Truck @.565 per mile	7,850	$4,435
Depreciation Expense (depreciation on truck not allowed, mileage method used)		$7,000
Total Expenses		$42,045
Net Profit		$18,599
Nondeductible items:		
Drawing Account	$11,700	
Asset Purchases	$45,000	
Loan Payments	$8,640	

1. **Daily Summary of Cash Receipts.** This summary is a record of cash sales for the day. It accounts for cash at the beginning and end of the day. The cash sales entry is from a cash register tape and equals the total of the daily cash sale slips and any other cash received that day. The total cash receipts for April 3 of $267.80 including cash sales of $263.60 and sales tax collected of $4.20, is then entered on the Monthly Summary of Cash Receipts.
   - **Petty cash fund.** Petty cash is used to make payments without having to write checks for small amounts. Each time a payment is made from this fund, a petty cash slip is made out and attached to the receipt as proof of payment. The petty cash fund has a fixed amount of $50. The total of the unspent petty cash and the total of the petty cash slips should always equal the fixed amount of the fund.

When the total of the petty cash slips approach the fixed amount, the fund is replentished by writing a check to "Petty Cash" for the total of the outstanding slips. This restores the fund to its fixed amount of $50 and records the expenses in the monthly check disbursements journal. (See the **Check Disbursements Journal** entry for check number 92.)

2. ***Monthly Summary of Cash Receipts.*** This shows the income activity for the month. The total monthly net sales shown in this summary are included in the Annual Summary.

   - To figure total monthly net sales, Patrick reduces the total monthly receipts by the sales tax imposed on his customers and turned over to the state. He cannot take a deduction for sales tax turned over to the state because he only collected the tax. He does not include the tax in his income.

3. ***Check Disbursements Journal.*** Patrick enters checks written on the business checking account. Each entry includes the date, payee check number, and amount. The amount is then allocated among the various expenses in the columns provided in the journal.

   - Frequent expenses have their own headings across the sheet. He enters in a separate column expenses that require comparatively numerous or large payments each month, such as materials, gross payroll, and rent. Under the *General Accounts* column, he enters small expenses that normally have only one or two monthly payments, such as licenses and postage.
   - Patrick does not pay personal or nonbusiness expenses by checks drawn on the business account. If he did, he would record them in the journal, even though he could not deduct them as business expenses.
   - The total of all the monthly expenses are included in the Annual Summary.

4. ***Bank Reconciliation.*** Patrick reconciles his checkbook with his bank statement and prepares a monthly bank reconciliation.

   - The starting point is the bank statement balance.
   - Patrick compares the deposits listed on the bank statement with deposits shown in his checkbook. Two deposits shown in his checkbook— $701.33 and $516.08—were not on his bank statement. He enters these two amounts on the bank reconciliation. He adds them to the bank statement balance of $1,458.12 to arrive at a subtotal of $2,675.53.
   - After comparing each canceled check with his checkbook, Patrick found four outstanding checks totaling $526.50. He subtracts this amount from the subtotal in (2). The result of $2,149.03 is the adjusted bank statement balance.
   - Patrick enters his checkbook balance on the bank reconciliation.
   - Patrick discovered that he mistakenly entered a deposit of $600.40 in his checkbook as $594.40. He adds the difference of $6.00 to the checkbook balance of $2,153.03. The $10.00 bank service charge on his bank statement is subtracted from the checkbook balance. The result is the adjusted checkbook balance of $2,149.03. Since this equals his adjusted bank statement balance computed, the account is reconciled and no further analysis is required.
   - The only book adjustment Patrick needs to make is to the Check Disbursements Journal for the $10 bank service charge. He does not need to adjust the Monthly Summary of Cash Receipts because he correctly entered the January 8 deposit of $600.40 in that record.

5. ***Employee Compensation Record.*** This record includes the employee's Gross and Net Pay for the period. The deductions withheld in computing the employee's net pay.

6. ***Depreciation Worksheet.*** This worksheet shows the information used to compute the depreciation allowed on the business assets. The depreciation expense is computed using the modified accelerated cost recovery system (MACRS). He purchased and placed in service several used assets that do not qualify for the Code Sec. 179

deduction or the special depreciation allowance. Patrick uses the information in the worksheet to complete Form 4562, *Depreciation and Amortization* (not illustrated).

7. ***Annual Summary.*** This annual summary of monthly cash receipts and expense totals provides the final amounts to enter on Patrick's tax return. He figures the cash receipts total from the total of monthly cash receipts shown in the *Monthly Summary of Cash Receipts.* He figures the expense totals from the totals of monthly expense items shown in the *Check Disbursements Journal.* As in the journal, he keeps each major expense in a separate column.

- Patrick carries the cash receipts total shown in the annual summary to Part I of Schedule C (not illustrated). He carries the total for materials to Part II of Schedule C.
- A business that keeps materials and supplies on hand generally must complete the inventory lines in Part III of Schedule C. There are no inventories of materials and supplies in this example since parts and supplies are purchased on a per-job basis.
- Annual totals for interest, rent, taxes, and wages on the appropriate lines in Part II of Schedule C. The total for taxes and licenses includes the employer's share of social security and Medicare taxes, and the business license fee. He enters the total of other annual business expenses on the "Other expenses" line of Schedule C.
- The auto expense for the pick-up truck is based upon the 2013 standard mileage rate of $.565 cents per mile. Patrick has records showing that the truck was driven for 7,850 business miles. Any operating expenses relating to the pick-up truck were omitted from the cash expenses reported above.
- The depreciation expense is taken from the Depreciation worksheet. However, the depreciation expense on the truck was omitted since the mileage method was used.
- Note that the cash withdrawn from the business (Drawing Account) and the loan payments are not deductible in computing net profit on Schedule C.

This concludes our discussion of the record keeping requirements of individual and business taxpayers.

¶10,011   Tax Preparer Workpapers

Workpapers are written records kept by the tax return preparer to document the procedures applied, the tests performed, the information obtained, and the conclusions reached in the preparation of the tax return. Workpapers may include information obtained from the taxpayer or third parties. Workpapers create a record of the relevant evidence, procedures, tests, and analyses to support positions taken on the tax return. Workpapers must include safeguards to protect confidential information. Workpapers include the following:

- Work performed before, during, and after contact with the taxpayer.
- Research activities.
- Summaries of telephone conversations and other contacts with the taxpayer and third parties.

Research activities should be documented with a "Memo to the file" which summarizes the facts, identifies the issues to be researched, gives a conclusion (recommendation) for each of the issues, and provides a summary of the authority or authorities used in making the recommendation. A sample template for a memo to the file is shown in **Figure** 1.

Figure 1:

TEMPLATE FOR TAX RESEARCH MEMO TO THE FILES

MEMO TO:	The Files
FROM:	[person preparing memo]
SUBJECT:	[taxpayer name and identifying number]
DATE PREPARED:	[date memo prepared]
REVIEWED BY:	[person reviewing memo]
DATE REVIEWED:	[date memo reviewed]

Relevant Facts:

[Relevant facts are summarized]

Specific Issues:

(1)

[Identify issue to be researched]

(2)

[If more than one issue, identify each issue separately]

Conclusion:

(1)

[Make a recommendation for action to be taken on issue researched]:

(2)

[If more than one issue, make a recommendation
for action to be taken on each issue separately]

Support (Authority):

(1)

[Summarize authority or authorities used to make the recommendation for issue (1)]

(2)

[If more than one issue, summarize authority or authorities used to make the recommendation
for each issue]

Actions to be taken:
- Prepare letter, review results with client.
- Place copy of tax and legal documents in the client file
- [List other actions as appropriate]

  - *Identifying Relevant Facts*. The practitioner must make reasonable efforts to deter-mine all relevant *facts* and disclose them with the opinion. Any *factual assumptions* made need to be disclosed with the opinion, and any factual assumptions that are unreasonable (for example, a projection from a nonqualified person) must be ignored. All *factual representations* must also be disclosed, and any opinion on such should not be based on the opinion of taxpayers and others, particularly with regard to such concepts as business purpose and showing a profit independent of tax benefits.

- ***Relating the Law to Facts***. The opinion must include a discussion of the law as it relates to the facts of the case. The discussion must be based on and supported by reasonable legal assumptions and conclusions, and must not rely on diminished chances of an IRS audit.
- ***Evaluating and Discussing Significant Tax Issues***. The practitioner must evaluate and discuss all significant tax issues. A *significant tax issue* is one in which the IRS would have a reasonable basis for a successful challenge, and its resolution could have a significant tax impact. Exceptions to the general requirement are provided for limited scope opinions and reliance opinions (where issues are evaluated by another person). Detailed supporting reasons must be discussed for (1) significant issues concluded in the taxpayer's favor (i.e., "more likely than not"), (2) significant issues with no conclusion, and (3) significant issues that are not in the taxpayer's favor (a separate disclosure is required for these issues). *Conclusions should **never** be influenced by the taxpayer's odds of having the return selected for audit (i.e., the audit lottery).*
- ***Overall Conclusion***. The opinion must contain the practitioner's overall conclusion regarding the treatment of significant tax issues, a statement that the treatment is proper, and the reasons for that conclusion. If the practitioner is unable to reach a conclusion, a similar discussion is required.

Individual Tax Return Preparation Workpapers. When preparing an individual tax return, the first step is usually to send the taxpayer a client organizer in which the taxpayer can list all sources of income and deductions and provide descriptive information pertaining to dependency exemptions and credits. The organizer should also contain questions regarding asset acquisitions and dispositions made during the year including sales or purchase prices. Unless the tax return preparer has reason to doubt the veracity of the information included in the organizer, the tax return can be prepared using "information provided by the taxpayer without verification." However, if the tax return preparer has a reasonable doubt regarding the validity of the information he or she should request additional information and include appropriate copies of supporting documents in the workpapers. Copies of third party documents, such as 1099s, W-2s etc. should be retained. In addition, the tax workpaper file should include copies of prior year's tax returns and workpapers relating to loss and credit carryforwards and any other information needed to prepare the next year's tax return. The file should also contain copies of e-mails and other written communications between the tax return preparer and the taxpayer. Contemporaneous records of telephone conversations should be included in the file, including the date, time, and summary of the phone conversation and the name of the person in the firm who handled the phone call. Most client organizers can be up to 60 pages or more. Thus, it is not feasible to reproduce a complete organizer in this chapter. **Figure 2** lists the Table of Contents for a typical individual tax organizer.

Figure 2:

ORGANIZER			Page 1
1040	**US**	**Topical Index**	

TOPIC	FORM	TOPIC	FORM
Adoption expenses	37	Medical and dental expenses	25
Alimony paid	24	Miscellaneous income	14.1
Alimony received	14.1	Miscellaneous itemized deductions	25 p3, 25 p4
Business income and expenses	16	Mortgage interest expense	25 p2
Business use of home	29	Moving expenses	17, 27
Capital gains/losses	17	Partnership information	20.1, 20.2
Charitable contributions	25 p2, 25 p3, 26	Pension distributions	10, 13.1, 13.2
Child and dependent care expenses	33.1, 33.2	Purchase of business assets	22 p2
Children's interest/dividend income	44	Qualified Plan (Keogh) contributions	24
Client information	1	Qualified tuition programs	14.3
Dependents	2	Railroad retirement benefits	14.1
Direct deposit of refund	3, 6, 7.1	Real estate taxes paid	25
Dividend income	11, 12	REMIC information	20.3, 20.4
Education expenses	38	Rental & royalty income & expenses	18
Education Savings Accounts	14.3	S corporation information	20.1, 20.2
Employee business expenses	30 p1	Sale of business assets	22
Estate information	20.3, 20.4	Sale of home	17, 27
Estate tax	25 p4	Sale of stocks and bonds	17
Estimated taxes	3, 6, 7.1	Sales and use taxes paid	25
Farm income and expenses	19	Self-employed elective deferrals	24
Foreign information	31.1	SEP contributions	24
Foreign wages and other income	31.2	SIMPLE contributions	24
Gambling income/losses	10, 13.1, 13.2	Social security benefits received	14.1
Health insurance premiums (self-employed)	24	State and local tax refunds	14.2
Health savings accounts	32.1	Student loan interest paid	24
Household employment taxes	42	Taxes paid	25
Installment sales	17 p2	Tax return preparation fee	25 p3
Interest income	11, 12	Trust information	20.3, 20.4
Interest paid	25 p2	Unemployment compensation	14.2
Investment expense	25 p3	Vacation home	18, 18 p2
Investment interest expense	25 p2	Vehicle information	22 p3, 30 p2
IRA contributions	24	Wages, salaries, tips	10, 13.1, 13.2
IRA distributions	10, 13.1, 13.2		

The AICPA also offers many useful Tax Practice Guides and Checklists to ensure that the appropriate and timely information is obtained from the taxpayer. These guides and checklists can be obtained in electronic format from the Tax Section of the AICPA. **Figure 3** lists the Table of Contents for the AICPA's Guides and **Figure 4** lists the available organizers.

Figure 3:

Main Contents

Tax Organizers

Tax Practice Management Forms

Tax Form Preparation Guides

User Inserts

U.S. Estate Tax Return (706)

U.S. Gift Tax Return (709)

Return of Organization Exempt From Income Tax (990)

Exempt Organization Business Income Tax Return Checklist (990-T)

Return of Private Foundation (990-PF)

Individual Tax Return (1040)

Estate and Trust Tax Return (1041)

Partnership Tax Return (1065)

C Corporation Tax Return (1120)

S Corporation Tax Return (1120S)

Employee Benefit Plan Return (5500 Series)

State and Local Tax Practice Guides

Miscellaneous Practice Guides

For additional practice guides and other informative and useful tax division products please visit the Tax Division Web site at tax.aicpa.org

Figure 4:

Tax Organizers

These tax organizers have been designed to assist in compiling the information needed to prepare the respective returns for 2009. The following pages contain many of the common income items, expenses, deductions, and credits, as well as questions that determine the proper handling of these items.

The organizer can be completed by the client or staff who is preparing the tax return. Download the files in Word or PDF format. The Word format allows you to easily modify the files to suit your needs.

	Adobe (.pdf)	Word (.doc)
Estate Tax (706)	Download Now	Download Now
Gift Tax (709)	Download Now	Download Now
Tax-Exempt Organization (990)—Expanded Version	Download Now	Download Now
Individual (1040)	Download Now	Download Now
Fiduciary (1041)	Download Now	Download Now
Partnership (1065)—Short Version	Download Now	Download Now
Partnership (1065)—Expanded Version	Download Now	Download Now
Corporation (1120 and 1120S)—Short and Expanded Versions	Download Now	Download Now
Qualified Retirement Plan (5500)	Download Now	Download Now

If the taxpayer is comfortable with entering information into a computer, an on-line tax organizer can be used. **Figure 5** summarizes the features of TaxNotebook, an online tax organizer from CCH, a Wolters Kluwer business. One of the major benefits of an online organizer is the ability to import the data into compatible tax preparation software, reducing data entry errors and saving hours of data entry time. Tax Notebook can automatically provide input to capture third party documents such as closing statements. The data from Tax Notebook can be imported into the ProSystem *fx* Tax Engagement system discussed later. Tax Notebook runs on any PC with Internet access. A client's progress can be tracked so that the tax preparer will know exactly when the Tax Notebook is complete. The information can be reviewed online and downloaded to a server for seamless integration into ProSystem *fx* Tax. In this case, the completed organizer can then be printed out, or stored electronically if the tax preparer is using an electronic document management system (discussed later).

Figure 5:

■ ONLINE TAX ORGANIZER

Revolutionize the way you collect your clients' tax data, process their tax returns, and promote your firm's services.

Tax
Document
Engagement
Fixed Assets
Outsource
Planning
Practice
Profit Driver
Site Builder
Trial Balance
Write-Up

Tax Notebook

Eliminate the administrative and mailing costs associated with paper tax organizers, and enjoy a secure transfer of data with your clients.

Tax Notebook, our online tax organizer, delivers expanded levels of convenience and technology that will improve your interaction with existing clients and help you reach potential new ones. Tax Notebook is a dynamic web application – not just a static electronic copy of the paper organizer – which means the program can automatically adapt to your client's changing tax situation. For example, if a client has a new rental property, the system will automatically provide input to capture all of the new information.

The following are just a few of the many benefits Tax Notebook offers your firm:

■ Import Tax Notebook data seamlessly into ProSystem *fx* Tax and save hours of data entry time.

■ Drive clients to your website where they'll quickly learn the full scope of services offered by your firm.

■ Enhance your professional image with a fully customized Tax Notebook, complete with a personalized Welcome Page that includes your firm name and logo.

■ Populate Tax Notebook with last year's Pro Forma information, quickly and accurately.

■ Monitor and quickly track the status of each client's Tax Notebook through the powerful status system included within the Tax Notebook Toolkit.

■ Marketing materials (postcards, flyers, sample letter and email text) are available to help you promote Tax Notebook to your clients.

■ Provides for import of W-2 data from a variety of payroll providers.

■ Import Schedule D and 1099-B data from GainsKeeper®Pro™.

THE TAX NOTEBOOK PROCESS IS AS EASY AS...

1 Using any PC with Internet access, your clients conveniently access their personalized Tax Notebook directly from a link on your firm's website (optional) and are guided through a streamlined tax interview.

2 Use the powerful online status system to track your clients' progress so you know exactly when their Tax Notebooks are complete.

3 Review completed Tax Notebooks online, and then download the information to your local system for seamless integration into ProSystem *fx* Tax.

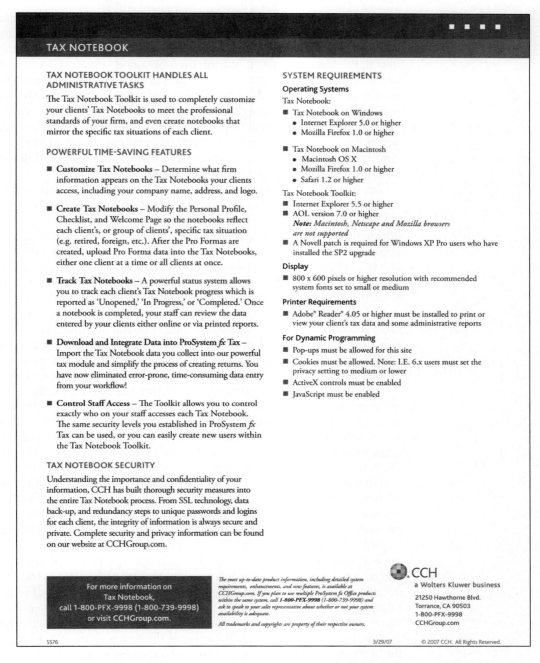

TAX NOTEBOOK

TAX NOTEBOOK TOOLKIT HANDLES ALL ADMINISTRATIVE TASKS

The Tax Notebook Toolkit is used to completely customize your clients' Tax Notebooks to meet the professional standards of your firm, and even create notebooks that mirror the specific tax situations of each client.

POWERFUL TIME-SAVING FEATURES

- **Customize Tax Notebooks** – Determine what firm information appears on the Tax Notebooks your clients access, including your company name, address, and logo.

- **Create Tax Notebooks** – Modify the Personal Profile, Checklist, and Welcome Page so the notebooks reflect each client's, or group of clients', specific tax situation (e.g. retired, foreign, etc.). After the Pro Formas are created, upload Pro Forma data into the Tax Notebooks, either one client at a time or all clients at once.

- **Track Tax Notebooks** – A powerful status system allows you to track each client's Tax Notebook progress which is reported as 'Unopened,' 'In Progress,' or 'Completed.' Once a notebook is completed, your staff can review the data entered by your clients either online or via printed reports.

- **Download and Integrate Data into ProSystem fx Tax** – Import the Tax Notebook data you collect into our powerful tax module and simplify the process of creating returns. You have now eliminated error-prone, time-consuming data entry from your workflow!

- **Control Staff Access** – The Toolkit allows you to control exactly who on your staff accesses each Tax Notebook. The same security levels you established in ProSystem fx Tax can be used, or you can easily create new users within the Tax Notebook Toolkit.

TAX NOTEBOOK SECURITY

Understanding the importance and confidentiality of your information, CCH has built thorough security measures into the entire Tax Notebook process. From SSL technology, data back-up, and redundancy steps to unique passwords and logins for each client, the integrity of information is always secure and private. Complete security and privacy information can be found on our website at CCHGroup.com.

SYSTEM REQUIREMENTS

Operating Systems

Tax Notebook:

- Tax Notebook on Windows
  - Internet Explorer 5.0 or higher
  - Mozilla Firefox 1.0 or higher

- Tax Notebook on Macintosh
  - Macintosh OS X
  - Mozilla Firefox 1.0 or higher
  - Safari 1.2 or higher

Tax Notebook Toolkit:

- Internet Explorer 5.5 or higher
- AOL version 7.0 or higher
  Note: *Macintosh, Netscape and Mozilla browsers are not supported*
- A Novell patch is required for Windows XP Pro users who have installed the SP2 upgrade

Display

- 800 x 600 pixels or higher resolution with recommended system fonts set to small or medium

Printer Requirements

- Adobe® Reader® 4.05 or higher must be installed to print or view your client's tax data and some administrative reports

For Dynamic Programming

- Pop-ups must be allowed for this site
- Cookies must be allowed. Note: I.E. 6.x users must set the privacy setting to medium or lower
- ActiveX controls must be enabled
- JavaScript must be enabled

For more information on Tax Notebook, call 1-800-PFX-9998 (1-800-739-9998) or visit CCHGroup.com.

The most up-to-date product information, including detailed system requirements, enhancements, and new features, is available at CCHGroup.com. If you plan to use multiple ProSystem fx Office products within the same system, call 1-800-PFX-9998 (1-800-739-9998) and ask to speak to your sales representative about whether or not your system availability is adequate.

All trademarks and copyrights are property of their respective owners.

CCH
a Wolters Kluwer business

21250 Hawthorne Blvd.
Torrance, CA 90503
1-800-PFX-9998
CCHGroup.com

5576   3/29/07   © 2007 CCH. All Rights Reserved.

Corporate Tax Workpapers. Tax workpapers for the corporate taxpayer can be much more complex than those for the individual taxpayer. Corporate tax data usually originates with the financial accounting trial balance which has been prepared using Generally Accepted Accounting Principles (GAAP). Adjusting journal entries, and if applicable, consolidating entries are made to arrive at the information disclosed on the tax return. These workpapers also include a reconciliation which ties the tax return to the general ledger, as well as other analyses that are necessary to complete the tax return. Ordinarily, tax reconciliation workpapers are prepared and provided by the taxpayer. However, in some cases they are prepared by the taxpayer's accountant. The term "tax workpapers," as used in the Internal Revenue Manual, refers to tax reconciliation workpapers. This term is also defined as workpapers other than audit workpapers or tax accrual workpapers.[8]

---

[8] IRM §34.12.3.13.1.

Audit workpapers. Audit workpapers, in contrast to tax workpapers, are retained by the independent accountant. Unlike tax workpapers, audit workpapers may not be requested at the beginning of an IRS examination. Audit workpapers concern the procedures followed, the tests performed, information obtained, and the conclusions reached pertinent to the accountant's examination. Workpapers may include analyses, work programs, memorandums, letters of confirmation and representation, abstracts of organization or plan documents, and schedules or commentaries prepared or obtained by the auditor. These workpapers provide an important support for the independent certified public accountant's opinion as to the fairness of the presentation of the financial statements, in conformity with generally accepted accounting principles and demonstrate compliance with the generally accepted auditing standards.[9]

Tax accrual workpapers. Ordinarily, tax accrual workpapers are prepared by a corporate taxpayer or an independent third party other than the firm's auditor. They are used to evaluate the sufficiency of a taxpayer's accrual for additional tax liabilities that may result during the ordinary course of an IRS audit. Many factors can be considered, including the taxpayer's books; records; tax returns; and relevant statutory, administrative, and judicial law used to evaluate uncertain positions taken on the tax return that may result in an audit adjustment. In exploring the tax consequences of these transactions, often the "worst case" scenario is used to ensure that the taxpayer is recording an adequate tax accrual. For each uncertain transaction the potential tax cost and the probability that additional liability will arise is determined. The workpapers might contain information on the taxpayer's financial transactions, as well as identification of questionable positions the taxpayer may have taken. Even if these workpapers are not used to prepare a tax return, they may still be relevant to an IRS investigation.[10] Chapter 17 offers a detailed explanation of the tax accrual process.

Effective Tax Rate workpapers. Effective tax rate reconciliation workpapers are not prepared for the purpose of determining the proper amount of the reserve for contingent tax liabilities. Thus, they are not audit workpapers in the sense that they are retained by the auditor to document the performance of the audit. Instead, the workpapers are prepared by the taxpayer, and do not reflect procedures followed or tests performed by an auditor in reviewing the taxpayer's financial statements. Effective tax rate reconciliation workpapers do not fall within the category of tax accrual workpapers as defined in the IRM. Under Section 4.10.20 of the current IRM, tax accrual workpapers are defined as a subset of audit workpapers that relate to the tax reserve for current, deferred and potential or contingent tax liabilities, whether prepared by the taxpayer, the taxpayer's accountant, or the independent auditor.

IRM Section 4.10.20.2(2). This section of the Internal Revenue Manual defines tax accrual workpapers as "those audit workpapers, whether prepared by the taxpayer, the taxpayer's accountant or the independent auditor, that relate to the tax reserve for current, deferred and potential or contingent tax liabilities, however classified or reported on audited financial statements, and to footnotes disclosing those tax reserves on audited financial statements".[11] Workpapers prepared as part of the tax preparation process are not immune from being requested by the IRS agent in the course of an IRS audit of the taxpayer. Thus, the workpapers should include sufficient documentation, usually supplied by the taxpayer, to substantiate the various income and expense items shown on the tax return, including the reconciliation of financial net income to taxable income as reported on either the Schedule M-1 or M-3. These workpapers include both paper and electronic files.

Electronic Workpapers. Electronic workpapers provide many features and have many benefits, including:

- *Replication of information.* An automated environment requires the acceptance of electronic communication, which can be accomplished in a secure dial-up environment. This "replication" process allows multiple users to access the information from any location. The benefits include improved communication and real-time workpaper review.

---

[9] IRM §§4.71.1.14.5, 7.6.2.3.1.1.
[10] *Arthur Young*, SCt, 84-1 USTC ¶9305, 465 US 805, 104 SCt 1495.
[11] IRS Advice Memorandum AM 2007-012, June 8, 2007.

- *Standardization.* A standard workpaper template provides structure while allowing flexibility for the tax return preparer. Workpapers are pre-formatted, and required administrative workpapers are pre-composed. This helps achieve consistency in the preparation process.
- *Convenience.* Never again will staff have to spend time heading-up workpapers. This process is handled through the software which keeps a log of users and the ability to route workpapers through the tax preparation process, including input, review, and filing of the tax return.
- *Doclinks.* Documents can be electronically connected so that the preparer can move from one workpaper to another and back again. No numbering of workpapers is required and flipping between multiple workpapers is simple.
- *Views.* A groupware solution allows staff, managers, and partners to view the entire process at any point in time. Different views allow supervisors to see what percent of the return is finished and how much remains to be done. Multiple views display all current year workpapers, all permanent file workpapers, findings forms, and other information.
- *Imaging.* Imaging, as well as optical character recognition (OCR), is accomplished via optical scanning. This allows for the incorporation of non-electronic media into the automated workpapers.
- *Communication.* E-mail, which is built directly into the application, helps improve communication throughout the process and alerts staff and reviewers when the tax return is ready for their attention.
- *Server as Central Point.* With a groupware solution, all work is stored on a server. Workpapers won't be lost, and workpapers are available on a local basis for everyone working on the tax return.
- *Timeliness.* The groupware solution allows for real-time management review, which means that workpapers and portions of the tax return can be reviewed as they are completed. The review process is finished sooner and the return preparer receives more timely feedback.
- *Application Integration.* Groupware has expanded the capabilities with tax preparation software. Data can be maintained in its original application, and the link between the data and the tax workpapers is seamless.
- *Access Rights Security.* The electronic world allows implementation of additional security controls over the tax workpapers. Through access rights, only those people who need to read, edit, or delete workpapers can do so. This allows for more security than that provided in a paper environment.

¶10,013   Best Practices for Tax Advisors

.01   GENERAL GUIDELINES FOR TAX ADVICE [IRS CIRCULAR 230].

Tax advisors should provide clients with the highest quality representation concerning federal tax issues by adhering to best practices. These best practices include:
- Communicating clearly with the client regarding terms of the engagement,
- Establishing the facts,
- Relating the applicable law,
- Arriving at a conclusion supported by the law and the facts, and
- Advising the client of the import of the conclusions reached (e.g., avoiding penalties, etc.).

Tax advisors with responsibility for overseeing a firm's practice of providing advice should ensure that all firm procedures are consistent with best practices. A practitioner may not sign a tax return as a preparer if the practitioner determines that the tax return contains a position that does not have a *realistic possibility* of being sustained on its merits, unless the position is not frivolous and is adequately disclosed to the IRS. As for *advice* to the taxpayer, any position recommended must meet the *realistic possibility standard* or be not frivolous and the practitioner advises the client of any possible penalties that may apply, as well as any opportunity to avoid the accuracy-related penalty by adequately disclosing the position. The practitioner may rely in good faith without verification on information furnished by the client in providing such advice, unless such information is incomplete or inconsistent with other facts; in that case, follow-up is required.

A tax practitioner is expected to provide his/her clients with the highest quality representation regarding federal tax issues. Section 10.33 of Circular 230 states that a practitioner should adhere to best practices when providing advice and preparing or assisting a taxpayer in the preparation of a submission to the IRS.

A practitioner is under a duty to take reasonable steps to ensure that his/her firm maintains and adheres to procedures for all members, associates, and employees that are consistent with best practices.

.03   BUILDING THE TAXPAYER'S CASE: REPRESENTATION ISSUES

Before accepting an engagement, a tax practitioner should ascertain if he or she possesses the competence and expertise to handle the matter and is able to devote the time and energy the task will require. If for any reason the tax practitioner cannot provide high quality representation to the client, the practitioner should decline to accept the engagement. The practitioner should determine if a conflict of interest currently exists or may develop. If a conflict does exist or may develop or if the facts create an appearance of a conflict, the practitioner should decline to accept the engagement. After ascertaining that he/she is competent and able to represent the taxpayer, the practitioner should establish a clear understanding with the client.

- Explain whether the fee structure is based upon hourly charges, a flat fee, or invoice billing on an interim basis or at the end of the job.
- Explain the likely procedural steps—how the process is likely to unfold
- Provide a best estimate of how long the matter may take
- Explain the client's role. Let the client know exactly what is expected—what the client will be asked to provide in the way of documentation

The practitioner should explain the taxpayer's rights. The practitioner should prepare and have the taxpayer sign a power of attorney, making sure that the taxpayer understands both the need for a power of attorney and the provisions contained in the power of attorney document.

Income and Expense Information. After identifying the issues and obtaining a clear understanding of the IRS inquiry and what the Service seeks from the taxpayer, the tax practitioner should review the returns in question. The practitioner should review not only the return for each year under examination, but also other years for which the statute of limitations remains open. The IRS may expand the examination to cover any or all open years and the practitioner needs to be familiar with the taxpayer's the returns for those periods. The practitioner's review should be complete. It should include the entire return, not just sections specifically targeted by the IRS for examination. The practitioner should be alert for any errors, unusual items, or potential omissions.

Example 10-1. Taxpayer Bruce Scott has asked Michele Lawson, an enrolled agent, to represent him regarding an audit examination of his 2011 federal income tax return. During her review of the return, Michelle notes that Bruce, a public school teacher, claimed no deduction for educator expenditures (maximum allowable amount of $250). Michele should discuss the matter with Bruce to ascertain if he is eligible for the deduction. If so, Michelle may want to raise the issue during the examination.

The practitioner should inquire regarding all income items and should make an initial determination whether items appear to have been correctly reported.

Example 10-2. During Michelle's review of Bruce's return, she notes that the return listed $1,000 of income from director's fees as other income, but omitted it from Schedule SE. Michelle should inform Bruce and explain his duty to report the error.

The practitioner should also review all deductions claimed on the return, including personal and exemption deductions and all expenditure deductions, whether personal (medical, etc.), business, or investment. The practitioner should ascertain if items appear reasonable in amount and are claimed in the appropriate place on the return.

Documentation. The tax practitioner should explain the client's basic documentation and substantiation requirements. As a general rule, a taxpayer has no inherent right to claim a deduction. Each taxpayer is expected to maintain accounting records sufficient to enable the taxpayer to file an accurate and complete return.

Code Sec. 446(b) specifically grants the IRS the authority to compute the income of a taxpayer who has maintained no records or whose records are inadequate and fail to clearly report the taxpayer's income. The practitioner should examine the taxpayer's documentation in support of all items reported on the return, ascertaining that documentation exists, is reliable, is adequate to verify the item and agrees in amount to what was reported on the return

Indirect Verification for Amounts in Dispute. A tax practitioner should understand and advise his/her clients regarding the options available to the IRS to ascertain if a taxpayer has reported all income. In addition to direct methods, such as W-2 and Form 1099 data, the IRS may employ various indirect methods to detect unreported income. When, for example, a taxpayer has maintained inadequate or no financial records, the IRS has in its arsenal a number of indirect audit techniques available to detect unreported income or to verify amounts in dispute. Although each method typically requires special adjustments and the facts in a particular case may affect the computation, the essential mechanics of the most common indirect methods appear below.

One option is the **"Cash-T Account"** method. When using a Cash-T Account, the IRS focuses squarely on the taxpayer's receipt and expenditure of cash. Essentially, the IRS creates a "T-Account." On the left side, the IRS lists the taxpayer's sources of cash for the year; on the right side it lists the taxpayer's uses or expenditures of cash. If the taxpayer has used and accumulated more cash than reported on the tax return or otherwise accounted for by the taxpayer, the IRS will presume that the difference represents understated income. Refer to Chapter 8 for a discussion and illustration of the Cash-T method.

OBSERVATION   Are these indirect methods of estimating income legal, especially when the taxpayer produces books and records for the audit? The answer is yes, according to the U.S. Supreme Court in *Marion L. Holland vs. U.S.*[12] In that case, the Court specifically noted that the IRS was "auditing the taxpayer, and not his or her books and records."

Another common indirect method is the **"Bank Deposit"** or **"Receipts and Disbursements"** method. When using this approach, the IRS focuses on the taxpayer's bank statements for the year. The IRS first establishes that the taxpayer is engaged in a trade or business or other income producing activity that would be expected to generate regular and periodic deposits into a bank account. The IRS adds the bank deposits for the year. The total of bank deposits for the year is assumed to represent taxable income unless the taxpayer can show otherwise. The IRS then adjusts the deposit total by adding to it

---

[12] *Holland*, SCt, 54-2 USTC ¶9714, 348 US 121, 75 SCt 127.

expenditures made in cash (since the cash is assumed never to have been deposited into the bank account) to arrive at taxable income.

Another indirect method available to the IRS to detect unreported income is the "**Net Worth Method**." When using the net worth method, the IRS establishes an estimate of the taxpayer's net worth at both the beginning of the year and the end of the year. Any resulting increase in net worth is then adjusted by adding nondeductible expenditures and losses, deducting nontaxable receipts to arrive at the taxpayer's apparent taxable income for the year.

OBSERVATION	If a case appears to be headed to a criminal proceeding, the IRS will most likely convert any indirect analysis to the net worth method, since this method was specifically sanctioned by the U.S. Supreme Court. Such a method might also be the easiest to explain to a jury.

The IRS will sometimes use third party research to verify amounts in dispute. The IRS will sometimes verify data through municipal tax property assessment data. Deed records will provide information regarding property dales. Other state and local tax information may be available. In limited situations, *Code Sec. 6103*, which governs confidentiality of tax returns, permits sharing of information between the IRS and state tax authorities.

OBSERVATION	A practitioner may consider performing his or her own indirect T-account analysis on the taxpayer's records *before* the IRS agent arrives. This can point out particular vulnerabilities, and also provide an opportunity to follow up with the client. Question: can the IRS subpoena such an analysis? The answer would appear to be no, since this analysis was not performed "in connection with the preparation of the return." Therefore, it should be protected by accountant/client privilege.

Other Supporting Documentation. In addition to the records to keep identified earlier in Table 1, a myriad of other supporting documentation may support entries on a tax return, and the tax practitioner should be alert to the need to obtain and review any other documents which may be beneficial in the representation of a taxpayer before the IRS. The tax practitioner should review prior and subsequent year tax returns. Returns filed for other years will often contain information relevant to the year in question.

Example 10-3. Marge Sloan, an enrolled agent, is representing David Smith, whose 2008 federal income tax return is being audited by the IRS. The IRS has requested verification of the basis of 100 shares of Ajax, Inc. common stock that David sold during the year. David doesn't remember purchasing the shares, but Marge recalls that David's 2007 return reported the sale of 50 shares of Ajax stock and that Schedule D reported that the stock was obtained by inheritance. Marge now has a lead to follow and will ask David to provide appropriate probate documentation which will likely indicate the value of the stock on the date of the decedent's death, which amount will become David's stepped-up basis for the shares inherited.

Other substantive and contemporaneous documentation (i.e., documentation made at the time of the expenditure) may support entries on a taxpayer's return.
- Mileage logs—deduction amounts (e.g., employee business expense for business use of a personal automobile)
- Corporate minutes—payment of dividends, adoption of employee benefit plans, and the like

Employment reimbursement policies may support entries (or the absence thereof) on a return.

Example 10-4. Dana Cromwell, an employee of the Acme Corporation, received significant reimbursement of employee business expense during 2011. Brian Lawson is an enrolled agent representing Dana before the IRS. Brian has obtained a copy of Acme's employment reimbursement policy, which permits reimbursement only upon receipt of an expense report which itemizes expenditures and includes evidence of payment. Brian also has copies of Dana's expense reports which comply in all respects with Acme's reimbursement policy. Brian should have no problem convincing the IRS that Dana properly omitted reimbursement amounts from her income tax return for the year in question.

Business entity documents (e.g., corporate by-laws or a partnership agreement) will sometimes support a return position. A partnership agreement may, for example, indicate the existence and mechanics of a guaranteed payment arrangement in support of a Form 1065 K-1 position relied upon by a partner when preparing his/her personal income tax return.

Using Tax Software. Most tax practitioners now use commercial software for the preparation of federal income tax returns. Are practitioners who use software for the preparation of income tax returns considered to be tax return preparers? Code Sec. 7701(a)(36)(A) defines a tax return preparer as "any person who prepares for compensation, or who employs one or more persons to prepare for compensation, any return of tax imposed by this title or any claim for refund of tax imposed by this title." Code Sec. 7701(a)(36)(B)(i) provides, however, that a person who merely provides typing, reproducing, or other mechanical assistance in the preparation of an income tax return is not a "tax return preparer." Clearly, the use of software in the preparation of an income tax return encompasses conduct beyond the scope of mere typing, reproduction, or other mechanical assistance, and a tax practitioner using software is deemed to be a "tax return preparer." Thus a practitioner using tax return preparation software will be subject to the same procedural duties and responsibilities imposed on other income tax return preparers, as discussed earlier in this Part. These include the duty to:

- Sign the return.[13]
- Provide his/her identifying number and address.[14]
- Provide the taxpayer a copy of the completed return.[15]
- Retain a copy or qualifying record of the return.[16]
- Retain records regarding employee preparers.[17]
- Exercise due diligence in the determination of taxpayer eligibility for the earned income credit.[18]

Example 10-5. Lauren Barrett, an enrolled agent, prepares a federal income tax return for her best friend, Sandy Lewis, using her firm's commercial software package. Lauren does not charge Sandy for the service and refuses Sandy's offer of compensation. Is Lauren a "tax return preparer" regarding Sandy's return? Because Lauren did not prepare Sandy's return for compensation, she is not a tax return preparer and technically not subject to the above listed duties and responsibilities, although common sense, professional care, and prudence would seem to dictate that Lauren comply in all respects.

[13] Reg. §1.6065-1(b)(1).
[14] Code Sec. 6109(a)(4), Reg. §1.6109-2(b)(1).
[15] Code Sec. 6107(a).
[16] Code Sec. 6107(b)(1).
[17] Code Sec. 6060.
[18] Reg. §1.6695-2(a).

OBSERVATION

A tax return preparer can file returns electronically after becoming an **Electronic Return Originator (ERO).** An ERO may originate the electronic submission of income tax returns that are either prepared by the ERO firm, or collected from a taxpayer. A preparer can register to become a user on the Internal Revenue Service's (IRS) e-services web site. The registration process involves collecting personal and taxpayer data for the sole purpose of authenticating the preparer's identity. The IRS will compare the information provided with the information received from the Social Security Administration (SSA) and with the tax return information previously filed. A registration confirmation code is mailed to the preparer via the U.S. Postal Service, if the information provided matches IRS data.

The following information must be provided to become an ERO:
- Legal name (verified with IRS & SSA records)
- Social Security Number (verified with SSA records)
- Date of birth (verified with SSA records)
- Telephone number
- E-mail address
- Adjusted Gross Income (AGI) from either your current year or prior year filed tax return (verified from IRS records)
- Username. Select your preferred username. Please read the rules for selecting your username
- Password and PIN. Select your password and PIN. Please read the helpful hints on selecting a secure, unique password and PIN
- Reminder question to recover a forgotten username
- Home mailing address (verified from IRS records)

To learn more about e-filing visit the IRS website, and follow the link for tax professionals, *http://www.irs.gov/taxpros/article/0,,id=109646,00.html*

Accuracy Issues. Tax practitioners using software for the preparation of federal income tax returns are also subject to the same duties and responsibilities regarding accuracy, due diligence, etc. applicable to all income tax return preparers. The Internal Revenue Code imposes a number of civil and criminal penalties against income tax return preparers who violate standards of care. These were discussed in Chapter 9.

A tax practitioner must use the same standard of care regardless of the method used to prepare a return—manual or via software. The practitioner using software must be alert for inconsistencies with source data, miscalculations, duplicate entries, and the like, and should carefully review the printed return or summary print-out to ascertain that source data has been entered correctly. Many practitioners use *control sheets* when summarizing data and entering information into the software program. A good control sheet provides for the preparer to record expected amounts for each category of income, deduction, credit, and tax payment. The practitioner should compare control sheet amounts with data per the printed return or summary print-out and investigate any variance.

The alternative minimum tax presents a special issue due to its complexity. A practitioner should take special care to enter all data (*e.g.*, depreciation or K-1 data) that might impact a taxpayer's potential liability for alternative minimum tax. The practitioner should never simply accept the software's computation of alternative minimum tax, but should review Form 6251 to verify that the amounts are consistent with source data and make sure that any available credit has been included and computed correctly. Good tax return preparation software will always include a diagnostics feature designed to alert the preparer to issues or errors that the software has been designed to detect. The practitioner should review the diagnostic print-out and address every item on it prior to moving forward with the return preparation process.

Example 10-6. George Irving, an enrolled agent, is preparing the federal income tax return of Donald Lee. While entering data into the computer software program, George failed to include the social security number of Donald's dependent son, Donald, Jr. As a result, the return has not allowed a dependency exemption deduction. Although George would eventually discover the error when he compares return data per his control sheet with the computer generated tax return or summary printout, an examination of the diagnostic printout will immediately alert him to the problem.

Before printing the final version of a return, a return preparer should review the return for overall completeness and consistency. Always compare inputs and outputs across forms. For example, is the itemized deduction amount appearing on Schedule B the same amount that has been carried to and deducted on the second page of Form 1040? Whenever possible, every return should be subjected to review by someone other than the actual preparer. The reviewer should check all entries on the return and compare entry amounts with supporting documentation. Many firms conduct a second review which focuses on the face of the return itself, checking for inconsistency, missing items, and the like.

A tax practitioner's client responsibility extends beyond the duty to prepare a complete and accurate return. A practitioner should strive to educate his/her clients. A taxpayer is under a duty to maintain accounting records sufficient to enable the preparation of an accurate and complete return and to retain supporting records and documentation. During the tax return preparation process, a practitioner usually examines and reviews client documentation in support of entries on the tax return. The practitioner is therefore in a unique position to judge the adequacy of a client's record-keeping efforts and should make certain that the client understands exactly what is expected.

Significance of Signature (*e.g.*, Joint & Several Liability, Penalty of Perjury). Code Sec. 6061(a) states, "Except as otherwise provided…, any return, statement, or other document required to be made under any provision of the internal revenue laws or regulations shall be signed in accordance with forms or regulations prescribed by the Secretary." The IRS requires income tax returns to be signed under penalty of perjury. Special signature rules apply to electronic filings. A taxpayer filing an electronic income tax return uses a Self-select PIN to:

- Authenticate the electronic portion of the income tax return
- Send any required paper forms
- Authorize the electronic return originator to transmit via a third-party transmitter
- Consent to directly deposit any refund and/or authorize electronic funds withdrawal for payment of tax

The tax return must be signed under penalty of perjury. The signature line on Form 1040 states, *"Under penalties of perjury, I declare that I have examined this return and accompanying schedules and statements, and to the best of my knowledge and belief, they are true, correct, and complete."* A practitioner who has prepared an income tax return should make certain that the client is aware of the import and consequences of his/her signature. The client needs to understand that the signature is not a simple formality, but a statement under penalty of perjury that:

- He or she has examined the return (including schedules and statements), and
- The return and schedules and statements (to the best of the taxpayer's knowledge and belief) are true, correct, and complete.

The IRS takes the position that an *unsigned return* is not a valid return. Accordingly, the taxpayer needs to understand the significance and consequences of the signature and the practitioner should advise the taxpayer to review the return prior to signing. In addition to the taxpayer declaration under penalty of perjury, the signature on a return carries with it responsibility for payment of tax liability. *Code Sec. 6013(d)(3)* provides that each spouse is jointly and severally liable for the full amount of income tax, penalty, and interest arising out of the return, meaning that the IRS may generally seek full payment from either party. A special innocent spouse rule, set out in Code Sec. 6015 provides relief from joint and several liability to those for whom it is available. An innocent spouse may seek relief from liability under the *innocent spouse relief* provision (by filing **Form 8857**) if certain requirements are satisfied.

An innocent spouse seeking relief under the *separation of liability* option must show that the spouses filed a joint return for the year in question and that the innocent spouse is legally separated from, or is no longer married to the other spouse, or has not been a member of the same household occupied by the other spouse for a twelve month period. An innocent spouse may also seek *equitable relief*—arguing that it would be unfair, considering all of the facts and circumstances, to hold the individual responsible for the understatement of tax.

Consequences of Dishonesty. Taxpayers filing incorrect returns are subject to a variety of penalties and sanctions, both civil and criminal in nature and the tax practitioner should determine that clients understand both the duty to be honest in all dealings with the IRS and the consequences which may result from noncompliance. The consequences are severe. Code Sec. 6663(a) imposes a penalty equal to 75 percent of any underpayment of tax that is due to fraud. Generally, the burden of proof is on the IRS to show by clear and convincing evidence that the taxpayer's conduct was fraudulent. One the IRS proves that any portion of an understatement is due to fraud, however, the entire underpayment is presumed to be due to fraud and the taxpayer must establish by a preponderance of the evidence what portion of the underpayment should be exempt from the fraud penalty. Taxpayer dishonesty may also lead to criminal sanctions, including imprisonment. The Internal Revenue Code (Title 26 of the United States Code) sets out a number of tax crimes. These penalties were discussed in Chapter 9.

Criminal statutes other than those contained in the Internal Revenue Code may also be applicable to tax filings. Provisions of ***Title 18 of the United States Code*** which may apply to tax prosecutions include:

- Conspiracy[19]
- Falsification, concealment or cover-up of a material fact or making of a false statement[20]
- Making of a false claim for refund[21]
- Mail fraud/Wire fraud[22]
- Money laundering[23]

Again, the tax practitioner should help keep his/her clients honest by making them aware of the potential consequences of their actions especially if taxpayers fail to keep appropriate records in order to verify the information contained on their tax returns.

¶10,015 Summary

- The key to tax communications is the creation and retention of documents supporting the items of income and expense reported on the tax return.
- For individual taxpayers recordkeeping is often an informal and haphazard process.
- For business taxpayers, especially corporate clients who maintain their books and records using Generally Accepted Accounting Principles, the recordkeeping process is a much more formal and complex process.
- Retention of documents in a format that permits their easy retrieval is essential to the tax practitioner and a key element in defense of possible tax preparer penalties.
- Most tax preparation firms are either in the process or have converted their traditional tax workpapers into electronic format.
- Safeguarding this electronic data from loss, destruction or theft is the new security threat of the 21st century.
- Tax practitioners should ensure that "best practices" are in place so that tax returns filed are as accurate and complete as possible.

---

[19] Code Sec. 371.
[20] Code Sec. 1001.
[21] Code Sec. 287.
[22] Code Secs. 1341 and 1343.
[23] Code Sec. 1956.

Review Questions for Chapter 10

True or False

Indicate which of the following statements are true or false by circling the correct answer.

1. Any person required to file a tax return must keep permanent records.   T   F
2. Books and records must be retained as long as their contents are material to the   T   F
    administration of any internal revenue law.
3. If you file a claim for a loss from a worthless security, you must retain the documents   T   F
    substantiating the loss for six years.
4. Businesses are required to maintain a double-entry system of books.   T   F
5. Records maintained in an electronic format are not accepted by the IRS as docu-   T   F
    mentation of an expense.
6. The term "tax workpapers" as used in the Internal Revenue Manual refers to tax   T   F
    reconciliation workpapers.
7. Even though it is a legal document, there is no reason to retain a copy of a divorce   T   F
    decree for tax purposes.
8. The taxpayer is required to mail a signed copy of the return to the IRS within 10   T   F
    days of filing electronically.
9. The IRS takes the position that an unsigned tax return is not a valid return.   T   F
10. Taxpayer dishonesty may lead to criminal sanctions, including imprisonment.   T   F

Fill in the Blanks

Fill in each blank with the appropriate word or phrase that completes each sentence.

11. A taxpayer must be able to provide the tax return preparer with _____ and _____ tax informa-
    tion in order to comply with tax law reporting.
12. Good _____ will help you to monitor the progress of your business.
13. Specific recordkeeping rules apply to _____ expenses.
14. Business transactions are ordinarily summarized in books called _____ and _____
15. The checking account should be reconciled _____.
16. A(n) _____ system of bookkeeping is the simplest to maintain, but is not suitable for most
    businesses.
17. The _____ fund is used to make payments without having to write checks for small amounts.
18. A(n) _____ is used to collect data from a taxpayer regarding all sources of income and
    deductions and to provide descriptive information pertaining to dependency exemptions and credits.
19. If for any reason the tax practitioner cannot provide _____ of a client, the practitioner
    should decline to accept the engagement.
20. A(n) _____ account method of verifying income lists the taxpayers sources and uses of cash
    for the year.

Multiple Choice

Circle the best answer for each of the following questions.

21. The "best practices" process of a tax practitioner should include all of the following except:
    a. communicating clearly with the client regarding the terms of the engagement
    b. establishing the facts and relating the applicable law
    c. arriving at conclusion supported by the law and facts and advising the client
    d. all of the above

22. Which of the following is not a "best practice" as that term is used in Circular 230?
    a.   Reasonable fee structure
    b.   Conduct marked by fairness and integrity
    c.   Clear communication with the client regarding the terms of the engagement
    d.   All are best practices

23. Circular 230 states that a practitioner who maintains a good faith belief on reasonable grounds that a record is privileged
    a.   Must nevertheless promptly submit the record to the IRS upon proper request
    b.   May to refuse to submit the record to the IRS only if the practitioner also believes that the request is of doubtful legality
    c.   May refuse to submit the record or information to the IRS
    d.   May refuse to submit the record or information to the IRS but must provide the IRS with a written summary of information contained in the record within twenty-one days after demand for the written summary.

24. If it appears that the IRS may pursue a criminal investigation against a taxpayer, the tax professional should
    a. Withdraw from the case immediately
    b. Inform the taxpayer to retain an attorney, as no accounting-client privilege exists on this matter
    c. Document the strengths and weaknesses of the IRS case in a memo to the file
    d. Immediately request a meeting with the IRS agent's supervisor

25. The tax practitioner's understanding with the client should not include an explanation of the:
    a.   Probable procedural steps likely to follow
    b.   Client's role in the matter
    c.   Fee structure
    d.   All of the above explanations should be included

26. Which of the following should a tax practitioner review before representing a client before the IRS?
    a.   Only those items on the taxpayer's return for the year under examination that the IRS has targeted for examination
    b.   Only the returns for the years under examination, but all items on those returns
    c.   All items on all of the taxpayer's returns which remain open under the statute of limitations
    d.   All of the taxpayer's returns which remain open under the statute of limitations, but only as to those items that the IRS has targeted.

27. Code Sec. 6001 of the Internal Revenue Code requires each taxpayer to
    a.   Maintain and keep accounting journals and a general ledger
    b.   Maintain and keep such records as required by the IRS
    c.   Carry the burden of proof in any civil tax matter
    d.   Maintain and keep duplicate accounting records at the office and at home

28. The IRS has the statutory authority to
    a.   Imprison taxpayers who have failed to file federal income tax returns
    b.   Ignore the statute of limitations and conduct an audit examination for any year in which a taxpayer has failed to maintain adequate accounting records
    c.   Deny a taxpayer a deduction on the grounds that the taxpayer filed a delinquent return for the year in question
    d.   Compute the income of a taxpayer who has maintained no accounting records

29. The use of indirect methods of estimating income may be used by the IRS
    a. in any audit situation
    b. only when criminal fraud is suspected
    c. only when the taxpayer does not produce books and records
    d. none of the above

30. Occasionally in the past, the IRS would use a taxpayer's lifestyle or living patterns in contending that unreported income exists. This practice
    a. is a valuable IRS tool that is used frequently
    b. is no longer allowed under the Code
    c. can be used in civil cases only
    d. none of the above

31. Which of the following documents supporting a taxpayer's case is not a legal document?
    a.   Cancelled check
    b.   Birth certificate
    c.   Will
    d.   Divorce decree

32. Which of the listed items would most likely be an application of contemporaneous documentation?
    a.   Corporate minutes
    b.   A partnership agreement
    c.   An employer's reimbursement policy
    d.   None of the above

33. A tax practitioner who uses software to prepare an income tax return for a client must
    a.   Sign the return
    b.   Provide the client a copy of any computer input sheets used to prepare the return
    c   Obtain a signed statement from the CEO of the company that designed the software attesting that the software complies in all respects with IRS guidelines for use of commercial software
    d.   None of the above

34. A practitioner using software to prepare a federal income tax return is subject to imposition of which Internal Revenue Code civil penalty?
    a.   Code Sec. 7201—Tax evasion
    b.   Code Sec. 6694(b)(2)(A)—Willful attempt to understate tax liability
    c.   Code Sec. 7206—Willfully aiding, assisting, advising or counseling in the preparation of a return
    d.   All of the above

35. Which of the following statements is false?
    a. A tax practitioner should review client documentation in support of entries on the return.
    b. A tax practitioner should strive to educate his or her client regarding the client's duty to maintain and keep adequate accounting records.
    c. A taxpayer is under a duty to maintain accounting records sufficient to enable the preparation of an accurate and complete return.
    d. None of the above

36. Criminal charges other than those specifically provided for in the Internal Revenue Code which may apply to a taxpayer include
    a. Failure to pay tax on time
    b. Conspiracy
    c. Tax evasion
    d. None of the above

Review Problems

37. Mary and Paul Smith are married and file a joint return. They have two children, ages four and seven. Paul works for the Angle Corporation and receives a salary of $45,000 per year. In addition, he receives an auto allowance of $200 per month since his employer requires him to visit clients. Mary works for the Straight Corporation and receives a salary of $45,000 per year. In addition, her company has a cafeteria plan from which Mary elected to receive child care reimbursement payments of $300 per month for the pre-school that her children attend while she is working. List and describe the basic records that Mary and Paul should keep when filing their individual income tax return.

38. David Morning, age 67, is retired and receives Social Security of $2,000 per month, and a pension of $1,000 per month. The pension distribution is from a qualified Code Sec. 401(k) plan that Paul contributed to while he was working. To occupy his time, Paul opened up an on-line brokerage account and transferred $10,000 of his personal savings to the account. During the year, he bought and sold various stocks based upon research he did on the internet. List and describe the basic records that David should keep when filing his individual income tax return.

39. Connie is a nail technician at the Hard-As-Nails Salon. She is paid a minimum wage of $3.00 per hour and is allowed to keep any cash tips that her clients give her. List and describe the basic records that Connie should keep when filing her individual income tax return.

40. Mary Henry uses electronic banking. She has her payroll checks deposited electronically and uses on-line banking to pay all her expenses, including medical expenses, mortgage payments, property tax payments, charitable contributions and investment expenses. List and describe the basic records that Mary should keep to provide proof of payments for t income and deductions.

41. James Grow, owner of Grow, Inc. is a die-hard Maryland Terrapin fan. During the current tax year, Grow, Inc. leased the largest skybox. The cost for the box was as follows:

Payment to the Terrapin Athletic Foundation for the right to lease the skybox	$150,000
Lease payment for the skybox (6 home games, 30 seats in the box)	$120,000
Food and beverages (billed based on actual consumption)	$15,000
Total cost of skybox	$285,000

James is a very talented businessman. The skybox was so much better than just having good seats (the best seats cost $50 per game). James took 29 customers to every football game and actually spent 45 minutes presenting the latest product information to them before he let them eat and drink. The $285,000 was included in advertising expense. List and describe the basic records that James should keep to justify his deduction for business use of the skybox. Write a memo to the files explaining the tax deductible portion of the skybox.

42. During the year, GiantPanda, Inc. paid the Environmental Protection Agency $500,000 related to the clean-up of leaking underground storage tanks. The EPA fixed the tanks and cleaned up the leak. Following the clean-up, the EPA initially assessed a $2,000,000 fine against the company representing the $25,000 per day penalty for noncompliance for the 80 days the company was not in compliance. GiantPanda ultimately settled the assessment for $500,000. During the settlement discussions, the EPA disclosed that actual clean-up costs incurred were $300,000. List and describe the basic records that GiantPanda should keep to justify the amount and the tax year of the deduction for the environmental cleanup. Write a memo to the files explaining the proper tax treatment of the payment including in which tax year the deduction can be taken.

Web-Based Research Problems

43. Search the internet for an on-line tax organizer that tax practitioners can use to obtain data from a taxpayer in order to prepare their tax return. (Hint: You may want to start with TaxNotebook the on-line tax organizer from CCH, a Wolters Kluwer business.) Write a one page summary of the advantages/disadvantages of using an on-line tax organizer.

44. Go to the IRS website at, *www.irs.gov/efile*. Write a one page summary of the material contained in the IRS Handbook for Authorized IRS e-file providers of individual income tax returns.

45. Visit the IRS website, and follow the link for tax professionals, *www.IRS.gov/taxpros*. Write a one page summary of the various authorized e-file providers.

Tax Compliance Problem

46. Use the worksheets illustrated in the chapter for Patrick Evans, the sole proprietor of an auto body repair shop, to prepare his Schedule C and Schedule SE. If you do not have access to tax preparation software, you can download the forms from the IRS website, *www.irs.gov.*

CHAPTER 11

Tax Planning for Individuals

Learning Objectives

1. Describe the purposes of the alternative minimum tax (AMT), and define the major components, such as adjustments, preferences, exemptions, and the AMT credit.
2. Summarize the major business, investment, and personal planning strategies for minimizing the effects of the AMT.
3. Describe how taxpayers can minimize the effects of the passive activity limitations by applying the activity, material participation, and residential real estate exception rules.
4. Summarize the investment interest deduction limitations, and the special election available for long-term capital gain and dividend incomes.
5. Describe at least one basic tax planning strategy for each of the following: tax-exempt income and fringe benefits, capital gains and losses, real estate investments, and alimony and charitable deductions.
6. Summarize the Code Sec. 280A limitations on vacation rental homes, and describe the tax planning opportunities with the expense allocation procedures.
7. Describe the following vehicles as tax-favored methods of accumulating funds for college education: educational savings bonds, educational individual retirement accounts, and Code Sec. 529 plans.

¶11,001 Introduction

This chapter represents the first of six chapters devoted to tax planning strategies. As the compliance side of the typical tax office has become more automated, and as more and more electronic tax research materials are available, it seems that tax planning has in some respects become the final frontier of contemporary tax practice. But good planning strategies must be constructed hand in hand with thorough tax research and solid compliance reporting, as evidenced by the current maze of penalty provisions applicable to taxpayers and tax professionals alike. For that reason, research and compliance issues are also addressed in the discussion and in the problem materials.

The discussion of tax planning strategies begins with the individual taxpayer, and a number of tax planning ideas applicable to individuals are discussed in this chapter. Along the way, the coverage also reviews a good bit of tax law applicable to individuals. This chapter does not address retirement planning and wealth transfer issues related to individuals; separate planning chapters addressing those topics follow this chapter.

The first part of this chapter examines three major constraints on tax planning for individuals: the alternative minimum tax, the passive activity rules, and the investment interest limitations. Planning strategies for avoiding or at least minimizing these limitations are also discussed.

The second part of the chapter examines specific planning strategies related to various topics. These include tax-exempt income and fringe benefits, capital gains and losses, rental investments as tax shelters, certain personal deductions, vacation rental homes, and sales of a personal residence. In some cases, the analyses are supplemented with tax planning problems based on EXCEL spreadsheet analyses. These planning problems are included in the end-of-chapter materials.

¶11,003   Tax Planning Constraints: The Alternative Minimum Tax

Historically, the **alternative minimum tax (AMT)** was designed to require taxpayers who owe little or no regular tax liability through the use of various tax incentives to pay some minimum amount of tax. Although Congress occasionally discusses a gradual repeal of this "shadow tax," it appears that perceived equity considerations virtually guarantee its continuance for years to come.

As more and more individual taxpayers are subject to the AMT, it is critical for taxpayers and tax professionals to understand how the AMT works and how to plan to avoid or minimize the imposition of the AMT. A recent Joint Committee on Taxation study noted that while only 140,000 individual returns reported an AMT in 1987, 856,000 were expected to report some AMT liability in 1998, and 8,830,000 were expected to report some AMT liability by 2008.[1] The following comprehensive example illustrating the AMT and the related AMT computation serves as a starting point for a discussion of a number of strategies for either avoiding the imposition of the AMT or minimizing its impact.

¶11,005   The Individual AMT Computation: A Comprehensive Example

Figure 1 and **Figure 2** display the 2013 regular tax (RT) and alternative minimum tax (AMT) computations for a hypothetical married couple, Howard and Martha Jones. Howard is an employee, and Martha is self-employed. **Figure 1** displays the regular tax computation, with accompanying notes, and **Figure 2** displays the AMT computations.

Figure 2 has two columns of computations to facilitate the explanation of the AMT credit. Howard and Martha were surprised to discover that instead of receiving a small refund, they had a significant tax liability because they had failed to take into consideration their alternative minimum tax liability when computing their estimated tax payments. In reviewing this example, several observations about the AMT can be made.

---

[1]   For an excellent article on why more and more individual taxpayers are subject to the AMT, see Beth B. Kern, "The AMT Trap," *Journal of Accountancy* (October, 1999), pp. 87-94.

Taxable Income Starting Point. Although the alternative minimum tax is technically a second tax computation with its own set of income and deduction rules, normally the AMT is computed by converting taxable income to alternative minimum taxable income (AMTI). This is accomplished by isolating only those items whose treatment differs between the regular tax and AMT computations.

AMT Adjustments. AMT adjustments involve the substitution of special AMT treatment for the regular tax treatment of certain items specified in Code Secs. 56 and 58. In general, most of these adjustments as shown in **Figure 2** either (1) accelerate income recognition, (2) tax income that is not subject to the regular tax, (3) decelerate expense recognition, or (4) deny certain deductions altogether. These items are designed to ensure that a taxpayer with substantial economic income cannot avoid tax through the use of special regular tax exclusions, deductions, and credits. The **adjustments**, unlike "preferences," may be positive or negative.

- The $5,000 depreciation adjustment "slows down" MACRS and ACRS depreciation for AMT purposes.
- The $50,000 unrealized gain from the bargain element of the stock option is accelerated to the date of exercise for AMT purposes, rather than the date the stock is sold.
- The private activity bond income is taxable for AMT purposes and is also AMT "investment income." The ceiling on the AMT investment interest deduction is thus increased by $7,000.
- Additional interest expense of $3,000 is deductible for AMT purposes because tax-exempt private activity bond interest is also AMT "investment income."
- A number of itemized deductions are adjusted for less favorable AMT rules.
- The personal exemption deduction is not allowed for the AMT.

AMT Preferences. **Preferences** are somewhat similar to adjustments, with one major difference; preferences are taken into account only when they are positive (negative preference items are ignored). With the exception of tax-exempt interest on certain private activity bonds ($7,000 in the example), the preference items specified in Code Sec. 57 represent a few holdovers from the old add-on minimum tax that preceded the alternative minimum tax computation instituted in 1978. This is the case for the $3,000 depreciation adjustment for pre-1987 real estate shown in the example.

AMT Exemption. In 2013, individual taxpayers are allowed an initial AMT exemption of $80,800 on a joint return, $51,900 on a single return, or $40,400 on a married filing separately return. The initial deduction is reduced $.25 for each $1.00 of AMTI before exemption that exceeds $150,000 (joint return), $112,500 (single return), or $75,000 (married-filing separately return). Thus, in Figure 2 the exemption is reduced by 25 percent of AMTI exceeding $150,000, which results in a net AMT exemption deduction of $56,425. As part of the American Taxpayer Relief Act of 2012, AMT exemption amounts are adjusted for inflation for years after 2013.

Tentative Minimum Tax. A two-tier AMT rate structure applies to noncorporate taxpayers. In computing the **tentative minimum tax** the first $175,000 of AMT for married filing jointly is taxed at a 26-percent rate, and any excess AMTI is taxed at a 28-percent rate. However, any long-term capital gains included in AMTI are taxed at the appropriate regular-tax capital gains rates (which could be 15-, 20-, 25-, or 28-percent). Note in the example that the $20,000 long-term capital gain is taxed at a 15-percent rate for both regular tax and AMT purposes.

Alternative Minimum Tax. The AMT is the excess of the tentative minimum tax (TMT) less the regular tax liability (RT). If such excess exists, the assumption is that the taxpayer has unfairly benefited from various tax-favored treatments in the Code and must increase the regular tax liability. The AMT so computed is added to the regular tax liability; in effect, the taxpayer "pays" the larger of the regular tax liability (RT) or the tentative minimum tax (TMT). Thus, in the comprehensive example, the Jones's 2013 tax liability is increased from $23,970 to $47,480 because of the $23,510 alternative minimum tax.

Figure 1
Howard and Martha Jones—Regular Tax Computation—2013

Salaries		162,000
Long-term Capital Gain (stock investment)		20,000
Interest Income (taxable bond)		15,000
Private Activity Bond Interest (a)		0
Incentive Stock Option (ISO) Exercise (b)		0
Sole Proprietorship Income (c)		<u>58,000</u>
		255,000
SEP-IRA and 1/2 Self-Employment Tax Deductions		(5,000)
Adjusted Gross Income (AGI)		250,000
Personal Exemptions (2 @ 3,900) (d)		(7,800)
Itemized Deductions:		
Medical ($25,000 less 7.5% of AGI)	6,250	
Interest—Qual. Acquisition Indebtedness	7,900	
Interest—Home Equity Indebtedness (e)	3,000	
Interest—Investment Activities (f)	15,000	
Taxes—State and Local	31,000	
Contributions—Cash and FMV of Property	41,600	
Casualty and Theft ($0 less 10% of AGI)	0	
Miscellaneous ($6,000 less 2% of AGI)	<u>1,000</u>	
Total Itemized Before Reduction	105,750	
Reduction (d)	(____0)	
Net Itemized Deductions		(105,750)
Regular Taxable Income—2013		136,450
Regular Tax Liability (Joint tax return):		
Regular tax on ($136,450 – $20,000 long-term capital gain)		20,970
Tax on long-term capital gain ($20,000 × .15)		3,000
Regular tax liability (RT)		23,970
Add: Alternative Minimum Tax (see Table 2)		23,510
Self-Employment Tax on $58,000 Proprietorship Income		8,195
Less: Credits		(0)
Prepayments of Tax (Assumed Withholdings and Estimated Tax)		(50,000)
Net Tax Liability		5,675

(a) Total received on 2007 private activity bond issue, $7,000
(b) On 2/1/2013, Howard exercised an incentive stock option, purchasing 1,000 shares of his company's stock at $10 per share (FMV of $60 per share). No restrictions were placed on the stock.
(c) Includes the following cost recovery deductions for 2013:
   $20,000 MACRS on post-86 property (AMT ADS is $15,000)
   $15,000 ACRS on pre-87 realty (straight-line is $12,000)
(d) There is no phase-out of the personal exemption deduction or itemized deductions in 2013, since the married-filing jointly phase-outs begin at $300,000 of AGI.
(e) Loan on personal automobiles secured by personal residence
(f) $18,000 investment interest paid, limit to $15,000 net investment income (interest income above)

Figure 2
Howard and Martha Jones—AMT Computation—2013

Items (T = timing, P = permanent)	All	Permanent
Taxable Income per Return (from page 1)	136,450	136,450
Less Disallowed Itemized Deductions (page 1)	(_____0)	(_____0)
Taxable Income as Adjusted	136,450	136,450
AMT Adjustments (may be positive or negative):		
[T] Post-86 Depreciation (MACRS – ADS)	5,000	- -
[T] Res. & Exp. Expenses (Ded. – 10-yr. amort.)	0	- -
[T] Amort. Of Pollution Control (5-yr – ADS recovery)	0	- -
[T] Mining Exploration & Develop (Exp – 10-yr amort.)	0	- -
[T] Circulation Expenditures (Exp – 3-yr amort.)	0	- -
[T] Passive Losses (Recompute with AMT rules)	0	- -
[T] Pct. of Completion Method (PCM – Comp. Cont.)	0	- -
[T] Net Operating Loss Ded. (Reg. NOL – AMT NOL)	0	- -
[T] Adj. Gain (Loss) (Regular Tax – AMT Amount)	0	- -
[T] Incentive Stock Option Exercise (FMV – Ex Price)	50,000	- -
[T] Adj. Expenses for AMT (Add'l Invest. Int Expense)	(3,000)	- -
[P] Disallowed Standard Deduction (if taken)	0	0
Disallowed Itemized Deductions:		
[P] Medical (7.5% ded. – 10% ded.)	6,250	6,250
[P] Interest Expense (Home Equity Disallowed)	3,000	3,000
[P] State and Local Taxes (none allowed)	31,000	31,000
[P] Miscellaneous Itemized (none allowed)	1,000	1,000
[P] Personal Exemption Deductions (none allowed)	7,800	7,800
Taxable Income as Adjusted	237,500	185,500
Preferences (Plus Only):		
[T] Pre-87 Deprec. (Excess – realty & leased per.)	3,000	- -
[P] Tax exempt Interest (Post 8/7/86 private act.)	7,000	7,000
[P] Excess Pct. Depletion (amt exceeding adj basis)	0	0
Alternative Minimum Taxable Income (AMTI)	247,500	192,500
AMT Exemption *	(56,425)	(70,175)
Net Alternative Minimum Taxable Income	191,075	122,325
Tentative Minimum Tax (TMT):		
All [(171,075 × .26) + (0 × .28) + (20,000 × .15)]	47,480	
Permanent Only [(102,325 × .26) + (20,000 × .15)]		29,604
Less Regular Income Tax Liability (see Page 1)	(23,970)	(23,970)
Alternative Minimum Tax Liability [AMT] (to page 1)	23,510	5,634
AMT Credit ("All" – "Permanent Only")	- -	17,876
	23,510	23,510

* Exemption amounts are:
  Joint Ret. (M)—$80,800, less 25% × (AMTI – $150,000) [$473,200 phaseout is complete]
  Single (or HH)—$51,900, less 25% × (AMTI – $112,500) [$320,100 phaseout is complete]
     MS—$40,400, less 25% × (AMTI – $75,000) [$236,600 phaseout is complete]

** When considering only permanent adjustments and preferences ("exclusions"), those items that will not reverse in the future, there would be $5,634 AMT due in 2013. Thus, $17,876 ($23,510 – $5,634) of AMT payable in 2013 is due solely to timing ("deferral") items; this $17,876 may be carried over to 2014 as an AMT credit, reducing 2014 regular tax (but not below the 2014 computed TMT). Thus, if the 2014 regular tax (RT) is $32,000 and the TMT is $27,000, only $5,000 of the 2014 AMT credit may be used to reduce the 2014 RT to $27,000. The remaining AMT credit would then be carried forward to 2015.

Alternative Minimum Tax Credit. When Congress lowered the regular tax rates for individuals in 1986, the regular tax rates and the AMT tax rates were not substantially different. This led to concerns that the AMT would create double taxation on the same items, i.e., once as part of the AMT and later as part of the regular tax liability when the items were reported for regular tax purposes. For example, gain on the exercise of the incentive stock options would be reported at the date of exercise for the AMT and then reported again for regular tax purposes when the stock was sold. To provide some "rough justice" in reducing this double taxation possibility, Congress came up with the idea of a **minimum tax credit** and enacted Code Sec. 53.

The basic theory of the minimum tax credit is that a portion or all of the AMT paid during a tax year may be used in future years as a credit against regular tax liability in those years. However, in no case can such a credit reduce the carryover year's regular tax liability below the tentative minimum tax liability for that year. There is no limit on the number of years that an AMT credit may be carried forward.

For individual taxpayers, only that portion of the current year's AMT that relates to **"timing differences"** (**deferral items** of adjustment and preference, in Code terms) is eligible to be carried forward as an AMT credit; any portion of the AMT related to **"permanent differences"** (**exclusion items** of adjustment and preference, in Code terms) is not eligible for AMT credit treatment. In order to apportion the AMT between timing and permanent differences, the normal procedure is to compute the AMT including both timing and permanent differences (the normal AMT computation), and then recompute the AMT with only permanent differences. The difference in the two AMT numbers is the AMT credit, since it relates solely to timing differences.

The "permanent" adjustment items are listed in Code Sec. 56(b)(1), and the "permanent" preference items are listed in paragraphs (1), (5), and (7) of Code Sec. 57(a). All other items of adjustment and preference are presumed to be "timing" items of adjustment and preference. Thus, the computed $17,876 AMT credit in **Figure 2** may be used in future years to offset regular tax liability (but *not* tentative minimum tax liability). Understanding the nature of the AMT credit is critical to applying some of the planning strategies discussed in the following section.

OBSERVATION   Recent legislation provides for a "refundable AMT credit" for any *long-term unused AMT credit* (more than three years old). The refundable amount is limited to the greater of (1) the lesser of $5,000 or unused long-term credit, or (2) 20 percent of the long-term credit. Thus, the computed refundable amount can reduce tax liability below the computed minimum tax liability for the year. This provides some relief to taxpayers who are constantly in an AMT position.

Credits Against Tentative Minimum Tax Liability. **Figures 1 and 2** do not show any credits as allowable against the tentative minimum tax. Traditionally, only the foreign tax credit was allowed as a credit against tentative minimum tax liability; other credits (including all personal credits) are not part of the AMT computation. Stated differently, personal credits only offset the regular tax liability to the point that the net tax liability equals the tentative minimum tax liability.

OBSERVATION   The various child and education credits enacted in recent years may subject a significant number of taxpayers to the AMT. To remove these taxpayers from possible imposition of the AMT, Congress, as part of the American Taxpayer Relief Act of 2012, modified Code Sec. 26(a) to make permanent the use of all nonrefundable personal credits as credits against the AMT liability.[2] Prior legislation had continually extended these waivers for several years to prevent this ticking time bomb from exploding.

[2]   *See* Code Sec. 26(a).

¶11,005

.01 AMT PLANNING FOR BUSINESS ITEMS

Acceleration of Income and/or Deceleration of Expenses. In certain circumstances, it may make sense for individuals to consider the acceleration of income (or deceleration of expenses) when faced with the AMT in the current tax year. This may be the case, for example, for taxpayers with little or no AMT credit because most or all of the preferences/adjustments are permanent in nature. In such a case, a taxpayer who accelerates income (or defers expense deductions) would pay an effective tax rate of 26 or 28 percent on the additional income, rather than regular tax rates as high as 35 percent.

Note that for Howard and Martha Jones, acceleration of income makes little sense since their marginal regular tax rate is 25 percent and their marginal AMT rate is 26 (near 28) percent. Also, a portion of the AMT credit can be used in the next year, which would argue against the acceleration of income (or deceleration of expenses). But what about taxpayers in the highest regular tax brackets with little or no AMT credits? Would accelerating income into the AMT year make sense? Caution is in order here. For one thing, the tax is being prepaid, and consideration of the time value of money should be made. Also, if the taxpayer's AMTI is in the phase-out range for the AMT exemption, an additional $1 of income will also cause a $.25 loss in the AMT exemption (in effect, increasing the marginal AMT tax rate on each additional dollar of AMT income by 25 percent, from 28 to 35 percent).

More importantly, if an AMT credit is generated, it makes little sense to accelerate income, since this represents nothing more than an acceleration of the tax liability. **Figure 3** provides a two-year comparison of the acceleration of income question for a 39.6-percent regular tax rate taxpayer when an AMT credit is created and when an AMT credit is not generated.

In **Figure 3**, based on the facts of Example 11-1, it is assumed that the timing adjustments occur only in the first year; the taxpayer is subject to the regular tax in the second year in each case. Note in **Figure 3** that if present value factors are ignored, the total taxes paid over the two years when the credit is generated are the same ($291,290 versus $291,292, $2 difference due to rounding) regardless of whether or not the income is accelerated:

Example 11-1. A married couple with $500,000 taxable income expected in the current year and the following year is considering accelerating $50,000 of the income from the next year (Year 2) into the current year (Year 1). AMT *timing adjustments* of $80,000 are expected only in the first year; none are expected in Year 2. This acceleration would actually *increase* the present value of the total taxes paid over the two tax years by more than $1,000, as illustrated below.

As illustrated in **Figure 3**, the taxpayer with timing adjustments as a component of the AMT is actually *worse off* with the acceleration of income in a present-value sense, since tax is needlessly paid one year ahead of time. Taxes would be saved only when *no* AMT credit is present, as in the case of the taxpayer having only permanent adjustments.

Determining the RT/AMT "Breakeven Point." At some point, the additional regular tax generated by accelerated income will overtake the additional tentative minimum tax generated, and from that point on any additional income will be taxed at the higher regular tax rates. To determine the amount of additional income that will roughly equate the two taxes (BEAI, or "breakeven additional income") divide the AMT by the difference in the marginal regular and AMT tax rates. This approximation is fairly accurate if the additional income does not change the marginal tax bracket, and the exemption phase-out does not apply.

Figure 3
Acceleration of Income and the AMT

Income Accelerated?	No		Yes	
	Year 1	Year 2	Year 1	Year 2
Regular Taxable Income	500,000	500,000	550,000	450,000
AMT Timing Adjustments	80,000	0	80,000	0
Adjusted Income	580,000	500,000	630,000	450,000
Tent. Min. Tax (TMT)	158,900	136,500	172,900	122,500
Regular Tax (RT)	(145,645)	(145,645)	(165,446)	(125,846)
AMT	13,255	0	7,454	0
Larger of RT or TMT	158,900	145,645	172,900	125,846
AMT Credit	0	(13,255)	0	(7,454)
Total Tax Liability	158,900	132,390	172,900	119,392
NPV @8%	158,900	122,583	172,900	109,622
NPV Years 1 and 2	281,483		282,522	

For **Figure 3**, this computation yields an additional amount of income of 190,895 as the break-even point, as illustrated below:

BEAI = (TMT – RT)/(Marginal RT Rate – Marginal AMT Rate)
BEAI = (158,900 – 145,645)/(.396 – .28)
BEAI = *$114,267*

Regular Tax Liability on ($500,000 + $114,267) = *$190,895*
Tentative Minimum Tax Liability on (500,000 + $80,000 + $114,267) = *$190,895*

OBSERVATION   Under the Pension Protection Act of 2006, taxpayers who converted a traditional IRA into a Roth IRA in the year 2010 could elect to include the resulting taxable distribution ratably in income in the tax years 2011 and 2012, unless they opted out of this provision by including the entire amount in income in 2010. For taxpayers already in an AMT situation in 2010, the question of accelerating the recognition into 2010 involved the same analysis discussed above. Unless the taxpayer's AMT was caused primarily by permanent differences, or the taxpayer expected to be in an AMT situation for the foreseeable future, the acceleration election was probably not the wise choice.

Cost Recovery Issues. A taxpayer may minimize AMT problems caused by positive depreciation adjustments by slowing down the regular tax cost recovery deductions for depreciable assets. However, since depreciation is a "timing" item, and if the resulting AMT credit can be used in the following year, the only tax "cost" of accelerated depreciation is one year of interest. On the other hand, if the taxpayer is likely to be in an AMT situation for the foreseeable future, then steps to minimize the exposure to the AMT should be taken so that accumulated AMT credits can be utilized against the regular tax liability. These include electing straight-line or ADS recovery, where the taxpayer can "fine tune" the result because Code Sec. 168(b)(5) provides that such elections are made on an asset-class-by-asset-class basis, and on a year-to-year basis.

A taxpayer may also consider leasing property rather than owning it, since such lease deductions are allowed for both regular tax and AMT purposes. But then again, lease pricing policies probably build in this consideration, and with the recent narrowing of cost recovery differences between regular tax and AMT, all economic factors should be considered when leasing alternatives exist.

A taxpayer should remember that *negative* AMT adjustments always result when the property is sold, exchanged, or abandoned before the end of its recovery life. This is because the adjusted basis of the property for AMT purposes is *higher*. If Howard and Martha Jones sold a business asset near the end of its recovery life, a negative adjustment (equal to the sum of all net prior positive depreciation adjustments on the asset) would reduce alternative minimum taxable income. This factor encourages a judicious choice of timing asset dispositions and abandonment. Specifically, such actions may be accelerated to a year when the taxpayer is already in an AMT position. The resulting negative adjustments will offset, or possibly eliminate, any AMT liability.

OBSERVATION	One advantage of an abandonment is that such transactions are not sales or exchanges for tax purposes. As a result, any loss recognized is reported as ordinary loss and not Code Sec. 1231 loss.

Credit versus Deduction Issues. Taxpayers are allowed the option of deducting certain items rather than utilizing a credit. This is true for the research credit,[3] the work incentive credit,[4] and the orphan drugs credit.[5] Such credits cannot be used to reduce the tentative minimum tax; however, if reported as expenses, such amounts are deductible for both regular tax and AMT purposes. If a taxpayer has a possible AMT problem looming, it may make sense to elect the expensing option. A taxpayer may also consider an election to reduce the Research and Experimentation (R&E) credit and forego the R&E expense reduction for research credits taken. If the taxpayer is already subject to the AMT, this election may make sense, since the deduction is allowed for both regular tax and AMT purposes, while the credit is allowed only for regular tax purposes.

Net Operating Loss Issues. Code Sec. 172 requires a regular tax and AMT consistency on the issue of foregoing a net operating loss carryback period. Taxpayers should carefully consider the impacts on both regular tax liability and TMT liability in carryback years if no AMT benefit is derived in the carryback years (i.e., there is no AMT liability in those years). Electing to forego the carryback would preserve the AMT net operating loss (NOL) benefits for carryforward years. Since an AMT NOL carryback *must* offset any AMTI in a carryback year, even if the taxpayer did not owe any AMT for that year, the tax benefit of the AMT NOL may be lost.

.03   AMT PLANNING FOR INVESTMENT ITEMS

Private Activity Bond Interest. Taxpayers should be aware of the negative AMT consequences associated with private activity bond interest. Such interest, though not subject to the regular tax, is subject to the AMT. More importantly, this is a permanent preference item, so no AMT credit is generated. Thus, for Howard and Martha Jones, the $7,000 private activity bond interest is effectively taxed at 28 percent (the AMT rate), with no prospect of recovering such taxes through an AMT credit in future years. If the bond paid a 6-percent rate of return, this would decline to only 4.32 percent in the current year when the AMT applies. Actually, if the $7,000 is treated as marginal income, the effective tax rate is 35 percent (28% × 1.25%), since Howard and Martha are in the phase-out range of the AMT exemption deduction. This lowers the effective rate on the 6-percent bond to 3.90 percent.

---

[3]   *See* Code Sec. 41.
[4]   *See* Code Sec. 51.
[5]   *See* Code Sec. 28.

OBSERVATION	If interest income is generated in an AMT year, care should be taken to ensure that any related expenses are deducted for AMT purposes. And since such interest is investment income for purposes of the investment interest limitation rules, the ceiling on the AMT investment interest expense deduction is increased. Thus, Howard and Martha Jones were able to deduct $3,000 additional interest that was disallowed for regular tax purposes.

Evaluating the Impact of Capital Gains. As mentioned earlier, the AMT rate applicable to long-term capital gains cannot exceed the preferential regular tax rate applicable to such gains (15-, 20-, 25-, or 28-percent). Although this somewhat lessens the exposure to the AMT, there is another potential problem lurking just beneath the surface: the gain may be subject to *state* income taxes (and recall that state and local tax adjustments do not generate AMT credit). The combination of large amounts of additional income from capital gains and the loss of the state tax deduction for purposes of the AMT may create an AMT problem.

OBSERVATION	Recall that *all* state and local taxes are disallowed for the AMT, and not just state and local income taxes. So the problem is not mitigated if state and local sales taxes exceed state income taxes, and the larger of the two is deductible under current law.

This problem is also magnified if state law does not recognize the Code Sec. 121 exclusion on the sale of a personal residence. The possible interplay of capital gains income and the state income tax deduction on the AMT should be examined before large capital gains are recognized. Problems may be avoided by spreading the gain over more than one year.

The same capital gains/state income tax considerations also apply to sales of qualified small business stock under Code Sec. 1202, with one other worrisome factor: seven percent of the excluded gain is a tax preference item for AMT purposes. This preference amount may reduce the attractiveness of Code Sec. 1202 stock. The state tax effects may not be disastrous in states that follow the federal tax inclusion rules for such capital gains, since only half the gain is includible in gross income. One planning strategy is to make sales across several years to minimize the effects of the AMT. Another possibility would be to rollover the stock tax-free into other Code Sec. 1202 stock under Code Sec. 1045.

Incentive Stock Option Exercise. For Howard and Martha Jones, the largest adjustment was for the bargain element in the stock option at exercise. In effect, the AMT rules accelerate recognition of such gain. For regular tax purposes, gain is recognized only when the stock is sold. Since this is a timing adjustment, an AMT credit is available in the following year to offset the negative current year effects, and once again the analysis simplifies to a time-value of money analysis. Thus, if this year's AMT is a one-time event, Howard and Martha will recover most of the tax benefit in the following year when the AMT credit offsets regular tax liability.

But what if Howard and Martha reasonably anticipate more AMT situations in the future? In this case, it may make sense to limit the number of stock options exercised. For example, a breakeven analysis can be used to determine the number of options that could be exercised to equate the regular and the AMT tax liabilities (see the Case Study in the problem materials for this chapter). In some situations, an AMT liability would still exist even if no options were exercised, so this suggestion is of little help to such taxpayers.

One strategy would be to sell the optioned shares in the same year as the exercise. Although this accelerates recognition of ordinary income gain for regular tax purposes, it does remove the adjustment item from the AMT computation.[6] And if this leaves the taxpayer in a regular tax situation for the current year, any accumulated AMT credits from prior years could possibly be utilized.

Capital Gains Election for Investment Interest Expense Deductions. For purposes of determining the Code Sec. 163(d) limit on investment interest expense, the definition

---

[6]　Code Sec. 56(b)(1)(3).

of "investment income" does not include long-term capital gains or dividends qualifying for the 15-percent rate. However, Code Sec. 163(d)(4)(B) permits a taxpayer to include such gains in the determination of investment income, but only at the expense of foregoing any lower capital gains rates otherwise applicable to such gains.

From the perspective of minimizing exposure to the AMT, the election to treat such gains as investment income may make sense. The additional investment interest expense deductible with the higher level of net investment income would be a deduction against both regular tax and alternative minimum tax, whereas the long-term capital gain, now reportable as ordinary income in both computations, would further narrow the difference between regular tax liability and the AMT. However, time value of money considerations should factor into such an analysis, as excess investment interest expense in any one year may be carried forward indefinitely as a deduction in future years.

Deducting Foreign Taxes Paid and Foregoing the Credit. The foreign tax credit is different from other tax credits related to businesses in that it may offset the tentative minimum tax liability. At one time, this credit was limited in any one year to 90 percent of alternative minimum taxable income. Thus, if that limit was likely to apply, then the deduction election would have been a more attractive alternative for lessening exposure to the AMT if it is anticipated that the credit will not be fully utilized in the foreseeable future. But with 100 percent of the foreign tax credit now allowed as an offset against the AMT, the credit probably is the better option.

.05 AMT PLANNING FOR PERSONAL ITEMS

Postponing Property Tax and Miscellaneous Itemized Deductions. Property tax and miscellaneous itemized deductions offer no benefits to a taxpayer in a year that the AMT applies; such deductions are wasted since they are not allowed for AMT purposes. Therefore, it may make sense for the taxpayer to postpone these deductions until the next year when perhaps they can be used to offset regular tax liability. This is true for Howard and Martha Jones. Since they are in an AMT situation, the property tax and miscellaneous itemized deductions are wasted in the year 2013. If a portion of either expenditure could be postponed to 2014, these expenses may be utilized fully against regular taxable income.

OBSERVATION	In some cases, this strategy may not save taxes. See the Case Study at the end of the chapter for an illustration of this point. Also, a taxpayer may make a negative adjustment for any state income tax refund reported as for regular tax purposes due to a prior-year regular tax deduction, since a deduction for state and local income taxes is never allowed for the AMT in any year.

Changing the Character of Unreimbursed Employee Expenses. Miscellaneous itemized deductions exceeding two percent of adjusted gross income are deductible for regular tax purposes, but as explained above, are not deductible for AMT purposes. For many taxpayers, unreimbursed employee expenses make up the bulk of this potential deduction. This is true for Howard and Martha Jones. Employees may prefer an employer-sponsored accountable reimbursement plan, so that such expenses would not fall in this category.

Evaluating Home Equity Loans. Howard and Martha Jones incurred $3,000 interest expense on a home-equity loan used to buy an automobile. This interest is not deductible for AMT purposes, and is a permanent adjustment in computing the AMT. Thus, the tax deductibility of a home equity loan is negated for any year that the taxpayer is in an AMT position.

Electing Out of an Installment Method. Electing out of the installment method does not provide any real advantage for AMT purposes, since only gain qualifying as capital gain can be reported as installment sale gain. Thus, nothing is gained because the capital gain is now taxed at the same rate for both regular tax and AMT purposes.

If a taxpayer sells depreciable property on an installment basis, Code Sec. 453(i) provides that any depreciation recapture must be reported in the year of sale. This may not necessarily be a bad thing for a taxpayer in a constant AMT situation since the recapture income is taxed at ordinary income rates. In effect, a taxpayer in an AMT situation pays at most a 26- or 28-percent rate on the ordinary income.

.07   CONCLUSION

Many commentators refer to the AMT as a largely symbolic tax, in that its existence gives the impression that all taxpayers pay some amount of income tax. However, the AMT is also a politically expedient way for Congress to require taxpayers to pay some (or more) tax without having to deal with the real causes of the problem—the tax incentives that give rise to the AMT. Since it is unlikely that the AMT will be repealed (although yet another proposal is before Congress now), it is important for taxpayers and tax professionals to be aware of strategies for avoiding or minimizing its impact. The previous analysis has proposed a number of ideas for implementing these strategies.

ON THE WEB   For more information on the AMT, enter the following web address into your internet browser:
http://www.finance.cch.com/text/c60s20d110.asp

¶11,007   Tax Planning Constraints: The Passive Activity Limitations

.01   PALS: THE GENERAL RULES

Many individual taxpayers invest in various activities, and this may invoke a significant planning constraint: the **passive activity limitations (PAL)** of Code Sec. 469. The passive activity limits were enacted in 1986 to limit losses from certain tax-shelter activities labeled as "passive activities" in the legislation. The typical tax shelter investment (such as a rental property) was characterized by little risk to the owner, net losses for tax purposes, and positive cash flows (because of such large noncash deductions as depreciation).

In general, Code Sec. 469 groups all activities of a taxpayer into one of three "baskets" of income: active, passive, and portfolio. Passive losses may only offset passive incomes in the same basket; any unused passive losses are carried over to future years (subject to the same netting). Suspended losses may finally be deducted when there is passive income in the basket, or, as explained below, when the activity is sold.

The Three "Baskets" of Income as Defined by Code Sec. 469

a.   **Active** (Trades or businesses in which the taxpayer "materially participates").
b.   **Passive** (Trades or businesses in which the taxpayer does not "materially participate").
c.   **Portfolio** (Investment activities income, such as interest, dividends and royalties).

Code Sec. 469 operates in a straight-forward manner: deductions from passive activities (those without "**material participation**") are limited to the incomes from passive activities. In other words, net passive losses may not offset active or portfolio incomes.

Example 11-2. Susan Beale had $100,000 salary and $30,000 interest income in 2013. Susan also invested in passive Activity A, which generated a net loss of $38,000, and passive Activity B, which generated a profit of $20,000. Susan can deduct only $20,000 of the loss from Activity A in 2013, that is, limited to the $20,000 passive income from Activity B. The remaining $18,000 loss is suspended as a loss from Activity A.

Any losses from passive activities that are not currently deducted ("suspended losses") may be carried over indefinitely and used when (1) passive income exists or (2) the activity that generated the losses is disposed of in a taxable transaction.

Example 11-3. Assume the same facts as the previous example, and that Susan has a net profit of $2,000 in Activity A and a net profit of $3,000 from Activity B in 2014. Susan may now offset the $18,000 suspended loss of Activity A by the profits generated in both passive activities in 2014. As a result, the suspended loss carried over to 2015 (all attributable to Activity A) is $13,000.

Example 11-4. Assume the same facts as the previous example, and that Susan sells Activity A in 2015. Susan may now deduct the $13,000 Activity A suspended loss from 2014, as well as any losses generated by Activity A in 2015.

The passive activity rules placed a significant constraint on the economics of certain investments, particularly real estate. However, there are two aspects of the Code Sec. 469 rules that may be planned around: (1) establishing material participation and (2) qualifying for the $25,000 residential real estate exception. Each is discussed below.

.03   PLANNING AROUND THE MATERIAL PARTICIPATION RULES

Two of the most important concepts necessary to apply the passive activity limitations are the definitions of an **"activity"** and **"material participation."** Interestingly, Congress defined neither one, leaving that task to the IRS to accomplish through regulations. An understanding of both concepts is critical to planning under Code Sec. 469.

Reg. §1.469-4 states that the primary focus in defining an "activity" should be on grouping trade or business activities, or rental activities, into "appropriate economic units," using a facts and circumstances approach. The key factors in determining such groupings should be (a) type of business, (b) common control, (c) common ownership, (d) geographic location, and (e) business interdependencies. These 1992 regulations also provide a few examples. One example involves a taxpayer who owns bakeries and movie theaters in both Philadelphia and Baltimore. In demonstrating the flexibility of the activity regulations, the example notes that the taxpayer could choose one of four options in grouping the interests: (1) two activities (bakeries and movie theaters); (2) two activities (Philadelphia and Baltimore); (3) four activities (two separate bakery activities and two separate movie activities); or (4) one activity (movies and bakeries).

OBSERVATION   Under the Affordable Care Act of 2010, a new 3.8% tax on investment income was added for certain high-income taxpayers, beginning in 2013. Because passive activities may be subject to these rules, Congress provided a one-time opportunity for taxpayers to "regroup" their activities for purposes of planning for this new tax.

Once activities are defined, a second question must be answered: specifically, which basket does the income or loss from the activity belong in? Note that the critical difference between the active basket and the passive basket is "material participation." The IRS defined such participation in Reg. §1.469-1 as being met if the taxpayer meets any of the following seven basic tests:

Seven Ways a Taxpayer Can Materially Participate in an Activity:

1.   Participate more than 500 hours
2.   Provide "substantially all" the material participation

3. Participate more than 100 hours and no one else participated more (**"significant participation"**)
4. Participate more than 100 hours in each of several activities, and the total participation in these "more-than-100-hour" activities exceeds 500 hours (the aggregation rule)
5. Materially participate in the activity in 5 of the preceding 10 years
6. Materially participate in any of the preceding three years of a personal service activity
7. Facts and circumstances (at a minimum more than 100 hours, no one else participates more, and a paid manager is not used in the activity)

Note that if a taxpayer materially participates in an activity, he or she will include such income or loss in the active basket. This is particularly important for losses, as such losses can offset *any* kind of income, including all sources of active, passive, and portfolio income. On the other hand, if the activity is profitable, the taxpayer may just as soon have the income to be in the passive basket, so that such income would be available to absorb other passive losses, such as certain rental losses (hence, the lookback tests five and six above, to prevent deliberately flunking material participation in profitable years or retirement years). The interplay of grouping activities and meeting (or failing) the material participation tests becomes paramount in planning for the individual.

Example 11-5. As of the end of November, Jane Beasley has worked 432 hours in an activity with two other individuals; Al Howdy worked 290 hours in the activity, and Jenny Ride worked 534 hours in the activity. The activity is expected to generate a significant loss in the current year. If Jane wants to be a "material participant" in the activity, she will need to work at least 69 more hours in the activity. This will give her 501 hours, which meets Test 1 (the 500 hour test); she does not have to work more hours than Jenny Ride.

.05   PLANNING WITH THE RENTAL REAL ESTATE EXCEPTION

A taxpayer who owns at least a 10-percent interest without limited liability in residential real estate may deduct the first $25,000 of such losses against any type of income; in other words, these losses "escape" the passive basket. However, the $25,000 maximum is reduced $.50 for each dollar of AGI of the taxpayer (computed without considering passive activities) exceeding $100,000. Thus, the **rental real estate exception** is completely phased out for a taxpayer with AGI of $150,000 or greater.

Example 11-6. Assume the same facts as Example 11-2, except that Activity A is qualifying residential real estate. Susan's AGI before considering passive activities is $130,000 ($100,000 salary + $30,000 interest), so her maximum exception to the passive activity rules is $10,000 ($25,000 – .50[130,000 – 100,000]). Thus, Susan can deduct $10,000 of the otherwise disallowed $18,000 passive loss in 2013, and the suspended loss carried over to 2014 is only $8,000.

In order to qualify for the $25,000 exception, a taxpayer must be an "**active participant**" in the rental real estate activity. To qualify as an active participant, Code Sec. 469 requires that a taxpayer (1) own at least a 10-percent interest (by value) in the activity, (2) is not a limited partner (unless an exception is provided in the regulations), and (3) demonstrate regular, continuous, and substantial involvement in the operations.

The third requirement can be demonstrated by participating in such decisions as approving new tenants, deciding on rental terms, and approving repairs or capital improvements. Paying a fee to an individual or an agency to manage the property will not cause the taxpayer to fail "active participation," as long as the taxpayer participates in the major decisions related to the property. Code Sec. 469(i)(6)(c) specifically states that there is *no* active participation requirement in the case of the low-income housing tax credit and the rehabilitation tax credit. The $25,000 exception is also available for these credits that may be related to rental property; however, the $25,000 deduction is converted to an equivalent credit based on the taxpayer's marginal tax rate.

The $25,000 exception offers middle-income taxpayers with a rental property or two some relief from the Code Sec. 469 rules. It is important to understand how these rules work and how to analyze the effects of additional income or deductions on the results.

¶11,009   Tax Planning Constraints: The Investment Interest Limitations

Prior to 1969, taxpayers could deduct all interest expense except that related to tax-free income. This rule permitted taxpayers to voluntarily incur substantial interest expense on funds borrowed to acquire or carry investment assets. Often these funds were used to purchase stocks that had growth potential but returned little or no dividends currently. This gave rise to an immediate deduction and permitted the taxpayer to report gain on sale of the appreciated securities (at capital gains rates) at a much later date. Undeveloped real estate offered the same kind of tax parlay. In order to curtail excessive abuses of this tax break, tax laws now limit the amount of interest deductible on funds borrowed by noncorporate taxpayers to purchase investment property.

Code Sec. 163(d) currently limits the deduction for noncorporate taxpayers' **investment interest expense** to the amount of the taxpayer's **"net investment income."** Any amounts disallowed are carried forward as interest expense in the succeeding tax year (subject to the limitations). In effect, there is an unlimited carryover.

Example 11-7. During 2013, M had $28,000 of investment interest income and $21,000 of investment expenses, exclusive of investment interest of $20,000 paid during the year. Her investment interest expense deduction for 2013 is limited to $7,000, the amount of her net investment income ($28,000 − $21,000). The remaining $13,000 of investment interest expense will be carried over to 2014 and treated as investment interest expense in that year.

In 1993, Congress excluded net long-term capital gains on the sale of investment property from "investment income" because they believed that it was inappropriate to allow taxpayers to use income taxed at a lower rate as a means of deducting otherwise nondeductible investment interest. However, Code Sec. 163(d)(4)(B) provides an election to include such gains in investment income as long as the gain is excluded from gain qualifying for lower capital gains rates. To ensure consistency, Congress, as part of the 2003 Act, extended the election to include dividend income qualifying for the 15-percent rate.

In some cases, it may be beneficial for the taxpayer to make such an election, although it is less likely with the low 15- or 20-percent rates. The taxpayer is comparing the tax cost of postponing an interest deduction to a later year with the cost of losing the 15- or 20-percent capital gains ceiling.

Example 11-8. Assume the same facts as the previous example, except that taxpayer also had $8,000 long-term capital gains and $4,000 of dividend income qualifying for the 15-percent rate. If the taxpayer elects to do so, the $12,000 total (or either item alone) can be treated as investment income, increasing the investment interest deduction by $12,000 and reducing the carryover to $1,000. However, the $12,000 total will be taxed at ordinary income rates (up to 39.6 percent), as such amounts no longer qualify for the 15-percent rate.

With the recent changes in capital gains and ordinary income tax rates, should such an election be considered? The decision depends primarily on when the taxpayer believes that any investment interest otherwise disallowed in the current year will be deducted if the special election is not made. A simple algebraic analysis may be performed. Any analysis of the two options must consider the time value of money, since postponed interest expense would be deducted in future years. The "breakeven" number to be solved for in this case represents the interest rate that equates the two options.

In other words, at what interest rate must the tax savings generated by the election in the current year (created by offsetting income that would otherwise have been taxed at 15 percent) be invested to equal the tax savings that would have been generated by using the expense to offset ordinary income in the future? This may be expressed with the following equality:

Tax savings in current year with special capital gains election (15% of capital gain)	=	Present Value of tax savings deduction in Year 2 only (35% of ordinary income)

The number of present value factors incorporated in the formula depends on the number of years the taxpayer believes will be necessary to fully recover the carryover interest deductions. In a case where the taxpayer believes that postponed deductions will be utilized in the next taxable year, the comparison would appear as follows:

$$DED \times CGR = DED \times OTR \times R, \text{ where}$$

DED = Investment interest expense deduction
OTR = Ordinary income marginal tax rate
CGR = Capital gains marginal tax rate
$R = (1 + r)^n$, where r = breakeven interest rate and n = number of years in future

Example 11-9. Jim Barlow, a 35-percent bracket taxpayer, has $100,000 of net investment interest expenses and $80,000 of net investment income in 2013. Jim also has a $20,000 long-term capital gain on the sale of investments that qualifies for the 15-percent rate. Jim believes that any interest expense disallowed during the current year will be deducted in the next tax year (2014). Thus, Jim's two tax choices are: (1) save 15-percent tax on capital gain otherwise taxed in Year 1, or (2) save 35 percent on ordinary income in Year 2. His relevant comparison is as follows:

$$DED \times CGR = DED \times OTR \times R$$
$$20,000 \times .15 = (20,000 \times .35)/(1 + R)$$
$$3,000 = 7,000/(1 + R)$$
$$3,000 (1 + R) = 7,000$$
$$3,000R = 4,000$$
$$R = 1.33 \text{ (or 133\%)}$$

Thus, the additional tax savings generated by the election in Year 1 must be invested at an annual rate of return of 133 percent (an unlikely possibility!) to equal the foregone tax savings available by waiting one year. Clearly, the election does not make much sense in this example, since merely deferring the deduction one year yields $4,000 ($7,000 − $3,000) more tax savings.

ON THE WEB   For more information on investment interest expense, enter the following web address into your internet browser: *http://www.finance.cch.com/text/c60s10d534.asp*

¶11,011 Tax Planning: Tax-Exempt Income and Fringe Benefits

.01 TAX-EXEMPT INTEREST INCOME

With the low interest rates currently available on investments, many taxpayers are finding tax-exempt state, local and territorial bonds to be worthwhile investments. In many cases, the after-tax return is higher on these bonds than other investments.

Example 11-10. A taxpayer has a choice of investing in a 6.0-percent taxable bond or a 4.2-percent nontaxable state bond. The taxpayer's current tax rate is 35 percent. The after-tax rate of return on the taxable bond is 3.9 percent [6% − (6% × .35)], and the after-tax rate of return on the nontaxable state bond is 4.2 percent (4.2% − 0). The nontaxable bond fares slightly better.

Simple algebra can be used to determine a before-tax rate of return to be earned from a taxable investment to equal a given rate from a nontaxable investment:

$$\text{Breakeven Rate of Return for Taxable Investment} = \frac{\text{Rate of Return on Nontaxable Investment}}{(100\% - \text{Taxpayer's Marginal Tax Rate})}$$

Example 11-11. Using the above formula, what is the breakeven rate of return for a taxable investment for a taxpayer in the 33-percent tax bracket who can invest in a 4.2-percent nontaxable bond? The answer is 6.26 percent, or .042/(1.00 − .33). If the taxpayer's marginal tax rate was 25 percent, the answer would be 5.60 percent, or .042/(1.00 − .25).

.03 TAX-FREE FRINGE BENEFITS

The Internal Revenue Code provides for a number of tax-free fringe benefits for employees of corporations. A number of these are discussed in Chapter 12. The tax-free status of these benefits makes them worth even more than their monetary value, since the employee would otherwise have to earn even more taxable income to generate enough tax-exempt income to purchase the fringe benefit. Specifically, this amount of before-tax income can be determined by dividing the value of the benefit by the percentage of gross income that the taxpayer receives after considering all related taxes.

Example 11-12. Anna Marie Freeman has a 33-percent marginal federal income tax rate and a 5-percent marginal state tax rate. State gross income is defined the same as federal gross income. During the current year, Anna Marie is provided with group health insurance coverage by her employer for which the employer paid $3,100. If Anna had to purchase such coverage on her own, it would cost $4,800. What is the "real" value of this coverage by Anna's employer, if she otherwise had to purchase the coverage on her own with after-tax funds? The answer is $7,742, or $4,800/(1.00 − .38).

¶11,013 Tax Planning: Capital Gains and Losses

Tutorials provided online (*CCHGroup.com/ContemporaryTax*) with this text provide a review of the basic capital gain and loss netting process for individuals. Recall that net long-term capital gains could be taxed at preferential rates of 15 or 20 percent (25 percent for certain "unrecaptured

Sec. 1250 gain" and 28 percent for collectibles and gain on the sale of Code Sec. 1202 stock). Also recall that short-term capital gains are fully taxable, and net capital losses are limited to a maximum offset of $3,000 against ordinary income in any tax year (with unlimited carryovers).

Understanding how these netting rules operate can reveal several possible planning strategies. A few of these are discussed below.

.01   THE VALUE OF CAPITAL LOSSES

Because recent tax acts enhanced the tax rate differential for certain long-term capital gains, it becomes important to understand the possible impact of year-end capital transactions. The best use of a short-term capital loss is to either offset short-term capital gains (which are taxed at ordinary rates as high as 39.6 percent), or to a limited extent, offset ordinary income (the first $3,000 of capital losses can offset ordinary income of individuals). In general, these losses should not be recognized in years in which significant long-term capital gains have already been recognized, especially those in the 15-percent grouping.

The same general rule for short-term losses (offsetting short-term gains and/or ordinary income) also applies to long-term capital losses. If at all possible, taxpayers should minimize the recognition of long-term capital losses in the same year as long-term capital gains, since the loss offsets are less valuable than offsetting short-term capital gain and/or ordinary income.

.03   THE TIMING OF CAPITAL GAINS

Obviously, gains in the 15- or 20-percent grouping should be avoided if at all possible in years in which capital losses are present. However, if the taxpayer must sell stock at a gain and can choose between 28- and 15- or 20-percent gains, the 28-percent gains should be recognized first (at least in an amount to absorb the capital losses). Also, because of the netting process, 15-percent gains should be avoided if possible in years in which 15-percent losses are recognized since the 15-percent net losses will first offset 28-percent gains, and then offset 25-percent gains.

.05   HOW MUCH LOSS IN VALUE CAN A TAXPAYER AFFORD TO RECEIVE LONG-TERM CAPITAL GAINS TREATMENT?

With the volatile stock market, a common question for investors these days is whether they should (1) realize a certain gain today as short-term capital gain and pay the additional tax at ordinary rates, or (2) hold the stock until they have met the long-term holding period and pay lower capital gains tax rates (but at a price unknown today).

Given that less tax will be paid with the latter option, it would be useful to know what sales price would equate the two options on an after-tax basis. Breakeven analysis can be used to determine how much loss in stock value a taxpayer can afford in chasing a lower tax rate. The necessary breakeven formula is:

$$\text{After-tax proceeds from selling after achieving long-term status} = \text{After-tax proceeds from selling at the present time}$$

The breakeven formula may be expressed as follows:

BSP – [(BSP – AB) × CGR] = CSP – [(CSP – AB) × OTR], where

BSP = Break-even sales price of the stock (a sales price exceeding this amount favors waiting for long-term status)
AB = Adjusted basis of the stock
CGR = Capital gains tax rate
CSP = Current sales price of stock
OTR = Ordinary income marginal tax rate

Example 11-13. Tina Seago, who is in the 35-percent marginal tax bracket, holds a stock with an adjusted basis of $80,000 that would sell today for $140,000; however, the stock has been held for only eight months. How much decline in value can Tina afford to absorb and yet still be as well off on an after-tax basis in order to qualify the 15-percent long-term rate? The answer may be determined by using the formula as follows:

$$\text{BSP} - [(\text{BSP} - \text{AB}) \times \text{CGR}] = \text{CSP} - [(\text{CSP} - \text{AB}) \times \text{OTR}]$$
$$\text{BSP} - [(\text{BSP} - \$80,000) \times .15] = \$140,000 - [(\$140,000 - \$80,000) \times .35]$$
$$\text{BSP} - .15\,\text{BSP} + \$12,000 = \$140,000 - \$21,000$$
$$.85\,\text{BSP} = \$107,000$$
$$\text{BSP} = \$125,882$$

Thus, the stock could decline in value as much as $14,118 ($140,000 − $125,882) if the stock was held long-term and the taxpayer would realize the same after-tax cash from the sale as selling now for $140,000.

ON THE WEB   For more information on capital gains and losses, enter the following web address into your internet browser: *http://www.finance.cch.com/text/c60s10d405.asp*

¶11,015   Tax Planning: Rental Investments as Tax Shelters

Residential real estate has been among the most popular forms of tax shelter investments. In addition to significant tax advantages available in the Code, these investments may be justified by sound economic reasons as well. Among the most important of these reasons are the leveraging opportunities and the historic growth in value of real estate.

Such investments also benefit from depreciation deductions, the possibility of capital gains treatment of any gain upon disposition, and the dual benefits of tax losses and positive cash flows. As discussed earlier, the tax losses produce immediate benefits for small investors due to the relaxation of the passive limitations on the first $25,000 of losses.

The benefits of rental real estate investments to small investors can be best demonstrated with a comprehensive example. **Figure 4** and **Figure 5** present an analysis of the after-tax effects of a portfolio of three different investments, including residential real estate, for the first year and the last year (the sixth year) of the investment. Although our focus will be on the real estate investment, the taxable bond and tax-exempt bond investments are also included for comparison purposes.

Before analyzing the real estate alternative, it is important to note that the entire analysis depends on the accuracy of the projected inflows, outflows, and appreciation. Investment analyses sometimes seem to imply a much higher degree of accuracy than warranted by the underlying assumptions. It is very important to emphasize this point when making these calculations. Nonetheless, the margin of error may be an acceptable risk when compared with the alternative of making no projections at all.

A good starting point in analyzing this investment is to mention the concept of **leveraging**, the process of using limited cash outlays to acquire much larger benefits. In the example, the taxpayer has a $64,000 depreciable investment in the building ($80,000 total cost less 20 percent, or $16,000, allocated to the land) for an initial cash outlay of only $16,000, the down payment. The tax savings from the cost recovery deductions on 27.5-year property in the first year cover approximately five percent of this down payment. Furthermore, interest on the mortgaged amount is deductible. (Note: The spreadsheet used to develop this example, *Rental2013.xls*, is on the text website (*CCHGroup.com/ContemporaryTax*) and is used in a tax planning case in the problem materials.)

Perhaps the most frequently cited advantage of real estate investments is the opportunity to create deductible tax losses and yet receive positive cash flows from the investment.

Figure 4 above compares the taxable income (loss) and net cash flow of a proposed investment in the first year. (Mortgage interest and principal payments are taken from a monthly amortization schedule for a 30-year, eight-percent mortgage.)

Figure 4 shows a $2,012 deductible loss and a $455 after-tax positive cash flow. Note particularly the computation of the income tax savings; the $503 total amount (shown in the "Investments Summary" section) is calculated on a marginal basis, by comparing the tax due *without* the three investments with the tax due *including* the three investments (real estate, taxable bonds, and nontaxable bonds). Of this total, marginal allocations reveal that the real estate investment generated $503 positive tax savings and the taxable bond generated $375 total tax costs.

This analysis can be prepared for all years of the assumed investment. Note that in each year of the rental investment analysis, the non-cash flow rental items (depreciation of the furniture and the building) are ignored in converting the rental result to a cash basis. Negative cash flow adjustments are also made nondeductible mortgage principal payments.

In order to simplify the analysis, it is assumed that all cash flows occur at the end of the year. It is assumed in **Figure 4** that the taxpayer invests short-term rent cash flows in a taxable money market fund that is expected to pay an average three-percent interest rate over the period. Thus, the net cash inflow invested in the money market fund at the end of Year 1 ($455) earns $14 ($455 × .03) of taxable interest in Year 2. The same procedure is used for each year of the investment, with the fund balance increased each year by that year's net cash inflow.

Figure 4			
ANALYSIS	**Tax Year 1**	**Tax Inc (Loss)**	**Rent Cash Flows**
Gross Salary Income		125,000	
Taxable Interest Income		1,500	
Taxable Passive Income		0	
Taxable Interest on Short-term Rent Fund		0	0
Adjusted Gross Income Before Rental		126,500	
Rental Receipts		7,980	7,980
Property Taxes Paid		(1,800)	(1,800)
Repair Expenses Paid		(300)	(300)
MACRS Deduction - Furnishings		(572)	0
MACRS Deduction – Building		(2,230)	0
Mortgage Interest Paid		(5,090)	(5,090)
Disposal of Rental Property		0	0
Gross Rental Income (Loss)		(2,012)	
Prior Year Suspended Loss Used Currently		0	
Current Rental Loss Suspended (Carryforward)		0	
Net Rental Income (Loss) After Passive Limits		(2,012)	
Adjusted Gross Income Including Rental		124,488	
Personal Exemption Deductions		(10,950)	
Itemized Deductions		(15,000)	
Taxable Income		98,538	
Mortgage Principal Paid on Rental Property			(838)
Net Before-Tax Cash Flow From Rental Property			(48)
Tax on Noninvestment Income (Sal & Passive)	16,620		
Marginal Tax Cost - Taxable Bond Interest	375		Carryover
Marginal Tax Cost (Savings) – Rental	(503)		Suspended
			Rent Loss
Total Tax Liability – Current Year	16,492		0

INVESTMENTS SUMMARY:	Rent	Tax Int	Tx-Ex Int	Total
Before-Tax Cash Flow	(48)	1,500	1,500	2,952
Tax Savings (Cost) of Investment	503	(375)	0	128
Cash Flow - Year [1]	455	1,125	1,500	3,080
Investment Fund Balances	455	31,125	51,500	83,080

The Year 6 results in **Figure 5** include the after-tax effects of liquidating the investment at the end of the year. The original investment assumption was that the land and the building would increase in value at a rate of three percent per year. Under this assumption, the land has a value of $19,105 and the building has a value of $76,419 in Year 6. Note that the gain on the land and building qualifies as Code Sec. 1231 gain, which will be taxed as long-term capital gain (eligible for a 15-percent maximum rate after reflecting 25-percent rate recapture on the building).

Figure 5			
ANALYSIS	**Tax Year 6**	**Tax Inc (Loss)**	**Rent Cash Flows**
Gross Salary Income		152,082	
Taxable Interest Income		1,803	
Taxable Passive Income		0	
Taxable Interest on Short-term Rent Fund		76	0
Adjusted Gross Income Before Rental		153,960	
Rental Receipts		8,811	8,811
Property Taxes Paid		(2,297)	(2,297)
Repair Expenses Paid		(383)	(383)
MACRS Deduction - Furnishings		(357)	0
MACRS Deduction – Building		(2,327)	0
Mortgage Interest Paid		(4,679)	(4,679)
Disposal of Rental Property		31,281	37,742
Gross Rental Income (Loss)		30,048	
Prior Year Suspended Loss Used Currently		(391)	
Current Rental Loss Suspended (Carryforward)		0	
Net Rental Income (Loss) After Passive Limits		29,657	
Adjusted Gross Income Including Rental		183,616	
Personal Exemption Deductions		(10,950)	
Itemized Deductions		(16,561)	
Taxable Income		156,105	
Mortgage Principal Paid on Rental Property			(1,248)
Net Before-Tax Cash Flow From Rental Property			37,945
Tax on Noninvestment Income (Sal & Passive)	23,000		
Marginal Tax Cost - Taxable Bond Interest	451		Carryover
Marginal Tax Cost (Savings) – Rental	3,107		Suspended
			Rent Loss
Total Tax Liability – Current Year	26,558		0

INVESTMENTS SUMMARY:	**Rent**	**Tax Int**	**Tx-Ex Int**	**Total**
Before-Tax Cash Flow	37,945	1,803	1,739	41,487
Tax Savings (Cost) of Investment	(3,107)	(451)	0	(3,558)
Cash Flow - Year [6]	34,837	1,352	1,739	37,929
Investment Fund Balances	37,341	37,415	59,703	134,459

On the other hand, the gain on the furnishings is taxed as ordinary income under Code Sec. 1245. The analysis in **Figure 5** projects a net before-tax net cash inflow from liquidating the investment (after paying off the mortgage) of $37,742. The detailed computations of gain and loss on the various properties are summarized in **Figure 6**.

Of course, these projections are only estimates that depend entirely on the accuracy of the projected revenues, expenses, and appreciation. The real value of this evaluation technique is the opportunity to use the same procedure to evaluate other investment alternatives and compare the results. Based on the assumptions of this analysis, the rental property would yield an average 11.5-percent rate of return, compared to 4.1 percent on the taxable bond investment and 3.0 percent on the tax-exempt bond investment.

Figure 6				
Computation of Taxable Gain & Cash Flows on Disposal of Rental Property				
	Furnish	Land	Building	Total
Taxable Gain Computation:				
Selling Price (Net of Costs)	2,425	19,105	76,419	97,950
Less Adjusted Basis	(536)	(16,000)	(50,133)	(66,669)
Total Gain (Loss)	1,890	3,105	26,286	31,281
Secs. 1245 or 1250 Ordinary Gain	1,890	0	0	1,890
Sec. 1231 Gain	0	3,105	26,286	29,391
Net Cash Flow Computation:				
Selling price (Net of Costs)	2,425	19,105	76,419	97,950
Less Mortgage Payoff				(60,208)
Total Net Cash Inflow				37,742

Rate of Return on Cash Flows	Year	Rent	Tax Int	Tx-Ex Int	Total
	0	(20,000)	(30,000)	(50,000)	(100,000)
	1	455	1,125	1,500	3,080
Test Rate:	2	602	1,167	1,545	3,314
0.15	3	548	1,211	1,591	3,350
	4	511	1,256	1,639	3,406
	5	388	1,302	1,688	3,379
	6	34,837	31,352	51,739	117,929
	Rate of Return	11.5%	4.1%	3.0%	5.4%

The previous example illustrates the various tax advantages available to small investors who acquire and rent real estate. These advantages are curtailed in the case of investors with adjusted gross incomes exceeding $100,000, as mentioned earlier. However, examining a simple case where the restrictions do not apply assists in understanding some of the legislative limitations imposed on such investments.

Tax Planning

The analysis presented in **Figures 4, 5 and 6** is based on an EXCEL spreadsheet. Such a tool permits sensitivity analysis of the key variables via electronic tax planning. Sequentially varying the key inputs to the program provides insights into the key estimates used in the investment analysis. For example, the computed rate of return on the rental real estate investment in **Figure 6** is 11.50 percent. The following summary provides insight into how this expected return would change with increases or decreases in key variables (optimistic or pessimistic one at a time, holding all other inputs constant):

Input Variables			**Computed Rates of Return**		
Optimistic	*Current*	*Pessimistic*	*Optimistic*	*Current*	*Pessimistic*
Monthly Gross Rents					
$800	$700	$600	15.20%	11.50%	8.10%
Mortgage Interest Rate					
5%	8%	11%	16.40%	11.50%	6.50%
Down Payment on Mortgage					
$8,000	$16,000	$24,000	14.10%	11.50%	10.40%
Annual Appreciation in Value					
6%	3%	0%	18.30%	11.50%	3.60%
Annual Increase in Expenses					
1%	5%	9%	12.30%	11.50%	11.00%

ON THE WEB   For more information on the real estate investments, enter the following web address into your internet browser: *http://www.finance.cch.com/text/c60s10d276.asp*

¶11,017 Tax Planning: Selected Personal Deductions

Each year a taxpayer may choose to itemize his or her personal deductions or use a standard deduction. For taxpayers with itemized totals near the standard deduction, it may pay to defer some itemized deductions until the following year to ensure that the deductions will not otherwise be lost. Otherwise, there are not many planning opportunities related to itemized deductions. Two possibilities, however, relate to the tax treatment of alimony and the tax choices available for contributions of certain properties to charity.

.01 ALIMONY

Payments by a taxpayer to a former spouse that qualify as **alimony** are deductible by the payor spouse and are included in gross income of the payee spouse. However, a special provision in Code Sec. 72 allows former spouses to designate amounts as "not alimony", even though the amounts otherwise qualify as such under the law. For this reason, recipient spouses are likely to favor such a clause, while payor spouses are likely to favor the alimony label for such payments.

If the payor and payee spouses are in differing tax brackets, it may be possible to satisfy both parties' needs in some situations. This could be done by increasing the monthly payments that would otherwise be labeled as "not alimony" so that the after-tax cost of such payments are actually less. This is best demonstrated by the following example.

Example 11-14. Brad and Jen are currently negotiating a divorce agreement. Jen insists that she be paid a net minimum of $2,400 per month alimony, and that such payments not be subject to federal taxation. Brad wants to pay no more than $1,800 net cash outflow a month. Brad's marginal combined federal and state tax rate is 40 percent, and Jen's combined federal and state tax rate is 18 percent. Is it possible that the goals of both parties can be met if they just "split the difference?" Yes. Since Brad's marginal tax rate is 40 percent, he could pay as much as $3,000 alimony to Jen and have a net cash outflow of only $1,800, provided that such amount is deductible alimony. And since Jen's marginal tax rate is 18 percent, she would realize an after-tax cash flow from $3,000 taxable alimony of $2,460 ($3,000 × .82). Thus, the conditions of both parties are satisfied.

ON THE WEB   For more information on the alimony, enter the following web address into your internet browser: *http://www.finance.cch.com/text/c60s10d711.asp*

.03 CONTRIBUTIONS OF APPRECIATED CAPITAL GAINS PROPERTY

For purposes of the Code Sec. 170 charitable contribution rules, **capital gains properties** are those that would generate long-term capital gains if sold at fair market value. These are basically capital assets (personal assets and investment properties) held longer than one year.

For such capital gains properties, the taxpayer has a choice (with two exceptions noted below). The taxpayer can (1) deduct the fair market value of the property, limited to 30 percent of adjusted gross income (AGI) in any year [*the 30-percent method*], or (2) reduce the fair market value by the unrecognized gain and deduct up to 50 percent of AGI in any one year [*the 50-percent method*]. As illustrated below, decreasing tax rates may justify using the 50-percent method, even though a portion of the total potential deduction is forfeited in doing so.

The two exceptions are (1) tangible personalty not used in the tax-exempt function of the charity (the 50-percent rule must be used), and (2) contributions to private non-operating foundations (special rules limit the deduction to the lesser of 20 percent of adjusted gross income or the deduction allowable under the 50-percent rule).

Example 11-15. Samantha Green ($70,000 AGI) contributes stock to a university. The stock, bought 12 years ago for $32,000, is currently worth $35,000. Samantha may either (1) [30-percent method] deduct the $35,000 fair market value of the stock, but only $21,000 ($70,000 × .30) in the current year (with the $14,000 excess carried over five years), or (2) [50-percent method] deduct the entire $32,000 cost basis this year ($35,000 fair market value – $3,000 gain that would be recognized if sold), since it is less than 50 percent of AGI (with no carryover).

Example 11-16. Using the facts of the previous example, assume that Samantha's current-year marginal tax rate is 35 percent, and that this rate is expected to drop to 15 percent next year when she retires. In this case, it may make sense for Samantha to elect the 50-percent method. She will save an additional $2,200 in taxes by accelerating $11,000 of deductions into the current year [$11,000 × (.35 – .15)], at a cost of giving up only $3,000 deductions next year at a 15-percent rate, or $450.

¶11,019   Tax Planning: Vacation Rental Homes

.01   CODE SEC. 280A: THE BASIC RULES

Code Sec. 280A has three basic rules that govern vacation rental homes. The particular rule that applies to the vacation home is dependent on the number of days that the property is rented and the number of days the property is used for personal reasons. The Code Sec. 280A requirements related to vacation homes may be summarized in the following manner:

1. ***De Minimis Rule.*** If the vacation rental home is rented out for fewer than 15 days during the taxable year, both the income and the expenses attributable to the rental property are ignored in computing the owner's taxable income. However, deductions for interest, taxes, and casualty losses related to the vacation home are still allowed as itemized deductions.[7]

2. ***Insignificant Personal Usage.*** If the home is not used for personal reasons more than the *greater* of 14 days or 10 percent of the total days rented, then all rental expenses attributable to the rental days are deductible on Schedule E. In determining deductible rental expenses, an allocation must be made between rental days and personal days. For these purposes, the vacation rental home is treated as a *rental property*, and not as a personal residence.[8] However, allowable deductions may still be subject to the application of the passive activity rules of Code Sec. 469 and, although less likely, the hobby loss rules of Code Sec. 183.

3. ***Significant Personal Usage.*** If the home is used for personal reasons more than the *greater* of 14 days or 10 percent of the total days rented, Code Sec. 280A limits the rental deductions to the gross income from the property, as reported on Schedule E. In this case, the vacation rental home is treated as a *personal residence*. Thus, a loss limitation rule is applied automatically without reference to the three out of five-year test of the hobby-loss rules or the passive activity rules. Any unused losses may be carried forward to future years and may be used only against any rental income exceeding deductions in the carryover year.[9]

---

[7] Code Sec. 280A(g).
[8] Code Sec. 280A(c)(3).
[9] Code Sec. 280A(c)(5).

As explained above, rental expenses are limited to gross rental income when significant personal usage occurs. In this case, the taxpayer is not allowed to report a net loss based on the rental activity, although such losses may be taken in future years as an offset to net rental income. For purposes of applying the limitation on deductions, Code Sec. 280(c)(5) provides that items that are *otherwise deductible* (interest expense, property taxes and casualty losses) are deducted *first* from gross rental income, followed by rental expenses *not otherwise deductible* and not involving adjustments to basis, and finally expenses involving adjustments to basis. Of course, the reason for these specified "tiers" of deduction is to prevent taxpayers from deducting interest, taxes and casualty and theft losses *last*, since any of these deductions not used against rental income are generally deductible anyway on Schedule A as qualifying itemized deductions.

.03   THE EXPENSE ALLOCATION CONTROVERSY

In determining the appropriate deductions against rental income when a property has both rental and personal usage, it is necessary to first apportion all expenses between rental and non-rental use of the property. In this regard, Code Sec. 280A(e)(1) defines the rental allocation of each expense as a usage fraction *"which bears the same relationship to such expenses as the number of days during each year that the unit (or portion thereof) is rented at a fair rental bears to the total number of days during such year that the unit (or portion thereof) is used."*

However, Code Sec. 280A(e)(2) specifically notes that this provision does not apply to *"any deduction which would be allowable under this chapter for the taxable year whether or not such unit (or portion thereof) was rented."* This reference is to such items as interest, taxes, and casualty or theft losses, all of which were fully deductible as itemized deductions at the time the statute was drafted, even if the property was not rented at all.

In Prop. Reg. §1.280A-3(c)(4), the Internal Revenue Service (IRS) applies the Code Sec. 280A(e)(1) allocation procedure to *all* expenses related to a rental property, including interest, taxes and casualty losses (deductions that are "otherwise allowable, " which at that time included *all* interest expense, since this regulation was also drafted prior to 1986). Thus, the IRS suggests that interest and taxes should be apportioned between rental and personal days based on a ratio of the rental days (numerator) to the total number of days the vacation rental home was actually *used* for rental and personal purposes during the year (denominator).

However, there is another allocation method for interest expense and property taxes that is allowed by decisions of the Tax Court,[10] the 9th Circuit,[11] and the 10th Circuit.[12] This allocation method is often referred to as the **Bolton Method**.

Specifically, the courts in these cases noted that Code Sec. 280(e)(2) clearly *prohibits* applying the Code Sec. 280(e)(1) "usage" allocation to interest and taxes (items "otherwise deductible"). The court noted that the allocation based on usage was originally intended only to apply to items such as repairs and maintenance (items that were *not* "otherwise deductible"). Using this logic, the Court approved the taxpayer's allocation of interest and taxes based on the entire year (365 days), and not just the total number of days the vacation property was actually "used" during the year. The Tax Court's logic was simple: the vacation home owner pays interest and taxes based on 365 days a year, and not the actual number of days the property is used. The IRS adamantly opposes this allocation method.

In summary, the IRS method uses only the number of days that the vacation home is used (personal or rental) in the allocation, whereas the Bolton method uses the total number of days in the year (365 days, or 366 days in a leap year). For example, a taxpayer renting a property for 120 days and using the property for personal reasons for 30 days would use a denominator of 150 days for the IRS allocation and 365 days for the Bolton allocation of interest and taxes.

Figure 7 provides a comparison of the two methods when the deduction limitations apply (i.e., the assumed 30 days personal usage exceeds the larger of 14 days or 10 percent of the 120 days rented). Note that the only difference in the two allocation methods is the treatment of interest and taxes.

---

[10] *Bolton*, 77 TC 104.

[11] *Bolton*, CA-9, 82-2 USTC ¶9699, 694 F2d 556.

[12] *McKinney*, CA-10, 83-2 USTC 9655, 732 F2d 414.

The Bolton method provides the largest benefits to the taxpayer in cases where the deductions of these two classes of expenses would be limited ($6,880 more deductions in this case), as smaller interest and tax deductions are taken against rental income. This in turn allows more deductions against rental income from the other two categories of rental expenses.

The reduction in interest and tax deductions available to offset rental income are not a concern, since the unused amounts are available for deduction on the taxpayer's Schedule A as itemized deductions. The interest deduction is taken there because the rental property is treated as a (second) *personal residence*. This is so because the property has failed the test for rental treatment (personal use equal to or less than the greater of 14 days or 10 percent of the days rented). Recall that Code Sec. 163(h)(3) allows residential interest deductions on a total of $1,000,000 of qualified acquisition indebtedness on up to *two* homes of the taxpayer.

.05   INSIGNIFICANT PERSONAL USAGE: A CLOSER LOOK

As indicated above, if the vacation property violates the personal usage test, the property is treated a second residence for the allocated personal days of usage.[13] On the other hand, if the personal usage test is not violated, Code Sec. 163(h)(4)(A)(i)(II) denies "second residence" treatment to such a property for purposes of deducting residential interest, since the two qualifying residences are defined by reference to Code Sec. 280A(d)(1). Thus, interest expense related to personal use days is nondeductible consumer interest, since it cannot be residential interest.

If the vacation property is treated as a true rental (personal use is not significant and therefore rental deductions are not limited), at first blush it may seem to be advantageous for the taxpayer to use the IRS allocation method instead of the Bolton method. If the property is treated as a true *rental property*, the IRS method provides a larger interest deduction against rental income, and any interest allocable to personal use is not deductible, since the vacation home cannot be a rental property *and* a personal residence at the same time.

This preference for the IRS method in the rental scenario has long been advocated in the literature. However, a close reading of Code Sec. 280A as presently worded reveals that the IRS and Bolton allocation methods actually provide the *same tax result* when the property is treated as a true rental property. Here's why.

As noted by the Tax Court in *Bolton*, the Code Sec. 280(e)(1) allocation procedure applicable to such items as repairs and maintenance should not apply to "items otherwise deductible" under the Code such as interest and taxes.[14] But since the nondeductible consumer interest related to the personal usage is no longer considered to be a "deduction otherwise allowable" after 1986, such expenses by default *must* be allocated under Code Sec. 280(e)(1). And Code Sec. 280(e)(1) specifies the allocation generally used for such items as repairs, which is based on "the number of days during such year that the unit (or portion thereof) is *used*" [emphasis supplied].

Thus, a literal reading of the Code suggests that any interest expense related to a vacation home that is "primarily rental" property is not a "deduction otherwise allowable" and must therefore be allocated under the same Code Sec. 280(e)(1) procedure originally intended for repair and maintenance expenses (i.e., the IRS method). Even though theoretically a taxpayer might "elect" the Bolton method in the primarily rental scenario, the Bolton allocation based on 365 days will apply only to the taxes. And since any taxes allocated to personal usage are deductible anyway as itemized deductions, the total deductions available to the taxpayer under either the IRS or Bolton allocations are exactly the same!

---

[13] Code Sec. 280A(d)(1).
[14] *Bolton*, 77 TC 104.

Figure 7

Vacation Rental Home—Tax Computations with Significant Personal Usage

Janet Penn owns a cabin by the beach that was held out for rent for the entire year of 2013. Janet actually rented the cabin for 120 days and used the cabin for 30 days of personal vacation. Janet received $13,200 gross rents for the 120-day period and incurred the following expenses related to the property in 2010: interest, $10,950; taxes, $3,650; repairs, $1,500; utilities, $2,800; and depreciation, $8,500. Since Janet's personal usage (30 days) exceeds the greater of 14 days or 10 percent of the days rented (12 days) her expense deductions attributable to the rental period would be limited as follows under the two allocation methods:

	IRS Method	Bolton Method
Gross Rents	$13,200	$13,200
Less Expenses Otherwise Deductible:		
Interest ($10,950 total):		
Per IRS ($10,950 × 120/150)	(8,760)	
Per Bolton ($10,950 × 120/365)		(3,600)
Taxes ($3,650 total):		
Per IRS ($3,650 × 120/150)	(2,920)	
Per Bolton ($3,650 × 120/365)		(1,200)
Remaining Rental Income	$1,520	$8,400
Less Expenses Not Requiring Basis Reduction:		
Repairs ($1,500 × 120/150)	(1,200)	(1,200)
Utilities ($3,500 × 120/150)	(320)*	(2,800)
Remaining Rental Income	$ 0	$4,400
Less Expenses Requiring Basis Reduction:		
Depreciation ($8,500 × 120/150)	(0)	(4,400)
Net Rental Income	$ 0	$ 0
Interest and Taxes Deductible on Schedule A:		
Interest:		
Per IRS ($10,950 − $8,760)	$2,190	
Per Bolton ($10,950 − $3,600)		$7,350
Taxes:		
Per IRS ($3,650 − $2,920)	$730	
Per Bolton ($3,650 − $1,200)		$2,450
Total Deductions—Schedule A	$2,920	$9,800
Additional Deductions With Bolton Method	$6,880	
	$9,800	$9,800

This anomaly in the tax law can best be illustrated by example. Assume that a taxpayer incurs $3,650 interest, $3,650 taxes, and $3,650 of repairs on a vacation home that is rented for 190 days and is used for personal purposes for 10 days. Since the personal usage does not exceed the larger of 14 days or 10 percent of the days rented, the property is treated as a rental. Traditionally, in applying the IRS method and the logic of the Bolton method, the allocations of interest and tax deductions would be as follows:

	IRS Method	*Bolton Method*
Rent expense deductions (Schedule E):		
Interest (190/200 and 190/365, respectively)	$ 3,468	$ 1,900
Taxes (190/200 and 190/365, respectively)	3,468	1,900
Repairs (190/200 for both computations)	3,468	3,468
Itemized deductions (Schedule A):		
Interest (none allowed – personal)	0	0
Taxes ($3,650 – rental deduction)	182	1,750
Repairs (none allowed – personal)	0	0
Total deductions	$10,586	$ 9,018

In this scenario, the taxpayer would seemingly prefer the IRS allocation method, which produces $1,568 additional total deductions. However, the Bolton allocation of interest above ignores the plain language of Code Sec. 280(e), which requires that such interest (which after 1986 is not "otherwise deductible") be allocated under Code Sec. 280(e)(1) in a manner similar to repairs (based on usage). Thus, if the taxpayer "elects" Bolton, only the taxes would be allocated based on 365 days, and the results would be as follows:

	IRS Method	*Bolton Method*
Rent expense deductions (Schedule E):		
Interest (190/200 and 190/200, respectively)	$ 3,468	$ 3,468
Taxes (190/200 and 190/365, respectively)	3,468	1,900
Repairs (190/200 for both computations)	3,468	3,468
Itemized deductions (Schedule A):		
Interest (none allowed – personal)	0	0
Taxes ($3,650 – rental deduction)	182	1,750
Repairs (none allowed – personal)	0	0
Total deductions	$10,586	$10,586

It seems highly unlikely that either Congress or the Tax Court in *Bolton* would sanction one allocation method for interest (usage days) and another allocation method for taxes (365 days) in the same year. And yet the current wording of the Code produces this result. This identity of results of the two methods may actually work in the taxpayer's favor, since a taxpayer that switches back and forth between "primarily rental" and "primarily personal" classifications each year would need only to "adopt" the Bolton method. This would avoid the problem of seeking IRS permission to switch to the IRS method in years that the personal usage test was not violated (see the discussion below).

.07   PLANNING OPPORTUNITIES: *MORE* PERSONAL USAGE?

The anomaly in the allocation methods may provide a window of opportunity for some vacation homeowners near the end of the year. Some of those who have not yet met the significant personal usage test that would limit rental deductions may find that tax savings result from increasing their personal usage for the year. In such cases, the tax advisor must recognize that the taxpayer may have the ability to control the status of the property, and that the choice between rental and personal treatment of the vacation home can affect the tax savings in an unexpected direction. The taxpayer and his or her advisor need to compare potential tax savings under both scenarios (rental property and personal residence treatment). Refer to the Tax Planning Problems at the end of the chapter for exercises that demonstrate this anomaly.

.09   PLANNING OPPORTUNITIES: TEMPORARY RENTALS OF A PERSONAL RESIDENCE

The vacation rental home rules also apply to the rental of a principal residence. Although the intent of the Code Sec. 280A rules was to limit deductions, the *de minimis* rule may actually work to a taxpayer's advantage when exorbitant rentals are charged for rental periods of less than 15 days (e.g., a one-week rental during the Olympic Games). In such a case, the rental expenses *and income* are ignored. (However, it doesn't pay to be too greedy; a number of Los Angeles residents rented their residences for the entire 1984 Olympic games—*16* days!) Because of this unintended loophole, one of the bills considered by Congress in 1995 would have repealed the *de minimis* rule due to the Olympic games being scheduled for Atlanta. However, this bill was never enacted.

.11 PLANNING OPPORTUNITIES: REPAIR DAYS

Occasionally a taxpayer will be engaged in repair or maintenance work on the vacation rental home. For any day that the taxpayer devotes a majority of the day to repair work, the day will *not* count as a personal day in the Code Sec. 280A tests. Taxpayers should be able to document such days for purposes of a later audit by the IRS.

ON THE WEB   For more information on the vacation rental homes, enter the following web address into your internet browser: *http://www.finance.cch.com/text/c20s15d430.asp*

¶11,021 Tax Planning: College Education Expenses for Children

A major concern of many families is funding the college education expenditures of their children. Congress and the state governments have devised a number of tax incentives to help families achieve these goals. A few of the techniques are discussed below. But first, a significant constraint on such planning is discussed: the allocable parental tax.

.01 A SIGNIFICANT CONSTRAINT: THE ALLOCABLE PARENTAL TAX (A.K.A., THE "KIDDIE TAX")

Prior to the 1986 Act, the tax law indirectly encouraged transfers of income-producing properties to children, thus reducing the taxes paid on the related unearned income. Congress took four actions in 1986 to discourage such transfers: (1) eliminated the personal exemption deduction for a taxpayer eligible to be claimed as an exemption by another person, (2) limited the child's standard deduction to a minimum of $1,000 (in 2013) if less than earned income plus $350, (3) eliminated "Clifford trusts," whereby a taxpayer could transfer property temporarily to a trust (for a period of at least ten years and one day) and thus assign the related income to another person, and (4) instituted the **allocable parental tax** (commonly known as the "**kiddie tax**").

Under the kiddie tax rules, a child under the age of *19* (or a full-time student under age 24) who is eligible to be claimed as an exemption by a parent (or any one else) may have a portion of his or her taxable income taxed at the parent's marginal tax rate. The portion taxed as the parent's rate in 2013 is the excess of "**unearned income**" over *$2,000* (twice the minimum standard deduction of $1,000). The child's remaining taxable income is taxed at the child's rate. Special rules apply when the family has several children under age 19 (or full-time students under age 24) with unearned income, or if the child's parents are divorced.

Example 11-17. Ted, age 11, is claimed as a dependent by his parents and has $2,950 interest income in 2013. His parent's marginal tax rate is 33 percent. Ted's taxable income is $1,950 ($2,950 gross income less a $1,000 minimum standard deduction and $0 exemption deduction), and his tax is computed as follows:

Taxed at parents' marginal rate [($2,950 unearned – $2,000 exempt) × .33]	$ 314
Taxed at Ted's rate [($1,950 taxable – $950 at parents' rate) × .10]	100
Total tax due	$ 414

The most obvious strategy for the kiddie tax is to have the children grow older! Once they reach age 19 (or 24, if a full-time student), the first $8,925 of taxable income will be taxed at only the regular 10-percent rate, and the first $36,250 (in 2013) will be taxed at only a 15-percent rate. And of course if the child has earned income, such amounts may lead to a larger standard deduction, even if less than 19 (or 24) years of age. These amounts could also be contributed directly to retirement accounts as well.

Despite the limitations imposed by the kiddie tax, transfers of income-producing property will still generate some tax savings. And with current low interest rates, this may be an effective way to transfer large amounts of property to children while minimizing both income tax and unified transfer tax costs. The latter topic will be discussed later in this course.

OBSERVATION   Planning around the kiddie tax rules in order to accumulate funds for the college education of a child may create an unexpected trap. Specifically, if growth stocks or Series EE savings bonds are used as funding devices, there could be substantial assets or income held by the child when he or she turns 19 years of age. This could cause a significant loss in financial aid over the four years of college, and this loss could dwarf the tax savings of planning around the kiddie tax.

.03 OUTRIGHT GIFTS TO MINORS

In the past, parents and grandparents made gifts to minors under the Unified Gift to Minors Act. However, this involves several drawbacks. First, all earnings are taxed in the year earned, at the child's rate (with the possibility of the kiddie tax applying). Such transfers are subject to the gift tax. Also, the donor loses control over the property; the funds become the property of the beneficiary when he or she reaches maturity. And finally, since the accounts are treated as owned by the children, a portion of the balance of the account would be included in any needs assessment for financial aid.

Prior to 1986, a taxpayer could transfer property into a trust for a period of longer than 10 years and the income from such trust would be taxed to the beneficiary. After 10 years, the property would revert back to the owner. Thus, these trusts were often used to accumulate income for a child beneficiary, particularly since the allocable parental tax did not apply at the time. Under the 1986 Act, the income cannot be assigned to the beneficiary unless the donor's reversionary interest is less than five percent of the value of the trust assets (an unlikely possibility, unless the reversion occurs years down the road).

.05 EDUCATIONAL SAVINGS BONDS

A special exclusion applies to U.S. Savings Bonds that are used to pay qualified higher education expenses. The **educational savings bonds** must be issued to a person at least 24 years old. A pro rata portion of any accrued interest on such bonds redeemed for these educational purposes is excludable; however, the exclusion phases out proportionately over the *$15,000* of AGI exceeding $74,700 in 2013 (the *$30,000* of AGI exceeding $112,050 if a joint return is filed).

Example 11-18. Adams redeems $20,000 face value U.S. Savings Bonds ($15,000 cost), and uses $18,000 of the proceeds for qualified education expenses. Adams is single with an AGI of $84,700 in 2013. The excludable portion of the $5,000 interest component ($20,000 − $15,000) is:

$$Ex = \$5,000 \times (18/20) \times [1 - ((84,700 - 74,700)/15,000)] = \$5,000 \times .90 \times 1/3 = \$1,500$$

As a practical matter, the drop in interest rates has caused these plans to fall out of favor. The adjusted gross income limits also restrict the usage of these bonds to a relative small number of families who could otherwise afford to make such investments.

.07   EDUCATION INDIVIDUAL RETIREMENT ACCOUNTS (IRAS)

An Education IRA, now known as a **Coverdale Education Savings Account (CESA)**, was established in 1997 to assist low- and middle-income taxpayers with higher education costs. An individual may contribute up to $2,000 per year to a CESA for a designated beneficiary until the beneficiary reaches age 18. Total contributions on behalf of one child are limited in total to $2,000. Although the contribution is not deductible, earnings on the account are not taxable and distributions to the beneficiary are not taxable to the extent that they do not exceed the qualified education expenses of the individual. These expenses include not only tuition, books, and fees, supplies and equipment, but also room and board. (Beneficiary expenses related to elementary and secondary school may also qualify, but these costs are limited to academic tutoring and Internet access fees.) All distributions must be made by the time the beneficiary reaches age 30.

As was true with educational savings bonds, the benefits of a CESA are phased out at certain levels of adjusted gross income. The phaseout range for a married couple is from $190,000 to $220,000, and for all others it is $95,000 to $110,000. In addition, any educational expenses used for purposes of claiming the Hope or Lifelong Learning Scholarship credits will reduce the expenses qualifying for exclusion from a CESA.

.09   CODE SEC. 529 PLANS

Code Sec. 529 plans have become the vehicle of choice for funding college education of children because these plans are not subject to the same restrictions as the other options discussed above. Code Sec. 529 plans can be set up as either a prepaid tuition plan or a qualified savings plan. The prepaid plan is not as popular as the qualified savings plan, because it only covers tuition, and not fees, books, room and board, and other expenses. Only 18 states currently offer such plans, and many such plans limit the application of the funds to in-state schools (although lump sum payments for out of state or private schools may be included as an option in such plans).

The more popular Code Sec. 529 plans are the qualified savings plans. Contributions to such plans are on an after-tax basis, earnings are not currently taxed, and distributions are not taxable to the extent funds are used for qualified educational expenses (tuition, fees, supplies, equipment, and room and board). There is no ceiling on the amount contributed for a particular individual, other than a ceiling imposed by the state (the highest ceiling was recently $305,000). There are also no phaseouts based on adjusted gross income. More than one individual may establish a Code Sec. 529 plan for the same person; for example, both parents and grandparents may establish plans for the same child.

Distributions from a plan are classified as being either from principal (after-tax contributions) or account earnings; only the latter are taxed. The Code Sec. 72 annuity rules are applied for purposes of determining the taxable portion of each distribution, and this only occurs if some of the distribution is not used for qualified education expenses.

Example 11-19. At the end of the current year, a Code Sec. 529 plan for Sara Moore had a balance of $60,000 ($45,000 from contributions and $15,000 from earnings). During the current year, distributions of $20,000 were made to Sara, of which $18,000 were used for qualified education expenses. Sara's "exclusion ratio" for each distribution is 75 percent ($45,000 cost divided by $60,000 fund balance). Thus, 25 percent of the $20,000 distribution ($5,000) is from earnings, but only 10 percent of this total is taxable (the other 90 percent (18/20) was spent on qualified education costs).

Contributions to a Code Sec. 529 plan are subject to the federal gift tax. However, the contributions are treated as present interests in property, which means that such amounts qualify for the $14,000 annual exclusion per donee per year. And a special provision Code Sec. 529(c)(2)(B), allows a taxpayer to make a $70,000 gift at one time to a Code

Sec. 529 plan with no gift tax consequences ($140,000 for a couple if gift-splitting is elected). In effect, the one-time gift is treated as five years' worth of gifts at $14,000 per year. This election can only be made once each five years, and any other gifts on behalf of the beneficiary during the five year period do not qualify for the annual exclusion.

One final beneficial tax treatment accorded Code Sec. 529 plans is that such plans are not included in the estate of a donor decedent; they would be included in the estate of the beneficiary. This is true despite the fact that the donor retains control over the account up to the point of death. An exception would include in the gross estate a pro-rata portion of any $70,000 election described above if the donor dies within the five-year period.

Are there any state tax consequences associated with Code Sec. 529 plans? The rules vary greatly state by state. Some states allow deductions for contributions to such plans, and others do not. In addition, some states exempt the earnings portions of distributions, and others limit this option to students who attend in-state schools Therefore, checking the state law is important when considering Code Sec. 529 plans.

OBSERVATION	Code Sec. 529 plans are excellent tools for grandparents to fund the college education of their grandchildren, since, unlike parents, their payments do not adversely affect financial aid applications.

ON THE WEB	For more information on Code Sec. 529 Plans, enter the following web address into your internet browser: *http://www.finance.cch.com/text/c20s15d710.asp*

¶11,023   Summary

- The alternative minimum tax (AMT) is a second or "shadow" income tax, with its own special rules involving adjustments, preferences, and credits.
- Common strategies for dealing with the AMT include accelerating income, postponing deductions, selectively disposing of depreciable assets, avoiding private activity bond interest, and electing slower recovery periods.
- The passive activity limitations offer limited planning opportunities through defining an activity, meeting the material participation requirements, and taking advantage of the residential real estate exception.
- The investment interest limitations cap the interest deduction related to investments; however, a special election to treat long-term capital gains and/or dividend income may increase this deduction (at a cost of losing favored tax status for such income).
- Nontaxable fringe benefits are worth more than the actual dollar value of the benefit itself, since after-tax dollars would otherwise be spent by the taxpayer to purchase such benefits.
- Selective timing and special elections may provide tax savings on such personal items as capital gains and losses, alimony and charitable deductions.
- The Code Sec. 280A rules limit the tax deductions for second or vacation homes; however, the Bolton allocation method may increase such deductions.
- The "kiddie tax" is a significant constraint on planning for the college education expenses of children.
- Tax favored vehicles assisting in accumulating college education funds include educational savings bonds, Coverdale Education Savings Accounts, and Code Sec. 529 plans.

Review Questions for Chapter 11

True or False

Indicate which of the following statements are true or false by circling the correct answer.

1. The starting point for computing the alternative minimum tax is taxable income for   T   F
    regular tax purposes.

2. AMT adjustments may be either positive or negative in amount.   T   F

3. The presence of private activity bond interest may allow an investment interest expense   T   F
    deduction for AMT purposes that is larger than the deduction for regular tax purposes.

4. If a taxpayer foregoes the two-year net operating loss carryback for regular tax purposes,   T   F
    the taxpayer must also forego the carryback for AMT purposes as well.

5. A taxpayer is automatically deemed to be a material participant in a non-personal service   T   F
    activity if he materially participated in the activity in at least 3 of the preceding 10 years.

6. A nontaxable fringe benefit of $6,500 furnished to a taxpayer in the 35-percent marginal   T   F
    tax bracket by her employer is actually worth $10,000.

7. As the down payment on a mortgage for rental property increases, the expected rate of   T   F
    return from the investment also increases.

8. A taxpayer may omit rental income and receipts from his or her tax return if the per-   T   F
    sonal usage of the property is equal to or less than the greater of 14 days or 10 percent
    of the days rented.

9. The standard deduction for a child eligible to be claimed as a dependent by another in   T   F
    2013 is the lesser of $950 or the child's earned income plus $300.

10. Code Sec. 529 plans are less restrictive than other tax-saving vehicles for saving for a   T   F
    college education.

Fill in the Blanks

Fill in each blank with the appropriate word or phrase that completes each sentence.

11. AMT _____ may only be positive; negative amounts are ignored.
12. The maximum AMT tax rate is _____ percent.
13. An AMT computation for the current year will generate an AMT credit only if some of the adjustments
    or preferences are _____ differences.
14. Under the passive activity limitations, any losses from passive activities can only offset profits from
    _____ activities.
15. A taxpayer can always be sure to qualify as a material participant if he or she works more than _____
    hours in the activity.
16. Allen has worked 180 hours in Activity A, 82 hours in Activity B, and 300 hours in Activity C. If Allen
    desires that all three activities meet the material participation rules, he should work _____ more hours
    in Activity B.
17. A taxable bond pays a 10-percent annual rate of return. If a taxpayer is in the 31-percent marginal tax
    bracket, a nontaxable municipal bond must pay an annual rate of at least _____ percent to yield the same
    after-tax cash flow.
18. The concept of using as much financing as possible in a rental investment to generate immediate tax ben-
    efits is called _____.

19. The 50 percent of AGI "reduced deduction election" for charitable contributions of appreciated property may make sense if the taxpayer's marginal tax rate in the next year will _____ (increase, decrease) significantly.

20. A taxpayer rents his vacation home for 225 days, and uses the home for 30 personal days. In determining the deduction for interest and taxes on the rental usage with the *Bolton* method, the taxpayer will use a fraction of _____.

Multiple Choice

Circle the best answer for each of the following questions.

21. In determining her regular tax liability, Marsha Mason had $3,000 investment income and $12,000 of investment interest expense (of which only $3,000 was deductible due to the investment interest expense limitation rules). If Marsha also has $5,000 private activity bond interest during the year, then for AMT purposes she will
    a.   report a positive $5,000 adjustment and a positive $9,000 adjustment.
    b.   report a positive $5,000 adjustment and a negative $5,000 adjustment
    c.   report a positive $5,000 adjustment and a negative $9,000 adjustment
    d.   report a negative $5,000 adjustment and a positive $9,000 adjustment

22. The AMT exemption for a married couple with $600,000 of alternative minimum taxable income would be
    a. $0
    b. $80,800
    c. $83,750
    d. $150,000

23. In its second year of doing business, Axel Company has an AMT credit carryover of $20,000. Axel's regular tax liability for the current year is $67,000, and its tentative minimum tax liability is $56,000. Axel's AMT carryover to next year, after utilizing the maximum amount possible in the current year, will be
    a. $0
    b. $9,000
    c. $11,000
    d. $20,000

24. Tamara Boardman sold a machine in the current year that generated a $42,000 gain for regular tax purposes and a $30,000 gain for AMT purposes. Which of the following statements is true?
    a.   the sale will generate a negative $12,000 adjustment for AMT purposes
    b.   the resulting adjustment is a permanent ("deferral") difference
    c.   a negative AMT adjustment will result, and this amount is the sum of all prior positive AMT adjustments related to the asset
    d.   (a) and (c)

25. One of the key factors in determining whether several undertakings should be grouped together as an "activity" for passive activity purposes is
    a.   common ownership
    b.   type of business
    c.   location
    d.   all of the above

26. Mary and William Penn have adjusted gross income of $136,000 during the current year. If they incur an $18,000 loss in a residential real estate activity in which they "actively participate," their maximum loss deduction related to the rental activity is
    a. $7,000
    b. $11,000
    c. $18,000
    d. $25,000

27. Which of the following sources of income is not treated as "investment income" for purposes of the investment interest limitations unless the taxpayer makes a special election?
    a. long-term capital gains
    b. interest income
    c. dividend income
    d. (a) and (c)

28. The best use of a long-term capital loss is to offset
    a. long-term capital gains
    b. short-term capital gains
    c. limited amounts of ordinary income
    d. (b) and (c)

29. Which of the following items affects the cash flow from a rental property but not the taxable income or loss from the property?
    a. Principal payments on a mortgage
    b. Interest payments on a mortgage
    c. Depreciation
    d. Repairs

30. Rose Heinbaugh rented her second home, a cabin in the mountains, for a total of 290 days in the current year. The maximum number of personal days that Rose may use the cabin without violating the Code Sec. 280 limitation rules is:
    a. 14 days
    b. 15 days
    c. 29 days
    d. 30 days

Review Problems

31. The minimum tax credit provides a form of "rough justice" for taxpayers subject to the AMT; however, only certain types of AMT adjustments and preferences may be used to create this credit. Explain.
32. "Accelerating the recognition of income near the end of the year may not be a good idea for an individual taxpayer, even though the taxpayer is already subject to the AMT and is in the 35-percent regular tax bracket." Do you agree? Explain.
33. Long-term capital gains are taxed at the same 15-percent rate for both regular tax and AMT purposes. This has led some commentators to note that the impact of long-term capital gains is more or less neutral in regards to the AMT. Do you agree? Explain.
34. Why is the definition of an "activity" so important in applying the passive activity loss limitations?
35. As a general rule, should a taxpayer make the special Code Sec. 163(d)(4)(B) election to have long-term capital gains incurred during the year treated as investment income for investment interest limitation purposes? Explain.

36. Jan Allen is in the 35-percent federal tax bracket and the 5-percent state income tax bracket. Jan's state uses the federal definition of gross income for taxing purposes. Jan has a choice of having her employer pay her $5,000 annual child-care expenses, or receiving $7,500 additional salary. Which benefit should she choose?

37. Sara Long has owned 1,000 shares of Zebco Corporation common stock for nine months. She paid $4,000 for the stock, and the shares are currently selling for $10,000. One week ago, the shares were selling for $10,300, and she hopes to hold the stock for three more months in order to obtain long-term capital gains treatment. However, the recent dip has troubled her, and she wonders if she should sell the stock now to lock in the gain, albeit a short-term gain. If Sara's federal tax rate is 35 percent, what advice could you give to help Sara make this decision?

38. In general, the concept of leveraging helps explain why the expected rate of return from a rental real estate investment goes up as the down payment required on the property goes down. Explain.

39. A rental investment generates $17,200 gross rents, $6,800 depreciation, $7,600 interest paid on a mortgage ($1,300 payments on principal), $1,200 repairs, $700 advertising, $2,800 taxes, and $940 insurance. Assuming the taxpayer's marginal tax rate is 35 percent, what is the net cash flow of the property?

40. If a taxpayer's adjusted gross income exceeds $150,000, then the evaluation of a potential investment in rental property may be more dependent on nontax factors than such an evaluation with an adjusted gross income less than $150,000. Explain.

41. Explain how a divorced couple with significantly different marginal tax rates may solve a dispute over the tax treatment of alimony in the divorce agreement, so that the result is a "win-win" situation for both spouses.

42. Generally, a taxpayer contributing intangible property to a charitable donee would elect to deduct 30 percent of the fair market value of the property to the charity. Are there circumstances where it might make more sense to make the special election to reduce the deduction by the appreciation in value of the property in exchange for a 50-percent limit for such contribution? Explain.

43. Explain why the Bolton method of allocating taxes and interest of a vacation home may provide significant tax savings for a taxpayer caught by the Code Sec. 280A limitations. Does the IRS approve of this allocation method?

44. Are there circumstances where a taxpayer may be better off tax-wise to *increase* the number of personal rental days for a property before year-end? Explain.

45. The kiddie tax (allocable parental tax) eliminates any benefit of transferring income-producing property to minor children. Do you agree? Explain.

46. Explain the tax advantages and disadvantages of saving for a child's college education with each of the following vehicles: (1) education savings bonds, (2) Coverdale education IRAs, and (3) Code Sec. 529 plans.

Research Questions

47. Brief the following case: *M. Razavi, 74 F3d 125 (CA-6, 1996)*. Then draft a single-page letter to clients explaining the importance of this decision for anyone who owns a second property that offers a pooling arrangement for their tenants. Keep the explanation brief and in non-technical language.

48. Hank Allen realized a $40,000 gain upon exercising stock options in 2013, and this created an alternative minimum tax for the year. In 2014, the exercised stock became worthless, and Hank's loss from worthlessness is $15,000 (his exercise price in the stock). Hank has no other capital transactions during 2014. Since the AMT credit will not help Hank in the current year, he believes that he should be able to report the $15,000 loss for AMT purposes, even though his regular tax loss would be limited to $3,000 (since the stock is a personal investment). Do you agree with Hank?

Tax Planning Questions

49. Refer to the text website at *CCHGroup.com/ContemporaryTax*, and work Tax Planning Question 11-1. This case involves an analysis of the AMT credit and its effect on year-end planning strategies. You will analyze the facts of this case with the Excel file INDALT2013.xls, also provided on the webpage.

50. Refer to the text website at *CCHGroup.com/ContemporaryTax*, and work Tax Planning Question 11-2. This case involves an analysis of investments in residential real estate, and the impact of the passive activity rules on the projected rates of return. You will analyze the facts of this case with the Excel file RENTAL2013.xls, also provided on the webpage.

51. Joe and Jill Bean, married taxpayers, expect to be subject to the AMT again this year. Near the end of the year, their AMT liability exceeds their regular tax liability by $30,000. Currently, Joe and Jill have alternative minimum taxable income before considering the AMT exemption of $300,000. If Joe and Jill choose to accelerate $50,000 of additional income into the current year, how much will their (a) regular tax and (b) tentative minimum tax increase? Joe and Jill's marginal regular tax rate is 35 percent.

52. Near the end of the current year, Bill Ross has worked the following number of hours in each of several nonrental activities (the expected profit or loss of each activity for the year is also disclosed):

Activity	Hours Worked	Projected Profit (Loss)
A	168	($32,000)
B	92	$42,000
C	180	($13,000)
D	53	($22,000)
E	104	$18,000
F	98	$26,000

How would you recommend that Bill spend his time for the rest of the year? Explain. Assume that other individuals work more hours than Bill in each activity.

53. Near the end of the current year, Dana Milbank has $120,000 adjusted gross income before considering a $15,000 loss from a residential real estate investment in which she qualifies as an "active" participant. Dana received a sizable inheritance in November, and she has the opportunity to invest the amount in either a taxable bond fund that will pay her $10,000 interest this year or a nontaxable bond fund that will pay her $6,500 interest this year. If Dana expects roughly the same results in the next several years, what advice would you give her regarding the two investments? Explain.

54. Near the end of 2013, Sylvia Portman's only capital transaction realized during the year resulted in a $500 net short-term capital gain. Sylvia's adjusted gross income is expected to be $250,000. She is also considering the possible sale of two additional blocks of stock, either before the end of 2013 or at the beginning of 2014. These stocks are:

Stock	Date Purchased	# of Shares	Cost Per Share	Current Value
Tax Pro, Inc.	8/12/2006	300	$ 20	$55 per sh.
Hula Hoop, Inc.	3/14/2008	200	$ 35	$15 per sh.

What action would you recommend for Sylvia? Explain.

55. James Mason ($50,000 AGI) contributes stock to a church. The stock, bought seven years ago for $24,000, is currently worth $28,000. Mason's current marginal federal tax rate is 35 percent, and he expects that marginal tax rate to drop to 15 percent next year when he retires. What advice would you give Mason regarding this contribution?

56. Marcy Allen (40-percent combined federal and state tax rate) has an opportunity to rent her Manhattan condo to eager customers during the Olympic Games. If she could rent the condo for the full 16 days of the convention, a rental agency estimates that she could earn $3,000 per day. If she rents the property for only 14 days, she would have to pay $2,000 a day for a hotel room for tenants for the other two days. What is your advice to Marcy?

57. Refer to the text website (*CCHGroup.com/ContemporaryTax*) and work Tax Planning Problem 11-3, which examines special planning opportunities with the vacation home rules via Excel worksheets.

58. Seth and Alice Moore are married taxpayers with a 35-percent marginal income tax rate. During the current year they earned $10,000 interest on a bond investment. Seth and Sara have five minor children, ages 17, 15, 11, 8, and 5. If Seth and Sara transfer the bond investment into a trust so that each child is taxed on $2,000 interest income as a beneficiary, how much federal income taxes would such a move save?

Tax Compliance Question

59. Your client, Ace Drilling, asks for your advice. Specifically, they filed their return electronically three weeks ago (one month before the March 15 deadline). On that return Ace elected under Code Sec. 59(e) to amortize their research and experimentation costs over a 10-year period for regular tax purposes, since this would make it less likely that they would be subject to the alternative minimum tax (AMT). However, they have rethought their decision, since it turned out that they would not be subject to the AMT this year, even if the total amount of expenses were deducted on that return. Therefore, they ask you if they should file an amended return and change this election. What is your advice? (Hint: refer to PLR 9607001.)

CHAPTER 12

Tax Planning for Compensation and Retirement

Learning Objectives

1. Understand the benefits to the employer and the employee of providing nontaxable fringe benefits.
2. Understand which benefits qualify for statutory exclusions from income of the employee.
3. Understand which benefits can be part of an employer sponsored cafeteria plans.
4. Understand how to provide tax-free medical expense reimbursement plans for qualified employees.
5. Understand why the employer and employee benefit from deferred compensation plans.
6. Understand the differences between defined benefit and defined contribution retirement plans.
7. Understand why many employers have adopted Code Sec. 401(k) (Cash or deferred arrangement) plans.
8. Understand how the self-employer and employees whose employers do not have retirement plans can save for retirement with tax-favored plans, such as regular IRAs, Roth IRAs, SIMPLE, and SEP plans.
9. Understand how to develop a pension maximization strategy that benefits both the employer and employee.
10. Evaluate the benefits of nonqualified deferred compensation and qualified stock option plans.

¶12,001   Introduction

This chapter examines planning issues related to compensation and retirement. The first part of the chapter reviews the basics regarding nontaxable fringe benefits. The major categories of excludable benefits are reviewed, and certain planning strategies are discussed. The second part of this chapter examines issues involving deferred compensation. The basics of the various defined benefit and defined contribution plans are reviewed and related planning issues are examined. Other forms of deferred compensation that may be part of a retirement planning package are also examined.

¶12,003   Nontaxable Fringe Benefits: A Brief Review

The Code contains a number of exclusion provisions for specific employee fringe benefits that are deductible by the employer and excludable by the employee. As discussed later in the text, this is one of the major advantages offered by the C corporation as a tax entity. Only S corporation shareholders owning less than two percent of the S corporation stock qualify for these benefits.

.01   SPECIFIC STATUTORY EXCLUSIONS

The statutory benefits specifically provided in the Code include the following:
- *Code Sec. 104 Compensation for Injuries or Sickness.* Gross income does not include—
  - amounts received under workmen's compensation acts as compensation for personal injuries or sickness,[1]
  - the amount of any damages (other than punitive damages) received (whether by suit or agreement and whether as lump sums or as periodic payments) on account of personal physical injuries or physical sickness,[2]
  - amounts received through accident or health insurance.[3]
- The following payments are taxable: Supplemental unemployment benefits from a company-financed fund or a union-financed strike fund and disability pay.
- However, assistance payments from the state (for energy costs, for example) are not taxable.
- *Health Related Payments*. Employer payments of health insurance premiums are excludable by employees, as are contributions to a Medical Savings Account (discussed below) and payments for long-term care. Benefits received are also excludable, if related to an injury or sickness. Disability income payments are taxable if the policy is provided by the employer, excludable if the employee purchased the policy, and are prorated if jointly purchased by the employer and employee. In addition, payments received from a company-sponsored medical expense reimbursement plan are excludable.[4]
- *Educational assistance plan payments.* A maximum of $5,250 per year may be excluded by employees, provided the assistance is for *either* undergraduate or graduate courses. The course does not necessarily have to be work-related, although purely recreational courses may not qualify.[5]
- *Tuition Assistance.* Employees of educational institutions may exclude the value of free or reduced tuition for themselves and their spouses or dependents.[6]

---

[1] Code Sec. 104(a)(1).
[2] Code Sec. 104(a)(2).
[3] Code Sec. 104(a)(3).
[4] Code Secs. 105, 106.
[5] Code Sec. 127.
[6] Code Sec. 117(d)(2).

- *Dependent Care Assistance.* A maximum of $5,000 per year may be excluded by employees; any amount so excluded does not qualify for the child and dependent care credit.[7]
- *Group-term Life Insurance Coverage.* Premiums on the first $50,000 of group-term life insurance coverage provided by an employer are excludable by the employee; however, coverage in excess of $50,000 is taxed according to a uniform table in the Regulations that provides monthly rates based on the age of the employee.[8]
- *Meals and Lodging.* The value of meals and lodging provided by an employer may be excluded if meals or lodging are (1) for the convenience of the employer, (2) furnished on the business premises, and (3) in the case of lodging, accepting lodging is a requirement of the job. Options to receive cash, or in the case of lodging to live elsewhere, make these benefits taxable. Occasional payments of *supper money* (cash payments for meals while working late) are excludable. The value of on-campus housing provided to faculty is excludable if the rent paid by the faculty member equals or exceeds five percent of the value of the housing.[9]
- *Service and Safety Achievement Awards.* An employee may exclude up to $400 for the value of any non-cash award based on service (at least five years) or safety achievement (no more than 10 percent of employees receive the awards). If the employer has a qualified plan for these awards, individual awards may go as high as $1,600 to an employee, although the average award must be $400 or less.[10]
- *Employer Contributions to Pension Plans.* Within the general statutory limits discussed below, employer contributions to qualified retirement plans (including 401(k) and 403(b) plans) are excludable by the employee.[11]
- *Adoption Expenses Paid by the Employer.* Under Code Sec. 137, an employee may exclude up to $12,970 (for 2013) of adoption assistance expenses provided by an employer. These payments reduce the amount eligible for the Code Sec. 23 Adoption Credit[12] which is claimed on form 8839.

.03 TAX PLANNING WITH STATUTORY FRINGE BENEFIT PROVISIONS

Employer Cost vs. Employee Cost

The value of a fringe benefit is actually more than the dollar value, since a taxpayer would otherwise use after-tax income to purchase the same benefit. In some cases, a taxable portion of the benefit is actually worth more for a different reason: the employer is able to buy the coverage on a group basis for much less than individual policies purchased by the employee would cost. For example, group-term insurance coverage in excess of the $50,000 limit under Code Sec. 79 is taxed according to a uniform rate in the tax regulations that is in reality much cheaper than what the employee, or for that matter, the employer would pay.

Exclusion vs. Credit Options

Taxpayers who receive employer reimbursement for child care expenses have a choice of either using the exclusion for up to $5,000 or foregoing the exclusion and taking the child care credit.[13] Obviously, the taxpayer may not choose both. The child care credit is limited to the first $3,000 of expenses for one child ($6,000 of expenses for two or more children, and the credit rate ranges from 35 to 20 percent (as adjusted gross income increases from $15,000 to $43,000). Once adjusted gross income exceeds $43,000, the credit rate is a flat 20 percent (Form 2441). Generally, a taxpayer should compare his or her marginal tax rate to the credit rate, and use the exclusion only if the marginal tax rate exceeds the credit rate.

---

[7] Code Sec. 129.
[8] Code Sec. 79.
[9] Code Sec. 119.
[10] Code Sec. 74.
[11] Code Sec. 401.
[12] Code Sec. 137.
[13] Code Secs. 129 and 21.

.05   CODE SEC. 132 GUIDELINES FOR OTHER CLASSES OF FRINGE BENEFITS

In addition to the specific statutory exclusions mentioned above, Code Sec. 132 provides broad exclusion guidelines for seven other classes of fringe benefits. These include the following:

- *No additional cost services.* If an employer does not incur substantial costs (or forego revenue) in providing a service to employees, the value of the service is nontaxable (e.g., free flights for airline employees and free hotel room for hotel employees). This exclusion is available for employees, spouses, dependents, and retirees.[14]
- *Qualified Employee Discounts.* Employee discounts are excludable, limited to the gross profit percentage for goods and property, and 20 percent of the normal charge for services. This exclusion is available for employees, spouses, dependents, and retirees.[15]
- *Working Condition Fringe Benefits.* An exclusion is available for certain work-related expenditures that would otherwise be deductible by the employee, such as professional dues and subscriptions, and employer-furnished meals at its own subsidized eating facility (if the revenue exceeds the cost of operating the eating facility.) This expenditure may be discriminatory.[16]
- *De Minimis Fringe Benefits.* An exclusion is available for nominal expenditures by an employer on the behalf of an employee that are too small to account for, such as a Thanksgiving turkey or a ham.[17]
- *Qualified Transportation.* The monthly limitation for the aggregate fringe benefit exclusion amount for transportation in a commuter highway vehicle and any transit pass is $245 (2013).[18] The monthly limitation for the fringe benefit exclusion amount for qualified parking is $245 (2013).[19]
- *Moving Expense Reimbursement.* To the extent that moving expenses are otherwise deductible, any reimbursement received from the employer is excludable.[20]
- *Recreational and Athletic Facilities.* The value of company-provided recreational and athletic facilities on the business premises is excludable. This exclusion is available for employees, spouses, dependents, and retirees.[21]
- *Company Provided Eating Facilities.* The savings generated by eating in company-owned cafeterias and other facilities (when compared to market prices for the meals) are excludable, *provided* the revenue of the facility at least covers the costs.[22]
- *Qualified Retirement Planning Services.* The value of any retirement planning advice or information provided to an employee and his spouse by an employer maintaining a qualified employer plan is excludable.[23]

.07   TAX PLANNING WITH THE CODE SEC. 132 EXCLUSION GUIDELINES

The exclusions for no additional cost services and courtesy discounts were major victories for the airlines and clothing industries, respectively. The savings can be significant over the span of a year for employees in this industry, and once again the tax savings are more than the value of the benefit.

At first one might question why "working condition" benefits warrant exclusion, since these expenditures are deductible by the employee in any case. The answer is that

---

[14] Code Sec. 132(a)(1).
[15] Code Sec. 132(a)(2).
[16] Code Sec. 132(a)(3).
[17] Code Sec. 132(a)(4).
[18] Code Sec. 132(f)(2)(A).
[19] Code Sec. 132(f)(2)(B).
[20] Code Sec. 132(g).
[21] Code Sec. 132(j)(4).
[22] Code Sec. 132(e)(2).
[23] Code Sec. 132(m)(1).

unreimbursed employee expenses are miscellaneous itemized deductions subject to the two percent of adjusted gross income floor, so a deduction is not always guaranteed to otherwise net to the same result as an exclusion.

Some of the benefits covered by Code Sec. 132 represent items that would otherwise not be deductible by the employee, and thus the exclusion provision is worth even more. For example, an employee cannot deduct parking or transportation costs, so having that cost picked up by an employer can represent significant savings over a year's time.

.09   EMPLOYER DEDUCTION FOR FRINGE BENEFITS

Generally, an employer can deduct the cost of a fringe benefit in whatever expense category the benefit fits; for example, a car lease for an employee is deducted as a lease expense. The deduction is limited to the cost of providing the fringe benefit, which is not necessarily its fair market value.

The costs of meals and lodging furnished to employees is also deductible; however, only 50 percent of the meal costs are generally deductible unless the amounts are either reported as income by the employee, furnished by a company catering service at a work site, or furnished as a *de minimis* fringe benefit (such as a company picnic).

Some items, though excludable by the employee and deductible by the employer, must be reported on Form W-2 to the employee. Moving expense reimbursement is an example. If a fringe benefit plan, such as a cafeteria plan, discriminates in favor of certain employees, those employees will be taxed as though they had elected cash rather than excludable fringe benefits. This affects the income reporting by the employer.

¶12,005   Cafeteria Plans, FSAs, HRAs, and HSAs

.01   CAFETERIA AND FLEXIBLE SPENDING ACCOUNT (FSA) PLANS

In some cases, an employer may offer a **cafeteria plan**, where the employee can select from a variety of taxable and nontaxable benefits. Under Code Sec. 125, the taxability of each option is not affected by the fact that one of the options is cash; each benefit is judged on its own merits. If not for this specific provision, the constructive receipt doctrine would cause all benefits to be taxed if cash is one of the options offered by the plan.

A cafeteria plan can only include a choice between cash or qualified benefits that are specifically excluded from gross income under a statutory provision (including group-term insurance coverage exceeding excludable amounts). "Qualified benefits" do not include benefits of Archer Medical Savings Accounts,[24] scholarships and fellowships,[25] educational assistance benefits,[26] any benefit that is essentially long-term care insurance, or benefits excludable under the general guideline rules of Code Sec. 132. Generally, deferred compensation is not included in a cafeteria plan, although Code Sec. 401(k) contributions under a profit-sharing or stock-bonus plan will qualify.

Example 12-1. Drew Corporation permits each employee to select from a variety of benefits up to five percent of their annual salary. During the current year, Diana Wilson selected $3,000 of health insurance coverage for herself and her family, $2,000 of child care assistance, and $1,000 cash. Only the cash payment is taxable.

A cafeteria plan may also be cast as a **flexible spending account (FSA)** under the guidelines of Reg. §1.125-2. Under an FSA, an employee is provided coverage under which specified incurred expenses may be reimbursed, subject to certain reimbursement maximums and reasonable conditions. Under these arrangements, employees are permitted

---

[24] *See* Code Sec. 106(b).
[25] *See* Code Sec. 117.
[26] *See* Code Sec. 127.

to make pre-tax contributions to FSAs for reimbursement of health and/or dependent care expenses. Beginning with the 2013 tax year, there is an annual $2,500 cap on medical reimbursement plans.[27] However, the contributions to FSAs are subject to a "use it or lose it" rule, in that unused amounts at the end of the year are forfeited.

One of the advantages of an FSA is that benefits are not subject to payroll taxes. This offers two other tax benefits. First, the take-home pay of the employee is not decreased by the amount of the reduced salary, since the payroll tax liability is reduced. This is true for all employees, since the Medicare portions of the FICA tax are not capped. Obviously, even more benefits accrue to taxpayers below the maximum annual limits on the social security portion of the FICA (capped at $113,700 in 2013).

A second advantage related to the exclusion from payroll taxes is that the after-tax cost of sponsoring these programs to the employer is significantly reduced. In some cases, this reduction may cover a significant portion of the cost of funding the program. Note in **Figure 1** that the estimated payroll tax savings each year from an FSA for a hypothetical employer with 12 employees is $1,676 ($1,360 + $316), and that by Year 4 these savings overtake the costs of administering the program.

OBSERVATION	The facts in **Figure 1** assume that each of the employees elect to contribute four percent of their salaries to an FSA. In reality, it may be difficult to convince some employees to do this, so it is important to show the employees how much they are saving by making the election. For example, an employee who has two dental visits a year could at least set aside that amount without fear of losing contributions made during the year.

Figure 1 Flexible Spending Account Analysis					
Percentage of Current Salary Reduced for FSA					4.00%
One-time Setup Charge for Flexible Spending Account					$3,000
Continuing Monthly Maintenance Charge for Flexible Spending Account (per employee)					$5
FICA Maximum Wage					$113,700
FICA rate					6.25%
Medicare rate					1.45%
Marginal Tax Rate of Employer					34%
Employee	Current Salary	Expected Conversion	FICA Tax Savings	Medicare Tax Savings	Total Savings
A	$20,000	$800	$50	$12	$62
B	$25,000	$1,000	$63	$15	$77
C	$28,000	$1,120	$70	$16	$86
D	$34,000	$1,360	$85	$20	$105
E	$36,000	$1,440	$90	$21	$111
F	$44,000	$1,760	$110	$26	$136
G	$52,000	$2,080	$130	$30	$160
H	$55,000	$2,200	$138	$32	$169
I	$67,000	$2,500	$156	$36	$192
J	$79,000	$2,500	$156	$36	$192
K	$83,000	$2,500	$156	$36	$192
L	$98,000	$2,500	$156	$36	$192
Total Savings			$1,360	$316	$1,676

---

[27] Code Section 125(i), Notice 2012-40.

	Year 1	Year 2	Year 3	Year 4	Year 5
Prior-Year Unrecovered Cost/Saving	$ -	$(1,096)	$(213)	$671	$1,554
Employment Tax Savings	$1,676	$1,676	$1,676	$1,676	$1,676
One-time Set-up Charge	$(3,000)	$ -	$ -	$ -	$ -
Continuing Maintenance Charge	$(1,200)	$(1,200)	$(1,200)	$(1,200)	$(1,200)
Tax Savings—Deducting Adm. Costs	$1,428	$408	$408	$408	$408
Net Cumulative (Cost) Savings	$(1,096)	$(213)	$671	$1,554	$2,438

.03   HEALTH REIMBURSEMENT ARRANGEMENTS (HRAs)

Congress and the IRS have developed two other tax-advantaged options for employees and employers in dealing with health care issues. The IRS gave the go ahead to a special health reimbursement arrangement (HRA) between employers and employees, and Congress enacted legislation providing a new vehicle, a qualified health savings account (HSA).

.05   HEALTH REIMBURSEMENT ARRANGEMENTS (HRAs)

In Revenue Ruling 2002-41[28] and Notice 2002-2,[29] the IRS approved a health reimbursement arrangement between an employer and an employee. In approving this arrangement, the IRS extended the reach of Code Secs. 105 and 106 regarding the excludability of employer payments for insurance coverage, as well as benefits received by the employee from coverage. The essential characteristics of an HRA are:

1. the employer pays for the HRA, and the payment is not related to a salary reduction election by the employee;
2. the plan reimburses the employee for qualifying medical expenses of the employee and dependents; and
3. the plan provides for reimbursements up to a maximum dollar amount for a coverage period, and any unused portion is carried forward to increase maximum reimbursement in future periods.

When these conditions are met, coverage and reimbursement of medical expenses of the employee, spouse, and dependents are generally excludable from income.

.07   HEALTH SAVINGS ACCOUNTS (HSAs)

As part of the *Medicare Prescription Drug, Improvement, and Modernization Act of 2003*, Congress added Code Sec. 223.[30] This provision allows individuals to establish **Health Savings Accounts (HSAs)**, which largely replace the Archer Medical Savings Accounts (MSAs)[31] enacted years earlier. HSAs are available to individuals with high deductible health plans (HDHP). For 2013, the minimum deductible is $1,250 for individual coverage and $2,500 for family coverage. The out-of-pocket expense maximum is $6,250 for individuals and $12,500 for families.[32] Out-of-pocket expenses include deductibles, co-payments and other amounts (other than premiums) that must be paid for plan benefits.[33] No amounts can be paid from the HDHP until the family has incurred covered medical expenses in excess of the minimum annual deductible.

---

[28] Rev. Rul. 2002-41, 2002-2 CB 75, IRB 2002-28, 75.
[29] Notice 2002-2, 2002-1 CB 285.
[30] P.L. 108-173.
[31] *See* Code Sec. 138.
[32] Rev. Proc. 2012-26, 2012-20 IRB 933.
[33] Code Sec. 223(c)(2)(A); Notice 2004-2, IRB 2004-2.

An individual with an HDHP may take a tax deduction for an amount paid in cash to an HSA based upon the annual deductible amount under an HDHP. In 2013, the contribution limits are $3,250 for self-coverage and $6,450 for family coverage.[34] For taxpayers between age 55 and 65, the annual limit is increased by $1,000 in 2013.)

An eligible individual may establish an HSA with a qualified HSA trustee or custodian, in much the same way that an IRA is established. No permission is necessary from the IRS, and the employee may establish the HSA with or without the contributions being made by the employer. An employee may elect to have amounts contributed by the employer to an HSA on a salary reduction basis. Amounts are treated as employer-provided coverage for medical expenses under an accident or health plan and are excludable from the employee's income. Any amount distributed out of an HSA that is not used to pay for qualified medical expenses must be included in gross income and is subject to a 10-percent excise tax under Code Sec. 223(f)(4).

HSAs may be added as an option in a cafeteria plan. However, an employer cannot offer an HSA that covers medical expenses also covered under another cafeteria option, such as a flexible spending account (FSA). Both plans may be offered under a cafeteria plan provided each account does not pay the same medical expense.

.09   TAX PLANNING WITH FSAs, HRAs, AND HSAs

HSAs and HDHPs offer significant tax savings possibilities for taxpayers, and these programs could help reduce the total cost of health care. By offering HDHPs to their employees, an employer can significantly cut the premium costs associated with provided health insurance coverage to its employees. And the HSA can be used to provide enough cash for the employee to pay medical expenses until deductibles are met.

Currently, family coverage premiums for low-deductible, co-pay plans have increased substantially with premiums often exceeding $15,000 a year. Depending on how HSA group plans are eventually packaged and offered, insurance premiums could be 40–70 percent of traditional insurance coverage that has a low deductible and co-pay feature. And these savings from lower premium costs can be channeled to employees into an HSA, perhaps through a flexible spending arrangement or an HRA funded by the employer. Thus, it is possible and even likely that the net cost of health care could decline with no loss in coverage.

The same basic arrangement can also be used by a self-employed individual. The premium savings from converting to an HDHP could be invested in an HSA for the self-employed individual to cover the medical costs paid before the high deductible is satisfied.

It is also possible that the savings will continue to grow each year. Since an HSA is not subject to a "use it or lose it" feature, contributions may accumulate in each year that significant medical expenses are not incurred. This enables the participant to save for post-retirement health-related expenditures, and may permit the participant to choose a high-deductible catastrophic Medicare insurance plan since out-of-pocket costs can be withdrawn from the HSA.

Example 12-2. Mel Allen, age 42, is married and has one child. His current marginal tax rate is 15 percent. He is self-employed and currently has no health insurance, and his medical annual expenses are $1,500. If Mel purchases a traditional low-deductible, co-pay health insurance family policy, his health insurance premiums would be approximately $700 per month. Mel may also choose to purchase an HDHP with a $5,100 deductible for a monthly premium of $215. Mel's net after-tax cost of health insurance coverage for the two plans is computed as follows (recall that a self-employed individual can deduct 100 percent of the premiums for family coverage):

---

[34] Rev. Proc. 2012-26, 2012-20 IRB 933.

Traditional low-deductible insurance ($700 × 12 × .85) $7,140

HDHP plan ($215 × 12 × .85)   (2,193)

After-tax savings with HDHP   4,947

The after-tax cost of the contribution is $4,335 ($5,100 × .85), which is less than the $4,947 cost savings generated by choosing an HDHP. Assume that Mel's medical expenses for the first year are $1,500 and that the $612 cost savings ($4,947 − $4,335) remaining after contributing to the HSA are spent on the medical expenses, and that the HSA charges a $3 per month administrative fee. Given these facts, the balance in the HSA at the end of Year 1 would be $4,176 ($5,100 − $1,500 + $612 − $36). Over several years, this could provide a substantial sum in the HSA to cover future medical expenses.

Because the HSA is a tax-favored trust account, any interest earned is tax-free. Over a number of working years, the HSA will provide a substantial sum of cash available to meet medical expenses not covered by the high-deductible policy.

OBSERVATION   The previous example assumes a self-employed taxpayer. But the same type of analysis would work for a corporate employer: a switch to HDHP coverage for employees would generate significant cost savings for the corporation, which in turn could use part of those savings to offer assistance to employees for covering medical costs before the deductible limits are reached. This might be accomplished by an employer-funded HRA or by offering HSA group benefits as part of a salary-reduction election by employees through a cafeteria plan or flexible spending account. As indicated in the above analysis, the cost savings generated by the switch to an HDHP will most likely be enough for the employer to fund the costs of those medical costs below the deductible and still have cash left over.

¶12,007   Deferred Compensation: Qualified Plans

Over the years Congress has granted special tax treatment for amounts set aside for retirement. Congress has encouraged private saving through a variety of tax-favored vehicles, and the purpose of the following discussion is to review the key requirements for each type of vehicle. These include qualified pension plans and a variety of Individual Retirement Account arrangements. In addition, special rules have been enacted for stock options and other restricted property plans discussed later.

.01   QUALIFIED RETIREMENT PLANS IN GENERAL

Retirement plans may be classified in general as either defined benefit plans or defined contribution plans. The three main advantages of qualified retirement plans are:

(1) a current deduction for contributions to trusteed accounts,

(2) tax-free earnings on contributions,

(3) deferral of tax until withdrawal (usually at retirement).

A **defined benefit plan** determines by a specific formula the benefits an employee will receive. The formula will necessarily involve actuarial computations, and the employer assumes the risks associated with the plan (i.e., the employer has to "make good" on the promised benefit). The benefit is generally based on a combination of average compensation and years of service.

Example 12-3. Mason Corporation offers a defined benefit plan, promising to pay each participant a retirement benefit equal to their average salary for the three highest-earning years times two percent times the number of years of service. This is a defined benefit plan.

A **defined contribution plan** determines in advance the amount the employer will contribute. This contribution does not involve actuarial computations, and the risks associated with the plan are born by the employee (the retirement benefit depends entirely on the investment performance). A defined contribution plan may be structured as a profit-sharing plan (a fixed formula based on profits), a money purchase pension plan (a fixed formula not based on profits), or a stock bonus plan (employer contributions of stock).

Example 12-4. Hedrin Corporation contributes 10 percent of each employee's salary to a retirement plan each year. The final retirement benefit the employee receives depends on the investment performance of the trusteed contributions during the employee's working years. This is a defined contribution plan.

A **cash balance plan** is a relatively new type of hybrid pension plan. Under the arrangement, the plan is funded by employer contributions but the employee assumes both the investment risks and rewards (the retirement benefit depends entirely on the investment performance). Although the employer bears the mortality risk if the employee lives longer than expected, the actual benefit is based on the invested amounts, not a promised amount.

.03   QUALIFICATION REQUIREMENTS FOR QUALIFIED PLANS

Qualified retirement plans must meet certain requirements found in Code Sec. 401, Qualified Pension, Profit-sharing, and Stock Bonus Plans, in order to benefit from the three tax advantages discussed earlier. These requirements include the following:

Exclusive Benefit Requirement. The plan cannot discriminate in favor of select groups, must exclusively benefit employees and plan beneficiaries, and may not allow certain prohibited transactions between the plan and disqualified persons (e.g., loans from the plan to the employer).[35]

Nondiscrimination Requirements. The plan must satisfy a variety of Code-based tests to insure that the plan does not discriminate in favor of "highly compensated employees; for example, the plan should cover at least 70 percent of all "non-highly" compensated employees.[36]

OBSERVATION

A *highly compensated individual* includes any employee who during the current year or the preceding year was either (a) a 5-percent owner of company, or (2) received more than $115,000 compensation (for 2013). Alternately, the top group may be defined as those receiving more than the annual limit *and* are members of the "top paid" group (the top 20 percent of employees).

Participation and Coverage Requirements. All employees 21 years of age or older must be able to participate after one year of service (1,000 hours of service within 12 months). Alternately, participation can be delayed until the later of (1) age 21 or (2) two years of service, if the employee vests immediately upon entering the plan. Certain minimum coverage requirements are also included in the Code; for example, the plan must cover the lesser of 50 employees or 40 percent of all employees.[37]

---

[35] Code Sec. 401(a)(1).
[36] Code Sec. 401(a)(5).
[37] Code Sec. 410(a).

Example 12-5. Temple Corporation's pension plan provides coverage for an employee after two years of service or whenever the employee reaches age 21. This rule meets the participation requirements of the Code if the employee immediately vests all benefits when the test is met.

Vesting Requirements. Participants rights must vest (as nonforfeitable) under one of two possible schedules: (1) 100 percent upon completion of five years of service ("cliff vesting"), or (2) 20 percent after three years, with 20-percent increments each year (100 percent after seven years of service). A faster vesting schedule applies to employer matching contributions.[38]

Distribution Requirements. Distributions from qualified plans must begin by the *later* of (1) the calendar year in which the participant reaches 70½ years old, or (2) the calendar year in which the participant retires. A five-percent owner or a traditional IRA holder must begin receiving payments no later than April 1 of the year following the year the participant reaches age 70½. Minimum annual distributions must be based on the life expectancy of the participant and a designated individual beneficiary. A 50-percent nondeductible excise tax is imposed on the participant for any required distributions for a year that were not distributed.[39]

.05   TAX CONSEQUENCES OF QUALIFIED PLANS TO THE EMPLOYEE

Generally, amounts are not taxable to the employee until distributed at retirement, even though the employer generally takes an immediate deduction when the contributions are made. Amounts received by employees are generally taxed under the Code Sec. 72 annuity rules, where the employee can recover any "investment in contract" tax-free (i.e., employee contributions made by the employee with after-tax dollars).

Example 12-6. Debra White retires from Cal Corporation after 30 years of employment. Debra is covered by a defined benefit plan, and Cal Corporation made all contributions to the plan. Any benefits received are fully taxable, since her investment in the contract is $0.

Example 12-7. Janet Brown retires from Macy Corporation after 25 years of employment. Janet is covered by a defined contribution plan; each year Janet contributed 2.5 percent of her salary to the plan, and her employer contributed 7.5 percent of her salary each year to the plan. Janet may recover nondeductible contributions tax-free under the annuity rules. Her "investment in the contract" is the total amount she contributed of her own after-tax dollars to the plan. If her contributions are made in "before-tax" dollars, then 100 percent of the amount distributed to her is taxable.

An employee may elect to receive a lump-sum distribution at retirement. Generally, distributions are taxable. Taxpayers receiving lump-sum distributions may avoid current taxation by rolling over the distribution into another qualified plan or an **Individual Retirement Account (IRA)**. This rollover may be direct, from the old plan to the new, or it may involve a distribution of cash and then a transfer to the new plan. In the latter case, the employee has 60 days to transfer the funds, and 20 percent of the proceeds are generally withheld as income tax prepayments.

If a taxpayer receives an early distribution, it is taxable and also subject to a 10-percent penalty.[40] However, the following distributions, while still taxable, are not treated as early distributions if made:

---

[38] Code Sec. 411(a)(2).
[39] Code Sec. 401(a)(9)(C)(i).
[40] Code Sec. 72(q).

- after the participant reaches age 59½
- to a beneficiary due to the death of the participant
- attributable to disability
- in equal payments as an annuity based on life expectancy
- due to early retirement after participant reaches age 55
- to pay medical expenses deductible under Code Sec. 213
- from an IRA for qualified higher education expenses
- from an IRA up to $10,000 for first-time home buyers

Example 12-8. Mark Harmon retires early at age 56 and begins to receive a monthly pension payment. Since Mark has retired early and has reached age 55, the 10-percent early withdrawal penalty does not apply. However, benefits received are subject to taxation under the normal annuity rules.

.07   TAX CONSEQUENCES OF QUALIFIED PLANS TO THE EMPLOYER

Code Sec. 415 imposes certain limits on (1) the amounts that an employer may contribute on behalf of an employee and (2) the aggregate amount deductible by the employer. These are not the same numbers, and should not be confused. Employers may defer paying the contributions until the due date of the return. The maximum contributions and deductions, indexed annually for inflation, are:

2013 Tax Year		
Type of Plan	Maximum Amount Contributable on Behalf of Employee	Maximum Amount Deductible by the Employer
Pension Plan (Defined Benefit Plan)	The lesser of: (1) 100% of the employee's compensation (average of highest 3 years, limited to $255,000) or (2) the present amount to fund an annual retirement benefit of $205,000.	Actuarial calculation of the amount necessary to fund the normal stated contract benefit (plus up to 10% of past service costs if using the normal cost method, or over remaining employee service years if using level funding method)
Profit-Sharing, Stock-Bonus, or Money Purchase Plan (Defined Contribution Plan)	The lesser of $51,000, or 100% of the employee's compensation	25% of total annual aggregate compensation of employees ($255,000 maximum per employee)
More Than One Plan Existing at One Time	Individual Limits As Specified Above	Greater of (1) 25% of total aggregate compensation of employees, or (2) minimum funding standards of Code Sec. 412

Example 12-9. Zell Mooney is covered by his employer's defined benefit pension plan. During the current year and the past two years, Zell averaged $260,000 annual salary. The maximum amount Zell's employer may contribute on his behalf in the current year is the actuarially-determined present value amount, (using a $255,000 annual compensation maximum), that would fund a retirement benefit not exceeding $205,000.

Example 12-10. Alice Thomas is covered by her employer's defined contribution (money-purchase) pension plan. During the current year, Alice received a salary of $60,000. The maximum contribution that Alice's employer may make to the pension plan on her behalf during the current year is $51,000.

Example 12-11. During the current year Nixon Corporation paid its employees a total of $800,000 in salary. The maximum deduction permitted for contributions to a defined contribution pension plan for the current year is $200,000 ($800,000 × .25).

.09 TAX PLANNING WITH QUALIFIED RETIREMENT PLANS

From an employer perspective, the current trend is towards defined contribution plans, where the investment risk is shifted to the employee. The employer simply promises to contribute a predefined amount to the employee's retirement account each year, and the final retirement benefit is dependent on the investment performance of the trusteed contributions. In recent years a number of companies have converted their defined benefit plans to cash balance plans, where the employer maintains some risks but no longer promises a definite benefit (the benefit is based on contributions only). Some employers also consider stock-bonus or profit-sharing plans as a means of limiting promised outlays to retirement plans each year. If there are no profits, then there are no contributions.

OBSERVATION The tax-free accumulation of income on trustee contributions to a retirement account may offer a tempting investment vehicle for employers to park excess cash (any reversions for failure to meet vesting standards go back to the employer). However, Congress has imposed a 10-percent excise tax on excess contributions to discourage this type of behavior.

From an employee's perspective, a defined benefit program offers the advantage of shifting the investment risk to the employer. The employer promises a certain predefined benefit at retirement, and it is up to the employer to insure that this obligation is met. The preference for a defined benefit program is especially true for older employees participating in a retirement plan. In most cases, the retirement benefit is dependent on the average compensation received for the three highest years, and it is possible to fund higher benefits over a shorter period of time.

On the other hand, younger employees traditionally have preferred defined contribution plans, since the tax-free accumulation during a number of working years on these contributions will produce a considerable sum at retirement. In terms of simple math, if the maximum contribution was made each year under both a defined benefit plan and a defined contribution plan, studies have shown that at a starting age of approximately 55 or 56 the defined benefit plan produces the larger retirement stream. If an employee's first year of service in the plan is before this age, then the defined contribution plan produces a larger retirement benefit.

When an employee changes jobs, the employee's vested balance in the qualified plan may be rolled over tax-deferred into the employee's own IRS or another qualified employer retirement plan. This portability is a key advantage for most qualified plans.

¶12,009 Code Sec. 401(k) Cash or Deferred Arrangements (CODAs)

A participant in a qualified plan may elect under Code Sec. 401(k) to receive an amount either in cash or as a tax-deferred contribution on their behalf to a profit sharing or stock bonus plan. The arrangement is usually cast in the form of a salary reduction agreement with the employer. These plans are sometimes called **cash or deferred arrangements (CODAs)**, in that the employee can choose between receiving currently-taxable cash or voluntarily reducing salary by an amount that will be tax-deferred until retirement.

Amounts contributed to a Code Sec. 401(k) account are not included in the gross income of the employee and are 100 percent vested. Any contributions by an employer on behalf of the employee are tax-deferred as well. Earnings on the contributions accumulate on a tax-free basis. A taxpayer who has attained age 50 by the end of the year may make additional "catch-up" contributions of $5,500 (for 2012). Thus, the maximum contribution by a taxpayer age 50 or older in 2012 is $22,000. A 10-percent excise tax applies to any excess contributions not withdrawn within 2½ months of the close of the plan year.

2013 Tax Year		
	Maximum Allowable Contribution	Maximum Allowable Exclusion
All Code Sec. 401(k) Arrangements	Lesser of: (1) $17,500 ($23,000 if age 50 or older) or (2) lesser of 100% of compensation or $51,000, less other tax-favored contributions	Same as the maximum allowable contribution

Example 12-12. Hal Davis, age 54, elects to reduce his salary by $18,000 and have that amount contributed to the company Code Sec. 401(k) profit-sharing plan. The entire $18,000 may be excluded from income, since Hall is over age 50.

OBSERVATION Employees who perform services for an educational organization are offered essentially the same benefits of a Code Sec. 401(k) plan through the provisions of Code Sec. 403(b)(1)(A)(ii). These are also normally cast as salary reduction plans and the same Code Sec. 401(k) dollar limits apply.

.01 TAX PLANNING WITH CODE SEC. 401(k) PLANS

Code Sec. 401(k) plans, as well as Code Sec. 403(b) plans, are sometimes referred to as supplemental retirement annuities, in that these amounts supplement the primary retirement income stream. In some cases, the employer offers to match all or a portion of an employee's contributions to these plans. In this situation, the planning strategy is an absolute no-brainer: the employee should invest every penny he or she can into the plan, up to the Code limits, if possible. The accumulation feature is simply too attractive to ignore.

Example 12-13. Melody Duncan, age 41, elects to contribute $10,000 each year to a Code Sec. 401(k) plan. Assuming an average investment return of four percent a year, at age 65 she will have an accumulation of $390,800. If her employer matches her contribution dollar-for-dollar, her accumulation will be twice that amount, or $781,600. Even if her employer only matched her contribution $.25 on the dollar, the accumulated total would be $488,500.

In the past, a number of employees who are otherwise conservative with their regular retirement investments were willing to speculate more with supplemental investments, such as Code Sec. 401(k) accounts. And many individuals did benefit from the stock market run-up in the late 1990s. But in cases like Enron, employees saw their multi-million dollar Code Sec. 401(k) accounts vanish because they were invested solely in their firm's stock. A steady two to four-percent "conservative" return does not look too bad for supplemental annuities. As demonstrated by the previous example, a small supplemental investment can go a long way towards funding a secure retirement.

¶12,011 SEP and SIMPLE Retirement Plans

In recent years the deductibility of contributions to IRAs has been restricted for many middle- and upper-income taxpayers. As a result, a SEP-IRA or a SIMPLE plan may be a more attractive alternative for retirement planning. As discussed above, implementing a qualified retirement plan involves a number of continuing administrative and legal tasks. Plans must be constantly monitored to assure that the qualification requirements are being met. In recent years, Congress has developed two simplified versions that allow an employer to contribute directly to an IRA or, in the case of a SIMPLE plan, a Code Sec. 401(k) account, and avoid much of this administrative complexity. These plans are known as SEP and SIMPLE plans.

.03 SEP PLANS

Small businesses may avoid the administrative complexity of qualified plans by using a **Simplified Employee Pension (SEP)** plan,[41] where the employer makes contributions directly to IRAs established for its employees (and the owner as well). A SEP can be established even if the self-employed person is the only employee. Contributions can be made up to the due date of the return. The account may be established up until the *due date of the return (including extensions)*. This is the same rule applicable to regular IRAs.

A SEP must be set up for every "qualified employee," a person who (1) is at least 21 years of age, (2) worked for the employer three of the preceding five years, and (3) who received at least $550 in compensation. Employer contributions must be nondiscriminatory, that is, they do not favor "highly compensated employees."

OBSERVATION   An employer can set up less restrictive qualifications, but not more restrictive ones.

For 2013, deductible contributions for each participant in a SEP are limited to the *lesser* of (1) 25 percent of the participant's compensation (limited to a compensation ceiling of $255,000 or (2) $51,000. Employees are taxed on any excess contributions made to their accounts. Contributions may be made until the due date of the return, including extensions.

The self-employed person is an employee for SEP purposes, and the deduction on his or her own behalf is generally determined with the same rule. However, for these purposes "self-employed income" is used in place of compensation, and this amount is defined as net self employed earnings after reduction for the SEP deduction and one-half of any self-employment tax.

Employees may also contribute to a SEP, if contributions made on their behalf under the SEP are less than the normal $5,500 limit (in 2013) on IRA contributions. In other words, the employee can make up any amount less than $5,500, or $6,500 if age 50 or older. For each employee, this limit covers all contributions to a regular IRA, a Roth IRA, and a SEP.

.05 SIMPLE RETIREMENT PLANS

A **Savings Incentive Match Plans for Employees (SIMPLE)** plan is an alternative to the more complicated qualified corporate. A SIMPLE plan may be adopted by any employer that has 100 or fewer employees who received at least $5,000 in compensation from the employer in the preceding year.

OBSERVATION   All employees do not have to be covered by the plan; they merely are eligible to participate. In effect, SIMPLE plans may be discriminatory, and the top-heavy rules do not apply. However, the employees' rights to the pension benefits must be nonforfeitable.

---

[41] *See* Code Sec. 408(k).

An employer may establish IRAs[42] or Code Sec. 401(k) plans for employees (including the self-employed business owner). Employees are permitted to either take cash or make *elective contributions* (salary reduction) of up to $12,000 per year in 2013 (plus a $2,500 catch-up for employees age 50 or older), and employers are generally required to *match* the employee contributions up to three percent of compensation. If the employer chooses to make *nonelective contributions*, rather than matching contributions, the limit is two percent of compensation per year.

The normal 10-percent penalty on early distributions (discussed later) applies to SIMPLE plans. If the distribution occurs within the first two years of participating in the plan, the penalty is increased to 25 percent of the distribution.[43]

.07   TAX PLANNING WITH SEP AND SIMPLE RETIREMENT PLANS

A Simplified Employee Pension (SEP) is a popular option for employers who want an easy way to provide retirement savings for their employees.[44] A SEP is basically similar to a traditional IRA, which is set up for each employee. From the perspective of the SEP participant, a SEP is not much different from a traditional IRA, except that a SEP allows the participant to put away more money each year for retirement.

Employers like SEP plans because they are easy to establish and administer. Under a SEP plan, an employer sets up a traditional IRA for each qualifying employee. An employer with leased employees may also have to provide them with SEPs as well. A leased employee is generally a person who works for the employer, but was hired by a leasing organization.

> **OBSERVATION**
>
> Although an employer adopting either a SEP or SIMPLE plan must include all eligible employees in the plan, the employer may exclude the following employees:
> (1) those covered by a union agreement if their retirement benefits were a result of good faith bargaining between their union and the employer,
> (2) nonresident alien employees who have no U.S. source earned income from their employer.

A Savings Incentive Match Plan for Employees (SIMPLE) plan is also one of the easiest and most convenient methods for a small business to provide retirement income to its owner and employees. Under a SIMPLE plan, an employer and an employee make contributions to a savings account set up for the employee. Setting up a SIMPLE plan is very easy because many financial institutions will help an employer establish one. These plans are also fairly straightforward, inexpensive, and low-maintenance when it comes to administrating them.

An employer is required to make contributions to the SIMPLE plan, but there are two basic options for the employer to choose from. The employer can make nonelective contributions where *two percent* of an employee's compensation is automatically added to the employee's account, even if the employee doesn't otherwise participate in the plan.

An option is for the employer to match an employee's contributions dollar-for-dollar up to *three percent* of the employee's compensation. An employer can contribute a lower percentage, as low as one percent, for any year, but can't do so for more than two years during a five-year period ending the year for which a choice is effective.

> **OBSERVATION**
>
> Employers may also choose to set up a SIMPLE plan through the use of IRA accounts. **SIMPLE-IRAs** are a type of SIMPLE plan that deposits contributions into individual retirement accounts or *annuities* on behalf of employees. A SIMPLE-IRA

---

[42] *See* Code Sec. 219.
[43] Code Sec. 72(t)(6).
[44] *See* Code Sec. 408(k).

is created after the employer and employee complete IRS Form 5304-SIMPLE or Form 5305-A-SEP. Form 5304 is used if an employer allows each plan participant to select the financial institution that will receive contributions under the plan. Form 5305 is used if an employer requires that all contributions under the plan be deposited initially at a designated financial institution. A SIMPLE IRA account can be set up as either a *trust* account or a custodial account. A trust account is set up by filling out IRS Form 5305-S, *SIMPLE Individual Retirement Trust Account*. A custodial account is established by completing IRS Form 5305-SA, *SIMPLE Individual Retirement Custodial Account*.

¶12,013 Individual Retirement Accounts (IRAs)

.01 TRADITIONAL IRAs

Any individual under age 70½ with earned income may establish an Individual Retirement Account (IRA). The deductibility of the contributions depends on factors explained below. Contributions may be made up until the due date of the tax return. The maximum allowable contributions and deductions for the traditional IRA may be summarized as follows:

2013 Tax Year		
	Maximum Allowable Contribution	Maximum Allowable Exclusion
All Traditional IRA Plans	The lesser of: (1) $5,500 per spouse if married ($6,500 if age 50 or older), even if one spouse does not work, or (2) the taxpayer's earned income for the year (both spouses if married)	Same as the maximum contribution if neither spouse participates in a qualified plan. If covered by a retirement plan at work, the maximum is reduced when AGI exceeds $59,000 (single) or $95,000 (joint). There is no deduction when AGI exceeds $69,000 (single) or $115,000 (joint). If spouse is covered by a retirement plan at work the maximum is reduced when AGI exceeds $178,000. There is no deduction when AGI exceeds $188,000.

Example 12-14. Jim and Kathleen Wilcox (both age 45) report adjusted gross income of $97,000. Kathleen is covered by a qualified plan at work. Jim may still contribute and deduct the $5,500 maximum to his IRA. Kathleen may also contribute a maximum of $5,500 to her IRA; however, her deduction is limited to $4,950 ($5,500 − $2,000/$20,000 × $5,500), since their $94,000 AGI is $2,000 into the $20,000 phase-out of the deduction for someone covered by a qualified plan.

Example 12-15. Assume the same facts as the previous example, except that Kathleen is covered by a qualified plan at work and that their adjusted gross income was $183,000. In this case, Kathleen gets no deduction (but may still contribute $5,000 to her IRA), and Jim's deduction is $2,750 ($5,500 − $5,000/$10,000 × $5,500) since their AGI is $5,000 into the $10,000 phase-out when AGI exceeds $178,000.

Individuals not qualifying for deduction may still make nondeductible contributions to an IRA to retain the remaining two advantages of qualified retirement plans: tax-free accumulation of earnings and deferral of tax until withdrawal (usually at retirement). Because the taxpayer makes these contributions on an after-tax basis, he or she is entitled to recover the contribution tax-free upon withdrawal.

Before making nondeductible contributions to a traditional IRA, taxpayers should consider establishing a Roth IRA, if certain adjusted gross income limitations are met. As explained below, distributions from a Roth IRA after five years are generally tax-free.

OBSERVATION   Banks, savings and loans, and other financial institutions make IRAs available to customers. As a general rule, amounts are invested in conservative, long-term savings accounts. However, some brokerage firms offer self-directed plans where the taxpayer can specify how the contributions will be invested.

.03   ROTH IRAs

Nondeductible contributions for 2013 of up to $5,500 ($6,500 if age 50 or older) may be made to a "back-loaded" IRA known as a Roth IRA. Allowable contri-butions will be proportionately phased out over AGI ranges of $178,000–$188,000 for joint filers, $112,000–$127,000 for single filers, and $0–$10,000 for married-filing separately filers.

Qualified distributions from a Roth IRA will be tax-free following a five-year period, if made on or after age 59½, for disability, or for qualifying first time home-buying expenses. Deferred income on non-Roth IRAs, if rolled over to Roth IRAs, is ratably reported as income in the rollover year.

Example 12-16. Sonja Wilkinson, age 38, has adjusted gross income of $88,000. She contributes $5,500 to a Roth IRA. This amount is not deductible, but any subsequent qualifying withdrawals of this amount (plus any earnings) will be tax-free after a five-year waiting period.

Tax-free withdrawals from a Roth IRA are permitted after the five-year holding period under certain conditions. Qualified withdrawals include (1) distributions after age 59½, (2) death of beneficiary, (3) disability, or (4) up to $10,000 for qualified first-time home buying expenses.

OBSERVATION   A tax credit of up to 50% is available to individuals who contribute to a traditional or Roth IRA or a 401(k) or other qualified employer plan. For 2013 the credit is phased out when adjusted gross income exceeds $29,500 (single) or $59,000 (married filing jointly). The credit is claimed on form 8880, Credit for Qualified Retirement Savings Contributions. Query: At these low levels of income, is it realistic to expect a single or married couple to be able to save for retirement in order to benefit from the tax credit?

.05   PENALTY TAXES ON IRAs

A six-percent nondeductible excise tax penalty applies to any excess contributions to an IRA during the year (including *any* contribution after age 70½). In addition, a 10-percent penalty applies to premature distributions from an IRA before age 59½, unless for (1) medical expenses exceeding 7.5 percent of adjusted gross income, (2) qualified higher education expenses, or (3) $10,000 of first-time home buying expenses.[45]

---

[45] Code Sec. 72(t).

.07 TAX PLANNING WITH TRADITIONAL AND ROTH IRAs

The appeal of a traditional IRA was lessened in 1986 when Congress restricted deductibility of contributions to these accounts. However, even without the deduction, two of the three key benefits of a qualified plan still apply to traditional IRAs: tax-free accumulation of income during working years and deferral of tax until withdrawal. In particular, the tax-free accumulation of income feature can lead to rapid growth of the IRA value, even to the point that the rate of return is better than a taxable investment even if the 10-percent premature withdrawal penalty applies.

OBSERVATION   In general, the 10-percent early withdrawal penalty applies to withdrawals by a participant before age 59½ (and obviously, any income tax due on the withdrawal is taxable as well). However, exceptions to the 10-percent penalty exist for distributions due to death, disability, and certain non-lump sum distributions. Additionally, Congress added two new exceptions in recent years: (1) withdrawals to pay qualified higher education expenses for the taxpayer, spouse, children or grandchildren, and (2) up to $10,000 of the cost of constructing or buying a principal residence by a "first time homebuyer."

Several studies have shown that the "breakeven" period for accumulating funds in a nondeductible IRA to match the after-tax funds accumulated with a similar taxable investment is about seven years. In other words, after seven years the traditional non-deductible IRA could be liquidated, the appropriate income taxes and the 10-percent early withdrawal penalty paid, and the net balance would approximately equal the accumulation in an account with the same rate of return that was subject to income tax each year. Interestingly, that breakeven period drops to about five years if the contributions to the IRA are deductible.

Roth IRAs appeal to younger taxpayers, as the tax-free accumulation of income over a number of years will yield a sizable sum available for tax-free distribution at retirement. For taxpayers who cannot deduct contributions to a traditional IRA, the Roth IRA is clearly the better choice since distributions from the traditional IRA will be taxable to the extent of accumulated income in excess of nondeductible contribution cost recovery.

One of the key questions related to traditional IRAs is whether or not the taxpayer should convert the balance to a Roth IRA. The conversion will cause the immediate taxation of any untaxed accumulated income in the traditional IRA, as well as any contributions that were deducted (only the nondeductible contributions may be recovered tax free). Essentially, the question is whether or not it is advantageous to rollover amounts from a traditional IRA to a Roth IRA and pay the tax now or keep the traditional IRA and pay the tax when regular distributions begin.

Several factors influence this decision. The key variables to consider are (1) the age of the taxpayer, (2) the taxpayer's marginal income tax rate at retirement, and (3) the source of the funds used to pay the tax on the conversion. In general, the younger the taxpayer, the more a conversion makes sense, since they will have more years to accumulate income on a tax-free basis and they will not have to worry about taxes on distributions at retirement. A conversion loses some of its appeal if the taxpayer expects to be in a lower tax bracket at retirement; in this case, the deferral of tax offered by a traditional IRA has more of an influence on the projected outcome. If the tax on the conversion has to be paid with funds from the converted funds, then a conversion may not be desirable since the taxpayer will start with a smaller accumulation to justify tax-free treatment in the future.

Breakeven studies have also been done comparing traditional and Roth IRAs. In general, those studies provide confirmation of the obvious: the younger the taxpayer, the more appealing the Roth IRA. These studies also indicate a "breakeven age" of about 50; once the taxpayer reaches this age, the after-tax distributions under both plans are closer.

Thus far, the discussion has only compared traditional and Roth IRAs. But how do these vehicles compare to a Code Sec. 401(k) plan, for example? Because contributions to a Code Sec. 401(k) plan are on a before-tax basis (excluded from income), most financial advisors suggest contributing to the 401(k) plan first. If an employer matches the contributions, then by all means the employee should try to contribute the maximum amount subject to matching. Then the employee may want to consider the maximum contribution to a Roth IRA.

¶12,015   Pension Maximization Strategies

Most retirement plans offer several distribution choices for a participant when he or she retires. For example, the retiree may elect to (1) withdraw the account balance as a lump sum, (2) convert the account balance to a single annuity (monthly payments for the remainder of his or her life), or (3) convert the account balance to a joint and survivor annuity, whereby the retiree and his or her spouse received an annuity for the remainder of their lives. Obviously, the monthly benefit in the third option is less than the second option, as the annuity payments are guaranteed over two life expectancies. However, this choice does provide a measure of income security for the second spouse to die.

In recent years, financial planners have devised a strategy to provide income security to a surviving spouse. This technique is commonly called **pension maximization**, or pension-max for short. This strategy suggests that the retiree might be better off to elect the single annuity on retirement and then invest the after-tax monthly income in excess of what the joint and survivor annuity would have been in a universal term-life insurance policy on his or her life with his or her spouse as beneficiary. If the retiree dies first, the surviving spouse would then use the life insurance proceeds to purchase a lifetime income annuity. If the after-tax monthly income from this annuity exceeds what the joint and survivor benefit would have originally been from the retirement account, then the pension maximization strategy was successful.

Example 12-17. Upon retirement, Sara Moore (age 62) elects to convert her retirement account to a single lifetime annuity that pays $4,000 a month. If she had elected to take a joint and survivor annuity that paid the same amount to her husband Ralph (age 64) after she died, the monthly benefit would have been reduced to $3,200. Assuming that Ralph and Sara's combined marginal federal and state tax bracket is 30 percent, she will realize an additional after-tax income of $560 a month ($800 × .70) by electing the single annuity versus the joint annuity. Sara can then spend this $560 monthly amount to buy as much term life insurance as she can on her own life with Ralph as the beneficiary. For illustration purposes, assume that this amount will purchase a policy with a face value of $800,000.

Assume that Sara dies five years later. Ralph receives the $800,000 face value of the policy and then invests this amount in a single annuity on his own life. Based on his current life expectancy (Ralph is now 69 years old), the investment will produce a monthly lifetime annuity of $3,475. Since this amount exceeds the projected joint and survivor annuity benefit of $3,200 under Sara's retirement plan, the pension-max strategy has been successful.

Obviously, the preceding example is greatly simplified due to the number of assumptions (dates of death, investment returns, etc.). In reality, the evaluation of a pension-max strategy is much more difficult. For example, if the employee retires at a relatively old age, it may not be possible to buy term insurance at that time. Also, interest rates can change over the years, and inflation adjustments to both projected benefits may need to be considered. And finally, the relative dates of death of the retiree and his or her spouse (the ultimate unknowns) are obviously critical variables in these determinations.

OBSERVATION

Critics of our current retirement system lament that with so many pension plan options to choose from—401(k), SEP, SIMPLE, regular IRAs, and Roth IRAs—many workers choose not to contribute to a retirement plan due to the uncertainty of which retirement plan is right for them. Also, with the various contribution limits, ranging from $5,500 to $51,000 and the various income phase-out thresholds ranging from $59,000 to $188,000, a worker may not know if a contribution will be deductible or even permitted. There have been numerous proposals to combine the various pension plans into one set of uniform rules regarding the maximum amounts that can be contributed or deducted and to establish uniform income phase-out thresholds when determining the deductibility of a contribution.

¶12,017 Other Deferred Compensation Strategies

.01 NONQUALIFIED DEFERRED COMPENSATION PLANS

Nonqualified plans are those plans that do not meet the specific qualification requirements of the Code (usually because the plans benefit small groups of employees, violating the broad coverage requirements of qualified plans). While these plans may be more flexible, the employer does not receive a deduction until the employee reports the amount as income.

However, unless the funds are specifically set aside by the employer to meet this obligation, the employee is not taxed as the benefit accrues, since theoretically the employee is an unsecured creditor (and "in line" behind outside creditors of the company). As a result, the employee is taxed only when the compensation is received. The deferral of an employer deduction is also a disadvantage, but this may be a small price to pay in order to avoid the requirements associated with a qualified plan.

A nonqualified deferred compensation plan may be funded, unfunded, or a funded/unfunded Rabbi-trust arrangement. Each is defined as follows, and applications of the rules are illustrated in **Figure 2**.

a. *Unfunded.* The employee has only the employer's promise to pay in the future; as a consequence, the employee is not taxed until the funds are received.

b. *Funded.* The employer funds a trust with the compensation, and the employee holds a beneficial interest in the trust. Unless the trust is subject to a "*substantial risk of forfeiture*," the employee recognizes income in the year that the amounts are set aside (and the employer receives a deduction at this time). In effect, the employee is treated as having a legal interest in "property." A *substantial risk of forfeiture* is a reasonable risk that the employee will forfeit the compensation if certain conditions are not met, such as continuing employment for a period of time or certain performance goals.

c. *Funded/Unfunded ("Rabbi Trust").* This is the same as a funded trust, except that the trust funds are within reach of the outside creditors. Thus, for tax purposes, the employee is not taxed until the funds are received (when the employer receives a deduction for the amount).

Generally, payroll taxes are assessed in the year compensation is earned, even if these amounts are deferred for income tax purposes. An exception applies if the deferred amounts are subject to a "substantial risk of forfeiture."

Figure 2

Examples—Nonqualified Compensation Plans

Mason Corporation offers a nonqualified compensation plan for its employees. The company set aside $40,000 for Mary Poston this year in deferred compensation for services performed this year. Determine the tax consequences associated with this deferred compensation, assuming that:

a.   The promise to pay the $40,000 is an unsecured, unfunded promise by Mason.

Mary will not be taxed on the compensation until the amount is actually received, since the amount is within reach of the general creditors of the company. Mason Corporation will not receive a tax deduction until the amount is actually paid to Mary. [Note: payroll taxes will be assessed in the year the compensation is earned.]

b.   The promise to pay the $40,000 is funded in a trust beyond the reach of secured creditors, with Mary holding a beneficial interest in her own behalf.

The $40,000 is taxable to Mary in the year that it is set aside, since the trust interest is a beneficial interest in property. Mason Corporation may deduct the $40,000 in the year that it is set aside. [Payroll taxes are also assessed in the same year.]

c.   Same as (b), except that the trust is structured in a way to be within the reach of the general creditors of the corporation.

Since Mary now has the risk that if the company becomes insolvent the general creditors will be paid first. This risk defers recognition of income (and deduction by the corporation) until actual receipt. Trusts with these provisions are frequently termed "rabbi trusts." [Payroll taxes will be assessed in the year the compensation is earned.]

d.   Same as (b), except that Mary must remain an employee of Mason Corporation for the next two years in order to qualify for the compensation.

The employment requirement is a "substantial risk of forfeiture," which will defer recognition of income until the forfeiture risk lapses (i.e., in two years). Mason will be able to deduct the amount at the same time. [Since there is a substantial risk of forfeiture, payroll taxes are not assessed until the forfeiture risk lapses.]

OBSERVATION   Nonqualified deferred compensation plans (NDCP) can be useful tools for attracting executive talent. The principal advantage is that the employee can defer the recognition of compensation to future periods, hopefully at retirement when his or her tax bracket will be lower. The taxpayer can also defer taxation of any earnings on the deferred compensation until paid by the employer, and this may yield a substantial sum in the long run. However, income may become "bunched" when the deferral period expires, and it is always possible that tax rates will go up.

.03   RESTRICTED PROPERTY PLANS

Significant risks of forfeiture on the use of property as compensation (sometimes referred to as "golden handcuffs") will generally defer recognition of income until the conditions are satisfied (i.e., a certain number of years of service must be met or the stock will be forfeited). The stock may also be subject to significant lapse or nonlapse restrictions, as discussed below.

As mentioned earlier, stock compensation is taxed immediately if there are no restrictions on the transfer and the recipient employee has the right to transfer the stock. The amount of income reported by the employee (which is also the amount deductible by the company) is the difference between the fair market value of the stock and any amount paid by the employee (such as an option price). Any appreciation occurring after the income recognition may be taxed at favorable capital gains rates.

The stock may also be subject to significant lapse restrictions, defined as conditions before the property may be earned as compensation (such as length of employment or attainment of certain performance goals). Additionally, corporate insider trading rules may impose a six-month waiting period before certain employees sell stock; this is also a lapse restriction. These conditions will also defer income recognition until the restriction lapses (i.e., no longer applies). Examples are displayed in **Figure 3**.

Figure 3

Examples – Stock Compensation Plans

a. Harold acquires 1,000 shares of stock from his employer for $12 per share when the stock is worth $20 per share. There are no restrictions attached to the stock.

Harold must report $8,000 income at the time the stock is acquired, and his employer will deduct $8,000 as compensation.

b. Same facts as (a), except that Harold may not acquire the stock at the agreed upon price until his division increases gross profit by 20 percent over the prior year.

Harold will not report any income until the restriction lapses. When the profit goal is achieved, Harold will report $8,000 income, and his employer will deduct this amount.

c. Same facts as (b), except that Harold makes a Code Sec. 83(b) election when the stock is selling for $20 a share.

In this case, Harold will report $8,000 income in the year that the Code Sec. 83(b) election to accelerate the reporting on income is made (i.e., treating the restriction as having lapsed). Harold's employer will deduct the $8,000 in the same year.

The employment agreement may also provide for *nonlapse restrictions* (those that will never lapse, such as requiring that the stock be sold back to the company at a predetermined formula price, such as book value of the stock). Although these restrictions do not affect the timing of income, they do affect the amount of income reported (such as the formula price for repurchasing the stock from the employee).

A taxpayer receiving stock compensation with a lapse restriction may make a special election within 30 days of receipt under Code Sec. 83(b) to report income as if the restriction did not exist. This may be advisable if the stock is expected to appreciate substantially, since any income recognized on a later sale will probably qualify as capital gains income, taxed at a 15-percent rate. Another advantage of the election is that the five-year holding period for Code Sec. 1202 treatment does not begin until the income is recognized, and the election will accelerate the beginning of that holding period.

OBSERVATION   The Code Sec. 83(b) election is usually not elected, since it results in an immediate recognition of income and a subsequent forfeiture leads to unfavorable tax consequences. But in isolated circumstances, the election may make sense. For example, the bargain element may be relatively small, so that initial income recognition is minimized. The election may also make sense if substantial appreciation is expected in the future, or if it is highly likely that the restrictions will be met.

.05   STOCK OPTIONS

Generally, no income is recognized when a taxpayer receives an option to purchase the employer's stock, since the option usually does not have a readily ascertainable value until it is exercisable. When exercised, the excess of the fair market value of the stock over the option price paid by the employee must be reported as income. However, special tax treatment is available for **incentive stock options (ISOs)**.

If certain conditions are met (including a requirement that the option price equal or exceed the current market price), an employee may postpone recognition of gain until the date that the stock is sold, and the gain will qualify as long-term capital gain. To receive this preferential treatment, the stock sale must occur more than (1) two years after the date the option was granted and (2) more than one year after the option was exercised.

If either of these tests is failed, the excess of the fair market value of the stock over the option price is reportable as ordinary income when the stock is sold, with any remaining gain reported as capital gain. The employer may deduct this ordinary income portion as compensation; any gain reported as capital gain does not qualify for deduction. Examples are provided in **Figure 4**.

OBSERVATION	ISOs tend to be used by large publicly-held corporations, since valuation issues are a problem with closely-held companies and the owners of the family business may not want to dilute their ownership interests. In some respects, *nonqualified* stock options are more flexible: for example, the option price may be less than fair market value when granted. Also, the employer obtains a deduction with nonqualified options, and this might be passed along to the employee. There is also some question of the viability of using stock options for compensation since ASC Topic requires these amounts to be deducted in the financial statements of companies.

Figure 4

Examples – Stock Options

d.   Assume the same facts from Figure 5(a), except that Harold acquires the stock on 2/1/2012 by exercising incentive stock options received on 1/23/2011.

There are no regular income tax effects in the year that qualifying incentive stock options are granted or exercised; income recognition is deferred until the underlying stock is actually sold. However, the Alternative Minimum Tax impact of exercising the incentive stock options should also be considered.

e.   Assume the same facts as (d). Harold sells the stock on 3/12/2013 for $25 per share.

Harold's entire gain of $13,000 ($25,000 – $12,000 cost) is reportable as long-term capital gain, since the stock was held more than two years after being granted and more than one year after being exercised. Since the entire gain is capital gain, Harold's employer receives no deduction.

f.   Assume the same facts as (e). Harold sells the stock on 1/12/2013 for $25 per share.

In this case, Harold must report $8,000 ordinary income ($8 bargain element at exercise per share on 1,000 shares) and $5,000 short-term capital gain. This is due to the fact that Harold did not hold the stock longer than one year after exercise. The company may deduct the $8,000 as ordinary compensation.

¶12,019   Summary

- Both employers and employees benefit from compensation plans which include both taxable and nontaxable benefits.
- Employers can offer low-cost health insurance by utilizing Health Savings Accounts that can reimburse the employee for the medical costs not covered because of the high deductibles.
- While in the past, employers provided generous retirement benefits under either a deferred benefit or deferred contribution plan, today most employers rely upon Code Sec. 401(k) retirement plans in which the employee participates in funding the plan.
- For self-employed taxpayers and employees whose employers do not offer retirement plans, there are many options for saving for retirement including regular IRAs, Roth IRAs, and simplified employee plans.
- Retirement planning is more important now than ever because of the many options available.
- Where feasible, employers should offer stock option plans to retain and reward employees.

Review Questions for Chapter 12

True or False:

Indicate which of the following statements are true or false by circling the correct answer.

1. The value of meals provided by an employer may be excluded if meals or lodging are for the convenience of the employer or furnished on the business premises   T   F

2. One of the disadvantages of a Flexible Spending Account is that benefits are subject to payroll taxes.   T   F

3. HSAs are available to individuals with high deductible health plans (HDHP).   T   F

4. A *defined benefit plan* determines by a specific formula the benefits an employee will receive.   T   F

5. Qualified retirement plans cannot discriminate in favor of select groups, must exclusively benefit employees and plan beneficiaries, and may not allow certain prohibited transactions between the plan and disqualified persons.   T   F

6. Distributions from qualified plans must begin by the end of the year in which the employee reaches age 65½.   T   F

7. In a Simplified Employee Pension (SEP) plan the employer makes contributions directly to IRAs established for each employee.   T   F

8. A Savings Incentive Match Plans for Employees (SIMPLE) plan may be adopted by any employer that had 10 or fewer employees who received at least $5,000 in compensation from the employer in the preceding year.   T   F

9. For 2013 a nondeductible contribution of up to $5,500 may be made to a Roth IRA by a single filer whose AGI is $110,000.   T   F

10. ABC corporation promises to pay its president $50,000 when he retires in five years. This is an example of a nonqualified compensation plan.   T   F

Fill-in-the-Blanks

Complete the following statements with the appropriate word(s) or amount(s).

11. An exclusion is available for employer payments of up to $_____ per month (for 2013) for parking and qualified commuter transit costs combined, and $_____ per month (for 2013) for other qualified transportation, such as transit passes and tokens.

12. An employer may offer a(n) _____ where the employee can select from a variety of taxable and nontaxable benefits.

13. In 2013, the contribution limits to a high deductible health plan are $_____ for self-coverage and $_____ for family coverage.

14. Contributions to a Flexible Spending Account are subject to a(n) _____ rule, in that unused amounts at the end of the year are forfeited.

15. Retirement plans may be classified in general as either _____ plans or _____ plans.

16. A(n) _____ determines in advance the amount the employer will contribute.

17. A(n) _____ is funded by employer contributions but the employee assumes both the investment risks and rewards.

18. In a qualified retirement plan, all employees _____ years of age or older must be able to participate after _____ hours of service within _____ months.

19. An "early distribution," from a qualified retirement plan is generally _____ and subject to a(n) _____.

20. In a(n) _____ the employee can choose between receiving currently-taxable cash or voluntarily reducing salary by an amount that will be tax-deferred until retirement.

Multiple Choice:

21. Sue is employed by Montgomery Enterprises and will retire at the end of the current year after 18 years of service. Under the company's defined benefit plan, she can retire at 80 percent of the average of her three highest consecutive years' salary. Her average salary over these three years is $80,000. What is the maximum amount Sue can receive from Montgomery's pension plan?
    a. $16,000
    b. $64,000
    c. $80,000
    d. $185,000

22. Sylvia, an employee of Mylah Corp., earns $180,000 in 2013. The maximum amount Mylah can contribute to a qualified defined contribution plan on behalf of Sylvia is:
    a. $36,000
    b. $40,000
    c. $42,000
    d. $51,000

23. Betty is a 15-percent partner in the BED Partnership and has net self-employment income of $100,000 in 2013. The maximum amount that Betty can contribute to a SEP-IRA is:
    a. $3,000
    b. $13,045
    c. $20,000
    d. $25,000

24. Bob and Diane, both in their thirties, are married and file a joint return. In 2013 Diane earns $64,000 and Bob earns $1,800 working part time. Their adjusted gross income is $77,500. Diane participates in an employer-sponsored retirement plan. What is their maximum allowable IRA deduction?
    a. $1,800
    b. $5,500
    c. $7,300
    d. $11,000

25. Harry is 45 years old, single, self-employed, and has no qualified pension plan. His net self-employment income is $31,000. What is the maximum amount he can contribute to a SEP-IRA during the current year?
    a. $1,000
    b. $5,500
    c. $7,750
    d. $31,000

26. Sharon and Billy, both in their forties, file a joint return. Billy earns $59,000 and Sharon earns $18,000. Their adjusted gross income is $91,000. Billy is an active participant in his company's pension plan. Sharon's employer does not have a pension plan. What is the maximum combined IRA contribution and deduction amounts for 2013?

	Contribution	Deduction
a.	$5,500	$0
b.	$5,500	$5,500
c.	$11,000	$0
d.	$11,000	$11,000

27. Sue is self-employed. She established a simplified employee pension plan (SEP) for herself and her two full-time employees. Her net self-employment income before her SEP contribution and self-employment tax for the year is $70,000. The maximum amount she can contribute to her SEP is:
    a. $9,130
    b. $11,500
    c. $14,000
    d. $17,500

28. The GRAD Corporation maintains a SIMPLE-IRA retirement plan for its employees. GRAD matches each employee's contribution up to a maximum of three percent of the employee's salary. Brandon's salary is $50,000 and he contributed $2,000 to the plan. What amount must GRAD contribute on Brandon's behalf?
    a. $0
    b. $600
    c. $1,500
    d. $2,000

29. The GRAD Corporation maintains a SIMPLE-IRA retirement plan for its employees. GRAD matches each employee's contribution up to a maximum of two percent of the employee's salary. Charlie's salary is $240,000 and he contributes $2,800 to the plan. What amount must GRAD contribute on Charlie's behalf?
    a. $2,800
    b. $3,000
    c. $3,400
    d. $4,800

30. Linda is the only employee of the Best Corporation. Her annual salary is $80,000. The corporation makes a noncontributory profit-sharing plan contribution of $24,000 on her behalf. The Best Corporation is subject to an excess contribution penalty of:
    a. $0
    b. $400
    c. $1,000
    d. $2,000

31. On January 1, 2013, Tidal Corporation grants Twylah an option under its nonqualified stock option plan to acquire 300 shares of the company's stock for $12 per share. The fair market price of the stock on the date of grant is $18. The fair market value of the option is $4. How much must Twylah report as income at the date of grant?
    a. $1,200
    b. $1,800
    c. $3,600
    d. $5,400

32. On September 15, 2013, DeLand Corporation grants Granger an option to acquire 250 shares of the company's stock for $10 per share. The fair market price of the stock on the date of grant is $14. The option does not have a readily ascertainable fair market value. How much must Granger report as income at the date of grant?
    a. $0
    b. $1,000
    c. $2,500
    d. $3,500

33. On May 10, 2010, Optima Corporation granted Edward an option to acquire 500 shares of the company's stock for $10 per share. The fair market price of the stock on the date of grant was $12. The fair market value of the option at the date of grant was $3. Edward exercises the option on July 1, 2013, when the fair market value of the stock is $20. What is Edward's regular income at the date of exercise?
    a. $0
    b. $1,000
    c. $1,500
    d. $4,000

34. On January 1, 2011, Mayfair Corporation granted Tim an option to acquire 200 shares of the company's stock for $8 per share. The fair market price of the stock on the date of grant was $6. The option did not have a readily ascertainable fair market value. Tim exercises the option on July 1, 2013, when the fair market value of the stock is $20. How much must Tim report as income at the date of exercise?
    a. $0
    b. $1,200
    c. $2,400
    d. $2,800

35. On March 1, 2011, Suede Corporation granted Pamela an option to acquire 200 shares of the company's stock for $6 per share. The fair market price of the stock on the date of grant was $10. The option requires that Pamela remain with the company for one year after the date of exercise. The option did not have a readily ascertainable fair market value. Pamela exercises the option on June 1, 2012, when the fair market value of the stock is $15. On June 1, 2013, the fair market value of the stock is $20 per share. How much must she report as income in 2013 assuming no Code Sec. 83(b) election was made?
    a. $0
    b. $1,200
    c. $1,800
    d. $2,800

36. On February 1, 2011, Paulson Corporation granted Donald an option to acquire 200 shares of the company's stock for $10 per share. The fair market price of the stock on the date of grant was $16. The stock requires that Donald remain with the company for one year after the date of exercise. The option did not have a readily ascertainable fair market value. Donald exercised the option on September 1, 2012, when the fair market value of the stock was $19. He made a Section 83(b) election at the exercise date. On September 2, 2013, the fair market value of the stock is $25 per share. How much must he report as income in 2013?
    a. $0
    b. $1,200
    c. $1,800
    d. $3,000

37. Pamela receives the right to acquire 700 shares of Plus Corporation stock through the company's incentive stock option plan. The fair market value of the stock at the date of the grant is $8 and the exercise price of the option is $15 per share. The fair market value of the stock at the date of exercise is $19. Pamela will recognize income at the date of grant and the exercise date of

	Date of grant	Exercise date
a.	$0	$0
b.	$0	$2,800
c.	$0	$4,900
d.	$5,600	$0

38. Jennifer receives the right to acquire 400 shares of Union Corporation stock through the company's incentive stock option plan. The fair market value of the stock at the date of the grant is $15 and the exercise price of the option is $19 per share. The fair market value of the stock at the date of exercise is $22. At the date of exercise, the tax consequences to Jennifer and the Union Corporation are:

	Jennifer	Union
a.	$1,600	$1,600
b.	$1,600	$0
c.	$0	$0
d.	$0	$1,600

39. On October 1, 2013, Fran sells 700 shares of stock at $26 per share. Fran acquired the stock on June 1, 2012, when she exercised the option to purchase the shares through her company's incentive stock option plan. The exercise price was $12 per share and the fair market value of the stock at the date of exercise was $16 per share. For 2013, Fran must report:

	Ordinary Income	Capital Gain
a.	$0	$7,000
b.	$0	$9,800
c.	$9,800	$0
d.	$2,800	$7,000

40. On October 1, 2013, Vivian sold 1,000 shares of stock at $20 per share. Vivian acquired the stock on November 1, 2012, by exercising an option to purchase the shares through her company's incentive stock option plan. The exercise price was $11 per share and the fair market value of the stock at the date of exercise was $14 per share. For 2013, Vivian must report

	Ordinary Income	Capital Gain
a.	$3,000	$6,000
b.	$6,000	$3,000
c.	$9,000	$0
d.	$0	$9,000

Problems

41. Susan Beale is a single mother with two children, ages three and six. She pays a total of $7,000 each year to a neighbor to care for her children while she works. Her employer reimburses $4,000 of this amount. Before considering the child care payments and reimbursement, her adjusted gross income is $44,000, and her taxable income is $36,000. Assuming that Susan files as a head of household, how should she report the child care payments and any allowable child care credit? (Hint: Complete the form 2441 for Susan.)

42. Ted Turner's employer offers him a choice of reimbursing up to $600 of professional dues and subscriptions each year, or reimbursing up to $600 of parking costs at work. Ted, a computer specialist with the firm, expects to earn an additional $20,000 during the current year as part-time consultant, which will be reported on Schedule C. What advice would you give Ted concerning the choice, assuming the dues and subscriptions would also qualify as ordinary and necessary business expenses on his Schedule C?

43. Mary Giles participates in a flexible spending account (FSA) arrangement with her employer. She has a choice of receiving $2,000 of child care assistance or $2,000 of health cost reimbursements. Mary's adjusted gross income is approximately $80,000. What factors should Mary consider in making this choice?

44. Frank, age 59, and Mary, age 58, have a high deductible family health plan with an annual deductible of $6,000. How much may they contribute to a family HSA in 2013?

45. Janet has an FSA that covers dental and eye care to which her employer contributes $200 per month. Her employer has an HDHP medical insurance plan with a $2,750 deductible that covers medical expenses other than dental and eye care. Janet opened an HSA and contributed $2,750. Janet incurred the following medical costs during the year: $600 for dental care, $400 for prescription eye glasses, and $1,500 for doctor visits. How can Janet be reimbursed for these expenses? Explain.

46. Henry is covered by his employer's defined contribution pension plan. During the year, he received a salary of $120,000 and his employer made a contribution to the plan on his behalf of $20,000. What is the maximum contribution he can make to a regular IRA?, to a Roth IRA?

47. Bob and Zee Marley are married and both are age 56. During the current year Bob earned only $7,200 due to an injury at work, and Zee earned $3,100 from her job before she had to quit and assist Bob. How much may Bob and Zee contribute to their IRA accounts during the year, and how much (if any) of those contributions will be deductible?

48. Rob Taylor, a cash-basis, self-employed electrician, expects his Schedule C earnings to be slightly more than $100,000 during the current year. Rob is considering a conversion of his traditional IRA into a Roth IRA during the current year. What advice might you give Rob in regards to planning for this conversion?

49. Gill is an employee of the Best Corporation which maintains a money purchase plan for all its employees. Compute the maximum deductible contribution to the pension plan for 2013 if:
     a.   salary is $93,000.
     b.   salary is $200,000.

50. Henry's employer maintains a profit-sharing plan for all its employees. Compute the maximum deductible contribution in 2013 for each of the following situations:
     a.   salary is $88,000.
     b.   salary is $295,000.

51. Blaise is a partner in Sweet LLP, which maintains a SEP-IRA plan for its partners and employees. Compute the maximum deductible contribution in 2013 for each of the following situations:
     a.   net self-employment income is $75,000.
     b.   net self-employment income is $280,000.

52. Rachel, age 42, established a Roth IRA and contributed $5,000 per year for 20 years. Assume the account balance is $297,000 ($100,000 contributions, $197,000 earnings). Rachel plans to withdraw the entire amount. Her marginal tax rate is 25 percent. How much tax would be paid as a result of this decision?

53. On March 1, 2013, Tiny Inc., grants Tim a nonqualified stock option to acquire 1,000 shares of the company's stock for $12 per share. The fair market price of the stock on the date of grant is $15. The option does not have a readily ascertainable fair market value. On June 1, 2013, when the fair market value of the stock is $18, Tim exercises the stock option. Determine the tax consequences to Tim and Tiny Inc., on the grant date of the option and the exercise date.

54. On August 1, 2011, Chris is granted the right to acquire 500 shares of the Blue Corporation for $18 per share. The option qualifies under the company's incentive stock option plan. The current fair market value of the stock is $10. On September 1, 2012 when the stock is selling for $20 per share, Chris exercises his option to purchase the stock. He sells the shares on November 15, 2013, for $30 per share. Determine the tax consequences to Chris and Blue Corporation on the:
   a. Date of grant
   b. Date of exercise
   c. Date of sale

Internet Exercises

55. Do a key word search on "defined benefit plans." Identify several companies that have recently terminated their plans in favor of either a defined contribution plan or a 401(k) plan. Discuss the reasons given for making the change.
56. Locate articles discussing the U.S. personal savings rate. What percent of income does the typical American save? What types of savings investments do most individuals hold?
57. Locate the legislation permitting employers to automatically enroll new employees in employer sponsored 401(k) plans. What explanation was given in the explanation to the bill justifying this change? Do you think that younger employees will choose to "opt out" of the automatic enrollment? Justify your answer.
58. Locate some articles on the projected financial solvency of the Social Security System. How many years until the fund is projected to run out of money? Discuss various options to improve the solvency of the Social Security System. (Hint: visit the Social Security website, *www.ssa.gov.*

Excel Spreadsheet Problem

59. Tom, who is age 35 and single, is not covered by a pension plan at work He is currently in the 25% marginal tax bracket. He plans to retire at age 70. Should he make annual contributions to a regular IRA or a Roth IRA? He expects to earn an annual rate of return on his contributions of 4%, expects to be in the 25% bracket during his employment years, and expects to be in the 15% bracket during his retirement years. [Hint: assume the contribution to the Roth account equals the contribution to the regular IRA x (1-marginal tax rate).] How would your answer change if he expects to be in the 25% marginal tax bracket when he retires? How would your answer change if he expects to be in the 30% marginal tax bracket when he retires?

CHAPTER 13

Gift and Estate Tax Planning I—The Basics

Learning Objectives

1. Describe how the federal gift tax and the federal estate tax are merged into a single unified transfer tax system.
2. Define a "gift" for federal gift tax purposes, and list some of the common exceptions to this definition.
3. Summarize the basic gift tax rules related to the annual exclusion, charitable transfers, the marital deduction, and the gift-splitting election.
4. Describe in general the rules for including property in the federal estate, including the rules for jointly-held property, incomplete transfers, and life insurance policies.
5. Summarize the requirements for the alternate valuation date election for federal estate tax purposes.
6. List the common deductions and credits allowed in computing the federal estate tax.
7. Summarize the important transfer tax considerations in evaluating a program of lifetime gifts vs. death transfers, including the role of basis.
8. Define the probate estate, and describe methods of avoiding the probate process.
9. Describe the tax considerations involved in planning for the estate tax marital deduction, including the "reduce to zero clause" and the "QTIP election".

¶13,001 Introduction

A federal transfer tax applies to lifetime transfers (**the gift tax**) and transfers at death (**the estate tax**). The two taxable events are related through the operation of a single unified tax rate structure applicable to all transfers at life and at death, as well as a single unified credit. For this reason, technically, there is no "gift tax" or "estate tax", but only one tax: a **unified transfer tax**. But old habits are hard to break, so we will refer to the gift tax and the estate tax throughout the discussion. But remember that the same rate schedule and unified credit structure applies to both.

The purpose of this chapter is to introduce the basic components of the federal gift tax and federal estate tax computations, as well as to review some of the tax choices available under the unified transfer system. Some basic planning strategies related to gift and estate transfers are also discussed. Chapter 14 presents more sophisticated planning strategies applicable to trusts and family businesses.

¶13,003 The Unified Transfer Tax System in General

In general, only individuals who are citizens or residents of the United States are required to file a federal gift tax return or a federal estate tax return. Both tax returns are part of a "unified transfer system," whereby the same tax rate schedules and unified credit amounts apply.

Lifetime and death transfers are cumulative, and marginal taxes are determined with the same unified transfer tax schedule. Both taxes are based on the **fair market value (FMV)** of properties, generally defined as *"the price that the property would change hands between a willing seller and a willing buyer, with neither under the compulsion to buy or sell."*[1] This amount can be determined in a number of ways. For example, in many cases, this will be the comparable retail price of the property if available. For publicly traded securities, the trading price on the date of gift (or death) would be used. If only intermittent sales exist, a weighted average based on the days around the valuation date is used. This is illustrated in the example below. Finally, notes receivable should be valued at fair market value, taking into consideration terms, collateral, and other factors that could affect the negotiated price at which the note would likely sell.

Example 13-1. Rita Prizler made a gift of stock that was not traded on the day of the gift, but was traded at $100 four days earlier and traded at $80 six days later. The weighted average valuation for this stock would be:

$$\text{Value} = [(\$100 \times 4) + (\$80 \times 6)] / 10 \text{ days} = \$880/10 = \$88 \text{ per share}$$

¶13,005 The Federal Gift Tax

.01 THE FEDERAL GIFT TAX: AN OVERVIEW

The formula for determining the federal gift tax is displayed by means of a multi-year example for Tom and Jan displayed in **Figure 1**. The unified transfer tax rate schedule, used to compute the gift and estate tax liabilities, is reproduced in *Appendix A*. The various components of the computation are explained in the following sections of this chapter.

The gift tax is cumulative, in that current year gifts are added to all prior-year gifts, a tax is computed on these total "lifetime" gifts, and then prior gift taxes paid are subtracted from this total. The resulting tax is the current year gift tax related only to the gifts made during the current year. Thus, the gift tax is computed on a cumulative basis.

Example 13-2. Annie Apple had made taxable lifetime gifts of $4,950,000 prior to 2013. During 2013 she made taxable gifts of $1,000,000. In computing her gift tax liability in 2013, she would determine the tax on $5,950,000 of total lifetime gifts (including the current tax year), and then subtract any gift taxes paid in prior years on the $4,950,000 of transfers. The resulting tax is the marginal gift tax for the current year.

[1] *Newberry*, 39 BTA 1123.

```
┌─────────────────────────────────────────────────────────────────────────────┐
│                               Figure 1                                        │
│            Taxation of Lifetime Gifts – Tom's Gift Tax Return                  │
│                         Without Gift Splitting                                 │
│             (Assuming that Tom and Jan do not Elect to Gift Split)             │
└─────────────────────────────────────────────────────────────────────────────┘
```

Gifts Made by Tom Baker:	2013	2014	2015
Cash to daughter Jill	$ 2,183,000	$ 817,000	$ 2,353,000
Cash to charity (United Givers Fund)	24,000	32,000	40,000
Cash to wife Jan	60,000	40,000	100,000
Land to son Jack (fair market value)	$ 2,270,000	290,000	$ 2,466,000
Cash to granddaughter Alexandra	$ 1,580,000	320,000	14,000
Gross gifts	6,117,000	1,499,000	4,973,000
Gift splitting election (1/2 of all third-party gifts)	(0)	(0)	(0)
Annual exclusions (5, including United Givers Fund)	(70,000)	(70,000)	(70,000)
Charitable deduction (after reflecting exclusion)	(10,000)	(18,000)	(26,000)
Marital deduction (after reflecting exclusion)	(46,000)	(26,000)	(86,000)
Adjusted taxable gifts - current year	5,991,000	1,385,000	4,791,000
Add: Adjusted taxable gifts - prior years	0	5,991,000	7,376,000
Total taxable lifetime gifts	5,991,000	7,376,000	12,167,000
Tax on total taxable lifetime gifts	2,342,200	2,896,200	4,812,600
Less credit for prior gift taxes paid	0	(296,400)	(850,400)*
Less unified credit (maximum)	(2,045,800)	(2,045,800)	(2,045,800)
Net tax liability - current year	$ 296.400	$ 554,000	$1,916,400

*$296,400 paid in 2013 plus $554,000 paid in 2014

Example 13-3. In **Figure 1**, note in the year 2014 that the initial tax is computed on total lifetime gifts of $7,376,000, which includes the $5,991,000 lifetime gifts for all prior years (only 2013 in this case). Since gift taxes had been paid in prior years, the resulting tax of $2,896,200 is reduced by both the 2013 gift taxes paid of $296,400 and the unified credit of $2,045,800 (as explained below).

A special **unified credit** may be deducted from the gift tax liability each year. This credit reduces the gift tax liability dollar for dollar. Each individual has a lifetime unified credit of $2,045,800 in 2013, which is the equivalent unified transfer tax on a transfer of $5,250,000. Thus, a donor owes no gift tax until taxable transfers exceed $5,250,000.

Example 13-4. Assume the same facts as Example 13-2 for Annie Apple ($4,950,000 gifts in prior years and $1,000,000 gift in the current year). Using the unified tax rate schedule in Appendix A, the tax liability on $5,950,000 of gifts is $2,325,800. After subtracting her unified credit of $2,045,800, Annie will owe gift taxes of $280,000 for 2013. Annie will not subtract any prior year gift taxes from this total, since she did not pay any gift taxes in prior years (transfers were less than $5,250,000 in total).

Example 13-5. Refer to **Figure 1** again. Note that in the year 2015, the gift tax liability on total lifetime transfers of $12,167,000, or $4,812,600, exceeds the unified credit and the prior gift taxes paid. In the year 2015, Tom will be able to subtract the $296,400 and the $554,000 amounts from the computed tax on prior lifetime transfers in 2013 and 2014, in addition to subtracting the unified credit. (Note: the tax-payer will subtract the unified credit each year in this case, since prior gift taxes paid only include amounts actually paid in cash and do not include the unified credit.)

.03   THE FEDERAL GIFT TAX—TRANSFERS SUBJECT TO TAX

In general, the federal gift tax applies to any gift of real or personal property, whether tangible or intangible, that is made directly or indirectly, in trust, or by any other means to a donee. If the gift is incomplete or revocable, it will not be treated as a gift for tax purposes.

OBSERVATION   Generally, the courts define a gift as "a gratuitous transfer for less than adequate consideration that is motivated by generosity or like impulses."[2] The courts also note that intent to make a gift must be present. Most gifts occur in personal settings; gifts in a business setting are generally presumed to be transfers for a full and valuable consideration.

Gifts can take many forms. These include:
- Bargain sales or bargain purchases (i.e., at less than fair market value)
- Release of a **general power of appointment** (the power to appoint anyone to the enjoyment of the property, including the holder of the appointment)
- Forgiveness of debt, particularly in family situations
- Interest-free or below-market loans (actual interest provided for in the loan as compared to current rates of interest)
- Assignment of benefits under an insurance policy
- Certain property settlements in divorce cases
- Surrendering a single annuity for a reduced joint and survivor annuity

---

Example 13-6. Taylor loans Abby $500,000 on a 10-year note that provides for one percent annual interest. The market rate of interest at the time of the loan was five percent. The difference between market-rate interest ($25,000) and actual interest paid ($5,000), or $20,000 is treated as a taxable gift from Taylor to Abby.

A donee has the right to *disclaim* a gift (e.g., refuse to accept the gift). If this occurs, then there is no gift for federal gift tax purposes. Generally, the donor must receive the **disclaimer** in writing within nine months of the gift.

Example 13-7. Tamara Bacon disclaims a $30,000 gift in favor of her sister Ellen. Thus, Tamara is treated as not receiving the gift; it is assumed generally under Code Sec. 2518 that the original gift went directly to Ellen. Tamara is not treated as though she chose to make a $30,000 gift to Ellen.

The creation of a **joint tenancy** in property generally results in a taxable gift, equal to the portion of the value of the property gifted to the new joint tenant by the original (and sole) owner of the property. The creation of a joint bank account is not a completed gift, as the creator may withdraw the funds immediately. However, the withdrawal of any funds by a co-owner that exceeds the amount he or she deposited *is* a gift.

Example 13-8. Bob and Barbara purchase land that is held jointly. The total cost is $100,000, of which Bob contributes $80,000 and Barbara contributes $20,000. Bob has made a taxable gift of $30,000 to Barbara, the amount he paid in excess of 50 percent of the cost of the gift. If Bob and Barbara are married, the gift would qualify for the marital deduction (see below).

---

[2] *Robertson*, 343 US 711.

Example 13-9. Sally deposits $40,000 in a joint checking account with her daughter Alice. This transfer is not subject to the gift tax. However, if Alice withdraws $15,000 from the account, Sally is treated as making a $15,000 taxable gift to Alice.

In determining whether or not a gift tax return should be filed, it is important to realize that certain "gifts" do not require the filing of a gift tax return. These include:

- Tuition paid for anyone else
- Medical expenses paid for anyone else
- Gifts to a political organization
- Gifts to a qualifying charity

Gifts to spouses generally do not require that a gift tax return be filed, since such gifts are not subject to tax. See the marital deduction discussion below.

OBSERVATION   There is no "joint return" option for a married couple; each spouse files his or her own gift tax return. However, as discussed later, a married couple may elect to "gift split", whereby all gifts to third parties are treated as being made one-half by each spouse.

Even though a gift tax return may be required, that does not mean that gift taxes are actually due. Each individual is provided a unified credit (described below) that exempts a certain level of gifts from taxation. For 2013, the unified credit is fixed at $2,045,800, the exemption equivalent of $5,250,000 of lifetime gifts. This unified credit amount is now adjusted for inflation each year. (For simplicity, no inflation adjustment is assumed in the three-year examples of Figures 1, 2 and 3.)

.05   THE FEDERAL GIFT TAX—THE ANNUAL EXCLUSION

Current law provides an **annual exclusion** from the federal gift tax of up to *$14,000* per donee per year. This is adjusted periodically for inflation. If the gift to a donee is less than $14,000, the actual amount of the gift is used as the exclusion. The $14,000 annual exclusion is available for any taxable gift of a **present interest**. A present interest simply means that the donee can immediately enjoy the benefits of possessing and using the property.

Example 13-10. Sara Spanos made gifts of $40,000 to her daughter Anne, $8,000 cash to her son Bill, and $32,000 to her niece Alice. Sara may deduct annual exclusions totaling $36,000 ($14,000 for the gift to Anne, $8,000 for the gift to Bill, and $14,000 for the gift to Alice).

A gift of a **future interest** does *not* qualify for the exclusion. A future interest is one in which the enjoyment of the property and the income from the property will not begin until a future date. Future interests include reversions and remainder interests.

Example 13-11. Trevor Howard creates a trust by contributing $500,000 worth of securities. The income from the trust will go to his daughter Jill for the rest of her life (a **life interest,** also called a **life estate**) and the principal (corpus) will go to his granddaughter Jane on Jill's death (a **remainder interest**). The present value of the life estate gifted to Jill will qualify for the $14,000 annual exclusion, as it is a present interest. However, the remainder interest to Jane is a future interest and will not qualify for the exclusion.

OBSERVATION An interesting court test of the present interest requirement was the case of *D. Clifford Crummey*.[3] In this case, the Court ruled that the trust beneficiaries (minor children) have a present interest as a result of certain language in the trust instrument. That language, often referred to as a **Crummey power**, entitled each beneficiary of the life insurance trust to demand a distribution of the lesser of the amount transferred to the trust each year or the maximum annual gift tax exclusion. The amount was labeled as a present interest because the beneficiary was given reasonable notice of the availability of the funds for withdrawal and a reasonable time period for withdrawals (a window of approximately 30 days was provided). There is a possible downside to a Crummey power, however: the education fund a parent set up for a child may end up being spent on a new convertible!

.07   THE FEDERAL GIFT TAX—DEDUCTIONS

The primary deductions for the gift tax are the marital and charitable deductions. The **marital deduction** is unlimited and is allowed against any gift to a spouse that is not a "**terminable interest.**" This is an interest that extinguishes due to a lapse of time (such as a patent) or the death of the spouse (an income interest, or life estate, in property that passes automatically under the will to someone else, and the spouse cannot control the disposition). An exception is made for a transfer of *qualified terminable interest property*, which is discussed later in this chapter.

There is also an unlimited **gift tax charitable deduction** for gifts to recognized charities of present interests in property. Once again, a present interest means that the charity can enjoy the benefits of owning the property immediately.

Example 13-12. In **Figure 1**, Tom transferred $60,000 to his spouse Jan in 2013. The procedure used in the example of **Figure 1** is to first subtract the $14,000 annual exclusion for each donee, and then apply either the marital deduction or the charitable deduction to the remainder. Thus, the marital deduction for that year is $46,000. In a similar manner, the charitable deduction (after reduction for the annual exclusion) is $10,000.

.09   THE FEDERAL GIFT TAX—GIFT-SPLITTING ELECTIONS

A married couple may agree to split all gifts to third parties during the tax year. In this case, each spouse is treated as making one half of the value of the gift, and each reports such amounts on his or her gift tax return (there is no "joint gift tax return"). If a husband and wife elect **gift splitting** all gifts to third parties, this effectively doubles the annual exclusion to *$28,000* per year. Thus, if A and B elect to gift split a $17,000 gift to a third party, each spouse has made a gift of only $8,500 ($17,000/2), and neither has made a taxable gift for the year.

The election also utilizes both spouses' unified credits, which can save substantial taxes, as demonstrated below. To make this election, the couple must be married to each other at the time of the gift, and if divorced or widowed after the gift, did *not* remarry during the rest of the year.

Figure 2 repeats the facts of **Figure 1**, except that an assumption is made that Tom and Jan elect to split all gifts to third parties. A comparison of the two tables reveals that this results in substantial tax savings to Tom. Of course, Jan must file gift tax returns as well, and she will end up owing the same tax each year as Tom, since (1) they elect to split all third-party gifts and (2) any transfers between spouses are not subject to tax, and (3) neither Tom nor Jan had made any prior lifetime gifts.

---

[3]   22 AFTR 2nd 6023 (CA-9, 1968).

FIGURE 2
Taxation of Lifetime Gifts – Tom's Tax Return With Gift Splitting
(Assuming that Tom and Jan Elect to Gift Split)

Gifts Made by Tom Baker:	2013	2014	2015
Cash to daughter Jill	$ 2,183,000	$ 817,000	$ 2,353,000
Cash to charity (United Givers Fund)	24,000	32,000	40,000
Cash to wife Jan	60,000	40,000	100,000
Land to son Jack (fair market value)	2,270,000	290,000	2,466,000
Cash to granddaughter Alexandra	1,580,000	320,000	14,000
Gross gifts	6,117,000	1,499,000	4,973,000
Gift splitting election (1/2 of all third-party gifts)	(3,028,500)	(729,500)	(2,436,500)
Annual exclusions (5, including United Givers Fund)	(68,000)	(70,000)	(63,000)
Charitable deduction (after reflecting exclusion)	(0)	(2,000)	(6,000)
Marital deduction (after reflecting exclusion)	(46,000)	(26,000)	(86,000)
Adjusted taxable gifts - current year	2,974,500	671,500	2,381,500
Add: Adjusted taxable gifts - prior years	0	2,974,500	3,646,000
Total taxable lifetime gifts	2,974,500	3,646,000	6,027,500
Tax on total taxable lifetime gifts	1,135,600	1,404,200	2,356,800
Less credit for prior gift taxes paid	0	0	0
Less unified credit (maximum)	(2,045,800)	(2,045,800)	(2,045,800)
Net tax liability - current year	0	0	$ 311,000

Figure 3 illustrates the tax computations for Jan each year. Note that taxes paid by each spouse are the same, and that no actual payment is required until the third year. Also note that Jan had made no gifts to her spouse Tom during any of the years. The total taxes saved with gift splitting are significant, and can be computed as follows:

Total taxes without gift splitting ($296,400 + $554,000 + $1,916,400)	$2,766,800
Total taxes with gift splitting ($311,000 Tom + $311,000 Jan)	(622,000)
Taxes saved with gift-splitting election	$2,144,800

.11 THE FEDERAL GIFT TAX—COMPUTING THE TAX-

The gift tax is computed on a cumulative basis by using a unified rate schedule that is applicable to both lifetime gifts and transfers at death (the "estate tax"). Each year's taxable gifts are added to cumulative lifetime gifts, a gift tax is computed, and then this tax is reduced by any gift taxes previously paid during the donor's lifetime. The result is a marginal gift tax at the highest rates for the current year's tax.

Each individual is provided a special lifetime *unified credit* that can be used to offset the gift tax liability dollar for dollar. The amount for 2013 is *$2,045,800*, which is the tax on the first *$5,250,000* of lifetime transfers. In effect, no lifetime gifts will be taxable until total taxable transfers exceed $5,250,000. The unified credit is the primary credit against the federal gift tax. This amount is available until fully utilized against lifetime gifts.

FIGURE 3
Taxation of Lifetime Gifts – Jan's Tax Return With Gift Splitting
(Assuming that Tom and Jan Elect to Gift Split)

Gifts Made by Tom Baker:	2013	2014	2015
Cash to daughter Jill	$ 1,091,500	$ 408,500	$ 1,176,500
Cash to charity (United Givers Fund)	12,000	16,000	20,000
Cash to husband Tom	0	0	0
Land to son Jack (fair market value)	1,135,000	145,000	1,233,000
Cash to granddaughter Alexandra	790,000	160,000	7,000
Gross gifts	3,028,500	729,500	2,436,500
Gift splitting election (1/2 of all third-party gifts)	0	0	0
Annual exclusions (4, including United Givers Fund)	(54,000)	(56,000)	(49,000)
Charitable deduction (after reflecting exclusion)	(0)	(2,000)	(6,000)
Marital deduction (after reflecting exclusion)	(0)	(0)	(0)
Adjusted taxable gifts - current year	2,974,500	671,500	2,381,500
Add: Adjusted taxable gifts - prior years	0	2,974,500	3,646,000
Total taxable lifetime gifts	2,974,500	3,646,000	6,027,500
Tax on total taxable lifetime gifts	1,135,600	1,404,200	2,356,800
Less credit for prior gift taxes paid	0	0	0
Less unified credit (maximum)	(2,045,800)	(2,045,800)	(2,045,800)
Net tax liability - current year	0	0	$ 311,000

.13   THE FEDERAL GIFT TAX—PROCEDURAL CONSIDERATIONS

A federal gift tax return is generally due on or after January 1 of the year following the gift, but not later than April 15 of the year following the year of the gift. The federal gift tax return is Form 709, and must be filed whenever there are taxable gifts exceeding the annual exclusion, or if there are any gifts of a present interest (since these gifts do not qualify for an annual exclusion).

Example 13-13. Brett Favor made gifts of $11,000 to Bill and $9,000 to Alice in 2013. A gift tax return is not required for 2013, since the value of each gift did not exceed the $14,000 annual exclusion. If either gift involved a future interest, however, a gift tax return would be required.

¶13,007   The Federal Estate Tax

.01   THE FEDERAL ESTATE TAX—DETERMINING THE GROSS ESTATE

The gross estate of an individual includes the fair market value of all property owned at the date of death (whether or not in actual possession of the decedent). This includes any accrued interest in property or income owned by the decedent at death, as well as any loans due the decedent. The gross estate is defined broadly to include the following items as well:
- Life insurance proceeds if the policy is payable to the estate (or to another for the benefit of the estate), or the decedent had significant incidents of ownership at death, such as the power to change the beneficiary, the power to borrow against the policy, etc.
- Face value of any life insurance proceeds of a policy that was previously owned by the decedent and transferred to another person within three years of death
- Any property transferred within three years of death in which the taxpayer had a reversionary interest
- Gift taxes paid on any gifts within three years of death (see the discussion on the *gross-up rule* below)

- Any property that the decedent had a *general* power of appointment over
- One half of any jointly owned property with a spouse, including community property (see the discussion below)
- Value of jointly-held property with a non-spouse, as reduced by the percentage of total cost contributed by the non-spouse (see the discussion below)
- Accrued interest and declared dividends (even though not received)

Any property interest that extinguishes with the death of the decedent would not be included in the gross estate. For example, if the decedent had a life income interest (e.g., life estate) in property that will automatically pass to someone else at death, such an interest would not be included in the estate. However, if the decedent could control, through a general power of appointment, the person would succeed to the interest in the property, then such property would be includible in the decedent's gross estate.

.03   THE FEDERAL ESTATE TAX—THE ALTERNATE VALUATION DATE

Generally, property is included in the estate at its fair market value on the date of death of the decedent. However, a special election allows the estate to elect to value the property exactly six months after the date of death. This is called the **alternate valuation date**.

This election is only available if a return is *required to be filed*, although the return can be filed late as long as the election is made within one year of the due date. An estate is permitted to elect alternate valuation only when doing so will (1) decrease the gross estate and (2) decrease the estate tax due. Otherwise, small estates not subject to the estate tax (e.g., estates smaller than the $5,250,000 threshold, as discussed below) would elect alternate valuation to provide a *higher* income tax basis to the beneficiaries at no tax cost.

If alternate valuation is elected and the executor/executrix of the estate sells or distributes the property before the six-month valuation date, the basis of such property is presumed to equal its fair market value on the date of the disposition. The alternate valuation election, once made, is irrevocable.

Example 13-14. Mary White died on September 1, 2013. The fair market value of her estate was $7 million, which included land with a value of $520,000. Exactly six months after the date of death, the estate was valued at $6.8 million, and the land was valued at $475,000. The estate may elect alternate valuation for the properties, and the land will be valued at $475,000. The beneficiary who receives this land will have a tax basis of $475,000.

Example 13-15. Assume the same facts as above, except that the estate distributed the land on December 4, 2013, to Wanda White when it was worth $505,000. This value on the date of distribution will be the alternate valuation for the estate, and Wanda's basis in the land will be $505,000.

.05   THE FEDERAL ESTATE TAX—SPECIAL VALUATION PROBLEMS

Congress has devised special estate inclusion rules for a number of items. These include joint interests in property, life insurance policies, and various other properties.

Joint Interests in Property. The possible inclusion in the gross estate of the value of a joint interest owned by the decedent is dependent on the form of ownership. The four possibilities (and related estate tax consequences) are:

- *Joint Tenancy.* A right of survivorship exists with a joint tenancy; when one owner dies, the entire property passes to the remaining owner(s). In the case of owners *other than husband and wife*, the fair market value of the entire estate is included in the estate of the first to die, less a percentage equal to the percentage contribution to the property's cost by other parties. If the owners are *husband and wife*, Code Sec. 2040(b) provides an automatic 50 percent of total value inclusion in the estate of the first to die.

- *Tenancy by the Entirety.* A **tenancy by the entirety** is an expression used in some states to denote a joint tenancy between husband and wife. Code Sec. 2040(b) provides an automatic 50 percent of total value inclusion in the estate of the first spouse to die.
- *Tenants in Common.* The **tenants in common** form of ownership is different from a joint tenancy in that death does not defeat an owner's interest; rather, the interest is passed on to the decedent's heirs. Thus, only the value of the decedent's interest will be included in the gross estate.
- *Community Property.* Nine states recognize property rights acquired after marriage as being **community property**, whereby each spouse has an equal interest in the property. Once again, death does not defeat the owner's interest, so the value of the decedent's interest only will be included in the estate.

Example 13-16. Apple and Banana own property as joint tenants. The property originally cost $100,000, with Apple furnishing $75,000 of the cost and Banana furnishing $25,000 of the cost. In 2013, Apple died when the property was worth $150,000. Assuming that Apple and Banana are not husband and wife, 75 percent of the value of the property, or $112,500, will be included in Apple's estate, since Apple furnished 75 percent of the original cost.

Example 13-17. Assume the same facts as above, except that Apple and Banana are married. When Apple dies, Code Sec. 2040(b) provides that 50 percent of the value of the property, or $75,000, will be included in the estate. The original cost contributions of the two spouses are irrelevant.

Life Insurance Policies. If the decedent owned a policy at death on the life of another person, the equivalent replacement cost for such a policy is includible in the decedent's estate. In contrast, any life insurance proceeds on the death of the decedent are includible in the estate if:

- the policy is payable to the estate (or to another for the benefit of the estate),
- the decedent had significant incidents of ownership at death (power to change the beneficiary, power to borrow against the policy, etc.), or
- the decedent transferred the policy to another person within three years of death

---

Example 13-18. Tom Allen transferred all rights to his insurance policy on his own life to Betty Allen, his sister. Tom died two years after the transfer. Even though all rights to the policy were transferred, the face value of the policy will be included in Tom's estate, because he died within three years of the transfer.

Example 13-19. Assume the same facts as the previous example, except that Tom retained the right to change the beneficiary on the policy and Tom died five years after the transfer. Because significant rights were retained on the policy, the face value of the policy will be included in Tom's estate. This is true even though Tom lived more than three years beyond the original transfer.

Miscellaneous Items of Inclusion in the Estate. Special tax valuation rules have also been enacted for the following properties:

- *Pension Plans.* Generally, any distributions from a decedent's pension plan will be included in the gross estate, although the amount includible in the income of the beneficiary receiving the distribution may be different.

- *Community Property.* If the decedent resided in a community property state, the spouse's share of the community property will not be included in the estate.
- *Dower and Curtesy Interests.* If an individual dies without a will, state intestate laws related to **dower** and **curtesy** interests generally determine how the property is distributed to beneficiaries. The most common example is one third to the surviving spouse and the remaining two thirds to their children. But this does not change the fact that such amounts are initially included in the estate, although the share to the surviving spouse may qualify for the marital deduction.
- *Gifts Within Three Years of Death.* Earlier it was mentioned that life insurance proceeds are includible in the gross estate if the policy was transferred by the decedent within three years of death. This rule also applies to any incomplete gifts. And finally, any gift taxes paid within three years of death are added back to the gross estate under a special **gross up rule**; this rule is to prevent deathbed gifts designed to remove the gift tax paid from the gross estate owned at death.

Example 13-20. Harriet Beach paid a gift tax of $42,000 in 2009 and $35,000 in 2011. Harriet died in 2013. Her gross estate must include the $35,000 gift taxes paid in 2011, since such amounts were paid within three years of death.

- *Annuities.* A single-life annuity owned by a decedent at death is not included in his or her gross estate, since the annuity has no value after death. If the annuity has a survivorship factor (such as payments continuing to a surviving spouse), the amount includible in the estate is the equivalent cost of a policy that would provide such benefits to the survivor. If the survivor provided a portion of the cost of the annuity, an equivalent portion of the amount otherwise includible in the estate will be exempt from taxation.

Example 13-21. When Gwen Taylor died, she left an annuity that will continue to make monthly payments to her surviving spouse Ed. The equivalent cost of such an annuity is $36,000, and this amount will be included in Gwen's gross estate. If Ed had contributed 25 percent of the cost of the original annuity, only $27,000 ($36,000 × .75) would be included in the gross estate.

.07   THE FEDERAL ESTATE TAX—DEDUCTIONS AND EXCLUSIONS

A number of deductions are allowed against the gross estate in arriving at the taxable estate. The major deductions allowed against the gross estate are:

- *Marital deduction.* An unlimited marital deduction for bequests of non-terminable interest property to a surviving spouse (a non-terminable interest is one that does not terminate with the spouse's death, so that the spouse controls its ultimate disposition at his or her death).
- *Charitable Deduction.* An unlimited deduction for bequests to recognized charities.
- *Administrative Expenses.* Any legal and accounting costs associated with the estate. This deduction includes any state death taxes paid.
- *Liabilities.* A deduction is allowed for any debts of the decedent if the related property is included in the gross estate.
- *Losses.* Any casualty or theft losses incurred during the estate may be deducted.
- *Expenses of Last Illness.* These are deductible by the estate on either the estate tax return (Form 706) or the estate income tax return (Form 1041), but not both.
- *Funeral Expenses.* These are deductible by the estate.

.09   THE FEDERAL ESTATE TAX—COMPUTING THE TAX

The estate tax is computed on a cumulative basis, much like the annual gift tax computation discussed earlier. The gross estate is added to total adjusted lifetime gifts (those made after 1976), a tax is computed from the same unified rate schedule used for gifts, and any gift tax actually paid by the taxpayer offsets this tax liability as a credit.

A number of credits are available for use against the estate tax. Recall that these represent dollar-for-dollar offsets against the tax liability. The major credits that may be used are:

- *Unified Credit.* The same lifetime credit available to offset lifetime gifts that was discussed earlier may also be used to offset estate transfers at death. The current unified credit for estates in 2013 is *$2,045,800*, the equivalent of exempting *$5,250,000* of lifetime and death transfers in total from the unified tax.
- *Prior Gift Taxes Paid Credit.* Since the taxpayer must add prior lifetime gifts to the gross estate in determining the estate tax liability, it is only fair that the total tax liability can be offset by any actual prior gift taxes paid. This prevents taxing the same transfer amount twice.
- *Prior Transfer Taxes Credit.* If property included in the decedent's estate was also subject to another round of estate taxes within the past 10 years (or 2 years *after* death), a portion of the prior estate taxes paid may be taken as a **prior transfer tax credit** on the decedent's return. The credit is the lesser of the marginal estate taxes due on the decedent's current estate tax return or the prior estate tax return. Furthermore, the percentage of the credit allowed is 100 percent if the second death occurs within two years of the first death, and that percentage decreases by 20 percent for each additional two years separating the two deaths.
- *Foreign Death Tax Credit.* A credit may be taken for any foreign death taxes paid by the estate.

OBSERVATION

Several years ago, a credit against the estate tax (instead of the current deduction) was available for any state death taxes paid; however, the American Taxpayer Relief Act of 2012 permanently repealed this provision. This caused a number of states to "decouple" their state estate tax computation from the federal estate tax computation. Why? Because most states defined their estate tax liability as the greater of the tax computed under the normal state statute or the federal state tax credit. In most cases, the federal credit was greater, so states took a free ride by "soaking the federal credit," so that the money collected would go to the state, and not the federal government. (After all, if the tax is in effect paid only once, why not insure that it goes to the state?) But since the credit is now $0, many state laws will have to be rewritten if they intend to continue collecting the amounts that the federal credit generated in the past.

.11   THE ESTATE TAX—A COMPREHENSIVE EXAMPLE

Figure 4 provides a comprehensive example of the estate tax computation for an individual dying in the year 2013. In reviewing this example note the following:

- The gross estate includes the life insurance proceeds, since the decedent had retained significant rights as of the date of her death.
- The gift taxes paid within three years of death are added to the gross estate.
- The marital deduction is limited to property actually passing to the spouse.

.13   THE FEDERAL ESTATE TAX—PROCEDURAL MATTERS

Generally, an estate tax return (Form 706) must be filed (due nine months after the date of death) if the sum of the decedent's gross estate plus adjusted lifetime gifts *exceeds* the exemption equivalent of the unified credit for the year of death. This requirement applies to both citizens and resident aliens.

The exemption equivalent for the unified credit in 2013 is *$5,250,000*. Thus, this is the maximum size estate that would not be subject to the filing requirement for an estate.

Figure 4
Example – Estate Tax Computation

Facts: Lois Carter died in 2013, leaving property worth $9,064,000. She had made taxable lifetime gifts in 2011 totaling $1,250,000, on which gift taxes of $102,500 were paid (after reduction for the unified credit). Her will provides for the following dispositions:

Asset	Fair Market Value	Beneficiary
Cash	30,000	Ralph Carter (husband)
Personal residence	1,900,000	Ralph Carter (husband)
7,000 shares of IBM common stock	4,910,000	Jack and Jill (children)
700 shares of Xerox common stock	424,000	Virginia Commonwealth Univ.
Life ins. proceeds (Lois kept rights)	1,800,000	Jack and Jill (children)
Total estate	9,064,000	

Estate administrative costs other than state death taxes were $85,000, and the will specifies that any estate taxes will be paid out of the children's share of the assets. State death taxes actually paid totaled $25,000.

Fair market value of all property owned at death	9,064,000
Add: Incomplete gifts within three years of death	0
Gift taxes paid on any gifts with three years of death	102,500
Gross estate	9,166,500
Less: Administrative expenses	(85,000)
State Death Taxes Paid	(25,000)
Liabilities, Losses, etc.	0
Adjusted gross estate	9,056,500
Less: Marital deduction (actually transferred: 30,000 + 1,900,000)	(1,930,000)
Charitable deduction (unlimited)	(424,000)
Total taxable estate	6,702,500
Add: Adjusted lifetime taxable gifts after 1976	1,250,000
Total taxable transfers	7,952,500
Gross unified transfer tax on total taxable transfers	3,126,800
Less: Credit for prior gift taxes paid	(102,500)
Unified credit	(2,045,800)
Prior transfer credit (est. taxes paid on prop. w/i 10 yrs)	(0)
Foreign death tax credit	(0)
Net transfer (estate) tax liability	978,500

¶13,009 The Generation-Skipping Transfer Tax

In order to prevent family gifts that "skip" a generation and hence avoid a layer of possible estate taxes, Congress enacted a special **generation-skipping transfer tax (GSST)**. In general, a transfer tax is computed for the "skipped" generation, using the highest gift (or estate) rates applicable. For example, a taxpayer may make a direct gift to her grandson. By "skipping" her child (the grandson's parent), a transfer tax on an intervening generation is avoided. To prevent this possibility, the GSST would be imposed on the transfer at the highest estate tax rate (currently 40 percent).

An exemption from the generation-skipping tax is available in 2004 and later years. This exemption is equal to the exemption equivalent of the estate tax unified credit. The exemption for 2013 is $5,250,000. The donor can choose which transfers qualify for the exemption amount.

OBSERVATION   In addition to taxing the transfer at the highest estate tax rate, any GSST paid is also treated as a *gift* by the donor to the recipient. When these two elements are combined, the total taxes paid may exceed the value of the property received by the donor. Now that is truly a tax disincentive!

¶13,011   Planning Basics—Lifetime Gifts

Gift and estate tax planning involves the application of various instruments to minimize the tax consequences of intergenerational transfers of property, including transfers to a spouse and to children. Estate, gift, and income tax considerations all come into play, as well as various non-tax considerations. The remainder of this chapter reviews the advantages and disadvantages of several common planning strategies. Primary among these basic "tools" in the planner's kit are lifetime gifting strategies, minimizing probate costs, and optimizing the marital deduction. More sophisticated planning tools related to trusts and business entities are discussed in the next chapter.

.01   LIFETIME GIFTS—GENERAL PLANNING CONSIDERATIONS

Maximizing the Use of the Annual Exclusion and Unified Credits. A systematic program of lifetime gifting often involves tradeoffs between potential tax savings versus the question of relinquishing control over property. This is especially true when considering gifts to children, although any transfer that constitutes "support" under state law is not treated as a gift.

Lifetime gift-giving offers several tax reduction possibilities, such as maximizing annual exclusions by spreading gifts over several years. Also, a married couple may elect gift-splitting to double the value of the annual exclusion and use two unified credits.

Example 13-22. David and Cheryl Allison, both age 40, have five children and have never made any lifetime gifts. If David and Cheryl begin a program of transferring $28,000 of property to each child each year and elect gift splitting, by the time they are age 70 they will have transferred $4,200,000 of assets to their children with no tax cost; the annual exclusion wipes out any taxable gifts. Plus, each still has the exemption equivalent of a unified credit, currently $5,250,000 each, to use for further gifts and/or estate tax purposes.

OBSERVATION   Query: Are there times when a married couple would *not* want to gift split? Generally, gift splitting is considered advisable, since this utilizes both unified credits and delays the inevitable payment of tax. However, if the sizes of the spouses' estates are disparate, it may make little sense for the spouse with the smaller estate to gift split with the other spouse, since this would just be compounding the tax potentially due at a much higher rate at death for the wealthier spouse (if the gifts exceed $28,000 per donee), as some of the wealthier spouse's unified credit would be used up.

Removing Appreciation from the Estate. Gifting appreciated property will remove any future appreciation in value from the taxable estate. If the gift involves high-value property, such as real estate, it may make sense to gift partial interests each year in order to maximize the use of the annual exclusion. This is especially true for younger taxpayers, as illustrated by the previous example. Multiple appraisals across the years are advisable with such strategies.

When gifts are large enough to require an actual payment of the gift tax, time value of money considerations are important. This may be the case with an older taxpayer or an extremely wealthy taxpayer, where a longer planning horizon is not available or the estate is simply too large to avoid payment of taxes. Such variables as life expectancy, current interest rates, appreciation or depreciation potential of the gift property, and the amount of gift taxes paid are all important considerations. But the possibility of removing significant post-gift appreciation from the estate makes such gifts viable alternatives for many individuals.

Example 13-23. Myra Granger, age 60, gifts $9,264,000 of real estate to her daughter Ellen in 2013. The real estate is expected to appreciate in value at a rate of approximately six percent per year, and Myra's after-tax opportunity cost of alternative investments is five percent. Myra's life expectancy is 25 years. Myra will pay a gift tax of $1,600,000 on the net $9,250,000 gift after annual exclusion and subtraction of the unified credit. If Myra does live 25 years, the property would be worth $39,759,883 at the time of her death. Thus, Myra effectively transferred $39,759,883 out of her estate at a tax cost of $1,600,000. If Myra still owned the property at death, the estate tax on that property alone, even assuming that the unified credit tripled in 25 years, would be $9,712,353.

OBSERVATION   Actually, the savings in the above example are even larger: since Myra paid the $1,600,000 gift tax, this amount is no longer in her estate. Recall, however, that if Myra dies within three years of making the gift, the gift tax paid will be included in the estate under the gross up rule.

Lifetime gifts may also provide a means to avoid state taxes, as only five states have a gift tax (but most have some form of estate tax or inheritance tax). However, there is no credit available for state taxes paid on the federal gift tax return, if gifts are made in those states with a gift tax law. Of course, there is no longer a credit for such state taxes on the federal *estate tax return* either.

.03   LIFETIME GIFTS—BASIS CONSIDERATIONS

The determination of the adjusted basis of gift property and inherited property is quite a bit different under current law. Because of these differences, basis issues may be a key factor in considering a lifetime gifting strategy.

Basis of Gift Property. Property acquired by a gift can create a "dual basis" problem, in that the basis for loss may differ from the basis for gain. The basic rules are:

- the basis for gain is *always* the **donor's** adjusted basis;
- the basis for loss is the *lesser* of the donor's basis or the fair market value (FMV) of the gift on the date of the gift; and
- if the amount realized (sales price) is between the two possible bases, then *no* gain or loss is recognized; the basis is presumed to equal the amount realized.

If the donor's basis is used, the donor's holding period is added to the donee's holding period (this is referred to as a **"tacking" of holding periods**). On the other hand, if the fair market value is used as the basis, there is no tacking of holding periods. Note the consistency of these holding period tacking rules; the donor's holding period is included only if the donor's adjusted basis is used in the gain or loss computation.

Example 13-24. Tina Keys received a gift of stock from her father during the current year ($4,000 FMV, $7,000 father's adjusted basis). If Tina sells the stock for $9,000, her gain is $2,000 ($9,000 – $7,000); if she sells the stock for $3,000, her loss is $1,000 ($3,000 – $4,000); and if she sells the stock for $6,200, there is no gain or loss ($6,200 – $6,200). Note: if FMV of stock was $10,000, the $7,000 basis would always apply in determining both gain or loss (since the donor's basis is *less* than FMV).

In some cases, a donor may be required to pay a federal gift tax on gifted property. To mitigate multiple layers of taxation, the Code provides a special **gift tax add-on** to the donor's basis in determining the donee's basis. The addition to the donor's basis is determined as follows (in the latter calculation, the *taxable* gift is the denominator):
- *Pre-1977 Gifts.* 100 percent of the gift tax paid (as long as the total basis doesn't exceed the FMV of the gift on the date of the gift).
- *Post-1976 Gifts.* A portion of the gift tax related to appreciation in value: *Addition = Gift Tax Paid × (Appreciation in Value/FMV of Gift at Gift).*

Example 13-25. Butch Ryder received 100 shares of stock as a gift from his mother this year. His mother paid $20,000 for the shares in 1989, and they were worth $32,000 on the date of the gift. Butch's mother paid $4,000 gift taxes on the transfer. Butch may increase the donor's basis of $20,000 by $1,500, the portion of the gift tax related to the appreciation in value of the shares (i.e., $12,000/$32,000 × $4,000). Thus, Butch's basis for both gain and loss is $21,500 ($20,000 + $1,500).[4] Note that the add-on occurs only when the gift has appreciated in value; if the property has depreciated in value, this calculation is ignored.

Inherited Property. The adjusted basis of inherited property is generally the fair market value of the property at the date of death, or the fair market value exactly six months after the date of death if the estate elects the alternate valuation date that was discussed earlier. In either case, the decedent's original adjusted basis simply disappears. The Code automatically defines inherited property as having been held on a long-term basis, regardless of the actual holding period.

For jointly held property with a right of survivorship, the survivor's adjusted basis in his or her portion of the property is increased by the fair market value of the remaining portion of the interest received from the decedent. If the property is held in a community property state, the surviving spouse may step up the basis of *both* his or her interest and the inherited interest. This may provide an incentive for holding property as community property in states where the law applies.

If the estate elects the alternate valuation date, the date exactly six months after the date of death, then the fair market value of the property on that date is used as the basis. It is important to note that the alternate valuation date can be used only when the adjusted gross estate and the estate tax due are *less* when using the alternate valuation date. If the alternate valuation date is elected and the property is distributed prior to that date, then the FMV on the date of the distribution is used as the basis.

Example 13-26. Abe Anders died on 5/1/13. Abe's will left property (adjusted basis to Abe, $40,000) to his daughter Amber. The fair market value of the property was $56,000 on the date Abe died, $53,000 on 11/1/13, and $52,000 on 10/14/13, the date it was distributed to Amber. If the estate does not elect alternate valuation, Amber's basis in the property is $56,000; if alternate valuation is elected, Amber's basis is $52,000.

---

[4] In *Rev. Proc. 2007-66, IRB 2007-45*, the IRS ruled that if the gift was the first or only gift to the beneficiary, the $14,000 annual exclusion would reduce the $32,000 FMV to $18,000 in the computation. If multiple gifts are made to the donee, this reduction applies only to the first transfers made at that point in time.

OBSERVATION   With the increases in the exemption equivalent of the unified credit in recent years, Congress became concerned about a possible way to subvert the normal basis rules. For example, assume that A gifts land on 6/1/13 to his Uncle B, who is terminally ill, with the understanding that Uncle B will "will" the property back to A upon his death. The land cost A $10,000 in 1953 and is currently worth $500,000. If Uncle B's total estate at death (including the land) is less than the exemption equivalent of the unified credit (currently $5,250,000), then A would have effectively "laundered" basis up to $500,000 at no tax cost at all. Congress's solution to this problem is to deny a step-up in basis to A if B dies on or before 6/1/14, i.e., within one year of the original gift transfer. In this case, the adjusted basis of the land to A is simply the original $10,000.

Incorporating Basis Considerations in Planning. As a general rule, a beneficiary would prefer to inherit high-basis property in order to avoid a tax on the appreciation in value up to the date of death when the property is later sold. If the property has depreciated in value, the donor may prefer to first sell the property during his or her lifetime at a loss and realize income tax savings. If the property is gifted, the donor's basis (used for gain computations of the beneficiary) would be higher than if the property is held to death, where the lower fair market value will always be the basis.

OBSERVATION   The gift versus inheritance tradeoffs are not relevant for property that is considered to be **income in respect of a decedent**, since the beneficiary "steps in the shoes" of the decedent and uses the same adjusted basis and recognizes the same character of the income. Income in respect of a decedent is income accrued to the decedent but not recognized at the date of death because of the decedent's method of accounting (e.g., cash basis in most instances). This can include accrued interest or dividend income, as well as uncollected installment notes. Such income, though not recognized for income tax purposes, is includible in the decedent's estate at its fair market value, however.

.05   USING LIFETIME GIFTS AS INCOME-SHIFTING TOOLS

One method of lowering the overall tax burden for a family is to shift income-producing assets to family members in lower tax brackets. This strategy will not be successful for transfers to children under the age of 19 (age 24, if a full-time student), as the allocable parental tax ("kiddie tax") applies to any unearned income exceeding $2,000 during the year 2013. As discussed earlier in the course, the excess is taxed at the parent(s) rate.

Gifts of income-producing property usually do not create tax consequences to the donor. However, there are two possible exceptions. First, gifts of installment notes will accelerate recognition of deferred income to the donor by treating the transfer as if the notes were sold for their fair market value. Secondly, a transfer of U.S. Savings Bonds will involve reregistering the bonds and requires recognition of any deferred interest income.

Example 13-27. Jim Brown transfers by gift an installment note with $30,000 remaining to be collected to his daughter Alice. The note was originally issued for $100,000 (with a gross profit of $40,000), and the note was valued at $28,000 on the date of the transfer. Jim must report a gain on the disposition of $10,000, or the $28,000 fair market value of the note less $18,000 unrecovered cost of the $30,000 notes ($30,000 – $12,000 unrecognized gross profit using a 40-percent gross profit ratio).

¶13,011.05

If either of these items is transferred at death, rather than as lifetime gifts, the income tax consequences are shifted to the beneficiary as income in respect of a decedent. One beneficial effect of a transfer at death is that depreciation recapture disappears at death, whereas the recapture "taint" carries over with a lifetime gift.

Gifts of income-producing properties make sense when the donee does not plan to sell the gift property in the foreseeable future. If the property might be sold in a relatively short time by the beneficiary, it may make sense to gift high-basis property and hold low-basis, high-value property until death. The donor may want to sell depreciating property and gift the proceeds, since this may provide an income tax deduction to the donor.

.07   LIFETIME GIFTS TO CHARITY

A lifetime charitable contribution generally makes more sense than one at death, since an income tax deduction is usually available. This avoids the gift tax and reduces the gross estate. The status of the charitable organization on the date of the transfer controls, not the status as of the date the contribution is authorized, such as in a will. The terms of the bequest can be flexible enough to allow a substitute charity if the original charity does not qualify for deductions at the time of the transfer.

.09   LIFETIME GIFTS TO A SPOUSE

Should gifts be made to a spouse? Generally, such gifts are thought of as tax neutral, since an unlimited deduction is available for both gift and estate tax purposes.

As explained below, such transfers can be used to roughly equalize the relative sizes of the spouses' estates. Due to the progressive nature of the unified transfer tax schedule, married couples can generally reduce their combined estate tax liability by balancing the size of each spouse's estate. This will also insure that the unified credit of both spouses is eventually utilized. However, the new "Deceased Spouse Unused Exclusion Amount (DSUEA)" election, discussed below, may accomplish the same objectives.

OBSERVATION   Given that everyone would like to put off a final "tax reckoning" until tomorrow, would it make sense for an older spouse to gift most of his or her property to a younger spouse so that there would be no estate tax due if the older spouse dies first? To a degree, this might make sense, but only if the older spouse retains enough property to fully utilize his or her unified credit. If all property is transferred to the younger spouse, then the credit of the older spouse is simply wasted and a potentially huge tax reckoning awaits the second spouse. But once again, the DSUEA election discussed below may mitigate this problem.

.11   LIFETIME GIFTS OF LIFE INSURANCE

Life insurance is sometimes referred to as a vehicle for "buying time," in that the proceeds of such a policy can create an instant estate, provide liquidity, and offer protection and financial freedom. And as mentioned earlier in the chapter, such proceeds are also includible in the estate of the insured decedent under Code Sec. 2042 if (1) the proceeds are payable to the estate, (2) the proceeds are used for the benefit of the estate, or (3) the decedent had any incidents of ownership in the policy at death. Incidents of ownership include the power to change beneficiaries, revoke an assignment, pledge the policy on a loan, or surrender or cancel the policy.

OBSERVATION   Recall that the above rules only apply to a policy on the life of the decedent. If the policy was owned by the decedent but on the life of another person, only the equivalent replacement cost for such a policy would be included in the decedent's estate. This is the value of the property owned by the decedent at death; since the death of the insured has not occurred, the face value of the policy is irrelevant.

¶13,011.07

For a decedent to exclude the value of a policy from his or her estate, he or she must transfer all incidents of ownership to another person or entity, and the transfer must occur more than three years before the date of death; otherwise, the face value of the policy is brought back into the estate. And even though the policy proceeds are not going to the estate or do not benefit the estate directly, they may be used indirectly to provide liquidity since the beneficiary is relieved of other obligations not related to the estate and thus has more flexibility in dealing with estate finances.

One technique used for transferring insurance policy incidents of ownership is to create an irrevocable demand trust for the policy. This trust will hold the policy for the benefit of beneficiaries (usually children), and may be able to "sprinkle" some income to a surviving spouse. If the trust is truly irrevocable, the grantor can contribute the amount of the annual premiums to the trust and qualify such payments for the annual exclusion, provided the trust includes a *Crummey power* (discussed earlier), permitting the beneficiary a limited window of opportunity to withdraw the funds. One other possible advantage of such a trust is that the trustee may be authorized to purchase assets from the decedent's estate, thus providing some measure of liquidity.

OBSERVATION	It is important to note that merely purchasing an insurance contract on one's own life and designating someone else as a beneficiary does not constitute a "gift," since the purchaser still possesses "incidents of ownership" on the policy. However, designating another beneficiary means that the proceeds are automatically paid to the beneficiary and thus avoid probate.

¶13,013   Planning Basics—Minimizing Probate Costs

Any assets subject to disposition by the executor under the terms of the will, as well as any property passing under state **intestate laws** are part of the **probate estate**. As such, the probate estate is subject to various administrative, legal, accounting and court costs that may be as much as 5 to 15 percent of the gross estate.

Probate costs may be minimized by (1) creating joint tenancies or (2) creating a living trust. These techniques assure immediate possession of the property in most cases, and possibly avoid ancillary probate proceedings for properties located in multiple states.

OBSERVATION	When considering probate costs, it is important to note that reducing probate costs does not necessarily reduce the gross estate. Gifts of appreciating property may eventually accomplish both objectives, but avoiding probate does not involve any reduction at all in the estate tax liability.

.01   JOINT TENANCIES AS A MEANS OF AVOIDING PROBATE

The various methods of property ownership were discussed earlier in the chapter. When a *joint tenancy* is established, each tenant has an undivided interest in the property with a right of survivorship. Since the property passes automatically to the survivor as a matter of contract law, the property is not subject to the probate process. Of course, there are plenty of non-tax implications of creating a joint tenancy, and such factors as family relations, possible divorce or family discord, and other issues should be considered.

The creation of a joint tenancy may involve a taxable gift, unless the tenancy is between a married couple where the unlimited marital deduction applies. If the value of the jointly-held property is large enough, some gift tax may be due upon creation of the joint tenancy. However, this tax cost may be eventually recouped when that fraction of the property is not included in the estate of the original donor. For married couples, this is not really an issue, since current law requires inclusion of one half of the fair market value of the property in the estate of the first to die.

.03   THE LIVING TRUST AS A MEANS OF AVOIDING PROBATE

Much has been made in recent years about the advantages of establishing a living trust. Trusts will be discussed in detail in the next chapter, but this option is worth noting at this point.

A **trust** is simply a legal contract established by a **grantor** where the legal title and management of the property is handled by a **trustee** for the beneficial enjoyment of one or more **beneficiaries**. Trusts can be established during lifetime (**inter vivos**, or living trusts) or at death (**testamentary** trusts). Trusts may also be **revocable** (i.e., the trust can be revoked by the grantor at any time) or **irrevocable** (revocation is not possible).

A revocable **living trust** comes into being when a grantor transfers property to a trustee under a written arrangement that generally provides that all income is to be paid to the grantor for his or her remaining life, as well as any amounts of principal so designated by the grantor. Upon the death of the grantor, the trust becomes irrevocable, as the property passes directly to beneficiaries designated by the grantor. Since the property passes automatically under the terms of the trust, probate costs are avoided. This is especially helpful if the grantor owns property in several states where probate procedures would otherwise have to be initiated. And the living trust offers one other advantage: unlike the public process of probating a will, the terms of the trust remain private.

OBSERVATION	It is important to realize that the use of a living trust does not save any estate taxes; since the trust is revocable, the full value of all property will be included in the grantor's estate at death. What is saved is the probate and administrative costs that would otherwise be required with a will.

Generally, the legal and administrative costs of setting up a living trust are less than probate and administrative costs of passing property through a will. However, it must be remembered that the former costs are paid during lifetime, while the latter costs would not be paid until after death. If the decedent lived a number of years after establishing the living trust, the present value of the future probate costs that would otherwise apply might actually be less than the current cost of setting up and maintaining the trust.

OBSERVATION	Grantors who set up a living trust will usually not transfer all of their property to such a trust, and for that reason, it is often recommended that the grantor include a **pour-over provision** in the will. This is a will that transfers property owned by the grantor at death to the trust through the regular probate process. In effect, this provision "sweeps" any remaining assets outside the trust into the trust at death.

Finally, it should also be noted that joint tenancies and living trusts are not the only methods of avoiding probate. Any property that passes automatically outside of a will or state intestate law will avoid probate. Thus, beneficiary designations for pensions, annuities, life insurance policies, and other products will achieve essentially the same goal: to provide for transfers outside the probate process.

¶13,015 Planning Basics—Optimizing the Estate Marital Deduction

The gift tax and estate tax marital deduction provisions add much flexibility in family financial planning. The gift tax marital deduction offers a tax-free method of equalizing estates of spouses during their lifetimes. And even more flexibility is gained through the use of the estate tax marital deduction. But caution is in order; it is possible to underfund or, although less likely with the new DSUEA portability option, overfund the marital deduction. Either option can create later problems for the surviving spouse. The following discussion examines these issues.

OBSERVATION	One of the key unknowns in funding the marital deduction is the expected date of death of the surviving spouse. Obviously, in terms of the time value of money, the less tax paid on the estate of the first to die, the better. In the past, this idea can be taken to the extreme by leaving everything to the surviving spouse (commonly called the "I love you" option), which would waste the decedent's unified credit, as discussed below. The new "portability election" described below has somewhat minimized the potential disasterous effects of such a provision. As the time interval between the two deaths increases, even bad marital deduction decisions may be less harmful than expected.

.01 THE DANGERS OF UNDERFUNDING THE MARITAL DEDUCTION THROUGH INTESTATE SUCCESSION

If an individual dies without a will (e.g., "intestate"), state law will control the distribution of any assets not disposed of by trust, joint ownership, or beneficiary designation. The same law will also be applied to any properties not covered by an existing will. All states have intestate laws, and generally only the surviving spouse, surviving children, the decedent's blood relatives, and the decedent's legally adopted relatives will inherit under those statutes.

In most states, if there is a surviving spouse and children, the spouse will inherit one third of the estate and the children will inherit the other two thirds. These are sometimes referred to as the *dower* (widow) and *curtsey* (widower) statutes. One of the dangers of dying intestate is that these rules could lead to an underfunding of the marital deduction, and may create an estate tax liability that could have been easily avoided.

Example 13-28. Tom Jade died intestate in 2013, leaving an estate worth $10,500,000. He is survived by his wife Alice and two children. Under state law, one third of the property, or $3,500,000 will pass to Alice, and this qualifies for a marital deduction. However, this leaves a taxable estate of $7,000,000, which after the unified credit leaves an estate tax liability of $700,000 ($2,745,800 gross tax liability – $2,045,800 unified credit). If Tom had executed a will that left at least $5,250,000 to Alice, the remaining $5,250,000 taxable estate would not be subject to tax because of the unified credit.

All is not necessarily lost in this situation, however, as the children may be able to *disclaim* a portion of their inheritance in favor of their mother. A *disclaimer* is a legal refusal to accept benefits conferred by will or by operation of law. This refusal is irrevocable and the property must not have been accepted by the disclaimant. The refusal must be in writing, must generally be made within nine months of the date of the decedent's death, and must pass to someone other than the disclaiming party.

Example 13-29. In the previous example, assume that each child agrees to disclaim $875,000 of inheritance in favor of their mother Alice. In this case, the total property passing to Alice is $5,250,000 [$3,500,000 + ($875,000 × 2)], the marital deduction is $5,250,000, the taxable estate is $5,250,000, and no estate tax is due.

.03 THE DANGERS OF OVERFUNDING THE MARITAL DEDUCTION WITH EXCESSIVE TRANSFERS

Prior to 2010, there were potential problems when the marital deduction was overfunded. If a decedent leaves all of his or her property to his or her spouse, this potentially leads to a compounding of tax problems when the surviving spouse dies. And more importantly, it may mean that the decedent's unified credit is completely wasted, if the objective is to eventually transfer all the couple's assets to other family members.

Example 13-30. Sally Fowler died in 2013 and left her entire $6,500,000 estate to her husband Allen, whose estate was worth $1,500,000. The full amount qualifies as an estate tax deduction, and no estate tax is due. As a result, Allen will have to transfer an estate of at least $8,000,000 when he dies. More importantly, Sally's entire unified credit was wasted, unless the DSUEA election described below was made.

In the above example, the disclaimer could have been used by Allen to undo the mistake of leaving all of the property to the surviving spouse. But in 2010, Congress added a special "portability election" to the law that would deal with the problem in a more direct manner.

.04   THE "PORTABILITY ELECTION" OF CODE SEC. 2010(C)

As part of the Tax Relief and Job Creation Act of 2010, Congress amended Code Sec. 2010(c) to provide a special election whereby the estate of the second spouse to die could utilize any "unused" unified credit of the first spouse to die, i.e., the unused amount is "portable" to the second spouse. The formal Code term used to define this amount is the "deceased spouse unused exclusion amount," or DSUEA. The election must be made by the executor/executrix on the estate tax return (including extensions) of the first spouse to die; otherwise, it is assumed that the estate is not making such an election. An estate tax return must be filed with the election, even if an estate tax return would not otherwise be required for the first spouse's estate.

Example 13-31. Mary Hardin died in 2013, leaving a taxable estate of $3,000,000. If the executor of Mary's estate makes a portability election, the $2,250,000 of unused unified credit exemption amount from Mary's estate can be used by Mary's husband Allen's estate when he dies, along with Allen's unified credit when he dies. Thus, if Allen dies in 2015, when the exemption equivalent of the unified credit is $5,600,000, Allen's estate qualifies for a unified credit based on the credit equivalent of a $7,850,000 exclusion ($2,250,000 unused amount from Mary's estate, and Allen's normal $5,600,000 exemption equivalent in 2015).

OBSERVATION   When originally enacted in 2010, the portability election was scheduled to expire after 2012. Interestingly, *both* spouses had to die within this two-year time frame to qualify for the portability election. Fortunately, the 2012 legislation made the portability election permanent, and such time contraints were removed.

With the enactment of the DSUEA election, a number of commentators have noted that the need for such time-tested estate planning techniques as the reduce to zero formula clause and the bypass trust are no longer necessary. However, there still may be valid reasons to use these techniques rather than electing the DSUEA, as explained below after introducing these two techniques.

.05   FINE-TUNING THE MARITAL DEDUCTION: A "REDUCE TO ZERO" FORMULA CLAUSE IN A WILL

One of the methods of fine-tuning the marital deduction prior to the enactment of the portability election was the inclusion of a **reduce to zero** clause in a will.

This is essentially a statement that the actual amount transferred to the surviving spouse would be the amount that reduces the taxable estate to the amount of the exemption equivalent of the unified credit for the year of death, and thus the estate tax due is reduced to zero.

Generally, the language to be used in a will for this purpose refers to the portion transferred to the surviving spouse as either a *pecuniary share* (a specific dollar amount) or a *fractional share* (a percentage of the estate assets). A typical reduce to zero clause would read as follows (assuming the amount is transferred into a trust for the benefit of the surviving spouse):

> *From the remaining assets there shall then be allocated to the marital trust the [amount] [fractional share of the remaining assets] that is required to obtain the largest available marital deduction, after taking into account the value of all other items in the grantor's gross estate that qualify for the marital deduction. If however, the federal estate tax on the grantor's estate may be reduced to zero (after taking into consideration all other items deducted on the federal estate tax return and all of the applicable credits against federal estate tax) by a deduction that is less than the largest available marital deduction, the [amount] [fractional share] allocated to the marital trust shall be determined to produce that lesser deduction.*

Note that the language ensures that all other deductions and credits are taken into consideration in determining the amount allocated to the marital trust. The last sentence is the qualifier that restricts the deduction to the smallest amount possible to "zero out" any estate tax otherwise due.

.07   OPTIMIZING THE MARITAL DEDUCTION—THE BYPASS TRUST

One method of implementing a reduce to zero formula is to create a **bypass trust**, where a bequest equal to the value of the unified credit goes directly to the children, thus "bypassing" the surviving spouse's estate. Accompanying this transfer would normally be transfer of the remaining property to a **marital deduction trust**. These arrangements are sometimes referred to as "A-B trusts."

One of the objectives of creating trusts may be to provide an income interest for the surviving spouse, with the remainder interest in the marital deduction trust passing under the trust terms to the children at death. The bypass trust arrangement and the marital trust arrangement used in conjunction with one another may accomplish this objective.

However, since the surviving spouse's income interest is a terminable interest (one that does not survive the spouse's death), the property will not be included in the surviving spouse's estate. Because of this possible result, the Code requires that the property be included in the estate of the first spouse to die; otherwise, *both* estates would escape taxation. This result is accomplished by denying a marital deduction for any property that is *terminable interest* property. The same result occurs if the transfer is a lifetime gift; the marital deduction is disallowed.

Example 13-32 Dan Siego's will provides that $5,000,000 of his estate will pass to a trust, with an income interest to his wife Teena for life and the remainder interest to pass to their son Aaron after Teena's death. Since Teena's interest is a terminable interest, the transfer will not qualify for the marital deduction in Dan's estate.

Technically, a **terminable interest** in property is an interest that terminates or fails after the passage of time, upon the happening of some contingency, or upon the failure of some event to occur. There are two important exceptions to the terminable interest rules: the power of appointment trust and the qualified terminable interest property (QTIP) election.

Power of Appointment Trust. If the surviving spouse of a bypass trust is given a *general power of appointment* over the trust property, the surviving spouse could appoint anyone, including himself or herself, to the trust proceeds. As a result, the property is includible in the surviving spouse's estate. Because of this later inclusion, the estate of the first spouse to die is permitted to take the marital deduction for the original transfer to the trust. The same tax result would apply in the case of a lifetime transfer to the trust, as this transfer would qualify for the marital deduction.

Example 13-33. Assume the same facts as the previous example, except that Teena is given a general power of appointment over the trust property. Because of this power, the property transfer now qualifies for the marital deduction on Dan's estate tax return, and the property will be included in Teena's estate when she dies.

Qualified Terminable Interest Property (QTIP) Election. The one disadvantage of the power of appointment trust is that the first spouse to die has no control over the ultimate disposition of the trust property, since the surviving spouse has the general power of appointment. This may be overcome with a special election for "**qualified terminable interest property (QTIP)**". The executor of the estate (or the donor, in the case of a lifetime transfer) makes this election.

In order to qualify for the election, two conditions must be met: (1) the surviving spouse is entitled to income for life from the trust, payable annually or at more frequent intervals, and (2) no person may appoint the property to anyone other than the surviving spouse during his or her lifetime. If these conditions are met, the original transfer qualifies for the marital deduction, and yet the deceased spouse controls the ultimate disposition of the property.

Example 13-34. Assume the same facts as the previous example, except that Teena is not granted a general power of appointment over the property. Rather, the executor of Dan's estate makes a QTIP election. Teena will receive a life income interest from the property, but the property will pass automatically to their son Aaron at her death. The property now qualifies for the marital deduction on Dan's estate tax return, and the property will be included in Teena's estate at her death.

OBSERVATION   The QTIP election may make a lot of sense for a donor who has remarried and has children from a former marriage. In that case, the donor can provide an income stream for the former spouse, obtain a marital deduction for the transfer to the trust, and yet still rest assured that the property will eventually be transferred to his or her children. This is sometimes referred to as *control from beyond the grave.*

.09 BYPASS TRUST OR DSUEA ELECTION?

At first blush, the DSUEA Election may seem to be a much simpler and straightforward method to fully utilized the two unified credit amounts of spouses. However, the decision is not that simple, and the following factors should be considered:

If a bypass trust is used, the appreciation in value of the trust assets will not be taxed, since such bypass assets were included in the estate of the first spouse to die. On the other hand, if the assets pass directly to the spouse with a DSUEA election, any appreciation in value will be included in the estate of the second spouse to die. The additional tax on this appreciation may be larger than the savings with the DSUEA election, especially if the bypass trust assets are expected to appreciate in value rapidly. One caveat, however;

if the DSUEA election is made, all assets passing to the beneficiaries upon the death of the second spouse will receive a step-up in basis to FMV; such is not the case for bypass assets included in the estate of the first spouse to die. The possible ramifications of this issue are best illustrated with a comprehensive example.

Example 13-35. Facts: Jill dies in 2013, leaving her entire estate worth $10,500,000 to her husband Jack. When Jack dies in 2022 the property has doubled in value to $21,000,000. Jack's separate estate property is worth $7,000,000 at his death. Neither Jack nor Jill made any lifetime gifts, and it is assumed that the inflation adjusted exclusion amount in 2022 is $8,000,000 (yielding a unified credit of $3,145,800 in 2022). An annual discount rate of 5% is assumed.

Option 1 (DSUEA Election): Jill's will leaves the entire $10,500,000 estate to Jill. The executor of Jill's estate makes a DSUEA election, transferring the unused $5,250,000 exclusion amount to Jack. No tax is due when Jill dies, but $5,900,000 tax is due when Jack dies in 2022 (tax on $28,000,000 estate is $11,145,800 gross tax − $5,245,800 unified credit on an equivalent combined exclusion amount of $13,250,000). Net assets transferred to the Jill and Jack's children total $22,100,000 ($28,000,000 − $5,900,000).

Option 2 (Bypass Trust): According to the terms of Jill's will, $5,250,000 assets are placed in a bypass trust with lifetime income to Jack, and the principal passing to the children at Jack's death. Jack has a general power of appointment over the property, so the transfer to the trust does not qualify for the marital deduction. The remaining $5,250,000 assets are transferred directly to Jack through a marital deduction trust. Thus, only the $5,250,000 transfer to the trust is subject to an estate tax equal to the $2,045,800 unified credit, and no estate tax is due. When Jack dies, the property he received from Jill through the marital trust is worth $10,500,000, and when combined with Jack's $7,000,000 of separate assets, the taxable estate is $17,500,000. This results in an estate tax of $3,800,000, or $6,945,800 gross tax less the $3,145,800 unified credit for the year 2022, leaving net after-tax assets of $13,700,000. The total value of net assets left to the children is in 2022 is this $13,700,000 plus the $10,500,000 current value of the bypass assets, a total of $24,200,000. Recall that the original $5,250,000 transfer to the bypass trust was taxable in 2012, and thus escapes taxation in 2022 when it has doubled in value to $10,500,000.

Conclusion: The bypass trust arrangement yields $2,100,000 more assets for the children in 2022 because (1) the DUESA is not subject to inflation adjustment and (2) the $5,250,000 contributed to the bypass trust was included in Jill's estate in 2012, thus removing future appreciation in value of the property from taxation in Jack's estate. However, recall that the children will only have a $5,250,000 basis in this property, and not the $10,500,000 basis that they would have with a DUESA election. If the assets were sold for their fair market values in 2022 by the children, and all were 20% capital gains taxpayers, this would reduce the differential by $1,050,000 ($5,250,000 × .20). However it is unlikely that all children would sell such assets immediately.

Other factors may make the DSUEA election seem less appealing that the standard bypass trust. These include:
- State estate tax laws may not honor the DSUEA election
- The DSUEA election is not adjusted for inflation, whereas the surviving spouse's own exclusion amount is adjusted
- A bypass trust will ensure that the property passes to the individuals that it was intended to
- The bypass assets may avoid potential probate costs
- A bypass trust may offer more credit protection for the trust assets

¶13,017   Summary

- Lifetime gifts and transfers at death are taxed under one unified transfer tax rate schedule, with each tax computed on a cumulative basis and then reduced by any gift taxes paid.
- A gift is generally a gratuitous transfer not involving consideration, motivated by generosity or like impulses. Some "gifts" are not taxed under the gift tax laws; these include political contributions, education expenses, and medical expenses.
- Gifts are taxed at their FMVs, and each gift is eligible for a maximum $14,000 annual exclusion per donee per year. Gross gifts are further reduced by charitable deductions, marital deductions, and any gift splitting election.
- The gross estate for federal estate tax purposes includes all property owned at death, including incomplete transfers, life insurance proceeds under certain circumstances, and certain forms of jointly-held property.
- The alternate valuation date is exactly six months after the date of death, and may be used to value estate property only if both the gross estate and the estate tax due are reduced with such an election.
- The gross estate may be reduced by deductions for charitable transfers, marital transfers, administrative expenses, funeral expenses, and debts. The gross estate tax liability may be reduced by credits for the unified credit, prior gift taxes paid, and certain prior transfer taxes paid.
- As a rule, low-basis, high-FMV property should be retained until death (to receive a step-up in basis to FMV), while high-basis, low-FMV property should be used as lifetime gifts (since the donee uses the donor's basis).
- The probate estate includes all properties passing under a will and/or state intestate laws: such costs may be avoided by holding property in joint names or in trusts, where the passage of the property is outside the will.
- The estate tax marital deduction may be used to leave enough property subject to the estate tax equivalent of the decedent's unified credit ($5,250,000 in 2013). A "reduce to zero clause" and/or a combination of a bypass trust and a marital deduction trust may be used to accomplish this objective. As an alternative, the DSUEA portability election may achieve some of the same objectives, but such an election may pose other risks.

APPENDIX A—UNIFIED TRANSFER TAX RATE SCHEDULE (2013)

A Taxable Amount Over:	B Taxable Amount Not Over:	C Tax on Amount in Column A	D Rate of Tax on Excess Over Column A
$0	$10,000	$0	18%
$10,000	$20,000	$1,800	20%
$20,000	$40,000	$3,800	22%
$40,000	$60,000	$8,200	24%
$60,000	$80,000	$13,000	26%
$80,000	$100,000	$18,200	28%
$100,000	$150,000	$23,800	30%
$150,000	$250,000	$38,800	32%
$250,000	$500,000	$70,800	34%
$500,000	$750,000	$155,800	37%
$750,000	$1,000,000	$248,300	39%
$1,000,000	—	$345,800	40%

Review Questions for Chapter 13

True or False

Indicate which of the following statements are true or false by circling the correct answer.

1. The federal gift tax and the federal estate tax are computed on separate tax rate schedules.   T   F
2. A joint gift tax return must be filed in order for a married couple to elect gift-splitting.   T   F
3. The current unified credit for gift tax purposes is the exemption equivalent of an exclusion for   T   F
    the first $2 million of lifetime transfers.
4. A federal gift tax return is filed quarterly.   T   F
5. The alternate valuation date is generally nine months after the date of death of the decedent.   T   F
6. Under the dower and curtesy rules of most states, if a decedent dies without a will, the spouse will   T   F
    be entitled to two thirds of the property and the surviving children will be entitled to one third of
    the property.
7. Funeral expenses are deductible on the federal estate tax return.   T   F
8. A direct gift from a grandmother to her granddaughter is potentially subject to the generation-   T   F
    skipping transfer tax.
9. A donee's basis for loss on the sale of gift property is the lesser of the donor's cost or the fair   T   F
    market value of the gift on the date of the gift.
10. If a QTIP election is made, the property subject to the election will generally be included in the   T   F
    estate of the second spouse to die.

Fill in the Blanks

Fill in each blank with the appropriate word or phrase that completes each sentence.

11. The ability to obtain an annual exclusion for gifts to an insurance trust on the behalf of minors by providing
    a limited withdrawal opportunity to the children is commonly referred to as a(n) _____ power.
12. In order for a gift to be "disclaimed," the donor must receive a written disclaimer within _____ months
    of the date of the gift.
13. If gift-splitting is elected by a married couple, the first $ _____ of present interest transfers to a donee
    during the tax year will not be taxable.
14. Generally, a transfer to a spouse will not qualify for the marital deduction if the interest in the property is
    a _____ (terminable, nonterminable) one.
15. Gift taxes paid by a decedent will be included in the decedent's estate if paid within _____ years of
    the decedent's death.
16. In order to qualify for the prior transfer taxes credit on a federal estate tax return, the property included in
    the decedent's estate must have been subject to the estate tax within the prior _____ year(s).
17. A donee's basis for gain on the sale of gift property is always _____.
18. Corrine Adams received land from her aunt as a gift when the property was worth $20,000. Her aunt had
    paid $8,000 for the property 16 years earlier, and had paid a $1,600 gift tax on the transfer. Corrine's basis
    for gain for purposes of a later sale of the land is $_____.
19. A beneficiary of an estate will not receive a step-up in basis of property if the beneficiary had originally
    gifted the property to the donee within ____ year(s) of the date of death of the decedent.
20. Any assets subject to disposition by the executor under the terms of the will and any property passing
    under state intestate laws are always part of the _____ estate.

Multiple Choice

Circle the best answer for each of the following questions.

21. A closely-held corporation stock was valued at $20 per share eight days prior to a gift, and was valued at $25 five days after the gift. For gift tax purposes, the stock will be valued at
    a. $20 per share
    b. $21.92 per share
    c. $24.13 per share
    d. $25 per share

22. Prior to the current year, Ann Marks had made $5,850,000 of lifetime gifts. During the current year, she made $300,000 of taxable gifts. In computing her gift tax liability, Ann will
    a. compute the tax on $300,000 and add the tax on $5,850,000
    b. compute the tax on $5,850,000 and subtract the tax on $300,000
    c. compute the tax on $6,150,000 and add the tax on $300,000
    d. compute the tax on $6,150,000 and subtract the tax on $5,850,000

23. Sara James and her son Mark set up a joint checking account, with Sara contributing $18,000 and Mark contributing $2,000. As a result of this transfer, Sara has made a taxable gift of
    a. $0
    b. $6,000
    c. $16,000
    d. $18,000

24. Assume the same facts as Problem 23. If Mark withdraws $5,000 from the checking account, Sara is treated as making a taxable gift of
    a. $0
    b. $2,000
    c. $3,000
    d. $5,000

25. Which of the following interests in a trust qualify for the annual exclusion when the trust is established?
    a. a life interest (a life estate)
    b. a remainder interest
    c. both a. and c.
    d. none of the above

26. Life insurance proceeds on the life of a decedent will be included in the decedent's estate if
    a. the policy was transferred by the decedent within three years of death
    b. the policy proceeds are payable to the estate
    c. the decedent possessed significant incidents of ownership in the policy at death
    d. any of the above would require inclusion in the estate

27. Jim Allen died on February 1, 2013. The fair market value of his estate was $7.6 million, which included land with a value of $800,000 on that date. Exactly six months after the date of death, the estate was valued at $7.4 million, and the land was valued at $775,000. When the land was distributed to the beneficiary exactly eight months after the date of death, the land was valued at $760,000, and finally, the land was valued at $755,000 exactly nine months after the date of death. Assuming the estate elects the alternate valuation date, the land will be valued for estate tax purposes at
   a. $800,000
   b. $775,000
   c. $760,000
   d. $755,000

28. Al and Joan purchased property in a joint tenancy (with a right of survivorship) in 2000 for $500,000, with Al contributing $200,000 of the purchase price and Joan contributing $300,000 of the purchase price. If the property is worth $1 million when Al dies, and Al and Joan are husband and wife, the property will be included in Al's estate at a value of:
   a. $0
   b. $200,000
   c. $400,000
   d. $500,000

29. Assume the same facts as (28), except that Al and Joan are brother and sister. The property will be included in Al's estate at a value of
   a. $0
   b. $200,000
   c. $400,000
   d. $500,000

30. A general rule of thumb in considering lifetime vs. death transfers of property to family members is
   a. transfer appreciated property during lifetime and depreciated property at death
   b. transfer depreciated property during lifetime and appreciated property at death
   c. transfer both types of property during lifetime
   d. transfer both types of property at death

Review Problems

31. Explain the concept of a "unified transfer system," and how such a system always taxes gift and estate transfers at the highest tax rates.

32. Paula James made the following gifts in 2013 $42,000 cash to her son Bill, $76,000 cash to her daughter Alisha, $20,000 to the United Givers Fund, $60,000 to her spouse Thomas, and land worth $80,000 to her granddaughter Brenda. Determine Paula's taxable gifts for 2013.

33. Paula James made the following gifts in 2013: $42,000 cash to her son Bill, $76,000 cash to her daughter Alisha, $20,000 to the United Givers Fund, $60,000 to her spouse Thomas, and land worth $80,000 to her granddaughter Brenda. Determine Paula's taxable gifts for 2013, assuming that she elects gift-splitting with her husband Jerry.

34. What are the gift tax implications of establishing a joint checking account with your daughter? Explain.

35. Tom Wilson made a gift of $43,000 to his grand-daughter to pay for her college education during the current year. Will Tom be required to file a gift tax return? Explain.

36. Shortly before boarding a plane for Omaha, Jill Henning inserted $25 in an insurance vending machine at the airport. These funds purchased a $1,000,000 policy on her life should the plane crash. The vending machine automatically notified named beneficiaries of the policy, and Jill named her son Brandon as the beneficiary of the policy. The flight subsequently crashed while attempting to land in Omaha, and Jill died. Is the face amount of the policy includible in Jill's estate? Explain.

37. Explain the tax benefits and the possible drawbacks of establishing a life insurance trust for a taxpayer's children and structuring the agreement with a "Crummey power" which would provide annual exclusions on the taxpayer's gift tax return each year.

38. Loretta died on January 20, 2013. The assets included in her estate were valued as follows:

	1-20-13	7-20-13	10-20-13
• House	$900,000	$800,000	$700,000
• Stocks	$850,000	$600,000	$1,000,000

   The executor sold the house on October 20, 2013 for $700,000. The alternative valuation date was properly elected. What is the value of Loretta's estate?

39. Bob and Brenda McGraw own property as joint tenants. The property originally cost $800,000, with Bob furnishing $240,000 of the cost and Brenda furnishing $560,000 of the cost. In 2013, Bob died when the property was worth $1,200,000. What amount will be included in Bob's gross estate related to this property, assuming that (a) Bob and Brenda are married and (b) Bob and Brenda are not married?

40. Jennifer Bloom died in 2013, leaving the following assets: $4,900,000 of land to her daughter Alice, $800,000 stock to her son Brandon, $300,000 cash to the American Lung Association, and a personal residence and its contents worth $800,000 to her husband Allen. Jennifer also had transferred a $1,000,000 life insurance policy to her daughter Alice seven years ago, but Jennifer reserved the right to change the beneficiary on the policy. Jennifer's only lifetime gifts were in 2011, totaling $1,200,000 on which $82,000 of gift taxes were paid (after reduction for the unified credit). Determine the final estate tax liability (if any) owed by Jennifer's estate.

41. Jerrold and Dee Morgan are married and own property jointly that originally cost $200,000 (one-half of the consideration was furnished by each spouse). When Jerry died, the property was worth $350,000. What is Dee's adjusted basis in the property after Jerrold's death, assuming that (a) Jerrold and Dee reside in a common-law state and (b) Jerrold and Dee reside in a community property state?

42. Who makes a QTIP election, and when is such an election advisable? Explain.

43. Explain how the "deceased spouse unused exemption amount (DSUEA)" election can mitigate problems created when a decedent wills virtually all of his or her assets to his or her spouse. Who makes the election, and how is this accomplished?

Research Questions

44. Mary Benson is a widowed mother of three daughters: Ellen, Alice, and Wilma. Mary prepared a will, leaving, among other assets, all of her life savings in her savings account to be split equally by her three daughters. For convenience, Mary had the savings account as a joint account with Wilma, who lived in the same town as Mary. Who is entitled to the savings account when Mary dies?

45. Would a prenuptial agreement, under which each spouse waives all marital rights in the property of the other, prevent a husband and wife from taking advantage of the gift-splitting provisions in making gifts to third persons? Explain.
46. to the husband of a refund annuity in the event of her premature death. Would the computed value of the refund annuity be included in decedent's estate? Explain.

Tax Planning Questions

47. Hank and Wilma Allen are married taxpayers (both age 62) who desire to eventually transfer all of their property to their children after they die. Hank's estate is currently worth $9,000,000, and Wilma's estate is worth $6,000,000. What possible actions would you recommend for Hank and Wilma to take during lifetime and at death to accomplish this objective? Explain.

48. A married couple, both age 40, have six children. If they start a gift program maximizing the tax-free gifts that they can make each year, what is the dollar value of property that could be transferred out of their estates by age 75 without utilizing a penny of their unified credits? Explain.

Tax Compliance Questions

49. Refer to Problem 32 above. Assuming that Paula had made $6,000,000 of lifetime gifts prior to the current year, prepare a Form 709 gift tax return for Paula for the current tax year.

50. Refer to Problem 40 above. Prepare a Form 706 estate tax return for Jennifer for the current year.

51. Al Johnson died intestate, with his widow receiving $4,000,000 and his two children receiving $8,000,000 ($4,000,000 each) under state intestate laws. Is there anything the family can do to minimize the estate tax due upon Al's death? Explain.

CHAPTER 14

Gift and Estate Tax Planning II—Trusts and Closely-Held Business Strategies

Learning Objectives:

1. Distinguish general and limited powers of appointment, as they relate to gift and estate taxes.
2. Distinguish the tax consequences of revocable and irrevocable trusts.
3. Describe the estate planning advantages of insurance trusts, personal residence trusts, charitable remainder trusts, and charitable lead trusts.
4. Explain the use of the following techniques as a means of freezing the value of an estate: installment sales, grantor retained income trusts, grantor retained annuity trusts, and grantor retained unitrusts.
5. Explain how minority interest transfers and lack of marketability may justify substantial discounts in the transfer of a family business.
6. Describe the tax transfer benefits offered by a family limited partnership, and the legal arguments used by the IRS to counter such arrangements.

¶14,001   Introduction

As discussed in the previous chapter, trusts generally offer the non-tax advantages of reducing probate costs and securing privacy for the donor. Trusts may also offer several tax advantages, such as reducing the gross estate, maximizing the use of the marital deduction and the unified credit, and shifting income to other lower-tax bracket family members. But trusts are taxed at very steep rates (see Appendix A), so the objective in many cases is to shift income taxation to beneficiaries.

Trusts are analyzed below in terms of tax planning for minors, charitable contributions, and estate freezes. The use of family limited partnerships for estate freeze purposes is also discussed. But first, the use of general and special powers of appointment, a simple method of controlling the enjoyment of property, is discussed.

¶14,003   Powers of Appointment—Tax Considerations

.01   GENERAL VS. LIMITED POWER OF APPOINTMENT

A power of appointment is a power to determine who shall own or enjoy (now or in the future) property subject to the power. Such powers may be classified as either *general powers of appointment* or *limited powers of appointment*.

A **general power of appointment** allows the holder to appoint anyone to enjoy the property, including the holder himself or herself and his or her creditors, estate, or creditors of the estate. When the holder of a general power of appointment dies, the fair market value of the property subject to the power is included in his or her gross estate. Furthermore, the holder is deemed to own the property for income tax purposes as well, and is taxed on the income from the property each year even though he or she never exercises the power on his or her own behalf. If the holder exercises the power in favor of someone else, he or she has made a taxable gift of the property.

Example 14-1. Jill Arrington transfers her property to an irrevocable trust, naming her brother Seth as trustee. According to the trust instrument, the trustee has the power to determine who will receive the income (a "*sprinkling trust*") and who ultimately will receive the remainder interest based on a list of potential beneficiaries included in the trust instrument. If Seth dies or refuses to serve, the trustee will be Second Savings and Loan. Seth may appoint the property to himself. This is a general power of appointment, and the fair market value of the property is included in Seth's estate at death as long as he retained this power. In addition, Seth is taxed on the income from the trust each year. If Seth exercises the power in favor of another beneficiary, Seth has made a taxable gift.

A **limited power of appointment** allows the holder to appoint anyone but himself or herself (or his or her creditors, estate, or estate creditors) to enjoy the property. In this case, there are no gift or estate tax consequences to the holder of such a power.

Example 14-2. Assume the same facts as the previous example, except that Seth possesses only a limited power of appointment. There are no tax consequences to Seth due to the possession of this power, since he cannot exercise the power in favor of himself.

.03   LAPSE OF A POWER OF APPOINTMENT

A **lapse** of a general power of appointment is subject to the gift tax only if the value of the property that could be appointed exceeds the greater of $5,000 or five percent of the aggregate value of the property subject to potential appointment. However, this exception does not apply in the year of death.

.05   THE ASCERTAINABLE STANDARD EXCEPTION

An important exception to the limited power of appointment rules allows the holder of such power to consume or invade the property for his or her own benefit under an **ascertainable standard** provided in the trust instrument. An ascertainable standard must relate to the holder's *health, education, support, or maintenance*. However, a power to use the property for "comfort, welfare, or happiness" is not an ascertainable standard.

Example 14-3. Assume the same facts as the previous example (a limited power of appointment), except that Seth has the power under the trust to occasionally withdraw funds for his own support. Since this withdrawal power is based on an "ascertainable standard," the trust will not be included in Seth's gross estate when he dies.[1]

¶14,005   Trusts: Classification as Revocable and Irrevocable

.01   REVOCABLE TRUSTS—TAX CONSEQUENCES

A revocable trust is one in which the transferor has retained the power to revoke or terminate the trust. In such a case, (1) no gift occurs on the creation of the trust, (2) the trust is includible in the estate of the transferor, and (3) the transferor is taxed on the income of the trust. If another person receives this income, then the transferor has made a taxable gift that qualifies for the exclusion, since the income is a present interest.

In effect, the tax effects of a revocable trust are the same as if no trust was created. Revocable trusts still offer the advantages of (1) avoiding probate costs, and (2) providing privacy to the donor (trust instruments are private, while wills are publicly available).

If the transferor provides another person with the power to revoke the trust, and the transferor did not retain the right to assume these powers, then the trust property will not be in the transferor's estate. However, the property will be in the transferor's estate if such powers are relinquished within three years of the date of the transferor's death.

Example 14-4. Macy Blue transfers property to a trust in 2008, reserving the power to revoke the trust. In 2013, Macy alters the terms of the trust so that only her niece Allison can revoke the trust. If Macy dies in 2015, the trust property will be included in Macy's estate, because Macy did not survive more than three years after relinquishing the power.

.03   IRREVOCABLE TRUSTS—TAX CONSEQUENCES

Tax savings may be generated if the transferor is willing to relinquish all powers over the trust. A common irrevocable trust arrangement is for the trust instrument to provide an income interest for life to one beneficiary and the remainder interest to another benefi-

---

[1] Code Sec. 2038(a)(1).

ciary. In such a case, the transferor has made two gifts: a gift of the income interest (life estate), and a gift of the remainder interest.

The *remainder interest* is valued based on mortality tables that consider the age of the life (income) tenant and current interest rates (under the Code, 120 percent of the mid-term applicable federal rate (AFR)).[2] A portion of this interest table (Table S) is included as Appendix B. Since this is a gift of a future interest, it does not qualify for the annual exclusion.

Once the remainder interest is valued, the value of the *income interest* is simply the fair market value of the gift less the computed value of the remainder interest. The income interest so computed qualifies for the annual exclusion, since it is a gift of a present interest.

Example 14-5. Beth King transfers $500,000 to an irrevocable trust. Under the terms of the transfer, Beth's friend Roberta (currently age 50) will receive an income interest until her death, and then the corpus of the trust (the remainder) passes to Paul who is not related to Beth. At the time of the transfer, 120 percent of the AFR rate was 8.0 percent. The value of the gift of the remainder interest and the gift of the income interest are determined as follows (remainder interest factors taken from Table S, Appendix B, 8-percent rate, age 50):

Remainder interest ($500,000 × .16388)	$ 81,940
Income Interest ($500,000 − $81,940)	418,060
Total Gift	$500,000

Beth has made two taxable gifts with the creation of the trust: an $81,940 taxable gift to Paul of the remainder interest that does not qualify for the annual exclusion, and a $418,060 gift to Roberta that qualifies for the $14,000 annual exclusion.

The transferor must be careful not to retain any powers related to the trust, as it is conceivable that a transfer could be treated as a gift and yet still included in the estate because of a minor power retained. This would be the case, for example, if the transferor retains the power to determine if the income should be distributed each year or retained by the trust. This is a taxable gift that does not qualify for an annual exclusion, since there is no requirement that the income be distributed annually. If the transferor dies with this power intact, the property will be included in his or her estate.

¶14,007   Irrevocable Transfers with a Retained Life Estate: General Tax Consequences

For various reasons, a transferor may decide to retain an income interest for himself or herself when a trust is created. This provides a steady stream of income to the transferor, but produces severe tax consequences. Code Sec. 2036 brings such a trust back into the estate when the transferor dies, as long as the transferor retained the right to enjoy the income up to the time of death. Such "enjoyment" includes any discharge of a legal obligation of the transferor, including providing for the support of another person. If a person other than the transferor is given the life estate, this does not cause the estate to be included in the income beneficiary's estate, since he or she is not the transferor.

Example 14-6. Assume the same facts as the previous example, except that Beth King (age 50) retains a life estate (income interest) for herself, with the remainder passing to Paul, who is not related to Beth. At the time of the transfer, 120 percent of the AFR rate was 8.0 percent. The value of Paul's remainder interest is still deter-

---

[2]   Code Sec. 7520(a)(2).

mined as before, a total of $81,940 ($500,000 × .16388). This gift does not qualify for the annual exclusion since it is a gift of a future interest. There is no gift of the income interest, since Beth retained such interest for herself. The full fair market value of the property in the trust will be included in Beth's estate when she dies, since Beth had retained the right to the enjoyment of the income from the trust.

Code Sec. 2702 provides even more disastrous consequences when the remainder beneficiary is an *applicable family member* of the transferor (i.e., spouse, ancestor, descendant, sibling, or spouse of an ancestor, descendant or sibling). Such arrangements are known as grantor retained income trusts (GRITs), and as explained later in this chapter, Code Sec. 2702 requires that the retained income interest of the grantor be automatically valued at *zero*. The remainder interest is thus valued at the fair market value of the property on the date of the transfer, and this is the amount of the taxable gift.

Example 14-7. Assume the same facts as the previous example, except Paul, the remainder beneficiary, is Beth's brother. In this case, Beth's income interest is automatically valued at zero, which means the gift of the remainder interest to Paul must be valued at $500,000. This gift does not qualify for the annual exclusion since it is a gift of a future interest. There is no gift of the income interest, since Beth retained such interest for herself. The full fair market value of the property in the trust will be included in Beth's estate when she dies, since Beth had retained the right to the enjoyment of the income from the trust.

Suppose the transferor merely retains the power to determine which of two or more beneficiaries will receive the income from the trust. In this case, the tax result is the same as above, even though the transferor does not retain the interest for himself or herself.

¶14,009 Insurance Trusts and Trusts for Minors

.01 INSURANCE TRUSTS

A life insurance trust is often one of the key components of a comprehensive estate plan. Usually, the insured grantor creates an irrevocable trust, which in turn purchases insurance on the grantor's life. In the common case, the grantor's children are beneficiaries of the life insurance trust. When the insured dies, the trust owns the policy, and for that reason the policy proceeds are not generally included in the insured's estate. Recall, however, that the proceeds will be includible in the estate if (1) the insured retained "incidents of ownership" in the policy, (2) the insured transferred the policy within three years of death, or (3) the proceeds are payable to the estate or are available to pay taxes, debts or other expenses or charges of the insured's estate.

Most insurance trusts are designed to take advantage of the annual exclusion for premium payments. Such premium payments by the grantor will qualify for the annual exclusion if they provide limited withdrawal opportunities to the beneficiaries under the *Crummey* power rules mentioned earlier (and discussed below in reference to minors).

OBSERVATION   If the insurance trust has more than one beneficiary, providing withdrawal powers to each can dramatically increase the annual exclusion amounts available to cover insurance premiums each year. However, there is always the danger that beneficiaries may exercise this right.

Life insurance trusts may be created for a variety of reasons. For example, the creation may simply be an investment decision, in that the tax-free rate of return on "inside" policy buildup may exceed the after-tax rate of return available on a taxable investment outside the policy. The proceeds of the trust may be also used to replace wealth transferred to a charity with such vehicles as a charitable remainder trust discussed below. Finally, the proceeds may help provide estate liquidity in indirect ways, however, care must be taken not to cause inclusion of the proceeds in the estate of the insured.

.03   TRUSTS FOR MINORS

Creating trusts for minors may generate substantial tax savings, but these transfers come at a price; generally, control over the trust property must be surrendered in order to qualify the gift as a present interest eligible for the annual gift tax exclusion. However, Code Sec. 2503(c) provides three conditions that allow such transfers to qualify for the annual exclusion and yet provide the opportunity for the trust to accumulate the income on the minor's behalf.

The three conditions to qualify for the annual exclusion are:
- the property and income may be expended on the minor's behalf prior to reaching age 21,
- any amounts not expended pass to the minor at age 21, and
- if the minor dies before age 21, the property and income is payable to the minor's estate or to a beneficiary designated by the minor under a general power of appointment.

If these three conditions are met, the gifts to the trust will qualify for the annual exclusion. Spreading the gifts to the trust over several years and utilizing gift-splitting elections are techniques that may maximize the tax savings associated with such transfers. This can be an effective strategy for life insurance trusts.

Trusts may also be established for taxpayers of any age and qualify for the annual exclusion if they provide for a *"Crummey Power"* mentioned earlier. In *TAM 8712014* and *PLR 8004172*, the IRS indicated that if the trust instrument requires that the trustee provide notice of withdrawal availability within seven days of the contribution to the trust and the beneficiary has at least 30 days to exercise the withdrawal right, then the contribution should qualify for the exclusion.

Example 14-8. Tara Wright sets up a life insurance trust with her 25-year old daughter Elizabeth as beneficiary. Each year on December 31st, Tara contributes an amount to the trust sufficient to pay the premiums on the insurance policy. The trustee then notifies Elizabeth of her right to withdraw the lesser of the annual contribution or $14,000 within the following 30 days. The contributions to the trust qualify for the annual exclusion.

¶14,011   Trusts and Charitable Contributions

Normally, taxpayers who are considering substantial contributions of cash or property to a charity should make such contributions during their lifetime, since the transfers are not subject to gift taxes and an income tax deduction is available. Such transfers are also exempt from estate taxes as well, but the income tax deduction would be lost if the transfer is delayed until death. One advantage of waiting until death is simply that the taxpayer can provide for the testamentary transfer in the will and yet still have the power to change his or her mind at any time.

Trusts may be used to increase the viability of transfers to a charity. Two common techniques are the charitable remainder trust and the charitable lead trust. Each is discussed below.

.01   CHARITABLE REMAINDER TRUST

In a charitable remainder trust arrangement, a grantor makes a gift to a charity now, but reserves for himself or herself the income from the gifted property for life. The income from the property is paid to the grantor as either a (1) fixed dollar amount of income each year (a **charitable remainder annuity trust**) or (2) a percentage of the value of the assets (a **charitable remainder unitrust**). If the trust sells the property contributed to the trust, any resulting gain is not taxable. When the donor dies, the property passes outright to the charity designated by the donor. Planning with such a trust is illustrated in **Figure 1**.

Figure 1

Illustration—Charitable Remainder Trust

Taylor Martin, age 65, currently owns stock worth $1 million that was originally acquired under an incentive stock option plan for $100,000. The stock is in a technology company which pays little dividends. Taylor's marginal federal income tax rate is 35 percent and his marginal state income tax rate is 7 percent. Two options being considered by Taylor to generate a retirement stream of income are:

1. ***Sell the stock and invest the proceeds in eight-percent taxable bonds.***

    If Taylor elects this option, he will pay approximately $198,000 in income taxes ($900,000 gain × 22 percent combined federal and state rate on long-term capital gains). The remaining $802,000 is invested in eight-percent bonds, generating an annual taxable income of *$64,160* per year ($802,000 × .08).

2. ***Establish a charitable remainder trust that pays Taylor an eight-percent return each year.***

    If Taylor elects this option, he will contribute the stock to a charitable remainder trust, which in turns sells the stock on a tax-free basis for $1 million. The trust then pays Taylor an annual taxable income of *$80,000* per year ($1,000,000 × .08). Using IRS tables based on Taylor's life expectancy, the charity's remainder interest is valued at approximately $220,000. Taylor claims the $220,000 as a charitable deduction for income tax purposes, which will eventually save him $92,400 in taxes ($220,000 × .42), although this deduction may be spread over several years because of adjusted gross income limitations.

3. ***Summary***

    With the charitable remainder trust, Taylor's retirement income is $15,840 greater each year ($80,000 − $64,160), and he receives $92,400 of income tax savings that were not available under the taxable bond option.

4. ***But what about the kids?***

    Because of the gift of the remainder interest to the charity, Taylor's children will not inherit the $802,000 net proceeds that would have been available from an outright sale of the stock by Taylor. Assuming that Taylor's marginal estate tax twenty years from now (his current life expectancy) is projected to be 40 percent; the children would have inherited approximately $480,000. Taylor could purchase term life insurance coverage of this amount for the heirs for approximately $81,000 (*less* than the tax savings from the charitable contribution deduction generated earlier).

Note that because the property is not available for distribution to family members, the grantor elects to purchase a life insurance policy to make up this difference. In the end, the technique still increases the annual income of the grantor when income tax considerations are factored in.

.03   CHARITABLE LEAD TRUST

A **charitable lead trust** also involves a contribution of property to a trust. However, in this case the trust term is for a fixed period of years, and the income from the trust (after the asset is sold) goes to the charity. After the term of the trust expires, the remainder interest in the property passes directly to the grantor's children.

A lead trust offers the advantages of providing income immediately to the charity and providing a tax deduction (the present value of the income interest) to the grantor. And since the property passes directly to the beneficiary at the end of the term, there are no probate costs.

OBSERVATION	Note in the above two strategies the critical role of the current interest rate if the income tax charitable contribution deduction is a prime incentive for the transfer. The higher the interest rate, the higher the value of the income interest and the lower the value of the remainder interest. This may argue in favor of transferring the income interest to the charity to maximize the income tax deduction. On the other hand, if interest rates are low, the value of the remainder interest is higher, and this might tip the scales in favor of the charitable remainder trust.

¶14,013   Estate Freezes—An Introduction

.01   ESTATE FREEZES: A HISTORICAL PERSPECTIVE

Estate freezes were very popular planning tools for a number of years prior to the late 1980s. This technique was used mostly within the context of a family business, but the same principles applied to all properties.

In a business context, a small business owner who was approaching retirement would recapitalize the business by issuing two classes of stock: voting preferred and nonvoting common. The parent would keep the preferred stock, which would typically be most of the value of the business due to the voting preferences attached to the stock. The common stock would then be gradually gifted to the children to move appreciation out of the estate. Since the common stock had little present value due to the second-class status compared to the preferred, little gift tax was paid on the transfers. Thus, the appreciation potential of the business was shifted to the next generation at little transfer tax cost.

In a nonbusiness example, a parent would transfer property, perhaps real estate, to an irrevocable trust, retaining a life estate in the property with the property automatically passing to the children at death. Once again, the value of the remainder interest to the children (the taxable gift) was relatively small as the income interest was generally valued using a 10-percent assumed rate of return, and little transfer tax was paid. This technique effectively shifts future appreciation in value of the property to the children.

For years Congress wrestled with a method of combating these "freeze transfers." A first attempt in the late 1980s was a special "anti-freeze" provision of Code Sec. 2036(c), which involved a complex set of rules for bringing the value of the transferred property back into the estate. These rules were repealed in 1990 and replaced by the new Chapter 14 of the Internal Revenue Code, Secs. 2701 through 2704, which still applies today.

Despite these limitations, there are still ways to plan around these rules. The discussion in the next section highlights the various freeze techniques that utilize trusts. But first, another simpler freeze technique, the installment sale, is discussed.

¶14,015   Installment Sales as a Freeze Strategy

.01   REPORTING THE INSTALLMENT SALE

As an individual nears retirement, he or she may consider an installment sale under Code Sec. 453 of business or investment properties as a means of "freezing" the estate value of property. If the seller dies before collecting all of the installments, only the face value of the remaining installments (the "frozen" amount) is included in the estate.

The appreciation potential of the property has been effectively shifted to the purchaser, usually a family member. And assuming that the sale was for fair market value, there are no gift tax consequences attached to the sale. Finally, the family member's basis in the business is equal to the purchase price; a step up in basis is not possible if the parent had gifted the property during his or her lifetime to the family member.

Example 14-9. Sara Long, age 60, sells her sole proprietorship business ($1,200,000 adjusted basis) to her daughter Anna Marie in 2013 for a total consideration of $4,000,000, payable with $200,000 cash down payment in the year of sale and 19 annual payments of $200,000 plus six-percent interest on the unpaid balance beginning next year. Unless Sara opts out of the installment method, she will report 70 percent of each payment as taxable gain as each payment is received ($2,800,000 gross profit/$4,000,000 total contract price). The gain will be reported as Code Sec. 1231 gain each year (and eventually as long-term capital gain if no other Code Sec. 1231 transactions are present). However, any depreciation recapture would have to be reported as ordinary income in the year of sale. She will also report interest income each year as ordinary income.

Example 14-10. Assume the same facts as the previous example, except that Sara sells the property to Anna Marie for a total consideration of $3,000,000, payable $150,000 a year for 20 years beginning with a down payment in the year of sale. Assuming that the business is actually worth $4 million, Sara will report a taxable gift to her daughter Anna Marie of $1 million. She will then compute her gross profit percentage for installment sales purposes based on a $3 million total contract price.

Example 14-11. Assume the same facts as Example 14-9, and assume that Sara dies shortly after receiving the 10th payment under the installment sales contract. In this case, the face value of the notes remaining to be collected is $2,000,000, and this amount will be included in Sara's estate. Any appreciation in value of the business since the original sale of the business has no effect on this valuation, because Sara's asset is the installment note and not the business.

OBSERVATION   What about the unreported income on the remaining $2 million of notes to be collected? This is treated as "income in respect of a decedent" by the ultimate beneficiary of the note, and is reported in exactly the same manner as Sara would have reported the income had she lived. Thus, if Sara wills the note to her son David, David will "step in the shoes" of Sara and report 70 percent of each payment received as income. But what if Sara wanted to just cancel the note at death, so that Anna Marie's obligation is extinguished? Read on!

.03   SELF-CANCELING INSTALLMENT NOTES (SCIN)

In many installment sales involving family members, the terms of the installment note are amended to provide that the installment payments continue until the total sales price is received or the seller dies, whichever occurs first. This is a contingent payment installment sale that is often referred to as a **self-canceling installment note (SCIN)**. Because there is a risk that the seller would die before collecting all the payments, an arm's length installment sale should generally provide for a higher sales price and/or a higher interest rate to include a premium for this risk to the seller. This means that the seller will be collecting more from each installment payment, which of course means that there are more assets left in the seller's estate. Also, in *GCM 39503*, the IRS indicated that the installment period must be less than the seller's remaining life expectancy; otherwise, the transaction could be recast as a "private annuity." Treatment as a private annuity is not discussed here, but generally such treatment requires the seller to allocate each payment between a capital amount (recovery of basis and capital gain) and an annuity (taxed as ordinary income).

What are the tax consequences associated with a SCIN, assuming that the seller dies before collecting the note? First of all, there is no inclusion in the estate, since there is no property left to pass on to others (the installment note is cancelled and thus has no value). However, there is the matter of the unreported income at the time of death. As established in *Frane*,[3] this gain is reported as income in respect of a decedent on the estate's income tax return. *(Does that case sound familiar?)*

OBSERVATION   If the parties involved in the installment sale use IRS life expectancy tables in estimating the risk premium, this will usually satisfy the IRS. These tables reflect an increasing risk premium as the seller's age and the term of the note increases. However, if death is imminent, the IRS has ruled that the tables do not apply, and they will assess the reasonableness of such a premium.[4]

¶14,017   Using Trusts for Estate Freezes

Trusts have traditionally been used in various ways to achieve a freeze of estate assets, particularly in the case of a business interest. Typically, the grantor retains a life estate or a term-certain annuity from the contributed property, with the remainder interest automatically passing to other family members (usually a younger generation) at death. Three common uses of trusts for accomplishing this purpose are Grantor Retained Income Trusts (GRITs), Grantor Retained Annuity Trusts (GRATs), and Grantor Retained Unitrusts (GRUTs).

The main advantage of using these types of trusts is related to the transfer tax savings upon setting up the trust, i.e., the gift to the trust. When the assets are placed into the trust, only the actuarial value of what will pass to the remainder persons is deemed to be a taxable gift. However, there is a significant downside to all three strategies; if the grantor dies prior to the termination of the income interest, the value of the assets held in the trust are includible in the grantor's gross estate under Code Sec. 2036(a).

OBSERVATION   Although inclusion in the estate is a definite disadvantage if the grantor dies during the term of the income interest, such inclusion just restores the grantor to the same position he or she would have been in without making the transfer. And if the transfer is subsequently included in the estate, the grantor's estate would be allowed a credit for any gift tax paid on the original gift to the trust.

[3]   *Frane*, CA-8, 93-2 USTC ¶50,386, 998 F.2d. 567.
[4]   *See* Rev. Rul. 80-80, 1980-1 CB 194.

.01   GRANTOR RETAINED INCOME TRUSTS (GRITs)

In a **Grantor Retained Income Trust (GRIT)**, a grantor would typically transfer either investment property or a business interest to a trust, reserving an interest in all the income from the property for the trust term and leaving the remainder for family members at death. As part of the 1990 Act, Congress severely curtailed the use of a GRIT when the remainder interest is left to a close family member (e.g., a blood relative other than cousins, nieces and nephews). Code Sec. 2702(b) now states that the value of the interest retained by the transferor is *zero* unless the retained income interest is a "qualified interest" as defined in Code Sec. 2702(a)(2).

Example 14-12. Marvin Davis contributes land worth $3 million to a trust, reserving the income from the property for life and leaving the remainder interest to his five children. Since Marvin and the children are related parties as defined by Code Sec. 2702, the value of the income interest retained by Marvin is presumed to be zero. Thus, the gift of the remainder interest, by default, is valued at $3 million, and no transfer taxes are saved at all.

"Qualified interests" are essentially the GRATS and GRUTS discussed in the next section, but it is important to note that the GRIT crackdown does not apply to (1) cousins, nieces, and nephews, as well as any unrelated party or (2) a **Qualified Personal Residence Trust (QPRT)**. In both cases, the taxpayer may still determine the value of the remainder interest using IRS tables and generate significant tax savings.

Example 14-13. Assume the same facts as in the previous example, except the remainder interest will be left to Marvin's companion, Ivana. Since Ivana is not a related party, the value of the remainder interest is discounted using current interest rates under Code Sec. 7520(a); for example, assume that the present value factor for the remainder interest is .42000. Rather than reporting the gift of the land at its fair market value of $3 million, Marvin would report a gift at a discounted value of only $1.26 million ($3,000,000 × .42000).

Figure 2 provides an illustration of a how a QPRT may be used to generate such transfer savings.

Figure 2

Illustration—Qualified Personal Residence Trust

Facts: Sue Mason, age 70, transfers her personal residence ($5,000,000 fair market value) into a trust, retaining an income interest in the residence for a period of 10 years. The residence will go to Sue's two sons Al and Frank at the end of the 10-year period (or on the date of Sue's death, if earlier). The value of Sue's gift of the remainder interest in the residence to her sons, assuming that the current Code Sec. 7520(a) monthly interest rate is 7.2 percent, is determined as follows (using values from Tables B and 90CM of Appendix B):

Present value of the remainder interest (Table B, 10 yrs., 7.2% interest rate)	*.498944*
Probability that Sue will survive 10 years (Table 90CM: 47,084 / 71,357) ×	*.659837*
Percentage value of the gift allocable to the remainder interest	*.329222*

Thus, the taxable gift reportable by Sue is $1,646,110 ($5,000,000 × .329222), resulting in a gift tax of $604,244, which is much less than the unified credit. The reduction in taxable transfers is thus $3,353,890, plus any appreciation in value of the home that may occur in future years. For example, if the property increased in value to $7.3 million after 10 years, the estate tax owed on the home if the QPRT was not formed would be $2,865,800 (before reflecting the unified credit). *But there is an important caveat; if Sue dies during the 10-year period, the fair market value of the residence will be included in her estate.*

In the illustration of **Figure 2**, the grantor Sue Mason was able to transfer $5,000,000 of property by reporting a taxable gift of only $1,646,110. What if the "right" Sue retained in the property was simply to live there for the rest of her life, rather than receiving any income from the property? The answer is that the computations would be made in exactly the same manner; the "right" would still be valued using the Code Sec. 7520(a) interest rates.

.03   GRANTOR RETAINED ANNUITY TRUSTS

As mentioned above, a **Grantor Retained Annuity Trust (GRAT)** is a qualified interest that is not subject to the zero valuation rule for any retained income interest. As a result, such a trust still offers potential tax savings when the property contributed to the trust is expected to appreciate at a rate higher than the discount rate used in valuing the remainder interest.

A GRAT is an irrevocable trust to which the grantor transfers an asset, retaining the right to receive a fixed annuity for a stated term of years or for the shorter of the stated term or the grantor's earlier death (a contingent term). The annuity amount to be paid can be expressed as either a fixed dollar amount or as a percentage of the initial value of the trust. Code Sec. 2702 requires that the annuity amount must be payable to the grantor for each taxable year of the stated term and must be paid in cash or in the form of assets held in the trust. At the expiration of the stated term or the death of the grantor, the trust property passes to or is held in further trust for persons designated by the grantor.

OBSERVATION

The key difference between a GRIT and a GRAT is that a GRAT is based on a fixed annuity for a definite period of time, whereas a GRIT was an interest in all income from the underlying property. As was true with a GRIT, if the grantor dies before the term of the GRAT expires, the value of the property in the trust is included in the grantor's estate. Under Proposed Regulations (Reg. §20.2036-1), this inclusion would equal the amount of corpus necessary to produce the annuity based on the Code Sec. 7520 rate in effect on the valuation date. This amount cannot exceed the amount of the corpus.

Figure 3 provides an illustration of the basis GRAT computations.

Figure 3

Illustration—Grantor Retained Annuity Trust (GRAT)

Sam Burger, age 60, transfers $1,000,000 worth of property to a trust for the benefit of his daughter Helen while retaining an annuity interest of $100,000 per year for 10 years. The current Code Sec. 7520(a) rate is 7.2 percent. The value of Sam's retained income interest in the trust is computed as follows, using Table B of Appendix B for a term certain:

Required annual trust annuity payment	$100,000
Annuity factor for 10 years at 7.2-percent interest (Table B)	× 6.9591
Present value of the annuity (income) interest	$695,910

Thus, the value of the remainder interest is $304,090 ($1,000,000 – $695,910). If the trust property provides a return greater than 7.2 percent, then significant transfer tax savings will be recognized. In effect, the gift transfer *freezes* a 7.2-percent implied rate of return.

OBSERVATION   The above calculation is the normal calculation of a straight-term interest of 10 years, which is traditionally used for such purposes. However, the IRS in *Reg. §25.2702-3, Example 5*, implies that the retained interest must be valued for the *shorter* of the stated term or the prior death of the grantor. Using complicated annuity factors to reflect this "shorter of term or life" condition would result in an increase in the remainder interest to $347,497. Although the IRS continues to insist on including this contingency condition in the computations, thus preventing a complete "zeroing out" of a GRAT, taxpayers recently won a major victory that permitted a "zeroed-out" GRAT.[5]

A simple spreadsheet may be developed to analyze the potential tax savings of a GRAT under different assumed interest rates, transfer amounts, and terms. Such a spreadsheet is illustrated in **Figure 4**. (This spreadsheet is used with a tax planning exercise in the end of chapter materials.) Note that significant transfer tax savings are generated with the GRAT because the expected appreciation rate on the GRAT property (six percent) is significantly higher than the expected rate of appreciation on other estate properties (three percent).

Also note that by reporting a discounted value of the remainder interest of $881,878 as a gift in the current year, the taxpayer's estate will not include any appreciation beyond the 3% Sec. 7520 rate on the $6,000,000 of GRAT property. This property is projected to be worth $10,745,086 10 years later when the term of the GRAT expires. In contrast, the taxable estate with the GRAT transfer would include only the cash returned to the grantor under the terms of the trust ($600,000 × 10 payments, or $6,000,000). The $6,000,000 is assumed to still be held by the grantor at the end of ten years, so that a fair comparison of the two options can be made.

The real value of such a simple spreadsheet is to perform sensitivity analysis, that is, to vary the key inputs to see the effects on projected tax savings or costs. For example, if the expected appreciation rate in the GRAT property is eight percent rather than six percent, the projected tax savings increase from $1,149,836 to $1,807,158. On the other hand, if the expected rate of appreciation is only four percent, the projected tax savings fall to $595,152.

OBSERVATION   What if the term of the GRAT is shortened to five years, with payments of $1,200,000 each year? In this case, the projected tax savings drop to $526,192. In general, the longer the term of the GRAT, the more the potential tax savings. On the other hand, as the term of the GRAT increases, the probability that the grantor will die during the term of the GRAT also increases, and if this happens the fair market value of the underlying GRAT property will be included in the grantor's estate. For that reason, most GRATs are for short durations, such as two years, with renewals every two years.

There is no limit on the number of GRATS that a grantor may create, and the larger the number of GRATS, the more diversified the portfolio. There is an even more practical reason to use short terms: it is generally easier to "beat" the IRS rate of return in a short period rather than a long period.

Generally, a GRAT is more attractive when the Code Sec. 7520 interest rate is low. As the Code Sec. 7520 rate decreases, the value of the retained interest in a GRAT will

---

[5]   *See Walton*, 115 TC 589.

increase because a decrease in the assumed rate of return makes the right to receive fixed amounts in the future more valuable.

For example, assuming the same facts as the GRAT in **Figure 4**, except that the Code Sec. 7520 interest rate for present value computations is two percent rather than three percent, the estimated tax savings from the GRAT increase to $1,230,623. Likewise, if the interest factor increases to five percent, the estimated tax savings drop to $1,074,955.

Figure 4

Estimated Tax Savings—Grantor Retained Annuity Trust		
Current Asset Holdings and Unified Transfer Totals:		
Total estate assets exclusive of GRAT transfer		12,000,000
Estimated appreciation rate per year for other estate assets		0.03
Estimated appreciation rate per year for GRAT assets		0.06
Total lifetime gifts to date		4,000,000
Total gift taxes paid to date		0
Current year		2013
Interest factor for present value computations		0.03
GRAT Transfer Information:		
FMV of property transferred to GRAT		6,000,000
Retained annuity income stream each year		600,000
Term (in years) of the GRAT		10
Current Code Sec. 7520(a) interest rate		0.03

Projected Tax Liabilities With and Without the GRAT Transfer:		
	No Transfer to GRAT	Transfer to GRAT
Gift Tax Liability on GRAT Transfer:		
Value of remainder interest in GRAT	0	881,878
Prior lifetime gift transfers		4,000,000
Total taxable transfers with GRAT		4,881,878
Gross unified transfer tax		1,898,551
Gift taxes paid in prior years		0
Unified credit for transfer year		(2,045,800)
Net gift taxes paid on GRAT transfer	N/A	0
Estate Tax Liability at Death (Assuming Death Occurs After Term Expires):		
FMV of GRAT property	10,745,086	6,000,000
FMV of other estate property at death	20,126,997	20,126,997
Prior Lifetime Transfers	4,000,000	4,881,878
Total taxable transfers	34,872,083	31,008,875
Gross unified transfer tax	13,894,633	12,349,350
Gift taxes paid in prior years	0	0
Unified credit for transfer year	(2,749,384)	(2,749,384)
Net estate taxes due at death	11,145,249	9,599,966
Present value factor　　　　　x	0.74409	0.74409
Present value of estate taxes paid	8,293,112	7,143,276
Present Value of total transfer taxes	8,293,112	7,143,276
NPV Tax savings with GRAT transfer		1,149,836

.05   GRANTOR RETAINED UNITRUSTS (GRUTs)

A **Grantor Retained Unitrust (GRUT)** is just a variation of a GRAT. In a GRUT, the amount paid to the grantor is expressed as a percentage of the fair market value of trust assets each year as recalculated by the trust. Otherwise, the same valuation principles illustrated above also apply to a GRUT.

OBSERVATION   Which should a grantor use, a GRAT or a GRUT? Generally, a GRAT should be used for property that will produce a reliable income stream, such as a high-end rental property. On the other hand, a GRUT might be a better choice for a portfolio of speculative or growth stocks, where a reliable cash flow is not assured.

¶14,019   Minority Discount Strategies for Family-Held Businesses

In valuing property for estate tax purposes, certain assets such as real estate or publicly-traded securities are relatively easy to value since there is a ready market of buyers and sellers for the property. Such is not the case with closely-held companies, since only a few people own them and those owners are frequently family members who do not regularly sell or trade the shares.

In recent years, taxpayers have won victories in the courts in valuing closely held stock by applying a "**minority discount**." This valuation rests on the simple theory that the sum of the fractional shares of a business does not necessarily equal the whole. A person with a minority interest has little or no control over the business, and a minority shareholder (or partner) also has little or no say about whether dividends are declared, how cash flows are distributed, or whether the company should be sold or liquidated. Thus, for example, if the total assets of a company were valued at $12 million, it does not follow that a decedent's one-third share in this business should be automatically valued at $4 million. In this case, a Court might approve a valuation "discount" of around 25 to 30 percent from the $4 million. In some cases, minority discounts up to 40 percent have been allowed.

OBSERVATION   Owners of closely-held businesses can increase the benefits of discounting by gifting interests in the closely-held business during lifetime to their children or other family members. As the owner's interest dropped below 50 percent, the "minority discounts" would be taken to reduce the valuations of the gifts. (Even when the interest was above 50 percent, a discount may be available for "lack of marketability" of the closely-held stock; see the discussion below.) Then, when the owner died, his or her interest in the business would also be a minority interest, thus generating more discount.

.01   MINORITY DISCOUNTS: A HISTORICAL PERSPECTIVE

One of the earliest cases to apply a minority discount was *Hooper*.[6] Noting that there were no recent sales of the closely-held family stock, and that the decedent controlled only one third of the shares, the Court stated that minority stock interests in a "closed" corporation are usually worth much less than the proportionate share of the assets to which they attach.

But what if the remaining shares of the closely-held business were held by close family members of the decedent? Could the IRS argue that the decedent could have "controlled" the votes of the close family members, and thus he or she really controlled a majority interest, rather than a minority interest? In one of the first cases on this issue, *Blanchard*,

---

[6]   *Hooper*, 41 BTA 114.

a taxpayer owned 1,048 of the 2,000 outstanding shares of a closely-held bank.[7] The taxpayer subsequently transferred 458 shares to six trusts in equal shares for the benefit of her grandchildren. Three weeks after the transfer, all 1,048 shares of the family were purchased by an unrelated party. The IRS contended that the gift of the 458 shares should not be discounted, since the "family" controlled all 1,048 shares (and obviously, they had knowledge of the impending sale). In this case, the Court sided with the IRS, noting that the gift transfer could not be divorced from the subsequent sale.

The IRS did not continue its success on this issue after the *Blanchard* decision, as the sale three weeks after the transfer was the key fact that produced a victory in that case. In subsequent cases, where there was no subsequent sale of the gifted interest, the Service generally failed to convince the courts that a "family attribution" rule should apply. However, the Service developed a more aggressive approach by arguing that if a donor transfers shares of a closely-held company to family members, the family essentially retains control of the stock and therefore a *premium* should be applied, not a discount!

One of the first cases in which the IRS tried to apply the premium theory was *Bright Estate*.[8] In this case, the decedent and her husband owned 55 percent of a closely-held company as community property. When she died, the IRS contented that a control premium should be applied to the value of the stock. Relying on the recent cases rejecting the stock attribution theory, the Fifth Circuit permitted a discount, noting that any attribution rule was inconsistent with a "willing-buyer, willing-seller" rule.

In a later case, *Ward*,[9] a husband and wife each owned 43.7 percent of the stock of a closely-held corporation. Each of them made gifts of minority interests to their three children. The IRS argued that the Wards "controlled" the corporation, and that no minority discounts should apply (but a premium should apply). The Courts sided with the estate, once again referring to the lack of consideration of a willing buyer and a willing seller. Following this loss, the IRS acquiesced to the *Ward* decision in *Rev. Rul, 93-12*,[10] announcing that they would no longer automatically apply family stock attribution rules in order to aggregate the shares owned by a family and value them as a controlling block of stock.

.03 CURRENT IRS STRATEGIES USED TO BLOCK MINORITY DISCOUNTS

Following the issuance of *Rev. Rul. 93-12*, planners have become more aggressive in arguing for even larger minority discounts. The Service continues to oppose such adjustments under various theories, such as "swing votes." For example, if in a closely-held business A owns 49 percent of the shares, B owns 49 percent of the shares, and C owns the remaining 2 percent of the shares, C has enough votes to "swing control" to one of the other two shareholders simply by selling the stock to him or her. Thus, the IRS would argue that the value of the two percent interest should not be discounted on a transfer. The service has had some success with these arguments.[11]

The Service has also attempted to apply a "step transaction doctrine" to disallow minority discounts. Under this strategy, the IRS would argue that several successive transfers in a very short period of time to the same donee should be collapsed into one transaction. In effect, the series of transfers is viewed as a tax-avoidance scheme solely to create a minority discount. For example, see *Driver*,[12] where transfers within days of one another to convert a majority interest into a minority interest were collapsed and the minority discount was disallowed.

---

[7] *Blanchard*, DC Iowa, 68-2 USTC ¶12,567, 291 F.Supp. 348.
[8] *Bright Estate*, CA-5, 81-2 USTC ¶13,436, 658 F.2d. 999.
[9] *Ward*, 87 TC 78.
[10] Rev. Rul, 93-12, 1993-1 CB 202.
[11] *See Estate of Winkler*, 57 TCM 373, TC Memo. 1989-231.
[12] *Driver*, DC Wis., 76-2 USTC 13,155.

A variation of the "step transaction doctrine" is a deathbed transfer of stock so that the stock owned at death would be a minority interest. For example, in *Murphy*,[13] a donor made a gift of .88 percent of her stock interest to each of her children 18 days before her death based on the advice of her tax advisor. These transfers reduced her holdings to 49.65 percent of the stock, which was transferred to a trust at her death. The Court denied the minority discount because the gift transfers were obviously in "contemplation of death."

.05   JUSTIFICATIONS FOR MINORITY DISCOUNTS

Despite these attempts by the IRS to control minority discounts, it appears that they are here to stay. Taxpayers have developed numerous rationales to justify a minority discount. These include:

- the stock is not registered for public sale
- the sale of stock is subject to SEC restrictions
- lack of marketability of the stock
- lack of voting rights

In an interesting twist, taxpayers have also argued that a minority discount should be allowed for the possibility that the hypothetical purchaser will sell the property later and such sale will be subject to capital gains taxes. These "built-in capital gains" could be caused, for example, if the property was potentially subject to a forced sale to a government authority later through eminent domain laws. This was the case in *Estate of P. Welch*,[14] where the city was contemplating eminent domain proceedings on real estate of a corporation subject to an estate transfer. In this case, the IRS argued that the taxpayer could always reinvest the proceeds tax-free under Code Sec. 1033, and a discount should not apply. The case was remanded back to the Tax Court for additional facts, following the IRS acquiescence in *I. Eisenberg*,[15] on a similar built-in gains issue (see below).

OBSERVATION   The minority discount procedure can also be used with a GRAT to achieve further tax savings. For example, the owner's retained interest could be a minority interest after a program of lifetime giving to his or her children. That reduced value would then be used in the GRAT computations to compute the value of the retained annuity interest and the remainder interest, both of which would be valued lower because of the initial application of the minority interest technique.

.07   LACK OF MARKETABILITY AS A BASIS FOR DISCOUNTS

In the discussion thus far, it has been assumed that the interest being transferred was a minority interest. However, a discount may apply to the transfer of a majority interest, if there is a lack of marketability for the interest. Such a discount can be justified because of an absence of willing buyers. The fact that stock is not actively traded does not necessarily mean that it has no fair market value, but that factor does affect its value.

For example, the Tax Court permitted a discount on a decedent's 94-percent interest in a corporation for estate tax purposes.[16] The Court noted that the decedent's controlling power to liquidate and sell the assets piecemeal was irrelevant to the issue of marketability because of the difficulty in finding a purchaser for the stock. Of much more relevance in the Court's view was the fact that willing purchasers would have preferred to buy the corporation's assets, rather than the underlying stock, so as to avoid any contingent or undisclosed liabilities of the corporation.

---

[13] *Estate of Murphy*, 60 TCM 645, TC Memo. 1990-472.
[14] *Estate of Welch*, CA-6, 2000-1 USTC 60,372.
[15] *Eisenberg*, CA-2, 98-2 USTC 60,322, 155 F3d 50.
[16] *See Estate of Andrews*, 79 TC 938.

The issue of a "built-in capital gains tax" has surfaced in the case of a majority owner of a business as well. In *I. Eisenberg*, the Second Circuit Court permitted a reduction in gift tax value for the potential capital gains tax that might be incurred if the corporation liquidated and sold its sole asset.[17] Even though the transaction was not contemplated by potential buyers, the Court said that this factor could affect the amount the potential buyer would be willing to pay.

> **OBSERVATION**
>
> It is important to remember that many of the issues that arise regarding minority discounts and marketability discounts in regards to partnerships are based on legal interpretations of the partnership agreement, rather than simple valuation questions. And these are questions that should be answered by attorneys in the valuation process, and not the CPA or the valuation expert. For an excellent summary of the process of valuing FLPs, see Linda B. Trugman, *"The Valuation of FLPs: What Does the Tax Practitioner Need to Know?"* **The Tax Adviser**, Vol. 41, No. 1 (January, 2010), pp. 38-45.

¶14,021   The Limited Partnership as an Estate Planning Tool

The concept of minority discounts applies to all types of entities, and not just closely-held corporations. One of the more popular entities used in recent years to effect transfer tax savings is the **family limited partnership (FLP)**.

.01   TAX BENEFITS OF AN FLP

In a typical FLP, a donor with business interests would form a limited partnership, transferring assets in exchange for both general and limited partnership units. (Because the entity is a partnership, at least one other family member, perhaps the donor's spouse, must also contribute assets in exchange for partnership units.) The general partnership units, traditionally a small fraction of ownership, are retained by the donor for control purposes.

The donor would then begin gifting the limited partnership interests to his or her children annually, utilizing the annual exclusion. And since the donor is transferring minority interests in a largely unmarketable entity, he or she should be able to take advantage of minority and lack of marketability discounts on these transfers. Given the tax stakes involved, the discounts should be supported by qualified appraisals or valuation reports. Finally, upon the donor's death, the donor's interest in the partnership may qualify for discount due to a lack of marketability or a minority interest.

> **OBSERVATION**
>
> In order to qualify the gifts for the annual exclusion, the limited partners must have the immediate use, possession, and enjoyment of the partnership, including the right to sell the interest at any time. However, the partner or partnership can retain a right of first refusal on a sale without disqualifying the "present interest" aspects of the transfers. The donor (general partner) would still control the timing and amount of the distributions to the limited partners as long as such decisions reflect the reasonable business needs of the partnership and the fiduciary duties to other limited partners are met.

FLPs can also be combined with a GRAT to achieve further tax savings. The donor could contribute his or her interest in the FLP to a GRAT in return for an annuity. A general lack of marketability of the partnership interest may justify discounts on this transfer as well.

---

[17] *Eisenberg*, 155 F3d 50.

.03   IRS ATTACKS ON FLPs

The IRS has mounted a serious attack against the use of FLPs, and one of President Clinton's budgets proposed elimination of valuation discounts altogether. Given this environment, FLPs are not for the faint-hearted. Among the weapons used by the IRS in this assault on FLPs have been (1) a lack of business purpose, (2) a failure to respect the partnership form, (3) a step-transaction, single testamentary theory, and (4) disqualification under Code Sec. 2036. Each is discussed briefly below.

Lack of business purpose. In some cases, the Service has argued that the FLP serves no business purpose and should be ignored for gift and estate tax purposes. If the Service is successful with this argument, the underlying business assets would be valued at fair market value for gift and estate tax purposes. This argument might be used to deny minority discounts for placing investment assets such as marketable securities into a partnership. What business purpose is served by that transfer, other than to obtain minority discounts? For example, in *Estate of Albert Strangi*, the Court, while not invalidating the FLP, agreed with the IRS's lack of business purpose argument to reduce the allowed discount.[18]

Failure to Respect the Partnership Form. A concept related to the business purpose test is the fundamental principle that if assets are placed into a partnership, then the partnership format should be respected. For example, commingling the general partner's assets with partnership assets would not be characteristic of a business-oriented partnership, and the IRS will likely use such a circumstance as evidence of a lack of business purpose. If the general partner continues to use and enjoy the assets transferred to an FLP, then the IRS would argue that such assets should be included in the transferor's estate under either Code Sec. 2036 (Transfers With a Retained Life Estate) or Code Sec. 2038 (Revocable Transfers). For the same reasons, personal assets such as a personal residence should never be transferred to an FLP.

Step-Transaction, Single Testamentary Theory. Under this theory, the IRS would argue that the formation of a partnership interest followed closely by a subsequent disposition of the interest should be combined and treated as though there was a single testamentary transfer through the estate. In effect, the partnership would be ignored for valuation purposes. For example, the IRS won with this theory in *Estate of Elizabeth B. Murphy*,[19] when the partnership formation was close in time to the grantor's death. But as the steps become "old and cold," it is questionable as to whether or not this theory would withstand scrutiny.

Disqualification Under Code Sec. 2036. Code Sec. 2036(a) reads as follows:

Abstract—Code Sec. 2036(a)

(a) General rule. – The value of the gross estate shall include the value of all property to the extent of any interest therein of which the decedent has at any time made a transfer (except in case of a bona fide sale for an adequate and full consideration in money or money's worth), by trust or otherwise, under which he has retained for his life or for any period not ascertainable without reference to his death of for any period which does not in fact end before his death –

(1)   the possession or enjoyment of, or the right to the income from the property, or

(2)   the right, either alone or in conjunction with any person, to designate the persons who shall possess or enjoy the property or the income therefrom.

To avoid the application of Code Sec. 2036(a), an estate must show that either (1) the decedent transferred the property in a bona fide sale for adequate and full consideration in money or money's worth (the "bona fide sale" exception) or (2) the decedent did not retain the possession or enjoyment of property or retain the right to designate persons who may possess or enjoy the property. Most challenges to FLPs under Code Sec. 2036(a) have been based on the theory that the decedent had retained an interest in the property.

---

[18] *Estate of Strangi*, 85 TCM 1331, TC Memo. 2003-145.
[19] *Estate of Murphy*, 60 TCM 645, TC Memo 1990-472.

In *J. G. Guyun*, the court ruled that Code Sec. 2036(a) applied in a case where there was an implicit agreement that the decedent would retain control or enjoyment of the transferred assets, even though the retained right was not legally enforceable.[20] Circumstances that may indicate the existence of such an implied agreement include:

- A transfer of a majority of the decedent's assets (usually by leaving amounts too small to provide a living for the grantor)
- Continued occupation of the transferred property by the grantor
- Commingling of personal and entity assets
- Use of entity funds for personal expenses
- Testamentary characteristics of the arrangement

The IRS has also had some success in attacking FLPs for the lack of a bona fide sale. For example, in *M.B. Harper Estate*, the decedent had formed an FLP by transferring the property in his revocable living trust; the trust received a 99-percent limited partnership interest in the FLP, and the decedent's son and daughter received .4-percent and .6 -percent interests, respectively, as general partners.[21] The Court ruled that the transfer was not a bona fide sale because the decedent independently formed the FLP, determined how the partnership would be structured and operated, decided what property would be contributed to the FLP, and declared what interest the trust would have therein. When combined with the fact that the decedent had also received disproportionately large distributions from the FLP, the Court stated that the decedent had "stood on both sides of the transaction," there was no bargaining or negotiation of any kind, and therefore there was no legitimate transfer.

Recent court tests of FLPs have produced mixed results. In *Estate of Albert Strangi*,[22] the IRS successfully contended that the decedent had retained sufficient rights to the beneficial enjoyment of FLP assets, and this caused the inclusion in the decedent's estate under Code Sec. 2036(a)(1). On the other hand, taxpayers won a major victory in the Fifth Circuit in *David A. Kimbell, Sr.*[23] In this case, the District Court disallowed a 49-percent discount on the valuation of the decedent's FLP interest, contending that there could not be an arm's length, "bona fide sale" in the original transaction creating the FLP because family members were involved. However, on appeal, the Fifth Circuit noted that such logic would in effect ignore the bona fide sale exception of Code Sec. 2036(a) whenever family assets were transferred to an entity, and that misconstrues Congressional intent.

OBSERVATION In ruling for the taxpayer in *Kimbell*, the Fifth Circuit noted that the lower Court had ignored five objective tests, each of which supported the fact that the transfer to the FLP constituted a bona fide sale. These factors are important, in that they provide a roadmap to a virtual "safe harbor" from a bona fide sale attack by the IRS. They are:

1. The decedent retained sufficient assets outside of the partnership to support herself;
2. Personal and partnership assets were not commingled;
3. All formalities were followed and the contributed assets were actually transferred to the partnership;
4. The contributed assets included oil and gas working interests that required active management (a business reason for the partnership form); and
5. There were valid nontax reasons for the transfer, such as legal protection from creditors, preservation of capital, reduction in administrative costs, and continuity of management.

[20] *Guyun*, CA-4, 71-1 USTC ¶12,742, 437 F2d 1148.
[21] *Estate of Harper*, 83 TCM 1641, TC Memo. 2002-121.
[22] *Estate of Strangi*, 85 TCM 1331, TC Memo. 2003-145.
[23] *Kimbell*, CA-5, 2004-1 USTC ¶60,486, 371 F3d 257.

Many tax professionals suggest that a client engage a personal financial planning specialist to estimate and document the annual income flow the taxpayer should have each year to maintain a desired standard of living. Such documentation may help overcome the first line of attack mentioned above.

¶14,023 Utilizing the Intentionally Defective Irrevocable Trust

A relatively new tool in the estate planner's arsenal is the **Intentionally Defective Irrevocable Trust (IDIT)**. This is not for the faint-hearted, as the technique has not been vetted by the Courts yet. But the strategy works like a GRAT and offers some advantages not available with a GRAT.

In general, the strategy involves setting up an irrevocable trust that is treated as a grantor trust (taxed to the grantor) for income tax purposes only. The basic steps involved may be summarized as follows:

- The grantor creates an irrevocable trust with beneficiaries (such as children) who will ultimately receive the trust assets upon his death.
- The grantor retains certain powers that cause the trust to be "defective" for income tax purposes, and as a result the trust is a grantor trust with all income taxed to the grantor under Code Sec. 691.
- The grantor gifts to the trust a small portion (at least 10 percent of the value) of the property ultimately to be transferred to the trust; this transfer is a taxable gift, and this initial transfer makes the trust economically viable.
- The grantor then sells the remaining appreciating property (such as marketable securities, closely-held business interests, real estate, etc.) to the trust in exchange for an interest-bearing note set at the current Applicable Federal Rate (AFR).
- No gain or loss is recognized on the sale, since it is between the grantor and the grantor trust; for the same reason, the grantor is not taxed on interest income received and the trust may not deduct interest payments.
- Other income earned by the trust will be taxed to the grantor.

The use of the IDIT offers several tax advantages when compared with a GRAT. First, there is little or no gift tax paid on the initial gift to the trust; with a GRAT, gift tax results in many cases. Secondly, the assets sold to the trust are removed from the estate as of the date of sale, so this effectively freezes the value of the assets in the grantor's estate to the fair market value of the promissory note at any time. All appreciation in value of the assets is now for the benefit of the beneficiaries. Recall that if the grantor dies before the term of a GRAT expires, the fair market value of all GRAT property would be brought back into the estate.

While a GRAT requires a fixed schedule of annuity payments, the installment note used in an IDIT offers more flexibility in structuring payments. And since the interest rate on the note of an IDIT is at the AFR, rather than the 120 percent of the AFR as required for GRATS under Code Sec. 7520, more property passes to beneficiaries.

| OBSERVATION | Although the grantor will be taxed on trust income, this does offer one further advantage. Specifically, such tax payments will further reduce the grantor's taxable estate. |

If the property transferred to the IDIT is a closely-held business interest, there is yet another tax advantage gained by using the IDIT. You guessed it—minority and marketability discounts would possibly be available for the transfers of interests, such as limited partnership interests in an FLP. Once again, caution is in order: combining an FLP and an IDIT is a tax parlay that just screams for IRS scrutiny!

Legislative Update

President Obama's 2013 budget proposal included several proposed "fixes" (think *revenue enhancers*) to popular estate planning tools discussed in this chapter. These include (1) imposing a minimum annuity term of ten years for GRATs, (2) disallowing any decline in the annuity, (3) requiring a non-zero remainder interest, and (4) establishing a category of "disallowed actions" that could not be used to allow minority discounts. These proposals would raise approximately $22 billion of revenue over the next ten years. However, to the relief of financial planners everywhere, none of these provisions were included in the 2012 American Taxpayer Relief Act. However, they are still out there and represent one of those handy "off the shelf" items that Congress may activate in attempting major tax reform legislation.

¶14,025　Documenting and Implementing an Estate Plan

In *60 Minute Estate Planner*, author Sandy F. Kraemer notes that every good estate plan requires two steps: (1) documentation and (2) implementation.[24] *Documentation* is defined as the preparation and execution of proper documents. *Implementation* is the process of correctly titling assets, transferring ownership of assets as necessary to achieve tax-planning goals, naming beneficiaries for life insurance, retirement benefits, and other financial arrangements, and various other details. The following case study borrows from some of the suggested documentation and implementation strategies discussed in this book.

The estate planning process can be illustrated by reference to a simple estate planning case. Assume that John and Mary Doe currently have an estate valued at $12,000,000, with $3,000,000 of the property in John's name and $9,000,000 of the property in Mary's name. They would like an estate plan that maximizes the eventual transfer of their properties to their two children, Audrey and Nancy. At the same time, they would like to ensure that after the first spouse dies, the second spouse has sufficient income to live on for the remainder of his or her life.

.01　IMPLEMENTING THE PLAN

Given these facts, a simple estate plan for John and Mary could include the following elements for the implementation phase:

- Mary should transfer enough property to John so that John's total estate, should he die first, is at least the amount of the unified credit exemption equivalent; otherwise, some of John's unified credit will be wasted. However, the DSUEA election can also be used to guarantee that John's unified credit amount will not be lost, although there can be some disadvantages with such an election, as discussed earlier.
- Consider implementing a lifetime gifting program, gifting a minimum of $28,000 each year to each child through gift-splitting elections (this may impact the equalization totals above if each spouse is making such gifts).
- Transfer as many assets as possible into living trusts to avoid probate, and provide in a "pour over" will that property still held at death is swept into the living trust.
- Consider having Mary establish a bypass trust and a marital deduction trust. The bypass trust would provide income to John for life, and pass to the children after John's death. The trust would be includable in Mary's estate, but would be set at the equivalent unified credit amount so that no estate tax would be due. The remaining assets would pass directly to John and qualify for the marital deduction.

---

[24] Sandy F. Kraemer, *60 Minute Estate Planner* (Paramus, New Jersey: Prentice-Hall, Inc., 1994). This work offers an excellent step-by-step guide for developing and implementing gift and estate plans.

.03   DOCUMENTING THE PLAN

The importance of good documentation cannot be overemphasized. Unless the decedent has made his or her wishes clear, someone else, such as the state, will determine the ultimate distribution of certain properties.

Among the many important instruments and documents that the couple should have established, completed, and/or retained are the following:

- Spousal transfer documents to support marital transfers
- A living trust with supporting documents (If John and Mary choose not to use a living trust and the related pour-over will, then a last will and testament must be prepared to provide for an orderly transfer of assets through the probate process)
- A pour-over will to transfer any remaining assets to the trust at death (assuming that a living trust is established)
- A bypass trust for assets passing directly to the children (and thus not qualifying for the marital deduction); this should be set up at a minimum for the exemption equivalent of the unified credit
- Gift tax returns evidencing transfers to children (if greater than the annual exemption)
- A QTIP marital deduction trust for providing income for the surviving spouse and a remainder interest for the children; this would generally be funded so that no estate tax would be due in the estate of the first to die
- Joint ownership documents for any jointly-held property (to avoid probate)
- Signed and up-to-date beneficiary designations on all life insurance policies, pensions, annuity contracts, and other financial arrangements (to avoid probate)
- Durable power of attorney for someone to act for the individual if John or Mary becomes incapacitated
- Medical durable power of attorney for someone to make health care decisions if John or Mary are unable to do so for themselves
- Living will expressing John and Mary's wishes as to being kept alive by machines in certain conditions
- Anatomical gift document if organ donation is desired
- Letters of instruction to help organize the estate and provide vital information and final instructions and communications to heirs

¶14,027   Summary

- A general power of appointment permits the holder to appoint anyone to enjoy the property in question, including the holder of the power; a specific power of appointment permits anyone but the holder of the power to enjoy the property unless an "ascertainable standard" is provided in the trust instrument.
- The typical irrevocable trust arrangement generally provides for an income interest (a life estate) and a remainder interest. The latter is valued first using 120 percent of the applicable federal rate, and the former is the residual after deducting the remainder interest from the fair market value of the trust property.
- A grantor retained income trust (GRIT) is valued under the general remainder interest computation described above, unless the remainder beneficiary is an applicable family member, in which case the retained income interest is valued at zero. An exception applies for certain qualifying personal residence trusts.
- A life insurance trust is a common estate planning tool, and premium payments made by the grantor may qualify for the annual exclusion if the beneficiaries (usually minor children) are given a limited right of withdrawal (often referred to as a "Crummey power").
- A charitable remainder trust is generally structured with a life estate to the grantor and a remainder interest to the charity; a charitable lead trust provides for a life estate to the charity (which qualifies for an annual gift tax exclusion) and a remainder interest to the grantor.

- Grantor retained annuity trusts (GRATs) and grantor retained unitrusts (GRUTs) are common estate planning tools used to "freeze" the underlying value of an estate. If the grantor dies during the term of the trust, the value of the trust property is included in the grantor's estate.
- Estate tax savings occur with a GRAT or GRUT when the annual rate of appreciation for the underlying trust property exceeds the discount rate used to value the remainder interest in the GRAT or GRUT.
- Taxpayers have been fairly successful in applying minority discounts and discounts for lack of marketability to the value of family business property transferred to other family members.
- A family limited partnership (FLP) has become the most popular vehicle for creating transfer tax savings. In such an arrangement, the donor usually retains the general partnership interest for control purposes, and begins gifting limited partnership interests to children annually and takes advantage of the annual gift tax exclusion, minority discounts, and discounts for lack of marketability.
- Arguments used by the IRS to attack FLPs include (1) lack of business purpose, (2) failure to respect the partnership form, (3) step-transaction doctrine, and (4) disqualification under Code Sec. 2036(a).
- Every successful estate plan requires good documentation and implementation

Appendix A

Estate and Trust Income Tax Rate Schedules—2013

If taxable income is:	The tax is:
Not over $2,450	15% of taxable income
Over $2,450 but not over $5,700	$367.50, plus 25% of the excess over $2,450
Over $5,700 but not over $8,750	$1,180.00, plus 28% of the excess over $5,700
Over $8,750 but not over $11,950	$2,034.00, plus 33% of the excess over $8,759
Over $11,950	$3,090.00, plus 39.6% of the excess over $11,950

Appendix B

Selected Partial Actuarial Values (IRS Publication 1457)

Table S
Single Life Factors Based on Life Table 90CM 8%

Age	Annuity	Life Estate	Remainder
50	10.4515	.83612	.16388
51	10.3407	.82725	.17275
52	10.2256	.81804	.18196
53	10.1061	.80849	.19151
54	9.9824	.79860	.20140

Table B
Annuity, Income, and Remainder Interests for a Term Certain 7.2%

Years	Annuity	Life Estate	Remainder
6	4.7373	.341082	.658918
7	5.3519	.385338	.614662
8	5.9253	.426621	.573379
9	6.4602	.465132	.534868
10	6.9591	.501056	,498944

Table 90CM Mortality Table

Age x	Lx	Age x	Lx	Age x	Lx
67	76,531	72	67,344	77	55,373
68	74,907	73	65,154	78	52,704
69	73,186	74	62,852	79	49,943
70	71,357	75	60,449	80	47,084
71	69,411	76	57,955	81	44,129

Review Questions for Chapter 14

True or False
Indicate which of the following statements are true or false by circling the correct answer.

1. Since trust tax rates are so steep, the objective in many cases is to shift income taxation to beneficiaries. T F

2. A limited power of appointment over trust property allows the holder to appoint anyone to enjoy the property, including himself or herself. T F

3. One possible advantage of a revocable trust is that the trust will be included in the probate estate. T F

4. Chapter 12 of the Internal Revenue Code was enacted to deal with the problem of "estate freezes." T F

5. A self-cancelling note between a father and his daughter should generally provide for an interest rate or sales price that is higher than would be the case if the sale was to an outside third party. T F

6. Minority discounts will not be successful if taken on transfers between family members. T F

7. GRATs are generally successful if the rate of appreciation on the transferred property exceeds the interest rate used to value the GRAT. T F

8. A charitable lead trust provides for an income interest to the charity. T F

9. Commingling business and personal assets in a family limited partnership may void any minority discount taken. T F

10. Potential capital gains taxes on a later sale of a business interest may justify a discount on the transfer price. T F

Fill in the Blanks
Fill in each blank with the appropriate word or phrase that completes each sentence.

11. A(n) _____ power of appointment trust allows the holder to appoint anyone to enjoy the property, other than the holder himself or herself.
12. A lapse of a general power of appointment is subject to the gift tax if the value of the property exceeds the greater of $_____ or _____ percent of the aggregate value of the underlying property.
13. A(n) _____ trust is one in which the transferor has retained the power to terminate the trust.
14. A transfer of the power to revoke a trust will not remove the underlying property from the original trust creator's estate unless he or she survives more than _____ years after the transfer of such power.
15. A(n) "_____ power" clause in an insurance trust set up for a minor may qualify the annual premium payments made by the donor for the gift tax annual exclusion.
16. In a charitable _____ trust arrangement, a grantor makes a gift to a charity now, but reserves for himself or herself the income from the gifted property for life.
17. The value of a retained income interest in a grantor retained income trust will be zero if the remainder interest is left to a(n) _____.
18. In a grantor retained annuity trust, the annuity amount to be paid to the grantor can be expressed as either a fixed dollar amount or a(n) _____ of the initial value of the trust.
19. In a(n) _____ trust, the donor deliberately structures the trust so that the trust income is taxed to the donor himself or herself.

20. The amount paid to a grantor each year from a(n) _____ trust is based on a percentage of the current fair market value of trust assets at the beginning of each year.

Multiple Choice

Circle the best answer for each of the following questions.

21. A holder of a general power of appointment over property will
    a. have such property included in his or her estate at death
    b. be taxed on the income from such property
    c. have a taxable gift if he or she exercises the power in favor of someone else
    d. all of the above.

22. An "ascertainable standard" in a trust instrument allowed the holder of a specific power of appointment to consume or invade the property for his or her own benefit. Which of the following may be a qualifying use for such a standard?
    a. the comfort of the holder
    b. the welfare of the holder
    c. the education of the holder
    d. none of the above

23. In valuing the income and remainder interest of a trust, the general procedure is to
    a. value the income interest first, and subtract this from the fair market value of the property in order to determine the remainder interest.
    b. value the remainder interest first, and subtract this from the fair market value of the property in order to determine the income interest.
    c. value both interests simultaneously
    d. none of the above

24. Rod Posey sold land to his daughter Alicia by using a 20-year self-cancelling note (i.e., if Rod dies before all payments are collected, the remaining payments are cancelled). In this case, the accumulated income that has not been reported as of the date of death will be taxable to
    a. Rod on his final income tax return
    b. Alicia on her tax return
    c. Rod's estate on Form 1041
    d. None of the above

25. Which of the following is not a typical trust arrangement aimed at "freezing" an estate?
    a. a GRIT
    b. a GROUT
    c. a GRAT
    d. a GRUT

26. A grantor retained income trust will be includible in the grantor's gross estate under Code Sec. 2036(a) if
    a. the grantor dies anytime before the termination of the income interest
    b. the grantor dies within five years of the original transfer
    c. the grantor remarries during the terms of the trust
    d. none of the above

27. The remainder interest in a grantor retained income trust will not be zero if
    a. the remainder beneficiary is a nephew
    b. the trust is a personal residence trust
    c. the remainder beneficiary is the grantor's spouse
    d. a and b only

28. Taxpayers who gift ownership interests in closely-held businesses often "discount" the fair market value of such interests due to
    a. lack of marketability of the interests
    b. transfer of a minority interest only
    c. either a or b
    d. none of the above

29. Which of the following is not among the weapons used by the IRS to attack the validity of a family limited partnership?
    a. step-transaction, single testamentary theory
    b. lack of a business purpose
    c. a sale of a partnership interest to a non-family member
    d. all have been used to attack such arrangements

30. Which of the following factors was identified in the *Kimbell* case as being indicative of a bona fide sale that would pass muster under Code Sec. 2036A?
    a. valid nontax reasons existed for the transfer, such as protection from creditors
    b. personal and partnership assets were not commingled
    c. grantor retained sufficient assets outside of the trust to support herself
    d. all of the above

Review Problems

31. Duke Anders transfers $800,000 to an irrevocable trust. Under the terms of the transfer, Duke's friend Mason (currently age 35) will receive an income interest for the remainder of his life, and then the corpus of the trust (the remainder) passes to Jennifer who is not related to Duke. At the time of the transfer, 120 percent of the AFR rate was 7.0 percent, yielding a present value factor of .09155. What are the gift tax consequences associated with the transfer?

32. Assume the same facts as Problem 31, except that Duke retains an income interest in the property for himself, rather than for Mason. What are the gift tax and estate tax consequences associated with the transfer? Duke is currently 35 years old.

33. Assume the same facts as Problem 31, except that Jennifer is Duke's daughter. What are the gift tax consequences associated with the transfer.

34. "A life insurance trust may provide a higher rate of return than many other investments set up for children." Do you agree? Explain.

35. Tony Joe White set up an insurance trust in 2013, and First Bank agreed to act as trustee. The beneficiary of the policy was Tony's daughter Michelle, age 17. The trust was set up to ensure an annual exclusion for benefit payments by notifying Michelle within 5 days of a contribution and providing 30 days to her to withdraw the contribution. In four different months since the trust was created, the bank forgot to enter the trust contribution on the books and notify Michelle, and in three other months Michelle was only given four days to make a withdrawal. Will the premium payments qualify for the annual exclusion?

36. Life insurance proceeds will be included in the estate if such proceeds are payable to the estate or are available to pay taxes, debts or other expenses or charges of the insured's estate. Given this fact, how can a life insurance trust help provide liquidity to the estate and yet avoid inclusion in the taxable estate?

37. Mike Hagen likes the potential tax savings of setting up a charitable remainder trust, but he is concerned that the stock that will be sold to fund the trust will no longer be available for his children to inherit. Can you suggest a possible strategy for Mike that would alleviate this concern?

38. What are the potential tax and non-tax benefits of establishing a charitable lead trust? Explain.

39. In a "pre-anti-freeze" world, explain and illustrate with an example the structure of a typical estate freeze strategy.

40. Anderson Looper, age 78, desires to establish a grantor retained income trust that has a term of 10 years. Do you foresee any problems with this strategy? Explain.

41. Jane Ishee owns a 70-percent interest in a closely-held corporation whose only asset consists of marketable securities in publicly-traded corporations. If Jane gifts these shares to her daughter, could she justify a marketability discount? Explain.

42. Explain the use of a family limited partnership as an estate planning tool. Include in your explanation the common steps used by the family in achieving their objectives.

43. Explain in general terms how an intentionally defective trust arrangement works, and why such an arrangement offers several advantages over a GRAT.

44. Determine the marital deduction (if any) for Martha Burke's estate under each of the following scenarios:
    a. Martha's will provides that $1,000,000 of her estate will pass to a trust, with an income interest to her husband Hootie for life and the remainder interest to pass to their son Arnold after Hootie's death.
    b. Assume the same facts as the previous example, except that Hootie is given a general power of appointment over the trust property.
    c. Assume the same facts as the previous example, except that Hootie is not granted a general power of appointment over the property. Rather, the executor of Martha's estate makes a QTIP election. Hootie will receive a life income interest from the property, but the property will pass automatically to their son Arnold after Hootie's death.

Research Questions

45. Describe the tax issues and court decision in the case of *L. Maxwell Est.,* CA-2, 3 F3d 591. Aff'g 98 TC 594, Dec. 48,212.

46. Betty and Alexander Nellis resided in the community property state of California. When Alexander died, he left a "Last Will And Testament" by which he intended to dispose of both his and Betty's interest in their community property. Under Alexander's will, Betty had the option to reject the will and receive only her share of the community property, or to transfer her portion of the community property into a trust consisting of the community property of both spouses from which she would receive all the income for life. Betty elected the latter. Approximately 15 months after making her election Betty died. Her son George, as executor, filed an estate tax return. The return referred to the trust established under Alexander's will, but it did not include any of the trust assets within Betty's taxable estate. Should the value of the property Betty contributed to the estate be included in her estate under Code Sec. 2036(a)? Explain.

47. A court has determined that a trust should be included in the decedent's estate because it was part of an incomplete transfer. Will the gross estate also include the accumulation of income on the trust assets? Explain.

Tax Planning Questions

48. The choice between establishing a charitable remainder trust and a charitable lead trust is sometimes influenced by the current interest rates. Explain the possible consequences if (1) current interest rates are high, and (2) current interest rates are low.

49. Explain the tax planning and "estate freezing" advantages of Jill Ward selling real estate to her son Mike through the use of a 20-year installment note. What are the gift, estate and income tax consequences associated with such a sale? What happens if Jill dies after collecting four annual payments, and (1) the note is willed to her daughter Ellen, or (2) the note is cancelled upon Jill's death?

50. Rita Jennings owns various investments in stocks, bonds, and rental properties. She wants to transfer the stocks to an FLP and take advantage of minority discounts. What advice might you give Rita to lessen the odds of having problems with the IRS later?

51. Refer to the text website (at www.CCHGroup.com/ContemporaryTax), and work the Case Study on GRATS that uses the Excel spreadsheet illustrated in this chapter.

Tax Compliance Question

52. Prepare hypothetical gift tax returns for the first year of implementing the suggested estate plan of Maynard and Meg Doe, discussed in the following case study at the end of the chapter. The returns should reflect gift-splitting and any intra-spousal transfers as well.

Case Study

53. Meg owns and operates a plastics manufacturing company, and Maynard is a teacher. Maynard and Meg's principal asset is stock in the family business (Meg owns 80 percent of the stock, and Maynard owns the other 20 percent); the business was recently appraised at $7.2 million. They have about $1 million of other assets, all jointly held. Meg has four children from a previous marriage: Tom (age 26, a lawyer), Martha (age 24, a manager in the family business), and twins Hal and Al, both college students age 20. Both Martha and Hal have indicated an interest in continuing the family business.

Neither Maynard nor Meg has made any lifetime transfers. They desire for their children to inherit all of their properties eventually. Since Meg is 10 years older than Maynard, she would like to ensure that Maynard has enough income to live on should he survive her, and she also would like to ensure that her children receive the entire estate after he dies. They would also eventually like to leave a gift of approximately $500,000 to State University to fund a scholarship program.

Assume that you have been asked to assist Maynard and Meg establish a family financial plan that would accomplish their wishes. List the basic steps that you would suggest that Maynard and Meg take in order to accomplish their wishes.

CHAPTER 15

Business Planning—Choice of Entity

Learning Objectives

1. Define a "business entity," and distinguish taxable, conduit, and not-for-profit entities.
2. Explain the "check the box" regulations as they relate to the choice of entity decision.
3. Compare the payroll tax computations and tax payment procedures for a self-employed individual and a corporate entity.
4. Distinguish the major tax and nontax advantages and disadvantages of the sole-proprietorship as a business entity.
5. Distinguish the major tax and nontax advantages and disadvantages of the partnership as a business entity.
6. Describe the major characteristics of a limited liability company (LLC) and a limited liability partnership (LLP).
7. Distinguish the major tax and nontax advantages and disadvantages of the S corporation as a business entity.
8. Distinguish the major tax and nontax advantages and disadvantages of the regular C corporation as a business entity.
9. Explain the concept of double taxation as it relates to (1) corporate distributions and (2) corporate liquidations.

¶15,001 Introduction

The **choice of entity** decision is one of the most important decisions facing tax professionals and their clients who own and operate businesses. There are several forms to choose from, each of which generates different legal and tax consequences. There is no single form of entity that is appropriate for every type of business owner or entity that a practitioner is likely to encounter.

Choosing the appropriate form of entity in which to operate is a complex decision. It depends upon many non-tax factors, including the owners' needs and desires and the particular characteristics and needs of the business in question. The federal tax consequences of each type of entity also play an important role, especially in closely held entities where the parties' combined tax liabilities should be analyzed as part of the decision-making process.

The purpose of this chapter is to review the key tax and non-tax factors involved in the choice of business entity. The major entity types reviewed are the sole proprietorship, the partnership (with special emphasis on limited liability entities), the S corporation, and the regular C corporation. A comprehensive case study is used to demonstrate the tax regime of each legal entity by using the same set of case facts.

The discussion of each entity also includes a summary of the key non-tax factors that should be considered for each type of entity. The chapter concludes with an examination of the tax consequences associated with a disposition of each entity type; this analysis extends the case study for several years into the future and assumes a sale of the business entity five years after formation.

¶15,003   Business Entities: An Introduction

.01   BUSINESS ENTITY DEFINED

A **business entity** carries on a trade or business. In order to do that, it must have: one or more associates, assets, and engage in some business activity. In *R.P. Groetzinger*, the U.S. Supreme Court noted the Code's "common-sense" concept of what constitutes a trade or business, noting that all the facts of a particular situation must be examined.[1]

Under *Groetzinger*, a taxpayer is engaged in a trade or business if the taxpayer is involved in the activity (1) with continuity and regularity, and (2) with the primary purpose of making income or a profit. A sporadic activity, a hobby, or an amusement diversion does not qualify as a business. Taxpayers who pursue an activity full-time, in good faith and with regularity, that produces income and that is not merely a hobby, are engaged in a trade or business.

.03   TYPES OF BUSINESS ENTITIES

One of the first decisions a business owner must make in setting up a business is the legal or tax entity to operate the business enterprise (the atom or unit of taxability). This is an important decision that affects the tax treatment given to subsequent business transactions. The entity is responsible for keeping separate records and reporting the results of operations to the taxing authority. Under the current U.S. taxation system, an entity can be classified as taxable, conduit, or tax-exempt.

Taxable entities are liable for the payment of tax on income. A taxable entity is any "person" as defined in Code Sec. 7701(a). Taxable business entities include the individual (doing business as a sole proprietorship), the regular C corporation, and some estates and trusts. We will limit our discussion of taxable business entities to individuals and corporations since these two are the dominant business entities.

Conduit entities are nontaxable reporting entities. All conduit entities are owned by one or more taxable entities. The income, deductions, losses, credits, and other tax attributes of conduit entities flow through to the tax returns of its owners. The two principal conduit entities are: the S corporation and the partnership. Both of these types of entities are examined in this chapter.

---

[1]   *Groetzinger*, SCt, 87-1 USTC ¶9191, 480 US 23, 107 SCt 980.

Not-For-Profit (NFP) entities are nontaxable reporting entities that have been organized to carry on a tax-exempt purpose. An NFP entity must apply for and receive tax-exempt status from the IRS. Most churches and civic associations are organized as NFPs. Many organizations organized for educational, scientific, or literary purposes apply for and are granted tax-exempt status. Some NFP entities also qualify as charitable organizations under Code Sec. 501(c)(3) so that donations to these organizations may be deductible as a charitable contribution. While NFP entities are occasionally taxed on their unrelated business income under the Unrelated Business Income Tax (UBIT), the taxation of NFPs is beyond the scope of this chapter and will not be discussed further. Refer to Chapter 8 for a brief introduction to tax-exempt entities and the UBIT in the discussion of *U.S. vs. American College of Physicians*.[2]

Taxable Entities: A Few Statistics

Based on IRS data, over 20 million businesses generate almost $13 trillion annually and report profits in excess of $500 billion. The most popular form of doing business is the sole proprietorship, followed by the regular C corporation, the S corporation, and lastly the partnership. As Limited Liability Companies (LLCs) become more popular, the number of partnerships is likely to surpass the S corporations.

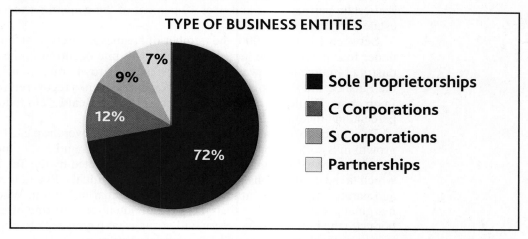

TYPE OF BUSINESS ENTITIES

- ■ Sole Proprietorships
- ■ C Corporations
- ■ S Corporations
- ☐ Partnerships

While sole proprietorships dominate the number of business entities, over one-half of the net business income is reported by regular C corporations, followed by partnerships, sole proprietorships, and lastly S corporations. Approximately four million corporate tax returns are filed annually, including over 1.7 million S corporations. Fewer than 67,000 consolidated returns are filed. Collectively, corporations own approximately $20 trillion in assets, generate almost $12 trillion in revenues and pay over $130 billion in federal income tax a year.

---

[2] *American College of Physicians*, 86-1 USTC ¶9339, 475 US 834, 106 SCt 1591.

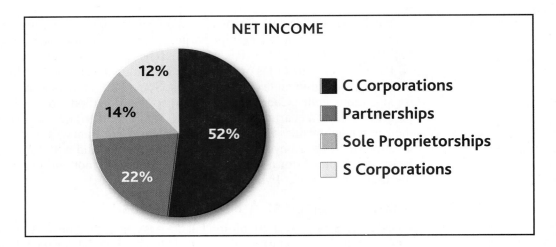

NET INCOME

There are approximately 1.5 million partnerships in the United States. Over 80 percent are general partnerships and fewer than 20 percent are limited partnerships. The real estate industry dominates all industrial groups. Over 62 percent of the limited partnerships are real estate partnerships, and over 40 percent of the general partnership returns are real estate partnerships.

Between 1980 and 2000, the number of businesses grew at an annualized rate of just under four percent. The largest annual growth rate occurred in the Communication industry (11 percent). However, the largest annual growth rates in net income occurred in the Finance and Banking industry (25 percent) as banks recovered from the Savings and Loan crisis. While the number of businesses in the Real Estate industry grew by over 2 percent, net income fell over 27 percent.

The number of corporations has increased steadily over the past 10 years. However, the growth in S corporations has outpaced the growth of regular C corporations since 1986. This is attributed to significant tax law changes enacted by the Tax Reform Act of 1986 which taxed corporations less favorably than individuals. Recall that both S corporation and partnership income are taxed on the individual tax return. When the top corporate marginal tax rate is higher than the top individual rate, shifting of income from the corporate to the individual tax return will occur as taxpayers seek to minimize their total tax liabilities by shifting income between related entities.

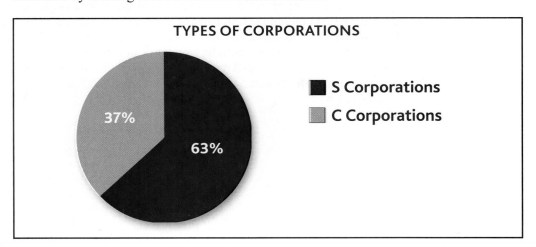

TYPES OF CORPORATIONS

¶15,005   Importance of the Choice of Entity Decision

.01   TAX ENTITY POSSIBILITIES

When a trade or business will be operated in a form other than the sole proprietorship, such as when there are two or more owners, the choice of entity decision requires a comparative assessment of these forms of business entities:

- Regular or "C" corporation;
- S corporation;
- Limited liability company; and
- General or limited partnership.

Performing this assessment requires an understanding of not only the major tax and non-tax aspects of each form of business, but also of how the comparative advantages and disadvantages of each relate to the needs of a specific client. Often, the decision revolves around two basic questions:

1. To what extent do the owners want to limit their personal liability for the debts and liabilities of the business?
2. Do the owners want the business to be taxed as a separate legal entity, or do they want the items of income, deduction, loss, and credit to "pass through" to them?

The following discussion examines the formation, operation, and liquidation of the four basic tax entities: sole proprietorship, partnership, S corporation, and C corporation. In general, limited liability companies and limited partnerships are taxed the same as regular partnerships, although a few differences exist. The limited liability company and limited liability partnership possibilities are discussed after the four basic forms.

.03   CHOICE OF ENTITY: THE "CHECK THE BOX" REGULATIONS

Prior to 1997, there was much confusion as to the circumstances that would cause an entity to be classified as a corporation. A four-factor test was often used by the IRS, and controversies inevitably arose. This procedure was greatly simplified by the "check the box" regulations issued by the IRS in 1997. Under these rules, if an entity is a separate entity (carrying on an active business) and is an "eligible" entity (certain special company statuses, such as insurance companies, banks, and joint-stock companies do not qualify), the business may choose its status under these rules:

- *If two or more owners.* The entity may elect to be a corporation or a partnership.
- *If one owner.* The entity may elect to be a corporation or elect to disregard the entity (i.e., elect to be treated as a sole proprietor).

If no election is made, the *default election* is specified in the Regulations as the entity offering the best federal income tax treatment. Thus, the default election for an entity with two or more owners is a partnership, and for one owner is a proprietorship.

.05   PAYROLL TAXES: AN IMPORTANT FACTOR IN ENTITY CHOICE

Before examining the income tax regimes of each entity, it is important to understand how payroll tax obligations are met for each type of entity. For this reason, **Figures 1 and 2** provide a review of the basic rules for the FICA taxes of employees and the self-employed taxes of sole proprietors and general partners.

In addition to these obligations for Social Security and Medicare taxes, an employer with more than one employee must also pay taxes under federal and state unemployment tax acts (usually refereed to as FUTA and SUTA taxes, respectively). This tax is imposed on the employer, and applies to the first $7,000 of wages earned by an employee during the year. Technically, the FUTA rate is 6.2 (or 6.0) percent, but this can be reduced in most states to .8 percent with a credit of up to 5.4 percent for state tax experience.

For simplicity, the following discussion will assume that the employer pays a full 6.2-percent tax in combined FUTA and SUTA taxes on the first $7,000 of income earned by each employee. Note that in some entities, owners are not employees and in other entities they are employees.

There is one additional payroll tax to worry about in 2013. For taxpayers receiving salary, sole proprietorship income, or partnership income and guaranteed payments, an additional 0.9% medicare tax applies to such amounts exceeding $200,000 on a single return and $250,000 (each) on a married-filing jointly return. And this is also the year that yet another tax not related to payroll kicks in: the 3.8% tax on net investment incomes, limited to 3.8% of modified adjusted gross income exceeding the same thresholds of $200,000 and $250,000.

Figure 1

FICA Tax and the Self-Employment Tax

FICA Tax Liability:

The FICA tax liability is shared equally by the employer and the employee. The 2013 tax is composed of the following two components and rates:

Social Security Tax: 6.2 percent on the first $113,700 of wages in 2013
Medicare Tax: 1.45 percent on all wages without limit

Since both employer and the employee pay the tax, the total tax collected will be at a 12.4-percent rate for the Social Security tax (6.2% × 2) and a 2.9-percent rate for the Medicare tax (1.45% × 2).

Example 15-1. Tad Was, an employee of Wake Corporation, was paid a salary of $50,000 in 2013. The FICA taxes payable by Wake and Tad in 2013 are as follows:

SS tax withheld from Tad's salary ($50,000 × .062)	$ 3,100
MC tax withheld from Tad's salary ($50,000 × .0145)	725
SS tax paid (matched) by Wake Corporation ($50,000 × .062)	3,100 *
MC tax paid (matched) by Wake Corporation ($50,000 × .0145)	725 *
Total FICA taxes due	$ 7,650

  * Deductible as expenses by Wake Corporation

Note that as long as the employee's salary is less than the FICA social security maximum for the year ($113,700 in 2013), both the employer and the employee will pay in a 7.65-percent share to the government (6.2% + 1.45%), resulting in 15.3 percent (7.65% × 2) of the gross salary being paid as FICA taxes.

Example 15-2. Assume the same facts as Example 15-1, except that Tad was paid a salary of $150,000 in 2013. The FICA taxes payable in 2013 is as follows:

SS tax withheld from Tad's salary ($113,700 × .062)	$ 7,049
MC tax withheld from Tad's salary ($150,000 × .0145)	2,175
SS tax paid (matched) by Wake Corporation ($106,800 × .062)	7,049 *
MC tax paid (matched) by Wake Corporation ($120,000 × .0145)	2,175 *
Total FICA taxes due	$18,448

  * Deductible as expenses by Wake Corporation

Figure 2

Self-Employment Tax Liability

Self-employed individuals and general partners do not have an employer to with-hold FICA taxes; thus, self-employed individuals must compute and pay their self-employment tax liabilities when filing their individual tax returns. The computation is made on Schedule SE, and the tax is added to the regular income tax liability. The self-employed individual must pay both the Social Security and Medicare portions, and the same FICA ceiling of $113,700 applies in 2013.

In order to provide approximately the same tax relief to self-employed individuals as corporations (who can deduct the 7.65-percent total share of FICA taxes that they pay), Congress enacted two special benefits: (1) self-employment income may be reduced by 7.65 percent (or, stated differently, only 92.35 percent of the self-employment income is subject to the tax), and (2) in computing the regular income tax liability, a self-employed person may deduct one-half of the self-employment tax liability as a deduction *for* adjusted gross income. Thus, the self-employment tax in 2013 has two components:

Social Security Tax: [*Lesser* of (a) $113,700 or (b) (SE income × .9235)] × .124
Medicare Tax: SE income × .9235 × .029

Example 15-3. Tad Was is self-employed in 2013, and his Schedule C discloses $50,000 of self-employed income. His self-employment tax liability is as follows:

SS portion: ($50,000 × .9235) × .124	$ 5,726
MC portion: ($50,000 × .9235) × .029	1,339
Total SE tax (added to income tax liability)	$ 7,065 *

    * One-half of this amount, or $3,533, is deductible for AGI for income tax purposes.

Example 15-4. Assume the same facs as Example 15-3, except that Tad's 2013 self-employment income is $150,000. His self-employment tax liability is as follows:

SS portion: $113,700 × .124	$14,099
MC portion: ($150,000 × .9235) × .029	4,017
Total SE tax (added to income tax liability)	$18,116 *

    * One-half of this amount, or $9,058, is deductible for AGI for income tax purposes.

If the self-employed individual also has salary from another source that was subject to FICA taxes, the $113,700 SS tax ceiling for purposes of the SE tax is reduced ac-cordingly. For example, if Tad in Example 15-4 above also received $40,000 salary from another job, only $73,700 ($113,700 − $40,000) would be subject to the SS tax.

OBSERVATION   In 2011 and 2012, Congress reduced the employee's share of the social security tax from 6.2% to 4.2%. This 2% reduction was designed to put more cash in the hands of taxpayers as a way of stimulating demand. However, Congress did not reduce the employer's 6.2% share. To provide parity to self-employed individu-als, the social security portion of the self-employment tax was also reduced 2%, from 12.4% to 10.4%. Although these provisions had some stimulative effect on the economy, Congress decided not to extend the reduction beyond 2012.

Case Study for Comparing the Tax Characteristics of Entities

Appendix B-1 presents a Case Study for taxpayers Dave and Ellen Davidson, illustrating the appropriate tax computations for the same set of facts assuming four different entities: sole proprietorships, partnerships, S corporations and C corporations, each of which is discussed below. In the following discussion, this same set of facts will be recast according to the tax regimes of the particular entity being discussed. The reader should pay particular attention to the tax treatment (if any) of the $50,000 "other payments" to the owner in each case.

In order to make the results roughly comparable, certain simplifying assumptions are made. For example, in the case of the partnership, an assumption is made that Dave Davidson is a 99.9-percent owner, with his wife Ellen owning the other .1 percent. And in the case of the S corporation and C corporation, an assumption is made that Dave is a 100-percent owner. Although the near 100-percent partnership ownership assumption may be somewhat unrealistic, it does provide a point of reference for comparisons to the other taxable entities.

OBSERVATION   Actually, the assumption that Ellen has a small partnership interest may be a realistic one, assuming that she contributed property or services for such interest. If her interest is limited, then her share of the income would not be subject to self-employment taxes and some tax savings would be generated. As discussed below, a limited partner is prohibited from participating in the affairs of the partnership, and thus does not have self-employment income.

The next sections of the chapter examine the non-tax and tax characteristics of the four major types of tax entities. The discussion for each entity concludes with an examination of the computed tax results for that type of entity as based on the facts of the Case Study. The following factors are discussed for each type of entity:
- Formation of the entity
- Ability to raise capital
- Liability issues
- The tax regime
- Payroll taxes of the owner
- Payments to the owner
- Liquidation of the entity

¶15,007   The Sole Proprietorship as a Business Entity

The **sole proprietorship** is the most common type of business entity in the United States. It also is the simplest to organize and to discontinue. No legal formalities are needed because the business and the individual are treated as one entity under tax law. The business owner has total control over all decisions. A sole proprietorship involves a lot less paperwork and expense in starting up the business; obtaining a license from the local government may be all that is required.

.01   FORMATION OF THE SOLE PROPRIETORSHIP

The formation of a sole proprietorship is not a taxable event, as the sole proprietorship entity is not distinguishable from the sole proprietor for tax purposes. The sole proprietor merely acquires assets and starts business; no formal transfer is required. If the sole proprietor uses assets that he or she already owns, then his or her adjusted basis in those assets carries over to the proprietorship.

OBSERVATION   If the property is a depreciable asset, the adjusted basis for depreciation is the *lesser* of adjusted basis or fair market value on the date of the conversion to business use. This prevents an indirect deduction (through depreciation) for a decline in value that occurred when the property was held for personal use.

.03 ABILITY TO RAISE CAPITAL

Of all the possible tax entities, the sole proprietor may have the most difficult time in raising capital. A sole proprietor will have unlimited liability, as the business and the business owner are indistinguishable in this environment. The proprietor may be able to acquire some properties with non-recourse financing, but that will not normally be the case.

.05 LIABILITY ISSUES OF A SOLE PROPRIETORSHIP

One of the major disadvantages of the proprietorship is the unlimited liability of the owner. Creditors of the business may attach the owner's personal assets since the owner is personally liable for the debts and liabilities of the business. However, this disadvantage can be overcome by electing single member LLC status, as discussed later.

.07 OPERATING A SOLE PROPRIETORSHIP: THE TAX REGIME

Sole proprietors are responsible for tax on the net income from self-employment. A sole proprietorship business is *not* a separate taxable entity; rather, the business income and expenses of the entity are reported on the sole proprietor's individual income tax return on Form 1040, Schedule C, which in effect serves as a tax "income statement" for the sole proprietor. Since the self-employment income relates solely to business operating income and expenses, items such as capital gains and losses, dividend income, interest income, and charitable contributions deductions are never reported on Schedule C, even though such items may be "run through the business checking accounts." The tax law does not distinguish the sole proprietor from the individual, and personal items such as charitable contributions should not be reported as a business expense.

.09 PAYROLL TAXES OF THE OWNER

The net income on Schedule C is treated as self-employment income, and the tax on this income is computed on Form 1040, Schedule SE. As mentioned earlier, one-half of this amount is deductible for adjusted gross income by the self-employed individual.

.11 PAYMENTS TO THE OWNER

Although sole proprietorships can hire employees and pay and deduct fringe benefits as proprietorship expenses, the owners cannot deduct any salary paid to themselves. Sole proprietors are allowed to withdraw cash from the business without tax, as though they were removing it from their own pockets since they have already paid tax on the profits. Sole proprietors can have retirement plans and may deduct wages or salary paid to a spouse or child, provided the family member actually works in the trade or business. There are no tax-free fringe benefits available to a sole proprietor, since he or she is an owner of the business and not an employee of the business.

.13 LIQUIDATION OF THE SOLE PROPRIETORSHIP

If the sole proprietor decides to liquidate the business, generally there are no tax consequences unless some of the proprietorship assets are sold. If assets are sold, gain or loss must be computed on each separate asset, and the character of the gain or loss on such sale depends on the type of asset (e.g., ordinary income for inventory and depreciation recapture, Code Sec. 1231 gain or loss for properties used in the business and held longer than one year, and capital gain or loss for investment properties). At most, there is a single layer of taxation at the individual level only. On the other hand, if the proprietor merely keeps all the assets used in the proprietorship, there is no gain or loss on this cessation of business; gain or loss would occur only if the sole proprietor sells the assets.

Case Study: The Sole Proprietorship (Appendix B-2)

In a sole proprietorship, the owner and the business are treated as one tax entity. The Schedule C net income includes only operating income and expenses; other "business items" such as dividend income, capital gains and losses on business investments, and charitable contributions are treated as items of an individual taxpayer and are not reflected on Schedule C. The "reasonable salary" withdrawn by Dave Davidson is not a business expense, but is merely treated as a nontaxable owner withdrawal (as is the $50,000 "other payment"). Likewise, Dave is not an "employee" for purposes of employment taxes; instead, Dave must pay self-employment taxes. As a sole proprietor, Dave is able to deduct one-half of the self-employment tax and 100 percent of health insurance premiums for adjusted gross income. Finally, Dave may establish a SEP-IRA retirement plan and deduct contributions on his own behalf for AGI each year.

¶15,009   The Partnership as a Business Entity

When two or more tax entities join together to operate a business for profit, they become partners. Although a partnership is an aggregate of other associates, it has a definite legal status and is treated as an entity separate from its partners under local law.

A **partnership** is defined as a syndicate, group, pool, joint venture, or other unincorporated organization through or by means of which any business, financial operation, or venture is carried on, and which is not a corporation, or a trust or estate. An entity may be a partnership for federal tax purposes but not for state law purposes.

A joint undertaking to share expenses is not necessarily a partnership for federal tax purposes. It is possible to co-own property and not be taxed as a partnership if no services are provided. For example, assume that two tenants in common of farm property lease it to a farmer for a cash rental or a share of the crops. Have they created a partnership?

There is a distinction between co-ownership of improved realty and a partnership. Customary tenant services such as heat, air conditioning, hot and cold water, unattended parking, normal repairs, trash removal, and cleaning of public areas can be provided by two or more co-owners without them necessarily becoming partners. However, the furnishing of additional services such as attendant parking, cabanas, and gas, electricity, and other utilities by the owners will result in a finding of a partnership relationship whether these services are provided directly or through an agent.

In many cases, it will make no difference whether persons are partners or not. If two persons share equally in the profits of a venture, each will be taxed on his or her share whether he or she is a partner or co-owner. It may, however, be beneficial for the parties to be taxed as a partnership. A partnership allows gains and losses to be specially allocated among partners. If there is only an employer-employee or creditor-debtor relationship, the employee or creditor is generally not allowed a deduction for any loss.

The associates in a **limited partnership** include one or more **general partners** who are responsible for the ongoing operations of the business and at least one limited partner, who is only an investor and does not participate in management. As explained below, only the general partner(s) are fully liable for the debts of the partnership. In exchange for giving up the right to direct partnership activities, the limited partner's liability for partnership debts is limited to what that partner has invested in the partnership. The limited partnership has been a popular choice for investors in risky activities, such as real estate, oil and gas exploration, and mining.

.01   FORMATION OF THE PARTNERSHIP

Generally, Code Sec. 721 provides that no gain or loss is recognized when a partner transfers property to a partnership in return for an interest in the partnership. Unlike the tax treatment of corporate formations under Code Sec. 351 discussed below, there is no 80-percent ownership requirement for nontaxable treatment to apply to the contribution.

The contributing partner's adjusted basis in the partnership interest is simply a carry-over of the basis in the property transferred. This amount is also the basis of the property to the partnership.

Example 15-5. Sue Mason exchanges land ($20,000 adjusted basis, $30,000 fair market value) for a one-third interest in MNO Partnership worth $30,000. Sue has a realized accounting gain of $10,000, but since no liabilities are involved in the trans-fer, Sue has no taxable gain or loss on the contribution, and her basis in the partnership interest is $20,000. The partnership's basis in the property received is also $20,000.

An exception to nontaxable treatment occurs in some cases when the partnership as-sumes liabilities on the property transferred. Specifically, if the share of the liabilities assumed by the *other partners* exceeds the basis of the property contributed, the contribut-ing partner is taxed on the excess as **boot** received. This prevents a negative basis in the new partner's interest, which becomes $0 after the gain is recognized.

Example 15-6. Assume the same facts, except that the land is subject to a $36,000 liability which is assumed by MNO Partnership. In this case, Sue is being relieved of $24,000 liabilities ($36,000 × ⅔, the amount assumed by N and O). Sue, as a one-third partner, is still liable for the remaining $12,000 of liabilities. Since the $24,000 liabilities assumed by N and O exceed Sue's $20,000 basis in the property, she must report a gain of $4,000. Her basis in her partnership interest will be $0 ($20,000 basis of property contributed + $4,000 gain recognized − $24,000 boot received with liabilities assumed by other partners). The partnership's basis in the property will be $20,000.

OBSERVATION   Even though a contributing partner is not taxed on the appreciation in value of contributed property, Code Sec. 704(c) requires *mandatory* allocation of that "built-in gain" to the contributing partner on a later sale of the property by the partnership.

.03   ABILITY TO RAISE CAPITAL

The unlimited liability aspect of a partnership interest may make it difficult for the part-nership to raise capital. However, unlimited liability applies only to general partners, so the partnership may be able to raise additional funds by selling a few limited partnership interests. Although limited liability is assured with such interests, such a restriction pre-vents the limited partner from taking an active role in the business.

.05   LIABILITY ISSUES AS A PARTNERSHIP

A major disadvantage of a general partnership is that the partners are jointly liable for the partnership's debt. This is not always a problem since personal liability may be mitigated by insurance or other means. However, when the liability of partners for the debts of the partnership is a problem, a limited partnership may be a solution, but at a cost. Limited partners are generally not liable for debts of the partnership, but they must restrict participation in management of the partnership or risk loss of limited liability.

A limited partnership requires at least one general partner. Use of a corporate general partner provides a solution to these problems, but it also introduces complexity.

.07   OPERATING A PARTNERSHIP: THE TAX REGIME

Partners in a partnership are not employees of the partnership; thus, they do not qualify for any of the special fringe benefit rules (described below) that may be available to employees of C corporations. The partnership offers the principal tax advantage of being a conduit. Profits and losses of the partnership are not taxed at the entity level, although such amounts are reported to the IRS on Form 1065; rather, such items flow through to the individual owners, and only a single level of tax is paid.

Each partner includes in income his or her share of (1) **guaranteed payments** (payments such as salary that are guaranteed without reference to the profitability of the partnership) and (2) the partnership's *ordinary income or loss* (after deducting any guaranteed payments as salary expenses). These amounts are identified on a Schedule K-1 that is furnished to each partner to disclose his or her share of the various partnership items. The totals of the K-1s must match the Schedule K that is part of the partnership tax return, Form 1065. Any guaranteed payments are deducted in determining partnership ordinary income and then allocated directly to the partner receiving them.

The **partnership's ordinary income** includes only those items of income and expense that could *not* vary in treatment across the individual partner's tax returns (i.e., sales revenue, cost of goods sold, advertising expense, etc.). Items that could vary across the tax returns are reported separately on Schedule K-1 as "specially allocated items"; these include such items as capital gains and losses and contribution expenses. See **Figure 3** for an explanation of ordinary income and specially allocated items. Non-guaranteed payments, such as withdrawals, are generally nontaxable distributions.

Example 15-7. During the current year, XY Partnership (owned equally by X and Y) had $150,000 ordinary business revenues, a $2,000 capital gain, $70,000 ordinary business expenses, and a $10,000 charitable deduction. In addition, XY made a guaranteed salary payment of $30,000 to X, and each partner withdrew $10,000 of non-guaranteed payments. The "ordinary income" of the partnership is $50,000 ($150,000 − $70,000 − 30,000), and each partner will report half of this amount, or $25,000, as income on his or her individual tax return. In addition, X must also report the $30,000 guaranteed payment as income. Each partner will also report one-half of the capital gain and one-half of the charitable contributions on their individual returns as separately reported items (from the K-1). This is because these two items can vary in treatment on the individual partner's return. Finally, as explained below, the $10,000 withdrawals by each partner are ignored for tax purposes, since these payments were not guaranteed.

Partnerships also offer the advantage of passing any losses through to the owners for immediate tax benefits. As explained below, this is not the case with a C corporation, where such losses stay in the separate corporate legal entity and can be used only as net operating loss carryovers. A major advantage of a partnership is that it can specially allocate items of income, deductions, and losses among partners non-pro rata. A contributor of money or property to a partnership can be allocated a disproportionate amount of the losses that the contribution has financed. However, the allocation must have **substantial economic effect** in order for it to be respected for tax purposes.

Figure 3

Treatment of "Specially Allocated Items" for Flow-Through Entities

Partnership (or S corporation) items of income and expense that could never vary in treatment on the individual owners' tax returns are included as part of the "ordinary income" divided among the partners. An example of "ordinary income" would be sales revenue (always taxable) or advertising expense (always deductible). On the other hand, items that may end up being treated differently by partners (or S shareholders) are not part of "ordinary income," but instead are allocated separately to each partner. Three such items are capital losses, charitable deductions, and dividend income. The rationale for each may be explained in terms of the following examples involving two equal partners in the AB Partnership.

Capital Losses

Tax Treatment. Capital losses may be deducted against any capital gains, and up to $3,000 of such losses may be offset against ordinary income (e.g., non-capital gains income) in a tax year.

Example 15-8. Partner A has $6,000 capital gains during the year, and Partner B has no capital gains. If the ABC Partnership has $10,000 capital losses during the year, Partner A may deduct her entire $5,000 share against the $6,000 of capital gains; however, Partner B may only deduct $3,000 of his $5,000 share against ordinary income. Since the capital losses can be treated differently across each partner's return, the losses must be reported as separately stated items.

Charitable Contributions

Tax Treatment. Contributions to recognized charities are itemized deductions, limited in total in any one year to 50 percent of the taxpayer's adjusted gross income (AGI).

Example 15-9. Partners A and B each have $60,000 AGI for the year. Partner A's charitable contributions for the year total $22,000, and Partner B's contributions total $29,000. If the AB Partnership has charitable contributions of $10,000 during the year, Partner A can deduct her full $5,000 share (since total contributions of $27,000 are less than 50 percent of AGI). On the other hand, Partner B can deduct only $1,000 of his $5,000 share, since his overall deduction is limited to $30,000 (50 percent of AGI). Since the charitable contributions can be treated differently across each partner's return, the contributions must be reported as separately stated items.

Dividend Income

Tax Treatment. Dividends are included in gross income and included in the definition of "investment income" that forms the upper limit on the amount of investment interest expense deductible in one year.

Example 15-10. Partner A has no investment income or expenses during the year, while Partner B has $40,000 investment income and $48,000 investment interest expense (thus limiting Partner B's investment interest deduction to $8,000 this year). If the AB partnership has $20,000 dividends during the year, Partner A will simply increase her gross income by $10,000. However, Partner B can increase gross income by $10,000 and at the same time deduct $8,000 more investment interest expense, since the $10,000 is included in "investment income." If the dividends were buried in partnership ordinary income, this would not be possible; they must be separately stated.

One unique aspect of a partnership interest is that the adjusted basis of such interest includes the partner's share of any partnership liabilities. This adjustment is made because the partner is liable for his or her share of partnership liabilities, and is thus permitted to include this in basis. This in turn increases the potential loss deduction of a partner.

Appendix B-3 recasts the facts of the Davidson Case Study in the form of a partnership entity. Once again, a simplifying assumption is made that Dave is a 99.9-percent partner (and Ellen owns the other .1 percent), so in effect all items of income and expense are allocated to Dave. This produces results that may be compared with the other types of entities.

Note specifically in Appendix B-3 the treatment of the dividends, capital gains, and contributions from the "business." These items, though related to the business entity, must be reported as separately stated items, for the reasons explained earlier. And even though these items are from the "business," they flow through to the Davidsons' Form 1040 as separately stated items that are not included in the "ordinary partnership income" that is reported on Schedule E of Form 1040.

.09   PARTNERSHIP: PAYROLL TAXES OF THE OWNER

General partners must pay self-employment taxes on their share of the ordinary income of the partnership, as well as any guaranteed payment received. *Limited partners* are not required to pay self-employment tax on their share of the ordinary income of the partnership, since by definition they cannot be active in the day to day management of the entity.

.11   NONLIQUIDATING CASH DISTRIBUTIONS TO THE OWNER

As a general rule, as long as nonliquidating cash distributions to a partner are less than the partner's basis in the partnership interest, no gain or loss is recognized. If the distributions do exceed basis, the gain is usually capital gain unless the partnership has certain Code Sec. 751 recapture properties known as "hot assets." With this exception, nonliquidating distributions are not income, since the net income of the partnership is reported when it is earned and not when it is distributed. Income shares increase a partner's adjusted basis in the interest, and distributions decrease that basis.

.13   LIQUIDATION OF THE PARTNERSHIP

A partnership may be liquidated by either distributing the partnership assets directly to the partners or by first selling the assets and then distributing the cash to the partners. In either case, there is a single layer of tax, recognized at the partner level. If the partnership distributes the assets directly to the partners, gain is recognized only to the extent that *money* (e.g., cash and marketable securities) distributed exceed the partner's basis in the partnership interest. If the money received is less than basis, the money reduces basis dollar for dollar, then basis is allocated first to unrealized receivables and inventory, and then any remaining assets received. Although gain is not recognized, it may be postponed because the basis allocation to some properties may be lower than the partnership relative basis.

If the partner receives cash from the partnership exceeding basis, then the excess is taxed as capital gain in most cases (subject to the existence of "hot assets"). But recall that if the partnership sold the assets first at a gain and then distributed the cash to the partners, the partners would not likely recognize gain because the gain on the sale by the partnership is taxed to the partners, which increases their adjusted bases in the partnership interests. Finally, a "retiring" partner may be required to report some payments as ordinary income if such payments are for "other than the partner's relative interest in partnership properties." These above-market payments are treated like compensation.

Case Study: The Partnership (Appendix B-3)

When assuming that Dave Davidson is essentially a 100-percent partner, the total tax liabilities under the sole proprietorship and partnership entities are the same. This is because all "business" items flow through to the individual return and retain their character. Items included in the computation of partnership "ordinary income" are those items of operating income and expense that cannot vary in treatment across the individual partners' returns. The $75,000 "reasonable salary", the $3,000 health insurance premium payment, and the $7,500 contribution to the SEP-IRA by the Partnership on Dave's behalf are all treated as guaranteed payments and are deducted in determining partnership ordinary income. The dividend income, the capital loss on the sale of the "business investment", and the partnership charitable contributions are all reported as separate items. Dave, a general partner, is subject to the self-employment tax liability.

¶15,011   The S Corporation as a Business Entity

An **S corporation** is a special-status corporation for tax purposes, in that it is essentially treated as a partnership for federal tax purposes (a conduit, thus avoiding the double taxation problem of a C corporation). But since the entity is a corporation in all other respects, the entity offers limited liability for its owners.

The Internal Revenue Code specifies a number of requirements for electing S status. For example, an S corporation may have no more than 100 shareholders; for these purposes, certain family members are counted as one shareholder. An S corporation may generally also have only one class of outstanding stock. S status must be affirmatively elected by *all* shareholders in order to be valid.

An S corporation gives shareholders the benefits of a pass-through entity for tax purposes (earnings are taxed only once) and the corporate advantage of limited liability. Although publicly held corporations cannot qualify for a Subchapter S election, there are no limits with regard to the size of an eligible corporation. Thus, very large closely held corporations may qualify as S corporations. An S corporation is created under state law in the same manner as a regular or **C corporation**.

A corporation qualifies as an S corporation if a valid election (Form 2553) is filed with the IRS. This election may be made during the year in which it is to become effective, but must be made on or before the fifteenth day of the third month of such year (e.g., March 15, for calendar year corporations that were in existence on January 1).

Alternatively, the election may be made during the year preceding the year for which it is to be effective. All current shareholders and the corporation itself must consent to the election. If the election is filed during the taxable year for which it is to become effective, any persons who are not currently shareholders, but who owned stock during that year, must also consent to the election.

.01   FORMATION OF THE S CORPORATION

When an S corporation is formed, it is treated as a regular corporation and is thus subject to the special rules of the Internal Revenue Code and state law. As a separate business entity, corporations must follow certain business formalities when forming; these include articles of incorporation, bylaws, and electing directors. This can be quite time-consuming and costly.

As for tax consequences on formation, Code Sec. 351 states that no gain or loss is recognized by either the contributing shareholder or the recipient corporation if three conditions are satisfied: (1) there is a transfer of property (and not services), (2) solely in exchange for corporate stock, and (3) after the exchange the contributing shareholder(s) is (are) in control of the corporation (e.g., own at least 80 percent of the voting and 80 percent of the outstanding stock).

If all conditions are met, no gain is taxed, and the basis of the shares to the shareholder equals the basis of the property transferred to the corporation (and the corporation has the same basis in the property). In essence, the transaction is treated as if nothing has changed.

Example 15-11. In exchange for 70 percent of the stock of Hamilton Corporation (an S corporation) valued at $70,000, James contributed land with an adjusted basis to him of $36,000 and a fair market value of $70,000. The other 30 percent of the stock was issued to Jane for property that she contributed to the corporation at the same time. Since the combined transfers for property provided at least 80-percent control, James will not recognize gain or loss on the transfer, his basis in the shares is $36,000 (a carryover basis), and the corporation's basis in the land is also the $36,000 carryover basis.

If the 80-percent control test is not met, the exchange will be fully taxable. In such a case the fair market value of the stock received is compared with the tax (adjusted) basis of the property contributed to the corporation. Any excess is reported as capital gain under the normal gain recognition rules, and there is no tacking of holding periods.

Example 15-12. Assume the same facts as the previous example, except that the 30-percent stock interest received by Jane was for services she performed for the corporation, and not for property. In this case, James has a $34,000 realized accounting gain ($70,000 – $36,000), and this must be recognized for tax purposes since only 70 percent of the stock was received for property. His basis in the shares will be $70,000; since the exchange was fully taxable, he receives fair market value as the basis of his shares. Likewise, the S corporation's basis in the land received is also $70,000.

OBSERVATION   In the above example, if Jane had also contributed some property with her services, would the transaction qualify for nonrecognition under Code Sec. 351? According to the Regulations, the answer is yes, but only if the value of the property contributed was worth at least 10 percent of the value of the services Jane contributed.

As was true with partnerships, a corporation will sometimes assume outstanding liabilities of the shareholder on contributed property. To prevent this from being a tax barrier to incorporation, Code Sec. 357 states that liabilities assumed by the corporation are not treated as boot received for purposes of determining gain on the contributing transfer. However, if the liabilities assumed exceed the tax basis of the property, such excess must be recognized as taxable gain; this prevents a negative basis in the stock received.

Example 15-13. Assume the same facts as Example 15-11, except that Hamilton stock was worth $40,000 and the land was subject to a $30,000 mortgage, to be assumed by Hamilton Corporation. In this case, the $4,000 excess of the mortgage assumed by the corporation ($40,000) over the adjusted basis of the property contributed ($36,000) must be reported as gain by James. James's adjusted basis in the stock is zero ($36,000 basis of the old + $4,000 gain – $40,000 liabilities assumed that are treated as boot received). The corporation's basis in the property is $40,000 ($36,000 basis to James + $4,000 gain recognized by James on the transfer).

.03   ABILITY TO RAISE CAPITAL

Normally, the corporate form is the best entity type for raising capital, since the company can potentially raise such capital by selling additional shares of stock. However, if an S election is in effect, this potential may be more limited due to the 100-shareholder limit on such entities. A family corporation is not likely to bring in outside owners in this case. Also, the S corporation can issue only one class of stock, and this can affect the flexibility of the company in raising capital as well.

.05   LIABILITY ISSUES OF AN S CORPORATION

One of the major nontax advantages of an S corporation is the limited liability of its owners. Creditors may only seek repayment from the S corporation itself; they may not pierce the corporate shell and attach the personal assets of the owners.

OBSERVATION   As a practical matter, the advantage of limited liability may have very little value to a new S corporation. Because such a company has little or no credit history when it is formed, it may be impossible for the owners of the business to obtain a business loan without cosigning the note or guaranteeing the note as shareholders. As a result, the "limited liability" trait effectively becomes "unlimited liability" until a credit history and solid corporate asset base is established.

.07   OPERATING AN S CORPORATION: THE TAX REGIME

After legislative changes in 1982, an S corporation is taxed in a manner similar to a partnership. All items of S corporation income, deduction, gain and loss are separated into "ordinary income" and specially allocated items. Each shareholder will pick up his or her share of S corporation income at the end of the year based on their weighted stock ownership percentage for the year. Although this allocation is similar to a partnership, there are no special allocations of profit or loss with an S corporation.

Like a partnership, the S corporation passes losses through immediately to shareholders. However, unlike partners in a partnership, an S corporation shareholder's basis in the ownership interest (stock in this case) does not include a share of the corporate liabilities. Recall that an S corporation shareholder is not liable for corporation debts, so such liabilities may not be included in basis of the stock.

OBSERVATION   If an S corporation shareholder's share of a loss exceeds his or her basis, such excess loss may be used to offset any loans from the shareholder to the S corporation. But this is technically not basis in the stock; the offset simply recognizes that the shareholder has a recoverable tax basis in such loans.

Appendix B-4 recasts the facts of the Davidson Case Study in the form of an S corporation entity. In this case, a simplifying assumption is made that Dave is a 100-percent shareholder so that the results may be compared to other entities. As was true with the partnership, all items of income and expense are allocated to Dave.

One key difference should be noted in Appendix B-4. Since the S corporation is treated as a regular C corporation in most respects other than federal taxation, Dave is considered to be an employee of this separate entity. Thus, the "reasonable salary payments" of $75,000 are treated as salary income, and Dave is treated as an employee in the company pension plan.

.09   S CORPORATION: PAYROLL TAXES OF THE OWNER

Generally, the income shares allocated to S corporation shareholders are not subject to the self-employment tax, since investor/shareholders are not treated as self-employed persons. But what if a shareholder is also an employee, a typical situation for a family business organized as an S corporation? In this case, any wages paid to a shareholder/employee are subject to the normal FICA rules whereby the corporation matches the amounts withheld from the employee's salary. This is because the S corporation is a separate legal entity, apart from its owners.

OBSERVATION

S corporations enjoy a distinct advantage when it come to payroll/self-employment taxes over partnerships and LLC's that are taxed under the partnership rules. A shareholder's share of S corporation flow-through income is not subject to the self-employment tax—only wage income is subject to payroll taxes. Because S corporations have wide discretion to characterize earned business profits as either salary or flow-through income, S shareholders can mimimize the employment tax obligations by paying themselves low salaries, thus increasing the amount that flows through to them as income not subject to self-employment tax. In the case study, note that Dave limited his salary in the S to $75,000, and this factor resulted in the total taxes paid by the S being lower than those of the partnership or sole proprietorship.

Paying low salaries to S shareholder/employees may also help avoid the .9% medicare tax on wages exceeding the same thresholds. And if the taxpayer is a material participant in the S corporation, the taxpayer will avoid the new 3.8% net investment income tax on any non-salary flow-through income allocation for the year. Obviously, this ability to avoid both the 0.9% medicare tax and the 3.8% net investment tax is probably not what Congress envisioned, and this may be corrected with future legislation.

.11   PAYMENTS TO THE OWNER

As was true with the partnership entity, no gain or loss is generally recognized on non-liquidating distributions to S shareholders. Such distributions are not income, since the net income of the S corporation, like a partnership, is reported when it is earned and not when it is distributed. Income shares increase an S shareholder's adjusted basis in the interest, and distributions decrease that basis.

An S corporation employee can exclude from tax the value of fringe benefits provided by the corporation only if the employee owns less than *two percent* of the outstanding stock. Thus, owner/employees in most small S corporations cannot exclude the value of the fringe benefits, since they own two percent or more of the outstanding stock.

OBSERVATION

In *Watson v. Commissioner, 668 F3d 1008 (CA-8, 2012)*, the courts offered a guide to determining an S corporation shareholder/employee's "reasonable salary." In this case a CPA was the sole shareholder of the S corporation, which in turn was a 25% shareholder in a very successful accounting firm. In 2002 and 2003, Watson set his compensation from the S corporation as $24,000 per year, an amount less than first-year employees were earning at the firm. The remaining S share of firm revenue was recognized as flow-through income, not subject to payroll taxes. Watson actually received distributions of $203,651 and $175,470 in total in 2002 and 2003. The IRS contended that the salary should be set at $93,000 per year, based on surveys conducted by the AICPA, which indicated such a salary for comparable CPAs for this firm size, as adjusted upwards for the fact that Watson was a shareholder rather than a non-director. This victory by the IRS reinforces the the point that the IRS is willing to take a formal, quantitative approach towards determining reasonable compensation for S shareholders/employees.

.13 LIQUIDATION OF THE S CORPORATION

An S corporation is treated just like a regular C corporation when liquidated. If the S corporation sells the assets and then distributes the proceeds to the shareholders, any gain recognized by the company on the asset sales is allocated to the shareholders as taxable gain, which increases their adjusted basis in their stock. As a result, the eventual distribution of cash to the shareholder usually produces no gain, thus resulting in a single layer of taxation at liquidation.

If the S corporation distributes property directly to the shareholders in liquidation of their interests, the result is basically the same. That is because the S corporation must recognize gain on any appreciation in value of such properties distributed, this gain is passed through and taxed to the shareholders, and there is no other gain from the liquidating distribution at the shareholder level. Once again, there is only a single layer of tax.

Case Study: The S Corporation (Appendix B-4)

The total tax liability under the S corporation is different, since Dave Davidson is an employee for federal tax purposes and subject to withholding. Because Dave's "reasonable salary" is assumed to be only $75,000, this results in some payroll tax savings. Recall that with a sole proprietorship, the lesser of $113,700 or 92.35 percent of Schedule C earnings are subject to the self-employment tax. Otherwise, the reporting for an S corporation is similar to a partnership, in that both apply a conduit approach.

¶15,013   The C Corporation as a Business Entity

A C ("regular") corporation is a separate legal and taxable entity, subject to a graduated income tax schedule from 15 to 35 percent. If such a corporation pays dividends to its owners, these amounts are also subject to taxation at the individual shareholder level. This is the primary disadvantage of a corporation—the same amount of income is taxed twice (the "double taxation" dilemma). However, as part of the 2003 Act, the tax rate applicable to most sources of dividend income is limited to a maximum tax rate of 15 percent, the same rate applicable to long-term gains. Under the Taxpayer Relief Act of 2012, this rate is increased to 20% for taxpayers in the 39.6% tax bracket.

01   FORMATION OF THE CORPORATION

When a C corporation is formed, it is treated as a separate legal entity and is thus subject to the special rules of the Internal Revenue Code and state law. As a separate and distinct legal entity, corporations must follow certain business formalities, such as drafting articles of incorporation, bylaws, and electing directors. As is true with an S corporation, this process can be quite time-consuming and costly.

The C corporation is subject to the same tax rules of Code Sec. 351 that are applicable to an S corporation upon formation (see the discussion above). Thus, no gain or loss is recognized when property is transferred solely in exchange for corporate stock and after the exchange the transferor is in control of the corporation (e.g., at least an 80 percent interest in voting and outstanding stock). Control can also be established by being part of a group of contributing shareholders who obtain at least an 80-percent controlling interest. As illustrated earlier, the receipt of boot or the assumption of liabilities exceeding basis by the corporation can create taxable gain to the contributing shareholder.

.03   ABILITY TO RAISE CAPITAL

The C corporation offers maximum flexibility in terms of the ability to raise capital. Different types of stock and securities may be offered as a means to raise such capital, and there are no limitations on the size or type of ownership interest offered.

Corporations may also issue bonds, with the added benefit of being able to deduct the interest expense (recall that dividends paid on stock are not deductible by the corporation). There is, however, a possible danger of having some debt reclassified as stock because the corporation is "thinly capitalized," i.e., the bondholders are also stockholders in the same relative proportions. In such a case, the IRS may argue that the bondholders are really stockholders, and that the classification as a debtor was solely for purposes of deducting interest expense.

Two other special tax-related provisions may assist the corporation in raising capital. First, Code Sec. 1244 allows a corporation to designate the first $1 million of original issue capital stock as "**Code Sec. 1244 stock**." With this designation, any individual or partner owner(s) may deduct the first $50,000 of losses each year ($100,000 on a joint return) as ordinary losses; any excess losses on such stock each year are capital loss.

Under Code Sec. 1202, a noncorporate taxpayer can exclude from gross income 50 percent of any gain from the sale or exchange of qualified small business stock held for more than five years. Qualifying corporations issuing **Sec. 1202 stock** must have aggregate gross assets not exceeding $50 million at the time of the issue. Corporations engaging in personal services do not qualify.

.05   LIABILITY ISSUES AS A C CORPORATION

The primary nontax advantage of a C corporation is the limited liability of the owners; creditors may only look to the corporate entity for payment. However, a C corporation without a credit history is likely to find that the only way they can borrow money is to cosign or guarantee the loans as individuals, so this advantage may be somewhat illusionary early in the life of the entity.

.07   OPERATING THE C CORPORATION: THE TAX REGIME

The C corporation is a separate legal and tax entity, and the tax scheme applicable to corporations is different from that of individuals in several important respects. These include the following:

- The corporate tax rates range from 15 to 35 percent, and may temporarily apply at a 38-percent tax rate (see Appendix A)
- There is no distinction between deductions "for AGI" and "from AGI"; all legitimate expenses of the corporation are deductible
- There is no preferential rate for long-term capital gains, and capital losses can only offset capital gains and not regular income (unused capital losses can be carried back three years and forward five years as *short-term* capital losses)
- Charitable contribution deductions are limited to 10 percent of taxable income *before* considering the contribution itself, any dividends received deduction, and any capital loss or net operating loss carryback (but *not* carryforward)
- Any dividend income received by the corporation qualifies for a 70-percent (if ownership interest is less than 20 percent) or 80-percent (ownership interest of 20 percent or more) dividends received deduction

One of the key tax differences between a C corporation and the other entities is the treatment of operating losses and capital losses. Since the C corporation is a separate taxable entity, these losses remain in the corporate entity and can only be used by the corporate entity; they do not flow through to the owners of the business. This can be a distinct disadvantage of the C corporation in early years when losses are likely.

.09   CORPORATION: PAYROLL TAXES OF THE OWNER

As a separate taxable entity, the C corporation must withhold payroll taxes from all employees' salaries, including shareholder-employees. The C corporation will then match the amounts withheld (only this portion of the FICA taxes forwarded to the IRS is deductible by the corporation).

Any shareholder who also works for the corporation is treated the same as other employees. There are no self-employment tax issues for a C corporation, since the corporation is a separate legal entity.

.11 PAYMENTS TO THE OWNER

Historically, the primary tax disadvantage associated with the C corporation is the double taxation of income. When the corporation earns an income, it pays an income tax, and when such earnings are distributed to the owners, they pay a second layer of income tax. The reduction in tax rates applicable to dividends to a maximum rate of 15 or 20 percent lessens but does not completely eliminate this double taxation.

Some closely held businesses can mitigate the double taxation problem by paying salaries, interest, or rents to their owners; such amounts would be deductible by the corporation and would thus eliminate the first layer of taxation. However, such payments must be reasonable based on the facts and circumstances of the case; otherwise, excessive amounts may be reclassified by the IRS as dividends, which are not deductible by the corporation but are nonetheless still taxable to the shareholders.

One of the primary advantages of a C corporation is that the Code provides for a number of fringe benefits that are not taxable to employees (who frequently are the owners of the business, if it is a small family corporation), even though they are deductible by the corporation. These include employer payments for health insurance coverage, medical reimbursement plans, childcare (up to $5,000), and group-term life insurance coverage (up to $50,000).

.13 LIQUIDATION OF THE CORPORATION

The specter of double taxation raises its head once again upon liquidation of the corporate entity. If the corporation sells its assets and distributes the proceeds to the owners, any gain recognized on the sale is taxable to the corporation. And when the cash is distributed to the shareholders, any amounts received in excess of the shareholder's basis in the stock are taxable gain. Thus, double taxation occurs upon the liquidation of a corporation.

The double tax cannot be avoided by distributing the assets directly to the shareholders. This is because the Code requires the distributing corporation to recognize gain or loss on distributions of property as though the properties were first sold at their fair market values and then distributed to the shareholders. Prior to 1986, it was possible to avoid such taxation through a special one-month liquidation procedure.

Case Study: The C Corporation (Appendix B-5)

At first, it may appear somewhat surprising that the corporate tax liability is not much higher than the proprietorship, the partnership, and the S corporation. This is true even though the total tax liability under the C corporation includes the $50,000 of "other compensation" that is treated as dividend income and is double taxed (once at the corporate level and then again at the individual shareholder level when distributed). But recall that such amount is taxed at only a 15-percent rate as a qualifying dividend. Also, note that the corporate tax rate was only 15 percent, since corporate taxable income was less than $50,000. However, the tax liabilities under the C corporation would increase in future years when (1) larger dividend distributions are made, (2) larger operating incomes are reported that cause the marginal tax rate to increase, and (3) a large double-tax is possible upon liquidation (see the analysis later in this chapter). Also note that the capital loss remains in the corporate entity and may not be passed through to the shareholders; the same would be true for operating losses. One beneficial tax treatment under the C entity is the treatment of tax-free fringe benefits, such as the health insurance premiums paid by the Company for Dave. These are deductible by the company and are excludable by Dave.

¶15,015   A Note on Personal Services Corporations (PSCs)

Because of the marginal tax rate differential between individual and corporate marginal tax rates, some service-providing taxpayers, such as doctors, lawyers, accountants, and other professionals, may be tempted to incorporate to take advantage of the lower corporate marginal tax rates on the first $75,000 of corporate taxable income.

To stop this tax minimization scheme, the IRS requires personal service corporations to pay tax at the *highest* corporate marginal tax rate, currently 35 percent, on the first as well as the last dollar of corporate taxable income. For purposes of the rules, the term "personal service corporation" has the same definition as under the rules permitting the IRS to reallocate income and deductions of personal service corporations.

A **personal services corporation (PSC)** is a corporation whose principal activity is the performance of personal services that are substantially performed by employee-owners. Under this rule, a taxpayer is a personal service corporation if it meets all of the following four tests:

1. It must be a C corporation for the tax year;
2. Its principal activity during the testing period for the tax year must be the performance of personal services;
3. During the testing period for the tax year, those services must be substantially performed by employee-owners; and
4. More than 10 percent of the fair market value of its outstanding stock must be owned by employee-owners on the last day of the testing period for the tax year.

OBSERVATION   Assuming the business can avoid being classified as a personal service corporation, the business owners should take advantage of the lower corporate marginal tax rates until a reasonable amount of income has been retained. Then the corporation could elect S corporation status to avoid the accumulated earnings tax.

¶15,017   Limited Liability Companies and Limited Liability Partnerships

.01   OVERVIEW

The **limited liability company (LLC)** or **limited liability partnership (LLP)** is a relatively new type of tax entity available in all the states. It combines the flow-through characteristics of the partnership with the limited liability of the corporation. In the LLP, no partner is personally liable for the debts of the partnership. In the LLC, liability relief is somewhat restricted in that the partner can be held personally liable for claims arising from malpractice by the partner. A single member LLC is taxed as a sole proprietorship.

Under the "check-the-box" system of entity classification, if a limited liability company (LLC) is not *automatically* classified as a corporation, the LLC is an "eligible entity" that may elect to be classified for tax purposes either as a partnership or as a corporation. An LLC may be *automatically* classified as a corporation if the statute under which it is organized does not refer to it as a corporation or joint stock company, if it is not an insurance company or one of certain kinds of banks, and if specified other characteristics are avoided.

OBSERVATION   Wyoming was the first state to come up with the idea of a limited liability entity with enough noncorporate characteristics that it would be taxed as a partnership. The "market" in state governments for new ways to attract business (read: steal businesses from other states in a "race to the bottom") is very efficient,

---

and soon every state had some variation of the limited liability entity statute. Wyoming's statute was soon copied by Florida. These two statutes have provided the pattern for most state statutes since these were the first such laws and both laws have passed judicial (and IRS) muster. All states now have some form of limited liability entity.

State laws vary on the requirements for qualifying as an LLP or an LLC, and for this reason electing LLP or LLC status may create special administrative burdens for companies with multi-state operations. In addition, not all states with LLC statutes permit professional service providers, such as lawyers, physicians, architects, and accountants, to organize as LLCs, although there is an increasing tendency to do so. For those states that do not permit professional service providers to form LLCs, or require a majority of the shareholders to be certified in the profession, a preferable alternative may be to elect S corporation status.

OBSERVATION   If an LLC is characterized as a partnership for federal tax purposes, the limited liability company form will offer the flow-through of tax attributes, as well as limited liability. Pass-through of tax attributes and limited liability are also available to S corporations. S corporations are, however, subject to many restrictions, including restrictions on the number of and kind of shareholders, which do not apply to limited liability companies. Additionally, unlike a limited partnership, a member of an LLC *can* participate in day-to-day management without losing limited liability.

.03   SUBTLE DIFFERENCES IN THE TREATMENT OF LLCS AND LLPS

For federal tax purposes, limited liability partnerships and limited liability companies are taxed as partnerships (conduits). However, the special legal status of such an entity may lead to a few subtle but important tax and nontax differences in applying the partnership taxation scheme to such an entity. These include the following:

- *Code Sec. 465 at-risk rules.* An LLP member will be able to increase his or her at-risk amount (as defined in Code Sec. 465) by his or her share of general entity debt, but an LLC member may not because the party ultimately liable under state law is usually the LLC and this provides a personal liability shield for the member.
- *Self-employment tax.* Proposed regulations provide that a partner or LLC member will not be subject to self-employment taxes unless (1) the partner or member has personal liability for the debts of the partnership, (2) the partner or member has the authority to contract on behalf of the partnership, or (3) the partner or member participates more than 500 hours in the entity activity during the year. Most members of a nonprofessional LLC will not be subject to the self-employment tax under these rules, but a partner in an LLP may be because of participation in the business.
- *Transition to a regular C corporation.* Often the owners of a limited liability entity desire to eventually take the company public. If this is the case, an LLC may be the better choice because this would greatly ease the administrative burden of going public.
- *Multi-state operations.* In some cases, there may be some question concerning the risk of personal liability when business is carried on in a state other than the one under whose laws the LLC was created. This could be a very important consideration for businesses engaged in multi-state operations.

.05 OTHER FACTORS TO CONSIDER WITH LIMITED LIABILITY ENTITIES

There are a number of other factors that should be taken into account when considering a limited liability entity. These include the following:

- **Making the Election.** The election for limited liability status is made on Form 8832 any time within the period 75 days before the beginning of the tax year until 100 days into the tax year.
- **Conversion from a Regular Partnership.** Any recourse liabilities of the regular partnership at the time of conversion remain recourse liabilities after the conversion; likewise, any "built-in gain" of a partner retains such status for later distributions to other members of the limited liability entity.
- **Conversion from a Regular C Corporation.** It is often tempting for a C corporation to consider converting to an LLC in order to avoid the double taxation dilemma. However, it is important to note that such a conversion is treated as a "deemed liquidation" of the C corporation and a corresponding "deemed distribution" of the hypothetical sales proceeds of the deemed liquidation to the C corporation shareholders. Thus, the price of converting to an LLC is one final round of double taxation through a deemed liquidation and distribution. One the other hand, in the current economic downturn asset values are at historical lows, so the tax costs may be minimal. And if the C corporation has any unused net operating losses, such losses may be used to offset the deemed gain.
- **Insurance.** Although the limited liability company statute may protect a member from tort and contract liability, the state statute may nonetheless require members to acquire certain minimum levels of insurance, usually from $100,000 to $1,000,000.
- **Participation in Management.** Unlike a limited partnership interest, members of a limited liability company may participate in the management of the company.
- **Reciprocity.** Most states honor the limited liability entity classification of other states.
- **Withdrawal of a Member.** The withdrawal of a member may mean the dissolution of the limited liability entity; state law should be checked in this regard.
- **Contribution of Services.** Some states may not allow such contributions by members to a limited liability entity.
- **Revocation or Loss of Limited Liability Status.** Most states require a five-year waiting period before such status may be elected again (unless a dissolution was due to a greater than 50-percent change in ownership interests).

¶15,019 Miscellaneous Considerations in Choice of Entity

.01 CHOICE OF TAX YEAR

Generally, a sole proprietorship and a C corporation are free to choose a calendar or a fiscal year. On the other hand, partnerships and S corporations are subject to significant restrictions in the choice of a tax year. A partnership must generally determine its tax year according to three tests, each applied sequentially until the appropriate year is determined: (1) the majority interest rule; (2) the principal partners rule; or (3) a tax year determined under a "least aggregate deferral" computation. Generally, an S corporation must use a calendar year unless a special prepayment election under Code Sec. 444 is made.

.03 ALTERNATIVE MINIMUM TAX

Alternative minimum tax (AMT) considerations are somewhat alike for the sole proprietor, the partnership, and the S corporation, since all items of income, deduction, and credits flow through the partnership and S corporation directly to the owners and retain their character. The sole proprietor has the most control over items that may affect the AMT, since he or she makes all tax elections as opposed to being one of possibly many owners. The regular C corporation is also subject to an AMT, but only if average gross receipts for the preceding three years exceed $7.5 million. The corporate AMT rate is only 20 percent (as opposed to 26 percent and 28 percent for individuals); however, the C corporation has one major adjustment that does not apply to the other entities: the adjusted current earnings ("ACE") adjustment. In general, ACE is a rough surrogate for financial accounting income, and to the extent this "accounting" number exceeds alternative minimum taxable income, 75 percent of the excess is reported as an AMT adjustment.

.05 MULTI-JURISDICTIONAL OPERATIONS

As a family business grows, the possibility of expanding beyond state (or national borders) may be a viable business option. This raises a host of tax issues; for example, has the business in the new jurisdiction established "nexus" (i.e., are there sufficient operations in the new location to justify that location imposing a tax for goods and services used in the new jurisdiction?). If the answer is yes, then some type of apportionment of income may be required. The type of entity in the new jurisdiction will determine the ultimate tax burden; for example, some states do not recognize the existence of an S corporation. Also, state tax rates, rules, and "tax holidays" may vary in today's competitive environment.

.07 TRANSFER OF THE FAMILY BUSINESS

The owner(s) of a family business must constantly give attention to the possible value of the business at their deaths, who will receive such interests, and who will eventually control the business. Depending on the size and complexity of the business, useful tax planning tools could include outright transfers to survivors or simple buy-sell agreements (where the decedent's ownership interest is purchased by surviving owners or is redeemed by the business). Leaving the entire interest to a surviving spouse eliminates estate tax considerations at death of the first spouse, but may create terrible tax consequences to the family when the second spouse dies.

A popular family transfer planning technique currently used is the "discounted transfer" discussed earlier, which eliminates post-transfer appreciation from the decedent's estate and limits the original amount subject to the gift or estate transfer. Court decisions have allowed minority interest and lack of marketability discounts when valuing shares of stock (or partnership interests).

.09 CORPORATE NOMINEES

It is often desirable for an individual or partnership to be considered the owner of property for tax purposes. Unlike a C corporation, if the property is deemed to be owned by an individual or partnership, profits arising from ownership thereof are taxed only once and losses are directly deductible by the beneficial owners. Although there is some danger of a corporate nominee being reclassified as an owner by the IRS, the Supreme Court decision in *Comm'r v. Bollinger,*[3] may be relied upon to refute this position. In Bollinger, the court held that the corporate owner was merely an agent for partnerships who were in fact the owners for tax purposes.

¶15,021 Choice of Entity: Final Summaries

Appendix C contains one-page summaries of the significant tax and nontax considerations for each of the four basic entity types. These summaries permit quick comparisons of the major characteristics of each entity.

---

[3] *Bollinger,* SCt, 88-1 USTC ¶9233, 485 US 340, 108 SCt 1173.

¶15,023   A Multi-year Spreadsheet Model for Assessing the Tax Consequences of Each Entity Type

The authors have developed a comprehensive, multi-year spreadsheet model that rolls forward the results for the Case Study for several years and projects total tax costs of each entity type after considering the liquidation of the entity. This spreadsheet is also used for Tax Planning Problem 1, and the initial inputs for the model are shown on the next page.

As a business entity grows, the tax effects may change significantly, especially with regards to the corporate entity. As the entity's income increases, the double taxation of C corporations will have a more pronounced effect, since the corporate rates eventually rise to 35 percent. And as dividend payments potentially increase, the double taxation effects will be even more prevalent. And given the budget deficit situation, it is by no means certain that the special 15-percent or 20-percent rate applicable to dividends will remain in the tax law.

In three of the four business entities, the sole proprietorship, the partnership, and the S corporation, there is only a single layer of taxation at liquidation. However, the problem of double-taxation crops up again on the liquidation of the C corporation entity. These tax consequences may be explained as follows:

- **Sole Proprietorship.** When the sole proprietor sells his or her business, the gain or loss is reported only once, on Form 4797 with the taxpayer's Form 1040 in the year of sale.
- **Partnership.** When the partnership sells the business, the gain will flow through to the partners, whose tax basis in the partnership increases by the amount of the gain. Then, when the partnership interests are liquidated, the gain is not taxed a second time because of these basis increases. If the partnership distributes the assets directly to the partners in liquidation of their interests, then each partner recognizes gain on the exchange (but only once).
- **S Corporation.** The tax consequences are essentially the same as the partnership, except that rather than liquidating the partnership interests of the partners, the distributions will liquidate the stock investment of the shareholders.
- **C Corporation.** If the corporation sells the assets in liquidation, the corporation must report any gain on Form 4797, and such gain is taxed at the normal corporate rates. Then, when the corporation distributes the cash to the shareholders in return for their stock, the gain is in effect taxed a second time (note that the shareholders could not increase their stock basis by the gain recognized by the corporation).

Davidson Company—Initial Input Variables

Initial Year 1 Business Incomes:		Assumed Growth Rates:	
Sales Revenues	645,000	*Business Items:*	
Consulting Fees	30,000	Sales and CGS	20%
Business Dividend Income	4,000	Consulting Fees	15%
		Business Dividend Inc	2%
Initial Business Expenses:		Business Expenses	5%
Cost of Goods Sold	142,200	Owner Reason. Comp.	10%
Interest, Supplies, Rents, Utilities	84,930	Other Owner Payments	10%
Salaries for Each of 5 Employees	50,000		
Health Insurance Cost per Person	3,000	*Personal Items:*	
Charitable Contributions	13,300	Ellen's Salary	5%
Short-term Capital Losses—Year 1	5,000	Other Income (Int & Div)	5%
Initial Payments to Owner:		Personal Expenses	5%
Reasonable Compensation	75,000		
Other Payments/Withdrawals	50,000	**Pension Plan Contrib:**	
		Employees (pct. Salary)	10%
Business Assets—Original Costs:		Owner (pct. reas. Comp)	10%
Cash	130,000		
Equipment (5/1 acq)	55,014	**Asset Ann. Apprec/Depr:**	
Buildings (11/1 acq)	400,000	Buildings and Land	10%
Land (11/1 acq)	20,000	Other Business Assets	5%
Computer (5/1/acq)	5,043		
Total Original Contribution Basis	610,057	**Analysis PV Disc. Rate**	5%
Less: Building and Equip Loans	(380,000)		
Assumed basis in C corp shares	230,057	**Building Loan:**	
		Principal	320,000
Ending Inventory at Year 5:		Term (Years)	30
		Interest Rate	8%
Estimated Cost	50,000		
Estimated Liquidation	70,000	**Equipment Loan:**	
		Principal	60,000
Initial Personal Information:		Term	10
		Interest Rate	9%
Ellen Davidson's Salary	71,300		
Interest Income	1,400	**Dividends Taxed at a**	
Dividend Income	1,200	**Maximum 15% Rate:**	1
Long-term Capital Gains—Year 1	6,100	0 = No, 1 = Yes	
Interest Paid on Home Mortgage	8,300		
State and Local Taxes Paid	14,000	**Exemption Amount**	3,900
Charitable Contributions (Cash)	3,900	**Number of Exemptions**	2
Unreimbursed Employee Exp (Ellen)	4,181	**Exemption Phase-out**	300,000
2013 Social Security limit	113,700	**Itemized Ded Phase-out**	300,000
2013 forward Social Security limit	113,700		

¶15,023

If the corporation instead distributes the assets to the shareholders directly in liquidation of their stock investments, the corporation MUST report any hypothetical gain as though the assets were sold by the corporation. Then, the shareholders will report a gain on liquidation of their shares (by comparing the fair market value of the assets received with the adjusted basis of their stock investments). Thus, there is always double taxation on the liquidation of the corporate entity, regardless of whether the assets are first sold and cash is distributed to the shareholder, or if the assets are distributed directly to the shareholder.

The spreadsheet available on the webpage essentially rolls the results of the Davidson Case Study forward for five years and then liquidates the business entity at the end of Year 5, by assuming that all assets are sold for their projected fair market values. This model assumes certain rates of appreciation in assets, distributions, incomes and expenses, and assumes that the net "cash flow" of the corporation is retained until the business is liquidated later.

The initial set of inputs for the spreadsheet is summarized on the preceding page. These include assumptions relating to the growth of sales and expenses, as well as assumptions regarding the appreciation rates of business assets.

Based on these inputs, the present value of tax liability results (including discounted value for Year 1 as well) of applying these values for five years, liquidating the business, and paying all taxes are as follows:

Final Entity Comparison—Original Facts						
Total Taxes Paid (By Year)						
	Year 1	Year 2	Year 3	Year 4	Year 5	Totals
Sole Proprietorship	39,969	57,745	89,944	110,735	231,557	529,949
Partnership	39,969	57,745	89,944	110,735	231,557	529,949
S Corporation	35,664	53,101	84,339	104,073	223,399	500,577
C Corporation	42,121	55,628	87,532	127,053	364,453	676,687

Analyzing Changes in Input Variables. It is interesting to examine how the relative tax liabilities of the four types of entities change as certain input variables are changed. Specifically, the following iterations are somewhat revealing. For example, here are the results if the projected growth rate for sales increases from 20 to 30 percent per year:

Final Entity Comparison—Increase Sales Growth Rate						
Total Taxes Paid (By Year)						
	Year 1	Year 2	Year 3	Year 4	Year 5	Totals
Sole Proprietorship	39,969	72,889	130,862	193,473	192,377	629,569
Partnership	39,969	72,889	130,862	193,473	192,377	629,569
S Corporation	35,664	67,412	122,962	182,645	177,598	566,281
C Corporation	42,121	71,141	129,312	196,179	553,160	991,912

In this case, note that as the tax liabilities increase, the results for the C corporation are much worse, in relative terms. This is because the excess cash generated will cause a second round of tax when distributed as dividends or as a final distribution upon liquidation. Tax Planning Problem #1 of this chapter varies other key factors in this model in order to analyze the sensitivity of the results across different assumptions, including an assumption that the preferential rate for dividends is eliminated.

¶15,025   Summary

- A business entity requires that a taxpayer be engaged in the activity with continuity and regularity, and with the primary purpose of making a profit.
- Under the check the box regulations, a taxpayer may choose the entity type for business; the default choices for a single owner is a sole proprietorship, and for multiple owners is a partnership.
- Employers other than self-employed individuals match their employees' 6.2% contributions for Social Security taxes (maximum $113,700 base for 2013) and 1.45% contributions for Medicare taxes; sole proprietors must pay both shares (12.4% and 2.9%).
- The sole proprietorship offers the advantages of simplicity and a single layer of taxation, while having the disadvantages of limited capital-raising potential and unlimited liability.
- The partnership offers the advantages of a single layer of taxation and a limited ability to allocate incomes among partners, while having the disadvantages of unlimited liability for general partners and prohibition on participation in the business activities by limited partners.
- Limited liability companies (LLCs) and limited liability partnerships (LLPs) are state-sanctioned entities that offer the advantages of being taxed as a partnership (a single layer of taxation) and limited liability (except in LLPs where personal negligence is a factor).
- The S corporation offers the advantages of a single layer of taxation and a limited liability for its owners, while having the disadvantages of a 100-shareholder limitation and the organizational complexities of a regular C corporation.
- The regular C corporation offers the advantages of tax-free fringe benefits for shareholder-employees, limited liability for its owners, and ease of raising capital and transferring interests, while having the disadvantages of double taxation and no flow-through of entity losses.
- Only the C corporation has double taxation, in that income is taxed when earned and then taxed a second time when distributed to shareholders, either as a dividend or a liquidating distribution; all other entity forms involve a single layer of taxation.

APPENDIX A

TAX RATE SCHEDULES

Tax Rate Schedule—Ordinary Corporations

If taxable income is

Over	But not over	The tax is:	of the amount over
$ 0	$ 50,000	15%	$ 0
50,000	75,000	$ 7,500.00 + 25%	50,000
75,000	100,000	13,750.00 + 34%	75,000
100,000	335,000	22,250.00 + 39%	100,000
335,000	10,000,000	113,900.00 + 34%	335,000
10,000,000	15,000,000	3,400,000.00 + 35%	10,000,000
15,000,000	18,333,333	5,150,000.00 + 38%	15,000,000
18,333,333	....	6,416,667.00 + 35%	18,333,333

2013 Tax Rate Schedule—Married Filing Jointly—Individual Tax Rate Schedule

If taxable income is

Over	But not over	The tax is:	of the amount over
$ 0	$ 17,850	10%	$ 0
17,850	72,500	$ 1,785.00 + 15%	17,850
72,500	146,400	9,982.50 + 25%	72,500
146,400	223,050	28,457.50 + 28%	146,400
223,050	398,350	49,919.50 + 33%	223,050
398,350	450,000	107,768.50 + 35%	398,350
450,000		125,846.00 + 39.6%	450,000

2013 Standard Deduction for Married Filing Jointly (in lieu of itemizing) $12,200

2013 Exemption Amount (per Exemption) $ 3,900

2013 FICA Tax Rates:

Social Security Portion   12.4% of the first $113,700 of FICA wages *

Medicare Portion   2.9% of all FICA wages *

* Liability shared equally by employer and employee (6.2% and 1.45% each)

2013 Self-Employment Tax Rates:

Social Security Portion   12.4% of the *lesser of:*

a) the first $113,700 of self-emp. income

b) self-employment income × .9235

Medicare Portion   2.9% of [self-employment income × .9235]

Appendix B

CASE STUDY

CHOICE OF ENTITY

FACTS OF THE CASE STUDY (B-1)

SOLE PROPRIETORSHIP (B-2)

PARTNERSHIP (B-3)

S CORPORATION (B-4)

C CORPORATION (B-5)

APPENDIX B-1—ENTITIES TAXATION CASE

COMPARISON OF THE FORMS OF DOING BUSINESS
(ASSUMING A 2013 TAX YEAR)

Facts:

Davidson Co. is in its first year of operations as a hardware and software retailer (with occasional consulting jobs). Davidson reports the following 2013 results (without respect to the type of entity):

"Business" Income:	
Sales (net of returns and allowances)	$ 645,000
Gross Consulting Fees Collected	30,000
Dividend Income (5% investment in Surreal Software Co.)	4,000
Loss on Sale of Surreal Stock ($28,000 – $33,000, held 9 months)	(5,000)
"Business" Expenses and Costs:	
Cost of Goods Sold	(142,200)
Salaries of five employees other than owner Dave Davidson ($50,000 each)	(250,000)
Payroll taxes paid on employees [($250,000 × .0765) + ($35,000 × .062)]	(21,295)
Health insurance coverage for employees ($3,000 × 5)	(15,000)
Retirement plan contributions for employees (10% of salaries)	(25,000)
MACRS depreciation on various company assets	(10,155)
Interest, utilities, insurance, supplies, deliveries, and miscellaneous expenses	(84,930)
Contributions to public charities	(13,300)
Compensation to Owners of "Business":	
Reasonable salary compensation to Dave Davidson	(75,000)
Other cash payments to owners	(50,000)
Health insurance coverage for Dave Davidson	(3,000)
Retirement plan contribution for owner (10% of "reasonable salary")	(7,500)

Dave and Ellen Davidson (both age 43) file a joint federal income tax return in 2013. They do not have any dependents. In addition to any compensation/income from the business described above, Ellen received a salary of $71,300 from ED Industries. Dave and Ellen also received $1,400 personal interest on a joint account, $1,200 personal dividends from jointly-held Thomson Co. stock, and $9,200 from the sale of 100 shares of Thomson stock (originally acquired five years ago for $3,100).

Dave and Ellen's personal expenses for 2013 include $2,600 personal property taxes, $11,400 state income taxes, 9,300 charitable contributions (not including the amounts mentioned above), $8,300 interest on personal home mortgage, and $4,181 of unreimbursed employee expenses by Ellen.

Required:

a. Assuming that Davidson Co. is operated as a sole proprietorship, determine the Davidsons' final federal income tax liability (including any self-employment tax).

b. Assuming that Davidson Co. is operated as a partnership (assuming that Dave Davidson is essentially a 100-percent partner, with a minimal interest held by Ellen), determine the Davidsons' final federal income tax liability (including any self-employment tax).

c. Assuming that Davidson Co. is operated as an S corporation (with Dave Davidson as essentially a 100-percent shareholder), determine the Davidsons' final federal income tax liability and any FICA taxes and unemployment taxes paid on Dave's compensation by Dave and by Davidson Co.

d. Assuming that Davidson Co. is operated as a C corporation (with Dave as a 100-percent shareholder), determine the final corporate income tax liability of Davidson Co., the Davidsons' final federal income tax liability and any FICA and unemployment taxes paid on Dave's compensation by Dave and by Davidson Co.

APPENDIX B-2

TAX RESULTS ASSUMING THAT DAVIDSON CO. IS A SOLE PROPRIETORSHIP (OWNED 100% BY DAVE DAVIDSON)

Schedule C Sole Proprietorship Income:

Gross profit – sales ($645,000 – $142,200)		$ 502,800
Consulting fees collected		30,000
Expenses:		
Salaries paid to **5** employees other than Dave Davidson ($50,000 each)		(250,000)
Payroll taxes paid on employees [(**$250,000** × .0765) + (**$35,000** × .062)]		(21,295)
Pension plan contribution on behalf of employees ($250,000 × .10)		(25,000)
Health insurance coverage for employees ($3,000 × **5**)		(15,000)
MACRS depreciation on company assets		(10,155)
Rent, utilities, insurance, supplies, deliveries, and miscellaneous expenses		(84,930)
Schedule C Sole Proprietorship Income		$126,420
Self-employment tax [(113,700 × .124) + (126,420 × .9235 × .029)]		**$ 17,485**

Form 1040 Personal Tax Return:

Schedule C income (see above)			**$126,420**
Salary (Ellen Davidson)			71,300
Interest (joint savings account)			1,400
Dividend income ($1,200 personal **plus $4,000 business**)			5,200
LT Gain on sale of Thomson Publishing Co. stock ($9,200 – $3,100)		$ 6,100	
ST Loss on sale of Surreal Stock (business – $28,000 – $33,000)		(5,000)	1,100
Gross Income			$205,420
Deductions for Adjusted Gross Income:			
SEP-IRA retirement plan contribution ($75,000 × .10)		7,500	
One-half of self-employment tax paid ($17,485 × .50)		8,742	
100% of self-employed health insurance ($3,000 × 1.00)		3,000	(19,242)
Adjusted Gross Income			$ 186,178
Personal Exemption Deductions ($3,900 × 2)			(7,800)
Itemized Deductions (greater than the 2013 standard deduction):			
Medical		$ 0	
State and local taxes [$2,600 + $11,400]		14,000	
Qualifying home mortgage interest		8,300	
Charitable contributions ($9,300 personal **plus 13,300 bus**)		22,600	
Miscellaneous expenses [$4,181 – ($186,178 × .02)]		458	(45,358)
Taxable Income			$ 133,020
Gross federal income tax liability [per 2013 tax rate schedules]			$ 24,483*
Self-employment tax			17,485
Total taxes paid as a sole proprietor entity			$ 41,968

* Tax includes regular tax liability on $126,720 ($133,020 – $1,100 – $5,200) plus 15% rate on the $1,100 net long-term capital gain and $5,200 dividend income.

APPENDIX B-3—TAX RESULTS ASSUMING THAT DAVIDSON CO. IS A PARTNERSHIP
(OWNED 99.9% BY DAVE DAVIDSON AND .1% BY ELLEN DAVIDSON)

Partnership Ordinary (Operating) Income:

Gross profit – sales ($645,000 – $142,200)	$ 502,800
Consulting fees collected	30,000
Expenses:	
Salaries paid to **5** employees other than Dave Davidson ($50,000 each)	(250,000)
Payroll taxes paid on employees [(**$250,000** × .0765) + (**$35,000** × .062)]	(21,295)
Pension plan contribution on behalf of employees ($250,000 × .10)	(25,000)
Health insurance coverage for employees ($3,000 × **5**)	(15,000)
MACRS depreciation on company assets	(10,155)
Interest, utilities, insurance, supplies, deliveries, and miscellaneous expenses	(84,930)
Salary (guar. payments) to Dave Davidson ($75,000 + $3,000 + $7,500)	**(85,500)**
Partnership Ordinary (Operating) Income	$ 40,920

Special Partnership Items (reported separately):

Dividend income (5% investment in Surreal Co.)	$ 4,000
Loss on sale of Surreal Co. stock ($28,000 – $33,000, held 9 months)	(5,000)
Contributions to public charities	(13,300)
Self-employment tax [(113,700 × .124) + (126,420 × .9235 × .029)]	**$ 17,485**

Form 1040 Personal Tax Return:

Shares of partnership ordinary income (see above)		**$ 40,920**
Guaranteed payment to David Davidson (salary, ins., and pension contr)		**85,500**
Salary (Ellen Davidson)		71,300
Interest (joint savings account)		1,400
Dividend income ($1,200 personal **plus $4,000 partnership share**)		5,200
LT Gain on sale of Thomson Publishing Co. stock ($9,200 – $3,100)	$ 6,100	
Share of partnership short-term capital loss ($28,000 – $33,000)	**(5,000)**	1,100
Gross Income		$ 205,420
Deductions for Adjusted Gross Income:		
SEP-IRA retirement plan contribution ($75,000 × .10)	7,500	
One-half of self-employment tax paid ($17,485 × .50)	8,742	
100% of self-employed health insurance ($3,000 × 1.00)	3,000	(19,242)
Adjusted Gross Income		$ 186,178
Personal exemption deductions ($3,900 × 2)		(7,800)
Itemized Deductions (greater than the 2013 standard deduction):		
Medical	$ 0	
State and local taxes [$2,600 + $11,400]	14,000	
Qualifying home mortgage interest	8,300	
Charitable contributions – ($9,300 pers **plus $13,300 p'ship**)	22,600	
Miscellaneous expenses [$4,181 – ($186,178 × .02)]	458	(45,358)
Taxable Income		$ 133,020
Gross federal income tax liability [per 2013 tax rate schedules]		$ 24,483
Self-employment tax		17,485
Total taxes paid as a partnership tax entity		$ 41,968

APPENDIX B-4—TAX RESULTS ASSUMING THAT DAVIDSON CO. IS AN S CORPORATION
(OWNED 100% BY DAVE DAVIDSON)

S Corporation Ordinary Income

Gross profit – sales ($645,000 – $142,200)	$ 502,800
Consulting fees collected	30,000
Expenses:	
Salaries paid to employees **and to Dave Davidson** (5@$50,000 + **$78,000**)	(328,000)
Payroll taxes paid on employees **[($328,000 × .0765) + ($42,000 × .062)]**	(27,696)
Health insurance coverage for employees ($3,000 × 5)	(15,000)
Pension plan contribution for employees and Davidson **($325,000 × .10)**	**(32,500)**
MACRS depreciation on company assets	(10,155)
Rent, utilities, insurance, supplies, deliveries, and miscellaneous expenses)	(84,930)
S Corporation Ordinary (Operating) Income	$ 34,519

Special S Corporation Items (reported separately):

Dividend income (5% investment in Surreal Co.)	$ 4,000
Loss on sale of Surreal Co. stock (held 2 years)	(5,000)
Contributions to public charities	(13,300)

Form 1040 Personal Tax Return:

Shares of S corporation ordinary income (see above)		**$ 34,519**
Salary from S corporation (David Davidson ($55,000 + $3,000)		**78,000**
Salary (Ellen Davidson)		71,300
Interest (joint savings account)		1,400
Dividend income ($1,200 personal **plus $4,000 S corp. share**)		5,200
LT Gain on sale of Thomson Publishing Co. stock ($9,200 – $3,100)	$ 6,100	
Share of S corp. short-term capital loss ($28,000 – $33,000)	**(5,000)**	1,100
Gross Income		$191,519
Deductions for Adjusted Gross Income:		
100% of self-employed health insurance ($3,000 × 1.00)	**3,000**	(3,000)
Adjusted Gross Income		$ 188,519
Personal exemption deductions ($3,900 × 2)		(7,800)
Itemized Deductions (greater than the 2013 standard deduction):		
Medical	$ 0	
State and local taxes [$2,600 + $11,400]	14,000	
Qualifying home mortgage interest	8,300	
Charitable contributions – ($9,300 pers **plus $13,300 S corp**)	22,600	
Miscellaneous expenses [$4,181 – ($188,519 × .02)]	411	(45,311)
Taxable Income		$135,408

Gross federal income tax liability [per 2013 tax rate schedules]	$ 25,080
Self employment tax	0
FICA taxes paid by Dave Davidson on salary ($78,000 × .0765)	5,967
FICA taxes paid by the S corporation on Dave Davidson's salary (matching)	**5,967**
Unemployment taxes paid by the S corporation on Dave Davidson's salary	**434**
Total taxes paid as an S corporation	$ 37,448

APPENDIX B-5—TAX RESULTS ASSUMING THAT DAVIDSON CO. IS A REGULAR C CORPORATION (OWNED 100% BY DAVE DAVIDSON)

C Corporation Taxable Income and Tax Liability:

Gross profit – sales ($645,000 – $142,200)	$ 502,800
Consulting fees collected	30,000
Dividend Income (5% investment in Surreal Software Co.)	**4,000**
Capital loss on sale of Surreal Stock (not deductible against ord income)	**0**
Gross Income	$ 536,800

Expenses:

Salaries paid to employees **and to Dave Davidson** (5@$50,000 + **$75,000**)	(325,000)
Payroll taxes paid on employees [(**$325,000** × .0765) + (**$42,000** × .062)]	(27,466)
Health insurance coverage for employees ($3,000 × **6**)	(18,000)
Pension plan contributions for emp and Davidson ($325,000 × .10)	(32,500)
MACRS depreciation on company assets	(10,155)
Interest, utilities, insurance, supplies, deliveries, and miscellaneous expenses	(84,930)
Income before charitable deduction and dividends rec'd deduction	$ 38,749
Charitable Contributions [$13,300, limited to $38,749 × .10]	**(3,875)**
Dividends received deduction ($4,000 × .70)	**(2,800)**
C Corporation Taxable Income	$ 32,074

C Corporation Tax Liability ($32,074 × .15)	$ 4,811

Form 1040 Personal Tax Return:

Salary from C corporation (David Davidson (**$75,000 + $0 ins**)		$ 75,000
Salary (Ellen Davidson)		71,300
Interest (joint savings account)		1,400
Dividend income ($1,200 **plus $50,000 C corporation distribution**)		51,200
Long-term gain on sale of Thomson Publishing Co. stock ($9,200 – $3,100)		**6,100**
Gross Income		$205,000
Deductions for Adjusted Gross Income		(0)
Adjusted Gross Income		$205,000
Personal exemption deductions ($3,900 × 2)		(7,800)
Itemized Deductions (greater than the 2013 standard deduction):		
Medical	$ 0	
State and local taxes [$2,600 + $11,400]	14,000	
Qualifying home mortgage interest	8,300	
Charitable contributions (**$9,300 personal only**)	9,300	
Miscellaneous expenses [$4,181 – ($205,000 × .02)]	81	(31,681)
Taxable Income		$ 165,519

Gross federal income tax liability [per 2013 tax rate schedules]	$ 27,507
Self employment tax	0
FICA taxes paid by Dave Davidson on salary ($75,000 × .0765)	5,738
FICA taxes paid by the C corporation on Dave Davidson's salary (matching)	**5,738**
Unemployment taxes paid by the S corporation on Dave Davidson's salary	**434**
Federal income tax liability of C corporation	**4,811**
Total taxes paid as a regular C corporation	$ 44,228

Appendix C

SUMMARY

KEY FACTORS IN CHOICE OF ENTITY

SOLE PROPRIETORSHIP

PARTNERSHIP

S CORPORATION

C CORPORATION

SOLE PROPRIETORSHIP ENTITY
KEY FACTORS ANALYSIS

Nontax Factors:

- *Formalities of Existence.* Few legal formalities are necessary when forming a sole proprietorship, since the business and the owner are treated as a single entity under the law. An employment identification number must be secured if employees will be used in the business.
- *Limited Liability of Owners.* A sole proprietor has unlimited personal liability in regards to business debts. This is a primary disadvantage of this entity type; creditors can attach personal assets.
- *Ability to Raise Capital.* A sole proprietor may face difficulty in raising capital for the business, since other owners are not involved. Bringing in partners or incorporating may be the only practical means of raising additional capital.
- *Participation in Management.* The sole proprietor has total control in managing the business, as there are no other owners to answer to.
- *Transferability of Interests.* The sole proprietor can easily transfer the business through sale or exchange. A sole proprietorship may be easily dissolved, with assets converted to personal use.

Tax Factors:

- *Tax Aspects of Formation.* The formation of a sole proprietorship is not a taxable event; the basis of assets contributed to the business is generally the proprietor's adjusted basis (unless the fair market value of converted assets is less than the adjusted basis at contribution).
- *Taxation as a Separate Entity vs. Pass-Through Entity.* The sole proprietorship business and the owner are treated as a single entity for tax purposes. The net income of the business is determined on Schedule C, and this amount is included in gross income on the Form 1040. Net losses would generally be deductible by the sole proprietor unless the hobby loss rules apply. Cash withdrawals generally have no effect on tax liability. Liquidation of the business by sale or exchange would involve a single layer of tax, with gains and losses reported on the individual tax return.
- *Taxation of Owner Compensation.* The sole proprietor is always taxed on the net income of the business (as reflected on Schedule C), regardless of withdrawals. Thus, the designation of a salary as "reasonable compensation" is meaningless in the sole proprietorship, and any other cash withdrawals have no effect on the final tax liability. The sole proprietorship is always subject to a single level of tax at the owner level. As to deferred compensation, a sole proprietor may establish a Keogh (HR-10) plan that provides benefits similar to corporate plans; immediate deductions for contributions, tax-free accumulation of income on the trusteed contributions, and deferral of tax until withdrawals (presumably at retirement). However, employees must be covered under the qualified plan rules.
- *Ability to Provide Tax-Favored Fringe Benefits.* The sole proprietorship entity does not provide a vehicle for tax-favored fringe benefits. However, in a limited attempt to provide parity with corporate entities with regards to health insurance coverage, a sole proprietor may deduct *for* adjusted gross income 100 percent of insurance premiums for health coverage for the sole proprietor and his or her family.

PARTNERSHIP ENTITY
KEY FACTORS ANALYSIS

Nontax Factors:

- *Formalities of Existence.* A partnership entity generally requires a partnership agreement that specifies the rights and responsibilities of the partners, including profit and loss sharing ratios. This agreement would need to be modified each time additional partners are added.

- *Limited Liability of Owners.* General partners (those who participate in the management of the partnership) have unlimited personal liability. The partnership may also be structured to offer limited partnership interests, where such partners' liability is limited to invested capital. However, limited partners may not actively participate in the management of the business.

- *Ability to Raise Capital.* Partnerships offer increased flexibility as to ability to raise capital when compared to sole proprietorships. Additional partnership interests may be offered as a means of raising additional capital; however, this entails changes in the underlying partnership agreement.

- *Participation in Management.* General partners are free to participate actively in managing the business, but limited partners are prohibited from managing the day to day affairs of the business. Because of this prohibition, limited partners are likely to be subject to the passive activity limitations.

- *Transferability of Interests.* Transfers of partnership interests can be somewhat complex, as other partners may have to agree to the transfer and the underlying documents will need to be amended. Transfers of more than 50 percent in interests will terminate the partnership for federal tax purposes.

Tax Factors:

- *Tax Aspects of Formation.* The formation of a partnership is generally not a taxable event unless the interest received is compensation for services or the liabilities assumed by other partners exceed the adjusted basis of the property to the contributing partner. In general, taxable transfers are less likely to occur with partnership formation; there is no 80-percent control requirement. Another positive aspect of a partnership is that a partner's tax basis includes is his or her share of partnership liabilities.

- *Taxation as a Separate Entity vs. Pass-Through Entity.* The partnership is a conduit entity for federal tax purposes; the single layer of tax is applied at the individual partner level. (The same rules apply for limited liability entities.) Items of partnership income, deductions, and credits retain their character and generally flow through to the partners based on profit and loss sharing ratios (this is also true of losses); however, special allocations having "substantial economic effect" may be made. Guaranteed payments are deductible in determining partnership ordinary income and are allocated directly to recipient partners. Distributions need not be pro rata in a partnership entity.

- *Taxation of Owner Compensation.* A partner is always taxed on his or her share of the "ordinary income" of the business, his or her share of any guaranteed payments, and his or her share of "separately stated items". Any cash withdrawals ("other cash payments") generally have no effect on the final tax liability. General partners may also establish Keogh accounts for deferred compensation, and these operate much like the Keogh account of a self-employed individual described above.

- *Ability to Provide Tax-Favored Fringe Benefits.* The partnership entity does not provide a vehicle for tax-favored fringe benefits. However, like a sole proprietor, general partners may deduct 100 percent of insurance premiums for health coverage for the sole proprietor and his or her family.

S CORPORATION ENTITY
KEY FACTORS ANALYSIS

Nontax Factors:

- *Formalities of Existence.* An S corporation is a separate entity for purposes other than tax, and as such, must conform to various legal and/or state requirements for incorporation. Additionally, strict election requirements must be met for federal tax purposes.

- *Limited Liability of Owners.* Since the S corporation is a separate legal entity, it offers the regular corporate advantage of limited liability for its owners. However, this advantage may be somewhat mitigated by the fact that creditors may require the owners of a startup S corporation (particularly in the case of family businesses) to personally guarantee notes for the initial financing of the business.

- *Ability to Raise Capital.* The 100 shareholder limit for S corporation status may cause some minor problems in raising capital. However, the company can issue as many shares as it desires, as the limit is stated in terms of the number of shareholders and not the number of shares.

- *Participation in Management.* Because of the limited number of shareholders in an S corporation, it may be possible for the owners to participate more in company management than in a regular C corporation.

- *Transferability of Interests.* Transfers of S corporation interests are generally easier to accomplish than transfers of partnership interests, since the S corporation shareholder can sell his or her shares. However, care must be taken so that the sale is not to a disqualified shareholder or that the sale causes problems with the 100 shareholder limit.

Tax Factors:

- *Tax Aspects of Formation.* The formation of an S corporation involves the same tax consequences as the formation of a regular C corporation. Thus, nontaxable treatment is assured only if the shareholder receives no boot, performs no services, does not transfer assets with liabilities exceeding basis, and most importantly, meets the 80-percent control requirement. Although liabilities are not added to a shareholder's basis, the tax basis of any unpaid loans to the S corporation may be recovered

- *Taxation as a Separate Entity vs. Pass-Through Entity.* The S corporation is a conduit entity for federal tax purposes; the single layer of tax is applied at the individual shareholder level. Items of S corporation income, deductions, and credits flow through to the shareholders of record at the end of the tax year and retain their character. Any distributions must be pro rata. Any operating losses would also flow through to the individual S corporation shareholders. It is important to note that some states may not recognize S corporation status for state income tax purposes.

- *Taxation of Owner Compensation.* The S corporation shareholder who is also an employee is treated as an employee of the separate corporate entity. Thus, such owner/employee is taxed on any compensation received, is subject to the normal FICA withholding rules, and is treated as an employee for pension plan purposes. Other distributions to an S shareholder/employee are treated as nontaxable withdrawals (as long as the amounts do not exceed basis).

- *Ability to Provide Tax-Favored Fringe Benefits.* The normal tax-favored treatment of fringe benefits available to shareholder/employees in regular C corporations (deduction for the corporation and exclusion for the employee) is generally not available to shareholder/employees in S corporations. The only exception is for those S shareholder/employees who own a two-percent or less interest in the S corporation. This seldom occurs in most closely-held family businesses.

C CORPORATION ENTITY
KEY FACTORS ANALYSIS

Nontax Factors:

- *Formalities of Existence.* A C corporation is a separate entity for tax and nontax purposes, and as such, must conform to various specific legal and/or state requirements for incorporation.

- *Limited Liability of Owners.* Since the C corporation is a separate legal entity, it offers the advantage of limited liability for its owners. However, as mentioned earlier with S corporations, this advantage may be somewhat mitigated by the fact that creditors may require the owners to guarantee personally any loans used to start the business.

- *Ability to Raise Capital.* The C corporation offers maximum flexibility in terms of the ability to raise capital. Different types of stock and securities may be offered as a means to raise such capital; limitations are not imposed by the Code (other than the possible danger of having some debt reclassified as stock because the corporation is too "thinly capitalized.")

- *Participation in Management.* In most cases, the stock of a C corporation is widely held, which effectively limits the ability of owners to participate in the management of the company. Most major decisions of the business are in the hands of an independent Board of Directors.

- *Transferability of Interests.* The C corporation offers maximum flexibility in transferring interests. A shareholder may sell his or her shares without any disruption to the ongoing business of the corporation.

Tax Factors:

- *Tax Aspects of Formation.* Nontaxable treatment in forming a C corporation is assured only if the contributing shareholder receives no boot, performs no services, does not transfer assets with liabilities exceeding basis, and most importantly, meets the 80-percent control requirement. The strict requirements of Code Sec. 351 must be satisfied before the entity formation is tax-free.

- *Taxation as a Separate Entity vs. Pass-Through Entity.* The major disadvantage of a C corporation is the double taxation possibility, since the corporation is treated as a separate tax entity. Income is taxed once at the corporate level and then again when distributed to shareholders at a 15-percent tax rate (unless in the form of deductible salary, rent, or interest). Also, capital losses and operating losses may not be passed through to the owners; they remain at the corporate level. If losses are expected for several years after formation, an S election should be considered if at all possible.

- *Taxation of Owner Compensation.* The C corporation shareholder/employee is treated as an employee of the separate corporate entity. Thus, such owner/employee is taxed on any compensation received, is subject to the normal FICA withholding rules, and is treated as an employee for pension plan purposes. Other distributions to a C shareholder/employee are treated as taxable dividends (taxed at a 15-percent rate) unless payments represent deductible rent or interest paid to the shareholder.

- *Ability to Provide Tax-Favored Fringe Benefits.* The tax-favored treatment of fringe benefits available to shareholder/employees is a major advantage offered by regular C corporations. Such benefits as health and insurance, group-term life insurance, reimbursement plans, meals and lodging, child care payments, educational benefits, and other items are deductible by the corporation and are excludable from income by the employee.

Review Questions for Chapter 15

True or False

Indicate which of the following statements are true or false by circling the correct answer.

1. One of the requirements for "engaging in a business activity" is that the entity must have a primary purpose of making income or a profit.   T   F

2. To be a taxable entity, the entity must be a "person" as defined in Code Sec. 7701(a).   T   F

3. A sole proprietorship is a conduit entity.   T   F

4. The default entity for a business having only one owner is a single-owner C corporation.   T   F

5. FUTA and SUTA taxes apply to the first $6,000 of income earned by each employee during the tax year.   T   F

6. Ace Hardware has an employee who earns $10,000. Ace Hardware may deduct $1,530 of employment taxes related to this employee, since that was the amount paid in total to the government.   T   F

7. If two co-owners of a rental property provide any services at all, the entity must be classified and taxed as a partnership.   T   F

8. A net Code Sec. 1231 gain would be included in partnership "ordinary income."   T   F

9. An S corporation must have no more than 75 shareholders, after counting certain family members as one shareholder.   T   F

10. A transfer consisting solely of property to a C corporation by a shareholder is not taxable if all contributing shareholders in the transaction receive at least 80 percent of the outstanding stock for property or services.   T   F

Fill in the Blanks

The table below lists the primary nontax and tax considerations in the choice of entity decision. For each factor, provide a ranking of from 1 to 4 as to which entity fares best. If you believe that two or more entities are roughly equal, then you may provide them the same ranking (e.g., the rankings for one factor might be 1, 2, 2, 4, for example). The first factor is illustrated with a subjective ranking.

	Sole Proprietor	(G & L) * Partnership	S Corporation	C Corporation
Nontax Factors:				
11. Formalities of Forming the Entity	1	2	3	3
12. Limited Liability of Owners				
13. Ability to Raise Capital for the Entity				
14. Participation in Management				
15. Transferability of Interests				
Tax Factors:				
16. Tax Aspects of Entity Formation				
17. Taxation as a Separate Entity vs. Pass-Through				
18. Taxation of Owner Compensation				
19. Providing Tax-favored Fringe Benefits				
20. Tax Consequences of Liquidation				

* A partnership with both general and limited partners (primary owner is a general partner)

Multiple Choice
Circle the best answer for each of the following questions.

21. In order to "carry on" a business, an entity must:
    a. have one or more associates
    b. have assets
    c. engage in some business activity
    d. all of the above

22. Under the check the box regulations, a business entity with two or more owners may elect to be taxed as a:
    a. sole proprietorship
    b. C corporation
    c. Partnership
    d. (b) or (c)

23. A sole-proprietorship business reports $100,000 of self-employment income on Schedule C. The amount of such income subject to the Social Security portion of the self-employment tax will be:
    a. $50,000
    b. $92,350
    c. $100,000
    d. $102,000

24. A sole-proprietorship business reports $100,000 of self-employment income on Schedule C. The amount of such income subject to the Medicare portion of the self-employment tax will be:
    a. $50,000
    b. $92,350
    c. $100,000
    d. $102,000

25. Bill Small, a self-employed plumber, made $2,500 of contributions to a local university by writing a check from his business account. This contribution will be reported by Bill on:
    a. Schedule A, Form 1040
    b. Schedule B, Form 1040
    c. Schedule SE, Form 1040
    d. Either (a) or (b), at the option of the taxpayer

26. In exchange for a one-third interest in a partnership, Ally Harris contributed land worth $80,000 (Ally's adjusted basis in the land was $60,000). Ally's gain recognized on the contribution of the land to the partnership, and her basis in the partnershjp interest, would be:
    a. $0 and $60,000
    b. $0 and $80,000
    c. $20,000 and $60,000
    d. $20,000 and $80,000

27. During the current year, ABC Partnership had $300,000 ordinary business revenues, $180,000 ordinary business expenses, a $60,000 guaranteed payment to A and a $30,000 guaranteed payment to B, and $10,000 dividend income. Partner C's one-third share of the ordinary income of the partnership, before considering specially allocated items, is:
    a. $10,000
    b. $20,000
    c. $30,000
    d. $40,000

28. Which of the following items would be part of ordinary partnership income, and thus not treated as a separately stated item?
    a.   Charitable contributions
    b.   Depreciation recapture under Code Sec. 1245
    c.   Short-term capital gains
    d.   None of the above (all are separately stated items)

29. Allen Ross is a shareholder-employee in a qualifying S corporation. For payroll tax purposes, Allen will be:
    a.   treated as a self-employed person
    b.   treated as a partner in a large partnership
    c.   treated as an employee of the S corporation
    d.   none of the above

30. Bleaker Corporation, a regular C corporation, incurred a $40,000 loss in its first year of doing business. This amount includes a $36,000 operating loss and a $4,000 short-term capital loss. Bob Bleaker owns 100 percent of Bleaker Corporation. As a result of this loss, Bob Bleaker will report on his Form 1040 for the year:
    a.   only the capital loss
    b.   only the operating loss
    c.   both the capital loss and the operating loss
    d.   neither the capital loss nor the operating loss

Problems

31. Melva Rhymer, a self-employed electrician, has Schedule C income of $200,000 during the year 2013. What is Melva's self-employment tax liability?
32. Refer to Problem 31. What may Melva deduct on her Form 1040 in regards to the self-employment tax paid? Where is this amount reported?
33. Sam "22" Elliott gambles full time solely for his own account. May he deduct his gambling losses as a deduction from gross income?
34. Susan Whitley purchased 500 acres of land in a rapidly growing part of the county. She anticipates holding the land for five years and selling it at a large profit. Her only expenditure is for annual real estate taxes on the land. Is Susan carrying on a trade or business?
35. The ABC Partnership is owned equally by Apple, Banana, and Citrus. During the year ABC has ordinary partnership income of $300,000 before considering a $60,000 payment to Apple for his services and a $30,000 payment to Banana as interest on his capital investment. What is each partner's share of partnership income for the year, including any guaranteed payments?
36. During 2013, Larry Ramis had the following items of income and expenditures in his sole proprietorship business: $450,000 gross receipts, $20,000 dividends on business stock investments, $4,000 capital gain on the sale of stock of a supplier, $260,000 cost of goods sold, $40,000 utilities expenses, $70,000 salaries expenses, $40,000 withdrawals by Larry, and $4,000 cash given from the business account to a local charity. What is Larry's Schedule C business income or loss, a figure that is also used to compute the self-employment tax liability?
37. Joyce Woodward owns land with an adjusted basis of $200,000 and a fair market value of $300,000. The land is also subject to a $240,000 loan. Which, if any, of the following transactions would require Joyce to report gain on contributing such property to the specified entity: (a) the contribution is to Corporation A for 90 percent of the outstanding stock of A; (b) the contribution is to WXY partnership for a one-third partnership interest.
38. Sandra Barnett owns 70 percent of the outstanding stock of Belco Corporation; the remaining shares are owned by her children. During the current year, Belco paid a salary of $130,000 to Sandra. If Belco is a regular C corporation, the IRS is likely to argue that the salary payment is too *large*. On the other hand, if Belco is an S corporation, the IRS is likely to argue that the salary payment is too *small*. Explain this paradox.

39. During 2013, Larry Barlow had the following items of income and expenditures in his sole proprietorship business: $380,000 gross receipts, $12,000 dividends on business stock investments, $14,000 capital loss on the sale of stock of a supplier, $210,000 cost of goods sold, $40,000 advertising expenses, $100,000 salaries expenses (which includes a $36,000 salary paid to himself), and $7,000 cash given from the business account to a local charity. What is Larry's self-employment income and self-employment tax liability for 2013?

40. Sally Wilkinson contributes land (adjusted basis of $55,000 and fair market value of $100,000) to WXY Partnership in exchange for a one-third partnership interest. In addition, the partnership assumes Sally's $90,000 liability on the land. Determine the following: (1) taxable gain (if any) reported by Sally, (2) tax basis of Sally's partnership interest, and (3) tax basis of the land to WXY Partnership.

41. During the current year, DEF Partnership (owned equally by D, E and F) had $150,000 ordinary business revenues, a $3,000 capital loss, $80,000 ordinary business expenses, a $20,000 charitable deduction, and $20,000 of dividend income. In addition, DEF made a guaranteed salary payment of $40,000 to D, and each of the three partners withdrew $10,000 of non-guaranteed payments. Determine each partner's share of ordinary partnership income, guaranteed payments, and specially allocated items.

42. Sue McCain is a 35-percent owner/employee in Baker Company, a qualifying S corporation. During the current year, the S corporation reported $100,000 of ordinary income. Determine Sue's self-employment tax liability for the year, assuming that Sue's "salary" is $50,000.

43. Malvern Company has a net income in 2013 of $180,000, before considering the $130,000 payments to its owner, Melva Malvern. Melva is married to Jim Malvern, and they do not have any children or other dependents; thus, they qualify for two exemption deductions worth a total of $7,800. Melva and Jim are both 45 years of age. Their itemized deductions for the year total $17,200 under all scenarios.

    Required: Determine the following amounts, assuming that Malvern is a self-employed individual. Ignore any federal unemployment tax liability (FUTA), but do consider any allowable expense deductions for the FICA and/or self-employment tax. (See hints below.)

Self-employment taxes paid	$ _____
Federal income taxes paid by Melva & Jim Malvern	_____
Total taxes paid	$ _____

44. Assume the same facts as Problem 43, except that Malvern Company is a corporation, and Melva and Jim are the only shareholders. Assume that $80,000 of the $130,000 payment to Melva is a reasonable salary, and the remaining $50,000 is a taxable dividend.

FICA taxes paid in by Melva as an employee	$ _____
FICA taxes paid by Malvern Co. on Melva's salary	_____
Federal income taxes paid by Malvern Co.	_____
Federal income taxes paid by Melva & Jim Malvern	_____
Total taxes paid	$ _____

45. Assume the same facts as Problem 43, except that the entire $130,000 payment to Melva represents a reasonable salary; there are no dividend payments.

FICA taxes paid in by Melva as an employee	$ _____
FICA taxes paid by Malvern Co. on Melva's salary	_____
Federal income taxes paid by Malvern Co.	_____
Federal income taxes paid by Melva & Jim Malvern	_____
Total taxes paid	$ _____

Hints: Do not forget that (1) one-half of the self-employment tax paid is a deduction in determining the taxable income of the sole proprietor, (2) the corporation and the employee share the FICA tax liability, and (3) the corporation's $180,000 income has not been reduced by the salary deduction or the company's share of the FICA taxes paid. Ignore FUTA and SUTA taxes for purposes of all computations.

Compliance Problems

46. Hunter Solutions is a computer consulting company that reports the following in 2013:

Gross Consulting Fees Collected	$434,650
Expenses:	
Office equipment rental fees	$32,400
Office rent	76,480
Supplies	23,120
Salaries to Employees (4 @ $40,000 each)	160,000
Miscellaneous expenses	57,650
Contributions (cash)	1,000
Reasonable compensation to Owner (Karen Hunter)	60,000
Other cash withdrawals by Karen Hunter	10,000

Karen Hunter is married to Bob Hunter, who earned a salary of $62,000 during 2013 (with $6,100 withheld as federal income taxes). Karen and Bob's only other income during the year was $450 interest, and their only deductible personal expenses are $9,600 state income taxes, $900 charitable contributions (cash), and $6,500 mortgage interest on their home. Karen made estimated federal income tax payments of $18,000 during 2013. Assuming that Hunter Solutions is operated as a sole proprietorship, prepare a Form 1040 for Bob and Karen Hunter, with accompanying Schedules A and B (if necessary), C, and SE. On the Schedule C, be sure to deduct FICA taxes paid by Hunter on the four employees and federal and state unemployment taxes paid on the four employees (at a 6.2-percent rate on the first $7,000 of earnings per employee).

47. Refer to Problem 46 above. Assuming that Hunter Solutions is operated as a corporation, prepare a Form 1120 (front page only) for Hunter, and prepare a Form 1040 for Bob and Karen Hunter, with accompanying Schedules A and B (if necessary). (In this case, the FICA taxes and the federal unemployment taxes paid by the corporation will be on the four employees and Karen Hunter.)

48. Refer to Problem 46 above. Assuming that Hunter Solutions is operated as a partnership (and for simplicity, assume that Karen Hunter is a 100-percent partner), prepare a From 1065 for the Hunter partnership, a Schedule K-1 for Karen Hunter, and a Form 1040 for Bob and Karen Hunter, with accompanying Schedules A and B (if necessary), E, and SE. (In this case, the partnership pays FICA tax and federal and state unemployment tax on the four employees.)

Planning Problems

49. Refer to Tax Planning Case 15-1 on the textbook website (*CCHGroup.com/ContemporaryTax*). This case involves manipulating additional variables in the Entity spreadsheet discussed earlier in the chapter, and analyzing the effects of changes in such inputs. The Entities-2013 Excel comprehensive spreadsheet is used to solve this case.

Research Problems

50. An S corporation converted to a limited partnership and also concurrently elected to be treated as an association taxable as a corporation. Will such actions terminate its S corporation election? Explain.

51. Upon audit, a two-member limited liability compa ny (LLC) was reclassified as a single-member LLC because one of the members held no economic interest in the entity. Under the LLC agreement, all decisions were made by one of the members, and all profits, losses, and credits were allocated to that member. Upon dissolution of the LLC, that member was to wind up the LLC's affairs. Since the LLC was considered a single-member entity, and the fact that the active member had not elected to be treated as a separate entity, could the IRS disregarded the LLC entity for tax purposes? Explain.

52. An oil and gas partnership incurred $230,000 of intangible drilling and development costs. Are these costs part of the ordinary income of the partnership, or are the costs treated as separately stated items? Explain.

CHAPTER **16**

Tax Planning Strategies— Business Entities

Learning Objectives

After completing this chapter you will gain a better understanding of the following issues of special importance to business entities:

1. Adopting and changing methods of accounting
2. Inventory method issues and planning possibilities
3. Planning for the acquisition, use and disposal of business property
4. Corporate Planning ideas for the Alternative Minimum Tax and Dividends Received Deduction

¶16,001 Introduction

This chapter covers several diverse, but important, issues relating to business entities. When a business entity's gross profit includes a deduction for Cost of Goods Sold, several important accounting method issues must be considered. These issues include how to compute ending inventory using Last-in-First-Out (LIFO) and the impact on the Uniform Capitalization rules of Code Sec. 263A on the Cost of Goods Sold Deduction. Likewise, a business entity that purchases personal and real property has several tax planning opportunities that can maximize the tax savings from depreciating these items using accelerated methods. The chapter concludes with a discussion of two additional tax planning strategies applicable to the corporate taxpayer: how to minimize the corporate Alternative Minimum Tax and how to maximize the corporate Dividends Received Deduction. The next section begins with a review of permissible accounting methods and what steps to take when a business entity discovers that it is using an impermissible or erroneous accounting method.

¶16,003   Adopting and Changing a Method of Accounting

Recent years have produced an upsurge in tax planning ideas involving accounting methods. As Congress looks to restrict accounting method choices as a means of raising additional revenue, tax professionals must be diligent in planning how to mitigate the adverse effect of these changes on their clients.

.01   SIGNIFICANCE OF "ACCOUNTING METHODS"

As Congress continues to broaden the income base, changes in the various accounting method rules are tempting revenue-raisers, since these changes typically invoke little or no political reaction. Over half of the revenue-raising provisions in The Tax Reform Act of 1986 related to changes in accounting methods. The IRS takes the position that it has virtually unlimited discretion in the accounting methods area with a number of court cases supporting this contention.

There may be significant costs of not using the best possible accounting method for a client (for example, taking advantage of certain income deferral opportunities, such as Rev. Proc. 2004-34 for service providers). Possible penalties may arise because of the use of an improper method of accounting, and in this regard, the IRS may go back to the earliest year to compute cumulative adjustments if improper methods are being used. Changing methods is not costless; the minimum costs include a $2,500 user fee ($625 if gross income is $250,000 or less) and the fees associated with preparing the change application (Form 3115). Accounting methods issues currently have a high priority with the Treasury; for example, many items on the IRS list of Coordinated Issues in its Industry Specialization Program relate to accounting methods.

.03   ACCOUNTING METHOD DEFINED

The Term "method of accounting" is not defined in either the Code or the Regulations. Code Sec. 446 states only that *"taxable income shall be computed under the method of accounting on the basis of which the taxpayer regularly computes his income in keeping his books."* And Reg. §1.446-1(a) (1) states that "[t]he term 'method of accounting' includes not only the over-all method of accounting of the taxpayer but also the accounting treatment of any item."

A workable definition of an accounting method is simply *any consistently applied practice of recognizing income or expense.* A "method of accounting" determines the timing of when an item of income or expense is to be recognized. This was specifically noted by the U.S. Supreme Court in *Indianapolis Power and Light,* where it was noted that a method of accounting involves a question of "timing" over the lifetime of the business (in this case, the timing for recognizing deposits from utility customers as income).[1]

This "timing requirement" was subsequently incorporated in IRS guidance on accounting methods.[2] In contrast, a question involving an improper deduction is *not* an accounting methods issue where an arbitrary practice of always writing off bad debts in one year and including them in income in the next year was no method at all.[3]

.05   ADOPTING AN ACCOUNTING METHOD

Three court cases that have shaped the law as to exactly when an accounting method is adopted are:

- *Pacific National Co.* The court held that once an accounting method is chosen on an initial return, the taxpayer is bound by the choice and may not file an amended return to change the election.[4]

---

[1]   *Indianapolis Power and Light*, SCt, 90-1 USTC ¶50,007, 493 US 203, 110 SCt 589.

[2]   For example, *see* Rev. Rul. 97-27, the current guidance for changing accounting methods, 1997-1 CB 680.

[3]   *See W.A. Holt*, CA-5, 66-2 USTC ¶9720, 368 F2d 311.

[4]   *Pacific National Company*, SCt, 38-1 USTC ¶9286, 304 US 191, 58 SCt 857.

- ***Silver Queen Motel***. The IRS disallowed a method of accounting when auditing the first year in which the method was used. The court determined the method was not adopted due to a lack of consistency and the taxpayer was free to change the method without receiving the permission from the IRS.[5]
- ***Robert and Shirley Foley***. The court found the petitioner had not previously regularly used the double declining-balance method in depreciating the items to which the method was erroneously applied. As a result, he can adopt the 150 percent declining-balance method for those items. The court further held that since utilization of the straight-line method for the remaining depreciable items was a correct application of an acceptable method, the petitioner could not change from that method without first obtaining consent of the Commissioner.[6]

Previously, the IRS took the view that a taxpayer could change from an erroneous accounting method without permission provided the statute of limitation was open for the first year that an erroneous method was used. The IRS has since modified its view by adapting the framework based upon the decisions cited above. This view was first espoused in *Rev. Rul. 90-38*,[7] and has been repeated in subsequent guidance on accounting methods. As a result:

a. A taxpayer using a *permissible* method of accounting is considered to have adopted that method by filing a tax return;
b. A taxpayer using an *impermissible* method of accounting is considered to have adopted that method by filing *two* returns.

Taxpayers desiring to change an accounting method after the appropriate return has been filed under the above rules must first request permission from the IRS to do so.

.07 WHEN DOES A CHANGE OF ACCOUNTING METHOD OCCUR?

Code Sec. 446 (e) states: "Except as otherwise expressly provided in this chapter, a taxpayer who changes the method of accounting on the basis of which he regularly computes his income in keeping his books shall, before computing his taxable income under the new method, secure the consent of the Secretary." In addition, Reg. §1.446-1(e)(3)(i) provides that "in order to secure the Commissioner's consent to a change of a taxpayer's method of accounting, the taxpayer must file an application on Form 3115 within the taxable year in which it is desired to make the change."

Reg. §1.446-1(e)(3)(ii) notes that "the Commissioner may prescribe administrative procedures, subject to such limitations, terms, and conditions as he deems necessary to obtain his consent...[these procedures] shall include those necessary to prevent the omission or duplication of items includible in income or deductions." Over the years, the IRS has prescribed such administrative procedures in a series of revenue procedures: Rev. Procs. 64-16, 70-27, 80-51, 84-74, 92-20, and (most recently) *Rev. Proc. 97-27*.[8]

The IRS has issued simplified and uniform procedures for obtaining automatic consent to make an accounting method change. A taxpayer complying with all of the requirements will be considered to have obtained the consent of the IRS to change its method of accounting.[9] In addition, the Instructions for Form 3115 list all available automatic changes.

Some transactions not treated as a change of accounting method include:

- ***Correction of an Error***. Examples include math or posting errors and errors in the computation of tax liability (e.g., an error in computing a credit).
- ***Correction of an Estimate.*** Changes to bad debt estimates and depreciation useful lives are not accounting methods changes; such changes are corrections of estimates and are reflected in revised deductions for the current and future years.

5 *Silver Queen Motel*, 55 TC 1101.
6 *Foley*, 56 TC 765.
7 Rev. Rul. 90-38, 1990-1 CB 57.
8 Rev. Proc. 97-27, 1997-1 CB 680.
9 Rev. Proc. 2002-9, as modified by Rev. Proc. 2002-19, Rev. Proc. 2002-33, Rev. Proc. 2002-54, Rev. Proc. 2004-11, and Rev. Proc. 2005-43.

- ***Correction of an Item Not Involving a Timing Issue.*** An example would be excessive compensation that is treated as a constructive dividend, or a deduction for a personal expense that is treated as a constructive dividend.

OBSERVATION   In *Diebold, Inc.,*[10] a taxpayer accidentally selected the wrong method of accounting on its first return (albeit an acceptable method). The taxpayer contended that IRS permission to switch to the correct method was not required because the transaction involved the "correction of an error." However, the Court ruled that a mistake in selecting a method of accounting is *not* treated as a correction of an error.

Reg. §1.446-1(e)(2) states that "[a] change in the method of accounting includes a change in the overall plan of accounting for gross income or deductions or a change in the treatment of any material item used in such an overall plan." The expression "material item" used above does not refer to the size of an item; rather, it refers to "any item which involves the proper time for the inclusion of the item in income or the taking of a deduction."

OBSERVATION   In *Lewis Corp.,* the Tax Court ruled that a $5,500 item was *material* to a corporation with $4 million of net assets.[11]

The slightest change that affects the timing of an item may be viewed by the IRS as a change of accounting method. For example, Reg. §1.446-1(c)(ii) allows a taxpayer engaged in manufacturing to account for a sale of an item when it is shipped, when it is delivered, when it is accepted by the buyer, or when title passes to the buyer. The IRS maintains that any change in this point of recognition is a change of accounting method.

.09   TAX PLANNING WHEN THERE IS A "CHANGE IN UNDERLYING FACTS"

Some taxpayers have been creative in avoiding the consent requirement by *changing the underlying facts* applicable to a transaction, rather than changing the accounting method itself. Two prominent court cases illustrate this type of a transaction:

In *Hallmark Cards,*[12] the company changed its policy of shipping Valentine's day cards in October of each year to shipping the cards in December, while retaining title until January 1 of the next tax year (as opposed to the time of the shipment, as used earlier). Thus, Hallmark was deferring recognition of income on the cards until the following year. The Tax Court ruled that the change in reporting Valentine card sales resulted from a *change in underlying facts* and not a change of accounting method (the passage of title was more than a ministerial act) so there was no change in the accounting method.

In another interesting case involving a change in the underlying facts, *Decision, Inc.,*[13] an accrual-basis, calendar-year taxpayer, was a publisher of employment directories. For many years the company billed customers in early November and shipped the directories the following January. However, when required by the Tax Court to report any advance payments as income when received, Decision changed its billing date to January. This resulted in a deferral of revenue until January, the same year the directories were published. The Tax Court ruled that this was a *change in underlying facts* (the billing system), and not a change in the accounting system.

---

[10] *Diebold, Inc.,* CA-FC, 90-1 USTC ¶50,003, 891 F2d 1579.
[11] *Sheperd Construction Co.,* 51 TC 890.
[12] *Hallmark Cards,* 90 TC 26.
[13] *Decision, Inc.,* 47 TC 58.

.11   PROCEDURES FOR CHANGING ACCOUNTING METHODS

Taxpayers desiring to change accounting methods *must* follow the procedures specified in Rev. Proc. 97-27.[14] Taxpayers may not attempt to change methods on their own, even if they are currently using an improper accounting method. The IRS District Director may make the change (under the "clearly reflects income" standard), even if the taxpayer does not.

The emphasis of the revenue procedure is on "fostering voluntary compliance." This is accomplished by rewarding voluntary changes by (1) providing longer spread periods for positive Code Sec. 481 adjustments, (2) providing audit protection, and (3) waiving penalties attaching to the use of improper methods. In addition, the document provides several windows of opportunity to change to acceptable accounting methods, even after contact with the IRS is made.

Code Sec. 481(a)(2) requires that any change of an accounting method takes into account those adjustments "which are determined to be necessary solely by reason of the change in order to prevent such amounts from being duplicated or omitted". Such adjustments prevent income or expenses from permanently escaping recognition because of a change of accounting method.

Exactly when this positive Code Sec. 481 adjustment is recognized as income depends on a finding under Rev. Proc. 97-27 as to whether the change is a *voluntary change* (initiated by the taxpayer) or an *involuntary change* (initiated by the IRS).

Example 16-1. Assume a cash-basis taxpayer switches to the accrual method on January 1, 2012. Given the following facts, the taxpayer would have a positive Code Sec. 481 adjustment based on the balances in accounts receivable, accounts payable, and merchandise inventory as of the day before the new method was adopted:

12/31/11 Accounts receivable balance	$78,000
12/31/11 Accounts payable balance	(61,000)
12/31/11 Merchandise inventory	35,000
Total Code Sec. 481 adjustment	$52,000

The beginning accounts receivable balance is a positive adjustment (additional income), since this was not reported under the old (cash) method and would not be reported as income when collected under the new (accrual) method. Similar logic justifies a *negative* adjustment in the taxpayer's favor for the beginning accounts payable balance (expenses not deducted under either the old method or the new method). Finally, the beginning inventory is a positive adjustment, since purchases were either deducted when paid for or are reflected in the account payable adjustment.

- *Voluntary Change.* In general, a taxpayer that voluntarily changes accounting methods is given a four-year spread forward period to report a positive adjustment beginning with the "year of change" (the tax year in which the new method is first used) and a one-year spread forward period to report a negative adjustment.

Example 16-2. Aaron Corporation voluntarily changes its accounting method in 2012, resulting in a $36,000 positive Code Sec. 481 adjustment. Aaron will increase its gross income by $9,000 a year ($36,000/4), beginning with the 2012 return.

- *Involuntary Change.* If the IRS initiates the change, no spread forward period is available; the entire adjustment is reported as income in the year of change.

---

[14] Rev. Proc. 97-27, 1997-1 CB 680 (and as modified by Rev. Proc. 2002-19, 2002-1 CB 696).

> **Example 16-3.** Assume the same facts as the previous example, except that the change is involuntary. The entire $36,000 Code Sec. 481 adjustment will be added to gross income in the year of change (the year audited).

- **Cutoff Adjustment Method.** In some cases (usually for LIFO inventories), Rev. Proc. 97-27 permits a so-called "cut-off method" for Code Sec. 481 adjustments. Under this procedure, the old method applies to items on hand and the new method applies to new items. This is in lieu of attempting to compute a complex Code Sec. 481 adjustment for such items.
- **De Minimis Adjustments.** Under Rev. Proc. 97-27, a taxpayer may elect a one-year adjustment period in lieu of the period otherwise provided by the revenue procedure if the entire Code Sec. 481 adjustment is less than $25,000 (either positive or negative).

It is extremely important to realize that the Code Sec. 481 adjustment is not barred by the statute of limitations; cumulative adjustments will reflect cumulative income and deductions related to both open and closed years. However, the Code provides that the IRS may not adjust for years prior to 1954 if the change is an involuntary one (initiated by the IRS). On the other hand, changes initiated by the taxpayer (voluntary changes) will open up the pre-1954 years. Thus, it becomes extremely important to determine who initiated the accounting change.

OBSERVATION In *Brookshire*, a taxpayer was deemed to have initiated the change when the IRS agent suggested that it would "be a good idea to change" and the taxpayer subsequently did so![15] A similar result was reached in *Irving Falk*.[16] However, in *Commissioner v. Welch-Thompson*, the Court of Appeals ruled that an agent's aggressive actions resulted in more than a suggestion when the agent stated orally and in writing that the taxpayer's grain business should use the accrual method.[17] In this case, pre-1954 adjustments were barred.

The pre-1954 Code rule may work to a taxpayer's advantage. In *Walter Potter*, a builder insisted that a forced change in the method of including the face amount of mortgages as income (less an arbitrary "reduction") was a change of accounting method.[18] If the Court had agreed, the taxpayer would have reaped large benefits from favorable pre-1954 cumulative adjustments. In an interesting twist, the IRS successfully argued that this was *not* a change of accounting method but a "correction" of an improper reporting procedure!

¶16,005 Inventory Method Issues—Planning Possibilities

.01 PLANNING WITH LIFO INVENTORIES AND SIMPLIFIED LIFO METHODS

LIFO—An Introduction. Generally, a taxpayer may be able to use actual costs when the taxpayer is able to identify the particular goods in inventory through accounting or production records. For example, a reseller of heavy construction equipment may be able to trace original cost by referring to serial and invoice numbers. Such an inventory

---

[15] *Brookshire*, CA-4, 60-1 ustc ¶9200, 273 F2d 638.
[16] *Irving Falk*, CA-5, 64-2 ustc ¶9528, 332 F2d 922.
[17] *Welch*, CA-5, 65-2 ustc ¶9450, 345 F2d 939.
[18] *Walter Potter*, 44 TC 159.

system is usually referred to as a specific identification system, in that the exact cost of the item can be matched with the inventory item. Reg. §1.471-2(d) specifically allows this approach in valuing year-end inventories.

On the other hand, specific identification would not be economically feasible for a parts dealer who handles literally hundreds of similar items. In these cases, a taxpayer must assume an order of cost flow. Three possible assumptions are *FIFO* (first-in, first-out), *LIFO* (last-in, first-out), and *average cost*. **FIFO** is authorized by Reg. §1.471-2(d), and **LIFO** is authorized by Code Sec. 472. Although average cost methods are not specifically mentioned in the Code or Regulations, there is no express authority that denies the use of these methods.

Although a FIFO assumption may more realistically represent the actual physical flow of the goods, a taxpayer is nevertheless permitted to elect the last-in, first-out LIFO method. This inventory method was incorporated into the tax law in order to cushion the impact of price increases in an inflationary economy. The LIFO method matches the current inventory costs more realistically against current revenues. Because of this economic incentive for electing LIFO, Congress has established specific requirements for its usage.

LIFO is considered to be a cost method of inventory valuation; therefore, lower-of-cost or -market procedures may not be used in conjunction with this method. If a taxpayer has used lower-of-cost or -market procedures before electing LIFO, any previous write-downs related to the beginning inventory in the year when LIFO is elected must be restored to income. Code Sec. 472(d) permits taxpayers to spread such an adjustment over three years (beginning with the year of change).

OBSERVATION   The decision in the *Thor Power Tool Company* case may actually be an incentive to switch to LIFO. Recall that in that case write-downs for excess or obsolete inventories were disallowed.[19] A taxpayer who has made such improper write-downs to inventory will be required to restore these adjustments to income, thus in effect writing up the inventory value to cost. Since the restoration of previous write-downs is a necessary prerequisite to adopting LIFO, one of the major barriers to electing LIFO for taxpayers making such write-downs will be removed. In cases such as these, it may make sense for the company to voluntarily make the change to LIFO and write up the inventory values to cost. This way, the company can spread the additional income caused by the write-up over three years; if they wait until the IRS audits them to make the change, the entire adjustment will be taxed immediately.

Applying LIFO inventory procedures to each different item of inventory is a difficult, if not impossible task for many businesses. Such an item method may be sufficient for a taxpayer with one type of inventory (such as the earlier example), but this procedure would be quite cumbersome for a manufacturer of hundreds of household products. To overcome this deficiency, Congress amended the tax regulations to allow the use of **dollar-value inventory methods**.

Dollar-value methods simplify inventory calculations by determining inventory cost on the basis of total dollars (for a base year) rather than the quantity and price of each inventory item. The primary advantage of these methods is that the inventory is viewed as a pool, not as a series of individual items. In addition to minimizing the laborious calculations associated with LIFO, the use of pools can lessen the possible tax impact of liquidation of the oldest and lowest cost layers of one particular inventory item.

Perhaps the most commonly used method of dollar-value LIFO valuation is the **double-extension inventory valuation method**, a procedure sanctioned by the Regulations. The following example illustrates the double-extension technique for a company with four products in its inventory. (In practice, a company may have literally hundreds

19   *Thor Power Tool Co.*, SCt, 79-1 USTC ¶9139, 439 US 522, 99 SCt 773.

of products in applying such a system, but the technique can be illustrated with only a few items.) Only by following the numbers can you see the two real advantages of the double-extension method: (1) detailed purchase records for each inventory item throughout the year are not necessary (only year-end prices and quantities are needed), and (2) decrements in one inventory item can be offset by increments in other inventory items through the aggregation procedure.

The Double-Extension Method Illustrated. Assume that Little Company adopts the double-extension, dollar-value LIFO method of inventory valuation for its pool of four products on December 31, 2012, when the inventory consisted of the following:

2012 Base Prices

2012 Base Inventory Prices			
Item	Quantity	Cost Per Unit	Total Cost
A	3,000	$ 7.00	$ 21,000
B	1,000	$12.00	12,000
C	6,000	$ 4.00	24,000
D	4,000	$ 8.00	32,000
Total Base Period Inventory at Cost			$ 89,000

The following sections of the chapter illustrate the double-extension procedure in terms of three basic steps each year: (1) determine the overall increment or decrement in inventory when both beginning and ending inventories are valued at base-period prices; (2) if an increment is present, determine the current-year price index for that increment by dividing the current aggregate price of the ending inventory by the aggregate base price of the same ending inventory; and (3) if an increment is present, add a layer to the ending inventory by multiplying the increment by the current price index; if a decrement is present, subtract the decrement (in terms of base period prices), starting with the newest layers first.

Reviewing the computations below discloses an increment (in terms of base period prices) of $8,000 in 2013, and this is valued at the 2013 price index of 112.4 percent. Similarly, there is an increment (in terms of base period prices) of $33,000 in 2014, and this is valued at the 2014 price index of 115.3 percent. Finally, there is a decrement of $31,000 (in terms of base period prices) in 2015, and this is "peeled off" the most recently added layer from 2014. Since the decrement was $31,000 in terms of base period prices and the 2014 layer was $33,000 in base period prices, there is no need to dip into any earlier layers.

OBSERVATION	It is sometimes easy to lose sight of the forest for the trees when examining these computations. The reason layers are added each year is to maintain a LIFO order; when there is a decrement, such as in 2015 in the illustration, the layers are "peeled off" from the most recently added layers to maintain the LIFO flow.

2013 Computations

Item	Base Prices		12/31/12 Current Price	
A	(3,000 @ $ 7)	$ 21,000	(3,000 @ $ 10)	$ 30,000
B	(2,000 @ $12)	24,000	(2,000 @ $ 7)	14,000
C	(7,000 @ $ 4)	28,000	(7,000 @ $ 5)	35,000
D	(3,000 @ $ 8)	24,000	(3,000 @ $ 10)	30,000
Totals		$ 97,000		$ 109,000

Increment (Decrement) at Base-Year Prices ($97,000 – $89,000) = $8,000
Current Year Price Index (if applicable) = $109,000/$97,000 = 112.4%

12/31/2013 Ending Inventory (by Layer)	
2012 Base Layer (Given)	$ 89,000
2013 Layer ($8,000 x 1.124)	8,992
Ending Inventory	$ 97,992

2014 Computations

Item	Base Prices		12/31/13 Current Price	
A	(5,000 @ $ 7)	$ 35,000	(5,000 @ $ 8)	$ 40,000
B	(2,000 @ $12)	24,000	(2,000 @ $ 15)	30,000
C	(4,000 @ $ 4)	16,000	(4,000 @ $ 8)	32,000
D	(7,000 @ $ 8)	56,000	(7,000 @ $ 7)	49,000
Totals		$ 131,000		$ 151,000

Increment (Decrement) at Base-Year Prices ($131,000 – $97,000) = $34,000
Current Year Price Index (if applicable) = $151,000/$131,000 = 115.3%

12/31/2014 Ending Inventory (by Layer)	
2012 Base Layer (Given)	$ 89,000
2013 Layer ($ 8,000 x 1.124)	8,992
2014 Layer ($34,000 x 1.153)	39,202
Ending Inventory	$137,194

2015 Computations

Item	Base Prices		12/31/14 Current Price	
A	(4,000 @ $ 7)	$ 28,000	(4,000 @ $ 8)	$ 32,000
B	(1,000 @ $12)	12,000	(1,000 @ $ 13)	13,000
C	(5,000 @ $ 4)	20,000	(5,000 @ $ 4)	20,000
D	(5,000 @ $ 8)	40,000	(5,000 @ $ 10)	50,000
Totals		$ 100,000		$ 115,000

Increment (Decrement) at Base-Year Prices ($100,000 – $131,000) = ($31,000)
Current Year Price Index = Not Applicable (Net Decrement)

12/31/2015 Ending Inventory (by Layer)	
2012 Base Layer (Given)	$ 89,000
2013 Layer ($ 8,000 x 1.124)	8,992
2014 Layer ($ 3,000 x 1.153)	3,459
Ending Inventory	$101,451

The Advantages of Pooling. As mentioned earlier, one of the advantages of pooling inventory items under the dollar-value method is that it neutralizes the possible adverse tax effects of significantly depleting the stock of one particular inventory item. Note in the example above that although the quantity of Product C dropped from 7,000 units in

2011 to 4,000 units in 2012, the overall result was an increment in the ending inventory for 2010; the drop in C was offset by increases in quantities of the other products in the "pool." Remember all increments, decrements, and price indexes are based on aggregate numbers which reflect all four inventory items. This simple example used only four items in the pool; in practice, a much larger number of items may constitute a pool.

As a general rule, it is to the taxpayer's advantage to group as many inventory items as possible into one pool. Reg. §1.472-8(e) requires that inventory be grouped into homogeneous pools. For manufacturers, a pool is usually defined as a natural business unit, which consists of the raw materials, work-in-process, and finished goods of one or more related product lines. For wholesalers and retailers, a pool is generally a major line, type, or class of goods.

Items of inventory in the hands of wholesalers, retailers, jobbers, and distributors electing the dollar-value method must be placed into pools by major lines, types, or classes of goods. In determining these groupings, customary business classifications of the particular trade in which the taxpayer is engaged is an important consideration, e.g., the department in the department store. In that case, practices are relatively uniform throughout the trade, and departmental grouping is peculiarly adapted to the customs and needs of the business. However, in appropriate cases, the principles relating to pooling by natural business units, may be used, with the IRS's permission.

Simplified Dollar-Value LIFO Procedures. Congress established an alternative **simplified dollar-value inventory method** in the Economic Recovery Tax Act of 1981, which was simplified even further by Congress in 1986. Code Sec. 474 allows a taxpayer to group inventories into multiple pools in accordance with either the 11 major categories of the Consumers Price Index (retailers) or the 15 major categories of the Producers Price Index (producers).

Changes in the published indexes are used to value the ending inventories, using what amounts to a link-chain procedure. The advantage of this method is that year-end prices of individual products do not need to be determined; price indexes are used in their place. This is particularly helpful for businesses that have a constantly changing inventory mix, where some items are dropped and new items are added.

The simplified dollar-value procedure is available only for an eligible small business, defined in Code Sec. 474(c) as a business with average annual gross receipts for the three preceding tax years of $5 million or less. The election to use this simplified method does not require IRS consent. A taxpayer must establish which month of the year is to be used to measure that annual change in the index, and that month must be used for all future computations (unless IRS approval is received to change the month of measurement).

The simplified dollar-value procedure is illustrated in **Figure 1** below. Note that the calculations do not require base-period prices for any of the inventory items, which means less paperwork for the taxpayer. Note also that the LIFO cost flow is retained because none of the base-period inventory of $100,000 is depleted.

Figure 1

Simplified Dollar-Value LIFO Procedure

On January 1, 2012, Quasar Company decides to elect LIFO procedures using the simplified dollar-value method. Quasar's 2011 ending inventory of Product A was valued at $100,000, and the 2012 inventory was valued at $120,000. The appropriate Producer Price Indexes for Product A were 110 percent for 2011 and 115 percent for 2010. (Note that the price index increased 4.55 percent over 2010, i.e., 1.15/1.10 = 1.0455%.) Quasar's 2012 ending inventory will be valued at $115,455 and consists of the following two layers:

2011 (Base Period Layer)	$100,000
2012 Increment ($14,778* × 1.0455)	15,450
2012 Ending Inventory	$115,450

* Determination of 2012 Incremental Layer:

Ending inventory at base prices ($120,000/1.0455)	$114,778
Beginning inventory at base prices ($100,000 × 1.0000)	(100,000)
2010 increment at base prices	$ 14,778

IPIC Simplified Methods per the Regulations. As an alternative to the double-extension or simplified methods, any taxpayer, regardless of size, may elect to use a special *Inventory Price Index Computation (IPIC)* method available in Regulations issued in 2002. The IPIC method is a mechanical method that based indexes on published inflation indexes from the Bureau of Labor Statistics (BLS): either the Consumer Price Index or the Producer Price Index Reports.

Since the IPIC method is based on external BLS indices, there is no need to "double extend" the year-end inventories of the taxpayer. In simplifying the use of such indices, the IRS provided the following advantages to electing IPIC methods:

- Unlike prior Regulations on the use of indices, where only 80 percent of an inflation price adjustment was allowed, the IPIC method provides for 100-percent inflation adjustments.
- The BLS indices often reflect greater inflation than a taxpayer's own internally computed indices using the double-extension method, which leads to additional tax savings.
- Generally, the IPIC method requires fewer pools, which increases the possible tax savings of offsetting decrements in one product with increments in another product in the same pool.
- The IPIC method allows taxpayers to select an index for a month prior to year end, such as November, which allows the taxpayer to make the necessary computations quickly at year end, rather than waiting for the publishing of the December index.

.03   UNICAP PLANNING ISSUES

UNICAP—General Applicability. The Tax Reform Act of 1986 modified the absorption costing rules with a single comprehensive set of *uniform capitalization rules* specified in Code Sec. 263A. These capitalization rules have become commonly known as the UNICAP rules. The 1986 provision, sometimes referred to as the "super absorption method," reclassifies as product (inventoriable) costs many indirect costs which were previously expensed as period costs. In addition to applying to property produced or constructed by a taxpayer, the rules also apply to property acquired for resale.

Congress exempted certain taxpayers from the application of the UNICAP rules. The principal exception is provided in Code Sec. 263A(b)(2), which exempts any reseller of personal property with average gross receipts of $10,000,000 or less during the preceding three taxable years. A reseller is a taxpayer who acquires property for resale, as opposed to a producer who manufactures property for resale. Also exempt from the UNICAP rules under Code Secs. 263A(c) and (d) are certain farming businesses, personal use property, research and experimentation expenditures deductible under Code Sec. 174, certain costs associated with oil and gas properties, and certain timber and ornamental trees. Additionally, Code Sec. 263A(c)(4) notes that the UNICAP rules do not apply to any long-term construction contracts covered by Code Sec. 460.

Although most producers are covered by the UNICAP rules, the IRS did provide a *de minimis* rule for producers in Reg. §1.263A-2(b)(3)(iv). This provision states that producers who elect the simplified production method (discussed later) and who incur $200,000 or less of indirect costs in a tax year are treated as having no additional Code Sec. 263A costs. Recall that indirect costs include those factory costs other than direct materials or direct labor.

UNICAP Rules as Related to Code Sec. 471 Inventory Costing. Although virtually all manufacturers and many resellers are now subject to the Code Sec. 263A UNICAP rules, it is still important to understand the previous inventory capitalization rules under Code Sec. 471 and the related Regulations. First of all, these rules are still applicable to all taxpayers exempted from the UNICAP rules, as discussed above. Secondly, many elements of the full absorption Regulations are still relevant in applying the Code Sec. 263A UNICAP rules.

Finally, and perhaps most importantly, the IRS has provided simplified allocation procedures for Code Sec. 263A costs that permit the taxpayer to continue to use the regular absorption costing rules of Code Sec. 471 and then add a computed amount of additional Code Sec. 263A costs to the Code Sec. 471 determination. One of the practical (and unfortunate!) effects of the Code Sec. 263A UNICAP rules was to create a costing requirement that frequently goes beyond the generally accepted accounting principles used by most firms in reporting financial accounting income. The practical effect of this change would have been to require many taxpayers to adjust their accounting systems to capture the additional costs to be capitalized.

To understand how UNICAP requirements affect normal inventory procedures, assume that CAP Corporation began operations this year and had total production costs of $1,200,000 in producing 100,000 units of its product, the AbRoller Plus. The production costs consisted of $300,000 direct materials, $400,000 of direct labor, and $500,000 of indirect costs (factory overhead), as measured using generally acceptable accounting principles. The costing method used for financial accounting purposes would also be acceptable under the Code Sec. 471 costing rules applicable prior to the enactment of the UNICAP rules and still applicable to taxpayers exempted from the UNICAP rules.

During the current year, 90,000 of the units were sold for a total of $1,800,000.

Assume that CAP Corporation has determined that $200,000 additional indirect manufacturing costs (overhead) treated as period costs in their financial accounting records (e.g., expensed) should be treated as manufacturing costs under Code Sec. 263A. Assuming that equal amounts of overhead were applied to each of the 100,000 units produced, the cost per unit for financial accounting purposes would be $12 ($1,200,000/100,000), and the cost per unit including Code Sec. 263A costs would be $14 ($1,400,000/100,000). Thus, their reportable gross incomes with and without Code Sec. 263A UNICAP rules would be:

	Without Code Sec. 263A Costs		With Code Sec. 263A Costs	
Gross Sales		$1,800,000		$1,800,000
Cost of Goods Sold:				
Beginning Inventory	$ 0		$ 0	
Current Product Costs	$1,200,000		1,400,000	
Costs to Account for	$1,200,000		$1,400,000	
Ending Inventory	(120,000)		(140,000)	
Costs of Goods Sold		(1,080,000)		(1,260,000)
Gross Income		$ 720,00		$ 540,000
Less Period Costs per Books		(200,000)		0
Gross Income Less Period Costs		$ 520,000		$ 540,000

Note that the UNICAP rules require CAP Corporation to treat an additional $200,000 of costs as inventoriable manufacturing costs. Of this total, $20,000 is presumed to relate to the ending inventory, and that creates the $20,000 difference in the final profit figures for books and tax purposes. As we shall see in the following discussion, the Code Sec. 263A Regulations would allow CAP to continue to use their financial accounting inventory methods and then pick up a portion of the additional Code Sec. 263A costs as inventoriable costs through the use of a simplified method based on estimates.

Such major changes in an accounting system would have created an administrative nightmare for many taxpayers, and this led the IRS to create a Simplified Production Method and a Simplified Retail Method that allow taxpayers to retain their present accounting systems that were largely based on Code Sec. 471 and the related Regulations. Taxpayers would account for any additional costs required to be capitalized under Code Sec. 263A separately, and then add this total to the Code Sec. 471 costs.

Exactly what costs are reclassified from period costs (for financial accounting purposes and Code Sec. 471 normal inventory procedures) to product costs under Code Sec. 263A? Under Code Sec. 471, direct materials, direct labor, and indirect costs related to production activities only ("factory overhead") were required to be capitalized; most other expenses related to sales, office, or management activities were expensed. Some of the more common costs deducted for financial accounting and under Code Sec. 471 as period costs that are now subject to capitalization are:

- Engineering and design costs (other than research and experimentation)
- Percentage depletion in excess of cost
- Excess tax depreciation and amortization
- Past service pension costs
- Taxes other than state and local taxes (e.g., property taxes)
- Employee benefits associated with production labor
- Rework, labor, scrap, and spoilage
- Factory administrative expenses
- Production officer salaries
- Insurance costs
- Incidental purchasing costs (including wages of purchasing agents)
- Processing costs, such as assembling and repackaging
- Costs associated with storage (e.g., wages, rent, insurance, taxes, etc.)
- Allocable general and administrative costs related to above
- Bidding expenses

Three Simplified Methods for Applying the UNICAP Rules While Retaining the Basic Code Sec. 471 Inventory Costing System. The detailed Code Sec. 263A provisions and accompanying regulations provide three simplifying computations that allow a taxpayer to retain the basic financial accounting inventory system and convert those inventory numbers to UNICAP-compliant numbers. These computational "assists" are for mixed service costs,

Simplified Service Cost Method for Mixed Service Costs. Reg. §1.263A-1(h)(4) and (5) provide a *simplified service cost method* for allocating mixed service costs. *Mixed service costs* are costs related to services that are partly allocable to production or resale activities (capitalizable) and partly allocable to nonproduction and nonresale activities (deductible). An example would be the costs of a personnel department that deals with recruiting factory workers (a capitalizable cost) and with developing fringe benefit policies (a deductible period cost). Under this simplified method, a producer can elect to use either a labor-based allocation method or a production-cost allocation method (resellers can use only a labor-based allocation). The two methods may be expressed in formula form as follows (in both cases, any costs included in the mixed service costs are excluded from both the numerator and denominator):

$$\begin{array}{c}\text{Capitalizable service costs}\\\text{(Labor method)}\end{array} = \frac{\text{Total Code Sec. 263A labor costs}}{\text{Total labor costs}} \times \begin{array}{c}\text{Mixed service}\\\text{costs}\end{array}$$

$$\begin{array}{c}\text{Capitalizable service costs}\\\text{(Production cost method)}\end{array} = \frac{\text{Total Code Sec. 263A production costs}}{\text{Total costs*}} \times \begin{array}{c}\text{Mixed service}\\\text{costs}\end{array}$$

*Excluding interest

For these purposes, total Code Sec. 263A labor costs are total labor costs allocable to all production activities, and total labor costs are total wage costs of the company (including both production and non-production activities). Likewise, total Code Sec. 263A production costs are total costs related to production activities, and total costs are all costs incurred by the company during the year.

Example 16-4. Deron Co., a producer, incurs total mixed service costs of $50,000. Its total labor costs for the year, excluding labor costs included in mixed service costs, is $750,000. Deron's labor costs allocable to production activities (Code Sec. 263A labor costs), excluding labor costs included in mixed service costs, is $450,000. The amount of mixed service costs that must be allocated to production activities (and subject to capitalization as inventory) under the labor-based cost ratio is $30,000, computed as follows:

Capitalizable service costs = ($450,000/$750,000) × $50,000 = $30,000

The remaining $20,000 of the mixed service costs is presumed to be related to nonproduction functions and is therefore deductible as a period cost.

Simplified Production Method. Producers who elect the **simplified production inventory method** initially calculate their inventory balances without regard to the Code Sec. 263A UNICAP rules (i.e., applying Code Sec. 471 and the related Regulations). Then, they determine the amount of additional Code Sec. 263A costs (other than interest) to be capitalized for the year and allocate a portion of this amount to the ending inventory based on an absorption ratio. The final ending inventory balance is thus the sum of the Code Sec. 471 costs (capitalized costs in ending inventory), and the Code Sec. 263A additional capitalized costs allocable to the ending inventory. (Note: If a taxpayer uses the LIFO method, the absorption ratio is multiplied by the Code Sec. 471 costs that relate solely to the LIFO increment; for simplicity, our discussion is limited to taxpayers using FIFO.)

Additional Code Sec. 263A costs are defined as those costs (other than interest) that were not capitalized under the taxpayer's method of accounting prior to the effective date of Code Sec. 263A (those items that were treated as expenses under Code Sec. 471 and related Regulations), but which now must be capitalized under Code Sec. 263A. The portion of these additional costs that must be inventoried is determined by the following formula that uses year-end totals for additional Code Sec. 263A costs and total Code Sec. 471 costs to determine an *annual absorption cost ratio*:

$$\begin{array}{c}\text{Inventoriable additional}\\\text{Code Sec. 263A costs}\end{array} = \frac{\text{Additional Code Sec. 263A costs incurred}}{\text{Total Code Sec. 471 costs incurred}} \times \begin{array}{c}\text{Code Sec. 471}\\\text{costs in ending}\\\text{inv.}\end{array}$$

Example 16-5. Assume that the controller of Melchon Corporation has determined that the company's ending inventory should be valued under Code Sec. 471 and related Regulations at $132,000. The controller has also determined that Melchon's actual overhead costs for the current year were $680,000. Assume that the controller has also determined that the following additional indirect costs are capitalizable under Code Sec. 263A and are not reflected in the $680,000 of Code Sec. 471 costs:

Tax depreciation in excess of financial accounting depreciation	$34,000
Past service pension costs	31,000
Insurance costs applicable to the factory	8,000
Warehousing costs (wages, depreciation, insurance, and taxes)	21,000
Mixed service department costs (using the simplified service cost method)	8,000
Total additional Code Sec. 263A costs incurred	$102,000

The portion of the $102,000 additional indirect costs to be allocated to the ending inventory is determined to be $19,800, based on an annual absorption cost ratio of 15 percent:

$$\frac{\text{Inventoriable additional Code Sec. 263A costs}}{(\$102,000/\$680,000) \times \$132,000} \quad \$19,800$$

Thus, Melchon's ending inventory will be valued under Code Sec. 263A at $151,800 ($132,000 Code Sec. 471 inventoriable costs plus $19,800 allocable additional Code Sec. 263A costs). By electing the simplified production method, Melchon may continue to use their financial accounting records (based on Code Sec. 471 and the related Regulations) as their tax records for inventories, as long as they compute the additional Code Sec. 263A costs at the end of the year using the procedure illustrated above.

OBSERVATION

In Example 16-5, Melchon used the actual additional Code Sec. 263A costs and Code Sec. 471 costs incurred during the current year in computing the absorption ratio of 15 percent ($102,000/$680,000). Reg. §1.263A-2(b)(4) provides a *special historic absorption cost ratio* election for taxpayers who have used a simplified production method for at least three preceding years based on an actual absorption ratio. If elected, the historic absorption ratio is calculated by dividing the taxpayer's additional Code Sec. 263A costs incurred during the test period (the three-year period immediately prior to the taxable year that the historic absorption ratio is elected) by the total Code Sec. 471 costs during the same period. In some cases, this ratio may be smaller than the annual ratio, and would therefore require a smaller portion of additional Code Sec. 263A costs to be capitalized at the end of the year.

Simplified Resale Method. Reg. §1.263A-3(a)(3)(d) provides a special *simplified resale method* for resellers subject to the UNICAP rules. This method is very similar to the previously discussed simplified production method for producers, in that either an actual or a historic absorption ratio can be used to determine the portion of the taxpayer's additional Code Sec. 263A costs to be added to its ending inventory based on Code Sec. 471 costs. Generally, this method is available only to resellers that do not engage in production activities (subject to a de minimis rule discussed later). The following is a brief overview of how this method is applied; the Code Sec. 263A Regulations should be consulted for examples of the detailed computations.

In applying the simplified resale method, a combined absorption ratio must be determined. This combined ratio is the sum of a storage and handling costs ratio (current year's storage and handling costs divided by beginning inventory plus current year purchases) and a purchasing costs absorption cost ratio (current year purchasing costs divided by current year's purchases). (Recall that both storage and handling costs and purchasing costs were not required to be capitalized under Code Sec. 471, so these represent "additional Code Sec. 263A costs.")

For example, if the storage and handling costs ratio is 6 percent and the purchasing costs ratio is 5 percent, then 11 percent of the Code Sec. 471 costs in ending inventory will be added to those Code Sec. 471 costs as capitalizable additional Code Sec. 263A costs. In determining the current year's storage and handling costs and purchasing costs, the taxpayer must allocate any amounts of service costs related to these functions. In determining this allocation, the taxpayer may elect to use the simplified service cost method, based on the labor cost ratio discussed earlier.

OBSERVATION	The Code Sec. 263A rules provide several opportunities to minimize the effects of the UNICAP rules. Two planning possibilities included in the Regulations are:

Purchasing Activities Safe Harbor. As mentioned earlier, resellers must now capitalize the costs associated with purchasing activities. However, Reg. §1.263A-3(c)(ii) provides a special exception one third to two thirds rule for allocating labor costs of associating with purchasing activities. Specifically, if less than one third of a person's activities are related to purchasing, none of that person's labor costs are allocated to purchasing; on the other hand, if more than two thirds of the person's activities are related to purchasing, then all of that person's labor costs are allocated to purchasing. In all other cases (between one third and two thirds), an allocation must be made. Taxpayers should keep detailed job descriptions for employees that are only marginally involved in the purchasing function so that their labor costs may be excluded under the one third to two thirds rule.

Noncapitalizable Costs. Reg. §1.263A-(3)(c)(4)(vi) specifically notes that distribution costs (those costs incurred outside of a storage facility) are not required to be capitalized. For example, this would include all activities associated with a loading dock. Also, Reg. §1.263A-3(c)(4)(vi) specifically excludes costs associated with pick and pack activities from the UNICAP rules. These are activities undertaken at a retail sales facility in preparation for imminent shipment to a particular customer after the customer has ordered the specific goods in questions (i.e., moving from storage, packing or repacking, etc.).

Another planning possibility related to the UNICAP rules should be noted. Specifically, taxpayers subject to the UNICAP rules may decide to forego the simplified computations and go ahead and build into their overhead application rates all additional costs required to be capitalized under Code Sec. 263A. In many cases, these actual allocations will produce larger cost of goods sold than the simplified methods. And with today's sophisticated inventory software, testing the actual numbers versus the "simplified" numbers should not be a difficult task.

¶16,007 Tax Planning—Acquisition, Use and Disposition of Property

A number of tax planning issues arise with the acquisition, use and disposition of property. The acquisition of property may offer potential tax credits and special expensing options. The use of property involves elections as to cost recovery methods, and possible changes in cost recovery methods through cost segregation studies. And finally, the disposition of property can involve recapture considerations and possible abandonment issues.

.01   TAX PLANNING ISSUES: PERSONALTY

Acquisition of Personalty. Personalty is defined simply as tangible property other than realty (which in turn is defined as land, buildings, and permanent structural components of buildings). There is only one permanent credit available for the acquisition of personalty, and that is the business energy credit. A credit is generally available for 10 percent of any energy conservation expenditures involving *solar* or *geothermal* energy property. The basis of the energy property is reduced by 50 percent of any allowable credit.

Example 16-6. A company that spends $40,000 on a solar heating panel may take a credit of $4,000 ($40,000 × .10), and its basis in the solar heating panel will be $38,000 [$40,000 – ($4,000 × .50)].

Since the credit is the equivalent of a dollar for dollar reduction in tax liability, it makes sense to take the business energy credit on any qualifying property. The loss of a small amount of basis is a small price for such instant tax savings.

The acquisition of personalty also offers an opportunity for small businesses to immediately expense part of all of its cost under Code Sec. 179. However, the maximum deduction is reduced dollar for dollar once total personalty placed in service during the tax year exceeds a specified maximum amount. For the 2012 tax year, the maximum Code Sec. 179 deduction is $500,000, with a dollar for dollar reduction in the maximum for personalty placed in service during the year exceeding $2,000,000.[20] In addition, there is a temporary bonus depreciation deduction of 50 percent for original use property with a MACRS recovery period of 20 years or less placed in service after December 31, 2007, and before January 1, 2014.

Example 16-7. A taxpayer placing $850,000 of personalty in service in 2012 will be limited to a Code Sec. 179 deduction of $500,000. If instead of qualifying for the Sec. 179 deduction, the machine qualifies for the temporary bonus depreciation deduction, that is, its original use commences with the taxpayer, a 50 percent bonus depreciation deduction of $425,000 ($850,000 × 50%) is allowed.

The Code Sec. 179 deduction is further limited to the taxable income derived from the active conduct by the taxpayer of any trade or business during such taxable year *before* considering any MACRS or Code Sec. 179 deduction. Any amount not deducted in the current year may be carried over to the next year and added to both total acquisitions that year and also to the dollar limit in that year. The limit is only on the Code Sec. 179 deduction; taxpayers may still deduct regular MACRS during the year, including any bonus depreciation, even if a loss is created).

OBSERVATION   The trade or business of an individual taxpayer is broadly defined to include wage income in addition to self-employment income. For taxpayers filing a joint return, the earned income of the spouse, including wage income and self-employment income may be used when computing the taxable income limit.

Example 16-8. John has Schedule C net self-employment income of $100,000. His wife, Mary has wage income of $75,000. For purposes of the taxable income limit under Code Sec. 179, John may expense up to $175,000 in qualifying personalty acquired during the year.

In some cases, it may be better for a taxpayer to forego the Code Sec. 179 deduction. For example, assume that a taxpayer has $12,000 taxable income for 2012 before considering cost recovery deductions on a $100,000 item of personalty placed in service during the year. The taxpayer's two options are (1) elect Code Sec. 179, with a $12,000 limit on the deduction and no MACRS deduction in the current year (but with a carryover of $88,000 added to next year's limit), or (2) forego the Code Sec. 179 deduction and take normal MACRS deductions (assuming a five-year property) of $20,000 (Year 1 MACRS rate of 20 percent multiplied by the $100,000 of cost). The second option creates an $8,000 net operating loss (NOL) that could be carried back to prior tax years for a potential immediate tax refund.

---

[20]   American Taxpayer Relief Act of 2012. (HR 8 as amended by the Senate).

OBSERVATION	Which option should the taxpayer choose? Among the key variables to consider are (1) profit prospects for the next taxable year, (2) marginal tax rates in the carryback or carryforward year for the NOL, (3) the likelihood of purchasing additional Code Sec. 179 assets in the next year, and (4) the estimated number of years it would take to use the Code Sec. 179 carryover.

Use of Personalty. The taxpayer has a myriad of choices for recovery methods on personalty (24 are available for a single item of personalty!). Generally, there is little reason not to use the maximum MACRS rates for regular tax. There is an adjustment for the **alternative minimum tax (AMT)** on personalty (use 150 percent declining balance for AMT rather than 200 percent declining balance). However, there is no AMT adjustment when the Code Sec. 179 deduction is taken.

There is an interesting interaction between the Code Sec. 179 deduction and the application of the half-year or mid-quarter convention on personalty. When a taxpayer places in service more than 40 percent of his or her personalty in the last quarter of the year, the mid-quarter convention must be used to compute the MACRS deduction. However, when the personalty placed in service in the last quarter is *expensed* under Code Sec. 179, it is left out of both the numerator and denominator when applying the 40-percent test.

Another interesting possibility regarding depreciable personalty is the possible reclassification of certain realty as personalty. By performing a cost segregation study, discussed later, the taxpayer may be able to shorten the useful life of components of a building by reclassifying them as personalty rather than as realty.

OBSERVATION	What if a taxpayer fails to take depreciation; is there any hope of reclaiming such deductions for years already closed by the statute of limitations? The answer is yes, according to Reg. §1.446-1. This authority allows a taxpayer to "change" the recovery period of ACRS and MACRS properties and treat such change as a change of accounting method under the automatic change procedures. Rev. Proc. 2004-11 allows a taxpayer to change the cost recovery period within a limited period of time even *after* the asset has been sold or exchanged.[21]

Disposition of Personalty. A disposition of personalty at a gain is subject to ordinary income recapture under Code Sec. 1245 to the extent of depreciation taken on the personalty; the remaining gain, if any, is Code Sec. 1231 gain. But depreciation recapture is not quite the draconian tax provision it is sometimes portrayed to be. In fact, in most cases the worst result of depreciation recapture is that the taxpayer has received an interest-free loan from the government, in that the taxpayer is swapping current deductions for future income. This view changes somewhat if the taxpayer is in a higher tax bracket when the income is recognized or if the installment sale recapture rules apply. Otherwise, the tax savings from a current deduction can be viewed as an "investment" that should exceed the future cost of the tax to be paid when the asset is sold at a gain.

.03   TAX PLANNING ISSUES: REALTY

Acquisition of Realty. Two tax credits are available on the purchase of realty: a rehabilitation tax credit and a low-income housing tax credit. Each is discussed briefly from a tax planning perspective.

Rehabilitation Tax Credit. The purpose of this tax credit when enacted in 1986 was to "bring business back downtown" by offering a 10- or 20-percent credit on qualified expenditures of rehabilitating old buildings. Qualifying expenditures must be incurred

---

[21] Rev. Proc. 2004-11, IRB 2004-3.

¶16,007.03

within a 24-month consecutive period and exceed the *larger* of $5,000 or the cost of the building. In addition, at least 75 percent of the external walls must be retained (as either external or internal walls) and at least 50 percent of the external walls must be retained as external walls.

The credit rate is either (1) 20 percent (for certified historic structures, as determined by the Department of Interior) or (2) 10 percent (other structures that were placed in service prior to 1936). The depreciable basis of the building includes the rehab expenditures; however, the basis is reduced by 100 percent of the credit allowed.

A portion of the credit may be *recaptured* if the building is held for less than five years (the credit is "earned" at the rate of 20 percent of the total for each full year that the property is held). Any credit recaptured may be added to basis.

Example 16-9. Morris Co. paid $80,000 for an old building in Shockhoe Slip, a certified historic district. Morris incurred $120,000 expenditures in rehabilitating the building. Morris's rehab credit is $24,000 ($120,000 × .20), and its depreciable basis in the building is $176,000 ($80,000 + $120,000 – $24,000). If Morris sells the building after holding it for three full years, the rehab credit recapture is $9,600 ($24,000 × .40), and this amount may be added to the basis of the building when computing the gain or loss on the sale.

This credit provides several planning possibilities. Assume that a building in a certified historic district costs $100,000 and an architect states that it can be rehabbed for only $96,000. In this case, it is preferable to increase the remodeling costs to more than $100,000 since this would yield a $20,000 credit against tax liability (rehab costs must exceed the cost of the building). Assuming that the passive activity rules do not apply, rehabilitation expenditures of $100,001 would be only $80,001 after the credit.

But what if the plan does not qualify for the credit because, for example, the wall requirement is not met? How much more could the taxpayer spend in attempting to qualify for the credit and still have the same after-tax cost? Up to 25 percent more could be spent on a historic structure (for the 20-percent credit), and up to 11.1 percent more could be spent on a non-historic structure (for the 10-percent credit). This is best illustrated by the following example.

Example 16-10. Axel Company received an estimate of $400,000 to remodel a certified historic structure that cost $300,000, but this would involve taking down two walls and the structure would no longer qualify for the rehabilitation credit. How much more could Axel spend in attempting to qualify for the credit and yet have the same after tax cost. The answer is $100,000 more ($400,000 × 25%). By spending $500,000 in total and receiving a 20-percent credit of $100,000, their after-tax cost would be only $400,000, the same as the estimate not qualifying for the credit. If the building qualifies for the 10-percent credit, Axel could spend up to $44,444 more in attempting to qualify for the credit.

Low-Income Housing Tax Credit. The low-income housing credit is designed to increase the supply of affordable housing for low-income individuals by providing developers of such housing a tax credit on that portion of a building (but not land) rented to a qualified low-income tenant. *Unlike other credits, this credit may be taken repeatedly over a 10-year period.* The credit is roughly either nine percent (new, nonfederally-subsidized housing or substantially rehabilitated (>$3,000 rehab per unit) housing or four percent (new housing financed with government or tax-exempt subsidies). Actual credit rates are adjusted monthly to current interest rates to yield either a 70-percent (9-percent credit) or 30-percent (4-percent credit) present value return on the investment.

The credit may be taken for 10 consecutive years, as long as the units remained occupied by qualifying low-income individuals. Recapture possibilities exist for a 15-year period, and owners have to sign commitments to keep the housing as low-income housing for a 30-year period (with certain exceptions). There is no basis reduction for the credit.

Finally, qualifying housing must meet an occupancy test and a rent test. For example, one occupancy test (the 40/60 test) requires that at least 40 percent of the units be rented to qualified low-income families, those having incomes less than 60 percent of the area median gross income as provided by government statistics (a 20/50 test is an alternative). The gross income test limits the rent to be charged on such low-income units to 30 percent of the 60-percent area median gross income figure computed above (or 50-percent figure, if the 20/50 test is used).

Example 16-11. Assume that a developer constructs a new 10-unit apartment complex for $1,200,000 ($200,000 for land and $1,000,000 for the building), and rents six of the units to qualified low-income individuals. Assuming that no government or tax-exempt financing is involved, the project will qualify for the "nine-percent" credit. The credit is computed as follows:

$$\text{Credit} = \$1,000,000 \times .60 \times .09 = \$54,000$$

As long as the six units are occupied by qualifying low-income individuals, the developer may take the $54,000 credit against taxes *for 10 consecutive years*.

The low-income housing credit offers a significant tax incentive for developers and investors. Generally, the lower rents to be charged are more than offset by the fact that a tax credit is available for 10 consecutive years. Most developments are 100-percent low-income housing units, because the cash flows incorporating the generous credit are much greater than the cash flows from units rented at market rates but not qualifying for the credit.

Developers have discovered another interesting tax parlay by locating qualifying housing projects in non-metropolitan areas and accepting government financing through the FHA program. Although this reduces the credit rate from roughly nine to four percent, the loan is a 50-year loan with a three-percent down payment and a one-percent interest rate. The interest savings generated by such generous loan terms more than offset the loss from a reduced credit.

Investors have found a bonanza in these housing developments. This is particularly true for C Corporations, that do not have to worry about the passive activity limitations. Wealthy individuals can get in on the action to a limited extent because the $25,000 real estate exception discussed earlier also applies to credits: the $25,000 is converted to an equivalent dollar amount. And unlike the $25,000 loss exception, the credit exception has no phase-out based on adjusted gross income.

OBSERVATION   Because Congress chose not to put a phase-out on the $25,000 credit exception for low-income housing, a number of developers have been selling smaller units of investment to take advantage of this opportunity. For example, a taxpayer in the 35-percent bracket would have a $25,000 deduction equivalent of $8,750. Thus, the first $8,750 of credits allocated to the taxpayer could offset any kind of income, and would not be restricted to tax liability on passive incomes only.

Use of Realty. Real estate is presently subject to straight-line recovery over either 27.5 years (residential realty) or 39 years (nonresidential realty). Thus, there are not many planning choices to take advantage of when depreciating a building. However, it may be to the taxpayer's advantage to undertake a cost segregation study, which may generate tax savings by reclassifying a portion of the building as personalty or 15-year land improvements.

The decision of the U.S. Tax Court in *Hospital Corporation of America* revolutionized the reporting of cost recovery deductions.[22] In this case, acquiesced to by

---

[22] *Hospital Corporation of America*, 109 TC 21.

the IRS in 1999,[23] the taxpayer allocated specific portions of a building's cost that would have qualified for the investment credit under prior law and assigned shorter depreciable lives than those assigned for realty. The court ruled that such allocations did not violate the ban on component depreciation established by the Economic Recovery Tax Act of 1981. This decision led to a flood of "cost segregation" analyses, where taxpayers would isolate certain elements of a building's cost, reclassify them as either depreciable personalty or realty with a class life of less than 27.5 years, resulting in not only a shorter useful life but also an accelerated cost recovery method for these assets.

The incentive to segregate costs has been facilitated by a series of IRS pronouncements that allow a taxpayer to treat a change in an asset's cost recovery period as a change in accounting method. Taxpayers making such a change are allowed to accelerate the remaining depreciation deductions on the reclassified properties as part of a Code Sec. 481 cumulative adjustment associated with a change of accounting method. Rev. Proc. 2002-9,[24] permits a taxpayer to treat such a change as an automatic change of accounting method and avoid the effort and costs of securing IRS permission through the normal procedures. Additionally, Rev. Proc. 2002-19[25] changed the Code Sec. 481 adjustment period for voluntary negative adjustments from four years to one year. As a consequence, a taxpayer will immediately realize some of the tax benefits of shorter recovery periods with a "catch-up adjustment" of depreciation.

The IRS provided two additional incentives to segregate costs. First, Reg. §1.446-1 was rewritten to clarify that a change in the recovery period of ACRS and MACRS properties will be deemed to be a change of accounting method under the automatic change procedures. Second, the Service issued Rev. Proc. 2004-11,[26] which allows a taxpayer to change the cost recovery period within a limited period of time even *after* the asset has been sold or exchanged. Common properties subject to reclassification to a shorter useful life, usually 15 or 20 years, are listed in Table 1.

---

[23] AOD CC-1999-008.
[24] Rev. Proc. 2002-9, 2002-1 CB 327.
[25] Rev. Proc. 2002-19, 2001-1 CB 696.
[26] Rev. Proc. 2004-11, IRB 2004-3.

Table 1
Code Sec. 1250 Properties Other Than Residential and Nonresidential Realty

Asset	Description	Authority
Land Improvements, Generally (Asset class 00.3, MACRS Life of 15)	Includes improvements directly to or added to land, whether such improvements are Code Sec. 1245 property or Code Sec. 1250 property, provided such improvements are depreciable. Examples of such assets might include sidewalks, roads, canals, waterways, drainage facilities, sewers (not including municipal sewers in Class 51), wharves and docks, bridges, fences, landscaping, shrubbery, or radio and television transmitting towers. Does not include land improvements that are explicitly included in any other class, and buildings and structural components as defined in section 1.48-1(e) of the regulations. Excludes public utility initial clearing and grading land improvements as specified in Rev. Rul. 72-403, 1972-2 CB 102.	Rev. Proc. 87-56, 1987-2 CB 674 (see also IRS Pub. 946).
Concrete Foundations and Footings	Foundations or footings for signs, light poles, canopies and other land improvements.	Restaurant Directive 2003
Concrete Footings	Footings that support gasoline pump canopies	Rev. Rul. 2003-54, IRB 2003-23, 1982
Concrete Silos	Constructed by a taxpayer on the site of a cement manufacturing facility and used to store finished cement are class 00.3, Land Improvements	Rev. Rul. 78-177, 1978-1 CB 65
Dredging & Excavating	The costs of excavating water canals and dredging channels in harbors and slips, like clearing and grading costs, are construction costs for land improvements.	Rev. Rul. 75-137, 1975-1 CB 74
Dredging—general	Initial dredging of a canal or other waterway can create a depreciable asset in and of itself if there is evidence of silting which indicates that the canal has a determinable useful life.	Tunnel, 367 F Supp 557, 11/28/1973, acq. AOD 1976-93
Dredging—specific facilities	Rev. Rul. 66-71 1966-1 CB 44 (dredging costs incurred to deepen a portion of a harbor), Rev. Rul. 68-280, 1968-1 CB 20 (cost of dredging a river bottom at a marine terminal facility), Rev. Rul. 68-483, 1968-2 CB 91 (costs of dredging a slip), and Rev. Rul. 69-78, 1969-1 CB 61 (excavation costs of a cooling water canal), are modified to the extent they hold that the costs considered there were for intangible assets. Rev. Rul. 69-606, 1969-2 CB 33, which holds that earthen tanks had indeterminable useful lives, is clarified to the extent it implies that the tanks were intangible property.	Rev. Rul. 75-137 (above)
Driveways	Associated with apartment complex	PLR 8848039
Electrical Distribution System	By taxpayer not in the business of selling electricity. Specifically, those associated with apartment complex including poles, aerial lines, transformers, meters, street lighting	PLR 8848039

Table 1		
Code Sec. 1250 Properties Other Than Residential and Nonresidential Realty		
Asset	**Description**	**Authority**
Electrical Light Fixtures—Exterior	Pole mounted or freestanding outdoor lighting system to illuminate sidewalks, parking, or recreation areas.	Restaurant Directive 2003
Excavating & Backfilling	Required for the construction of laundry facilities and the storm sewer system at a mobile home park. Replacement of the underground components of these facilities will require excavation and backfilling.	Rev. Proc 80-93, 1980-1 CB 50
Fencing	Associated with apartment complex	PLR 8848039
Gas Station Convenience Stores	Specifically, any Code Sec. 1250 property that is a retail motor fuels outlet (whether or not food or other convenience items are sold at the outlet).	P.L. 104-188 Code Sec. 168(e)(3) (E)(iii)
Golf Course—Irrigation System	Underground water pipe and valve system is a land improvement.	Rev. Rul. 69-273, 1969-1 CB 30
Golf Course—"Modern" Greens	Land preparation undertaken by a taxpayer in the construction or reconstruction of modern greens that is so closely associated with depreciable assets, such as a network of underground drainage tiles or pipes, that the land preparation will be retired, abandoned, or replaced contemporaneously with those depreciable assets.	Rev. Rul. 2001-60, 2001-1, CB 587
Grading	The costs of grading for roadways may be depreciable where it can be established that the grading is associated with a depreciable asset and that the grading will be retired, abandoned, or replaced contemporaneously with that asset.	Rev. Rul. 68-193, 1968-1 CB 79
Grading, Clearing & Excavating	Clearing, grading, excavating and removal costs directly associated with the construction of sidewalks, parking areas, roadways and other depreciable land improvements are part of the cost of constructing the improvements.	Restaurant Directive 2003
Landscaping	Associated with apartment complex. Top soil and hydromulch of all yards, a shade tree and deciduous shrubs at each house.	PLR 8848039
Parking Lot	At headquarters 100 miles away from electricity producing plant are not included in the activity asset class for an electric utility steam production plant.	Rev. Rul. 2003-81, IRB 2003-30, 126
Poles and Pylons	Light poles for parking areas and poles used in concrete footings for signage.	Restaurant Directive 2003
Recreation—Fishing	The fish preservation facilities constructed at a hydroelectric dam including, access roads, fixed wharves, landings, an entrance pool, a fish ladder, a holding pool, a fish collection channel, a mechanism for lifting the fish out of the holding pool into trucks, and piping for a supply of water. Those facilities not are inextricably associated with the land are depreciable land improvements.	Rev. Rul. 73-466, 1973-2 CB 52.

Table 1		
Code Sec. 1250 Properties Other Than Residential and Nonresidential Realty		
Asset	**Description**	**Authority**
Recreation—Playground	Outdoor playground constructed with an apartment complex. Swing set, climber, slide, bouncers, see-saw 1, enclosed merry-go-round, picnic tables, benches, basketball backboards, football/soccer goal posts, thirty foot flagstaffs, softball backstop, jogging trail, and stationary aerobic equipment.	PLR 8848039
Reservoir— In General	Preparation of the reservoir site, constructed by an electric utility for use with a steam turbine generating plant.	Rev. Rul. 72-96, 1972-1 CB 67
Reservoir—Timber Farm	Constructed on timber farm.	Kurzet, 222 F.3d 830, (CA-10, 2000)
Roads—Logging	The parts of logging truck roads constructed by the taxpayer are depreciable if the parts have useful lives to the taxpayer that are determinable.	Rev. Rul. 88-99, 1988-2 CB 33.
Roads & Trails—Ranch	Depreciable because they would be abandoned if the improvements to which they led were to be abandoned	Rudolph Investment, TC Memo 1972-129
Roads & Trails—Ski Area	Some costs associated with construction and maintenance of roads and trails at ski resort may be depreciated.	FSA 200021013
Sidewalks	In apartment complex. 3 foot wide concrete service walkway leading from the driveway to each house and 4 foot wide concrete walkway at the curb	PLR 8848039
Signage	Score boards and message board not attached to the building. Internal components like equipment and circuitry are Code Sec. 1245 property.	Rev. Rul. 69-170, 1969-1 CB 28
Signage	A casino's outdoor sign is part land improvement, part equipment.	FSA 200203009
Site Work	Site work includes site drainage, sewers, roads, sidewalks, paving, curbing, general site improvements, landscaping not adjacent to the building, site fencing and enclosures, playground fencing, and all other site improvements not directly related to the building.	Restaurant Directive 2003
Snowmaking System	Buried pipelines and electrical lines, components of a snowmaking system, are similar to a golf course irrigation system.	PLR 8036009
Stone Work	Includes patio stonework imbedded in the ground and applied to exterior half walls that are not an integral part of the building's structural shell.	Restaurant Directive 2003
Streets	Ruling describes 28-foot wide hot-mix asphalt streets with concrete curbs and gutters with 6 inch limestone base material over 6 inch stabilized sub base.	PLR 8848039
Water Distribution System	By taxpayer not in the business of selling water utilities. Specifically, those associated with apartment complex.	PLR 8848039

Disposition of Realty. A sale of realty at a gain may require Code Sec. 1250 recapture, where generally any excess of accelerated recovery deductions over straight-line recovery is reported as ordinary income. However, taxpayers using straight-line recovery have no recapture, because there is no "excess depreciation." Since Code Sec. 1250 applies only to properties placed in service prior to 1987, and these properties had a maximum MACRS recovery period of 19 years, they were fully depreciated by 2007. Since 2008 there is no "excess depreciation" and hence no Code Sec. 1250 gain. For corporations, Code Sec. 291 requires that 20 percent of the accumulated straight line depreciation will be treated as ordinary income (Refer to Chapter 7).

¶16,009 Corporate Planning Ideas

.01 PLANNING FOR THE CORPORATE ALTERNATIVE MINIMUM TAX (AMT)

Although the threat of the corporate AMT has been lessened for most small corporations, this "shadow tax" can generate significant tax consequences for corporations that fail to plan for it. One measure of how well a tax provision works is the lobbying pressure to repeal it. If that is an appropriate measure, the AMT was working very well. Beginning in 1993, Congress began slowly repealing the corporate AMT in a stealth-like manner. Perhaps the most important step in the "stealth repeal" of the corporate AMT was the enactment of Code Sec. 55(e) in the Taxpayer Relief Act of 1997, which eliminated the requirement for many small business C corporations to compute the AMT, for tax years beginning in 1998. To be exempt from the AMT, a corporation must have average gross receipts of not more than $7,500,000 for the prior three years ($5,000,000 in the case of a start-up company).

Many of the same principles applicable to individuals subject to the AMT also apply for corporations. For example, the same considerations on accelerating income (or decelerating expenses) to take advantage of lower AMT rates apply. But there are a few differences in strategy, due mainly to the fact that the corporate AMT computation differs from the individual AMT computation in these important respects:

- The corporate AMT rate is a flat 20-percent rate
- The corporate AMT exemption is $40,000 less any alternative minimum taxable income (AMTI) exceeding $150,000
- The AMT credit carryover equals the AMT for the year; there is no requirement to limit the AMT credit to "timing differences," as was true for individuals
- Corporations have a unique adjustment for 75 percent of the excess of "adjusted current earnings (ACE)" over alternative minimum taxable income

OBSERVATION   The ACE adjustment bears special mention. In the original version of the corporate AMT in 1986, Congress instituted a "BURP" adjustment ("Business Unreported Profits). Essentially, a corporation had to include 50 percent of the excess of financial accounting ("book") earnings over AMTI. In effect, Congress was telling taxpayers that they could not have their cake and eat it too; high profits shown to shareholders and little profit shown to the government. The BURP adjustment was so unpopular that Congress repealed it and replaced it with the "ACE adjustment." Under this concept, *adjusted current earnings* were defined as a modification of book income, but with some tax breaks retained. Much of the ACE rules slow down certain cost recoveries, speed up certain incomes, and perhaps tax certain incomes that were not taxed for regular tax or AMT purposes. A few deductions allowed for the AMT and regular taxes are also denied for ACE purposes.

Table 2 illustrates the regular tax liability and the AMT for the Bruno Corporation.

Table 2	
Bruno Corporation—Regular Tax Computation	
Gross sales revenue	8,220,409
Cost of goods sold [a]	(5,199,320)
Gross Profit	3,021,089
Gross dividends received (5% interest in domestic ACE Corporation)	200,000
Gross dividends received (22% interest in domestic BC Corporation)	100,000
Interest income - U.S. Treasury Notes	30,400
Interest income - State of Ohio Bonds ($200,000) [b]	0
Interest Income - 1996 private activity bond issue ($400,000) [c]	0
Life insurance proceeds - death of company officer ($1,000,000) [d]	0
Gain (ordinary) on the sale of depreciable property [e]	115,520
Gain (capital) on installment sale of land [f]	250,000
Gross Income	3,717,009
Depreciation cost recovery [g]	(77,567)
Other ordinary operating expenses	(1,579,300)
Income before charitable contributions deduction	2,060,142
Contributions	(128,620)
Income before dividends received deduction	1,931,522
Dividends received deduction [h]	(220,000)
Taxable income	1,711,522
Gross tax liability	581,917
Alternative minimum tax (see AMT computation attached)	118,743
Credits against regular tax liability	0
Estimated federal income tax payments for the year	(640,000)
Net regular tax liability	60,660

[a] Zeno uses LIFO. Current year LIFO layer was $60,000.
[b] Expenses of $12,000 related to these bonds were incurred
[c] Expenses of $18,000 related to these bonds were incurred
[d] Life insurance proceeds received from the death of a key company employee. Premiums of $60,000 were paid on the policy during the current year, and the cash surrender value of the policy at the date of death was $80,000. (There is no cash surrender value increase for the current year.)
[e] A cement mixer (personalty) was sold on June 1st of the current year for $210,000. Refer to Cost Recovery Schedule.
[f] Five hundred acres of business land was sold at the end of the current tax year for a total gain of $970,000, of which $250,000 was reported for regular tax purposes in the current tax year using the installment method.
[g] Refer to Cost Recovery Schedule,
[h] Deduction is [$200,000 × .70) + ($100,000 × .80)]

Alternative Minimum Tax Computation		
Corporate taxable income (before any net operating loss deduction)		1,711,522
Adjustments to taxable income (+ or -):		
Excess depreciation on post-86 property (see Asset Schedule)		(14,202)
Gain (loss) adjustments on asset sales (AMT gain – regular tax gain)		(66,136)
Expense adjustments (expenses on private activity bonds)		(18,000)
Taxable income plus or minus adjustments		1,613,184
Tax preference item:		
Tax-exempt interest income on post-8/7/86 issue private activity bonds		400,000
Alternative minimum taxable income before ACE adjustment		2,013,184
Adjusted current earnings (ACE) adjustment:		
Adjustments to current earnings:		
E&P income - tax-exempt interest on State of Ohio bonds	200,000	
E&P expense - expenses related to interest on State of Ohio bonds	(12,000)	

Alternative Minimum Tax Computation	
E&P income - life insurance proceeds - net cash surrender value	920,000
E&P expense - life insurance policy premiums paid	(60,000)
E&P income - disallowance of the installment method for non-dealers	720,000
E&P income - disallowance of current-year layer of LIFO inventory	60,000
E&P income - disallowance of 70% dividends received deduction	140,000
Total adjustments to current earnings	1,968,000
	× .75
Adjusted current earnings (ACE) adjustment	1,476,000
Alternative minimum taxable income (AMTI) before AMT exemption deduction	3,489,184
AMT exemption [phased-out $40,000 – [(AMTI – $150,000) × .25]]	0
Alternative minimum taxable income (AMTI)	3,489,184
AMT tax rate	× .20
Tentative minimum tax (TMT)	697,837
Less regular tax liability	(581,917)
Alternative minimum tax (AMT) - add to regular tax liability *	115,920

* Current-year AMT can be used as an AMT credit against regular tax liability of future years, not to exceed the tentative minimum tax liability of the carryover year

Asset	Cost	Class Life	MACRS Life	Cost Recovery Deductions		
				MACRS	AMT	Difference
Cement Mixers *	400,000	20	15	11,810	8,923	2,887
Machinery & Equip	350,000	10	7	31,237	42,871	(11,634)
Drill Equipment	450,000	10	7	20,081	27,560	(7,479)
Nonresidential realty	300,000	N/A	31.5	9,525	7,500	2,025
Nonresidential realty	200,000	N/A	39	4,915	4,915	0
Total				77,568	91,769	(14,201)
AMT Adjustment					(14,201)	

* The cement mixers were sold in the current year, creating gain/loss adjustments for AMT and ACE purposes

While the AMT has been repealed for small corporations, larger corporations must continue their tax planning efforts to minimize their AMT liability. The following strategies should be considered when other AMT preferences and adjustments apply in order to mitigate the impact of the AMT:

- **Carefully Scrutinize Private Activity Bond Investments.** Both corporate and noncorporate taxpayers are faced with a tax preference item for interest earned on private activity bonds. For corporate taxpayers, this may just be a temporary time value of money problem because of the guaranteed AMT credit.

  However, if the amounts that would have been invested in private activity bonds are in turn invested in taxable sources, the regular tax liability may quickly overtake any TMT liability because of the higher regular tax rates. Investing in other tax-exempt bonds may be a solution, but corporate investors have to consider possible ACE complications, since other sources of tax-exempt interest income are treated as positive ACE adjustments.

- **Assess the Effects of the Tax Benefit Rule of Code Sec. 59(g).** Code Sec. 111(a) states that gross income for regular tax purposes does not include income attributable to the recovery during the current year of any amount deducted in a prior year to the extent the amount did not reduce the amount of tax imposed. This seems to imply that if the AMT applied in the deduction year, the subsequent recovery would not be included in income for regular tax purposes. For example, this would exclude a state income tax refund for a corporate taxpayer if the AMT applied in the year of original deduction.

- **Avoid Investments that Generate ACE Income.** Investments in tax-exempt securities other than private activity bonds generate positive adjustments for ACE purposes. The same is true for less than 20-percent investments in corporate stock, as the 70-percent dividends received deduction (allowed for regular tax and AMT purposes) is not allowed for ACE. Even if an AMT is generated because of such investments, an AMT credit is always generated for the corporate taxpayer. Thus, the only "cost" of such investments may be the time value of paying additional tax in one year before it is returned in a future year as an AMT credit. Corporations with stock investments approaching the 20-percent threshold for the 80-percent dividends received deduction may want to increase the investment so as to avoid the ACE adjustment.

- *Time Recognition of Negative ACE Adjustments.* Corporations should always keep in mind the relationships between positive and negative ACE adjustment years. Negative ACE adjustments are only allowed in a tax year to the extent of post-1989 positive adjustments. This rule does not work in reverse; positive ACE adjustments in the current year may not be used to offset net negative adjustments of prior years. Therefore, a company headed toward a negative ACE adjustment in the current year may want to avoid this if there are no positive ACE adjustments in prior years. Otherwise, the negative adjustment will simply be lost.

- *ACE Installment Sales Adjustments and the "Applicable Percentage" Rule.* Corporate taxpayers with large dollar installment sales of nondealer property should be familiar with Code Sec. 56(g)(4)(D)(iv). Although the installment method is not allowed for ACE purposes, this provision states that the prohibition does not apply the "applicable percentage" of such sales as defined in Code Sec. 453A. The applicable percentage is that portion of total installment sales (including only those exceeding $150,000) that exceeds $5 million. This percentage of the installment sales will qualify for installment sale treatment for ACE purposes. For example, if installment sales total $20,000,000, the applicable percentage is 75 percent (15/20), and no ACE adjustment is required for the gross profit on $15,000,000 of the sales.

.03   PLANNING FOR THE DIVIDENDS RECEIVED DEDUCTION

Code Sec. 243(a)(1) permitted a deduction of 85 percent of the gross dividends received from domestic, nonaffiliated corporations until 1986. In 1986 the Dividends Received Deduction (DRD) was reduced to 80 percent by the Tax Reform Act of 1986. A year later, the Revenue Act of 1987 amended Code Sec. 243(a)(1), reducing the DRD to 70 percent of the gross dividends except for certain "20-percent owned corporations" to which the 80-percent rule continued to apply. A 20-percent owned corporation is defined as any corporation in which 20 percent or more of its outstanding stock is owned by the corporate shareholder that receives the dividends.

The two tiers of dividends qualifying for different amounts of DRDs (hereafter referred to as D7 for dividends eligible for the 70-percent deduction, and D8 for dividends eligible for the 80-percent deduction) will cause few problems as long as the corporation is profitable. When the corporation suffers losses, however, calculation of the DRD taxable income limitation and planning to minimize or eliminate the loss of that deduction certainly becomes more complex and is invariably confusing.

One-Tier Dividend Analysis. The taxable income limitation on the DRD is most easily explained where a corporation has a single class of dividend income. For purposes of the following explanation of the taxable income limitation, reference is made to **Figure 2**, which involves a hypothetical corporate shareholder that has a single class of dividends eligible for the 80-percent DRD. The discussion is equally applicable to a corporation with a single class of dividends from non-20-percent owned corporations that qualify for the 70-percent DRD.

Before discussing the taxable income limitation, it is important to note that the limitation (and the accompanying exception to the limitation) are relevant only when the corporate shareholder has a net loss from business operations (taxable income exclusive of the gross dividends and the DRD). If the corporate shareholder has a positive operating income, the limitation will not apply. For purposes of the following discussion, the positive operating income situation is referred to as the "*general rule.*"

Code Sec. 246(b)(1) limits the DRD to 80 percent [70 percent] of taxable income, computed without regard for the deductions allowed for net operating losses,[27] capital loss carrybacks,[28] or the DRD itself.[29] In the following discussion, this result is referred to as the "*taxable income limitation*," or simply the "limitation."

Code Sec. 246(b)(2) provides an exception to the limitation; the full DRD is allowed if the full 80- [70-] percent deduction would create or add to a net operating loss (NOL) for the year. This result is hereafter referred to as the "*exception to the taxable income limitation*," or simply the "exception."

In summary, the general rule is that the DRD is allowed in full as long as the corporate shareholder has a positive operating income. However, the DRD is subject to limitation in any situation in which the corporation suffers a loss from operations (using that phrase loosely to encompass all taxable income and loss other than dividends), and that loss is insufficient to trigger the NOL exception.

The cumulative effect of these rules is to cause the corporation to lose 80 [70] cents of dividends received deduction for every dollar of loss over a certain range of taxable income. The general rule, the limitation, and the exception to the rule can be illustrated by the calculations set out in **Figure 2**. The only item that is varied is the level of operating profit (OP) or operating loss (OL), defined as all items of taxable income for the year exclusive of dividends, and not including net operating loss deductions or capital loss carryovers. The following discussion assumes an 80-percent DRD in the cases of **Figure 2**, but the same logic would apply with a 70-percent DRD.

The interaction of the taxable income limitation and the exception to such limitation can sometimes lead to what is referred to as the DRD trap, where a few dollars more of expenses would generate significant tax savings. For example, assume that the operating loss in **Figure 2** was $80,000. In this case, the net income before the DRD would be $320,000 (–$80,000 + $400,000), the full DRD would not create an NOL ($320,000 – $320,000 = $0), and the DRD would thus be limited to $256,000 ($320,000 × .80). This leaves taxable income of $66,000, which taxed at corporate rates would be $11,500 of tax due.

However, if expenses were just $1 more, a $1 NOL would be created with a full 80-percent DRD, the taxable income limit would not apply, and no tax would be due. In short, $1 more of expense would save $11,500 of taxes! Therefore, in this case, a corporate taxpayer would want to check the DRD status near year end to see if it makes sense to "purchase tax savings" with a minimal increase in expenses.

Figure 2—The Dividends Received Deduction

Anderson Company owns a 26-percent stock interest in Bell Corporation common stock. During the current year, Anderson received $40,000 of gross dividends on the Bell Corporation stock. Anderson's dividends received deduction, assuming operating incomes (losses) of $180,000, ($5,000), and ($15,000) would be computed as follows:

	(a) General Rule	(b) Limitation	(c) Exception
Operating Income (Loss)	$1,800,000	($ 50,000)	($ 150,000)
Dividend Income	400,000	400,000	400,000
Taxable Income Before DRD	$2,200,000	350,000	250,000
DRD	(320,000)	(280,000)	(320,000)
Taxable Income (NOL)	$1,880,000	$ 70,000	($ 70,000)

---

[27] *See* Code Sec. 172.
[28] *See* Code Sec. 1212(a)(1).
[29] *See* Code Sec. 243(a)(1).

In column (a), the general rule states that the DRD is the lesser of $320,000 (80 percent of the $400,000 dividend) or $1,760,000 (80 percent of $2,200,000 taxable income before DRD). The exception to the general rule does not apply because there is no possible net operating loss. Thus, the DRD is $320,000.

In column (b), the general rule states that the DRD is the lesser of $320,000 (80 percent of the $400,000 dividend) or $280,000 (80 percent of $350,000 taxable income before DRD). The exception to the general rule does not apply because a $320,000 DRD would not create or increase a net operating loss (i.e., $35,000 – $32,000 = $30,000 positive income). Thus, the DRD is $280,000 under the limitation to the general rule.

In column (c), the general rule states that the DRD is the lesser of $320,000 (80 percent of the $400,000 dividend) or $200,000 (80 percent of $250,000 taxable income before DRD). However, the exception to the general rule applies in this case because a $320,000 DRD would create a $70,000 net operating loss (i.e., $250,000 – $320,000 = $70,000 loss). Thus, the DRD is $320,000 under the exception to the limitation.

Tax professionals are often cautioned to be alert for this possibility near the end of the tax year so that "tax savings" can be generated by increasing total expenses for the year by a few more dollars. Alternatively, it may make more sense to increase income, rather than deductions.

OBSERVATION   If the loss of the DRD is important enough to warrant action, there is also a second option open to the taxpayer or tax professional before year-end. Specifically, consideration should be given to reducing or eliminating the operating loss with the realization of additional income prior to year end. Of the two strategies, the realization of additional taxable income may be the better choice.

Additional taxable income will be taxed at only 20 to 30 percent of the corporation's marginal tax rate as long as additional income serves to validate D7 or D8 DRDs in the case of one-tier dividend situations. In the case of solely D8 dividends (**Figure 2**), note that as the operating loss is decreased from $20,000 (Case D) to $0 (Case B), the marginal tax rate on each additional dollar of income is only 3 percent, or 20 percent of the normal 15-percent first-bracket corporate rate. In the case of solely D7 dividends (**Figure 2**), as the operating loss is decreased from $30,000 (Case D) to $0 (Case B), the marginal tax rate on each additional dollar of income is only 4.5 percent, or 30 percent of the normal 15-percent first-bracket corporate rate. Also, assuming the corporation is eligible for the 15 percent introductory bracket, additional amounts of income will be taxed at very low rates. Once the tax year has passed, the opportunity to employ the first tier rates for that year are gone forever.

By contrast, a net operating loss may be employed to recover previous tax paid at relatively high rates of 34 or 35 (perhaps even 39) percent. That tax savings is, however, presumably offset by equivalent future income taxed at similarly high rates when the corporation returns to profitability. Thus, absent significant rate bracket differentials, the value of this strategy is limited primarily to the time value of the refund for the period between receipt and subsequent tax payments. Since loss increasing strategies typically borrow the majority of increased deductions from the immediately succeeding year, the savings are usually short term and as a result, of modest value.

In summary, the one-tier dividend situation (e.g., dividends are all 80-percent dividends, or dividends are all 70-percent dividends) may be expressed as a simple rule. Specifically, if operating losses are present and are less than 20 percent [30 percent] of the gross 80-percent [70-percent] qualifying dividends, the income limitation will apply.

Two-Tier Dividend Analysis. As mentioned earlier, current law establishes two tiers of dividends eligible for the dividends received deduction and subject to the taxable income limitation. The first class of dividends is allowed an 80-percent DRD if the corporate owner holds 20 percent or more of the outstanding stock. Dividends from non-20-percent owned companies are eligible for a 70-percent DRD.

If a corporation receives dividends from both 20-percent owned and non-20-percent corporations, the Code provides that the taxable income limitation and the accompanying exception to the limitation are to be applied sequentially. First, the limit is applied separately to the dividends qualifying for the 80-percent deduction (i.e., 20-percent owned corporations). For these computations, any non-20-percent owned dividends are included in taxable income for purposes of applying the taxable income limitation and the exception.

Second, the limitation is then applied separately to dividends from non-20-percent owned corporations to potentially limit the 70-percent DRD to 70 percent of taxable income. In applying the second limitation, taxable income does not include the gross dividends received from 20-percent owned corporations, or the related deduction. The two-tier dividend analysis for the dividends received deduction is not only more complex, it increases the maximum amount of deduction that can be lost. The six cases illustrated in **Figure 3** are used to analyze the two-tier dividend case.

Operating under a two class system of dividends does not change the general rule that the taxable income limitation does not apply if the corporate shareholder has any positive operating income (or $0 income). This is illustrated in Cases A and B of **Figure 3**. As was true in the one tier dividend case, adding a nonnegative operating income figure to positive gross dividends means that neither DRD limitations will apply.

General Rule. If the corporation has any positive operating income (or even $0 operating income), there is no taxable income limitation on either the D8 or D7 dividends received deductions.

The two percentages require a modest alteration of the one-tier NOL exception rule, however. In this case, the operating losses must exceed the sum of 20 percent of D8 and 30 percent of D7. This is because the net operating loss exception is "tested" by subtracting both the D7 and D8 DRDs from taxable income to see if a net operating loss is created or increased. This is the result in Case F of **Figure 3**; the operating loss of $20,001 exceeds the sum of 20 percent of D8 ($18,000, or $90,000 × .20) and 30 percent of D8 ($3,000, or $10,000 × .30). By subtracting the full DRDs for both classes of dividends, a $1 net operating loss is created and the taxable income limitations are irrelevant.

Net Operating Loss Exception. If operating losses are present and exceed the sum of 20 percent of D8 and 30 percent of D7, there is no income limitation on the dividends received deduction (because the DRD must create or add to an NOL for the year).

The taxable income limitation rule is substantially modified, however, to impose order on the application of the limitation to the two classes of dividends. The apparent intent of this rule is to assure that a $1 change in operating loss will affect only one class of dividends at a time (avoiding the possibility that $1 of additional loss could cost $1.50 in lost DRDs).

As mentioned earlier, the Code provides that the D8 DRD taxable income limitation is computed first. The D8 DRD is limited to 80 percent of the sum of D7 and D8 dividends reduced by the operating loss resulting from all other taxable activities during the year (henceforward, OL). Thus, the formula for the income limitation on the D8 DRD is:

D8 DRD limit = 80% × (D8 + D7 − OL)

Figure 3

Dividends Received Deduction—Two Tiers (D7 and D8) of Dividends

	A	B	C	D	E	F
	A	B	C	D	E	F
D8	90,000	90,000	90,000	90,000	90,000	90,000
D7	10,000	10,000	10,000	10,000	10,000	10,000
OP (OL)	10,000	0	(5,000)	(10,000)	(21,000)	(21,001)
Total	110,000	100,000	95,000	90,000	79,000	78,999
D8DRD	(72,000)	(72,000)	(72,000)	(72,000)	(72,000)	(72,000)
D7DRD	(7,000)	(7,000)	(7,000)	(7,000)	(7,000)	(7,000)
Taxable	31,000	21,000	16,000	11,000	0	(1)
Limit?						
D8DRD	No	No	No	No	Yes	No
D7DRD	No	No	Yes	Yes	Yes	No
Before DRD	110,000	100,000	95,000	90,000	79,000	78,999
D8 DRD	(72,000)	(72,000)	(72,000)	(72,000)	(63,200)	(72,000)
D7 DRD	(7,000)	(7,000)	(3,500)	(0)	(0)	(7,000)
Taxable	31,000	21,000	19,500	18,000	15,800	(1)
Tax Due	4,650	3,150	2,925	2,700	2,370	0
Change OP/OL		10,000	5,000	5,000	11,000	1
Change Tax		1,500	225	225	330	1,650
Tax Rate on Change		15%	4.5%	4.5%	3%	1,650%

The taxable income limitation for the D7 DRD is calculated second. It is equal to 70 percent of D7 dividends reduced by the operating loss. D8 is ignored for these purposes. Thus, the income limitation on the D7 DRD is:

D7 DRD limit = 70% (D7 – OL)

The different bases and interaction between the two types of dividends make it impossible to develop a simple rule of thumb when both classes of dividends are received by a corporation. A more complex but easily applied year-end estimation procedure is apparent when examining each formula.

The Taxable Income Limitation can be restated as follows for two-tier dividends:

Taxable Income Limitation. If operating losses are present and are less than the sum of 20 percent of gross D8 dividends plus 30 percent of gross D7 dividends, the following taxable income limitations will apply:

a. The D8 DRD will be limited only when the operating loss is greater than D7 dividends, and there is no D7 DRD at this point; and

b. The D7 DRD will always be limited when operating losses are present but are less than the D7 dividends.

OBSERVATION   The taxable income limitation on the DRD was a questionable policy choice when originally enacted. The DRD was intended to minimize multiple levels of federal income tax on a single stream of corporate income as it passed from corporation to corporation and finally from corporation to non-corporate shareholder. The taxable income limitation does nothing to meet this objective. Rather it places a premium on planning and professional advice and lays a trap for the unwary where no significant policy or revenue objective is served. Further, the establishment of a second tier of 70-percent DRD dividends was driven by revenue needs and appears to be completely free of either theoretical or policy considerations. The additional complexity that has resulted cannot be justified. If the policy rationale for the income limitation was in doubt before the 1987 Act, it now must be viewed as wholly unjustified.

.05   PLANNING FOR OTHER LIMITATIONS FOR CERTAIN DIVIDENDS

In addition to the taxable income limitation on the DRD, other limits on the ability to minimize the tax liability on dividend income should be considered. Limitations apply when the stock is held for a short holding period, when the dividend is an "extraordinary" dividend, or when the purchase price of the stock is debt financed. A discussion of these limitations follows:

Short Holding Period.

Corporations cannot take a deduction for dividends received if common stock was held less than 46 days during the 91-day period beginning 45 days before the stock became ex-dividend with respect to the dividend. Ex-dividend means the holder has no rights to the dividend. If the stock is preferred stock, no dividends received deduction is allowed for stock held less than 91 days during the 181-day period beginning 90 days before the stock became ex-dividend with respect to the dividend if the dividends received are for a period or periods totaling more than 366 days.

Example 16-12. SDF Corporation declared a dividend on February 1 to shareholders of record on February 28, payable on March 10. QET Corporation purchased stock in SDF Corporation on Feb 15. The dividends received deduction is not allowed since the stock was held for less than 46 days before the ex-dividend date.

Extraordinary Dividends.

If a corporation receives an extraordinary dividend on stock held two years or less before the dividend announcement date, it generally must reduce its basis in the stock by the nontaxed part of the dividend. The nontaxed part is any dividends-received deduction allowable for the dividends. An extraordinary dividend is any dividend on stock that equals or exceeds a certain percentage of the corporation's adjusted basis in the stock. The percentages are:

- 5% for stock preferred as to dividends, or
- 10% for other stock.

All dividends received that have ex-dividend dates within an 85-consecutive-day period are treated as one dividend. All dividends received that have ex-dividend dates within a

365-consecutive-day period are treated as as extraordinary dividends if the total of the dividends exceeds 20% of the corporation's adjusted basis in the stock.

Any dividend on disqualified preferred stock is treated as an extraordinary dividend regardless of the period of time the corporation held the stock. Disqualified preferred stock is any stock preferred as to dividends if any of the following apply.

- The stock when issued has a dividend rate that declines (or can reasonably be expected to decline) in the future.
- The issue price of the stock exceeds its liquidation rights or stated redemption price.
- The stock is otherwise structured to avoid the rules for extraordinary dividends and to enable corporate shareholders to reduce tax through a combination of dividends-received deductions and loss on the disposition of the stock.

Example 16-13. XCV Corporation purchased stock in JKL Corporation on November 1 of the prior tax year for $50,000. On January 15 of the current tax year, XCV received a dividend of $10,000. Assuming that the dividend otherwise qualified for the 70% dividends received deduction, the basis in the JKL stock must be reduced by $7,000 ($10,000 × 70%) because the dividend exceeds 10% of the basis in the stock and the stock was owned less than two years.

Debt Financed Stock.

If any portion of the purchase price of stock was debt financed and any portion of the debt remains unpaid during the period dividends are received, the dividends received deduction will be limited. The dividends received deduction equals the percentage of the stock price that is NOT debt financed. As the corporation reduces the debt, the dividends received deduction will increase.

Example 16-14. ABC Corporation purchased 1,000 shares of DEF Corporation stock for $50,000. ABC borrowed 80% of the purchase price. Assuming that a $5,000 dividend paid to ABC by DEF otherwise qualifies for the 70% dividends received deduction, the deduction will be limited to $700 [$5,000 × 70% × 20% (1 - .8)].

When acquiring stock in another corporation which is otherwise eligible for the DRD, the corporation should be aware of the above limitations on the DRD and take steps to avoid transactions what would limit the ability of the corporation to use the maximum DRD or would require a reduction in the corporation's basis in the stock.

¶16,011   Summary

- Although the term "method of accounting" is not defined in either the Code or the Regulations, business entities should ensure that they are using an appropriate accounting method.
- When a business entity discovers that it is using an incorrect or inappropriate accounting method, it should file an application to voluntarily correct its method of accounting.
- There are many tax planning issues relating to adopting and using a permissive method of valuing inventory. There are many planning opportunities to consider when the business entity is using LIFO as an inventory valuation method.
- The Uniform Capitalization rules specified in Code Sec. 263A, require capitalization of certain period costs into ending inventory. These rules are quite complex and firms may want to consider using the various permissible simplified methods.

- Cost segregation studies generally permit a taxpayer to accelerate the write-off of certain components of a building.
- The corporate AMT requires large corporations to consider tax planning strategies to minimize the impact of the AMT and to maximize AMT credit carryforwards.
- The dividends received deduction requires a two-tier dividend analysis. In some cases, it may be preferable to defer recognition of expenses or to accelerate recognition of income in order to maximize the DRD. Other limitations restricting the benefits of the DRD should be considered when purchasing and holding corporate stock as an investment.

Review Questions for Chapter 16

True or False

Indicate which of the following statements are true or false by circling the correct answer.

1. The term "method of accounting" is defined in Code Sec. 446.   T   F
2. The IRS has issued simplified and uniform procedures for obtaining an automatic consent   T   F
    to make an accounting method change.
3. The emphasis of Rev. Proc. 97-27 is to "foster voluntary compliance."   T   F
4. The Code Sec. 179 deduction is limited by taxable income derived from the active   T   F
    conduct of the trade or business in which the asset will be used.
5. The low-income housing tax credit may be taken repeatedly over a 10-year period.   T   F
6. The corporate AMT has been repealed for small corporations that have average gross   T   F
    receipts of not more than $10,000,000 for the prior three years.
7. The 80-percent dividends received deduction applies only to corporation in which the   T   F
    taxpayer owns more than 50 percent of the stock.
8. An advantage of pooling inventory items under the dollar-value method is to neutralize   T   F
    the possible adverse tax effects of a significant reduction in the stock of a particular
    inventory item.
9. Manufacturers who incur $200,000 or less of indirect costs in a tax year are treated as   T   F
    having no Code Sec. 263A costs in that year.
10. The dividends received deduction on debt financed stock is allowed in full.   T   F

Fill in the Blanks

Fill in each blank with the appropriate word or phrase that completes each sentence.

11. A workable definition of an accounting method is simply "_____
     _____."
12. In the _____ court case, the court held that once an accounting method is chosen on
     an initial return, the taxpayer is bound by the choice.
13. An example of _____ is a math or posting error.
14. A voluntary change in an accounting method permits the taxpayer to spread the increase in income over
     _____ years.
15. Under Rev. Proc. 97-27 the taxpayer may elect a one-year adjustment period if the entire Code Sec. 481
     adjustment is less than $_____ (either positive or negative).
16. A disposition of personalty at a gain is subject to _____ under Code Sec. 1245
     to the extent of depreciation taken.
17. A taxpayer who undertakes a(n) "_____" analysis is attempting to isolate certain elements
     of a building's cost as either personalty or realty with a shortened class life.
18. The corporate AMT rate is currently a flat _____ percent rate.
19. Under the two-tier dividend analysis, the first class of dividends is allowed a(n) ____-percent dividends
     received deduction and the second class of dividends is allowed a(n) ____-percent dividends received
     deduction.
20. When specific identification is not a feasible method for valuing inventory, the taxpayer must assume one
     of three cost flow assumptions: _____, _____, or _____.

Multiple Choice

21. Lario's LLC purchased a building for $150,000 that was built in 1935 and incurred qualifying rehabilitation expenditures of $200,000 to convert the building into a restaurant. What is the qualifying tax credit for rehabilitation expenditures, and the basis in the building after the renovations are complete?
    a. $20,000 credit, $330,000 basis.
    b. $20,000 credit, $200,000 basis.
    c. $20,000 credit, $350,000 basis.
    d. $40,000 credit, $310,000 basis.

22. Lario's LLC purchased a structure for $150,000 that was built in 1935 and spent $200,000 on qualifying rehabilitation expenditures of $200,000 to convert the building into a restaurant. After operating the restaurant for three years, the building was sold to a developer who plans to convert the building into loft-condominiums. What is the recapture, if any, in the year the building was sold by Lario's?
    a. None
    b. $8,000.
    c. $20,000.
    d. $40,000.

23. Henry Corporation acquired the following two used machines each costing $500,000 in a tax year in which the maximum Code Sec. 179 deduction is $500,000:
    Machine A (5 year property) on January 1
    Machine B (7 year property) on September 1

    Compute the maximum deduction assuming Henry elects the maximum Code Sec. 179 deduction and the maximum MACRS cost recovery deduction (assume the bonus depreciation deduction does not apply).
    a. $35,700
    b. $50,000
    c. $535,700
    d. $550,000

24. Jonas Corporation purchased a new apartment building on July 1 of the current year for $500,000. A cost segregation analysis was performed and it was determined that $100,000 of the cost could be classified as land improvements. As a result of this analysis which of the following statements is correct regarding the $100,000 in land improvements?
    a. Depreciate over 27.5 years using 200% DB
    b. Depreciate over 27.5 years using 150% DB
    c. Depreciate over 15 years using 150% DB
    d. Depreciate over 15 years using 200% DB

25. Purple Corporation purchased an office building on November 1 of the current year for $2,000,000. A cost segregation analysis revealed that $80,000 of the cost could be reclassified as signage (seven-year property). What is the maximum deduction for the signage assuming no other personalty assets were acquired in the year?
    a. $80,000
    b. $2,856
    c. $256
    d. $364

26. Tom Swift is married and files a joint return. His wife Mary earned $35,000 as a school teacher. Tom purchased a new five-year property asset for $95,000 during the year to be used in his sole proprietorship business. The net income from his business before taking the asset acquisition into account is $50,000. What is the maximum allowable Code Sec. 179 deduction based on the income limitation?
    a. $0.
    b. $50,000.
    c. $85,000.
    d. $95,000.

27. Swift Corporation, a calendar year taxpayer, has alternative minimum taxable income [before adjustment for adjusted current earnings (ACE)] of $600,000. Swift's (ACE) is $1,500,000. What is its tentative minimum tax?
    a. $1,275,000.
    b. $1,500,000.
    c. $255,000.
    d. $242,000.

28. In the current year, Pedro Corporation discovered that it had been capitalizing as production costs expenses that should have been deducted as administrative expenses resulting in an overstatement in its ending inventory of $200,000. What should the company do?
    a. The company should amend its prior year tax return.
    b. The company should change its accounting method in the current year and reduce its taxable income by a $200,000 Code Sec. 481 adjustment.
    c. The company should change its accounting method in the current year and reduce its taxable income by a $50,000 Code Sec. 481 adjustment.
    d. The company should change its accounting method in the current year and increase its taxable income by a $200,000 Code Sec. 481 adjustment.

29. Pedro Corporation has consistently, but incorrectly, used an allowance for bad debts rather than the specific write-off method. At the beginning of the year, the balance in the allowance account is $100,000. What should the company do?
    a. Pedro should wait until the IRS examines the taxpayer's return. The agent will then require the company to change its accounting method. There will be a two-year audit adjustment of $50,000 per year.
    b. Pedro should voluntarily change its method by increasing its income by $25,000 per year in the current and three following tax years.
    c. Pedro should voluntarily change its method by not making any future additions to the reserve and using the balance to absorb future bad debts until the account balance reaches zero.
    d. Pedro should voluntarily change its method by increasing its income by $100,000 in the current tax year.

30. The IRS is requiring Pedro Corporation to change an accounting method. Which of the following are correct statements?
    a. Pedro may be subject to penalties and interest.
    b. Pedro may elect to make the change as of the beginning of the current tax year.
    c. Pedro may spread the adjustment over three future tax years.
    d. All of the above are correct.

31. Piñata Corporation voluntarily changed from the cash to the accrual method of accounting because it discovered inventories were material to its business. The change resulted in a positive $50,000 adjustment to income.
   a. Piñata must increase its income by $50,000 in the year the erroneous method is discovered.
   b. Piñata must amend all prior open tax years and recomputed its gross profit based upon the correct beginning and ending inventories.
   c. Piñata must increase its income by $12,500 in the year of the change and increase its income by $12,500 in each of the three preceding tax years.
   d. Piñata must increase its income by $12,500 in the year of the change and increase its income by $12,500 in each of the three following tax years.

32. At the beginning of the current year, Blaize Corporation voluntarily changed from the cash to the accrual method of accounting. The relevant account balances as of January 1, are as follows:

Accounts receivable	$ 85,000
Inventory	125,000
Accounts payable for merchandise	90,000

   Which of the following statements is correct?
   a. Blaize has a positive adjustment to income of $120,000 that must be recognized in the current tax year.
   b. Blaize has a negative adjustment to income of $120,000 that must be recognized in the current tax year.
   c. Blaize has a $30,000 positive adjustment to income that can be recognized in the current year and in each of the three following tax years.
   d. Blaize has a $40,000 positive adjustment to income that can be recognized in each of the three following tax years.

Problems

33. Mayan Corporation purchased the following new seven-year class personalty. Mayan plans to make the maximum Code Sec. 179 deduction of $500,000 for the current tax year. Mayan will not be subject to the income limitation for making the Code Sec. 179 deduction. Which asset(s) should Mayan include in its Code Sec. 179 election?

Asset	Acquisition Date	Cost
A	January 1	$306,000
B	May 1	90,000
C	July 1	70,000
D	November 1	234,000
Total		$700,000

34. Progressive LLC spent $1,000,000 to build qualified low-income housing in Chicago. The units are occupied on January 1 of the current tax year by qualified low-income tenants. Compute the low-income housing credit available to the partners of Progressive assuming the units continue to meet the required conditions over a 10-year period and the applicable credit percentage is 8.12 percent.

35. Azure Corporation has the following gross receipts:

	Gross receipts
2006	4,600,000
2007	4,300,000
2008	4,200,000
2009	6,000,000
2010	7,200,000
2011	8,500,000
2012	9,800,000

When will Azure first be subject to the AMT?

36. PriceCutters Corporation has the following tax return information:

Taxable income	$100,000
Regular corporate tax liability	22,250
AMT adjustment (excluding ACE adjustment)	80,000
ACE adjustment (prior positive adjustments are $40,000)	100,000

Calculate its AMT, if any, based upon the above information assuming the company's average annual gross receipts for the prior three-year period is $8.2 million.

37. In filing its first tax return, Max Corporation checked the "cost" box as to inventory method. At the end of the year, the cost and market value of their inventories was the same. In the second year, the market value of the inventories dropped significantly, and Max desires to use the "lower of cost or market" method. Max argues that checking the "cost" box was a mistake, and that since they essentially applied the lower of cost or market method in the first year, they should be permitted to use the lower of cost or market method without asking the permission of the IRS. Do you agree? Explain.

38. Blaine Corporation, a calendar-year taxpayer, filed its first tax return on February 4, 2012, electing to capitalize research and experimentation (R&E) costs and amortize them over five years. On March 14, 2012, Blaine filed a corrected 2011 return and elected to deduct currently the R&E costs. Both methods of reporting the R&E costs are proper tax accounting methods. Is Blaine allowed to arbitrarily change this method or reporting R&E costs, or must they request permission from the IRS to do so? Explain.

39. A taxpayer entered the wrong MACRS asset code for an asset that produced smaller deductions than intended. The taxpayer contended that the correction was the correction of an error, and not a change of accounting method. Is this a change of accounting method? Explain.

40. The Tax Court just ruled on an inventory method, and their decision runs contrary to IRS regulatory advice. Mecan Company changes their inventory method to conform to the Tax Court decision, stating that this is not an accounting change but a change in the underlying facts (a new major source of authority). Do you agree? Explain.

41. Bell Company has been using an improper inventory method since it was incorporated in 1923. Bell is afraid to change the accounting method now for fear of an IRS audit. The IRS has audited Bell in the past, but said nothing about the improper method. Bell has come under some criticism from other companies in the industry for using a method that does not clearly reflect income, but since Bell is not a publicly traded company, it has not really worried about such criticism. Is it possible that the IRS knows about the bad method but simply chose not to make the adjustment? Explain.

42. During the year, Mallard Company placed in service $550,000 of personalty, including $240,000 in the last quarter of its tax year. What acquisition year convention will Mallard use if (1) no Code Sec. 179 election is made, (2) the maximum Code Sec. 179 election is made on personalty placed in service in the first three quarters of the year, or (3) the Code Sec. 179 election is made on personalty placed in service in the last quarter of the year? Explain. [Assume the maximum Sec. 179 deduction is $500,000 for the year.]

43. Tina Seago, president of Global Manufacturing, has a custom of spending the first hour at work each day touring the factory, saying hello to all the workers and listening to any complaints. Her remaining hours at work are devoted to long-range planning and financing for the company. Should Global treat a portion of Tina's salary and a portion of all other costs related to the president's office (secretarial support, depreciation, supplies, etc.) as capitalizable Code Sec. 163A costs? Explain.

44. Travis Trammell, controller of Shortstop Corporation, has just given up on his latest attempt to determine the total additional Code Sec. 263A costs allocable to Shortstop's manufacturing operation. He believes that if he were able to trace each additional cost down to the last penny, the total would be no more than 10 percent of the normal financial accounting (and Code Sec. 471) inventoriable costs. So Travis made an arbitrary decision to simply increase Shortstop's ending inventory at the end of each year by 10 percent. Is this an acceptable method of accounting for Code Sec. 263A costs, given that the Regulations refer to any other acceptable method? Explain.

45. The GHJ Corporation received dividends qualifying for the DRD from the SDF Corporation. Compute the GHJ Corporation's taxable income based upon the following operating income (losses):

	a	b	c
DRD %	70%	70%	70%
Operating Income	$100,000	$(10,000)	$(70,000)
Dividend Income	$60,000	$60,000	$60,000

d. How would your answer change to part a, if the stock was purchased 30 days before the SDF stock became ex-dividend with respect to the dividend?
e. How would your answer change to part a, if the stock purchase was debt financed and the por-tion of the debt that remains unpaid when the dividend was received equals 75% of the purchase price?
f. How would your answer change to part a, if GHJ purchased the stock last year for $200,000? What effect, if any, would the dividend have on the basis in the stock?

Research Problems

46. The HotChili Investors, LLC, a limited partnership, purchased a fire house built in 1925 from the city of Moline, IL with the intention of renovating the building and turning it into a restaurant. The building has two exterior walls each approximately 50 feet long and two exterior walls each approximately 40 feet long. The structure was purchased from the city for $85,000 with the stipulation that the building be moved to a new location so a new and larger fire house could be built at the old location. The partnership moved the old structure at a cost of $125,000 and spent $815,000 renovating the building, including increasing the size of the building by approximately 40 percent and installed restaurant furniture and equipment costing $500,000. During the renovation process, it was necessary to remove 85 percent of one of the longer exterior walls in order to add on additional eating space for the restaurant portion of the facility, with the remaining 15 percent of the wall becoming an interior wall in the restaurant portion of the facility. Will the renovation and expansion qualify for the rehabilitation credit? What are the total costs that qualify for the credit?

47. Able Manufacturing Corporation makes water pumps that are used in residential and commercial building. The company uses the FIFO inventory method for the manufacturing process of its basic commercial water pump and the LIFO inventory method for the costs associated with conversion of the core pumps into pumps suitable for residential installation. Is the company using a proper method of accounting for its inventory in accounting for its inventory costs? Why or why not? Assuming the company is using an incorrect method, what should the company do?

48. The local Acura dealer offers new car customers a 36-month bumper to bumper service package for a one time payment of $1,800. The package includes all costs associated with the recommended servicing costs required by the warranty which the manufacturer provides on each new auto. The car owner who purchases the service package is entitled to regularly scheduled oil changes and other services recommended at three month or 4,500 mile intervals. The dealership deposits the fees from sales of the service package into an escrow account and recognizes service income of $200 (1,800 × 1/9) each time the auto is serviced. Is the dealer's method of recognizing income from the service contracts a permissible method of accounting? Explain.

49. BountifulSnow, Inc., a calendar year, accrual method taxpayer, received permission from the U.S. Forest Service to operate a snowboarding facility on five acres of forest land near Boise, Idaho. The corporation had the terrain graded to accommodate snowboarding activities and installed lift equipment to carry the snowboarders to the top of the recreation area. The total cost of grading the land was $175,000; the cost of the lift equipment was $285,000 and the cost of a portable modular building to be used as a ticket booth and warming house for its patrons was $145,000. The facility was ready for business on November 1 of the current year. Because of an unusually warm winter, the facility did not have its first customers until January 15 of the following year. The corporation had $0 gross income in the current year and $495,000 net income on the subsequent year before considering any Code Sec. 179 or cost recovery deduction. From October 1 to January 15, Bob Brown, the manager of the facility, used the modular building as his personal residence while his permanent residence was under construction. In which tax year is the corporation entitled to take the Code Sec. 179 deduction and depreciation expense for the assets it acquired to operate the snowboarding facility? Compute the maximum Code Sec. 179 deduction and maximum MACRS depreciation expense for the current year and the subsequent tax year.

50. The A-1 Auto Salvage corporation purchases autos that have been damaged in auto accidents, or stolen and later recovered with significant damage as a result of the thefts. All of these autos have been declared a total loss by the insurance companies and have been sold to A-1 at a price that estimated their scrap value. The scrap autos are delivered to A-1's salvage lot and placed in rows based upon the make and model of the auto. As the autos are stripped of anything of value and these parts are resold to both retail and wholesale customers, it has been the policy of A-1 to compute a cost of goods sold equal to 85 percent of the sales price of the salvaged part. The company has never taken a complete physical inventory of all parts in its salvage yard that have future value. In order to obtain a bank loan to obtain additional working capital, the bank required A-1 to obtain a certified audit. The auditors required A-1 to make a 100-percent physical count of the salvageable parts in its salvage yard. The ending value of this physical inventory resulted in an increase in its ending inventory of $50,000. When it filed its tax return, A-1 increased both its beginning and ending inventory by $50,000. How should A-1 account for the change to its ending inventory on its tax return?

Internet Exercise

51. Use your favorite search engine to locate the websites of three companies that specialize in cost segregation studies for businesses. Write a one-paragraph summary for each web-site describing the services offered and the touted benefits of having their consulting firm prepare an analysis for your firm.

Spreadsheet Exercise

52. Download the cost segregation study spreadsheet from the website. Change the inputs to correspond with the facts of a hypothetical client you are advising. Write a one-page memo explaining your analysis.

CHAPTER 17

The Tax Accrual: An Introduction to Financial Accounting Issues

Learning Objectives

In this chapter you will learn:

1. The differences between financial income and taxable income, including temporary and permanent differences.
2. How book-tax differences are disclosed in the financial income statement and the footnotes to the financial statements and the impact that ASC Topic 740, formerly FAS 109 and FIN 48, has on the disclosure of these differences.
3. How book-tax differences are disclosed on the tax return through preparation of the Schedule M-3.
4. How to report uncertain tax positions using the Schedule UTP.

¶17,001 Introduction

Book-tax differences are the result of the divergence of taxable income and financial income which has occurred primarily since the Tax Reform Act of 1986. This Act significantly broadened the tax base in order to accommodate a significant reduction in the top individual and corporate tax rates. This base broadening caused a shift away from recognition of income and expense items based upon generally accepted accounting principles (GAAP) to rule-based principles incorporated into the Internal Revenue Code. This resulted in significant differences in when income and expense items are recognized and in some cases the amount of the income or expense to be recognized. Book-tax differences that result in permanent differences, that is the item of income or expense will never be reported for tax purposes, are reflected in the effective tax rate, while differences that result only in a timing difference impact only on when (the tax year) the item will be recognized. Significant footnote disclosure is now required to identify and explain these differences and their impact on the financial net income of the firm, including the current and noncurrent for tax expense.

In addition, the IRS also requires regular corporations, S corporations, and partnerships with Assets of $10,000,000 or more to complete the Schedule M-3 which provides a detailed explanation of these differences and to identify whether these differences are temporary or permanent differences. This re-quires not only a basic understanding of tax accounting principles but also of financial (GAAP) accounting principles. The tax professional must become well-versed in how and when these book-tax differences arise and how to measure these differences. In addition, the tax professional must keep detailed records from year to year so that the appropriate entries can be made when a timing difference reverses.

This chapter will help you to gain a basic understanding of the differences between financial and tax accounting.

¶17,003   Book-Tax Differences

A significant difference may exist between a corporation's federal income tax liability as reported on its Form 1120 and its financial statements prepared using GAAP. There are three main explanations for these differences.

.01   DIFFERENT REPORTING ENTITIES

A corporate group must consolidate all U.S. and foreign subsidiaries within a single financial statement for book purposes when the parent corporation controls more than 50 percent of the voting power of those subsidiaries. For financial accounting purposes, the parent uses the equity method to account for the earnings of a subsidiary where the parent corporation owns between 20 and 50 percent of another corporation. If the corporation owns less than 20 percent of another corporation, the cost method is used to account for its investment in the corporation. Income is reported only when dividends are received.

For federal tax purposes, a U.S. corporation may elect to include any domestic subsidiary that is 80 percent or more owned in its consolidated U.S. tax return. The income of a foreign subsidiary may not be included on a consolidated return. If less than 80 percent is owned in a domestic subsidiary, it may not be included on the U.S. tax return of the parent.

Example 17-1.

- ACL, a domestic corporation, owns 80 percent of BCL, a domestic corporation, 80 percent of CCL, a foreign corporation, and 40 percent of DCL, a domestic corporation.
- ACL's consolidated financial statements must include the financial information for BCL and CCL. On its balance sheet, ACL accounts for its investment in DCL using the equity method.
- ACL may elect to file a consolidated tax return only with BCL.

.03   DIFFERENT TAXES

The income tax expense reported on a corporation's financial statement is its combined federal, state, local, and foreign income tax expense. The financial tax expense includes both current and deferred tax expense amounts. The income tax expense shown on the Federal income tax return is based on the corporation's taxable income. State and local taxes are reported as deductions in arriving at taxable income.

Example 17-2. Michael Corporation has net income from operations of $50,000. In addition, Michael paid $6,000 in state income tax and $4,000 in local property tax. Michael's federal income tax liability is computed as follows:

Net income from operations	$50,000
State income tax	–$6,000
Local property tax	–$4,000
Taxable income	$40,000
Federal income tax @15%	–$6,000
Net income after tax	$34,000

.05 DIFFERENT ACCOUNTING METHODS

Many differences exist between book and tax accounting methods. Some differences are temporary and are due to timing differences as to when the item is reported for financial and tax purposes. Examples of temporary differences which will eventually reverse include:
- The difference between financial and tax depreciation methods
- Accrual of expenses that give rise to a tax deduction only when they are actually paid
- Recognition of income for tax purposes before the item is accrued for book purposes
- Carryforward or carryback of net operating losses
- Intangible assets amortized for tax purposes, but written down to their current value for book purposes.

Some differences are permanent and occur when items appear in the financial statement or the tax return, but not both. Examples of permanent differences include:
- Income which is recognized for book purposes but not for tax purposes
- Expenses which are deductible for book purposes but not for tax purposes
- Tax credits, which reduce federal income taxes but have no corresponding book treatment, such as the Alternative Minimum Tax Credit, the Research and Development Credit, and the Foreign Tax Credit.

Note: To reconcile taxable income to book income both permanent and timing differences are taken into account. These items may be either positive or negative adjustments. This reconciliation is made on either Schedule M-1 or M-3 of the Form 1120. The Schedule M-3 is discussed later.

Some of the more frequently encountered differences are:

Temporary Differences	Permanent Differences
Income	**Income**
Deposits	Life insurance proceeds
Installment Gains	Municipal bond interest
Prepaid Income	
Deductions	**Deductions**
Accrued vacation pay	50% disallowance of meals and entertainment
Amortization Expense	Expenses to carry tax-exempt income
Capital losses	Fines and penalties
Charitable contributions	Premiums on life insurance policy
Depreciation expense	
Health Insurance, future benefits	
Inventory write-downs	
Net operating losses	
Pension Benefits	
Warranty expenses	

¶17,005   Income Taxes in the Financial Statements

The ASC Topic 740, formerly FAS 109, approach follows the matching principle with all expenses related to earning income reported in the same period the income is recognized. The date that the expenses are actually paid is disregarded for financial statement purposes. The total book tax expense is made up of both current and deferred components. The current tax expense represents the taxes actually payable (refundable) to the government in the current period. However, the current portion of the book income tax expense rarely matches the taxpayer's actual tax liability.

ASC Topic 740-10-25 Principles

The following basic principles are applied in accounting for income taxes at the date of the financial statements:

a.   A current tax liability or asset is recognized for the estimated taxes payable or refundable on tax returns for the current year.

b.   A deferred tax liability or asset is recognized for the estimated future tax effects attributable to temporary differences and carryforwards.

c.   The measurement of current and deferred tax liabilities and assets is based on provisions of the enacted tax law; the effects of future changes in tax laws or rates are not anticipated.

d.   The measurement of deferred tax assets is reduced, if necessary, by the amount of any tax benefits that, based on available evidence, are not expected to be realized.

The deferred component of the book tax expense is called the deferred tax expense or deferred tax benefit. It represents the future tax cost (savings) associated with income reported in the current-period financial statement. ASC Topic 740-10 adopts a balance sheet approach to measuring deferred taxes. The deferred tax expense is reported as a deferred tax liability. A deferred tax liability is the expected future tax liability related to current income. It occurs when:

- An expense is deductible for tax purposes in the current period but is not deductible for book purposes until some future period.
- Income is includible currently for book purposes but is not includible in taxable income until a future period.

Example 17-3.   Computation of Deferred Tax Liability: Depreciation

Consider the following timing differences between financial depreciation (straight line) and tax depreciation (DDB). Note that over the useful life of the asset, the total depreciation expense is the same under both methods. In the first four years tax depreciation exceeds financial depreciation, while in the next six years, financial depreciation exceeds tax depreciation.

DEPRECIATION EXPENSE

Cost	$50,000			
Salvage	$ 0			
Useful Life	10 years			
Tax Rate	35%			
Period	Straight Line	Double Declining Balance	Difference	Deferred Tax Liability
1	$5,000	$10,000	($5,000)	($1,750)
2	$5,000	$8,000	($3,000)	($2,800)
3	$5,000	$6,400	($1,400)	($3,290)
4	$5,000	$5,120	($120)	($3,332)
5	$5,000	$4,096	$904	($3,016)
6	$5,000	$3,277	$1,723	($2,412)
7	$5,000	$3,277	$1,723	($1,809)
8	$5,000	$3,277	$1,723	($1,206)
9	$5,000	$3,277	$1,723	($603)
10	$5,000	$3,277	$1,723	$0
	$50,000	$50,000	$ 0	

Assume the company has $1,000,000 in net income annually before considering the depreciation deduction.

Year 1	Financial	Taxable
Net Income	$1,000,000	$1,000,000
Depreciation Expense	$(5,000)	$(10,000)
Net Income before tax	$995,000	$990,000
Tax Expense	$348,250	$346,500
Deferred Tax Liability		$1,750
		$348,250

Year 1 Entry to Record Tax Liability		
Financial Tax Expense	$348,250	
Deferred Tax Liability		$1,750
Taxes Payable		$346,500

Year 9	Financial	Taxable
Net Income	$1,000,000	$1,000,000
Depreciation Expense	$(5,000)	$(3,277)
Net Income before tax	$995,000	$996,723
Tax Expense	$348,250	$348,853
Deferred Tax Liability		$(603)
		$348,250

Year 9 Entry to Record Tax Liability		
Financial Tax Expense	$348,250	
Deferred Tax Liability	$603	
Taxes Payable		$348,853

Example 17-4. Computation of Deferred Tax Asset: Charitable Contributions

Consider the following timing difference regarding a charitable contribution made by the Best Corporation. The deduction is allowable for financial accounting in the year in which it is made. For tax purposes, the deduction is limited to 10 percent of the taxable income before the charitable contribution. Assuming the corporation has net income of $60,000 per year, it will take nine years for the contribution to be deducted for tax purposes. The difference between financial and tax accounting treatment gives rise to a deferred tax asset.

CONTRIBUTION DEDUCTION

Net Income before contribution	$60,000			
Contribution Deduction	$50,000			
Tax deduction % limit	10%			
Tax Rate	35%			

Period	Financial Statement Deduction	Tax Deduction	Difference	Deferred Tax Asset
1	$50,000	$6,000	$44,000	$15,400
2	$0	$6,000	($6,000)	$13,300
3	$0	$6,000	($6,000)	$11,200
4	$0	$6,000	($6,000)	$9,100
5	$0	$6,000	($6,000)	$7,000
6	$0	$6,000	($6,000)	$4,900
7	$0	$6,000	($6,000)	$2,800
8	$0	$6,000	($6,000)	$700
9	$0	$6,000	($6,000)	$603
10	$0	$2,000	($2,000)	$0
	$50,000	$50,000	$ 0	

Assume the company has $60,000 in net income annually before considering the contribution deduction.

Year 1	Financial	Taxable
Net Income	$60,000	$60,000
Contribution Expense	$(50,000)	$(6,000)
Net Income before tax	$10,000	$54,000
Tax Expense	$3,500	$18,900
Deferred Tax Asset	$15,400	
	$18,900	

Year 1 Entry to Record Tax Asset

Financial Tax Expense	$3,500	
Deferred Tax Asset	$15,400	
Taxes Payable		$18,900

Year 6	Financial	Taxable
Net Income	$60,000	$60,000
Contribution Expense	$ -	$(6,000)
Net Income before tax	$60,000	$54,000
Tax Expense	$21,000	$18,900
Deferred Tax Asset		$2,100
		$21,000

Year 6 Entry to Record Tax Asset

Financial Tax Expense	$21,000	
Deferred Tax Asset		$2,100
Taxes Payable		$18,900

¶17,007 Valuation Allowance

Much of GAAP is based on the conservatism principle, which provides assurance that assets are not overstated and liabilities are not understated. Under ASC Topic 740-10-30, deferred tax assets are recognized only when it is *more likely than not* (more than 50 percent) that the future tax benefits will be realized. When a deferred tax asset does not meet the *more likely than not* threshold, a **valuation allowance** must be established. The valuation allowance is a contra-asset account that offsets all or a portion of the deferred tax asset and is made separately from the tax accrual. The deferred tax asset is the reported net of the valuation allowance in the financial statements, much like the Accumulated Depreciation account, which is also a contra account.

Example 17-5. Refer to the previous example for the Best Corporation. Assume a valuation allowance of $5,000 is recorded due to the uncertainty that the company will have taxable income beyond year five. In addition to the above journal entry for Year 1, Best must make the following additional journal entry:

Dr. Income tax expense (provision)	$5,000	
Cr. Valuation allowance		$5,000

To determine whether a valuation allowance is required, both positive and negative evidence must be considered, including:

- History of losses
- Expected future losses
- Strong earnings history
- Unrealized appreciation in assets
- Sales backlogs

Once facts and circumstances giving rise to the valuation allowance have changed, the balance in the valuation allowance can be reversed.

Example 17-6. Refer to the previous example for the Best Corporation. Assume in Year 4 that the uncertainty the company will have taxable income beyond Year 5 no longer exists. Best makes the following journal entry to reverse the valuation allowance:

Dr. Valuation allowance	$5,000	
Cr. Income tax expense (provision)		$5,000

¶17,009 Earnings of Foreign Subsidiaries

Since foreign corporations cannot be included as part of a U.S. consolidated tax return, it is possible to achieve deferral of current U.S. taxes on foreign income earned by a foreign subsidiary. Although the actual U.S. tax on profits earned by a foreign corporation are deferred, the reported effective tax rate for financial statement purposes may not reflect this deferral. ASC Topic 740-10-45 requires that the corporate group report both current and deferred income tax expense. ASC Topic 740-30 permits a U.S. corporation that is permanently reinvesting the earnings of its foreign subsidiary outside the United States to not record as an expense the U.S. income tax on foreign earnings. If the foreign tax rate is greater than or equal to the U.S. tax rate, there is no deferral potential.

Example 17-7. USA Corporation has a wholly owned foreign subsidiary. It must report consolidated net income for financial statement purposes as shown below, but reports only the income of the U.S. parent for tax purposes. Its applicable tax rate is 35 percent. If it can meet the permanent reinvestment exception, its effective tax rate after rounding is 28 percent (($245,000 + $30,000)/$1,000,000) = 27.5%). The company saves $75,000 in tax ($105,000 – $30,000) since the income of its subsidiary is taxed at the foreign tax rate of 10 percent rather than the U.S. tax rate of 35 percent.

EARNINGS OF A FOREIGN SUBSIDIARY

	U.S. Corp.	Foreign Corp.	Consolidated
Income	$700,000	$300,000	$1,000,000
U.S. Tax @ 35%	($245,000)	($105,000)	($ 350,000)
Foreign tax credit @ 10%		$ 30,000	$ 30,000
Net Income After Tax	$455,000	$225,000	$ 680,000
Current U.S. tax			$ 245,000
Current foreign tax			$ 30,000
Deferred U.S. tax			$ 75,000
Total Tax Expense			$ 350,000
Effective Tax Rate on Global Income			35%
Effective Tax Rate on global income assuming a permanent reinvestment of earnings in foreign country			28%

¶17,011   Uncertain Tax Positions

When a company records a deferred tax liability, there is no corresponding valuation allowance to "increase" this liability for potential tax increases resulting from an examination of a current or prior tax return by the taxing authorities. These potential tax increases can include additional tax liabilities relating to both permanent and timing differences. A multinational company may also face additional taxes imposed by taxing authorities outside the United States.

For fiscal years ending after December 15, 2006, specific guidance for accounting for uncertainty in income taxes is governed by ASC Topic 740-10-50, formerly FASB Interpretation No. 48. A tax position can result in a permanent reduction of income taxes payable, a deferral of income taxes otherwise currently payable in future years, or a change in the expected realizability of a deferred tax asset. The term tax position includes, but is not limited to:

- a decision not to file a tax return,
- an allocation or a shift of income between jurisdictions,
- the characterization of income,
- the decision to omit income from a tax return,
- a decision to classify a transaction, entity, or other position in a tax return as tax exempt.

Under this interpretation a two-step process is used to evaluate a tax position:[1]

1. *Recognition Step*. The enterprise determines whether it is *more likely than not* (likelihood of more than 50 percent which is a lower threshold than the 75-percent probable standard) that a tax position will be sustained upon examination, including the appeal process, based upon the technical merits of the position.

---

[1]   ASC Topic 740-10-50, formerly FAS Interpretation No. 48, ¶¶6, 8.

2. *Measurement Step*. A tax position meeting the *more likely than not* threshold is measured to determine the amount of benefit that is greater than 50 percent likely of being realized upon ultimate settlement.

Differences between tax positions taken in a tax return and amounts recognized in the financial statements will generally result in:
- An increase in taxes payable or a reduction in taxes receivable;
- A reduction in a deferred tax asset or an increase in a deferred tax liability; or
- Both of the above.

Whether the accrual is to a current or long-term liability depends upon when the enterprise anticipates making a payment. Potential interest and penalties can be accrued separately as interest/penalty expense or added to the tax expense.[2]

Example 17-8. Company A has net income of $1,000,000. It took a position on a tax return in which it excluded $100,000 from taxable income while reporting the income in its financial statements, creating a temporary book-tax difference. The company uses an applicable tax rate of 35 percent. Since the income was not excluded from its financial statements, the company records a financial tax expense and a deferred tax liability of $35,000 ($100,000 × 35%). The journal entry to record this transaction is:

Year 1	Financial	Taxable
Net Income	$1,000,000	$1,000,000
Excluded Income		$(100,000)
Net Income before tax	$1,000,000	$900,000
Tax Expense	$350,000	$315,000
Deferred Tax Liability		$35,000
		$350,000

Year 1 Entry to Record Tax Liability		
Financial Tax Expense	$350,000	
Deferred Tax Liability		$35,000
Taxes Payable		$315,000

If, however, the company concludes that it is *more likely than not* the taxing authorities would require $40,000 of this amount to be included in current taxable income, the company will also recognize a tax liability of $14,000 ($40,000 × 35%). The journal entry to record the tax accrual is:

Deferred Tax Liability	$14,000	
Tax Liability (for uncertain tax position)		$14,000

This would reduce the deferred tax liability to $21,000 ($35,000 – $14,000).

An approximation of interest payable based upon all the available evidence is accrued in each subsequent reporting period after which the position was taken on the tax return.

Example 17-9. Assume that the company has accrued interest of $7,350 by the time the issue is resolved three years after the return is filed. Assuming Management agrees with the IRS determination to include the $40,000 in income, the following journal entry is made when the issue is resolved and the deficiency is paid:

Tax Payable	$14,000	
Tax or Interest payable	$ 7,350	
Cash		$21,350

The deferred tax liability of $21,000 remains on the books and will be reversed when the remaining $60,000 is reported for tax purposes.

---

[2] ASC Topic 740-10-50, formerly FAS Interpretation No. 48, ¶19.

OBSERVATION   ASC Topic 740-10-50, formerly FASB Interpretation No. 48, requires that each item in both the deferred tax asset and deferred tax liability accounts be evaluated as to whether or not it represents an uncertain tax position. By proscribing that this evaluation be made as part of the tax accrual process, firms will no longer be able to accrue a "tax cushion" as a contingent liability, but will instead record a liability based upon increases/decreases in its deferred tax asset/liability accounts using the *more likely than not* standard.

Tax Disclosures in the Financial Statements. Once the company has determined it has a deferred tax asset or a deferred tax liability, these amounts must be classified as either current or noncurrent. If the deferred tax liability or asset cannot be related to any asset, then the classification is based on the expected reversal period. A company may have current and noncurrent deferred tax assets and liabilities.

Example 17-10. Refer to the deferred tax asset for the Best Corporation (Example 2). Since the company expects to receive a tax benefit in the next tax year from deducting $6,000 of its charitable contribution carryover, $2,100 ($6,000 × 35%) of the tax benefit is treated as a current asset. The Year 1 journal entry is:

Dr. Current deferred tax assets	$ 2,100	
Dr. Noncurrent deferred tax assets	$13,300	
Cr. Income tax expense (provision)		$15,300

Additional disclosures are required in the notes accompanying the financial statements, including:

- A breakdown of income between domestic and foreign sources
- A detailed analysis of the provision for income tax expense
- A detailed analysis of the deferred tax assets and liabilities
- An effective tax rate reconciliation
- A discussion of significant tax matters.

OBSERVATION   These disclosures are illustrated in the General Electric Annual Report which can be found at: http://www.ge.com/en/company/investors.   What is the total of GE's net deferred tax liability for the current reporting period? What is the largest change in the net liability from the prior year? What is GE's effective tax rate? What is the net change in the effective tax rate from the prior year?

Demonstration Problem.

Computation of deferred tax asset (liability). Open the Excel file from the book's website at *CCHGroup.com/ContemporaryTax*, Ch17DefTaxes.xls, which computes the financial accounting tax expense, the tax payable, and the deferred tax asset (liability) for the Small Corporation. What-if analysis.

1. Change the following amounts in the input variables:

Capital losses > capital gains:	$ 0
Charitable contributions:	$ 5,000
Tax depreciation > financial depreciation	$18,000

2. Why did the change in the input variables result in a Deferred Tax Liability rather than a Deferred Tax Asset?

¶17,013　Tax Reporting Requirements for Book-Tax Differences and Uncertain Tax Positions

.01　REPORTING BOOK TAX DIFFERENCES

The Schedule M-3 expands the current Schedule M-1 that had not been updated in several decades. Schedule M-3 is required for regular C corporations and for U.S. consolidated groups, S corporations and partnerships with total assets of $10 million or more.

> **OBSERVATION**　The stated goals of Schedule M-3 are to increase the transparency of transactions to allow the IRS to analyze tax return data more efficiently in order to identify returns containing the highest compliance risk, to avoid examining returns with low compliance risk, and to improve the audit cycle time. Schedule M-3 will also facilitate the use of Limited Issue Focused Examination (LIFE) audits through greater transparency.

In speeches delivered on January 28, 2004, four IRS executives clearly stated the intention of the new Schedule M-3 filing requirements:

"The proposed Schedule M-3 will make differences between financial accounting net income and taxable income more *transparent*. We see benefits to taxpayers and the IRS from the new Schedule: a reduction in unnecessary audits and a swifter focus on those differences that are more likely to arise when taxpayers take aggressive positions or engage in aggressive transactions. In addition, the increased *transparency* will have a deterrent effect." Pam Olsen, Assistant Secretary for Tax Policy.

"These changes will enable us to focus our compliance resources on returns and issues that need to be examined and avoid those that do not. Increasing the *transparency* of corporate tax returns is critical to our objective to provide certainty to taxpayers sooner and to improve overall compliance." Deborah Nolan, IRS Large and Mid-Size Business Division Commissioner.

"The purpose of this project has been to make differences between financial accounting net income and taxable income more *transparent*. Schedule M-3 provides information that will identify taxpayers that may have engaged in aggressive transactions and therefore should be audited." Greg Jenner, Acting Assistant Secretary for Tax Policy.

"The Schedule M-3 will help us better distinguish between high-risk and low-risk returns, thereby improving our ability to focus our examination resources where they are needed most. Increasing *transparency* and disclosure of tax issues are important elements in the Treasury and IRS strategy to improve tax compliance." Donald Korb, IRS Chief Counsel.[3]

Schedule M-3 provides much greater detail because it requires the taxpayer to state separately each transaction giving rise to a book-tax difference, irrespective of the size of the difference, and to identify whether the difference is permanent or temporary. Schedule M-1 has only 10 lines, while Schedule M-3 has over 90 lines. The lines are not consistent with the way financial

---

[3]　John Everett, Cherie Hennig, and William Raabe, *Practical Guide to Schedule M-3 Compliance* (Chicago: CCH Inc., 2007).

information is classified for financial accounting purposes. The corporation's financial accounting database, which may contain thousands of income and expense accounts, will have to be reconfigured so transactions can be summarized in accordance with the specific lines on Schedule M-3. This may significantly increase the compliance burden for many taxpayers. In many cases, Schedule M-3 requires additional disclosure on supporting schedules to provide detailed information for specific transactions. There are three parts to the Schedule M-3.

.02   PART I. FINANCIAL INFORMATION AND NET INCOME OR LOSS RECONCILIATION

Information about the corporation's financial statements is reported in Part I. The following information is disclosed:
- General information;
- Information on public filings, if any;
- Elimination of income from entities not included in the consolidated income tax return;
- Consolidated net income or loss of all includible corporations listed on Form 851 of the consolidated tax return.

Parts II and III disclose temporary and permanent differences in income and expense/deduction items. If the corporation prepares GAAP financial statements, any item treated as temporary under GAAP is treated as a temporary difference. All other items are treated as permanent differences. If a corporation does not follow GAAP, an item is treated as a temporary difference if it will reverse in a future year or if it is a reversal from a prior year; otherwise it is treated as a permanent difference. If it is not possible to determine whether the item is a temporary difference, it is treated as a permanent difference.

.03   PART II. RECONCILIATION OF NET INCOME OR LOSS PER THE INCOME STATEMENT OF EACH INCLUDIBLE CORPORATION WITH INCOME REPORTED ON THE TAX RETURN

This part has 30 lines with eight subparts, so there are 38 specific line items. All items relating to a listed transaction in which Form 8886 is filed must be disclosed on line 12, even if there is no book-tax difference. A schedule explaining each disclosure must be attached if more than one Form 8886 is filed. Line 25 is used to disclose differences not included in the first 24 lines. Line 28 is used for items that have the same treatment for tax accounting as they have for financial accounting.

.04   PART III. RECONCILIATION OF NET INCOME OR LOSS PER THE INCOME STATEMENT OF EACH INCLUDIBLE CORPORATION WITH EXPENSES AND DEDUCTIONS REPORTED ON THE TAX RETURN.

This part has 38 lines for specific items of expense/deduction. Line 37 is used to report all other differences not disclosed in the first 36 lines. Line 28 on Part II is used to report all items with no differences in book-tax treatment that have not been included in lines 1 through 38 of Part III.

Schedule M-3 Demonstration Problem

Facts: CJH Wonderful Goods, Inc. was organized as a C corporation on January 1, 2012. The corporation incurred organization expenses of $8,600 during January 2012. During the month of January, the corporation purchased a commercial building for $1,400,000 (ignore land) and equipment for $650,000. Ending inventory is $700,000. The reserve method is used to accrue bad debts for financial statement purposes. The specific write-off method is used for tax purposes.

The trial balance as of December 31, 2012, is found in the Excel Worksheet, CJH-WonderfulGoodsTB.xls. The unadjusted trial balance is found in Columns B and C. The adjusting journal entries for financial statement purposes are entered in Columns D and E which flow to Columns F through I of the spreadsheet. The latter will be used to prepare the GAAP financial statements. Columns J and K show the adjusting entries for tax purposes which flow through to Columns L through O.

The completed Schedule M-3 is found in the file, SchM3.pdf on the book website *CCHGroup.com/ContemporaryTax*. Print outs of the worksheet and Schedule M-3 are also found on the website.

IRS Website. More information can be found about the Schedule M-3 by visiting the IRS website, *www.irs.gov*, and typing Schedule M-3 in the search box. The site has an FAQ page, a list of articles published regarding schedule M-3 compliance and links to all the tax forms required of Schedule M-3 filers.

OBSERVATION   Will IRS Policy of Restraint When Requesting Tax Accrual Workpapers Change in Light of Schedule M-3 Disclosures?

- Chief Counsel Donald Korb stated:

  "The IRS will continue its policy of requesting the tax accrual workpapers when a taxpayer has engaged in more than one listed transaction, first with an Information Document Request (IDR), then with a summons if the workpapers are not forthcoming."[4]
- If the taxpayer fails to honor the summons, the IRS can go to court for enforcement of the summons.
- The question of whether disclosure of Temporary Differences in column (b) of Schedule M-3 waives protection under the work product doctrine of the tax accrual workpapers is yet to be determined. Until this uncertainty is resolved, taxpayers should segregate workpapers used to report temporary differences from opinion work product workpapers.
- The IRS is considering requiring certain Schedule M-3 filers to attach a new tax form to their 2010 tax return in which they would be required to list and describe all uncertain tax positions.

.05   REPORTING UNCERTAIN TAX POSITIONS ON SCHEDULE UTP.

With the 2010 tax year the IRS began implementation of the new Schedule UTP (Uncertain Tax Positions) which will require corporations to voluntarily identify and provide extensive disclosures of uncertain tax positions taken on the federal income tax return. The IRS estimates that the tax gap included underreported income from corporations in 2006 of $67 billion, an increase of $37 billion over 2001, a 123% increase. The IRS may view using the information provided on UTP schedules as one way of slowing the tax gap expansion. IRS Commissioner Douglas Shulman asserted that collecting information about uncertain tax positions will improve IRS's efficiency by sharpening its focus on potential noncompliance associated with specific issues However, corporate taxpayers have reason to be concerned—not only about self-identifying audit issues—but about the burden of complying with these required disclosures. Since 2010, corporate taxpayers that issue audited financial statements

---

[4]   BNA Daily Tax Report, Aug. 31, 2007, p. K-1.

and have assets of $100 million or more have been required to include Schedule UTP with their corporate return. For the 2012 tax year, the requirement was extended to corporate filers with assets of $50 million or more and will apply to corporate filers with assets of $10 million or more for the 2014 tax year, ultimately impacting approximately 50,000 corporations. These mid-sized corporations may encounter some unique compliance challenges. Many corporations of this size have limited tax staffs and relatively few of the taxpayers in this asset range are regularly examined by the IRS. As a result, this next wave of affected taxpayers may be less familiar with the requirements related to Schedule UTP.

In addition to the Schedule M-3, a corporate taxpayer or related party that has prepared audited financial statements covering all or portion of the corporation's tax year will now be required to file a Schedule UTP. The term "audited financial statements" is defined as financial statements on which an independent auditor has expressed an opinion under GAAP, IFRS, or other country-specific accounting standard. Compiled or reviewed financial statements are not audited financial statements. A corporate taxpayer without audited financial statements is required to file a Schedule UTP if it is a related party (described in Sec. 267(b), Sec. 318(a), or Sec. 707(b)) to a corporate taxpayer or is an entity that is included in the consolidated audited financial statements in which a corporation with audited financial statements is also included.

Example 17-11: Blue Corporation has $60 million in assets. Black Corporation is a foreign corporation not doing business in the US but is a related party to Blue Corporation. The corporations issue separate audited financial statements. Blue Corporation took a tax position on its tax return and Black Corporation recorded a reserve with respect to the tax position. The position must be reported on Blue Corporation's Schedule UTP (Schedule UTP instructions, example 2, page 2).

An uncertain tax position is a tax position taken on a tax return that would result in an IRS audit adjustment and the corporation or a related party has recorded a reserve with respect to all or part of that tax position in audited financial statements. If multiple tax positions affect a single line item on the tax return, each tax position is treated as a separate tax position The corporation must also report on Schedule UTP a tax position taken on its return for which no reserve for income tax was recorded because the corporation or a related party determines that the probability of settling the position with the IRS is less than 50% and the corporation expects to litigate the position and has determined that it is more likely than not to prevail on the merits in the litigation.

Example 17-12: Purple Corporation entered into a cost sharing arrangement with a foreign subsidiary and deducted its proportionate share of the costs as re-search and development costs. Management has determined that the probability of sustaining the full deduction upon an IRS audit is less than 50%. No reserve was recorded for the potential tax liability because management expects to litigate the issue and believes it is more likely than not to prevail upon litigation of this issue. The tax position must be disclosed on the Schedule UTP even though no reserve was made in its audited financial statements.

The Schedule UTP is divided into three parts. In Part I the corporate taxpayer reports tax positions taken in the current year that meet the definition of a UTP Disclosure Position. Part II of the Schedule UTP reports tax positions taken by a corporation in a prior year that have not been reported on a prior year's Schedule UTP. Part III of the Schedule UTP provides a concise description of each uncertain tax position reported in Parts I and II. Consider the following examples illustrating the application of these rules:

Example 17-13: Brown Corporation deducted an expense for warranty costs for financial accounting but not on its tax return. A deferred tax asset was recorded for the deferred tax benefit. If management believes that a por-tion of the warranty costs may not be deductible based on current US tax law, the deferred tax asset is reduced and current financial tax expense is increased by an amount that reflects the uncertain tax position. The un-certain tax position is not disclosed on the Schedule UTP because the de-duction has not yet been taken on the US federal tax return.

Example 17-14: White Corporation deducted the full amount of an expenditure incurred in the current tax year. The corporation determines it is uncer-tain whether the expenditure is currently deductible or should be amortized over 5 years. It records a reserve with respect to the position taken. If the deduction is not sustained on the current year tax return an amortiza-tion deduction would be allowed on its subsequent tax returns. The position must be disclosed on Part I of the Schedule UTP for the current year and al-so in subsequent tax years.

The following information must be provided for each UTP Disclosure Position:

- Internal Revenue Code sections (up to three) relating to each UTP Disclosure Position.
- Whether the position is a temporary difference, a permanent difference, or both. Categorization must be consistent with the accounting standards used to prepare the audited financial statements.
- The taxpayer identification number of the pass-through entity must be provided if applicable.
- Whether the relative size (by amount of the dollar reserve) is greater than or equal to 10% of all tax positions listed on Parts I and II of the Schedule UTP for that year (referred to as "Major Tax Positions").
- The rank based on size of all tax positions on Parts I and II combined with the number 1 being assigned to the largest, the number 2 to the next largest, and so on. In addition, the rank is to be preceded by the letter "T' for all transfer pricing positions or the letter "G" for all other tax positions.

The size of each tax position is determined on an annual basis and is the amount of the federal income tax reserve for accounting purposes. Positions that are disclosed on the basis of an expectation to litigate are not included in the ranking or in the determina-tion of Major Tax Positions since a reserve has not been established for these items for financial statement purposes.

A concise description of each uncertain tax position must be provided in Part III of the Schedule UTP, including a description of the relevant facts affecting the tax treatment of the position and information that reasonably can be expected to apprise the IRS of the identity of the tax position and the nature of the issue. It is not necessary to provide an assessment of the hazards of a tax position or an analysis of the support for or against the position. A complete and accurate disclosure of a tax position on the Schedule UTP will be treated as if the corporation filed a Form 8275, Disclosure Statement, or a Form 8275-R, Regulation Disclosure Statement, regarding the tax position and can be used to avoid certain accuracy-related penalties with respect to that position and satisfy the disclosure requirement of Section 6662(i). The following examples from the IRS instruc-tions describe what would be an acceptable disclosure:

- Taxpayer incurred costs of completing one business acquisition and investigating and partially negotiating potential business acquisitions that were not completed. The issue is whether the allocation of costs between completed and uncompleted acquisitions is appropriate.
- Taxpayer is a member of an LLC which is treated as a US partnership for tax purposes. Taxpayer received a cash distribution during the year from the LLC. The issue is the potential application of Sec. 707(a)(2) to recharacterize the distribution as a sale of a portion of the taxpayer's interest in the LLC.
- Taxpayer incurred costs to clean up environmental contamination caused by activities in prior tax years at a site which includes both its manufacturing facility and its corporate headquarters. The issue is the allocation of the cleanup costs between production and non-production activities under Sec. 263A.

Schedule UTP will burden corporate filers on two levels. Completing this schedule will require taxpayers to self-identify tax positions that may not be acceptable to the IRS. Compiling necessary information and satisfying disclosure requirements will likely require considerable expertise and effort.

¶17,015   Concluding Thoughts

Large corporations and partnerships (those with $10,000,000 or more in assets) must provide a detailed annual reconciliation of their book-tax differences to the IRS using the new Schedule M-3. Proper completion of this tax form requires an understanding and comprehension of those transactions that result in both temporary and permanent book-tax differences. It is now the responsibility of the tax accountant to have not only technical expertise in tax law but also a firm grasp and understanding of financial accounting issues giving rise to book-tax differences and to be prepared to explain how these book-tax differences were determined upon an IRS audit. In addition, the tax return preparer must consider whether the Schedule UTP should be filed to report uncertain tax positions taken on the tax return. This chapter has summarized the basic financial and tax issues necessary for understanding and reporting book-tax differences and uncertain tax positions.

¶17,017   Summary

- Differences between financial income and taxable income are either temporary or permanent.
- Temporary differences result in a deferred tax asset or a deferred tax liability and must be disclosed in a footnote to the financial statements. These differences reverse over time.
- Permanent differences generally reduce the effective tax rate and must be disclosed in a footnote to the financial statements. These differences never reverse.
- New disclosure requirements of uncertain book-tax differences must now be measured and recognized using the format proscribed in ASC Topic 740-10-50, formerly FIN 48. As the level of uncertainty changes on these positions, the firm must remeasure and reassess its impact on the financial statements.
- The IRS requires all corporations, including S corporations and partnerships, with Assets greater than $10,000,000 to make a detailed disclosure of book-tax differences on the Schedule M-3. Corporations with audited financial statements must report on Form UTP any uncertain tax positions for which an accrual has been made for an uncertain position that was taken on the federal tax return.
- The tax practitioner must understand not only tax accounting concepts but also financial accounting concepts in order to measure and disclose book-tax differences and uncertain tax positions.

Review Questions for Chapter 17

True or False

Indicate which of the following statements are true or false by circling the correct answer.

1. The reports prepared by managerial, financial, and tax accountants all rely on the same transactions-based data.   T   F

2. There may be differences between the income figures reported on the income statements prepared according to GAAP and those prepared in compliance with tax laws because the two disciplines have different purposes that require different rules be used to calculate income.   T   F

3. Temporary differences can arise because revenues are recognized in the same accounting period for tax purposes as they are for book purposes.   T   F

4. Permanent differences arise because expenses that are not deductible for tax purposes must still be deducted under generally accepted accounting principles.   T   F

5. The Schedule M-1 is used to analyze the difference between financial income and taxable income during the tax accounting period.   T   F

6. Deferred taxes arise because of permanent differences.   T   F

7. A corporation reporting a deferred tax asset expects to have lower taxes to pay in some future time periods.   T   F

8. The valuation allowance is a contra-account to the Income Tax Payable account.   T   F

9. If a corporation documents that it is permanently reinvesting the earnings of its foreign subsidiaries outside the United States, it does not record any future U.S. income tax on the income.   T   F

10. An uncertain tax position need not be disclosed on Schedule UTP if the position does not pertain to a federal tax liability.   T   F

Fill-in-the-Blanks

Complete the following statements with the appropriate word(s) or amount(s).

11. _____ accountants try to satisfy the informational needs of investors, while _____ accountants provide the information required by the tax authorities.

12. _____ differences exist because the goals and objectives of financial and tax accounting are different.

13. _____ differences arise when income is never recognized for tax purposes although it is recognized for book purposes.

14. Only _____ differences affect deferred taxes.

15. _____ differences reverse themselves over time.

16. A deferred tax asset occurs when book revenues are _____ than tax revenues or book expenses are _____ than tax expenses.

17. ASC Topic 740, formerly FAS 109, prescribes presentation and _____ guidelines for deferred tax information.

18. When a deferred tax asset does not meet the more likely than not threshold for recognition, ASC Topic 740, formerly FAS 109, requires that a(n) _____ _____ be created.

19. ASC Topic 740-10-50, formerly FIN 48, is a two-step process requiring both _____ and _____ when evaluating a tax position.

20. A corporation may have both _____ and _____ deferred tax assets and liabilities.

Multiple Choice

Circle the best answer for each of the following questions.

21. Which statement best describes the relationship between financial accounting income and tax accounting income?
    a. financial accounting and tax accounting are parallel independent reporting systems
    b. tax accounting principles take precedence over financial accounting principles
    c. since financial accounting statements are prepared according to generally accepted accounting principles and are audited pursuant to generally accepted auditing standards, they provide a validated baseline upon which to derive tax-adjusted statements
    d. both b and c

22. The foundations of financial accounting and tax accounting differ because:
    a. the primary focus of financial accounting is the balance sheet, while the primary focus of tax accounting is the income statement
    b. the primary objectives of financial accounting are broadly defined under generally accepted accounting principles, while the primary objectives of tax accounting are a proper measure of the tax base
    c. generally accepted accounting principles may not be used in computing taxable income
    d. all of the above

23. In computing tax accounting income, when the starting point is financial accounting income,
    a. positive adjustments to gross income per books are allowed
    b. positive adjustments to expenses per books are allowed
    c. negative adjustments to income per financial statements are allowed
    d. all of the above

24. If the depreciation tax expense is lower than the depreciation book expense in the first two years of the useful life of an asset, the total depreciation taken over the life of the asset for tax purposes
    a. will be less than the total depreciation for financial purposes
    b. will be more than the total depreciation for financial purposes
    c. will be the same as the total depreciation for financial purposes
    d. cannot be determined from the facts given

25. A company is in the business of selling pre-need funeral plans. During the year, it collected $120,000 from 10 customers, and paid out $50,000 in funeral expenses for 5 customers. For tax purposes, the company recognizes **gross** income of:
    a. $50,000
    b. $60,000
    c. $70,000
    d. $120,000

26. Which of the following is *not* a temporary difference between book income and tax income?
    a. capital losses in excess of capital gains
    b. capital gains in excess of capital losses
    c. charitable contributions in excess of the 10-percent limit
    d. all of the above are temporary differences

27. The HILow Corporation has a charitable contribution carryover from the prior tax year for tax purposes of $15,000. This amount must be:
    a. subtracted from book income to derive tax income
    b. added to book income to derive tax income
    c. neither added to nor subtracted from book income
    d. cannot be determined from the facts given

28. The ABC Corp., which uses the accrual method of accounting, received cash of $10,000 for interest earned during the prior year on a City of New York Port Authority bond. This income:
    a. is recognized as income under GAAP in the year the interest is accrued
    b. is recognized as taxable income in the year the interest is accrued
    c. is recognized as taxable income in the year the interest is paid
    d. both a and c

29. ASC Topic 740, formerly FASB Statement Number 109, Accounting for Income Taxes:
    a. applies only if the corporation has a deferred tax liability
    b. applies only if the corporation has a deferred tax asset
    c. requires an adjustment to a contra-asset account only if the deferred tax assets have a greater than 50-percent chance of not being realized
    d. measures current and non-current deferred taxes using the average tax rate

30. Corporation PQ has financial deprecation of $300,000 and tax depreciation of $150,000 for the current year. If the marginal tax rate for the current year is 40 percent, the corporation has:
    a. a deferred tax asset of $60,000
    b. a deferred tax liability of $60,000
    c. a deferred tax asset of $120,000
    d. a deferred tax liability of $120,000

31. Which of the following statements relating to Schedule UTP, uncertain tax positions, is true?
    a. All tax benefits involving income and non-income taxes must be disclosed.
    b. Only income tax benefits to be realized in the future must be disclosed.
    c. Only recognized tax benefits related to income tax positions claimed on a filed tax return must be disclosed.
    d. All recognized tax benefits related to income tax positions must be disclosed regardless of whether the item is take on a filed tax return.

32. Which of the following statements best describes the process for evaluating a corporation's uncertain tax positions?
    a. The corporation must complete a two-step analysis every time it evaluates its uncertain tax positions.
    b. The corporation must complete the recognition step in its evaluation of its uncertain tax positions only if it is more-likely-than-not that that its tax position will be sustained on its merits.
    c. The corporation must take into account the probability of audit by a tax authority in the measurement step when evaluating its uncertain tax positions.
    d. The corporation can record a tax benefit from an uncertain tax position only if it is probable the benefit will be sustained on audit by a tax authority.

33. What confidence level must management have that a tax position will be sustained on audit before it can recognize any portion of the related deferred tax asset?
    a. More likely than not
    b. Reasonable basis
    c. Substantial authority
    d. Probable

Problems

34. YDNet, Inc., is an accrual-basis taxpayer that publishes magazines. During the current year, it received $48,000 for prepaid subscriptions. At of the end of the year, the remaining balance in these prepaid subscriptions was $38,000. The company's federal marginal tax rate is 35 percent.
    1. What is the Schedule M-1 (M-3) adjustment?
    2. What is the deferred tax asset or liability?

35. Standout, Inc., is a construction company that uses the percentage-of-completion method for book purposes and the completed contract method for tax purposes. The corporation anticipates its newest project, which will be completed in three years, will generate total revenues of $2,000,000 and total costs of $1,400,000. It will be 20 percent complete at the end of Year 1. The company's federal marginal tax rate is 40 percent.
    • What is the Schedule M-1 (M-3) adjustment for Year 1?
    • What is the deferred tax asset or liability for Year 1?

36. The tax return of Grates, Inc., a calendar year C corporation, reported a net operating loss of $260,000 in the current year. It has an expected marginal tax rate of 35 percent. Taxable income in the first preceding tax year was $50,000 and it was $10,000 in the second preceding tax year. The marginal rate in both of the carryback years is 15 percent.
    1. What is the Schedule M-1 (M-3) adjustment for the current tax year?
    2. What is the deferred tax asset or liability balance?

37. On January 1, Starlight Corp. (a calendar-year taxpayer) recorded $600,000 of goodwill as a result of a business acquisition that it made. The corporation elected to amortize it over 15 years for tax accounting and uses the impairment method for financial accounting purposes. Assume the impairment write-offs are $15,000 in Year 1, $60,000 in Year 5 and $300,000 in Year 25.
    • What is the annual Schedule M-1 (M-3) adjustment for each year during the first 15 years of the amortization period?
    • What is the annual Schedule M-1 (M-3) adjustment for each year during the last 25 years of the amortization period?
    • What is the deferred tax asset or liability balance for Years 1, 5, and 25, assuming a 35-percent marginal tax rate?

38. Assume the President signs a stimulus package permitting businesses to expense $250,000 of equipment purchases in the current tax year, provided total equipment purchases do not exceed $750,000. Assume the ABC corporation purchased a machine for $500,000 during the qualifying time period. The machine has a 7-year MACRS life and a 10-year straight line write-off for financial accounting purposes.
    • What is the deferred tax liability balance for Years 1, 5, and 9, assuming a 35-percent marginal tax rate?
    • What is the journal entry to record the deferred tax benefit in Years 1, 5 and 9?
    • Assume a discount rate of 10 percent, what is the NPV of the tax savings from the additional Year 1 write off?

39. Corporation HHH's auditors prepared the following reconciliation between book and taxable income. Assume the marginal and effective tax rate is 34 percent.

Financial Net income before tax	$6,000,000
Permanent book/tax differences	–$1,500,000 (tax-exempt interest income)
Temporary book-tax differences	–$750,000 (depreciation expense)
Taxable Income	$3,750,000

    • Compute the financial tax expense
    • Compute the tax payable
    • What is the journal entry to record the tax accrual?

40. D Corporation, a calendar year accrual basis corporation, reported net income per books of $300,000 for the tax year ended December 31. Included in the calculation of net book income were the following items:

- Federal income tax expense $ 90,000
- Life insurance proceeds on officer who died in 2010   120,000
- Insurance premiums on key employee life insurance   6,000
- Net loss on sale of securities held for investment   4,000
- Depreciation expense per books ($86,000 per tax)   50,000

    Compute D Corporation's taxable income and regular tax expense. What is the marginal tax rate? What is the average tax rate?

41. For the year ended December 31 EFG, a calendar year accrual basis corporation, reported $479,900 net income after tax on its financial statements prepared in accordance with GAAP. The corporation's financial records include the following:

- EFG earned $314,800 from a qualified domestic production activity eligible for a 9% deduction.
- EFG earned $10,700 on an investment in tax-exempt municipal bonds.
- EFG's allowance for bad debts as of 1/1 was $21,000. Write-offs for the year total $4,400 while the addition to the allowance was $3,700. The balance in the allowance account on 12/31 was $20,300.
- EFG paid a $6,000 fine to a municipal government for violating a local zoning ordinance.
- Depreciation per books was $44,200 and MACRS depreciation was $31,000.
- EFT has an $8,800 capital loss carryover. This year, it has a Code Sec. 1231 gain on the sale of equipment of $31,000.
- EFG capitalized organizational costs of $6,900 and elected to amortize the costs over 180 months. For book purposes, it expensed the costs.
- EFG's federal income tax expense per books was $243,000.

    Required:

- Compute EFG's taxable income and regular income tax expense.
- Prepare the journal entry to record the tax accrual.

42. Wingo Inc. which has a 34-percent income tax rate (also assume this is the applicable tax rate) is considering making a substantial investment in marketable securities that will generate annual income of $400,000. Analyze each of the following four scenarios:

a. The income is from tax-exempt bonds and Wingo will pay regular income tax but no AMT.

b. The income is from dividends on publicly traded stock eligible for the 70-percent dividends received deduction and Wingo will pay regular income tax but no AMT.

c. The income is from tax-exempt bonds and Wingo is in an AMT position and has a positive ACE adjustment before consideration of the interest income.

d. The income is from dividends on publicly traded stock eligible for the 70-percent dividends received deduction and Wingo is in an AMT position and has a positive ACE adjustment before consideration of the interest income.

    For each scenario:

- What is Wingo's after-tax cash flow?
- How is this income reported for financial and taxable income?
- What is the journal entry to record the tax accrual?

43. BBY is a calendar year accrual method corporation with a marginal and effective tax rate of 34 percent. It had $5,000,000 of financial income before making the following cash payments on December 31, 2011:

a. $4,000 paid to a consultant for work to be performed in January 2012.

b. $600,000 for equipment delivered on December 1, 2011. The equipment has a useful life of 10 years for financial accounting and 7 years for tax accounting. This was the only asset purchased in 2011. (MACRS mid-quarter percentage is 3.57. The Sec. 179 deduction was not taken.)

c. $17,000 for property tax for the first six months of 2012.

d. $84,000 for a two-year office lease beginning December 1, 2011.

e. $230,000 for inventory purchases. $100,000 was on-hand at 12/31/11.

For each of these expenditures:
- How are these expenditures reported for financial and taxable income?
- What is the financial tax expense?
- What is the tax liability?
- What is the journal entry to record the tax accrual?

44. Cat Company purchased and placed in service on January 1 of the current year a building which cost $1,000,000. It has an applicable and marginal tax rate of 34%. The annual straight line financial depreciation expense is $50,000. Company A engaged a consulting firm to perform a component depreciation analysis which it plans to use to compute the year 1 de-preciation expense on the building and its component parts. Management is considering four alternatives, a through d and has made a determination of their impact on the company's federal income tax accrual. The accrual for the deferred tax liability and management's determination of the likelihood of success of sustaining the deduction in an IRS audit are given below:

Alternate Scenarios	Financial Depreciation Expense	Tax Depreciation Expense	Deferred Tax Liability	Probability of success
a	$50,000	$50,000	$ -	100%
b	$50,000	$100,000	$17,000	95%
c	$50,000	$150,000	$34,000	60%
d	$50,000	$200,000	$51,000	40%

For each scenario:
- What is the accrual for an uncertain tax position, if any?
- Explain why or why not an accrual for an uncertain tax position would be required.

Internet Exercises

45. Go to the IRS website, *www.irs.gov*. Type Schedule M-3 in the search box.
   a. Follow the link for Published Articles on Schedule M-3 by IRS/Treasury Authors. Write a one page summary of one of the articles listed.
   b. Follow the link for Frequently Asked Questions (FAQs) for Form 1120 Schedule M-3. Write a one paragraph summary of one of the FAQs.

46. Go to the IRS website, *www.irs.gov*. Follow the link for More Forms and Publications, Form and Instruction number.
   a. Select the most recent Inst 1120 (Schedule M-3) (PDF) Instructions. Save/download these instructions. Write a one paragraph summary describing the Schedule M-3 filing requirements for corporations.
   b. Select the most recent Form 8916-A (PDF) Reconciliation of Cost of Goods Sold Reported on Schedule M-3. Write a one paragraph summary describing the Interest Income/Expense reporting requirements for completing page two of this form.

47. Go the IRS website, www.irs.gov. Type Schedule UTP in the search box.
   a. Locate an article on Schedule UTP disclosures. Write a one page summary of what constitutes an adequate disclosure of an uncertain tax position on Schedule UTP.

CHAPTER 18

Tax Reform Proposals

Learning Objectives

1. Identify the deficiencies in the current income tax system.
2. Describe the basic elements of each of the five reform proposals.
3. Understand the advantages and disadvantages of each of the five reform proposals.

¶18,001 Introduction

Ever since our first constitutional income tax laws in 1913, there have been calls to "reform" the tax law. It seems virtually no one is happy with the current tax system, and yet proposals to change the law are generally dismissed quickly. Perhaps one of the reasons reform does not happen is that although many believe we need a simpler, fairer system more conducive to economic growth, few are willing to give up current tax incentives such as the state and local tax deduction or the home mortgage interest deduction in order to achieve those goals.

The Lighter Side—Today's *Top Ten Tax Quotes*, with apologies to David Letterman:

10. "A fine is a tax for doing something wrong. A tax is a fine for doing something right." *(Anonymous)*

9. "There is untold wealth in America—especially at income tax time." *(Anonymous)*

8. "If you drive a car, I'll tax the street. If you try to sit, I'll tax your seat. If you get too cold, I'll tax the heat. If you take a walk, I'll tax your feet. Taxman! Yeah, I'm the taxman. Yeah, I'm the taxman."*(John, Paul, George, and Ringo)*

7. "I want to find out who this FICA guy is and how come he's taking so much of my money." *(Nick Kypreos)*

6. "A tax loophole is something that benefits the other guy. If it benefits you, it is tax reform." *(Russell B. Long, U.S. Senator)*

5. "It's income tax time again, Americans: time to gather up those receipts, get out those tax forms, sharpen up that pencil, and stab yourself in the aorta." *(Dave Barry)*

4. "On my income tax [Form] 1040 it says 'Check this box if you are blind.' I wanted to put a check mark about three inches away." *(Tom Lehrer)*

3. "People who complain about taxes can be divided into two classes: men and women." *(Anonymous)*

2. "A government which robs Peter to pay Paul can always depend on the support of Paul." *(George Bernard Shaw)*

1. "The First Rule of Practicing Tax Law: If someone has to go to jail, make sure it's the client." *(Fred Drasner)*

Over the years there have been a number of serious tax reform proposals, but none seem to gain any traction. Why? The purpose of this chapter is to discuss the perceived deficiencies of the current tax system, examine the more popular proposals for reform, and discuss the advantages and disadvantages of each proposal.

¶18,003   Perceived Deficiencies of the Current Tax System

Proposals to reform the current federal income tax have been the subject of intense debate over the years. Inevitably, these proposals always point out the perceived deficiencies of the current tax system. Most criticisms fall into one of six major categories: (1) mind-numbing complexity, (2) significant compliance costs, (3) disproportionate benefits to the wealthy, (4) underground economy is untaxed, (5) bias against savings and investment, and (6) global competitive disadvantages. Each of these charges is discussed briefly in the following sections.

.01   MIND-NUMBING COMPLEXITY

There is little argument about the complexity of our current tax laws. A few simple numbers illustrate this complexity. For example, the following graph charts the *thousands* of words in the Internal Revenue Code (dark shaded area) and the Regulations (light shaded area) over the years:[1]

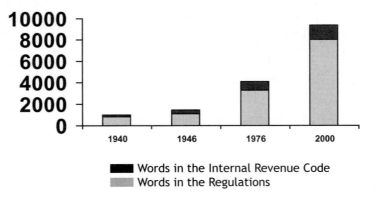

Yes, this graph indicates that the Code and Regulations contain over *9 million* words! In 1954, there were 103 sections in the Internal Revenue Code; by 2005, there were 736 income tax code sections, a 615 percent increase.

---

[1]   Michael J. Graetz, *A Fair and Balanced Tax System for the 21st Century*, May 11, 2005.

Since the 1954 codification, there have been approximately 35 major pieces of tax legislation and more than 450 other public laws that have modified the Code. Of all this legislation, only the Tax Reform Act of 1986 made any attempt to simplify the tax law, by reducing the tax rate structure to two brackets (which quickly grew back to six brackets within six years). Since 2001 there have been approximately 4,680 changes to the tax code, an average of more than one per day.[2]

One of the causes of this complexity is simply that our tax laws represent a blending of economic, social, and political objectives. There are so many stakeholders with vested interests in the tax law that major reform is extremely difficult. In addition, tax legislation is usually generated on a piece-meal basis, resulting in little concern for consistency or simplification.

COMMENTARY

Here is another possible explanation for the complexity of our current tax laws, courtesy of the *FreedomWorks Foundation:*[3]

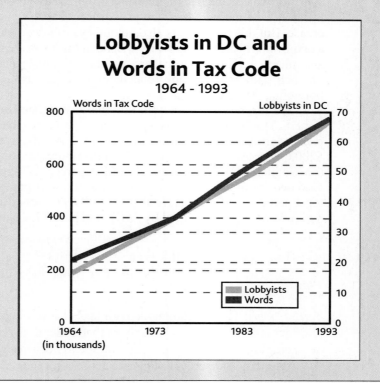

.03   SIGNIFICANT COMPLIANCE COSTS

Invariably, increases in the complexity of the tax law are accompanied by increases in the cost of complying with and administering the tax law. In 2010, it is estimated that individuals, businesses and nonprofits spent an estimated 6.1 billion hours complying with the tax law, with an estimated compliance cost of over $168 billion. This amounts to imposing a 15 cent tax compliance surcharge for every dollar collected.

The burden of tax compliance does not fall evenly on taxpayers. A 2005 study found that businesses bear the majority of the costs, estimated at nearly $148 billion in 2005 with individual compliance costs estimated at $111 billion. When examined by income level, compliance cost is found to be highly regressive, taking a larger toll on low-income taxpayers as a percentage of income than high-income taxpayers.[4]

---

[2] Taxpayer Advocate Service, 2012 Annual Report to Congress.

[3] *Freedomworks.org.*

[4] For additional information, *see Tax Foundation Special Report No. 183, The Rising Cost of Complying with the Federal Income Tax,* by Scott A. Hodge, J. Scott Moody and Wendy P. Warcholik at *http://www.taxfoundation.org/research/show/1281.html.*

.05   DISPROPORTIONATE BENEFITS TO THE WEALTHY

A common criticism of the current tax system is that it is slanted in favor of the wealthy. There is a popular notion that the rich simply are not paying their fair share, and that provisions such as the alternative minimum tax are largely ineffective in redistributing the tax burden.

When analyzing the distributional effects of a tax law, the notions of horizontal equity and vertical equity come into play. While both of these principles are worthy goals, the tax laws do not always adhere to these ideals.

The principle of **horizontal equity** states that equal incomes should pay equal taxes. For example, A, B, and C each have $100,000 of taxable income but they will pay vastly different taxes because A's income is from a salary, B's income is from a long-term capital gain, and C's income is from City of Dayton municipal bonds.

The principle of **vertical equity** states that higher incomes should pay higher taxes. This principle is the backbone of the progressive rate structure of the federal income tax laws; as income increases, the proportion of that income paid in taxes should also increase. But this principle is also not always followed in our tax laws either; for example, a taxpayer with $200,000 salary will be in the 33-percent tax bracket. But if this taxpayer also incurs a $100,000 long-term capital gain, he or she will pay only a 15 percent rate on such gain, even though total income is increasing. Such a differential rate causes horizontal inequities as well.

There can be little argument that there are indeed some inequities in the current tax system. The 2009 IRS Statistics of Income indicates that approximately 50 percent of the revenue from individual tax returns comes from taxpayers with adjusted gross income of $200,000 or less. Approximately 69 million individual returns report no income tax liability (45% of households). The top-earning 25 percent of taxpayers (AGI over $69,126) earned 67.6 percent of the nation's income, and paid 87.1 percent of the federal income tax. The top 1 percent of taxpayers (AGI over $369,691) earned approximately 18.9 percent of the nation's income (as defined by AGI), and paid 37.4 percent of all federal income taxes.

OBSERVATION

Impact of Payroll Taxes[5]
"Two-Thirds of Tax Units Pay More Payroll Tax Than Income Tax"
By Len Burman and Greg Leiserson

April 15 is synonymous with taxes in the United States, but most Americans actually pay more payroll taxes than federal income taxes. In 2006 workers and employers each paid 6.2 percent Social Security tax on the first $94,200 of earnings and 1.45 percent Medicare tax on all wages. While the statutory obligation to pay payroll taxes is split evenly between workers and employers, most economists believe that the employer tax usually translates into lower wages, so workers bear the full burden of the tax. Thus, the total payroll tax rate equals 15.3 percent of earnings for most workers.

About two-thirds of taxpayers owed more payroll taxes (including the employer portion) than individual income taxes in 2006. Many households (including most retirees) do not have any wage income and thus pay no payroll tax. Among households with wage earners, 86 percent have higher payroll taxes than income taxes, including almost all of those with incomes less than $40,000 and 94 percent of those with incomes less than $100,000. If only the employee portion of payroll taxes is considered, 44 percent of taxpayers and 56 percent of wage earners pay more payroll tax than income tax, including nearly 80 percent of earners with incomes less than $50,000.

---

[5] Len Burman and Greg Leiserson, "Two-Thirds of Tax Units Pay More Payroll Tax Than Income Tax," *TAX NOTES*, April 9, 2007: pg. 173.

The following table was also included in the article.[6]

Distribution of Federal Payroll and Income Taxes by Cash Income Class, 2006[1]									
Cash Income Class (thousands of 2006 dollars)[2]	Percent of Tax Units[3]	Percent of Tax Units With Positive:		Average Tax Rate (percent)[6]		Percent With Payroll Tax Greater Than Income Tax		Percent With Employee Share of Payroll Tax Greater Than Income Tax	
		Payroll Tax[4]	Income Tax[5]	Payroll Tax	Income Tax	All Tax Units	Wage Earners	All Tax Units	Wage Earners
Less than 10	13.0	52.5	1.9	7.7	-5.1	52.5	99.9	52.5	99.9
10-20	17.4	60.2	26.0	7.8	-4.4	59.7	99.3	59.4	98.8
20-30	13.5	76.5	46.6	9.8	-1.0	75.2	98.5	62.2	81.1
30-40	10.2	83.7	62.6	10.8	2.6	81.7	97.7	49.0	58.0
40-50	8.1	86.0	78.7	10.8	4.8	82.0	95.5	44.4	51.2
50-75	14.3	88.2	92.0	10.7	6.6	75.8	86.4	39.0	44.3
75-100	8.6	91.1	97.4	10.9	7.9	72.6	80.4	30.7	33.8
100-200	10.8	93.3	98.9	10.1	10.5	55.4	60.1	12.0	12.9
200-500	2.9	91.2	98.8	6.0	15.2	8.0	9.0	2.3	2.5
500-1,000	0.5	89.0	99.0	3.0	18.3	4.2	5.0	2.0	2.4
More than 1,000	0.3	88.7	99.2	1.2	19.3	1.1	1.3	0.8	0.9
All	100.0	77.2	59.7	8.3	9.7	65.9	85.5	43.9	56.2

Source: Urban-Brookings Tax Policy Center Microsimulation Model (version 1006-2), *available at* http://www.taxpolicycenter. org/t07-0115.
[1]Calendar year.
[2]Tax units with negative cash income are excluded from the lowest income class but are included in the totals. For a description of cash income, see http://www.taxpolicycenter.org/TaxModel/income.cfm.
[3]Includes both filing and nonfiling units but excludes those that are dependents of other tax units.
[4]Includes the employee and employer portion of Social Security (OASDI) and Medicare (HI) taxes and self-employment taxes.
[5]Income tax after refundable credits.
[6]Tax as a percentage of cash income.

.07 UNDERGROUND ECONOMY IS UNTAXED

The compliance costs of the current tax system to taxpayers were discussed earlier; however, there is also a considerable compliance cost on the governmental side of the equation as well. For example, the IRS budget in 2007 was $12 billion, and this agency will process over 200 million returns. Over one million tax returns are audited each year, and the IRS receives over *1.5 billion* supporting documents, such as Forms W-2, 1099, etc., to compare with the numbers reported on income tax returns.

Despite these daunting numbers, there is still a lot of cheating on income taxes, and the current system fails to collect all taxes that are owed. The estimate of the overall gross tax gap for tax year 2006—the difference between what taxpayers should have paid and what they actually paid on a timely basis—comes to $385 billion. Underreported income from the "cash economy"—taxable income from legal activities that is not subject to information reporting or withholding—is probably the single largest component of the tax gap, likely accounting for over $100 billion per year.[7]

OBSERVATION

What is the Tax Gap?[8]
Components of the Tax Gap
The tax gap can be divided into three components: nonfiling, underreporting and underpayment. Nonfiling occurs when taxpayers who are required to file a return do not do so on time. Underreporting of tax occurs when taxpayers either understate their income or overstate their deductions, exemptions and credits on timely filed returns. Underpayment occurs when taxpayers file their return but fail to remit the amount due by the payment due date.

Of these three components, underreporting of income tax, employment taxes and other taxes represents about 80 percent of the tax gap. The single largest sub-component of underreporting involves individuals understating their incomes, taking improper deductions, overstating business expenses and erroneously claiming credits. Individual underreporting represents about half of the total tax gap.

---

[6] *Id.*
[7] **IRS News Release, IR-2006-28, February 14, 2006.**
[8] **IRS Fact Sheet FS-2005-14, March 2005.**

.09   BIAS AGAINST SAVING AND INVESTMENT

Our tax system has always taxed most interest and other returns on capital. Many commentators contend that this represents a bias against saving and investment, and impedes any improvement in the country's long-run standard of living. In essence, today's savings by individuals become tomorrow's dollars of investment by business, and, in that sense, one is dependent on the other. By taxing interest and other returns, the pool of money available to fund long-term economic investment in machinery and equipment is reduced, and with less investment, there are fewer jobs to provide savings by workers in the first place. Therefore, savings and investment are both sides of the same coin.

The reduced rates on dividends to 15 percent is designed in part to deal with the savings disincentive, as well as the double-taxation of corporate income. The personal savings rate of U.S. citizens in 2010 was approximately 5 percent of income per year, as compared to over 10 percent in countries such as Belgium, Austria, Sweden, Switzerland, China and Germany. And as explained below, this factor is one of the powerful arguments put forth for some type of consumption tax as an adjunct or replacement to the income tax.

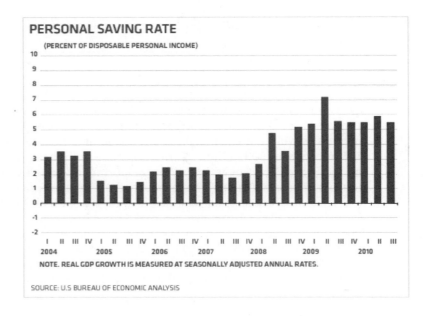

.11   GLOBAL COMPETITIVE DISADVANTAGES

U.S. income tax rates, as a generalization, are higher than the rates in other countries. Table 1 below provides the combined corporate tax rate in various OECD countries. The high corporate income tax rate is often cited as a reason that U.S. companies are at a disadvantage when trying to compete in global markets. For example, many commentators point out the positive features of certain European forms of the Value Added Tax (VAT), where the tax is levied on imports, but all taxes levied on exports are rebated to the exporter. Therefore, exports are essentially tax free. Of course, this argument ignores the fact that other countries may not buy U.S. goods because of the VAT imposed on *their* imports. Still, encouraging exports and discouraging imports is a worthy goal.

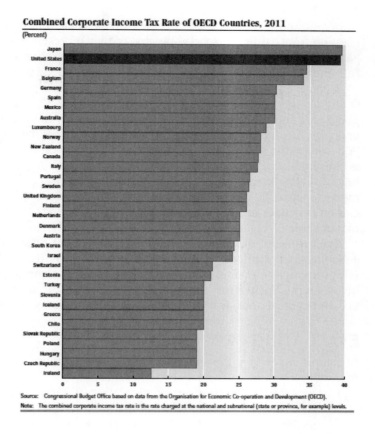

Combined Corporate Income Tax Rate of OECD Countries, 2011

Source: Congressional Budget Office based on data from the Organisation for Economic Co-operation and Development (OECD).

Note: The combined corporate income tax rate is the rate charged at the national and subnational (state or province, for example) levels.

Tax systems may also influence a U.S. taxpayer's decision to invest in this country versus another country. In a perfect world, the tax system should be neutral with respect to the location of an investment. However, if the tax rates are lower in another country than in the United States, this may be a factor influencing the location of the investment. The importance of this factor is mitigated with the availability of a foreign tax credit for taxes paid to other countries.

Example 18-1. Banyon Corporation is considering an investment that promises an 18-percent pre-tax rate of return, and is comparing the benefits of making the investment in the United States versus Sweden. If the U.S. tax rate applicable to the investment is 40 percent, and the Swedish tax rate is 28 percent, then Sweden might look like a better investment. But Banyon will be subject to tax in both the United States and Sweden, and the foreign tax credit allowed on the U.S. return will be limited to the 28-percent tax paid to Sweden. Thus, an additional tax of 12 percent will be paid to the United States, which means that total taxes paid are at a 40-percent rate, regardless of whether the investment is in the United States or in Sweden. In effect, the location decision will more likely depend on the projected pre-tax rate of return in each country.

¶18,005   Tax Reform Proposals: The View from 10,000 Feet

The following discussion examines five different reform proposals for the federal income tax: (1) the value-added tax, (2) the national retail sales tax, (3) the flat tax, (4) the personal consumption tax, and (5) the 2010 President's National Commission on Fiscal Responsibility and Reform proposals. Each of these plans is summarized in **Table 1**.

In examining these plans, it becomes obvious that most proposals shift the incidence of taxation from earnings to spending, that is, they represent to some degree a consumption-based tax. Most also propose major changes in the current income tax system, and the full implications of each system are somewhat unpredictable.

When examining a proposal, it is important to determine whether the proposed system is an *income tax* or a **consumption tax**. An income tax is based on revenue less cost of goods sold and allowable deductions, similar to financial accounting. The questions arising under an income tax may include: What is income? What expenses should be allowed? A consumption tax is a tax on spending rather than on income. Income is taxed when it is consumed, not when saved. Examples include sales tax and value-added tax (discussed below). Consumption taxes exempt savings and allow businesses to deduct capital investments (such as land, buildings, and equipment) immediately, rather than through depreciation (as under the income tax system). The questions arising under a consumption tax may include: Who is the taxpayer? What types of consumption, if any, should be exempt?

Keep in mind that annual income is either spent or saved: Income = Consumption + Savings. Consumption can be taxed either directly (through a sales tax) or indirectly (Consumption = Income – Savings). Measuring consumption as income less savings can be accomplished in two ways: a cash flow approach, income less amounts saved; or a tax-prepayment approach that exempts the income on savings from tax.

.01   EVALUATING PROPOSALS

In examining each of the alternative tax proposals, there are a few key questions to keep in mind:

1. Does the change produce simplification of our tax laws?
2. Does the reform proposal retain the progressive rate structure of current tax law?
3. Are the compliance burdens on taxpayers, both business and individuals, increased or decreased?
4. What are the potential administrative costs of adopting a reform proposal?
5. What are the income distributional effects of the proposed system on individuals, in terms of both horizontal equity and vertical equity?
6. How does the reform proposal affect major stakeholders in the current tax system, such as charities, financial institutions, and the construction industry?
7. How does the proposed reform affect savings and investments, two important economic factors?
8. Does the proposed reform provide export incentives?
9. How does the proposed reform affect plant and equipment investment decisions by businesses?

Table 1
Tax Reform Proposals
A Quick and Dirty Summary

The Value-Added Tax. A tax collected at each stage of the production/distribution cycle, based on the "value added to the product." Under the more widely-used credit invoice method, a credit is allowed at each stage of the process for all VAT paid in previous production levels, so that only the *value added* in that particular stage is taxed. Costs are expensed under a VAT, with the exception of labor costs. No VAT credit is available for the final retail sale to a customer. Investment incomes are exempt from the tax. Special rates, exemptions, and/or credits are usually provided for goods typically consumed by lower-income taxpayers.

The National Retail Sales Tax. A tax is collected only on the final retail sale of goods or services to customers, much like a state or local sales tax. Only business entities selling to end-use customers are affected. Investment incomes are exempt from the tax. Special rates, exemptions, or credits are usually provided for goods typically consumed by lower-income taxpayers.

The Flat Tax. The flat tax imposes a single tax rate to income, and specifically exempts all investment income from taxation. Most versions eliminate all deductions and credits of current law, and substitute a generous personal and/or dependency allowance for individual taxpayers.

The Personal Consumption Tax. This tax would retain many of the features of current law, such as deductions, credits, and a graduated rate structure. The major difference is that a new unlimited deduction would be allowed for a net savings increase by taxpayers (i.e., net investment increase). Savings increases must be reduced by borrowings, and any dissavings (spending from accumulated savings) will increase taxable income.

The President's 2010 National Commission on Fiscal Responsibility and Reform Plan. The Commission offered three plans. All three plans have many elements in common, such as (1) reducing tax rates, (2) eliminating the alternative minimum tax, and (3) eliminating a significant portion of current tax benefits and credits.

¶18,007   Tax-inclusive and Tax-exclusive Rates

As with any tax discussion, it is important to understand the terminology. Discussions of alternative tax systems often reference tax rates as being **tax-inclusive** or **tax-exclusive**. A tax-exclusive tax rate refers to the amount of tax paid as a proportion of the pretax value of whatever is taxed; sales tax rates are typically expressed in tax-exclusive terms. Conversely, a tax-inclusive rate refers to the amount of tax paid as a proportion of the after-tax value; income tax rates are often expressed in tax-inclusive terms. Thus the difference between the two definitions is whether or not the tax paid is included in the denominator when calculating the tax rate. The tax-inclusive rate will always be lower than the tax-exclusive rate, and the difference grows as the rates rise.

Example 18-2.

1) A 15-percent tax-inclusive sales tax rate on a sale of $2,000 yields a tax of $300 and a total sales price of $2,000; the equivalent tax-exclusive rate is 17.65 percent (of $1,700).
2) A 15-percent tax-exclusive sales tax rate on a sale of $2,000 yields a tax of $300 and a total sales price of $2,300; the equivalent tax-inclusive rate is 13.04 percent (of $2,300).

¶18,009   The Value-Added Tax

.01   SUMMARY

The **value-added tax (VAT)** is the primary source of revenue for most European countries. The VAT is a modified consumption-based tax, and is imposed and collected on the value added at each stage in the production and distribution cycles for goods and services. The tax base for the VAT, the "value added," is the difference between the value of a taxpayer's outputs (sales) and inputs (purchases). No deduction is allowed for labor costs, since this "value added" is the reason for the tax.

The value-added tax can be computed in either of several ways. The two most common methods used are the credit-invoice method and the subtraction method. The credit-invoice method is by far the most popular form, levied by over 150 countries worldwide and all 25 members of the European Union.

Under the **credit-invoice method**, a tax is imposed on all sellers of goods by multiplying the invoice sales price of goods or services, and then subtracting a credit for all VAT paid on purchases of taxable goods and services (this credit is shown on the top of the invoice from the vendor, much like state and local sales taxes are shown on a grocery receipt). In effect, a tax is collected at each stage of the production process. A credit is not available to the final nonbusiness consumer of the product. In such a system, a taxpayer will need to rely only on sales invoice records and purchase invoices to determine the VAT. For example, consider the production of canned tomatoes, where each stage of the process is subject to a 10-percent VAT:

	Grower	Cannery	Distributor	Retail Store	Total
Sales	$2,000	$2,600	$3,200	$4,400	
× VAT rate	× .10	× .10	× .10	× .10	
= VAT on sales	$ 200	$ 260	$ 320	$ 440	
- VAT credit – purchases	(0)	(200)	(260)	(320)	
= Net VAT owed	$ 200	$ 60	$ 60	$ 120	$ 440

OBSERVATION   When a sale is made to another business under the credit-invoice method, the seller must state the amount of the VAT so the purchaser can claim a credit. Since consumers do not qualify for the credit, this amount is not disclosed on the final sale.

Under the **subtraction method**, the VAT is calculated as the tax rate times the difference between a taxpayer's taxable sales and purchases of taxable goods (or services) from other taxpayers. In this case, the rate is applied to the net value added. Note that the taxpayer under this method will need to rely on financial accounting and/or tax accounting records to compute the tax. Using the facts of the previous example, the VAT computation under the subtraction method would appear as follows:

	Grower	Cannery	Distributor	Retail Store	Total
Sales	$2,000	$2,600	$3,200	$4,400	
- Purchases	(0)	(2,000)	(2,600)	(3,200)	
= Value added	$ 2,000	$ 600	$ 600	$ 1,200	
× VAT rate	× .10	× .10	× .10	× .10	
= Net VAT owed	$ 200	$ 60	$ 60	$ 120	$ 440

OBSERVATION   The subtraction method offers more flexibility, since numbers are determined from the firm's accounting system. Thus, such accounting method choices as expensing or capitalizing, inventory methods, installment elections, and matching conventions will influence the final result. On the other hand, the credit-invoice method effectively results in expensing all items, and avoids the accounting complexities.

For various economic, social, and political reasons, most VAT systems provide special exclusions (or deductions or credits) for certain goods and services. Most of these exclusions are for those goods and services thought to be consumed by lower-income taxpayers (e.g., food, rent, utilities, etc.). In addition, most VAT systems have special rules for imported goods or services (generally subject to the tax) and exported goods or services (generally tax-free). In some cases certain goods and services are excluded from the VAT simply because the value added or the element of consumption cannot be measured accurately. The various exclusions are provided through either the use of an exemption or a *zero-rated sale* (i.e., a sale with a tax rate of zero percent).

.03 ADVANTAGES AND DISADVANTAGES

Three advantages to the VAT are generally identified. The primary purpose of the VAT is to encourage investment and savings by taxing consumption. Two other touted advantages of such a system would be to relieve taxpayers of the task of complying with today's complex Code (*no* tax return would be required for individuals), and to bring the underground economy into the tax-paying net. Exports would also be encouraged, since they are not subject to tax. Many tax accounting controversies would also disappear if a credit-invoice VAT system is implemented.

A number of disadvantages are raised regarding the VAT. Since lower- and middle-income taxpayers spend the largest share of their income on consumption, they will likely bear the main burden of a VAT. The VAT is regressive in nature, in direct contrast to our current progressive income tax structure, so it is often said that the VAT favors the wealthy. It is also likely that the imposition of a new type of tax structure in the country will involve significant start-up and continuing administrative costs, although how such costs would compare to current IRS administrative costs is anyone's guess. One fear of taxpayers is that a VAT system might be instituted without an elimination of the income tax, and the net result might be that the VAT is just an additional tax, rather than a substitute for the income tax.

¶18,011 National Retail Sales Tax

.01 SUMMARY

A national retail sales tax would provide essentially the same economic benefits as a VAT. This proposal would impose a sales tax on the retail sales price of taxable goods and services. As investment incomes are not part of a retail sale, such income would be exempt from taxation. Since the tax is based only on the final retail sale, only those entities that sell to end users would be affected.

COMMENTARY Note in the two previous examples of a credit-invoice VAT and a subtraction method VAT that the total tax collected under each system was $200. By simply imposing a 10-percent national retail sales tax on the final sale to the customer, the same $200 of taxes would be collected. In effect, the VAT proposals simply carve this $200 into its various pieces as each part adds to the value of the property. In this respect, the national sales tax would be much easier to implement (but also easier to evade).

One of the key questions related to a national sales tax is exactly what tax rate would be used in such a system. Most serious proposals for implementing a national sales tax peg the tax rate at somewhere between 15 and 25 percent. Once again, the more goods and services used by lower-income taxpayers that are exempted, deducted, or credited, the higher the necessary rate. Recent proposals suggest that it would take a rate of approximately 19 percent to raise the same revenue as our current tax system.

.03 ADVANTAGES AND DISADVANTAGES

One of the main advantages of a national retail sales tax is that the startup and continuing administrative costs would likely be small. For one thing, such a tax could more or less piggy-back on a state tax sales system, or at least incorporate many of the same features. Business compliance costs should also be reduced, as only retail sellers would be burdened with significant record-keeping costs. The tax also offers the VAT advantage of simplicity for individual taxpayers; no tax return would be required.

A national retail sales tax suffers from some of the same disadvantages of a VAT system. Specifically, such a tax is also regressive in nature, and in that respect it can be said that the national sales tax proposal also favors the wealthy. Obviously, low-income individuals have little choice but to consume most of their incomes, while wealthy individuals have the wherewithal to choose to consume much less. Taxpayers will still fear that a national retail sales tax might be instituted without elimination of the income tax, and the net result will be a dual tax structure, rather than one or the other. The simplicity of a single point of collection (the retail sale) may also make such a tax easier to evade, as the tax collector gets only one opportunity to collect the tax.

COMMENTARY   As mentioned above, one of the key questions with a national retail sales tax is what rate will be adopted for the system. Most likely, the rate will have to be at least 19 percent to generate approximately the same revenue as the current system. And even though some purchases may be exempted to ease the burden of the tax on low-and middle income taxpayers, the total tax paid may be much larger for these taxpayers than current law. And it is lower- and middle-class taxpayers who do not have much discretion as to spending, since so much of the family budget is for such essentials as food, shelter, and clothing. The more of these goods exempted from the tax, the higher the tax rate will have to be.

¶18,013   Flat Tax

.01   SUMMARY

A flat tax system has one distinguishing characteristic: there is only a single tax rate. In order to encourage investment and savings, most flat tax proposals exempt investment income (e.g., interest, dividends, royalties, annuities, capital gains, etc.) from the tax base. In this respect, most flat tax proposals are essentially consumption-based systems.

Most proposed flat tax systems would scrap the current Internal Revenue Code and instead tax all personal and business income at one rate. One of the most popular flat tax proposals over the years has been the one espoused by Robert E. Hall and Alvin Rabushka in their book Low Tax, Simple Tax, Flat Tax.[9] Under the Hall/Rabushka proposal, all personal deductions and credits would be eliminated. The only deduction allowed would be a personal allowance and dependency exemptions so that most basic family expenses are covered before paying any tax to the government. Interest, dividends, capital gains, and other forms of investment income would not be subject to the tax; such amounts are only taxable at the source (i.e., taxed once, to the financial institution).

One of the key questions regarding the enactment of a flat tax is if Congress would leave it alone once enacted. Over the years, the Internal Revenue Code has been used as a tool of economic and social policy, and given Congress's propensity to enact targeted tax breaks, would a flat tax remain flat (and simple) for long?

The most appealing aspect of a flat tax to most taxpayers is its simplicity. This is one tax return that truly could be filed on a post card. For example, Form 1 below is a draft tax form for the 19-percent flat tax, as proposed by Robert Hall (Form 2 would be filed by businesses):

---

[9]   Robert E. Hall and Alvin Rabushka, *Low Tax, Simple Tax, Flat Tax*. New York: McGraw-Hill, 1983.

Form 1	Individual Wage Tax	2004

Your first name and initial (if joint return, also give spouse's name and initial)   Last name

Your social security number

Present home address (number and street including apartment number or rural route)

Spouse's social security number

City, town, or post office, state, and ZIP code

Your occupation

Spouse's occupation

1	Wages and salary	1
2	Pension and retirement benefits	2
3	Total compensation (*line 1 plus line 2*)	3
4	Personal allowance	
	(a) ❑ $27,000 for married filing jointly	4(a)
	(b) ❑ $14,000 for single	4(b)
	(c) ❑ $24,000 for single head of household	4(c)
5	Number of dependents, not including spouse	5
6	Personal allowances for dependents (*line 5 multiplied by $7,000*)	6
7	Total personal allowances (*line 4 plus line 6*)	7
8	Taxable compensation (*line 3 less line 7, if positive; otherwise zero*)	8
9	Tax (*19% of line 8*)	9
10	Tax withheld by employer	10
11	Tax due (*line 9 less line 10, if positive*)	11
12	Refund due (*line 10 less line 9, if positive*)	12

Form 2	Business Tax	2004

Business name

Employer identification number

Street address

County

City, state, and ZIP code

Principal product

1	Gross revenue from sales	1
2	Allowable costs	
	(a) Purchases of goods, services, and materials	2(a)
	(b) Wages, salaries, and pensions	2(b)
	(c) Purchases of capital equipment, structures, and land	2(c)
3	Total allowable costs (*sum of lines 2(a), 2(b), 2(c)*)	3
4	Taxable income (*line 1 less line 3*)	4
5	Tax (*19% of line 4*)	5
6	Carry-forward from 2003	6
7	Interest on carry-forward (3% of *line 6*)	7
8	Carry-forward into 2004 (*line 6 plus line 7*)	8
9	Tax due (*line 5 less line 8, if positive*)	9
10	Carry-forward to 2005 (*line 8 less line 5, if positive*)	10

Note that under the Hall/Rabushka proposal, there would be no personal deductions or credits. Instead, a taxpayer could deduct a personal allowance (based on filing status) and an additional allowance for each dependent. For example, a married couple with two children would deduct a $27,000 personal allowance and two dependency allowances of $7,000 each, for a total of $41,000.

What about businesses? These taxpayers (corporations, partnerships, and individuals with rental income and sole proprietorships) would complete "Form 2" (the alternative side of a postcard). Note that businesses would be able to immediately expense all capital expenditures.

COMMENTARY   In his presentation to President Bush's Tax Reform Commission, Robert Hall also floated the idea of an "X tax", which would be a flat tax with two rates for all taxpayers: 12 percent for the first $60,000 of taxable income, and 25 percent for income exceeding $60,000. This proposal might be more politically palatable, since the burden on middle-income taxpayers could be reduced with a higher tax rate applicable to larger incomes. Here is how the total tax liability (vertical axis) would compare as total earnings (horizontal axis) increase:

.03   ADVANTAGES AND DISADVANTAGES

The obvious advantage of a flat tax is its simplicity; although individual tax returns are required, they could be reduced to a post card, and the Internal Revenue Code would be obsolete. Since business expenditures are fully deductible, most accounting method issues would disappear—in fact, most businesses would simply report on the cash basis. The plan also encourages investment and savings, and may lead to a decrease in interest rates. The flat tax *appears* to offer fairness and equality—every taxpayer (individual or business) will pay the same tax rate.

A flat tax represents a dramatic change from our progressive tax rate structure, which has been the backbone of our tax system. Perhaps the major disadvantage associated with a flat tax is simply that the rate would need to be set fairly high; the 19 percent proposed by Hall/Rabushka would not raise the revenue that the current system does.

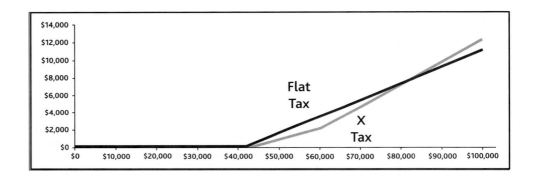

Setting the rate above 20 percent without any credits means that many low- and middle-income taxpayers will actually pay *more* tax under the flat tax than the current tax structure. Consider the following three examples, all assuming a married couple with two dependent children (both under age 17) taking the standard deduction under the current system:

	$75,000 Gross Income		$125,000 Gross Income		$175,000 Gross Income	
	Current System	**19% Flat Tax**	**Current System**	**19% Flat Tax**	**Current System**	**19% Flat Tax**
Gross Income	75,000	75,000	125,000	125,000	175,000	175,000
Standard Allowance	(10,300)	(27,000)	(10,300)	(27,000)	(10,300)	(27,000)
Exemption Allowance	(13,300)	(14,000)	(13,300)	(14,000)	(13,300)	(14,000)
Taxable Income	51,400	34,000	101,400	84,000	151,400	134,000
Gross Tax Due	6,955	6,460	18,465	15,960	31,796	25,460
Child Credit	(2,000)	N/A	(0)	N/A	(0)	N/A
Net Tax Due	4,955	6,460	18,465	15,960	31,796	25,460

Note in the above example that the loss of the child credit for a family of four with $75,000 income causes more tax to be paid under the flat tax, and as gross income increases, the effects of the graduated tax structure under current law causes the flat tax to produce smaller tax liabilities. However, since the vast majority of taxpayers at the higher income levels itemize, the average difference per income level is probably less than indicated above.

Additionally, there are a variety of other credits that taxpayers could use under current law, notably the earned income tax credit, the child and dependent care credit and the education credits. Finally, if any of the income is investment income (which is more likely the case with higher income taxpayers), the exclusion of such income from the flat tax will magnify this difference.

OBSERVATION   But wouldn't the flat tax save a lot of taxes for couples with incomes below $41,000, since there is *no* tax due under the flat tax? The answer, surprisingly, is not necessarily. Recall that the earned income credit is a refundable credit, and is only completely phased out once adjusted gross income (or earned income, if larger) exceeds $36,920 for one qualifying dependent and $41,952 for two or more. For families utilizing the earned income credit, $0 tax liability under a flat tax is a tax *increase* since no credits are allowed. For example, a family of four with $25,000 adjusted gross income would lose a refundable earned income credit of $4,662 in 2012.

A frequently cited disadvantage of the flat tax is that charitable giving may decrease significantly with the loss of the charitable deduction. (This is a common complaint of all consumption-based tax systems.) Although some economists make the argument that contributions are correlated with wealth and not taxable income, it is hard to isolate these two factors. Most charities and foundations are on record as opposing any type of consumption-based tax or flat tax.

¶18,015   Personal Consumption Taxes

.01   SUMMARY

A somewhat different type of consumption tax is the personal consumption tax, sometimes referred to as the "savings exempt tax." This tax is simply based on what an individual consumes—not by keeping track of every expenditure, but simply subtracting net increases in saving from total income.

OBSERVATION   Ed McCaffery of the University of Southern California, in testimony before the President Bush's Advisory Panel on Federal Tax Reform, defined the objective of a personal consumption tax rather succinctly with two statements:
"It's time to get the fair timing of tax down right."
"We should tax people when they spend, not when they work, save, give, or die."

The personal consumption tax initially includes all sources of income, similar to the present income tax system. Then, an unlimited deduction is provided for all new net savings. This deduction works like an unlimited deduction to an Individual Retirement Account; to the extent that the income is "saved," it is not included in the tax base. In order to insure that only net savings are deducted, any savings increases must be decreased by any borrowings. For example, if $20,000 is borrowed and immediately invested, the net increase in savings is simply $0. What if some of the previous savings are now spent? Savings reductions would be offset in the calculation of any increases in savings, so effectively income that is taxed is income *not* used to buy financial assets (i.e., savings) *plus* any net drawdown of existing savings.

OBSERVATION	Interestingly, most personal consumption tax proposals define "savings" to include investments in education. In effect, this allows a deduction for investments in human capital and would preserve the favorable tax treatment of education expenses under current law.

What tax rate(s) would apply in a personal consumption tax system? This system would not be constrained to one rate, and studies have indicated that a graduated rate structure topping out at 40 percent for individuals and 11 percent for businesses would generate approximately the same revenue as our current system.

.03   ADVANTAGES AND DISADVANTAGES

The primary advantage of the personal consumption tax is simply that it encourages saving and discourages consumptive debt, one of the common complaints about our current tax system. More savings equals more investment, which should have beneficial economic effects on a national and international trade scale. Supporters also note that, unlike the other consumption-based alternatives, the personal consumption tax can easily accommodate a graduated rate structure. This allows a more progressive distribution of the tax burden, a requirement often cited by tax reform proponents. The tax could generate enough revenue that a complicated second business tax, such as a VAT, might not be needed. Finally, since much of the current tax system is retained, there would be no need to impose new collection mechanisms or layers of tax administration.

Unlike the other consumption-based taxes discussed above, the personal consumption tax would complicate the tax reporting for individuals, rather than lessen or even eliminate this burden. Rather than just tracking realization transactions (as required under present law), taxpayer would also have to account for nonrealization events related to savings (e.g., borrowings and savings account withdrawals). This reporting is significantly more difficult than just reporting contributions to an IRA account. The personal consumption tax would also present information reporting and monitoring problems, as financial institutions do not report on "net borrowing" activities. Taxpayers would also have little incentive to report borrowings or withdrawals, and compliance issues would invariably arise.

¶18,017   Modifying the Current System: The President's 2010 National Commission on Fiscal Responsibility and Reform Plan

In February 2010, President Obama created the bipartisan National Commission on Fiscal Responsibility and Reform to address the nation's fiscal challenges. The Commission was charged with identifying policies to improve the fiscal situation in the medium term and to achieve fiscal sustainability over the long run. The Commission released their report, The Moment of Truth (the plan), on December 1, 2010. On December 3, 2010, 11 of the 18 commission members voted to support the plan, three votes shy of the 14 vote super majority needed to require Congressional action. Although the plan was never debated by Congress, it offers an alternative to the overly complex Internal Revenue Code while addressing the long term financial issues of the U.S. government.

The Commission's plan centers on six basic recommendations including discretionary spending caps, tax reforms, controlling the growth of health care costs, mandatory savings in the areas of farm subsidies, military, and civil service retirement, shoring up Social Security for the next 75 years and critically reforming the budget process to ensure control and adherence to the plan. The plan seeks to achieve long term financial solvency for the U.S. Federal Government through budgetary cuts (approximately 75%) and tax changes (approximately 25%).[10]

---

[10]   http://online.wsj.com/article/SB20001424052748703805004575606643067587042.html

The plan actually lowers tax rates, but at the cost of popular tax provisions such as the home mortgage interest deduction, child care tax credit, earned income credit, and preferential rates for dividends and capital gains. The Commission offered three tax reform options, starting with the elimination of all tax expenditures and then adding back certain credits and tax benefits. Table 2 summarizes the plan's three tax reform options and Table 3 compares current tax law to some of the specific provisions of Options 1 and 2.

Table 2
Tax Rate Scenarios from the Commission Plan

	Bottom Rate	Middle Rate	Top Rate	Corporate Rate
Current Rates for 2013	10% 15%	25% 28%	33% 35% 39.6%	35%
Option 1: Eliminate all Tax Expenditures	8%	14%	23%	26%
Option 2: Keep Child Tax Credit + EITC	9%	15%	24%	26%
Option 3: Additional Tax Benefits Retained	12%	22%	28%	28%

Option 1: Eliminate All Tax Expenditures: This plan calls for significantly lowering the individual and corporate income tax rates by eliminating most, if not all, of the tax breaks including the home mortgage interest deduction, earned income tax credit, child credit, etc. It also eliminates the preferential rate for dividends and capital gains.

Option 2: Keeping the Child Tax Credit and EITC: Under this variation, the Commission proposes three individual rates of 9%, 15%, and 24% along with the elimination of alternative minimum tax and the phase outs of personal exemptions and itemized deductions. The increased rates over option one pay for the current child tax credit and earned income tax credit.

Option 3: Additional Tax Benefits Retained: The Commission's report illustrates a third scenario which retains tax benefits for a greater number of individual expenditures including home ownership, health care, charity, and savings. By adding back the additional tax benefits, the individual rates are increased to 12%, 22% and 28% and the corporate rate is increased to 28%. The third variation eliminates itemized deductions and provides tax benefits for mortgage interest and charitable contributions through tax credits. The exclusion for employer provided health insurance is capped and the interest on newly issued state and municipal bonds is taxed.

Table 3
Comparison of Current Tax Law to
Option 2: Keep Child Tax Credit + EITC
and Option 3: Additional Tax Benefits Retained

	Current	Keep Child Tax Credit + EITC	Additional Tax Benefits Retained
Individual Tax Rates	15%, 25%, 28%, 33%, 35%, 39.6%	9%, 15%, 24%	12%, 22%, 28%
Capital Gains and Dividends	15%, 20%	Taxed as ordinary income, see above	Taxed as ordinary income, see above
Itemized Deductions	Numerous	All deductions are forgone	All deductions forgone but see credits below
Mortgage Interest	Restricted to interest on $1 million for 2 homes and $100,000 for home equity	None	12% nonrefundable credit only up to $500,000
Charitable Giving	Deductible if one itemizes	None	12% nonrefundable credit with a 2% floor

Retirement	Numerous Options	Unclear	Consolidate to lower of $20,000 or 20% of income
Employer-Provided Health Care	Generally fully deductible	Unclear	Capped at 75% of premium levels in 2014 and phased out by 2038. Excise tax of 12%
Municipal Bond Interest	Generally tax free	Tax interest on newly issued bonds	Tax interest on newly issued bonds
Other Tax Expenditures	Over 150 additional tax expenditures	Eliminate nearly all tax expenditures	Eliminate nearly all tax expenditures
Table adapted from "Reworking the Tax Code," *WSJ*, 12/2/10 and Commission Report, Figure 7, Illustrative Individual Tax Reform Plan.			

.01   ADVANTAGES AND DISADVANTAGES

All three options would simplify the current tax law for individuals including eliminating the alternative minimum tax. But these simplifications come at a price: the value of tax benefits, if available at all, is significantly smaller than current law. All three plans call for eliminating the tax exclusion for interest on newly issued municipal bonds, certainly resulting in a change in public financing.

The Commission's plan also outlined corporate tax reform proposals. The recommendations include eliminating industry specific subsidies, and moving to a territorial tax system for taxing foreign source income. Overall the Commission outlined a plan that would put the US government back on the path of fiscal responsibility but most found it a bitter pill with every group finding something to criticize.

¶18,019   Concluding Thoughts

Everyone complains about the current tax system, but little is done to change it. There are so many unknowns if a switch is made to a consumption-based tax. One of the biggest issues with reform proposals is that the high rates necessary to generate the same revenue as our current system will create a lot of pain for lower- and middle-income taxpayers. Trying to implement a credit/deduction/exclusion system for certain expenditures incurred primarily by these taxpayers is extremely difficult because everyone incurs food, clothing, shelter, and transportation expenditures.

But what if by some miracle, a new simplified system, such as the flat tax or the retail sales tax, was enacted? The question becomes how long the "simplicity" would last. Could politicians resist the urge to tinker with the new, simple tax system in order to benefit their special project or constituency?

¶18,021   Summary

- The current U.S. income tax system is criticized for its complexity, compliance costs, advantages for the wealthy, inability to tax the underground economy, bias against savings and investment, and global competitive disadvantages.
- Reform proposals include replacing the current system with a consumption based tax such as a value-added tax, a national retail sales tax, a flat tax, or a personal consumption tax. President Obama's National Commission on Fiscal Responsibility and Reform made recommendations to amend the current income tax system that include certain components of a consumption tax.
- All the alternative tax systems have advantages and disadvantages including the question of how long Congress would leave the new system untouched.

Review Questions for Chapter 18

True or False

Indicate which of the following statements are true or false by circling the correct answer.

1. The U.S. corporate tax rate is generally lower than other developed countries.   T   F
2. Our current tax system is biased against savings and investment.   T   F
3. Reasons for revamping our current federal income tax system include simplification and   T   F
    economic growth.
4. The complexity of the federal income tax system has remained fairly constant since the   T   F
    re-codification in 1986.
5. Noncompliance is highest among taxpayers whose income is not subject to third party   T   F
    information reporting or withholding.
6. If a $1,000 sale yields a tax of $200 and a total sales price of $1,200; the tax-exclusive rate   T   F
    is 20 percent.
7. The Hall/Rabushka Flat Tax will reduce taxes for most of the working poor.   T   F
8. The primary advantage of the personal consumption tax is simply that it encourages saving   T   F
    and discourages consumptive debt.
9. Both the National Retail Sales tax and the VAT offer an advantage of simplicity for indi-   T   F
    vidual taxpayers.
10. The value-added tax is the primary source of revenue for most European countries.   T   F

Fill in the Blanks

Fill in each blank with the appropriate word or phrase that completes each sentence.

11. The principle of _____ states that equal incomes should pay equal taxes.
12. The principle of _____ is the backbone of the progressive rate structure of the federal
    income tax system.
13. The _____ is the difference between the amount of tax that taxpayers should pay under the tax
    law and the amount they actually pay on time.
14. A(n) _____ tax provides the immediate deduction of equipment while a(n) _____ tax requires
    depreciation.
15. Under the _____ VAT, the rate is applied to the net value added.
16. The 2010 Presidential Commission proposed three alternative tax plans. Under option_____, home owner-
    ship results in tax benefits, but through the use of a tax credit rather than itemized deductions.
17. All three options from the President Obama's National Commission on Fiscal Responsibility and Reform
    retain the _____ tax rate structure of the current income tax system.
18. Post card size tax forms would be available under the _____.
19. An alternative version of the flat tax, called the _____, proposes two tax rates instead of one.
20. One of the benefits of the 2010 National Commission's plans would be the elimination of the
    _____, the complex, alternative second tax computation for individuals.

Multiple Choice
Circle the best answer for each of the following questions.

21. Recently, U.S. citizens have increased their average savings to approximately:
    a. 1 percent of their income each year
    b. 5 percent of their income each year
    c. 10 percent of their income each year
    d. 15 percent of their income each year

22. Under a VAT system, typically:
    a. exports are taxed and imports are not taxed
    b. imports are taxed and exports are not taxed
    c. both imports and exports are taxed
    d. neither imports or exports are taxed
    e. none of the above

23. A stapling widget went through five stages of production before finally being sold to a retail customer (an individual taxpayer) for $700. Under a VAT credit-invoice system, the prior five stages of production had reported total VAT paid of $115. Assuming a 20-percent VAT rate, the final retail customer will pay a VAT of:
    a. $0
    b. $14
    c. $25
    d. $115
    e. $700

24. In a credit-invoice VAT system, a prominent number will appear on each sales invoice generated by that system that is critical to the operation of the VAT. This number is:
    a. the total sales price of the item
    b. the VAT tax rate
    c. the VAT taxes paid by the previous step in the production chain
    d. the VAT taxes paid by all previous steps in the production chain
    e. none of the above

25. Which of the following types of income would not be subject to a national retail sales tax?
    a. Plumbing services by a plumber for a customer
    b. consulting services by a self-employed CPA for a client
    c. sale of hardware by a hardware store to a customer
    d. interest income earned by an investor
    e. sale of groceries by a supermarket to a customer

26. To make their flat tax proposal more palatable, Hall/Rubushka proposed an alternative "X tax," which involves:
    a. a single reduced tax rate compared to the regular proposal
    b. a dual tax rate structure, with a higher rate at lower income levels
    c. a dual tax rate structure, with a higher rate at higher income levels
    d. a higher tax rate for capital gains
    e. a lower tax rate for earned income

27. Under a personal consumption tax, an individual's taxable income is decreased by:
    a.   any excess of borrowings over savings
    b.   any excess of savings over borrowings
    c.   any amount spent on personal groceries, rent, and transportation
    d.   both a and c
    e.   both b and c

28. Which of the following items would no longer provide any tax benefit under any of National Commission options?
    a.   interest expense
    b.   state and local taxes expense
    c.   charitable contributions
    d.   all would be disallowed under the plan

29. Which of the proposals of the National Commission's options would be closer to a consumption-based tax?
    a.   Option 1
    b.   Option 2
    c.   Option 3
    d.   none of the above plans has elements of a consumption-based tax

30. A VAT (value added tax):
    a.   Is *not* regressive in its effect.
    b.   Has proven quite popular outside of the United States.
    c.   Is *not* a tax on consumption.
    d.   Is used exclusively by third world (less developed) countries.
    e.   None of the above.

Review Problems

31. Which of the National Commission's options include the following?
    a. Repeal of the alternative minimum tax
    b. Deductions for retirement savings
    c. Earned income tax credit
    d. A deduction for state and local taxes
    e. Lower tax rates on interest, dividends and capital gains.
    f. Progressive tax rates

32. Discuss the differences between an income and consumption tax and how to determine which type of system a reform proposal is based on.

33. Compute the tax-inclusive and tax-exclusive rates for the following products:
    a. The sales price of a widget without tax is $400. The tax equals $48.
    b. The sales price of a pool table is $3,000 without tax. The tax equals $540.

34. Complete the chart for the following single individuals with no dependents:

	$25,000 Gross Income		$50,000 Gross Income		$150,000 Gross Income	
	Current System	19% Flat Tax	Current System	19% Flat Tax	Current System	19% Flat Tax
W-2 Wage Income	25,000		50,000		150,000	
Interest Income	0		2,000		5,000	
Standard Allowance						
Exemption Allowance						
Taxable Income						
Gross Tax Due						

Discuss the impact of the proposed flat tax on each of the individuals.

35. Identify two reasons why evasion is likely to be higher under a National Retail Sales Tax than a Value Added Tax.

36. Jessica earns $50,000 a year as a CPA. Her yearly expenditures include:

Description	Amount	Description	Amount
Social Security/Medicare	3,800	Federal Income Tax	6,000
401(k) Contribution	3,000	Rent	12,000
Utilities	1,400	Groceries	4,500
Eating Out	6,000	Gasoline	2,100
Clothing, home furnishings, presents, etc.	3,000	Other car expenses (insurance, repairs, etc)	1,700
Cable, cell phone, etc	1,500	Doctor, prescriptions, other medical	2,000
Student loan payment	3,000		

Assume the Federal Income tax listed is equal to Jessica's tax under the current income tax system. Which of the items listed would be subject to a National Retail Sales Tax? Which items would you argue should be exempt? Why? Given the items you believe should be taxed, what rate would be required to replace the current tax revenue?

37. Choose a code section that you believe is overly complex. Develop three possible changes to the code section that would simplify the law without repealing it.

38. Travis, a single individual, reports the following items on his 2012 tax return:

Salary	$150,000	Mortgage interest	$15,000
Dividend income	10,000	Charitable contributions	3,000
Interest income	2,000	State & local taxes	5,000
Net long term capital gain	6,000	Real estate taxes	4,000

Using the summary information provided about Option 3 of the National Commission's Plan and the tax rate schedule below, determine Travis' tax liability under Option 3.

Tax Rates Under the Simplified Income Tax Plan
Tax would be computed using three marginal tax rates—12, 22 and 28 percent—instead of the seven rates that exist under current law.

Tax Rate	Married	Unmarried
12%	Up to $70,700	Up to $35,000
22%	$70,701-$217,400	$35,001-$178,600
28%	$217,401 or more	$178,600 or more

Based on the 2012 Tax Rate Schedules

39. Susan and Bob, a married couple with two school age children, report the following items on their 2012 tax return:

Salaries	$175,000	Mortgage interest	$20,000
Dividend income	12,000	Charitable contributions	7,000
Interest income	3,000	State & local taxes	10,000
Net long term capital gain	8,000	Real estate taxes	6,000

Using the summary information provided about Option 2 of the National Commission's Plan and the tax rate schedule below, determine Susan and Bob's tax liability under Option 2.

Tax Rates under the Growth and Investment Tax Plan
Under the Growth and Investment Tax Plan, wages, compensation, and other compensation would be taxed at three progressive rates of 15, 25, and 30 percent, instead of the six rates used in our current system. As summarized below, the rate brackets for married taxpayers are exactly twice the amounts for unmarried taxpayers, which would reduce the marriage penalties.

Tax Rate	Married	Unmarried
9%	Up to $70,700	Up to $35,000
15%	$70,701-$217,400	$35,001-$178,600
24%	$217,401 or more	$178,601 or more

Based on the 2012 Tax Rate Schedules

40. Stan is a financial advisor currently reporting his income on a Schedule C included in his Form 1040. Determine the tax on Stan's business income under the Hall/Rubushka flat tax, given his 2012 business income and expenses listed below. List any assumptions necessary to compute the tax.

Income:
Gross receipts $400,000
Expenses:
Employee wages 125,000   Computer equipment 15,000
Employee benefits   Travel and entertainment 10,000
(Simple IRAs, health insurance) 20,000
Operating expenses
(rent, professional fees, insurance) 45,000

Web-based research

41. Locate the Value Added Tax rates for the European Union member states. Which country has the highest rate? The lowest rate? The Sixth VAT Directive requires certain goods and services to be exempt from VAT. What items are exempt?

42. Locate a recent report on the tax gap. Provide two possible ways to reduce the gap and discuss at least two challenges of implementing the solution.

43. Locate the AICPA's Tax Policy Concept Statement 1, Guiding Principles of Good Tax Policy: A Framework for Evaluating Tax Proposals.
    a. Evaluate the current federal income tax system using the 10 guiding principles.
    b. Compare and contrast the flat tax and national retail sales tax using the principles of simplicity, transparency and minimum tax gap.

Glossary of Tax Terms

#

30-day letter

In general, a 30-Day Letter is issued in unagreed and partially agreed audit cases. The 30-Day Letter requests the taxpayer to either sign and return Form 870, a waiver of restrictions on assessment, if the taxpayer agrees with the findings, or exercise his/her appeal rights. If the taxpayer fails to respond within 30 days, the case is processed based on the proposed adjustments and a 90-Day Letter is issued.

90-day letter

The 90-Day Letter is the statutory notice of deficiency in the audit process. The letter offers the taxpayer the option of filing a protest in Tax Court within the 90 days before making any payment or signing the waiver form. Signing and returning the waiver permits the IRS to assess the deficiency. If the taxpayer does not sign and return the waiver or file a petition with the Tax Court, then the IRS will assess and bill the taxpayer for the deficiency after 90 days from the date of the letter (150 days if the letter is addressed to a taxpayer outside the United States).

A

"All events" test

An "all events" test was adopted by the Supreme Court in *Groetzinger*. This test is used for determining the existence of a trade or business. Such activities must be pursued "in good faith and with regularity."

"Away from home"

See *tax home*.

Accrual basis

See *accrual method*.

Accrual method

The accrual method of accounting is distinguished from the cash method. With the accrual method, income is generally reported when it is earned (even though not received), and expenses are reported when they are incurred (even though not yet paid). This tax reporting method is very close to the accrual method used for financial accounting reporting purposes, although some differences do exist. Under the accrual method, it is the right to receive income, and not the receipt of the income itself, that determines when the income is reported.

Action on Decision (AOD)
An Action on Decision recommends what action the IRS should take in response to an adverse court decision, such as acquiescence, non-acquiescence, or simply do nothing at the present time.

Active participant
An active participant in rental real estate activity is defined by Code Sec. 469 as a taxpayer that (1) owns at least a 10-percent interest (by value) in the activity, (2) is not a limited partner (unless an exception is provided in the regulations), and (3) demonstrates regular, continuous, and substantial involvement in the operations.

Activity
In regards to passive activity limitations, Reg. §1.469-4 states that the primary focus in defining an activity should be on grouping trade or business activities, or rental activities, into "appropriate economic units," using a facts and circumstances approach. The key factors in determining such groupings should be (a) type of business, (b) common control, (c) common ownership, (d) geographic location, and (e) business interdependencies.

Adjustments
For AMT purposes, adjustments involve the substitution of special AMT treatment for the regular tax treatment of certain items specified in Code Secs. 56 and 58. Generally, these adjustments either accelerate income recognition, decelerate expense recognition, or deny certain deductions altogether. These items are designed to ensure that a taxpayer with substantial economic income cannot avoid tax through the use of special regular tax exclusions, deductions, and credits.

Administrative authority
Administrative authority includes all pronouncements of the administration currently controlling the Presidency. Most tax administrative authority is drafted by the Department of Treasury and one of its major divisions, the Internal Revenue Service (IRS). The primary administrative authority is the tax Regulations, the official interpretations of the tax law by the Treasury and the IRS. Other sources of administrative authority are revenue rulings, revenue procedures, letter rulings, and various other notices and announcements.

Alimony
In a legal sense, alimony is support payment made after divorce or legal separation. In some respects, the income tax law definition is broader. It includes payments made under a decree of divorce or separate maintenance, under a decree for support if a wife is separated from her husband, or under a written separation agreement executed by the husband and wife if the wife is separated from her husband and they file separate returns. Payments that qualify as alimony are deductible by the payor spouse and are included in gross income of the payee spouse. However, a special provision in Code Sec. 72 allows former spouses to designate amounts as "not alimony", even though the amounts otherwise qualify as such under the law.

Allocable parental tax
The allocable parental tax is commonly known as the "kiddie tax." Under the kiddie tax rules, a child under the age of 19 (or a full-time student under age 24) who is eligible to be claimed as an exemption by a parent (or any one else) may have a portion of his or her taxable income taxed at the parent's marginal tax rate. The portion taxed as the parent's rate in 2008 is the excess of "unearned income" over

$1,800 (twice the minimum standard deduction of $900). The child's remaining taxable income is taxed at the child's rate. Special rules apply when the family has several children under age 19 (or full-time students under age 24) with unearned income, or if the child's parents are divorced.

Alternate valuation date

The alternate valuation date is a tool to minimize estate tax. Generally, property is included in the estate at its fair market value on the date of death of the decedent. However, this special election allows the estate to elect to value the property exactly six months after the date of death. This election is only available if a return is required to be filed, and if the election will decrease the gross estate and decrease the estate tax due.

Alternative minimum tax (AMT)

The alternative minimum tax was designed to require taxpayers who owe little or no regular tax liability through the use of various tax incentives to pay some minimum amount of tax. Althgouh Congress occasionally discusses a gradual repeal of this "shadow tax," it appears that perceived equity considerations virtually guarantee its continuance for years to come. A taxpayer's AMT for a tax year is the excess of the tentative minimum tax over the regular tax and must be paid in addition to year-end tax liability.

AMT exemption

Individual taxpayers are allowed an initial AMT exemption of $66,250 on a joint return, $44,350 on a single return, or $33,125 on a married filing separately return. The initial deduction is reduced $.25 for each $1.00 of AMTI before exemption that exceeds $150,000 (joint return), $112,500 (single return), or $75,000 (married-filing separately return).

Annual exclusion

Current law provides an annual exclusion from the federal gift tax of up to $12,000 per donee per year. This is adjusted periodically for inflation. If the gift to a donee is less than $12,000, the actual amount of the gift is used as the exclusion.

Arm's length

An arm's length transaction is any transaction between two unrelated people who are acting in their own best interest.

Ascertainable standard

An ascertainable standard provided in a trust instrument is an important exception to the limited power of appointment rules that allows the holder of such power to consume or invade the property for his or her own benefit. An ascertainable standard must relate to the holder's health, education, support, or maintenance. However, a power to use the property for "comfort, welfare, or happiness" is not an ascertainable standard.

B

Bank Deposit

The Bank Deposit method, also known as the "Receipts and Disbursements" method is an indirect method the IRS uses to detect unreported income. The IRS first establishes that the taxpayer is engaged in a trade or business or other income producing activity that would be expected to generate regular and periodic deposits into a bank account. The IRS then adds the bank deposits for the year. The total of bank deposits for the year is assumed to represent taxable income unless the taxpayer can show otherwise. The IRS then adjusts the deposit total by adding to it expenditures made in cash (since the cash is assumed never to have been deposited into the bank account) to arrive at taxable income.

Beneficiaries

Beneficiaries are those who benefit from a trust. The term is also used for individuals who inherit property from an estate.

Bolton method

The Bolton method is a method of allocating interest and taxes in regards to vacation rental property. The Tax Court, 9th Circuit Court, and 10th Circuit Court all approved this method of allocating interest and taxes based on the entire year (365 days) as opposed to just the total number of days the vacation property was actually "used" during the year. The Tax Court's logic was simple: the vacation home owner pays interest and taxes based on 365 days a year, not just the number of days the property is in use.

Book-tax differences

Book-tax differences are the result of the divergence of taxable income and financial income which has occurred primarily since the Tax Reform Act of 1986. This Act significantly broadened the tax base in order to accommodate a significant reduction in the top individual and corporate tax rates. This base broadening caused a shift away from recognition of income and expense items based upon generally accepted accounting principles (GAAP) to rule-based principles incorporated into the Internal Revenue Code.

Boot

Boot is a term that is sometimes used to describe the other property received in an exchange which, but for such other property, would be nontaxable. Partial gain may be recognized from the receipt of such boot, not to exceed the fair market value of the boot. Such boot or other property consists of money or property other than stock or securities (or other than like property in like-kind exchanges) which may be received tax free. The final tax result of a Code Sec. 1031 exchange depends on whether or not boot is involved in the exchange.

Business entity

A business entity is an entity that carries on a trade or business. In order to do that, it must have: one or more associates, assets, and engage in some business activity. In *R.P. Groetzinger*, the U.S. Supreme Court noted the Code's "common-sense" concept of what constitutes a trade or business, noting that all the facts of a particular situation must be examined. Under that case, a taxpayer is engaged in a trade or business if the taxpayer is involved in the activity (1) with continuity and regularity, and (2) with the primary purpose of making income or a profit.

Bypass trust

A bypass trust is a trust where a bequest equal to the value of the unified credit goes directly to the children, thus "bypassing" the surviving spouse's estate. Accompanying this transfer would normally be transfer of the remaining property to a marital deduction trust. This is one method of implementing a reduce to zero formula.

C

C corporation

A C corporation is a separate legal and taxable entity, subject to a graduated income tax schedule from 15 to 35 percent. If such a corporation pays dividends to its owners, these amounts are also subject to taxation at the individual shareholder level.

Cafeteria plan

A cafeteria plan is a separate written benefit plan maintained by an employer for the benefit of its employees, under which all participants are employees and each participant has the opportunity to select particular benefits. The participant may choose from among two or more benefits consisting of cash and qualified benefits.

Capital asset

The term capital asset in income tax law generally means all business and nonbusiness assets with the following exceptions: inventory, depreciable personal and real property, certain works created through personal efforts, business accounts and notes receivable, and certain U.S. publications. The term also excludes supplies, derivatives, and certain commodity and derivative instruments. Exclusions are laid out in Code Sec. 1221. Generally, any asset owned by an individual for personal or investment purposes is a capital asset.

Capital expenditure

A capital expenditure is one that is made for assets of a more or less permanent nature—those with a useful life of more than one year. Such an expenditure may not be deducted in the year made, even though made in connection with a trade or business. In other words, it is capitalized. But if the assets are wasting assets they may, in proper cases, be the subject of a depreciation deduction. Uniform capitalization rules require capitalization of certain costs and expenditures.

Capital gains properties

For purposes of the Code Sec. 170 charitable contribution rules, capital gains properties are those that would generate long-term capital gains if sold at fair market value. These are basically capital assets (personal assets and investment properties) held longer than one year.

Cash balance plan

A cash balance plan is a relatively new type of hybrid pension plan. Under this arrangement, the plan is funded by employer contributions but the employee assumes both the investment risks and rewards (the retirement benefit depends entirely on the investment performance). Although the employer bears the mortality risk if the employee lives longer than expected, the actual benefit is based on the invested amounts, not a promised amount.

Cash basis

See *cash method*.

Cash equivalent

A cash equivalent is the fair market value of property or services received as payment. This concept was developed in order to prevent cash-basis taxpayers from arranging to receive non-cash property or services in return for services rendered.

Cash flow analysis
A cash flow analysis is an indirect method used by the IRS to estimate underreported income. In this method, the Service basically tries to tie down all sources and uses of cash, both taxable and nontaxable. The Service uses numbers off the tax return whenever possible, and is especially careful in tying down the beginning and ending cash balances. Sometimes referred to as the Tennessee T-Account Method or Cash-T Account.

Cash horde defense
The cash horde defense is used to explain differences between income and spending to the IRS. The defense is that excess spending was from a cash stockpile built up from previous years.

Cash method
The cash method is one of the two principal recognized methods of accounting. It must be used by all taxpayers who do not keep books. It is elective as to all other taxpayers (except corporations, certain partnerships, and tax-exempt trusts); however, it may not be used if inventories are necessary in order to reflect income. On the cash basis, income is reported only as it is received, in money or other property having a fair market value, and expenses are deductible only in the year they are paid.

Cash or deferred arrangements (CODAs)
Cash or deferred arrangements are retirement plans in which the employee can choose between receiving currently taxable cash or voluntarily reducing salary by an amount that will be tax-deferred until retirement.

Cash-T Account
See *cash flow analysis*.

Charitable lead trust
A charitable lead trust involves a contribution of property to a trust. In this case the trust term is for a fixed period of years, and the income from the trust (after the asset is sold) goes to the charity. After the term of the trust expires, the remainder interest in the property passes directly to designated beneficiaries.

Charitable remainder annuity trust
In a charitable remainder annuity trust arrangement, a grantor makes a gift to a charity now, but reserves for himself or herself the income from the gifted property for life. The income from the property is paid to the grantor as a fixed dollar amount of income each year.

Charitable remainder unitrust
In a charitable remainder unitrust arrangement, a grantor makes a gift to a charity now, but reserves for himself or herself the income from the gifted property for life. The income from the property is paid to the grantor as a percentage of the value of the assets.

Check disbursements journal
A Check disbursements journal is a financial accounting book of original entry which summarizes and classifies all distributions of cash by the company.

Choice of entity
The choice of entity decision is one of the most important decisions facing tax professionals and their clients who own and operate businesses. There are several

forms to choose from, each of which generates different legal and tax consequences. There is no single form of entity that is appropriate for every type of business owner or entity that a practitioner is likely to encounter.

Claim-of-right

The claim-of-right doctrine is a judicially-based concept that holds that an amount is includible in income at the latest when it is received, provided that the taxpayer has an unrestricted right to the funds. This is so even if the amounts are received in error or the right to such income is contested and subsequent events require repayment. This doctrine reflects the basic principle that each tax year stands on its own.

Closed rule

The full House of Representatives generally debates a bill under a closed rule, whereby the only person who may amend the bill is a member of the Ways and Means Committee.

Closed transaction

A closed transaction is a transaction where all events to determine the tax consequences have occurred; in effect the item of income has been received, the expenditure has been made, or the transaction is otherwise closed.

Closing agreements

Closing agreements are binding agreements between the IRS and taxpayers authorized under Code Sec. 7121. Closing agreements finally and conclusively settle a tax issue between the IRS and a taxpayer unless there is a showing of fraud or malfeasance, or misrepresentation of a material fact.

Code Sec. 529 plans

Code Sec. 529 plans have become the vehicle of choice for funding college education of children because these plans are not subject to the same restrictions as the other options. Code Sec. 529 plans can be set up as either a prepaid tuition plan or a qualified savings plan. The prepaid plan is not as popular as the qualified savings plan, because it only covers tuition, and not fees, books, room and board, and other expenses. Only 18 states currently offer such plans, and many such plans limit the application of the funds to in-state schools. Contributions to the plan are not deductible, but benefits are not taxable if used for qualified educational purposes.

Code Sec. 1244 stock

Code Sec. 1244 allows a corporation to designate the first $1 million of original issue capital stock as "Code Sec. 1244 stock." With this designation, any individual or partner owner(s) may deduct the first $50,000 of losses each year ($100,000 on a joint return) as ordinary losses.

Code-based service

A Code-based service is a tax service tax that is organized by Internal Revenue Code section, from Section 1 to the end. All information relevant to that particular Code section is in a single location; this includes Regulations, committee report extracts, editorial explanations, and extracts of relevant cases and rulings. The coverage for each Code section is more or less in the form of short snippets, and is arranged to find answers to tax questions easily and quickly.

Community property

Community property is property owned by husband and wife in community, each sharing equally in the income therefrom. This concept of ownership is currently recognized by nine states.

COM

Compliance research

Compliance research, also known as after-the-event or closed transaction research, is any tax research performed after the fact. This is probably the most common type of research because the issues are typically identified during the preparation of the tax return or during an audit. In this type of research, the transaction has already taken place, so there is less flexibility because the facts are already certain. The tax advisor's goal is to find the optimal solution based on the given facts

Conduit entities

Conduit entities are nontaxable reporting entities. They pass through their income (loss) to owners (beneficiaries). All conduit entities are owned by one or more taxable entities. The income, deductions, losses, credits, and other tax attributes of conduit entities flow through to the tax returns of its owners. The two principal conduit entities are: the S corporation and the partnership.

Congressional Record

The Congressional Record is a record of all exchanges on the floor of Congress. The Congressional Record is the only source for determining legislative intent on amendments made on the floor of the House or Senate. The relevant discussion must be located by the day of the debate, no easy task. An important part of this document in regard to a discussion of tax law changes is the presence of colloquies and floor statements. These represent discussions between members of Congress and the managers (from the Joint Committee) of a tax bill that are intended to clarify specific provisions. These discussions are inserted into the Congressional Record.

Constructive receipt

Constructive receipt is a vehicle for preventing cash-basis taxpayers from avoiding recognition of income by delaying receipt. In general, income must be reported immediately when it can be reduced to the taxpayer's possession; a taxpayer may not delay recognition by avoiding receipt of the income. This doctrine is described more fully in Reg. §1.451-2(b). Under this doctrine, a taxpayer is taxed on interest income as it is earned, even though the taxpayer chooses not to withdraw the interest during the year.

Consumption tax

A consumption tax is a tax on spending rather than on income. Income is taxed when it is consumed, not when saved. Examples include sales tax and value-added tax. Consumption taxes exempt savings and allow businesses to deduct capital investments (such as land, buildings, and equipment) immediately, rather than through depreciation (as under the income tax system).

Contested liabilities

Contested liabilities include any liability that is subject to a legal dispute between the lender and the borrower. Code Sec. 461(h) provides a deduction for amounts placed into escrow while the dispute is being settled.

Correspondence audit

A correspondence audit is an audit that is conducted by either mail or telephone. These audits generally involve only one or two items on a return. The IRS generally sends a letter to the taxpayer questioning a single tax issue, such as charitable contributions, medical expenses or other itemized deductions. The letter will request additional information and ask the taxpayer to submit supporting documentation to the IRS. Supporting documentation may include receipts, cancelled checks, correspondence, etc. The IRS reviews the submitted documents and determines the necessary adjustments to the return, if any. The taxpayer is again notified by letter of any proposed changes and the resulting tax and interest.

Coverdale Education Savings Account (CESA)

Education IRAs, now known as a Coverdale Education Savings Accounts (CESAs), were established in 1997 to assist low- and middle-income taxpayers with higher education costs. An individual may contribute up to $2,000 per year to a CESA for a designated beneficiary until the beneficiary reaches age 18. Total contributions on behalf of one child are limited in total to $2,000.

Credit-invoice method

The credit-invoice method is a method of taxation where a tax is imposed on all sellers of goods by multiplying the invoice sales price of goods or services, and then subtracting a credit for all VAT paid on purchases of taxable goods and services (this credit is shown on the top of the invoice from the vendor, much like state and local sales taxes are shown on a grocery receipt). In effect, a tax is collected at each stage of the production process. A credit is not available to the final nonbusiness consumer of the product.

Crummey power

A Crummey power entitles each beneficiary of a life insurance trust to demand a distribution of the lesser of the amount transferred to the trust each year or the maximum annual gift tax exclusion.

Curtesy

Curtesy is a husband's legal right under state law to a portion or all of his wife's property upon her death.

D

Deceased Spouse Unused Exemption Amount (DSUEA)

The executor or executrix of the estate of the first spouse to die may elect to transfer to the second spouse any unused exemption amount (based on the unused unified credit) of the first spouse to die.

Deductions

Deductions are statutory reductions in gross income that are specifically granted in the Internal Revenue Code. They are to be distinguished from exclusions from gross income, which are not taken into income at all.

Deductions for adjusted gross income

Deductions for adjusted gross income are those deductions from gross income to compute adjusted gross income.

Deductions from adjusted gross income

Deductions from adjusted gross income are those deductions taken from adjusted gross income. These are generally personal or nonbusiness expenses.

Deferral items

Deferral items are those income items that are not taxable until a future year. Deferral items also describe temporary (timing) differences between regular tax and alternative minimum tax treatments of a particular item of income or deduction.

Defined benefit plan

A defined benefit plan is a retirement plan that determines by a specific formula the benefits an employee will receive. The formula will necessarily involve actuarial computations, and the employer assumes the risks associated with the plan (i.e., the employer has to "make good" on the promised benefit). The benefit is generally based on a combination of average compensation and years of service.

Defined contribution plan

A defined contribution plan is a retirement plan that determines in advance the amount the employer will contribute. This contribution does not involve actuarial computations, and the risks associated with the plan are born by the employee (the retirement benefit depends entirely on the investment performance). A defined contribution plan may be structured as a profit-sharing plan (a fixed formula based on profits), a money purchase pension plan (a fixed formula not based on profits), or a stock bonus plan (employer contributions of stock).

Determination Letter

A Determination Letter is issued by the office of a local IRS District Director in response to a request for a formal tax determination concerning a particular situation or transaction. Two of the most common uses for Determination Letters are questions regarding the tax-exempt status of an organization or questions regarding the qualification of a pension plan as a qualified plan under the Code. These letters are not published by the IRS.

Disclaimer

A disclaimer is a written refusal to accept a gift. A legal disclaimer must be given to a donor within nine months of a gift. If this occurs, then there is no gift for federal gift tax purposes.

Discriminant Function (DIF)

The Discriminant Function (DIF) system is a mathematical program used for identifying and selecting returns for examination. Mathematical formulas identify returns by assigning weights to certain return characteristics. The weights are then added together to produce a score for each return. Returns are then ranked in numerical sequence from the highest to lowest score. Generally, the higher the score, the greater the likelihood of a significant change on examination. The DIF mathematical formulas are kept confidential and examination departments are only provided the list of returns with high DIF scores, not the actual scores.

Dividends-received deduction

A corporation receives a 70 percent or 80 percent deduction—with limitations—for dividends it receives, unless it is an affiliated corporation which does not, or cannot, file a consolidated return. A 100-percent dividends-received deduction is allowed for dividends from a controlled subsidiary (at least an 80 percent interest).

Dollar-value inventory methods

Dollar-value inventory methods simplify inventory calculations by determining inventory cost on the basis of total dollars (for a base year) rather than the quantity and price of each inventory item. The primary advantage of these methods is that the inventory is viewed as a pool, not as a series of individual items.

Donor

The person giving a gift.

Double taxation

Double taxation occurs if a corporation pays dividends to its owners. These amounts are subject to taxation at the individual shareholder level as well as at the corporate level. This is the primary disadvantage of a corporation—the same amount of income is taxed twice (the "double taxation" dilemma).

Double-extension inventory valuation method

The double-extension inventory valuation method is perhaps the most commonly used method of dollar-value LIFO valuation. The two real advantages of the double-extension method are (1) detailed purchase records for each inventory item throughout the year are not necessary (only year-end prices and quantities are needed), and (2) decrements in one inventory item can be offset by increments in other inventory items through the aggregation procedure.

Dower

Dower is a wife's legal right under state law to a portion or all of her husband's property upon his death.

E

Economic performance

The point in time at which a liability is satisfied and the corresponding deduction is allowed (assuming that the "all events test" has been met). Economic performance occurs in one of four situations: (1) goods or services are provided to the taxpayer, (2) property is used by the taxpayer, (3) goods or services are provided by the taxpayer, or (4) the expenditure is classified as a payment liability.

Educational savings bonds

Educational savings bonds must be issued to a person at least 24 years old. A pro rata portion of any accrued interest on such bonds redeemed for these educational purposes is excludable; however, the exclusion phases out proportionately over the $15,000 of AGI exceeding $67,100 in 2008 (the $30,000 of AGI exceeding $100,650 if a joint return is filed). A special exclusion applies to U.S. Savings Bonds that are used to pay qualified higher education expenses.

Electronic Return Originator (ERO)

A tax return preparer can file returns electronically after becoming an Electronic Return Originator (ERO). An ERO may originate the electronic submission of income tax returns that are either prepared by the ERO firm, or collected from a taxpayer. A preparer can register to become a user on the Internal Revenue Service's (IRS) e-services web site. The registration process involves collecting personal and taxpayer data for the sole purpose of authenticating the preparer's identity.

En banc decision

An en banc decision is a decision that has been reviewed by the entire court.

Estate freezes

Estate freezes is a general expression for any estate planning technique that removes appreciation from an estate while retaining a non-appreciating controlling interest in the property or interest transferred.

Estate tax

The estate tax is a federal transfer tax that applies to transfers at death.

Exclusion items
Exclusion items are items of income specifically exempt from taxation under the Code. This is also a term used for permanent differences between regular tax and alternative minimum tax treatments of a particular item of income or deduction.

F

Fair market value
The fair market value of property is that amount which would induce a willing seller to sell and a willing buyer to buy the property. Market quotations are an acceptable measure of value, except where the quantity of property involved is so great that its sale would affect the market quotations before the sale is finished. Unlisted stocks sometimes are valued on the basis of the corporate assets, including goodwill, whether or not they are entered on the books. Real estate is valued on the basis of net earnings, location, etc., and this value is best proved by an expert appraisal.

Family limited partnership (FLP)
In a typical family limited partnership (FLP), a donor with business interests would form a limited partnership, transferring assets in exchange for both general and limited partnership units. (Because the entity is a partnership, at least one other family member, perhaps the donor's spouse, must also contribute assets in exchange for partnership units.) The general partnership units, traditionally a small fraction of ownership, are retained by the donor for control purposes. The donor would then begin gifting the limited partnership interests to his or her children annually, utilizing the annual exclusion. And since the donor is transferring minority interests in a largely unmarketable entity, he or she should be able to take advantage of minority and lack of marketability discounts on these transfers. Given the tax stakes involved, the discounts should be supported by qualified appraisals or valuation reports. Finally, upon the donor's death, the donor's interest in the partnership may qualify for discount due to a lack of marketability or a minority interest.

Field audit
A field audit is used mostly for business returns and larger, more complex individual returns and is conducted at the taxpayer's place of business or home. The revenue agents that perform field audits are the most experienced auditors. These audits usually involve tax issues that require a review of the taxpayer's books and records. The taxpayer may request that the audit be moved to the office of the taxpayer's representative (attorney or accountant). The agent will review the entire financial operations of the taxpayer, including the taxpayer's history, the system of internal controls, the location of business assets, and accounting methods. The audit will also include an examination of relevant business agreements or documents, a reconciliation of book income to taxable income, the testing of gross receipts, and verification of expense deductions.

Field Service Advice (FSA)
A Field Service Advice (FSA) is a memorandum issued by the National Office of the IRS to IRS Agents, Attorneys, and Appeals Officers who seek advice and guidance for either (1) developing an issue or (2) assessing litigation hazards.

Final Regulations
Final Regulations are published in the Federal Register as Treasury Decisions (TD), and then published in the weekly Internal Revenue Bulletin (and subsequently in the semi-annual Cumulative Bulletin). The date of publication in the Federal Register is the release date. Final regulations can be either interpretative or legislative.

First-in, first-out rule (FIFO)

This rule is generally applied to otherwise unidentifiable stocks where a number of shares of the same kind of stock have been bought at different times and different prices. If they cannot otherwise be identified, those which were purchased first are regarded as having been sold first in determining the cost price to be applied against the selling price for the purpose of determining any gain or loss on the sale. The term is also applied to inventory items where the LIFO method (see *Last-in, first-out rule,* below) is not used. As so used, the first-in, first-out rule is also referred to as the FIFO method.

Flexible spending account (FSA)

A flexible spending account (FSA) is a benefit described in Reg. §1.125-2. Under an FSA, an employee is provided coverage under which specified incurred expenses may be reimbursed, subject to certain reimbursement maximums and reasonable conditions. Under these arrangements, employees are permitted to make pre-tax contributions to FSAs for reimbursement of health and/or dependent care expenses. However, the amounts are subject to a "use it or lose it" rule, in that unused amounts at the end of the year are forfeited.

Future interest

A future interest is one in which the enjoyment of the property and the income from the property will not begin until a future date. Future interests include reversions and remainder interests. A gift of a future interest does not qualify for the exclusion.

G

General Council Memoranda (GCM)

General Council Memoranda (GCM) are generated by the office of the IRS Chief Counsel in response to a internal IRS requests for a legal analysis to be used in preparing such external pronouncements as Revenue Rulings, Private Letter Rulings, and Technical Advice Memorandums. GCMs generally provide an indication regarding the IRS position in an upcoming ruling, but since they are internal documents, they are not binding authority.

General partners

General partners are those partners who are responsible for the ongoing operations of the business. General partners are fully liable for the debts of the partnership.

General power of appointment

A general power of appointment allows the holder to appoint anyone to enjoy the property, including the holder himself or herself and his or her creditors, estate, or creditors of the estate. When the holder of a general power of appointment dies, the fair market value of the property subject to the power is included in his or her gross estate. Furthermore, the holder is deemed to own the property for income tax purposes as well, and is taxed on the income from the property each year even though he or she never exercises the power on his or her own behalf.

Generally accepted accounting principles (GAAP)

Generally accepted accounting principles are the standards used by the accounting profession to prepare financial statements for users outside of the reporting entity.

Generation-skipping transfer tax (GSST)

A generation-skipping transfer tax (GSST) was enacted by Congress in order to prevent family gifts that "skip" a generation and hence avoid a layer of possible estate taxes. In general, a transfer tax is computed for the "skipped" generation, using the highest gift (or estate) rates applicable. For example, a taxpayer may make a direct gift to her grandson. By "skipping" her child (the grandson's parent), a transfer tax on an intervening generation is avoided. To prevent this possibility, the GSST would be imposed on the transfer at the highest estate tax rate (currently 45 percent).

Gift tax
The gift tax is the tax on any transfer of assets between two taxpayers where no consideration for the transfer is provided to the donor.

Gift tax add-on
Gift tax add-on is the term for a portion of the gift tax paid by a donor that is added to the donor's basis to determine the donee's basis in the property. The portion is for any gift tax paid that is related to the appreciation in value of the property.

Gift tax charitable deduction
An unlimited gift tax charitable deduction exists for gifts to recognized charities of present interests in property.

Gift-splitting
Gift-splitting is a technique used by married couples to get around the gift tax. Each spouse is treated as making one half of the value of the gift, and each reports such amounts on his or her gift tax return (there is no "joint gift tax return"). If a husband and wife elect gift splitting all gifts to third parties, this effectively doubles the annual exclusion to $24,000 per year.

Grantor
A grantor is the person who establishes a legal contract where the legal title and management of his or her property is handled by a trustee for the beneficial enjoyment of one or more beneficiaries.

Grantor Retained Annuity Trust (GRAT)
A Grantor Retained Annuity Trust (GRAT) is a qualified interest that is not subject to the zero valuation rule for any retained income interest. A GRAT is an irrevocable trust to which the grantor transfers an asset, retaining the right to receive a fixed annuity for a stated term of years or for the shorter of the stated term or the grantor's earlier death (a contingent term).

Grantor Retained Income Trust (GRIT)
In a Grantor Retained Income Trust (GRIT), a grantor would typically transfer either investment property or a business interest to a trust, reserving an interest in all the income from the property for the trust term and leaving the remainder for family members at death.

Grantor Retained Unitrust (GRUT)
A Grantor Retained Unitrust (GRUT) is just a variation of a GRAT. In a GRUT, the amount paid to the grantor is expressed as a percentage of the fair market value of trust assets each year as recalculated by the trust. Otherwise, the same valuation principles illustrated above also apply to a GRUT.

Gross up rule
The gross up rule exists to prevent deathbed gifts designed to remove the gift tax paid from the gross estate owned at death. Any gift taxes paid within three years of death are added back to the gross estate under the gross up rule.

Guaranteed payments

Guaranteed payments are those payments made by a partnership to a partner such as salary that are guaranteed without reference to the profitability of the partnership.

H

Health reimbursement arrangement (HRA)

A health reimbursement arrangement (HRA) is a benefit plan that the employer pays for. The payment is not related to a salary reduction election by the employee; the plan reimburses the employee for qualifying medical expenses of the employee and dependents; and the plan provides for reimbursements up to a maximum dollar amount for a coverage period, and any unused portion is carried forward to increase maximum reimbursement in future periods. When these conditions are met, coverage and reimbursement of medical expenses of the employee, spouse, and dependents are generally excludable from income.

Health savings accounts (HSAs)

HSAs are available to individuals with high deductible health plans (HDHP). For 2008, the minimum deductible is $1,100 for individual coverage and $2,200 for family coverage, but the out-of-pocket expense maximum is $5,600 for individuals and $11,200 for families. Out-of-pocket expenses include deductibles, co-payments and other amounts (other than premiums) that must be paid for plan benefits. No amounts can be paid from the HDHP until the family has incurred covered medical expenses in excess of the minimum annual deductible.

Hobby

A hobby is (1) an ongoing personal effort of an entrepreneurial nature and (2) pursued in good faith and with regularity, yet the primary motive for the activity is personal enjoyment rather than making a profit. If the activity is profitable for at least three out of five years (seven years for racehorse activities), then the activity is presumed to be a business rather than a hobby. If the presumptive rule is met, the burden of proof is on the IRS to demonstrate that the taxpayer's primary intent is personal enjoyment rather than to make a profit.

Horizontal conflicts

Horizontal conflicts are conflicts of opinion between courts at the same level, for example, two different trial courts, including two different district courts, the Tax Court and the Court of Federal Claims, or the Tax Court and a district court. In many horizontal conflicts, the courts have equal authority and are not bound by the decision of the conflicting court.

Horizontal equity

The principle of horizontal equity states that taxpayers with equal incomes should pay equal taxes.

Hybrid method

A hybrid method of accounting is specifically permitted by Code Sec. 446(c)(4). A hybrid method is any accounting method where two or more permissible methods are combined into one method.

I

Incentive stock option (ISO)

The incentive stock option is a statutory employee stock option. No income tax consequences result from the grant or exercise of such an option, and, if holding and other requirements are met, gain on eventual sale of the employer's stock will be long-term capital gain.

Income in respect of a decedent

Income in respect of a decedent is income earned by a decedent but not reportable by the decedent at the time of his or her death. Instead, the beneficiary of such income reports such income by "stepping in the shoes" of the decedent.

Individual Retirement Account (IRA)

An Individual Retirement Account (IRA) is an account to which any individual may contribute 100 percent of earned income, up to $4,000 a year, ($8,000 on a joint return, i.e. $4,000 per spouse). Taxpayers over age 50 are allowed to contribute an additional $1,000. The contributions are deductible from gross income, except for individuals who participate in a qualified deferred compensation plan with AGI over a certain level ($53,000 in 2008, and for joint filers, $85,000 in 2008). The investment grows tax-deferred, but all withdrawals constitute gross income. A 10 percent penalty on gross income is levied on pre-age 59 1/2 withdrawals, except on account of disability, death, first-time home purchases (up to $10,000), insurance premiums for the unemployed, deductible medical expenses, as well as withdrawals in the shape of annuities. Withdrawals must start with respect to the year the participant reaches age 70 1/2. An IRA may receive tax-deferred rollovers from other qualified plans, including other IRAs. Distributions from IRAs are not subject to withholding.

Intentionally Defective Irrevocable Trust (IDIT)

An Intentionally Defective Irrevocable Trust (IDIT) is a relatively new tool in the estate planner's arsenal. This is not for the faint-hearted, as the technique has not been vetted by the Courts yet. In general, the strategy involves setting up an irrevocable trust that is treated as a grantor trust (taxed to the grantor) for income tax purposes only.

Inter vivos

An inter vivos trust, or living trust, is a trust created during the lifetime of the person setting up the trust. A testamentary trust is one set up under the will of the decedent.

Intestate laws

Intestate laws are the laws that determine what happens when a person dies without a will.

Investment interest expense

Investment interest expense is any interest expense incurred on funds borrowed to acquire investment property.

Involuntary conversion

An involuntary conversion of property results when property is destroyed in whole or in part, stolen, seized, requisitioned or condemned (or where there is a threat or imminence of requisition or condemnation) and, as a result, the property is converted into money or other similar property, through insurance proceeds, condemnation awards, etc. The law has special provisions on involuntary conversion only where the conversion results in gain—that is, where the amount recovered exceeds the cost or other basis of the property converted. The law permits the nonrecognition of gain on such an involuntary conversion.

Irrevocable

An irrevocable trust is a trust that is set up so that the grantor cannot revoke it at any time.

J

Joint Committee on Taxation Report (the Blue Book)

The Joint Committee on Taxation issues a final report on the tax legislative process commonly called the "Blue Book" due to the color of the cover on the paperback edition. The Joint Committee on Taxation Report includes the same four elements that the Ways and Means Committee and Senate Finance Committee reports: (1) a draft of the legislation, (2) reasons for the changes, (3) an explanation of the changes, and (4) an estimate of the revenue effects of the change. All of these elements change as a bill moves through the process, so in many respects the Blue Book is the most accurate and comprehensive explanation of a new law.

Joint tenancy

Where property is held in the names of two or more persons with the title passing from the first joint tenant to die to the other joint tenant (or joint tenants) upon death. The creation of a joint tenancy in property generally results in a taxable gift, equal to the portion of the value of the property gifted to the new joint tenant by the original (and sole) owner of the property.

Judicial authority

Judicial authority includes any decisions of the federal courts on tax matters.

K

Keogh (HR-10) plan

A Keogh (or HR-10) plan is a special retirement plan for self-employed individuals. These are much like qualified corporate plans; the maximum contribution and deduction amounts for contributions on behalf of employees are the same as for qualified corporate plans. Coverage and vesting rules are also the same. A plan must be established before the end of the tax year; however, contributions may be made up until the due date of the return and deducted for the earlier year.

Kiddie tax

See *allocable parental tax*.

L

Lapse

Lapse is the expiration of an option period specified in a contract. The term signifies that the option was not exercised.

Last-in, first-out rule (LIFO)

LIFO is the popular abbreviation for the last-in, first-out rule for identifying items in an inventory to determine their cost. By this method, goods remaining on hand at the close of the taxable year are treated as being, first, those included in the opening inventory to the extent thereof, and, second, those acquired during the taxable year.

Legislative authority

Legislative authority refers to tax authority enacted by the legislative body, the United States Congress. Tax bills passed by Congress are added to Title 26 of the U.S. Code and have the force and effect of law, unless they are found to be unconstitutional. Legislative authority also includes the various committee reports issued by the tax-writing committees in Congress, as well as tax treaties involving the United States.

Leveraging

Leveraging is the process of using limited cash outlays to acquire much larger benefits. Leveraging usually involves the use of debt.

Life estate

See *life interest*.

Life interest

Also called a life estate, a life interest is a legal right to the income from a property or trust for the holder's natural life.

Limited liability company (LLC)

A limited liability company (LLC) is an unincorporated entity which combines the flow-through characteristics of a partnership with the limited liability of a corporation. In the LLC, no member is personally liable for the debts of the entity.

Limited liability partnership (LLP)

A limited liability partnership (LLP) combines the flow-through characteristics of a partnership with the limited liability of a corporation. In the LLP, liability relief is somewhat restricted in that the partner can be held personally liable for claims arising from malpractice by the partner.

Limited partnership

A limited partnership is a partnership where one or more general partners are responsible for the ongoing operations of the business and at least one limited partner is only an investor and does not participate in management. The limited partner's liability for the debts of the partnership cannot exceed his or her investment in the partnership.

Limited power of appointment

A limited power of appointment allows the holder to appoint anyone but himself or herself (or his or her creditors, estate, or estate creditors) to enjoy the property. In this case, there are no gift or estate tax consequences to the holder of such a power.

Living trust

A living trust comes into being when a grantor transfers property to a trustee under a written arrangement that generally provides that all income is to be paid to the grantor for his or her remaining life, as well as any amounts of principal so designated by the grantor. Upon the death of the grantor, the trust becomes irrevocable, as the property passes directly to beneficiaries designated by the grantor.

Losses

Losses are expenditures that do not produce a benefit, as opposed to expenses that do produce a benefit. Such costs may be deductible under Code Sec. 165.

M

Marital deduction

A marital deduction is an unlimited deduction allowed against any gift or transfer at death to a spouse that is not a terminal interest.

Marital deduction trust

A marital deduction trust is a trust set up for property transferred to a spouse (either as a gift or a bequest) that will qualify for the unlimited marital deduction.

Material participation

The IRS defined material participation in Reg. §1.469-1 as being met if the taxpayer meets any of seven basic tests.

Memorandum Decision

A Memorandum Decision typically involves either a straightforward application of existing law or an interpretation of facts. These decisions are not published by the Court. There are approximately 500 to 600 Memorandum decisions each year.

Minimum tax credit

The basic theory of the minimum tax credit is that a portion or all of the AMT paid during a tax year may be used in future years as a credit against regular tax liability in those years. However, in no case can such a credit reduce the carryover year's regular tax liability below the tentative minimum tax liability for that year. There is no limit on the number of years that an AMT credit may be carried forward.

Minority discount

The minority discount valuation rests on the simple theory that the sum of the fractional shares of a business does not necessarily equal the whole. A person with a minority interest in a business has little or no control over the business, and a minority shareholder (or partner) also has little or no say about whether dividends are declared, how cash flows are distributed, or whether the company should be sold or liquidated.

N

Necessary

To be necessary an expense must be capable of making a contribution to a trade or business. Fortunately for the taxpayer, the courts and tax administrators do not insist that necessity be determined in retrospect; it is sufficient if the expense appeared to be appropriate and helpful at the time it was incurred. The "prudent person" test is applied; if, in the same circumstances, a prudent person would have incurred the expense in the expectation that it would be helpful in the taxpayer's business, it will likely be deemed "necessary."

Net investment income

Net investment income is the excess of investment income less investment expenses. This amount sets an upper limit on any investment interest deduction for the tax year.

Net worth method

The net worth method is an indirect method used by the IRS to estimate income. This technique compares a taxpayer's net worth based on comparative balance sheets using historical costs at the beginning and end of a tax year, and then adds all consumption expenditures for the year (which, of course, would not be reflected in the ending net worth figure). A taxpayer is given a chance to explain where the money came from to create a discrepancy between reported income and estimated income with the net worth method.

Nexus
Nexus is the necessary relationship between a state and the transaction, property, or party the state seeks to tax.

Nonqualified plans
Nonqualified plans are those benefit plans that do not meet the specific qualification requirements of the Code (usually because the plans benefit small groups of employees, violating the broad coverage requirements of qualified plans). While these plans may be more flexible, the employer does not receive a deduction until the employee reports the amount as income.

Not-for-Profit (NFP) entities
Not-for-Profit (NFP) entites are nontaxable reporting entities that have been organized to carry on a tax-exempt purpose. An NFP entity must apply for and receive tax-exempt status from the IRS.

O

Offers in compromise
An offer in compromise is a procedure for settling unpaid tax accounts for less than the full amount of the assessed balance due. The offer in compromise is made by the taxpayer and may cover all taxes, interest and penalties owed. Once an offer in compromise is accepted by the IRS, a contract exists whereby the taxpayer must comply with all the terms of the offer in compromise in exchange for the IRS's agreement to reduce the tax liability owed.

Office audit
An office audit is an audit conducted in a local IRS office. These audits are complex, usually involving issues that will require some analysis or judgment on the part of the examiner. The returns selected for office audit are generally individual returns that may or may not have a small amount of business income. The returns usually involve common items such as dependency exemptions, travel and entertainment expenses, casualty losses, income from rents and royalties, and income from partnerships and trusts. Once a return is selected for an office audit, the taxpayer will receive a letter in the mail (called an appointment letter) informing him/her of the audit and requesting the taxpayer to bring in documentation supporting the items on the tax return that are being questioned.

One-year rule
The one-year rule is an expression coined from the *Zaninovich* case, whereby any prepaid expense that will be incurred within one year of a prepayment is generally deductible.

Open rule
The Senate debates bills under an open rule, whereby any Senator may propose amendments to any bill.

Open transaction
See *open transaction doctrine*.

Open transaction doctrine

The open transaction doctrine was formally established in the case of *Edith Logan*. The doctrine allows for transactions where nothing is taxed until the taxpayer recovers his or her basis. The lack of an ascertainable value of the property received means that the transaction cannot be closed.

Ordinary

The essence of the ordinary criterion seems to be that the expense would be acceptable or commonplace among other taxpayers who find themselves in comparable circumstances.

P

Partnership

A partnership does not pay taxes. It is a conduit for nontaxable income, dividend income, partially taxable interest, ordinary income, and the capital gains and losses shares to be taken into the income of the individual partners. For income tax purposes, the term partnership is more comprehensive than when taken in its ordinary meaning. It includes a syndicate, group, pool and joint venture, as well as an ordinary partnership, in which two or more persons join their money and/or their skills in carrying on as co-owners a business for profit. If the organization of a limited partnership is more in the nature of an association than a partnership, it is deemed to be an association taxable as a corporation.

Partnership ordinary income

Partnership ordinary income includes only those items of income and expense that could not vary in treatment across the individual partner's tax returns (i.e., sales revenue, cost of goods sold, advertising expense, etc.).

Passive activity limitations (PAL)

A short-hand reference to the Code Sec. 469 rules which limit loss deductions from passive activities (those trades or businesses without material participation) to incomes from passive activities. The passive activity limits were enacted in 1986 to limit losses from certain tax-shelter activities labeled as "passive activities" in the legislation. The typical tax shelter investment (such as a rental property) was characterized by little risk to the owner, net losses for tax purposes, and positive cash flows (because of such large noncash deductions as depreciation). See Code Sec. 469.

Pension maximization

Pension maximization, or pension-max for short, refers to a strategy to provide income security to a surviving spouse. This strategy suggests that the retiree might be better off to elect the single annuity on retirement and then invest the after-tax monthly income in excess of what the joint and survivor annuity would have been in a universal term-life insurance policy on his or her life with his or her spouse as beneficiary. If the retiree dies first, the surviving spouse would then use the life insurance proceeds to purchase a lifetime income annuity. If the after-tax monthly income from this annuity exceeds what the joint and survivor benefit would have originally been from the retirement account, then the pension maximization strategy was successful.

Permanent differences

Permanent differences are those differences between financial and tax accounting income that will never reverse. "Permanent" adjustment items are listed in Code Sec. 56(b)(1), and the "permanent" preference items are listed in paragraphs (1),

(5), and (7) of Code Sec. 57(a). Permanent differences also describe temporary (timing) differences between regular tax and alternative minimum tax treatments of a particular item of income or deduction.

Personal service corporation (PSC)

A personal service corporation is a corporation whose principal activity is the performance of personal services that are substantially performed by employee-owners. It must be a C corporation for the tax year. Its principal activity during the testing period for the tax year must be the performance of personal services. During the testing period for the tax year, those services must be substantially performed by employee-owners. More than 10 percent of the fair market value of its outstanding stock must be owned by employee-owners on the last day of the testing period for the tax year.

Personalty

Personalty includes all tangible property that is not realty.

Planning research

Planning research (also know as before-the-event or open transaction research) is research performed before the client takes an action, before the facts are certain. This type of research allows the practitioner to clearly demonstrate the benefits of research by participating in the structuring of transactions and minimizing the associated taxes. The tax advisor's goal is to identify the optimal set of facts to achieve the client's desired business and tax outcomes. This type of research generally results from continued contact with the client throughout the year where the client shares thoughts and ideas about new directions for the company.

Pocket veto

A pocket veto occurs if Congress adjourns within the ten-day period after it passes legislation and the President does not sign the bill. The effect is the same as a veto.

Policy research

Policy research includes analyzing different tax reform proposals being considered by Congress. It may also involve research to influence legislation for clients or to promote a tax position for the profession. Policy-type research may also be performed for education purposes. Professionals must learn new law in order to stay current and this often requires research into the legislative history, the Joint Committee's blue book, and IRS notices.

Pour-over provision

A pour-over provision is a provision in a will that transfers property owned by the grantor at death to the trust through the regular probate process. In effect, this provision "sweeps" any remaining assets outside the trust into the trust at death.

Preferences

Preferences are items that must be added back to taxable income for AMT purposes. They generally originated from pre-1987 tax year concepts and activities (e.g., accelerated depreciation on real estate). Preferences are somewhat similar to adjustments, with one major difference: preferences are taken into account only when they are positive (negative preference items are ignored).

Present interest

A present interest simply means that the donee can immediately enjoy the benefits of possessing and using the property.

Primary authority

Primary authority is derived from the "official" body of tax law, consisting of the Internal Revenue Code as drafted by Congress, Regulations and other pronouncements of the Department of the Treasury, and judicial decisions devoted to tax issues.

Prior transfer tax credit

If property included in the decedent's estate was also subject to another round of estate taxes within the past 10 years (or 2 years after death), a portion of the prior estate taxes paid may be taken as a prior transfer tax credit on the decedent's return. The credit is the lesser of the marginal estate taxes due on the decedent's current estate tax return or the prior estate tax return. Furthermore, the percentage of the credit allowed is 100 percent if the second death occurs within two years of the first death, and that percentage decreases by 20 percent for each additional two years separating the two deaths.

Private Letter Rulings

Private Letter Rulings are issued by the IRS National Office in response to taxpayers' requests for the IRS's position on a particular tax issue. such requests receive a more limited review by the National Office of the IRS at the Group or Section levels only. Such rulings are not published (in print) by the IRS.

Probate estate

Probate estate refers to the legal process of administering a decedent's estate. Property subject to the probate process includes any property passing under the terms of the decedent's will or any property passing under terms of state intestate laws.

Progressive tax rate

A progressive tax rate is one where the tax rate increases as the taxpayer's income increases.

Proposed Regulations

At the beginning of the year, the Treasury schedules Regulation projects for the year. A task force is formed for each Regulation project, consisting principally of attorneys, economists, and CPAs in the Chief Counsel's office. Once the task force completes a draft of a regulation, it is published in the Federal Register as a Proposed Treasury Decision (TD). Interested parties are given 30 days to comment (in writing or orally) on the Proposed Regulations. As long as a Regulation is a Proposed Regulation, it does not have the force and effect of law of a Final Regulation. Nonetheless, the Proposed Regulation provides clues as to the IRS position on an issue, and should be considered when contemplating future transactions.

Q

Qualified Personal Residence Trust (QPRT)

A qualified personal residence trust (QPRT) is a trust funded by a grantor's personal residence, whereby the grantor retains an income interest in the property (or a right to use the property) for a limited period of time, with the remainder interest passing to a deemed beneficiary.

Qualified terminal interest property (QTIP)

Qualified terminal interest property (QTIP) is property transferred to a spouse in which all rights to the property terminate with the spouse's death (such as a life estate in the property). However, the transfer qualifies for the marital deduction because of a special QTIP election by the transferor spouse (if a lifetime gift) or his or her estate (if a transfer at death).

Question of fact

A question of fact is a question as to how the law applies when a particular set of facts is unclear.

Question of law

A question of law is a situation when an interpretation of a statute is unclear, the more important court decisions tend to focus on questions of law.

R

Reasonable

As a practical matter, the reasonableness criterion is typically at issue in the case of compensation of related taxpayers. Reasonable compensation is the amount that would ordinarily be paid for like services by like enterprises under like circumstances. Thus, every case of reasonable compensation must stand on its own facts and circumstances.

Receipts and Disbursements

See *bank deposit*.

Recurring item exception

Under the recurring item exception, a liability is treated as being incurred during the taxable year in question if (1) the all events test is met as of the end of the year, (2) economic performance occurs before the earlier of the due date of the return (including extensions) or the 15th day of the 9th month following the close of the tax year, (3) the item is recurring in nature, and (4) the liability is either not material or the accrual in the current year results in a better matching of income and expenses

Reduce to zero

A reduce to zero clause is a methods of fine-tuning the marital deduction in a will. This is essentially a statement that the actual amount transferred to the surviving spouse will be the amount that reduces the gross estate to the amount of the exemption equivalent of the unified credit for the year of death, and thus the estate tax due is reduced to zero.

Regular decision

A Regular decision generally involves an important new or unusual point of law. Such a decision is published by the Tax Court through the Government Printing Office. There are approximately 60 to 70 regular decisions per year.

Remainder interest

A remainder interest is a property interest passing to a beneficiary after the expiration of an income interest related to the property. The most common example is a marital trust, where the income from the trust property (a "life" interest) is assigned to a spouse for his or her lifetime, with the underlying property passing to designated beneficiaries at the spouse's death.

Rental real estate exception

A taxpayer who owns at least a 10-percent interest without limited liability in residential real estate may deduct the first $25,000 of such losses against any type of income; in other words, these losses "escape" the passive basket. However, the

$25,000 maximum is reduced $.50 for each dollar of AGI of the taxpayer (computed without considering passive activities) exceeding $100,000. Thus, the rental real estate exception is completely phased out for a taxpayer with AGI of $150,000 or greater.

Revenue Procedures

Revenue Procedures, as defined in Reg. §601.601 are "statements of procedure affecting the rights or duties of taxpayers or other members of the public under the Code and related tax laws, or of information that should be a matter of public knowledge." These pronouncements essentially describe the internal practices and procedures of the IRS in administering the federal tax laws. These include guidance on filing requirements and special requirements for elections under the Code.

Revenue Rulings

Revenue Rulings are official IRS interpretations of the tax consequences of the Code's application in a specific unnamed hypothetical taxpayer's situation (i.e., a specific set of facts). Unlike Regulations, they are not general statements of authority.

Revocable

A revocable trust can be revoked by the grantor at any time.

Roth IRA

A Roth IRA is a "back-loaded" IRA where allowable nondeductible contributions up to $4,000 will be proportionately phased out over AGI ranges of $159,000–$169,000 for joint filers, $101,000–$116,000 for single filers, and $0–$10,000 for married-filing separately filers.

S

S corporation

An S corporation is a special-status corporation for tax purposes, in that it is essentially treated as a partnership for federal tax purposes (a conduit, thus avoiding the double taxation problem of a C corporation). But since the entity is a corporation in all other respects, the entity offers limited liability for its owners.

Savings Incentive Match Plans for Employees (SIMPLE)

A Savings Incentive Match Plans for Employees (SIMPLE) plan is an alternative to the more complicated qualified corporate or Keogh plans. A SIMPLE plan may be adopted by any employer that had 100 or fewer employees who received at least $5,000 in compensation from the employer in the preceding year.

Sec. 1202 stock

Under Code Sec. 1202, a noncorporate taxpayer can exclude from gross income 50 percent of any gain from the sale or exchange of qualified small business stock held for more than five years. Qualifying corporations must have aggregate gross assets not exceeding $50 million at the time of the issue. Corporations engaging in personal services do not qualify.

Secondary authority

Secondary authority includes all unofficial sources of tax information that are helpful in clarifying complex tax issues. Examples of secondary authority are tax services (such as CCH's Standard Federal Income Tax Reporter, RIA's Federal Tax Coordinator, and BNA's Tax Management Portfolios), journals, textbooks, newsletters, and treatises.

Self-canceling installment note (SCIN)
A provision in an installment note that provides that the installment payments continue until the total sales price is received or the seller dies, whichever occurs first.

Significant participation
Significant participation in an activity occurs when a taxpayer participates more than 100 hours (but less than or equal to 500 hours) in an activity and no one else participated more.

SIMPLE-IRAs
A SIMPLE-IRA is a type of SIMPLE plan that deposits contributions into individual retirement accounts or annuities on behalf of employees. A SIMPLE-IRA is created after the employer and employee complete IRS Form 5304-SIMPLE or Form 5305-SIMPLE. Form 5304 is used if an employer allows each plan participant to select the financial institution that will receive contributions under the plan.

Simplified dollar-value inventory method
The Simplified Dollar Value Inventory Method is a dollar-value LIFO inventory method that groups inventories into various pools and uses price indices to value the ending inventories in a link-chain fashion.

Simplified Employee Pension plan (SEP)
A Simplified Employee Pension (SEP) plan is a retirement plan that small businesses may use to avoid the administrative complexity of qualified plans. For SEPs, the employer makes contributions directly to IRAs established for its employees (and the owner as well). A SEP can be established even if the self-employed person is the only employee. Contributions can be made up to the due date of the return; however, unlike a Keogh, the account may be established up until the due date of the return (including extensions).

Simplified production inventory method
The simplified production inventory method is an elective uniform capitalization (UNICAP) method for inventories, which assigns additional Code Sec. 263A unicap costs to traditional inventory values based on an absorption ratio. This ratio is the "normal" Sec. 471 costs in ending inventory divided by total "normal" Sec. 471 costs incurred during the year. The resulting ratio is multiplied by identifiable Sec. 263A costs incurred for the year, and the result is added to the Sec. 471 inventory total.

Sole proprietorship
The sole proprietorship is the most common type of business entity in the United States. It also is the simplest to organize and to discontinue. No legal formalities are needed because the business and the individual are treated as one entity under tax law.

Stare decisis
Translated literally, stare decisis means "let the decision stand." In other words, courts are hesitant to overturn their own decisions for fear of creating more ambiguity in the law. Therefore, any decisions of a court related to the issue at hand should be considered carefully for their value as a precedent. Each Circuit Court follows a doctrine of stare decisis, in that the Court will always follow its own decisions as precedents; however, one Circuit Court is not required to follow another Circuit Court's decisions (but they may choose to do so, in the interests of promoting consistency in the judicial system). A Circuit Court is bound only to follow decisions of the U.S. Supreme Court.

Substantial authority

Substantial authority is an objective standard involving an analysis of the law and application of the law to relevant facts. There is substantial authority for the tax treatment of an item only if the weight of the authorities supporting the treatment is substantial in relation to the weight of authorities supporting contrary treatment.

Substantial economic effect

Substantial economic effect is an expression related to the allocation of items of income, expense, gain, loss, and credits to partners by a partnership. In order to justify such allocations, the partnership agreement should provide that such allocations have real economic effects exclusive of tax benefits.

Subtraction method

Under the subtraction method, the VAT is calculated as the tax rate times the difference between a taxpayer's taxable sales and purchases of taxable goods (or services) from other taxpayers. In this case, the rate is applied to the net value added.

T

Tacking of holding periods

Tacking refers to the process of including the holding period of a prior owner or a prior property with the actual physical holding period of property. For example, in the case of gift property, if the donor's basis is used, the donor's holding period is added to the donee's holding period (this is referred to as a "tacking" of holding periods). On the other hand, if the fair market value is used as the basis, there is no tacking of holding periods. Note the consistency of these holding period tacking rules; the donor's holding period is included only if the donor's adjusted basis is used in the gain or loss computation.

Tax benefit

The tax benefit rule requires inclusion in income of any amount that was erroneously deducted in a prior year, but only to the extent that the deduction generated a tax benefit in that year. This rule is the reason, for example, that a taxpayer must include a state income tax refund in taxable income in the year received, but only if the taxpayer itemized in the prior year (i.e., benefited from a tax deduction). The same logic applies to unexpected reimbursement of a medical expense that was deducted in the previous tax year. the tax benefit is a largely judicially-defined concept; little is said about this doctrine in the Code, other than Code Sec. 111(a).

Tax home

For federal tax purposes, the IRS and the courts typically define a taxpayer's home as the taxpayer's work location (i.e., "post of duty"), and not the physical residence (the "taxpayer's abode").

Tax return preparer

A tax return preparer is any person who prepares for compensation or employs or engages another to prepare, all or a substantial portion of any tax return or refund claim. In order to be subject to the return preparer sanctions, a person must prepare a return for compensation.

Taxable entities

A taxable entity is any "person" as defined in Code Sec. 7701(a). Taxable business entities include the individual (doing business as a sole proprietorship), the regular C corporation, and some estates and trusts.

Tax-exclusive

A tax-exclusive tax rate refers to the amount of tax paid as a proportion of the pretax value of whatever is taxed; sales tax rates are typically expressed in tax-exclusive terms.

Tax-inclusive

A tax-inclusive rate refers to the amount of tax paid as a proportion of the after-tax value; income tax rates are often expressed in tax-inclusive terms.

Technical Advice Memoranda (TAM)

A Technical Advice Memorandum (TAM) is another type of letter ruling issued by the IRS. A TAM represents the IRS's response to a request by an IRS District Director or Appeals Officer regarding a technical question that develops during an audit. The response requires a high level of expertise and a consistent approach by the IRS. In contrast to a PLR, a TAM generally involves a completed transaction.

Temporary Regulations

Temporary Regulations are those Regulations issued by the IRS without the normal comment period. They are generally effective on the date of issuance. These Regulations are "fast lane" guidance, in that most are drafted in response to a law change or a judicial decision that requires immediate guidance. Generally, such Regulations are issued when the requirements for public notice are impracticable, unnecessary, or contrary to the public interest. Temporary Regulations must be issued as Proposed Regulations at the same time and automatically expire three years after issuance.

Tenancy by the entirety

Generally speaking, a tenancy by the entirety is a joint tenancy between husband and wife. A tenancy by the entirety cannot be terminated except by the joint action of the husband and wife during their lives. This is in contrast to a joint tenancy, which either party may terminate merely by conveying the interest to another party.

Tenancy in common

A tenancy in common is a form of ownership where title is held by two or more persons with each owning a fractional interest in the undivided property. Upon the death of one tenant in common, the interest will not pass to the surviving tenant in common but will become part of the deceased tenant's probate estate and will be distributed according to such tenant's will.

Tentative minimum tax

The tentative minimum tax, a component of the alternative minimum tax (AMT), is the sum of a taxpayer's regular taxable income plus or minus AMT adjustments, plus preferences, and less the AMT credit. The excess of the tentative minimum tax over the regular tax liability is the "alternative minimum tax".

Terminal interest

A terminal interest is an interest that extinguishes due to a lapse of time (such as a patent) or the death of the spouse (an income interest, or life estate, in property that passes automatically under the will to someone else, and the spouse cannot control the disposition). There are two important exceptions to the terminal interest rules: the power of appointment trust and the qualified terminal interest property (QTIP) election.

Testamentary trust

A trust which is set up under the will of the decedent. Conversely, an inter vivos trust is one set up during the lifetime of the person setting up the trust.

Timing differences

Timing differences is an expression for book-tax differences that are due solely to differing points of recognition, i.e., the differences eventually reverse over time. The expression is also used for certain regular tax/alternative minimum tax adjustments and preferences that also reverse over time.

Topics-based service

A topics-based service is a secondary tax service organized around logical tax topics, such as depreciation or partnerships, and not the Code. Thus, one topic may involve a number of different Code sections (e.g., partnerships). In contrast to a Code-based service, the coverage of the topic is in narrative form. Reading such a service is like reading a reference book; all relevant cases and rulings are discussed in the narrative and footnoted for reference. A topics-based service is designed for the tax professional who wants to learn more about a topic, in addition to just finding a simple answer to a question.

Trade or business

A trade or business consists of any activity that occupies the time, attention, and labor of individuals for the purpose of earning a livelihood or making a profit. It includes the rendering of services to others as an employee for compensation, the carrying on of a profession, and every business occupation carried on for subsistence or profit and into which the elements of bargain and sale, barter, exchange, or traffic enter.

Trust

A trust is a legal contract established by a grantor where the legal title and management of the property is handled by a trustee for the beneficial enjoyment of one or more beneficiaries.

Trustee

A trustee is the person whohandles the legal title and management of a trust for the benefit of one or more beneficiaries.

U

Unearned income

Unearned income is any income from activities in which the taxpayer does not material participate. This includes dividends, interest, and rent.

Unified credit

The unified credit is a direct reduction in the computed federal gift tax or estate tax liability. The maximum unified credit for gift transfers is frozen at $345,800 (the equivalent credit on transfers of $1 million). The maximum unified credit for estate transfers is $780,800 in 2008 (the equivalent credit on transfers of $2 million).

Unified transfer tax

The unified transfer tax includes both the gift tax and the estate tax. A single tax rate schedule applies to both types of transfers, and the tax is computed on a cumulative basis each year so that current transfers are taxed at the highest marginal tax rates.

Unitary principle

Under the unitary principle, a business engaged in multi-state activities is viewed as one unitary business unit, and each state should tax only a portion of the company's total income based on the proportion of value created in that state. Generally, that proportion was based on the three-factor test using payroll, property, and sales figures for the state in question as compared to the total figures for all states that the company did business in.

Unrelated business income tax (UBIT)

Congress instituted an unrelated business income tax (UBIT) in order to prevent tax-exempt entities from having an unfair competitive advantage to their for-profit counterparts. Any profits not related to an organization's tax-exempt purpose are taxable under the UBIT.

V

Valuation allowance

A valuation allowance is a contra-asset account that offsets all or a portion of a deferred tax asset when it is no longer "more likely than not" that future tax benefits related to the deferred tax asset will be realized.

Value-added tax (VAT)

The value-added tax (VAT) is the primary source of revenue for most European countries. The VAT is a modified consumption-based tax, and is imposed and collected on the value added at each stage in the production and distribution cycles for goods and services. The tax base for the VAT, the "value added," is the difference between the value of a taxpayer's outputs (sales) and inputs (purchases). No deduction is allowed for labor costs, since this "value added" is the reason for the tax.

Vertical conflicts

Vertical conflicts involve courts at different levels, for example, a Circuit Court of Appeals and the Tax Court. In vertical conflicts, the lower level court may be bound by the decision of a Circuit Court of Appeals.

Vertical equity

The principle of vertical equity states that higher incomes should pay higher taxes. This principle is the backbone of the progressive rate structure of the federal income tax laws; as income increases, the proportion of that income paid in taxes should also increase.

W

Water's edge election

A water's edge election is an election available in selected states such as California whereby the traditional three-factor formula used for apportioning a company's income will include only incomes from domestic operations (i.e.. within the "water's edge).

Wherewithal-to-pay

The wherewithal-to-pay concept is that the taxpayer should be taxed on a transaction when he or she has the means to pay the tax. For example, a taxpayer owns property that is increasing in value. The IRS does not tax the increased value until the taxpayer sells the property. At the time of sale, the taxpayer has the wherewithal to pay. This concept is a central tenet in much of the Code, and the application of this principle overrides any financial accounting or basis election of the taxpayer.

Work product immunity

Work product immunity is a legal doctrine denying access to certain client records due to a confidential relationship between the client and his or her representative. In essence, the 2nd Circuit decision carved out a work product immunity doctrine for a taxpayer and his or her accountant. And this was the taxpayer's argument: to allow the IRS access to accounting workpapers would violate privileged communications between the taxpayer and the accountant, particularly since such documents were not related directly to the preparation of the return (a condition imposed by the 10th Circuit). In particular, the taxpayer feared that the IRS would provide a roadmap to the "thought processes" of the accountants and the taxpayer in assessing the likelihood of having positions sustained on various tax issues.

Topical Index

All references are to paragraph (¶) numbers.

All references are to paragraph (¶) numbers

All references are to paragraph (¶) numbers

All references are to paragraph (¶) numbers

All references are to paragraph (¶) numbers

All references are to paragraph (¶) numbers

All references are to paragraph (¶) numbers

All references are to paragraph (¶) numbers

All references are to paragraph (¶) numbers

All references are to paragraph (¶) numbers

All references are to paragraph (¶) numbers

. amendments to ... 4005.07
. amount of text in, growth of ... 18,003.01
. audits by. *See* Audit, IRS
. authority of, to compute taxpayer income, scope of ... 10,013.03
. authority of, to deduct expenses and losses ... 6003.01
. codification of income recognition judicial decisions in ... 5001
. communications among taxpayer, tax return preparer, and ... 10,001
. complete reference to, citation format of ... 1009.05
. guidance on capitalization versus deduction of expenses by ... 6017.09
. history of ... 1005
. as legislative authority ... 1011.03
. tax act provisions not codified in, types of ... 1009.07
. tax authority of ... 4005.07; 4005.11
. as tool of economic and social policy ... 18,013.01
. Treasury Department charged with overall administration of ... 2003.01
. website of ... 10,013.03
Internal Revenue Manual (IRM) ... 2015.09; 8003.01
. guidelines for identifying tax returns for audit in ... 9007.09
Internal Revenue Service (IRS) ... 9001-9037
. access to taxpayer records by ... 8003-8003.01
. acquiescence/nonacquiescence policy for cases lost by ... 3017.05
. *Action on Decision* by ... 2015.07
. allocation method for vacation rental home expenses by ... 11,019.03-.07
. *Announcements* by ... 2015.01; 4005.07
. Appeals Division of ... 9013.03
. audit-related releases by ... 2019.01-.03
. audits by. *See* Audit, IRS
. budget of ... 18,003.07
. campuses (service centers) of, regional ... 9007
. closing agreements by ... 2019.01
. collection statistics of ... 9003
. Commission appointed by President as head of ... 2003.01
. compliance-related releases by ... 2021.01-.03
. compliance studies by ... 9007.05
. Coordinated Examination Program of, for examining large cases ... 9007
. *Cumulative Bulletin* by ... 2005.05; 2007.05; 2007.07; 2009.05
. Documenting Matching program of ... 9007.03
. Frivolous Return Program of, screening zero returns through ... 9007; 9007.07
. *General Council Memorandum (GCM)* by office of Chief Counsel of ... 2015.03
. informational releases by ... 2017.01-.05
. instructions to tax forms by ... 2021.03
. *Internal Revenue Bulletin* by ... 2005.05; 2007.05; 2007.07; 2009.05; 4005.07

. Math Error program of ... 9007.03
. National Research Program (NRP) of ... 9007.05
. News Releases by ... 2017.05
. *Notices* by ... 2015.01; 4005.07
. Office of Tax Shelter Analysis of ... 9031
. operating divisions of ... 9003.05
. practice before, best practices for ... 9033-9033.09
. private letter rulings by ... 2003.03; 2011-2011.05
. publications of ... 2021.01; 9005.03; 10,007.01
. regulations by. *See* Regulations, IRS
. as respondent in Tax Court cases ... 3005.03
. Revenue Procedures by ... 2003.03; 2009-2009.05
. Revenue Rulings by ... 2003.03; 2007-2007.07; 3017.05; 4005.07; 4005.11
. *Semi-Annual Agenda of Regulations* by ... 2005.09
. settlement opportunities with, prior to going to court ... 3003.05
. structure of ... 9003.03; 9003.07
. technical advice memorandums by ... 2003.03; 2013.01
. Technical Memoranda by ... 2015.05
Inventories
. capitalization rules for ... 16,005.03
. dollar-value methods for ... 16,005.01
. double-extension valuation method for ... 16,005.01
. excess or obsolete, GAAP versus tax regulations for ... 8005-8005.01
. FIFO system for ... 16,005.01
. identifying particular goods in ... 16,005.01
. Inventory Price Index Computation (IPIC) method for ... 16,005.01
. LIFO system for ... 16,005.01
. pooling ... 16,005.01
. property held for resale ... 7003.01; 16,005.03
. shrinkage estimate in computing year-end ... 8005.05
. Simplified Production Method (IRS) for ... 16,005.03
. Simplified Retail Method (IRS) for ... 16,005.03
Investment interest expense
. deductions of ... 11,005.03
. limitations on ... 11,009
Investment items, AMT planning for ... 11,005.03
Investment records ... 10,005
Involuntary conversions
. of business and income-producing properties ... 7009.03
. deferral of gain in, Code Sec. 1033 election for ... 7011.03
. of owner-lessor properties ... 7017.03
Irrevocable trusts ... 14,005.03
. GRATs as ... 14,017.03
. intentionally defective ... 14,023

All references are to paragraph (¶) numbers

All references are to paragraph (¶) numbers

All references are to paragraph (¶) numbers

All references are to paragraph (¶) numbers

All references are to paragraph (¶) numbers

All references are to paragraph (¶) numbers

All references are to paragraph (¶) numbers

All references are to paragraph (¶) numbers

All references are to paragraph (¶) numbers

All references are to paragraph (¶) numbers

All references are to paragraph (¶) numbers